Hymns Ancient & Modern Revised

TONIC SOL-FA

Canterbury Press
Norwich

Canterbury Press is an imprint of
Hymns Ancient and Modern Ltd
St Mary's Works
St Mary's Plain,
Norwich
Norfolk NR3 3BH

Hymns Ancient and Modern Revised
first published 1950

Tonic Sol-fa edition reissued 2010

© Compilation Hymns Ancient and Modern Ltd

All rights reserved. No part of this publication
may be reproduced, copied or transmitted in any
form or by any means without the prior permission of
Hymns Ancient and Modern Ltd

978 1 85311 011 5

Printed in the UK by
CPI William Clowes, Beccles, NR34 7TL

PREFACE

HYMNS ANCIENT AND MODERN was first published (in a form complete with music) in 1861. It was an attempt to consolidate the hymn-books, Anglican and others, which had appeared in the previous hundred years or more and had now become very numerous. It soon became something of a national institution. The Proprietors, a body of Church of England clergymen, found themselves almost embarrassed by the success of their undertaking. An appendix was added in 1868. A revised edition appeared in 1875, to which a Supplement was added in 1889. A new edition, published in 1904, did not succeed in replacing the old book, which with a Second Supplement (1916) has continued to be the most widely used Hymnal of the Church of England. The Standard Edition dates from 1922, when it was reset and many improvements were introduced.

The Proprietors, five in number, were appointed under a Trust Deed. They nominated Assessors to aid them. After certain deductions authorised by the Trust Deed, the whole of the profits on the book was paid to a body of Trustees who distributed them to charities in accordance with the instructions of the Proprietors. It was the custom of the Proprietors to make a donation to the Central Board of Finance of the Church of England a first charge on the sum available for charitable donations. The Rev. Sir Henry Baker was the first Chairman of the Proprietors. Among his successors, Bishop W. H. Frere and Sir Sydney Nicholson may be specially mentioned.

The Musical Editors have been as follows: Dr. W. H. Monk (helped by the Rev. Sir F. A. Gore-Ouseley) from 1861 to 1889; then Dr. C. Steggall for the 1889 Supplement. The music of the 1904 edition was edited by Mr. B. Luard Selby, the Supplement of 1916 by Sir Sydney Nicholson, who continued to be Musical Editor until his death in 1947. In the preparation of the edition now published Sir Sydney was assisted by Mr. G. H. Knight and Dr. J. Dykes Bower.

The shaping of Hymns Ancient and Modern Revised has been a task of much labour, and the Proprietors had a good hope that it will be welcomed by the large public for whom it is designed, as preserving the general tone and character which the book has always had and at the same time making it more serviceable both by what it adds and by what it omits.

The cumbrous device of two Supplements was inconvenient in itself and had made the book too large. It will be seen that the hymns are now arranged in one series of not much over 600 in all. In order to effect this reduction and to make room for new matter the Editors were obliged to leave out a good number of hymns. These soon fell into two distinct classes. The first was of those which had never really found favour. It was easy to cut them out, but there were not enough of them to meet the whole of the necessary reduction. The second class was of those which the Editors felt could well be spared, yet undoubtedly they were endeared to quite a number of congregations. Most of these had to go on the assumption that they were not likely to last much longer. They were bound in the end to be discarded, the Editors thought, and by a justifiable

PREFACE

anticipation might be discarded now. Sometimes a favourite hymn may therefore seem to be missing, but the Editors believe that prevailing tendencies would have swept it away before long. They have tried to respect the strong power of association which operates in the minds of hymn-singers by preserving, where possible, the old numbers in the earlier part of the book. A few hymns which have recently become popular are absent owing to copyright difficulties.

Of the hymns to be found in this book which have not appeared in previous editions of Hymns Ancient and Modern, the greater number are old hymns which have been successfully resuscitated in one place or another and have won a wide acceptance and so have become such as no hymn-book could well omit. The Editors have brought in a certain number of new hymns, mainly to satisfy a particular need or occasion, or to match a good tune with fitting words.

The book does not always adhere to the original text of the hymns. The Editors of the earliest editions made alterations to meet the requirements of a hymn-singing congregation, and the present Editors see no reason to go back upon the practice of their predecessors. Many of the great Charles Wesley's hymns have hardly ever been sung as he originally wrote them. Not a few authors, including Dr. Neale, have agreed that for the purpose of a hymn-book the version of their hymns in Hymns Ancient and Modern were, on the whole, improvements. The case for alteration has been considered on its merits, and in many hymns the author's text has been restored. In others, however, the emended text has been retained as more convenient and having the sanction of long usage.

The provision of hymns to be sung in Procession has been very much increased and make more methodical. On the other hand, from some hymns which seemed over-long for ordinary use one or more verses have been omitted where this appeared not to spoil the effect as a whole.

In concluding what has been the labour of many years, the Proprietors expressed a hope that in this new book the Church will find the same endearing and enduring qualities as in the old, the same heart-felt yet sober tone, so much in keeping with English-speaking Christianity. At the same time they believed that what is new in sense and sound will commend itself as a real augmentation of the rich treasury of hymns and hymn-tunes which are now employed in the divine praises and catholic teaching of the Christian Church. The new book does not aim at breaking fresh ground or exploiting novel ideas. The hope is that it may prove to be, as it was before, a consolidation of all that has been gained over many a long year since the wholesome practice of hymn-singing won an accepted place in Church, School and Home.

TABLE OF CONTENTS

Morning	1–11
Mid-day	12, 13
Evening	14–38
Sunday	39–44
Advent	45–56
Christmas	57–71
New Year	72, 73
Epiphany	74–82
Septuagesima	83
Lent	84–95
Passiontide	96–112
Good Friday	113–123
Good Friday Evening and Easter Even	124–127
Easter	128–143
Rogationtide	144
Ascensiontide	145–150
Whitsuntide	151–157
Trinity Sunday	158, 159
General Hymns:	160–382
God, Three in One	160–164
God Creator, Ruler, Father	165–184
Jesus Son of God:	185–229
His Incarnation and Earthly Life	185–187
His Holy Name	188–192
Lord of Light, Life, and Love	193–209
His Cross and Passion	210–215
His Power and Glory	216–226
His Second Coming	227–229
The Holy Spirit	230–239
The Family of God:	240–286
The House of God	240–249
The Word of God	250–252
General Hymns (contd.)	
The Family of God (contd.)	
The Church and the Kingdom	253–271
The Communion of Saints	272–274
The Church Triumphant	275–286
The Ministry of Angels	287, 288
The Christian Life: 289–316	
Pilgrimage	289–302
Warfare	303–309
Faith, Hope and Love	310–316
Prayer and Penitence	317–324
Discipleship and Work	325–341
Hymns of Personal Devotion	342–364
Praise and Thanksgiving	365–382
Holy Communion	383–423
Holy Baptism	424–428
For the Young	429–456
For School and College Use	457, 458
Confirmation	459–462
Holy Matrimony	463–465
The Departed	466–469
Ember Days	470–473
Dedication Festival	474–476
Hospitals: the Sick	477–479

TABLE OF CONTENTS

ALMSGIVING	480
HARVEST	481–486
FOR THOSE AT SEA	487
FOR ABSENT FRIENDS	488
FAREWELL SERVICES	489
IN TIME OF WAR	490–492
SERVICES, SOCIETIES, MEETINGS, ETC.	493–502
SAINTS' DAYS: GENERAL: 503–532	
APOSTLES	503–507
EVANGELISTS	508–511
THE BLESSED VIRGIN MARY	512–515
MARTYRS AND OTHERS	516–522
FOR ANY SAINT'S DAY	523–532
SAINTS' DAYS AND OTHER HOLY DAYS: PROPER: 533–576	
ST. ANDREW	533
ST. THOMAS	534
ST. STEPHEN	535
ST. JOHN THE EVANGELIST	536, 537
THE INNOCENTS' DAY	538
THE CIRCUMCISION	539
CONVERSION OF ST. PAUL	540–542
THE PURIFICATION	543, 544
ST. MATTHIAS	545
THE ANNUNCIATION	546, 547
ST. MARK	548
ST. PHILIP AND ST. JAMES	549
ST. BARNABAS	550
ST. JOHN BAPTIST	551–553
ST. PETER	554, 555
SAINTS' DAYS (*contd.*)	
ST. MARY MAGDALENE	556
ST. JAMES	557
THE TRANSFIGURATION	558–561
ST. BARTHOLOMEW	562
ST. MATTHEW	563
MICHAELMAS	564–566
ST. LUKE	567
ST. SIMON AND ST. JUDE	568
ALL SAINTS	569–572
ST. GEORGE	573
SAINTS, MARTYRS, AND DOCTORS OF THE CHURCH OF ENGLAND	574
ST. DAVID	575
ST. NICOLAS	576
NATIONAL	577–585
LITANIES	586–590
PROCESSIONAL HYMNS: 591–636	
CHRISTMAS	591–594
EPIPHANY	595, 596
PALM SUNDAY	597–599
EASTER DAY	600–605
ROGATIONTIDE	606, 607
ASCENSIONTIDE	608–611
WHITSUNDAY	612–615
TRINITY SUNDAY	616, 617
DEDICATION FESTIVAL	618–621
THANKSGIVING FOR THE INSTITUTION OF HOLY COMMUNION	622
SAINTS' DAYS	623–628
GENERAL	629–636

INDEX OF FIRST LINES

A

A charge to keep I have	328
A great and mighty wonder	68
A safe stronghold our God is still	183
A work hath Christ for thee to do	430
Abide with me; fast falls the eventide	27
Again the Lord's own day is here	40
All creatures of our God and King	172
All glory, laud, and honour	98
All glory, laud, and honour	597
All hail, adorèd Trinity	617
All hail the power of Jesus' name	217
All people that on earth do dwell	166
All praise be to God	566
All things bright and beautiful	442
All ye who seek for sure relief	104
Alleluia! Alleluia! hearts to heaven and voices raise	137
Alleluia! sing to Jesus	399
Alleluia, song of sweetness	82
Almighty Father, Lord most high	405
Almighty Father, who dost give	583
And did those feet in ancient time	578
And now another day is gone	36
And now, beloved Lord, thy soul resigning	123
And now, O Father, mindful of the love	397
And now the wants are told, that brought	32
Angels, from the realms of glory	64
Angel-voices ever singing	246
Approach, my soul, the mercy-seat	345
Around the throne of God a band	448
Art thou weary, art thou languid	348
As now the sun's declining rays	29
As pants the hart for cooling streams	314
As with gladness men of old	79
At even, ere the sun was set	20
At the Cross her station keeping	118
At the Lamb's high feast we sing	139
At the name of Jesus	225
At thy feet, O Christ, we lay	6
Author of life divine	394
Awake, my soul, and with the sun	3
Awaked from sleep we fall	9

B

Be thou my guardian and my guide	300
Before Jehovah's awful throne	370
Before the ending of the day	16
Behold, the Bridegroom draweth nigh	46
Behold, the great Creator makes	69
Behold the Lamb of God	212
Behold us, Lord, a little space	13
Blessèd city, heavenly Salem	474
Blessèd city, heavenly Salem	620
Blest are the pure in heart	335
Blest Creator of the light	44
Bread of heaven, on thee we feed	411
Bread of the world in mercy broken	409
Breathe on me, Breath of God	236
Brief life is here our portion	275
Bright the vision that delighted	161
Brightest and best of the sons of the morning	75
Brothers, joining hand to hand	294
By Jesus' grave on either hand	125

C

Captains of the saintly band	507
Children of the heavenly King	295
Christ is gone up; yet ere he passed	470
Christ is now risen again	601
Christ is our Corner-stone	243
Christ, the fair glory of the holy angels	564
Christ the Lord is risen again	136
Christ the Lord is risen to-day	131
Christ, who once amongst us	447
Christ, whose glory fills the skies	7
Christian, dost thou see them	91
Christian, seek not yet repose	308
Christians, awake! salute the happy morn	61
Christians, to the Paschal Victim	138
City of God, how broad and far	258
Come down, O Love divine	235
Come, gracious Spirit, heavenly Dove	232
Come, Holy Ghost, our souls inspire	157
Come, Holy Ghost, who ever One	11
Come, labour on	339
Come, let us join our cheerful songs	221
Come, let us join our friends above	628
Come, my soul, thy suit prepare	319
Come, O Creator Spirit, come	152
Come, O thou Traveller unknown	343
Come, pure hearts, in sweetest measures	508
Come sing, ye choirs exultant	509
Come, thou Holy Spirit, come	156
Come, thou long-expected Jesus	54
Come unto me, ye weary	350
Come, ye faithful, raise the anthem	222
Come, ye faithful, raise the strain	133
Come, ye thankful people, come	482
Conquering kings their titles take	191
Creator of the starry height	45
Creator of the world, to thee	83
Crown him with many crowns	224

D

Day of wrath! O day of mourning	466
Daystar on high, bright harbinger of gladness	604
Dear Lord and Father of mankind	184

ix

INDEX OF FIRST LINES

Dearest Jesu, we are here	408
Deck thyself, my soul, with gladness	393
Disposer supreme, and Judge of the earth	506
Do no sinful action	433
Draw nigh and take the Body of the Lord	386

E

Earth has many a noble city	76
Eternal Father, strong to save	487
Eternal Power whose high abode	621

F

Fair waved the golden corn	338
Faithful Shepherd, feed me	415
Far-shining names from age to age	576
Fast sinks the sun to rest	37
Father, hear the prayer we offer	182
Father, let me dedicate	72
Father most high, be with us	112
Father most holy, merciful and loving	158
Father of heaven, whose love profound	164
Father of mercies, in thy word	251
Father, whate'er of earthly bliss	180
Fierce raged the tempest o'er the deep	313
Fierce was the wild billow	312
Fight the good fight with all thy might	304
Fill thou my life, O Lord my God	373
Firmly I believe and truly	186
Fling out the banner! let it float	268
For all the saints who from their labours rest	527
For all thy saints, a noble throng	557
For all thy saints, O Lord	531
For ever with the Lord	346
For the beauty of the earth	171
For thee, O dear, dear country	277
For thy mercy and thy grace	73
Forgive them, O my Father	114
Forsaken once, and thrice denied	323
Forth in thy name, O Lord, I go	336
Forty days and forty nights	92
From all that dwell below the skies	630
From east to west, from shore to shore	57
From glory to glory advancing, we praise thee, O Lord	417
From Greenland's icy mountains	265
From heaven's height Christ spake to call	540
From out the cloud of fiery light	548
From the eastern mountains	595
From thee all skill and science flow	479

G

Gabriel to Mary came	547
Gentle Jesus, meek and mild	451
Give us the wings of faith to rise	571
Glorious things of thee are spoken	257
Glory and honour and laud be to thee, Christ, King and Redeemer	598
Glory be to Jesus	107
Glory to thee my God, this night	23
Go forth with God! the day is now	500
Go to dark Gethsemane	110
God be in my head	332
God be with you till we meet again	489
God from on high hath heard	63
God is working his purpose out as year succeeds to year	271
God moves in a mysterious way	181
God of mercy, God of grace	264
God of the morning, at whose voice	8
God save our gracious Queen	577
God, that madest earth and heaven	26
God the all-terrible! King, who ordainest	491
God the Father, God the Son	587
God the Father, God the Son	590
God, whose city's sure foundation	574
Good Christian men, rejoice and sing	603
Good Joseph had a garden	438
Gracious Spirit, Holy Ghost	233
Great mover of all hearts	316
Great Shepherd of thy people, hear	247
Guide me, O thou great Redeemer	296

H

Hail, gladdening Light, of his pure glory poured	18
Hail, glorious spirits, heirs of light	626
Hail, O Mary, full of grace	499
Hail! princes of the host of heaven	549
Hail the day that sees him rise	147
Hail the day that sees him rise	610
Hail to the Lord who comes	544
Hail to the Lord's Anointed	219
Hail, true Body, born of Mary	407
Hands that have been handling	494
Happy are they, they that love God	261
Hark! a thrilling voice is sounding	47
Hark! hark, my soul! angelic songs are swelling	354
Hark, my soul! it is the Lord	344
Hark the glad sound! the Saviour comes	53
Hark! the herald-angels sing	60
Hark! the sound of holy voices	526
Hearken, O Lord, have mercy upon us	586
He is risen, he is risen	143
He sat to watch o'er customs paid	563
He that is down needs fear no fall	301
He wants not friends that hath thy love	274
He who to Jesus manfully bore witness	519
Her Virgin eyes saw God incarnate born	513
Here, O my Lord, I see thee face to face	414
Here, while the cherubim within the veil	391
High let us swell our tuneful notes	592
Hills of the north, rejoice	269
His are the thousand sparkling rills	120
Holy Father, cheer our way	22
Holy Father, in thy mercy	488
Holy, Holy, Holy! Lord God Almighty	160
Holy Spirit, gently come	614

INDEX OF FIRST LINES

Hosanna in the highest	421
Hosanna to the living Lord	241
Hosanna we sing, like the children dear	453
How beauteous are their feet	510
How bright these glorious spirits shine	528
How glorious is the life above	420
How joyful 'tis to sing	493
How sweet the name of Jesus sounds	192
How vain the cruel Herod's fear	74
I bind unto myself to-day	162
I could not do without thee	353
I heard the voice of Jesus say	351
I hunger and I thirst	413
I love to hear the story	445
I praised the earth, in beauty seen	173
I sing the birth was born to-night	70
I vow to thee, my country, all earthly things above	579
Immortal, invisible, God only wise	372
Immortal love for ever full	208
In days of old on Sinai	559
In our day of thanksgiving one psalm let us offer	476
In our work and in our play	454
In the bleak mid-winter	67
In the Lord's atoning grief	105
In token that thou shalt not fear	424
It came upon the midnight clear	66
It is a thing most wonderful	435
It is finished! blessed Jesus	124
J	
Jerusalem, my happy home	282
Jerusalem, my happy home	623
Jerusalem on high	280
Jerusalem the golden	278
Jesu, gentlest Saviour	418
Jesu, grant me this, I pray	211
Jesu, lover of my soul	193
Jesu, meek and gentle	194
Jesu, meek and lowly	213
Jesu, my Lord, my God, my all	202
Jesu, our hope, our heart's desire	146
Jesu, Son of Mary	469
Jesu! the very thought is sweet	188
Jesu, the very thought of thee	189
Jesu, thou joy of loving hearts	387
Jesu, thy mercies are untold	201
Jesu, who this our Lenten-tide	85
Jesus calls us! o'er the tumult	533
Jesus Christ from death hath risen	605
Jesus Christ is risen to-day	134
Jesus, kind above all other	456
Jesus lives! thy terrors now	140
Jesus, Lord of life and glory	321
Jesus, Lord of our salvation	573
Jesus shall reign where'er the sun	220
Jesus, still lead on	206
Jesus, these eyes have never seen	347
Jesus, where'er thy people meet	245
Joy and triumph everlasting	523
Just as I am without one plea	349

K	
Kindly spring again is here	607
King of glory, King of peace	367
L	
Lead, kindly Light, amid the encircling gloom	298
Lead us, heavenly Father, lead us	311
Let all mortal flesh keep silence	390
Let all on earth their voices raise	504
Let all the multitudes of light	150
Let all the world in every corner sing	375
Let hearts awaken, now the night is ended	10
Let love arise and praise him	627
Let our choir new anthems raise	518
Let saints on earth in concert sing	272
Let us employ all notes of joy	423
Let us thank the Christ for all who did their duty	455
Let us, with a gladsome mind	377
Lift high the Cross, the love of Christ proclaim	633
Lift up your heads, ye gates of brass	306
Lift up your hearts! We lift them, Lord, to thee	341
Lift up your voice, ye Christian folk	297
Light of the lonely pilgrim's heart	209
Light's abode, celestial Salem	279
Light's glittering morn bedecks the sky	602
Lo, from the desert homes	552
Lo, God is here! let us adore	249
Lo, he comes with clouds descending	51
Lo, round the throne, a glorious band	525
Lord, accept the alms we offer	406
Lord and Master, who hast called us	495
Lord, as to thy dear Cross we flee	334
Lord, be thy word my rule	327
Lord, behold us with thy blessing	457
Lord, dismiss us with thy blessing	458
Lord, enthroned in heavenly splendour	400
Lord God the Holy Ghost	615
Lord, her watch thy Church is keeping	267
Lord, I would own thy tender care	443
Lord, in this thy mercy's day	94
Lord, in thy name thy servants plead	144
Lord, it belongs not to my care	342
Lord Jesus Christ, our Lord most dear	425
Lord Jesus, when we stand afar	109
Lord Jesus, think on me	200
Lord of beauty, thine the splendour	174
Lord of life and King of Glory	498
Lord of our life, and God of our salvation	253
Lord of the Harvest it is right and meet	378
Lord of the worlds above	248
Lord of the worlds, unseen or seen	492
Lord, pour thy Spirit from on high	473
Lord, teach us how to pray aright	317
Lord, through this Holy Week of our salvation	100

xi

INDEX OF FIRST LINES

Lord, thy word abideth	250
Lord, to our humble prayers attend	588
Lord, when thy Kingdom comes, remember me	116
Lord, while for all mankind we pray	581
Love divine, all loves excelling	205
Love of the Father, Love of God the Son	238
Love's redeeming work is done	141
Loving Shepherd of thy sheep	444

M

Magdalene, thy grief and gladness	556
May the grace of Christ our Saviour	636
Most ancient of all mysteries	159
My Father, for another night	5
My God, accept my heart this day	459
My God, and is thy table spread	396
My God, how wonderful thou art	169
My God, I love thee; not because	106
My God, my Father, while I stray	357
My Lord, my Master, at thy feet adoring	103
My song is love unknown	102
My soul, there is a country	286
My spirit longs for thee	89

N

Nearer, my God, to thee	352
New every morning is the love	4
Not a thought of earthly things	392
Not always on the mount may we	561
Not by far-famed deeds alone	562
Not for our sins alone	324
Now, my tongue, the mystery telling	383
Now thank we all our God	379
Now that the daylight fills the sky	1
Now the day is over	431
Now the labourer's task is o'er	467

O

O Christ our joy, gone up on high	611
O Christ, thou Lord of worlds, thine ear to hear us bow	505
O Christ, who art the Light and Day	95
O Christ, whom we may love and know	450
O come, all ye faithful	59
O come, all ye faithful	593
O come and mourn with me awhile	113
O come, O come, Emmanuel	49
O, David was a shepherd lad	449
O day of rest and gladness	41
O dearest Lord, thy sacred head	436
O Father, by whose sovereign sway	465
O Father, for this little life	426
O Father, we thank thee for Jesus thy Son	441
O food that weary pilgrims love	389
O for a closer walk with God	326
O for a heart to praise my God	325
O for a thousand tongues to sing	196
O God, before whose altar	340
O God, in this thine hour of grace	460
O God of Bethel, by whose hand	299
O God of grace, thy mercy send	589
O God of love, O King of peace	490
O God of truth, O Lord of might	12
O God of truth, whose living word	309
O God, our help in ages past	165
O God, the world's sustaining force	14
O God, thy soldiers' great reward	516
O God, unseen yet ever near	412
O God, whose mighty works of old	501
O happy band of pilgrims	289
O heavenly Jerusalem	569
O help us, Lord! each hour of need	320
O Holy Ghost, thy people bless	234
O Holy Spirit, Lord of grace	231
O Jesu, blessed Lord to thee	419
O Jesu, thou art standing	355
O Jesu, thou the virgins' crown	521
O Jesus, I have promised	331
O joy, because the circling year	151
O joy of God that comest in the morning	404
O King enthroned on high	237
O little town of Bethlehem	65
O Lord, how joyful 'tis to see	244
O Lord Jesus, I adore thee	388
O Lord of heaven and earth and sea	480
O Lord of Life, whose power sustains	585
O Lord, to whom the spirits live	468
O Lord, turn not thy face from me	93
O love divine, how sweet thou art	195
O love, how deep, how broad, how high	187
O Love that wilt not let me go	359
O Love, who formedst me to wear	203
O loving Father, to thy care	427
O Maker of the world, give ear	84
O martyrs young and fresh as flowers	538
O most merciful	410
O my Saviour, lifted	360
O perfect God, thy love	121
O perfect life of love	122
O perfect Love, all human thought transcending	463
O praise ye the Lord! praise him in the height	376
O quickly come, dread Judge of all	227
O Rock of ages, one Foundation	554
O sacred head, surrounded	111
O Sion, open wide thy gates	543
O Son of God, our Captain of Salvation	550
O sons and daughters, let us sing	130
O sorrow deep	126
O splendour of God's glory bright	2
O strength and stay upholding all creation	17
O thou, before the world began	395
O thou eternal King most high	145
O thou, from whom all goodness flows	117
O thou not made with hands	259
O thou, who at thy Eucharist didst pray	402
O thou who camest from above	329
O thou who gavest power to love	464
O thou who makest souls to shine	471
O Trinity, most blessed Light	15
O valiant hearts, who to your glory came	584
O what their joy and their glory must be	281
O wondrous type, O vision fair	558

INDEX OF FIRST LINES

O Word of God above	475
O word of pity, for our pardon pleading	115
O worship the King all glorious above	167
O worship the Lord in the beauty of holiness	77
Of the Father's love begotten	58
Of the Father's love begotten	591
Oft in danger, oft in woe	291
On Jordan's bank the Baptist's cry	50
On this day, the first of days	39
Once in royal David's city	432
Once, only once, and once for all	398
Once pledged by the Cross, as children of God	462
Onward, Christian soldiers	629
Our blest Redeemer, ere he breathed	230
Our day of praise is done	38
Our Father's home eternal	625
Our Lord, his Passion ended	155
Our Lord is risen from the dead	609
Our Lord the path of suffering trod	517
Out of the deep I call	322

P

Palms of glory, raiment bright	530
Paul the preacher, Paul the poet	542
Peace, perfect peace, in this dark world of sin	358
Pleasant are thy courts above	240
Praise, my soul, the King of heaven	365
Praise, O praise our God and King	481
Praise, O Sion, praise thy Master	622
Praise the Lord of heaven, praise him in the height	381
Praise the Lord! ye heavens, adore him	368
Praise to God, immortal praise	485
Praise to God who reigns above	565
Praise to the Holiest in the height	185
Praise to the Lord, the Almighty, the King of creation	382
Praise we the Lord this day	546
Put thou thy trust in God	310

R

Rejoice, O land, in God thy might	582
Rejoice! the Lord is King	216
Rejoice, ye pure in heart	635
Resting from his work to-day	127
Revive thy work, O Lord	362
Ride on! ride on in majesty	99
Ride on triumphantly! Behold, we lay	599
Rise at the cry of battle	497
Rise in the strength of God	302
Rock of ages, cleft for me	210
Round me falls the night	35

S

Saviour, again to thy dear name we raise	31
Saviour, when in dust to thee	86
Saviour, who didst healing give	567
See the Conqueror mounts in triumph	148
See the destined day arise	101
Shall we not love thee, Mother dear	515
Shepherd divine, our wants relieve	318
Shepherds, in the field abiding	594
Sinful, sighing to be blest	87
Sing Alleluia forth in duteous praise	283
Sing, my tongue, the glorious battle	97
Sing praise to God who reigns above	366
Sing to the Lord the children's hymn	446
Sing we the praises of the great forerunner	551
Sleepers, wake! the watch-cry pealeth	55
Soldiers of Christ, arise	303
Soldiers of the Cross, arise	305
Soldiers, who are Christ's below	524
Sometimes a light surprises	176
Son of God eternal Saviour	207
Songs of praise the angels sang	369
Songs of thankfulness and praise	81
Souls of men! why will ye scatter	364
Sound aloud Jehovah's praises	616
Spirit divine, attend our prayers	239
Spirit of Jesus, who didst move	511
Spirit of mercy, truth, and love	153
Stalwart as pillars bearing high their burden	520
Stand up, and bless the Lord	374
Stand up, stand up for Jesus	307
Stars of the morning, so gloriously bright	288
Still nigh me, O my Saviour, stand	90
Strong Captain, in thy holy ranks	461
Sun of my soul, thou Saviour dear	24
Sweet Saviour, bless us ere we go	28

T

Take my life, and let it be	361
Take up thy cross, the Saviour said	333
Teach me, my God and King	337
Ten thousand times ten thousand	284
That day of wrath, that dreadful day	228
The advent of our King	48
The ancient law departs	539
The Church of God a kingdom is	254
The Church's one foundation	255
The Church triumphant in thy love	624
The day is past and over	21
The day of Resurrection	132
The day thou gavest, Lord, is ended	33
The duteous day now closeth	34
The earth, O Lord, is one wide field	472
The eternal gifts of Christ the King	503
The God of Abraham praise	631
The God of love my Shepherd is	178
The God whom earth and sea and sky	512
The golden gates are lifted up	439
The great forerunner of the morn	553
The head that once was crowned with thorns	218
The heaven of heavens cannot contain	619
The heavenly Child in stature grows	78
The heavenly Word, proceeding forth	384
The heavens declare thy glory, Lord	252
The highest and the holiest place	545
The King of love my Shepherd is	197
The Queen, O God, her heart to thee upraiseth	580
The Lamb's high banquet called to share	129

INDEX OF FIRST LINES

The Lord is King! lift up thy voice	175
The Lord is risen indeed	142
The Lord my pasture shall prepare	179
The Lord will come and not be slow	52
The people that in darkness sat	80
The radiant morn hath passed away	19
The royal banners forward go	96
The saints of God! their conflict past	572
The saints who toiled from place to place	522
The Son of God goes forth to war	529
The sower went forth sowing	486
The spacious firmament on high	170
The strife is o'er, the battle done	135
The sun is sinking fast	30
The world is very evil	276
Thee, living Christ, our eyes behold	422
Thee we adore, O hidden Saviour, thee	385
There is a book, which runs may read	168
There is a green hill far away	214
There is a land of pure delight	285
There's a Friend for little children	452
They come, God's messengers of love	287
They whose course on earth is o'er	273
Thine arm, O Lord, in days of old	478
Thine for ever! God of love	330
This is the day of light	42
This is the day the Lord hath made	43
Thou art gone up on high	149
Thou art the Christ, O Lord	555
Thou art the Way: by thee alone	199
Thou didst leave thy throne and thy kingly crown	363
Thou gracious God, whose mercy lends	502
Thou to whom the sick and dying	477
Thou who sentest thine apostles	568
Thou whom shepherds worshipped, hearing	596
Thou, whose almighty word	266
Thou Wind of God, whose coming stirred	440
Three in One, and One in Three	163
Throned upon the awful Tree	119
Through all the changing scenes of life	290
Through the day thy love has spared us	25
Through the night of doubt and sorrow	292
Through the night thy angels kept	429
Thy hand, O God, has guided	256
Thy Kingdom come, O God	262
Thy Kingdom come! on bended knee	263
Thy way, not mine, O Lord	356
'Tis good, Lord, to be here	560
To Christ, the Prince of Peace	198
To the name of our salvation	190
To thee, O Comforter divine	613
To thee, O Father, lamp of all the living	428
To thee, O Lord, our hearts we raise	484
To thee our God we fly	606
To us a Child of royal birth	71
To you was given, O saint beloved	537
Trumpet of God, sound high	270
'Twas by thy Blood, immortal Lamb	634

U

Unchanging God, who livest	496
Up to the throne on high	315

V

Virgin-born, we bow before thee	514

W

We hail thy Presence glorious	403
We have a King who came to earth	434
We love the place, O God	242
We plough the fields, and scatter	483
We praise thee, Lord, for all the martyred throng	532
We praise thy name, all holy Lord	575
We pray thee, heavenly Father	401
We sing the glorious conquest	541
We sing the praise of him who died	215
We would extol thee, ever-blessed Lord	380
Welcome, morning of joy, glad feast that all ages shall hallow (*Easter*)	600
Welcome, morning of joy, glad feast that all ages shall hallow (*Ascension*)	608
Welcome, morning of joy, glad feast that all ages shall hallow (*Whitsun*)	612
Welcome, morning of joy, glad feast that all ages shall hallow (*Dedication*)	618
When all thy mercies, O my God	177
When came in flesh the incarnate Word	56
When God of old came down from heaven	154
When, his salvation bringing	437
When I survey the wondrous Cross	108
When morning gilds the skies	223
When wounded sore the stricken heart	88
Where high the heavenly temple stands	204
Wherefore, O Father, we thy humble servants	416
While shepherds watched their flocks by night	62
Who are these like stars appearing	570
Who dreads, yet undismayed	534
Who would true valour see	293
Word supreme, before creation	536
Worship, honour, glory, blessing	632

Y

Ye choirs of new Jerusalem	128
Ye holy angels bright	371
Ye servants of God, your Master proclaim	226
Ye servants of the Lord	229
Ye that know the Lord is gracious	260
Yesterday with exultation	535

ACKNOWLEDGEMENTS

THANKS ARE DUE to those who have given permission for the use of their copyright hymns. The present owners, so far as they can be ascertained, are:

Mr. Barclay Baron 500 — The Beacon Press, Boston, Mass., U.S.A. (from *Hymns of the Spirit*) 263 — Mrs. Boutflower 404 — The Proprietors of the *Church and School Hymnal* 449 — The Church Pension Fund (from *American Church Hymnal*) 126 — The Clarendon Press and the Executors of the late Robert Bridges 34, 152, 238, 261, 523, 566, 580, 582 — Miss M. Cropper 450 — J. Curwen & Sons Ltd. 172, 292, 431, 629 — Girls' Friendly Society (and Miss Cropper) 434 — Lord Gorell 428 — Mr. H. V. Lowry 207 — Marshall, Morgan & Scott Ltd. 237, 588, 589 — The Mothers' Union 498 — A. R. Mowbray & Co. Ltd. 302, 436, 594 — Mrs. Newman 573 — Novello & Co. Ltd. 604 — The Oxford University Press 254, 463 — E. H. Freeman Ltd. 294 — The Royal School of Church Music 297 — St. Christopher's College, Blackheath 438, 495 — Mr. C. R. Sedgwick 406 — Skeffington & Co. Ltd. 584 — The S.P.C.K. 155, 426, 430, 440, 455, 460, 461, 492, 499, 501, 585 — The Universities Mission to Central Africa 469 — Mr. E. M. S. Wood 408.

Also to the personal representatives of the authors for these:

150, 315, 380, 400, 402, 403, 496, 534, 560.

The following belong to *Hymns Ancient and Modern Limited*:

10, 37, 84, 85, 100, 115, 121, 145, 174, 260, 270, 340, 388, 391, 392, 401, 405, 419, 422, 423, 427, 441, 447, 465, 476, 486, 493, 494, 497, 511, 512, 519, 520, 522, 537, 538, 542, 547, 551, 556, 562, 564, 574, 576, 583, 586, 596, 598, 599, 600, 603, 608, 612, 618, 622, 627, 633.

Thanks are also due to those who have given permission for the use of copyright tunes and arrangements. The present owners, so far as they can be ascertained, are:

The Abbot of Downside 185*b* — Mr. H. A. Bate 180 — Mr. L. J. Blake 36 (arrangement) — The Cambridge University Press (descants) 167*a* and *b*, 190*a*, 506 — The Proprietors of the *Church and School Hymnal* 449 — J. Curwen & Sons Ltd. 182, 269, 431, 442*a*, 495 — The English Hymnal Co. Ltd. 65*a*, 326, 380, 416, 589 — The Faith Press Ltd. 385*b*, 547 — Mr. K. G. Finlay 33*a*, 433*a*, 494, 583 — The Girls' Friendly Society 476 — Sir William H. Harris 235, 528*a*, 614 — A. R. Mowbray & Co. Ltd. 594 — Novello & Co. Ltd. 36, 304*b*, 606*b* — The Oxford University Press 21, 120, 224*a*, 257*a*, 298*a*, 299*a*, 332*a*, 341, 450, 456, 500, 550, 596 — The Royal School of Church Music 79 (arrangement and descant), 143, 171 (arrangement and descant), 190*b*, 223*a*, 244, 245 (descant), 297, 319*b*, 332*b*, 441, 445*a*, 575, 576, 584*a*, 623, 627 — Schott & Co. Ltd. 312, 429 — The S.P.C.K. 492—Stainer & Bell Ltd. 162, 283, 527*a*.

Also to the personal representatives of the composers for these:

65*b*, 67, 102, 131*a*, 174, 230*b*, 247, 256, 271, 296*b*, 331, 339, 375, 386*b*, 417, 489, 496, 522, 555, 579, 590.

The following tunes belong to *Hymns Ancient and Modern Limited*:

9*a* and *b*, 46, 72*a*, 133, 155, 205*a*, 215, 237, 270, 302, 307*a*, 308*a* 315, 324*a*, 359, 369, 381, 392, 396*a*, 404, 407*b*, 421, 446, 453, 455, 486, 497, 532, 534, 562, 585, 607, 610, 616, 622, 633.

ACKNOWLEDGEMENTS

Also these arrangements:

1a, 2a, 10a and b, 14, 15a, 26a, 45a, 70, 96a, 97a and b, 105a, 129b, 138, 145b, 151a, 157, 158a and b, 164a, 188a, 211, 213a, 228, 239, 253a, 268, 277, 294, 304a, 319a, 337, 383a and b, 385a, 386a, 387a, 388a, 390, 391, 407a, 409a, 410, 423, 425, 428, 430, 448, 466, 474a, 477a, 479, 501, 504a, 505, 507a, 512a and b, 514, 516b, 519, 520, 523, 525, 538, 551a, 554, 558a and b, 564b, 567, 581, 586, 587, 588, 591 (alternative version), 598, 601, 602 (alternative version), 605, 608, 609, 612, 618. And (from the *Plainsong Hymn Book*) 16, 37, 74a, 82a, 84a, 95a, 129a, 145a, 384a, 503a, 516a, 564a, 600.

Also these descants:

3, 24b, 59, 108, 147a, 161, 165, 197, 222, 292b, 371, 593.

Apologies are offered to any authors or composers whose names have been omitted from the above lists, through inadvertence or inability to trace; mistakes will be rectified as soon as possible.

1 January, 1972

COPYRIGHT AND GRANTS

For permission to print copyright hymns and tunes belonging to the Company, whether in permanent or temporary form, application should be made to HYMNS ANCIENT AND MODERN LIMITED, c/o Messrs William Clowes & Sons, Ltd., Publishing Office, 31 Newgate, Beccles, Suffolk, NR34 9QB. For other copyright hymns and tunes, application must be made to the respective owners.

Liberal grants of any edition of HYMNS ANCIENT AND MODERN are made by the Company to help parishes in the intoduction of the book or in the renewal of existing supplies. An application form for a grant can be obtained from the Publishers, Messrs William Clowes & Sons, Ltd., Publishing Office, 31 Newgate, Beccles, Suffolk, NR34 9QB.

EXPLANATION OF MARKS

† signifies a slight alteration of the author's original; ‡ a more extensive alteration; * indicates that these verses may be omitted if so desired; (phrasing sign) indicates that there should be no break between the end of a line and that which follows it.

EXPLANATION OF MARKS

† signifies a slight alteration of the author's original; ‡ a more extensive alteration; * indicates that these verses may be omitted if so desired; ⌣ (phrasing sign) indicates that there should be no break between the end of a line and that which follows it.

MORNING

Hymn 1   FIRST TUNE

KEY C   Jam lucis orto sidere   Mode viii

SECOND TUNE

KEY F   Illsley (*or* Bishop)   J. Bishop, 1665–1737

Jam lucis orto sidere

(*Prime*)

1
NOW that the daylight fills the sky,
We lift our hearts to God on high,
That he, in all we do or say,
Would keep us free from harm to-day:

2
Would guard our hearts and tongues from strife;
From anger's din would hide our life:
From all ill sights would turn our eyes,
Would close our ears from vanities:

3
Would keep our inmost conscience pure;
Our souls from folly would secure;
Would bid us check the pride of sense
With due and holy abstinence.

4
So we, when this day is gone,
And night in turn is drawing on,
With conscience by the world unstained
Shall praise his name for victory gained.

[UNISON]
5
All laud to God the Father be;
All praise, eternal Son, to thee;
All glory, as is ever meet,
To God the holy Paraclete.

Tr. J. M. NEALE

MORNING

Hymn 2
FIRST TUNE

KEY **F** Splendor paternae gloriae Mode i

{| d d r m f m r m | m r s s r m f m—r— |

{| m m r m r d t₁ d | r m r d t₁ d r t₁ l₁ — ||

SECOND TUNE

KEY **B♭** Winchester New *Musikalisch Handbuch* (Hamburg, 1690)

	:s₁	d :s₁	l₁ :l₁	s₁ :f₁	m₁		m₁	f₁ :m₁	r₁ :s₁	s₁ :fe₁	s₁ :—	
	:m₁	s₁ :m₁	f₁ :d₁	d₁ :—.t₂	d₁		d₁	d₁ :d₁	t₂ :t₂	m₁ :r₁	r₁ :—	
	:d	d :d	d :f₁	s₁ :s₁	s₁		s₁	f₁ :s₁	s₁ :s₁	d :l₁	t₁ :—	
	:d₁	m₁ :d₁	f₁ :f₁	m₁ :s₁	d₁		d₁	l₂ :d₁	s₂ :m₁	d₁ :r₁	s₂ :—	

	:s₁	d :r	m :d	f :m	r		m	d :l₁	s₁ :d	d :t₁	d :—
	:s₁	s₁ :f₁	m₁ :s₁	f₁ :s₁	s₁		s₁	s₁ :f₁	s₁ :m₁	l₁ :s₁	m₁ :—
	:s₁	s₁ :l₁.t₁	d :d	l₁.t₁:d	t₁		d	d :d	d :d	r :r	d :—
	:s₁.f₁	m₁ :r₁	d₁ :m₁	r₁ :m₁.f₁	s₁		d₁	m₁ :f₁	m₁ :l₁	f₁ :s₁	d₁ :—	

Splendor paternae gloriae

O SPLENDOUR of God's glory bright,
Who bringest forth the light from Light;
O Light, of light the fountain-spring;
O Day, our days illumining;

2
Come, very Sun of truth and love,
Come in thy radiance from above,
And shed the Holy Spirit's ray
On all we think or do to-day.

3
Teach us to work with all our might;
Put Satan's fierce assaults to flight;
Turn all to good that seems most ill;
Help us our calling to fulfil.

4
O joyful be the livelong day,
Our thoughts as pure as morning ray,
Our faith like noonday's glowing height,
Our souls undimmed by shades of night.

[UNISON] 5
All praise to God the Father be,
All praise, eternal Son, to thee,
Whom with the Spirit we adore
For ever and for evermore.

ST. AMBROSE *Tr.* Compilers† (1904)

MORNING

HYMN 3 Morning Hymn   F. H. Barthélémon, 1741–1808
KEY G

(musical notation)

The Descant may be sung for the Doxology

PART 1

1
AWAKE, my soul, and with the sun
Thy daily stage of duty run;
Shake off dull sloth, and joyful rise
To pay thy morning sacrifice.

2
Redeem thy mis-spent time that's past,
And live this day as if thy last;
Improve thy talent with due care;
For the great day thyself prepare.

3
Let all thy converse be sincere,
Thy conscience as the noon-day clear;
Think how all-seeing God thy ways
And all thy secret thoughts surveys.

4
Wake, and lift up thyself, my heart,
And with the angels bear thy part,
Who all night long unwearied sing
High praise to the eternal King.

PART 2

5
Glory to thee, who safe hast kept
And hast refreshed me whilst I slept;
Grant, Lord, when I from death shall wake,
I may of endless light partake.

6
Lord, I my vows to thee renew;
Disperse my sins as morning dew;
Guard my first springs of thought and will,
And with thyself my spirit fill.

7
Direct, control, suggest, this day,
All I design or do or say;
That all my powers, with all their might,
In thy sole glory may unite.

The following Doxology may be sung at the end of either Part:

[UNISON]   **8**
Praise God, from whom all blessings flow,
Praise him, all creatures here below,
Praise him above, angelic host,
Praise Father, Son, and Holy Ghost.

BISHOP T. KEN†

MORNING

Hymn 4   Melcombe   S. Webbe, 1740–1816
KEY E♭

```
                           B♭. t.
{ :s  |s  :f  |m  :r  |d  :l  |s   ‖ s d  |f  :m  |r  :d  |d  :t, |d :—  ‖
{ :d  |s, :l,.t,|d :t, |l, :d |d     r s, |f, :s, |s, :m, |r, :r, |m, :—
{ :m  |m  :f   |s  :s  |m  :f |m     s d  |t, :d  |t, :d  |l, :s, |s, :—
{ :d  |m  :r   |d  :s, |l, :f,|d     t,m,|r, :m,.f,|s,:l,|f, :s, |d, :—  ‖

   f. E♭.
{ :¹,m|m  :f   |s  :m  |r  :—.m|f  ‖ f  |m :r  |s  :f  |m  :r  |d :—  ‖
{ :f,d|d  :t,.l,|s, :d |t, :—.d|r    r  |d :t, |d  :d  |d  :t, |d :—
{ :¹,m|s  :f   |m  :s  |s  :—.s|l    s  |s :s  |s  :l  |s  :—.f|m :—
{ :f,d|d  :r   |m  :d  |s  :—.m|r    t, |d :s, |m, :f, |s, :s, |d, :— ‖
```

NEW every morning is the love
Our wakening and uprising prove;
Through sleep and darkness safely brought,
Restored to life and power and thought.

2

New mercies, each returning day,
Hover around us while we pray;
New perils past, new sins forgiven,
New thoughts of God, new hopes of heaven.

3

If on our daily course our mind ⌣
Be set to hallow all we find,
New treasures still, of countless price,
God will provide for sacrifice.

4

The trivial round, the common task,
Will furnish all we need to ask,
Room to deny ourselves, a road ⌣
To bring us daily nearer God.

5

Only, O Lord, in thy dear love
Fit us for perfect rest above;
And help us, this and every day,
To live more nearly as we pray.

J. Keble†

Hymn 5   St. Timothy   Sir H. W. Baker, 1821–77
KEY A♭

```
                                   E♭. t.
{ :s, |d :—.d |t, :d  |r  :r  |d   ‖ d f  |m  :d  |r  :r  |d  :—  |—  ‖
{ :m, |m, :—.s,|s, :s, |l, :s, |m,   m l,.t,|d :d  |l, :t, |d  :—  |—
{ :d  |d :—.d |r  :d  |d  :t, |d    d f  |s  :s  |f  :f  |m  :—  |—
{ :d, |d, :—.m,|s, :m, |f, :s, |d,   ¹r  |d  :m, |f, :s, |d  :—  |— ‖

   f. A♭.
{ :s r|m :—.m |r  :d  |f  :m  |r  ‖ r  |s, :l,.t,|d :t, |d  :— |—  ‖
{ :r l,|se,:—.se,|t, :l, |s, :s, |s,   s, |s, :f, |m, :s,.f,|m, :— |—
{ :r l,|t, :—.t,|m :m  |r  :d  |t,   t, |d :d  |d  |d  :— |—
{ :ta,f,|m, :—.m,|se, :l, |t, :d  |s,   f, |m, :f, |s, :s, |d, :— |— ‖
```

4

MORNING

MY Father, for another night
  Of quiet sleep and rest,
For all the joy of morning light,
  Thy holy name be blest.

2
Now with the new-born day I give
  Myself anew to thee,
That as thou willest I may live,
  And what thou willest be.

3
Whate'er I do, things great or small,
  Whate'er I speak or frame,
Thy glory may I seek in all,
  Do all in Jesus' name.

4
My Father, for his sake, I pray,
  Thy child accept and bless;
And lead me by thy grace to-day
  In paths of righteousness.

SIR H. W. BAKER

HYMN 6   Sunrise   *Trier Gesangbuch*, 1695

KEY G

[tonic sol-fa notation]

---

mf AT thy feet, O Christ, we lay
Thine own gift of this new day;
Doubt of what it holds in store
Makes us crave thine aid the more;
Lest it prove a time of loss,
Mark it, Saviour, with thy Cross.

2
If it flow on calm and bright,
Be thyself our chief delight;
p If it bring unknown distress,
Good is all that thou canst bless;
Only, while its hours begin,
Pray we, keep them clear of sin.

3
mf We in part our weakness know,
And in part discern our foe;
Well for us, before thine eyes
All our danger open lies;
Turn not from us, while we plead
Thy compassions and our need.

4
Fain would we thy word embrace,
Live each moment on thy grace,
All our selves to thee consign,
Fold up all our wills in thine,
Think and speak and do and be
Simply that which pleases thee.

5
Hear us, Lord, and that right soon;
Hear, and grant the choicest boon
That thy love can e'er impart,
Loyal singleness of heart:
f   So shall this and all our days,
Christ our God, show forth thy praise.

W. BRIGHT

MORNING

Hymn 7 Ratisbon J. G. Werner, *Choralbuch*, 1815
Key D

```
{ | s  :s  | l  :t  | d' :d' | t  :-  || l  :d' | s  :m  | f  :r  | d  :-  ||
  | d  :d  | d  :f  | m  :m  | r  :-  || d  :m  | r  :d  | d  :t, | d  :-  ||
  | m  :s  | f  :f  | s  :s  | s  :-  || m  :m  | s  :s  | l  :s  | m  :-  ||
  | d  :m  | f  :r  | d  :d  | s, :-  || l, :l, | t, :d  | f, :s, | d  :-  || }

{ | m  :m  | r  :m  | f  :f  | m  :-  || m  :l  | se :l  | t  :t  | l  :-  ||
  | d  :d  | t, :d  | d  :r  | d  :-  || d  :m  | m.r:d  | f  :m  | d  :-  ||
  | s  :s  | s  :s  | l  :s  | s  :-  || s  :d' | t  :l  | l  :se | l  :-  ||
  | d  :d  | s, :d  | l, :t, | d  :-  || d  :l, | m  :f  | r  :m  | l, :-  || }

{ | d' :l  | s  :m  | f  :f  | m  :-  || l  :l  | s  :m  | r  :r  | d  :-  ||
  | d  :d  | t, :d  | d  :r.d|t, :-   || m  :d  | r  :d  | d  :t, | d  :-  ||
  | l  :f  | r  :l  | l  :t.l|se :-   || l  :m  | s  :s  | l  :s  | m  :-  ||
  | f, :f, | s, :l, | r  :r  | m  :-  || d  :l, | t, :d  | f, :s, | d  :-  || }
```

f CHRIST, whose glory fills the skies,
 Christ, the true, the only Light,
Sun of Righteousness, arise,
 Triumph o'er the shades of night;
Dayspring from on high, be near;
Daystar, in my heart appear.

2

p Dark and cheerless is the morn
 Unaccompanied by thee;
Joyless is the day's return,
 Till thy mercy's beams I see,
Till they inward light impart,
Glad my eyes, and warm my heart.

3

mf Visit then this soul of mine,
 Pierce the gloom of sin and grief;
Fill me, radiancy divine,
 Scatter all my unbelief;
f More and more thyself display,
Shining to the perfect day.

C. WESLEY

MORNING

HYMN 8 Hilderstone P. Hart (*c.* 1713)

KEY **G**

{| d :m.f |s :l | s :-.f |m || d |m :l |r :s | s :fe |s :— ||
 | s₁ :d.d |d :d | d :t₁ |d || d |d :d |r.d:t₁| d.t₁:l₁ |s₁ :— ||
 | m :s.l |s :f.m |r :s | s || m |s.f:m |s :s | m.r :d |t₁ :— ||
 | d :d.l₁|m₁ :f₁| s₁ :s₁|d || d |d :d |t₁ :m | l₁ :r₁ |s₁ :— ||}

f. C. G. t.

{|:r l|l :t |d' :t | d' :r'|m' || d'f|r :m.f|s :d | d :t₁ |d :— ||
 |:s r|m :m |m :s | s :-.f|m || m l₁|t₁ :t₁ |d :l₁ | s₁ :s₁|s₁ :— ||
 |:ta f|m :se|l :r' | d' :t |d' || d'f|s :s |s :f.m|r :r |m :— ||
 |:s r|d :m |l :s.f|m :s |d || l r|s₁ :f₁|m₁:f₁ | s₁ :s₁|d₁ :— ||}

GOD of the morning at whose voice
The cheerful sun makes haste to rise,
And like a giant doth rejoice
To run his journey through the skies;

2

O, like the sun, may I fulfil
The appointed duties of the day,
With ready mind and active will
March on, and keep my heavenly way.

3

Give me thy counsel for my guide,
And then receive me to thy bliss:
All my desires and hopes beside
Are faint and cold, compared with this.

I. WATTS

Alternative Tune, Truro, 220

MORNING

Hymn 9 FIRST TUNE

KEY D Veryan   G. H. Knight

[sheet music]

4. B♭.

[sheet music]

F. t.   D. 3.

[sheet music]

SECOND TUNE

KEY D Gerrans   A. H. Brown, 1830–1926

[sheet music]

A. t.

[sheet music]

MORNING

f. D.

```
{ s,r :r  |m :f  | f :—  |m :—  | d' :l  |se :t | l :—  |— :
  m,t,:t, |d :r  | r :—  |d :—  | d  :m |m :—.r| d :—  |— :
   d s :s |s :l  | s :—  |s :—  | l  :l |t :se | l :—  |— :
   d s :f |m :r  | t,:—  |d :—  | l, :d |m :m  | l :—  |— :  }

{ l :f  |m :r  | s :—  |d :—  | m :r  |d :t,  | d :—  |— :—
  d :r  |d :t, | d :—  |d :—  | t,:l, |s,:s,  | s,:—  |— :—
  l :l  |s :s  | s :—  |m :—  | s :f  |m :r   | m :—  |— :—
  f :r  |s :f  | m :—  |l,:—  | m,:f, |s,:s,  | d :—  |— :— }
```

ἐξεγερθέντες τοῦ ὕπνου

mf   AWAKED from sleep we fall⏝
        Before thee, God of love,
        And chant the praise the angels raise,
          O God of might, above:
        Holy, Holy, Holy! Thou art God adored!
p   In thy pitying mercy show us mercy, Lord.

2

mf   As at thy call I rise,
        Shine on this mind and heart,
        And touch my tongue, that I among⏝
          Thy choir may take my part:
        Holy, Holy, Holy! Trinity adored!
p   In thy pitying mercy show me mercy, Lord.

3

mf   The Judge will come with speed,
        And each man's deeds be known,
        Our trembling cry shall rise on high
          At midnight to thy throne:
        Holy, Holy, Holy! King of Saints adored!
p   In the hour of judgement show us mercy, Lord.

Tr. R. M. MOORSOM

MORNING

HYMN 10

FIRST TUNE

KEY B♭ Nocte surgentes   Mode vi

Nocte surgentes

{| l₁   d   t₁ l₁   d   d   l₁   t₁   s₁   l₁   d—   d— }
1 Let hearts a- wa- ken, now the night is end- ed,
2 So, with the an- thems of the blest u- ni- ting,
3 Grant this, O Fa- ther, Son, and Ho- ly Spi- rit,

{| d   d   d   r   d   d   d   d   r   m—   r— }
1 And raise their morn- ing psalm of ad- o- ra- tion,
2 May we find grace to win the courts ce- les- tial,
3 Tri- ni- ty bless- sèd who one God- head shar- est:

{| m   r   d   r   d   r   m d t₁   l₁d s₁— | l₁   s₁   l₁ d—d— ||
1 In sweet- est con- cert the Cre- a- tor's glo- ry Joy- ful- ly sing- ing.
2 And hymn the praise of heaven's high King e- ter- nal Through life un- end- ing.
3 Thine be the glo- ry through the whole cre- a- tion Now and for ev- er.

SECOND TUNE

KEY D   Christe sanctorum   La Feillée, *Méthode*, 1782

May be sung in Unison

{| s :— | m :f | m :r | d :— | m :—.f | s :s | l :— | s :— | s :— | l :t |
  d :— | d :r | t₁ :— | d :— | d :—.d | r :m | f :m | r :— | d :— | m :r |
  m :f | s :l | s :— | m :— | l :—.l | t :t | d' :— | d' :t | s :— | m :s |
  d :r | m :r | s₁ :— | d :— | l₁ :—.l₁ | s₁ :s | f :— | s :— | m :r | d :t₁ |

{| d' :— | s :— | d' :—.t | l :t | l :— | s :— | d' :— | s :l | s :f | m :— |
  d :— | r :— | m :s | r :s | fe :— | s :f | m :— | s :f | r :— | d :— |
  l :— | s :— | s :d' | r' :r' | r' :d' | t :— | d' :— | d' :d' | t :— | d' :— |
  l₁ :— | t₁ :— | d :m | fe :s | r :— | m :r | d :r | m :f | s :— | l :— |

{| f :—.m | f :s | f :m | r :— | s :— | d :f | m :— | r :— | d :— | — :— |
  r :d | r :r | d :— | t₁ :— | d :t₁ | l₁ :r | r :d | — :—.t₁ | d :— | — :— |
  l :l | l :s | s :— | s :— | s :— | l :l | s :— | — :— | m :— | — :— |
  r :l₁ | r :t₁ | d :— | s :f | m :— | f :r | s :— | s₁ :— | d :— | — :— ||

Nocte surgentes

LET hearts awaken, now the night is ended,
And raise their morning psalm of adoration,
In sweetest concert the Creator's glory
    Joyfully singing.

2

So, with the anthems of the blest uniting,
May we find grace to win the courts celestial,
And hymn the praise of heaven's high King eternal
    Through life unending.

MORNING

3
Grant this, O Father, Son, and Holy Spirit,
Trinity blessèd, who one Godhead sharest:
Thine be the glory through the whole creation
Now and for ever.

Tr. C. S. PHILLIPS

HYMN **11** FIRST TUNE

KEY **G** Jam lucis   G. Guidetti, *Directorium Chori*, 1582

DOH	r :-.d	d		DOH	d :t₁	r :-.r	m :—	
SOH₁	s₁ :-.s₁	s₁		SOH₁	s₁ :s₁	l₁ :s₁	s₁ :—	
ME	s :-.m	m		DOH	d :r	r :t₁	d :—	
DOH	t₁ :-.d	d		ME₁	m₁ :s₁	f₁ :s₁	d₁ :—	

ME	r :-.d	d		DOH	d :d	r :-.d	d :—	
DOH	t₁ :-.l₁	l₁		ME₁	s₁ :m₁	s₁ :s₁	m₁ :—	
SOH	s :-.m	m		DOH	d :d	d :t₁	d :—	
DOH	s₁ :-.l₁	l₁		LAH₁	m₁ :l₁	s₁ :s₁	d₁ :—	

SECOND TUNE

KEY **B♭** Warrington   R. Harrison, 1748–1810

s₁ :s₁ :f₁	m₁ :s₁ :d	d :—.r:t₁	d :—		m r :— :r	m :— :r.d
m₁ :m₁ :r₁	m₁ :r₁ :m₁	f₁ :— :r₁	m₁ :—		s₁ s₁ :— :s₁	s₁ :fe₁ :s₁.l₁
d :d :t₁	d :r :d	l₁ :— :s₁	s₁ :—		d d :t₁ :t₁	d :— :r .m
d₁ :m₁ :s₁	d :t₁ :l₁	f₁ :r₁ :s₁	d₁ :—		d₁ s₁ :— :s₁	d₁ :l₂ :t₂.d₁

t₁ :— :l₁	s₁ :— :—		d :d :s₁	l₁ :— :d	f :—.m :r.d
s₁ :— :fe₁	s₁ :— :—		m₁ :s₁ :m₁	f₁ :— :s₁	f₁ :—.s₁ :l₁
r :— :r.d	t₁ :— :—		d :d :d	d :— :d	r :l₁ :r
r₁ :— :r₁	s₁ :— :—		d₁ :m₁ :d₁	f₁ :— :m₁	r₁ :—.m₁ :f₁

d :t₁	l₁	s₁ :— :f₁	m₁ :s₁ :d	d :—.r:t₁	d :— :—	
s₁ :—	f₁	m₁ :— :r₁	m₁ :— :m₁.f₁	s₁ :l₁ :s₁	s₁ :— :—	
m :r	d.r	m :d :t₁	d :— :d.r	m :f :r	m :— :—	
s₁ :—	l₁.t₁	d :m₁ :s₁	d₁ :m₁ :l₁	s₁ :f₁ :s₁	d₁ :— :—	

(*Terce*)   Nunc Sancte nobis Spiritus

COME, Holy Ghost, who ' ever One   In will and deed, by ' heart and tongue,
Art with the ' Father and the Son,   With all our ' powers, thy praise be sung;
Come, Holy Ghost, our ' souls possess And love light up our ' mortal frame,
With thy full ' flood of holiness.   Till others ' catch the living flame.

3
Almighty Father, ' hear our cry
Through Jesus ' Christ our Lord most high,
Who with the Holy ' Ghost and thee
Doth live and ' reign eternally.

? ST. AMBROSE
Tr. Cardinal J. H. Newman‡

MID-DAY

HYMN 12 FIRST TUNE

KEY **G** Jam lucis G. Guidetti, *Directorium Chori*, 1582

```
{| DOH  |r  :-.d  |d    || DOH  |d  :t,   |r  :-.r  |m  :—  ||
 | SOH, |s, :-.s, |s,   || SOH, |s, :s,   |l, :s,   |s, :—  ||
 | ME   |s  :-.m  |m    || DOH  |d  :r    |r  :t,   |d  :—  ||
 | DOH  |t, :-.d  |d    || ME,  |m, :s,   |f, :s,   |d, :—  ||

{| ME   |r  :-.d  |d    || DOH  |d  :d    |r  :-.d  |d  :—  ||
 | DOH  |t, :-.l, |l,   || ME,  |s, :m,   |s, :s,   |m, :—  ||
 | SOH  |s  :-.m  |m    || DOH  |d  :d    |d  :t,   |d  :—  ||
 | DOH  |s, :-.l, |l,   || LAH, |m, :l,   |s, :s,   |d, :—  ||
```

SECOND TUNE

KEY **B♭** Warrington R. Harrison, 1748–1810

```
{|s, :s, :f, |m, :s, :d  |d :-.r :t, |d :—||m  |r :— :r  |m :— :r.d \
 |m, :m, :r, |m, :r, :m, |f, :—  :r, |m, :—||s, |s, :— :s, |s, :fe, :s,.l, |
 |d  :d  :t, |d  :r  :d  |l, :—  :s, |s, :—||d  |d :t, :t, |d :— :r.m  |
 |d, :m, :s, |d  :t, :l, |f, :r, :s, |d, :—||d, |s, :— :s, |d, :l2 :t2.d,/

{|t, :— :l, |s, :— :—  |d :d :s, |l, :— :d  |f :-.m :r.d \
 |s, :— :fe,|s, :— :—  |m, :s, :m,|f, :— :s, |f, :-.s, :l, |
 |r  :— :r.d|t, :— :—  |d :d :d  |d :— :d  |r :l, :r  |
 |r, :— :r, |s, :— :—  |d, :m, :d,|f, :— :m,|r, :-.m, :f, /

{|d :t, ||l, |s, :— :f, |m, :s, :d  |d :-.r :t, |d :— :—||
 |s, :— ||f, |m, :— :r, |m, :— :m,.f,|s, :l, :s, |s, :— :—||
 |m :r  ||d.r|m :d :t, |d :_ :d.r |m :f :r  |m :— :—||
 |s, :— ||l,.t,|d :m, :s,|d, :m, :l, |s, :f, :s, |d, :— :—||
```

(*Sext*)

Rector potens, verax Deus

O GOD of truth, O ¹ Lord of might,
Who orderest ¹ time and change aright,
Arraying morn with ¹ joyful gleams,
And kindling ¹ noonday's fiery beams;

MID-DAY

2

Quench thou on earth the ' flames of strife;
From passion's ' heat preserve our life;
Our bodies keep from ' perils free,
And grant our ' souls true peace in thee.

3

Almighty Father, ' hear our cry
Through Jesus ' Christ our Lord most high,
Who with the Holy ' Ghost and thee
Doth live and ' reign eternally.

? ST. AMBROSE
Tr. Compilers

HYMN 13 St. Peter   A. R. Reinagle, 1799–1877

KEY **D**

{ :s | d' :t | l :s | s :f | m ‖ m r :d | f :m | r :— |— ‖
  :d | m :m | d :d | r :t, | d ‖ d l, :s, | t, :d | t, :— |— ‖
  :m | s :s | f :s | s :s | s ‖ s f :s | s :s | s :— |— ‖
  :d | d :m | f :m | t, :s, | d ‖ d f :m | r :d | s, :— |— ‖ }

{ :m | f :m | l :s | s :f | m ‖ d m :r | d :t, | d :— |— ‖
  :d | d :d | d :d | l, :t, | d ‖ l, d :l, | s, :s,.f, | m, :— |— ‖
  :s | f :s | d :d | r :r | d ‖ m s :f | m :r | d :— |— ‖
  :d.ta, | l, :s, | f, :m, | r, :s, | l, ‖ l, m, :f, | s, :s, | d :— |— ‖ }

BEHOLD us, Lord, a little space
 From daily tasks set free,
And met within thy holy place
 To rest awhile with thee.

2

Around us rolls the ceaseless tide
 Of business, toil, and care;
And scarcely can we turn aside
 For one brief hour of prayer.

3

Yet these are not the only walls
 Wherein thou may'st be sought:
On homeliest work thy blessing falls,
 In truth and patience wrought.

4

Thine is the loom, the forge, the mart,
 The wealth of land and sea;
The worlds of science and of art,
 Revealed and ruled by thee.

5

Then let us prove our heavenly birth
 In all we do and know;
And claim the kingdom of the earth
 For thee, and not thy foe.

6

Work shall be prayer, if all be wrought
 As thou wouldst have it done;
And prayer, by thee inspired and taught,
 Itself with work be one.

J. ELLERTON

EVENING

HYMN 14 Optatus votis *Barking Hymnal*, Mode iv

KEY **D**

(None) Rerum Deus tenax vigor

{| m s l l s s f m | d r f }

1 O God, the world's sus-tain-ing force, Thy-self un-
2 O grant us light at ev-en-tide, That life may
3 Al-migh-ty Fa-ther, hear our cry Through Je-sus

{| m r f r m m— | m s s l s l t l }

1 moved, all mo-tion's source, Who, from the morn till
2 un-im-paired a-bide, And that a ho-ly
3 Christ our Lord most high, Who with the Ho-ly

{| s f m | f s f f m r d m — ||

1 eve-ning's ray, Dost through its chang-es guide the day;
2 death may be The door of im-mor-ta-li-ty.
3 Ghost and thee Doth live and reign e-ter-nal-ly.

? ST. AMBROSE
Tr. J. M. Neale and Compilers (1904)

Alternative Tune, Illsley, 1

HYMN 15 FIRST TUNE

KEY **D** O Lux beata Trinitas Mode viii

O Lux beata Trinitas

{| s l s f m f r m f s l l s s — | s l s f m f }

1 O Tri-ni-ty, most bles-sèd Light, O Un-
2 To thee our morn-ing song of praise, To thee
3 All praise to God the Fa-ther be, All praise,

{| r m f s l l s s — | s l d¹ t d¹ l s f }

1 i-ty of sove-reign might, As now the fie-ry
2 our eve-ning prayer we raise; Thee may our souls for
3 e-ter-nal Son, to thee, Whom with the Spi-rit

{| s l s f m m — | f s s f m f r m f s l l l s s — ||

1 sun de-parts, Shed thou thy beams with-in our hearts.
2 ev-er-more In low-ly rev-er-ence a-dore.
3 we a-dore, For ev-er and for ev-er-more.

EVENING
SECOND TUNE

KEY **F** Westminster   B. Cooke, 1734–93

{:s |s |s :l |s :-.f|m :r |d ||d |r :m |f :m |r :d |s :-||
 :d |d |d :d.r|m :-.r|d :t, |d ||l, |t, :d |r :d |r, :l, |t, :-||
 :m |m |m :f |s :l |s :-.f|m ||m.fe|s :s |s :s |s :-.fe|s :-||
 :d |d |d :f,|m, :f,|s, :s,|l, ||l, |s, :d |t, :d |r :r |s, :-||

{:s |s |s :l |f :s |m :f |r ||r |s :m |l :s.f |m :r |d :-||
 :r |m |m :de|r :t, |d :d |t, ||s, |s, :d.t,|l,.t,:d |d :t, |d :-||
 :t |t |t :l |l :s |s :l |s ||t, |d :d |f :s.l |s :s.f|m :-||
 :s.f|m |m :l,|r :s,|d :f,|s, ||s, |m, :l,.s,|f, :m,.f,|s, :s,|d :-||

O Lux beata Trinitas

O TRINITY, most blessèd Light,
O Unity of sovereign might,
As now the fiery sun departs,
Shed thou thy beams within our hearts.

2
To thee our morning song of praise,
To thee our evening prayer we raise;
Thee may our souls for evermore
In lowly reverence adore.

[UNISON] 3
All praise to God the Father be,
All praise, eternal Son, to thee,
Whom with the Spirit we adore,
For ever and for evermore.

? ST. AMBROSE
Tr. J. M. Neale and Compilers

HYMN 16 Te lucis   Mode viii
KEY **B♭**

{| l, d d d d r d t, | l, l, l, l, t, t, l, s, — }

{| t, t, l, s, m, s, l, l, | d d d d l, t, l, s, — ||

(Compline)   Te lucis ante terminum

BEFORE the ending of the day,
Creator of the world, we pray,
That with thy wonted favour thou
Wouldst be our guard and keeper now.

2
From all ill dreams defend our eyes,
From nightly fears and fantasies;
Tread under foot our ghostly foe,
That no pollution we may know.

3
O Father, that we ask be done,
Through Jesus Christ thine only Son,
Who, with the Holy Ghost and thee,
Doth live and reign eternally.

Tr. J. M. NEALE

Alternative Tune, St. Gregory, 83

EVENING

Hymn 17 — FIRST TUNE

KEY **F** Genevan Psalm xii L. Bourgeois, *Genevan Psalter*, 1551

```
{ |m :— |d :r   |m :— |s :—   |m :d |r :d    |t, :— |l, :—  ||
  |l, :— |l, :t, |d :— |s, :—   |s, :l, |t, :-.l, |l, :se, |l, :— ||
  |d :— |m :s   |s :— |r :—   |m :m |f :m    |m :— |d :—   ||
  |l, :— |l, :s, |d :— |t, :—   |d :l, |r :l,   |m, :— |l, :—  || }
```

C. t.

```
{ |m :— |m l :s |l :— |r' :—   |l :r' |d' :—  |t :— |l :— |— :— ||
  |l, :— |s d :d |f :— |f :—   |m :r |m :—  |m :r |d :— |— :— ||
  |d :— |m l :d'|l :— |t :—    |d' :l |l :—  |se :— |l :— |— :— ||
  |l, :— |d f :m |r :— |r :—   |d :f |d :r   |m :— |l, :— |— :— || }
```

f. F.

```
{ |ʳ l, :— |d :d  |t, :— |l, :—   |m :m |r :t, |d :— |t, :— ||
  |ta,f, :— |s, :s, |s, :— |m, :—  |m, :l, |t, :se, |m, :ba, |se, :— ||
  |f d :— |m :m  |r :— |d :—     |t, :d |f :m  |m :— |m :—  ||
  |ta,f, :— |d, :m, |s, :— |l, :—  |s, :d, |r, :m, |l, :— |m, :— || }
```

```
{ |m :— |s :m |d :— |r :—   |m :l, |d :— |t, :— |l, :— |— :— ||
  |s, :— |s, :s, |l, :— |t, :— |t, :l, |l, :— |se, :— |l, :— |— :— ||
  |m :— |r :d |m :— |s :—   |s :d |m :— |m :— |d :— |— :— ||
  |d :— |t, :d |l, :— |s, :— |m, :f, |d, :r, |m, :— |l, :— |— :— || }
```

SECOND TUNE

KEY **D** Strength and Stay J. B. Dykes, 1823–76

```
{ |m :— |m :f  |s :— |— :l   |s :m |d :f  |m :r |m :— ||
  |d :— |d :d  |d :— |— :l,  |t, :t, |d :d |d :t, |d :— ||
  |s :— |s :f  |m :— |— :f   |m :s |s :f  |s :— |s :— ||
  |d :— |t, :l, |s, :— |— :f, |s, :s, |l, :r |s, :— |d :— || }
```

EVENING

A. t.

[Tonic sol-fa notation]

f. D.

[Tonic sol-fa notation]

[Tonic sol-fa notation]

Rerum Deus tenax vigor

mf O STRENGTH and stay upholding all creation,
    Who ever dost thyself unmoved abide,
Yet day by day the light in due gradation
    From hour to hour through all its changes guide;

2

p Grant to life's day a calm unclouded ending,
    An eve untouched by shadows of decay,
The brightness of a holy death-bed blending
    With dawning glories of the eternal day.

3

mf Hear us, O Father, gracious and forgiving,
    Through Jesus Christ thy co-eternal Word,
Who with the Holy Ghost by all things living
    Now and to endless ages art adored.

? St. Ambrose
Tr. J. Ellerton and F. J. A. Hort

EVENING

Hymn 18 Sebaste
Key E♭

Sir J. Stainer, 1840–1901

φῶς ἱλαρὸν ἁγίας δόξης

Hail gladdening Light, of his pure glory poured / Who is the immortal Father, heavenly, blest, Holiest of Holies, Jesus Christ our Lord!

Now we are come to the sun's hour of rest, The lights of evening round us shine, We hymn the Father, Son, and Holy Spirit divine.

Worthiest art thou at all times to be sung With undefilèd tongue, Son of our God, giver of life, alone:

EVENING

ff rall.

d':d'.d'|t :l	s :d |s : f	m :— | r :—	d:—|—:—
m :m.m|m :f	d :d |m : r	d :— | t₁:—	d:—|—:—
There-fore in all the	world thy glo-ries,	Lord, they	own.
d' :d'.d'|d':d'	d' :s |l : l	s :— | f :—	m:—|—:—
d :l.l |s :f	m :m |f : f	s :— | s₁:—	d:—|—:—

3rd cent. or earlier
Tr. J. KEBLE

HYMN 19 St. Gabriel   Sir F. A. G. Ouseley, 1825-89

KEY E♭

:m	s :f |m :f	m :—.r|d	d	l :s |f :s	m :fe |s :—
:d	d :d |d :d	d :t₁ |d	ta₁	l₁.t₁:de|r :r	d :d |t₁:—
:d'	t :l |s :l	s :f |m	s	f :s |l :s	s :l |r :—
:d	d :d |d :f₁	s₁:s₁ |l₁	m	f :m |r :t₁	d.t₁:l₁ |s₁:—

f. A♭.

:ˢr	r :t₁ |d :l₁	t₁ :t₁ |d
:ᵗᵃf₁	m₁:m₁|m₁:l₁	l₁ :se₁|l₁
:ʳl₁	se₁:t₁|l₁:m	f :m |m
:ˢr₁	m₁:se₁|l₁:d₁	r₁ :m₁ |l₁

E♭. t.

tₗm	d :— |r :—	d :— |—
fe t₁	d :— |— :t₁	d :— |—
re se	l :m |f :—	m :— |—
tₗm	l₁:— |s₁:—	d :— |—

---

mf THE radiant morn hath passed away,
And spent too soon her golden store;
The shadows of departing day‿
 Creep on once more.

2

Our life is but an autumn day,
Its glorious noon how quickly past!
Lead us, O Christ, thou living Way,
 Safe home at last.

3

O by thy soul-inspiring grace
Uplift our hearts to realms on high;
Help us to look to that bright place‿
 Beyond the sky,

4

Where light and life and joy and peace
In undivided empire reign,
And thronging angels never cease‿
 Their deathless strain;

5

Where saints are clothed in spotless white,
And evening shadows never fall,
Where thou, eternal Light of Light,
 Art Lord of all.

G. THRING

EVENING

Hymn 20 Angelus   G. Joseph (1657)

KEY E♭

mf AT even, ere the sun was set,
    The sick, O Lord, around thee lay;
O in what divers pains they met!
    O with what joy they went away!

2

Once more 'tis eventide, and we
    Oppressed with various ills draw near;
What if thy form we cannot see?
    We know and feel that thou art here.

3

O Saviour Christ, our woes dispel;
    For some are sick, and some are sad,
And some have never loved thee well,
    And some have lost the love they had;

4

And some have found the world is vain,
    Yet from the world they break not free;
And some have friends who give them pain,
    Yet have not sought a friend in thee;

5

And none, O Lord, have perfect rest,
    For none are wholly free from sin;
And they who fain would serve thee best
    Are conscious most of wrong within.

6

O Saviour Christ, thou too art Man;
    Thou hast been troubled, tempted, tried;
Thy kind but searching glance can scan
    The very wounds that shame would hide;

7

f Thy touch has still its ancient power;
    No word from thee can fruitless fall:
mf Hear, in this solemn evening hour,
    And in thy mercy heal us all.

                                                         H. TWELLS

EVENING

HYMN 21 St. Anatolius   A. H. Brown, 1830–1926

KEY E♭

[tonic sol-fa notation]

By permission of the Oxford University Press

τὴν ἡμέραν διελθών

THE day is past and over;
  All thanks, O Lord, to thee;
  I pray thee now that sinless
    The hours of dark may be:
O Jesu, keep me in thy sight,
And guard me through the coming night.

2

The joys of day are over;
  I lift my heart to thee,
And ask thee that offenceless
    The hours of dark may be:
O Jesu, keep me in thy sight,
And guard me through the coming night.

3

The toils of day are over;
  I raise the hymn to thee,
And ask that free from peril
    The hours of dark may be:
O Jesu, keep me in thy sight,
And guard me through the coming night.

4

Be thou my soul's preserver,
  For thou alone dost know
How many are the perils
    Through which I have to go:
O loving Jesu, hear my call,
And guard and save me from them all.

Tr. J. M. NEALE‡

EVENING

HYMN 22 Vesper

Sir J. Stainer, 1840–1901

KEY E♭

```
{| m :f   |s :l   |t :d¹  |s :f   || m :r   |d :r   |m :f   |r :—  ||
 | d :t₁  |d :d   |f :m   |r₁:t₁  || d :t₁  |l₁:t₁  |d :r   |t₁:—  ||
 | s :s   |s :f   |f :s   |s :—   || s :f   |m :s   |s :l   |s :—  ||
 | d :r   |m :f   |r :d   |t₁:s₁  || d :s₁  |l₁:s₁  |d :f₁  |s₁:—  ||
```

B♭. t.   f. E♭.

```
{| ᵐl₁:—.l₁|s₁:d  |t₁:f   |m :r   || ᵈs :d  |f :r   |d :—   |— :—  ||
 | ᵈf₁:—.m₁|r₁:s₁ |f₁:l₁  |se₁:—  || ˡm₁:d  |l₁:t₁  |d :—   |— :—  ||
 | ˢd :—.d |t₁:d  |r :d   |t₁:—   || ˡm :m  |r :f   |m :—   |— :—  ||
 | ᵈf₁:—.f₁|f₁:m₁ |r₁:r₁  |m₁:—   || ᶠd :l₁ |f₁:s₁  |d :—   |— :—  ||
```

mf HOLY Father, cheer our way
   With thy love's perpetual ray;
   Grant us every closing day
      Light at evening time.

2

Holy Saviour, calm our fears
When earth's brightness disappears;
Grant us in our latter years
   Light at evening time.

3

p Holy Spirit, be thou nigh
   When in mortal pains we lie;
   Grant us, as we come to die,
      Light at evening time.

4

Holy, blessèd Trinity,
Darkness is not dark with thee;
Those thou keepest always see
   Light at evening time.

R. H. ROBINSON

Alternative Tune, Capetown, 163

EVENING

HYMN 23 Canon   T. Tallis, *c.* 1505–85

KEY **G**

f GLORY to thee, my God, this night
For all the blessings of the light;
Keep me, O keep me, King of Kings,
Beneath thy own almighty wings.

2

mf Forgive me, Lord, for thy dear Son,
The ill that I this day have done,
That with the world, myself, and thee,
I, ere I sleep, at peace may be.

3

Teach me to live, that I may dread
The grave as little as my bed;
Teach me to die, that so I may
Rise glorious at the awful day.

4

O may my soul on thee repose,
And may sweet sleep mine eyelids close,
Sleep that may me more vigorous make
To serve my God when I awake.

5

When in the night I sleepless lie,
My soul with heavenly thoughts supply;
Let no ill dreams disturb my rest,
No powers of darkness me molest.

[UNISON]
6

f Praise God, from whom all blessings flow,
Praise him, all creatures here below,
Praise him above, angelic host,
Praise Father, Son, and Holy Ghost.

BISHOP T. KEN

EVENING

HYMN 24   FIRST TUNE

KEY A♭   Abends   Sir H. S. Oakeley, 1830–1903

SECOND TUNE

KEY F   Hursley   Katholisches Gesangbuch, *c.* 1775

DESCANT

The Descant may be sung for verse 6

mf SUN of my soul, thou Saviour dear,
    It is not night if thou be near:
    O may no earth-born cloud arise
    To hide thee from thy servant's eyes.

2
p When the soft dews of kindly sleep
    My wearied eyelids gently steep,
    Be my last thought, how sweet to rest
    For ever on my Saviour's breast.

3
mf Abide with me from morn till eve,
    For without thee I cannot live;
    Abide with me when night is nigh,
    For without thee I dare not die.

4
If some poor wandering child of thine
    [divine,
Have spurned to-day the voice
Now, Lord, the gracious work begin;
Let him no more lie down in sin.

EVENING

5
Watch by the sick; enrich the poor
With blessings from thy boundless store;
Be every mourner's sleep to-night
Like infant's slumbers, pure and light.

[UNISON] **6**
f Come near and bless us when we wake,
Ere through the world our way we take;
Till in the ocean of thy love
We lose ourselves in heaven above.

J. KEBLE

HYMN **25** Dretzel   C. H. Dretzel, 1698–1775

KEY E♭

{| d :s |s :f |m :r |d :d || d¹ :t |l :t | l :l |s :— ||
 | s₁:s₁ |d :r |d :t₁|d :s₁ || d :r |r :r | m :r |t₁:— ||
 | m :r |d :s |s :—.f|f.m:m || m :s |fe :s | s :fe|s :— ||
 | d :t₁ |l₁:t₁|d :s₁|d :d || l₁ :t₁.d|r :t₁ | d :r |s₁:— ||}

{| d :s |s :f |m :r |d :d || d¹ :t |l :t | l :l |s :— ||
 | d :t₁ |d :r |d :t₁|d :s₁ || d :r |r :r | r :—.d|t₁:— ||
 | m :s.f|m :s |s :—.f|f.m:m || m.fe:s |fe :s | s :fe|s :— ||
 | d :s₁ |l₁:t₁|d :s₁|d :d || l₁ :t₁ |d :t₁.d|r :r₁|s₁:— ||}

{| s :s |l :l |t :t |d¹:— || s :s |f :m | r :r |d :— ||
 | r :d |d :r |r.m:f|f :m || r :d |l₁.t₁:d| d :t₁|d :— ||
 | s :m |m :f |s :s |s :— || s :m |f :s | l :s |m :— ||
 | t₁:d |l₁:r |s₁:s₁|d :— || t₁:d |r :m | f :s |d :— ||}

THROUGH the day thy love has spared us;
  Now we lay us down to rest;
Through the silent watches guard us,
  Let no foe our peace molest:
    Jesus, thou our guardian be;
    Sweet it is to trust in thee.

2
Pilgrims here on earth and strangers,
  Dwelling in the midst of foes,
Us and ours preserve from dangers;
  In thine arms may we repose,
    And, when life's sad day is past,
    Rest with thee in heaven at last.

T. KELLY

EVENING

HYMN 26

FIRST TUNE

KEY **G** All through the night Welsh Traditional Melody

[sol-fa notation]

SECOND TUNE

KEY **D** Nutfield W. H. Monk, 1823–89

[sol-fa notation]

GOD, that madest earth and heaven,
 Darkness and light;
Who the day for toil hast given,
 For rest the night;
May thine angel-guards defend us,
Slumber sweet thy mercy send us,
Holy dreams and hopes attend us,
 This livelong night.

2
Guard us waking, guard us sleeping,
 And, when we die,
May we in thy mighty keeping
 All peaceful lie:
When the last dread call shall wake us,
Do not thou our God forsake us,
But to reign in glory take us
 With thee on high.

1 BISHOP R. HEBER
2 ARCHBISHOP R. WHATELY

EVENING

Hymn 27 Eventide　　　　　　　　　　　　　　　W. H. Monk, 1823–89

KEY E♭

{ |m :— |m :r |d :— |s :— |l :s |s :f |m :— |— :— ‖ m :— |f :s |
  |d :— |t₁:t₁|d :— |d :— |d :t₁|d :r |d :— |— :— ‖ d :— |d :d |
  |s :— |s :f |m :— |d :— |d :s |s :s |s :— |— :— ‖ s :— |f :m |
  |d :— |s₁:s₁|l₁:— |m₁:— |f₁:s₁|l₁:t₁|d :— |— :— ‖ d :t₁|l₁:s₁| }

{ |l :— |s :— |f :r |m :fe|s :— |— :— ‖ m :— |m :r |d :— |s :— |
  |d :— |d :— |d :r |d :d |t₁:— |— :— ‖ d :— |t₁:t₁|d :— |d :— |
  |f :— |m :— |l :s |s :d |r :— |— :— ‖ m :f |s :f |m :— |d':t |
  |f₁:— |d :— |r :t₁|d :l₁|s₁:— |— :— ‖ d :— |s₁:s₁|l₁:— |m₁:— | }

{ |s :f |f :m |r :— |— :— ‖ r :— |m :f |m :r |d :f |m :— |r :— |d :— |— :— ‖
  |d :d |de:de|r :— |— :— ‖ t₁:— |d :t₁|d :t₁|d :r |d :— |t₁:— |d :— |— :— ‖
  |l :l |l :s |f :— |— :— ‖ s :— |s :s |s :f |m :l |s :— |— :f |m :— |— :— ‖
  |f₁:—.s₁|l₁:l₁|r :— |— :— ‖ f :— |m :r |d :s₁|l₁:f₁|s₁:— |— :s₁|d :— |— :— ‖ }

mf　ABIDE with me; fast falls the eventide:
　　The darkness deepens; Lord, with me abide:
　　When other helpers fail, and comforts flee,
　　Help of the helpless, O abide with me.

2

p　Swift to its close ebbs out life's little day;
　　Earth's joys grow dim, its glories pass away;
　　Change and decay in all around I see:
　　O thou who changest not, abide with me.

3

mf　I need thy presence every passing hour;
　　What but thy grace can foil the tempter's power?
　　Who like thyself my guide and stay can be?
　　Through cloud and sunshine, Lord, abide with me.

[UNISON]　　4

f　I fear no foe with thee at hand to bless;
　　Ills have no weight, and tears no bitterness.
　　Where is death's sting? Where, grave, thy victory?
　　I triumph still, if thou abide with me.

5

p　Hold thou thy Cross before my closing eyes;
　　Shine through the gloom, and point me to the skies:
f　Heaven's morning breaks, and earth's vain shadows flee·
　　In life, in death, O Lord, abide with me.

　　　　　　　　　　　　　　　　　　　　H. F. LYTE

EVENING

Hymn 28 St. Matthias   W. H. Monk, 1823–89

KEY **F**

[sol-fa notation]

mf SWEET Saviour, bless us ere we go;
   Thy word into our minds instil,
   And make our lukewarm hearts to glow
   With lowly love and fervent will.
f Through life's long day and death's dark night,
   O gentle Jesus, be our Light.

2

p The day is done, its hours have run,
   And thou hast taken count of all,
   The scanty triumphs grace hath won,
   The broken vow, the frequent fall.
f Through life's long day, etc.

3

mf Grant us, dear Lord, from evil ways,
   True absolution and release;
   And bless us, more than in past days,
   With purity and inward peace.
f Through life's long day, etc.

4

mf Do more than pardon; give us joy,
   Sweet fear, and sober liberty,
   And loving hearts without alloy
   That only long to be like thee.
f Through life's long day, etc.

EVENING

5

p For all we love, the poor, the sad,
　　The sinful, unto thee we call;
mf O let thy mercy make us glad:
　　Thou art our Jesus, and our all.
f Through life's long day, etc.

F. W. FABER

Alternative Tune, Stella, 203

HYMN 29 St. Columba   Traditional Irish Melody

KEY E♭

Labente jam solis rota

p AS now the sun's declining rays
　　At eventide descend,
　So life's brief day is sinking down
　　To its appointed end.

2

Lord, on the Cross thine arms were stretched
　To draw thy people nigh:
O grant us then that Cross to love,
　And in those arms to die.

[UNISON] 3

f All glory to the Father be,
　All glory to the Son,
All glory, Holy Ghost, to thee,
　While endless ages run.

C. COFFIN
Tr. J. CHANDLER‡

Alternative Tune, St. Peter, 13

EVENING

Hymn 30 St. Columba
H. S. Irons, 1834–1905

KEY **F**

{music notation}

Sol praeceps rapitur

p THE sun is sinking fast,
The daylight dies;
Let love awake, and pay_
Her evening sacrifice.

2
As Christ upon the Cross
His head inclined,
And to his Father's hands
His parting soul resigned,

mf So now herself my soul
Would wholly give_
Into his sacred charge,
In whom all spirits live;

4
So now beneath his eye
Would calmly rest,
Without a wish or thought
Abiding in the breast,

5
Save that his will be done,
Whate'er betide,
Dead to herself, and dead_
In him to all beside.

6
f Thus would I live; yet now_
Not I, but he,
In all his power and love
Henceforth alive in me.

7
One sacred Trinity!
One Lord divine!
May I be ever his,
And he for ever mine.

c. 18th cent.
Tr. E. CASWALL†

Hymn 31 FIRST TUNE
KEY **A♭** Ellers
E. J. Hopkins, 1818–1901

{music notation}

30

EVENING

HYMN 31   SECOND TUNE

KEY **D**   Pax Dei   J. B. Dykes, 1823–76

(At the end of Service)

mf SAVIOUR, again to thy dear name we raise
With one accord our parting hymn of praise;
We stand to bless thee ere our worship cease;
p Then, lowly kneeling, wait thy word of peace.

2

Grant us thy peace upon our homeward way;
With thee began, with thee shall end, the day:
Guard thou the lips from sin, the hearts from shame,
That in this house have called upon thy name.

3

Grant us thy peace, Lord, through the coming night;
f Turn thou for us its darkness into light;
From harm and danger keep thy children free,
For dark and light are both alike to thee.

4

mf Grant us thy peace throughout our earthly life,
Our balm in sorrow, and our stay in strife;
p Then, when thy voice shall bid our conflict cease,
Call us, O Lord, to thine eternal peace.

J. ELLERTON

EVENING

HYMN 32 Beulah G. M. Garrett, 1834–97

KEY E♭

(At the end of Service)

mf AND now the wants are told, that brought
Thy children to thy knee;
Here lingering still, we ask for nought,
But simply worship thee.

2
The hope of heaven's eternal days
Absorbs not all the heart
That gives thee glory, love, and praise,
For being what thou art.

3
For thou art God, the One, the Same,
O'er all things high and bright;
And round us, when we speak thy name,
There spreads a heaven of light.

4
p O wondrous peace, in thought to dwell
On excellence divine;
To know that nought in man can tell
How fair thy beauties shine!

5
mf O thou, above all blessing blest,
O'er thanks exalted far,
Thy very greatness is a rest
To weaklings as we are;

6
For when we feel the praise of thee
A task beyond our powers,
We say, 'A perfect God is he,
And he is fully ours.'

[UNISON]
7
f All glory to the Father be,
All glory to the Son,
All glory, Holy Ghost, to thee,
While endless ages run.

W. BRIGHT

HYMN 33 FIRST TUNE
KEY G Ardgowan K. G. Finlay

EVENING

[Tonic sol-fa notation for first tune]

HYMN 33   SECOND TUNE

KEY A♭   St. Clement   C. C. Scholefield, 1839–1904

[Tonic sol-fa notation for second tune]

mf THE day thou gavest, Lord, is ended,
    The darkness falls at thy behest;
To thee our morning hymns ascended,
    Thy praise shall sanctify our rest.

2

We thank thee that thy Church unsleeping,
    While earth rolls onward into light,
Through all the world her watch is keeping,
    And rests not now by day or night.

3

As o'er each continent and island
    The dawn leads on another day,
The voice of prayer is never silent,
    Nor dies the strain of praise away.

4

The sun that bids us rest is waking
    Our brethren 'neath the western sky,
And hour by hour fresh lips are making
    Thy wondrous doings heard on high.

[UNISON]

5

f So be it, Lord; thy throne shall never,
    Like earth's proud empires, pass away;
Thy Kingdom stands, and grows for ever,
    Till all thy creatures own thy sway.

J. ELLERTON

EVENING

HYMN 34 Innsbruck
KEY G
Volkslied (15th cent.)

mf THE duteous day now closeth,
Each flower and tree reposeth,
 Shade creeps o'er wild and wood:
Let us, as night is falling,
On God our Maker calling,
 Give thanks to him, the giver good.

2
Now all the heavenly splendour
Breaks forth in starlight tender
 From myriad worlds unknown;
And man, the marvel seeing,
Forgets his selfish being,
 For joy of beauty not his own.

3
His care he drowneth yonder,
Lost in the abyss of wonder;
 To heaven his soul doth steal:
This life he disesteemeth,
The day it is that dreameth,
 That doth from truth his vision seal.

4
p Awhile his mortal blindness
May miss God's loving-kindness,
 And grope in faithless strife:
cr But when life's day is over
Shall death's fair night discover
 The fields of everlasting life.

Yattendon Hymnal Based on
Nun ruhen alle Wälder, P. GERHARDT

HYMN 35 Thuringia
KEY G
A. Drese, 1620–1701

EVENING

mf ROUND me falls the night;
　Saviour, be my light:
Through the hours in darkness shrouded
Let me see thy face unclouded;
　Let thy glory shine
　In this heart of mine.

2

p Earthly work is done,
　Earthly sounds are none;
Rest in sleep and silence seeking,
Let me hear thee softly speaking;
　In my spirit's ear
　Whisper, 'I am near.'

3

mf Blessèd, heavenly Light,
　Shining through earth's night;
Voice, that oft of love hast told me;
Arms, so strong to clasp and hold me;
　Thou thy watch wilt keep,
　Saviour, o'er my sleep.

W. ROMANIS

HYMN 36　Twyford

L. J. Blake

KEY **G**

[sol-fa notation]

By permission of Novello & Co., Ltd.

mf AND now another day is gone,
　I'll sing my Maker's praise,
My comforts every hour make known,
　His providence and grace.

2

p I lay my body down to sleep;
　May angels guard my head,
And through the hours of darkness keep
　Their watch around my bed.

3

f With cheerful heart I close my eyes,
　Since thou wilt not remove;
And in the morning let me rise
　Rejoicing in thy love.

I. WATTS

35

EVENING

HYMN 37 Sol praeceps rapitur   *Paris Antiphonal,* 1681
KEY **C**   Mode iii

1. Fast sinks the sun to rest, Fast fall the shades of night;
   Fain would the weary heart Keep love's frail flame alight,
   End the day that fading dies With an offering of sacrifice.

2. E'en as the Crucified, Calm in the hour of death,
   Into his Father's hands Yielded his latest breath,
   So my spirit would repose Safe in God's mighty keeping close.

3. Meekly beneath his hand Lieth my helplessness,
   Thinking and caring naught Save what he purposes,
   And in utter calm abides, Dead to self and to all besides.

4. Be it not I who live But God who lives in me,
   Reigning and triumphing In love's sweet majesty;
   May he mine for ever be, God who One is in Trinity.

c. 18th cent.   Tr. C. S. PHILLIPS

HYMN 38 Allington   *J. Hopkins,* 1822–1900
KEY **G**

(For Festivals)

mf   1. OUR day of praise is done;
      The evening shadows fall;
      But pass not from us with the sun,
      True Light that lightenest all.

f   2. Around the throne on high,
      Where night can never be,
      The white-robed harpers of the sky
      Bring ceaseless hymns to thee.

p   3. Too faint our anthems here;
      Too soon of praise we tire:
mf But O the strains how full and clear
      Of that eternal choir!

4. Yet, Lord, to thy dear will
   If thou attune the heart,
   We in thine angels' music still
   May bear our lower part.

EVENING

5
'Tis thine each soul to calm,
Each wayward thought reclaim,
And make our life a daily psalm
Of glory to thy name.

f **6**
A little while, and then
Shall come the glorious end;
And songs of angels and of men
In perfect praise shall blend.

J. ELLERTON

Alternative Tune, Carlisle, 374

SUNDAY

HYMN 39 Lübeck   J. Freylinghausen, *Gesangbuch*, 1704
KEY D

```
{ |d :m |s :s |l :t |d' :— || t :d' |r' :t |l :l |s :— |
  |d :d |r :m |d :r |m :— || r :s |r :m |m :r |t₁ :— |
  |m :l |t :d' |l :f |s :— || s :s |s :s |s :fe |s :— |
  |d :l₁ |s₁ :d |f :r |d :— || s :m |t₁ :m |d :r |s₁ :— }

{ |m :f |s :s |r :m |f :— || m :f |s :m |r :r |d :— |
  |d :d |t₁ :d |r :de |r :— || d :r |r :d |d :t₁ |d :— |
  |s :f |r :s |l :s |l :— || l :l |s :s |s :—.f |m :— |
  |d :l₁ |s₁ :m |f :m |r :— || l₁ :r |t₁ :d |s₁ :s₁ |d :— }
```

(*Morning*)   **Die parente temporum**

f ON this day, the first of days,
   God the Father's name we praise,
   Who, creation's Lord and spring,
   Did the world from darkness bring.

4
mf Father, who didst fashion me
   Image of thyself to be,
   Fill me with thy love divine,
   Let my every thought be thine.

2
On this day the eternal Son
Over death his triumph won;
On this day the Spirit came
With his gifts of living flame.

5
Holy Jesus, may I be
Dead and risen here with thee,
And upon love's fire arise
Unto thee a sacrifice.

3
O that fervent love to-day
May in every heart have sway,
Teaching us to praise aright
God the source of life and light!

6
Thou who dost all gifts impart,
Shine, good Spirit, in my heart;
Best of gifts, thyself bestow;
Make me burn thy love to know.

7
God, the one God of my heart,
I am thine, and mine thou art;
Take me, blessèd One in Three,
Here I give myself to thee.

18th cent. *Tr.* SIR H. W. BAKER‡

SUNDAY

HYMN **40** Church Triumphant J. W. Elliott, 1833–1915

KEY B♭

En dies est dominica

AGAIN the Lord's own day is here,
The day to Christian people dear,
As, week by week, it bids them tell
How Jesus rose from death and hell.

2

For by his flock their Lord declared
His Resurrection should be shared:
And we who trust in him to save
With him are risen from the grave.

3

We, one and all, of him possessed,
Are with exceeding treasures blessed;
For all he did, and all he bare,
He gives us as our own to share.

4

Eternal glory, rest on high,
A blessèd immortality,
True peace and gladness, and a throne,
Are all his gifts, and all our own.

5

And therefore unto thee we sing,
O Lord of peace, eternal King;
Thy love we praise, thy name adore,
Both on this day and evermore.

Ascribed to THOMAS À KEMPIS
Tr. J. M. Neale and Compilers

SUNDAY

Hymn 41 Wordsworth   W. H. Monk, 1823–89

KEY E♭

[tonic sol-fa notation]

f. A♭.   E♭. t.

1
O DAY of rest and gladness,
  O day of joy and light,
O balm of care and sadness,
  Most beautiful, most bright;
On thee the high and lowly
  Before the eternal throne
Sing Holy, Holy, Holy,
  To the great Three in One.

2
On thee, at the creation,
  The light first had its birth;
On thee for our salvation
  Christ rose from depths of earth;
On thee our Lord victorious
  The Spirit sent from heaven;
And thus on thee most glorious
  A triple light was given.

3*
To-day on weary nations
  The heavenly manna falls,
To holy convocations
  The silver trumpet calls,
Where Gospel-light is glowing
  With pure and radiant beams,
And living water flowing
  With soul-refreshing streams.

4
New graces ever gaining
  From this our day of rest,
We reach the rest remaining
  To spirits of the blest:
To Holy Ghost be praises,
  To Father, and to Son;
The Church her voice upraises
  To thee, blest Three in One.

BISHOP CHR. WORDSWORTH†

Alternative Tune, Offertorium, 176

SUNDAY

HYMN 42 Dominica   Sir H. S. Oakeley, 1830–1903

KEY A♭

f   THIS is the day of light:
Let there be light to-day;
O Dayspring, rise upon our night,
And chase its gloom away.

3
This is the day of peace:
Thy peace our spirits fill;
Bid thou the blasts of discord cease,
The waves of strife be still.

2
mf   This is the day of rest:
Our failing strength renew;
On weary brain and troubled breast
Shed thou thy freshening dew.

4
This is the day of prayer:
Let earth to heaven draw near;
Lift up our hearts to seek thee there,
Come down to meet us here.

5
f   This is the first of days:
Send forth thy quickening breath,
And wake dead souls to love and praise,
O vanquisher of death.

J. ELLERTON

HYMN 43 Bishopthorpe   J. Clarke, *c.* 1659–1707

KEY G

SUNDAY

f THIS is the day the Lord hath made,
   He calls the hours his own;
Let heaven rejoice, let earth be glad,
   And praise surround the throne.

2
To-day he rose and left the dead,
   And Satan's empire fell;
To-day the saints his triumphs spread,
   And all his wonders tell.

3
Hosanna to the anointed King,
   To David's holy Son!
O help us, Lord, descend and bring
   Salvation from thy throne.

4
mf Blest be the Lord, who comes to men
       With messages of grace;
   Who comes, in God his Father's name,
       To save our sinful race.

[UNISON]
5
f Hosanna in the highest strains
      The Church on earth can raise;
   The highest heavens in which he reigns
      Shall give him nobler praise.

I. WATTS†

HYMN 44   Vienna   J. H. Knecht, 1752–1817
KEY **G**

(*Evening*)   Lucis Creator optime

mf BLEST Creator of the light,
   Making day with radiance bright,
Thou didst o'er the forming earth
   Give the golden light its birth.

2
Shade of eve with morning ray
Took from thee the name of day;
Darkness now is drawing nigh;
Listen to our humble cry.

3
p May we ne'er by guilt depressed
   Lose the way to endless rest;
Nor with idle thoughts and vain
Bind our souls to earth again.

4
mf Rather may we heavenward rise
   Where eternal treasure lies;
Purified by grace within,
Hating every deed of sin.

5
Holy Father, hear our cry
Through thy Son our Lord most high,
f Whom our thankful hearts adore
With the Spirit evermore.

Tr. COMPILERS

ADVENT

HYMN 45 FIRST TUNE

KEY **F** Conditor alme Mode iv

{| m d m s | l l f s | s l f s f m r m — }

{| s f r m f m r d | d m f s f m r m — ||

SECOND TUNE

KEY **A♭** Brockham J. Clarke, c. 1659–1707

[sol-fa notation]

Conditor alme siderum

1
CREATOR of the starry height,
Thy people's everlasting Light,
Jesu, Redeemer of us all,
Hear thou thy servants when they call.

2
Thou, sorrowing at the helpless cry
Of all creation doomed to die,
Didst come to save our fallen race
By healing gifts of heavenly grace.

3
When earth was near its evening hour,
Thou didst, in love's redeeming power,
Like bridegroom from his chamber, come
Forth from a Virgin-mother's womb.

4
At thy great name, exalted now,
All knees in lowly homage bow;
All things in heaven and earth adore,
And own thee King for evermore.

5
To thee, O Holy One, we pray,
Our Judge in that tremendous day,
Ward off, while yet we dwell below,
The weapons of our crafty foe.

[UNISON] 6
To God the Father, God the Son,
And God the Spirit, Three in One,
Praise, honour, might, and glory be
From age to age eternally.

Tr. J. M. NEALE and Compilers

ADVENT

HYMN 46 Geronimo   Sir C. V. Stanford, 1852–1924

KEY **D**

Ἰδοὺ ὁ Νυμφίος

f   'BEHOLD, the Bridegroom draweth nigh!'
       Hear ye the oft-repeated cry?
         Go forth into the midnight dim;
mf For blest are they whom he shall find
       With ready heart and watchful mind;
         Go forth, my soul, to him.

2
f   'Behold, the Bridegroom cometh by!'
       The call is echoed from the sky:
         Go forth, ye servants, watch and wait;
mf The slothful cannot join his train;
       No careless one may entrance gain:
         Awake, my soul, 'tis late.

3
p   The wise will plead with one accord,
       'O Holy, Holy, Holy Lord,
         On us thy quickening grace bestow,
       That none may reach the door too late,
       When thou shalt enter at the gate
         And to thy Kingdom go.'

4
f   'Behold, the Bridegroom draweth near!'
       The warning falls on every ear:
         That night of dread shall come to all:
       Behold, my soul, thy lamp so dim,
       Rise, rise the smoking flax to trim;
         Soon shalt thou hear his call.

Tr. R. M. MOORSOM

ADVENT

Hymn 47 Merton
W. H. Monk, 1823–89

KEY **F**

Vox clara ecce intonat

f HARK! a thrilling voice is sounding;
  'Christ is nigh,' it seems to say;
  'Cast away the dreams of darkness,
  O ye children of the day!'

2
Wakened by the solemn warning,
  Let the earth-bound soul arise;
Christ, her Sun, all ill dispelling,
  Shines upon the morning skies.

3
mf Lo, the Lamb, so long expected,
  Comes with pardon down from heaven;
Let us haste, with tears of sorrow,
  One and all to be forgiven;

4
That when next he comes with glory,
  And the world is wrapped in fear,
With his mercy he may shield us,
  And with words of love draw near.

5
f Honour, glory, might, and blessing
  To the Father and the Son,
With the everlasting Spirit,
  While eternal ages run.

Tr. E. CASWALL‡

Hymn 48
FIRST TUNE

KEY **G** St. Thomas
Adapted from A. Williams (1765)

ADVENT

Hymn 48 SECOND TUNE

KEY E♭ Franconia *Harmonischer Liederschatz*, 1738

Instantis adventum Dei

THE advent of our King
Our prayers must now employ,
And we must hymns of welcome sing
In strains of holy joy.

2
The everlasting Son
Incarnate deigns to be;
Himself a servant's form puts on,
To set his servants free.

3
Daughter of Sion, rise
To meet thy lowly King;
Nor let thy faithless heart despise
The peace he comes to bring.

4
As Judge, on clouds of light,
He soon will come again,
And his true members all unite
With him in heaven to reign.

[UNISON] 5
All glory to the Son
Who comes to set us free,
With Father, Spirit, ever One,
Through all eternity.

C. COFFIN
Tr. J. Chandler and Compilers

ADVENT

HYMN 49 Veni Emmanuel *Hymnal Noted*
From a French Missal

KEY **G**

UNISON

{ :l₁ | d:—:m | m:—:m | r:f | m:r | d:— || r | m:d | l₁:d | r:t₁ | l₁:s₁ | l₁:—|— ||

{ :r | r:l₁ | l₁:t₁ | d:t₁:l₁ | s₁:— || d | r:m | m:m | r:f | m:r | d:—|— || s | s:—: |m }
　　　　　　　　　　　　　　　　　　　　　　　　　　　　　　　　　　　　Re-joice!　Re-

{ |m:—| :m | r:f | m:r | d || r | m:d | l₁:—:d | r:t₁ | l₁:s₁ | l₁:—|— ||
joice!　Em-man - u-el⌣ Shall come to thee, O Is - ra-el.

Veni, veni, Emmanuel

O COME, O come, Emmanuel,
And ransom captive Israel,
That mourns in lonely exile here,
Until the Son of God appear.
　　Rejoice! Rejoice! Emmanuel⌣
　　Shall come to thee, O Israel.

2
O come, thou Rod of Jesse, free⌣
Thine own from Satan's tyranny;
From depths of hell thy people save,
And give them victory o'er the grave.
　　Rejoice, etc.

3
O come, thou Dayspring, come and cheer⌣
Our spirits by thine advent here;
Disperse the gloomy clouds of night,
And death's dark shadows put to flight.
　　Rejoice, etc.

4
O come, thou Key of David, come,
And open wide our heavenly home:
Make safe the way that leads on high,
And close the path to misery.
　　Rejoice, etc.

5
O come, O come, thou Lord of Might,
Who to thy tribes, on Sinai's height,
In ancient times didst give the law
In cloud and majesty and awe.
　　Rejoice, etc.

Tr. J. M. NEALE and Compilers

ADVENT

HYMN 50 Winchester New *Musikalisch Handbuch*
(Hamburg, 1690)

KEY **C**

```
{ :s  |d' :s  |l  :l  |s  :f  |m  ||m  |f  :m  |r  :s  |s  :fe |s  ·—
{ :m  |s  :m  |f  :d  |d  :-.t₁|d  ||d  |d  :d  |t₁ :t₁ |m  :r  |r  :—
{ :d' |d' :d' |d' :f  |s  :s   |s  ||s  |f  :s  |s  :s  |d' :l  |t  :—
{ :d  |m  :d  |f  :f  |m  :s   |d  ||d  |l₁ :d  |s₁ :m  |d  :r  |s₁ :—
```

```
{ 's  |d' :r' |m' :d' |f' :m' |r' ||m' |d' :l  |s  :d' |d' :t  |d' :—
{ :s  |s  :f  |m  :s  |f  :s  |s  ||s  |s  :f  |s  :m  |l  :s  |m  :—
{ :s  |s  :l.t|d' :d' |l.t:d' |t  ||d' |d' :d' |d' :d' |r' :r' |d' :—
{ :s.f|m  :r  |d  :m  |r  :m.f|s  ||d  |m  :f  |m  :l  |f  :s  |d  :—
```

Jordanis oras praevia

ON Jordan's bank the Baptist's cry
Announces that the Lord is nigh;
Awake, and hearken, for he brings
Glad tidings of the King of Kings.

2

Then cleansed be every breast from sin;
Make straight the way for God within;
Prepare we in our hearts a home,
Where such a mighty guest may come.

3

For thou art our salvation, Lord,
Our refuge, and our great reward;
Without thy grace we waste away,
Like flowers that wither and decay.

4

To heal the sick stretch out thine hand,
And bid the fallen sinner stand;
Shine forth, and let thy light restore
Earth's own true loveliness once more.

[UNISON] 5

All praise, eternal Son, to thee
Whose advent doth thy people free,
Whom with the Father we adore
And Holy Ghost for evermore.

C. COFFIN
Tr. J. Chandler and Compilers

ADVENT

Hymn 51 Helmsley   T. Olivers, 1725–99

KEY A♭

(tonic sol-fa notation)

2
f LO, he comes with clouds descending,
　Once for favoured sinners slain;
　Thousand thousand saints attending
　Swell the triumph of his train:
　　Alleluia!
　Christ appears on earth to reign.

p Every eye shall now behold him
　Robed in dreadful majesty;
　Those who set at naught and sold him,
　Pierced and nailed him to the Tree,
　　Deeply wailing,
　Shall the true Messiah see.

3
mf Those dear tokens of his Passion
　Still his dazzling body bears,
　Cause of endless exultation
　To his ransomed worshippers:
　　With what rapture
　Gaze we on those glorious scars!

[UNISON] 4
f Yea, Amen, let all adore thee,
　High on thine eternal throne;
　Saviour, take the power and glory,
　Claim the kingdom for thine own:
　　Alleluia!
　Thou shalt reign, and thou alone.

C. WESLEY and J. CENNICK

ADVENT

HYMN 52 St. Stephen   W. Jones, 1726–1800

KEY **A**

```
{:d  |s  :m  |d  :r.d |t, :d   |r       ||m.f |s  :d.r |m :r   |d :— |— ||
 :s, |s, :s, |l, :l,  |s, :s,.fe,|s,    ||s,  |s, :m,.f,|s, :s,.f,|m, :— |— ||
 :m  |r  :d  |m  :f   |r  :d   |t,      ||d   |d  :d   |d :t,  |d :— |— ||
 :d  |t, :d  |l, :f,  |s, :l,  |s,      ||d   |m, :l,  |s, :s, |d, :— |— ||

{:m  |f  :r  |m  :f   |s  :r.d |t,      ||l,  |s, :d.r |m :r   |d :— |— ||
 :s, |l, :s, |s, :f,  |m,.s,:l,|s,      ||r,  |m, :m,.f,|s, :s,.f,|m, :— |— ||
 :d  |d  :t, |d  :d.t,|d  :f   |r       ||t,  |d  :d   |d :t,  |d :— |— ||
 :d  |f, :s, |d, :r,  |m, :f,  |s,      ||f,  |m, :l,  |s, :s, |d, :— |— ||
```

[UNISON]

THE Lord will come and not be slow,
   His footsteps cannot err;
Before him righteousness shall go,
   His royal harbinger.

2

Truth from the earth, like to a flower,
   Shall bud and blossom then;
And justice, from her heavenly bower,
   Look down on mortal men.

[UNISON] 3

Rise, God, judge thou the earth in might,
   This wicked earth redress;
For thou art he who shalt by right
   The nations all possess.

4

The nations all whom thou hast made
   Shall come, and all shall frame
To bow them low before thee, Lord,
   And glorify thy name.

[UNISON] 5

For great thou art, and wonders great
   By thy strong hand are done:
Thou in thy everlasting seat
   Remainest God alone.

                                                         JOHN MILTON

ADVENT

HYMN 53 Bristol T. Ravenscroft, *Psalms*, 1621

KEY **G**

[Tonic sol-fa notation — first setting, key G, transitioning f.C. and G.t.]

ALTERNATIVE VERSION
(Melody in the Tenor part)

KEY **G** Harmonized by T. Ravenscroft (1621)

[Tonic sol-fa notation — alternative version, key G, f.C. and G.t.]

The Alternative Version may be used for verses 2 and 4

f HARK the glad sound! the Saviour comes,
    The Saviour promised long:
  Let every heart prepare a throne,
    And every voice a song.

2
He comes, the prisoners to release
    In Satan's bondage held;
The gates of brass before him burst,
    The iron fetters yield.

3
mf He comes, the broken heart to bind,
    The bleeding soul to cure,
  And with the treasures of his grace
    To bless the humble poor.

ADVENT

4
Our glad Hosannas, Prince of Peace,
Thy welcome shall proclaim;
And heaven's eternal arches ring
With thy belovèd name.

P. DODDRIDGE†

HYMN 54   Cross of Jesus   Sir J. Stainer, 1840-1901

KEY G

mf COME, thou long-expected Jesus,
Born to set thy people free;
From our fears and sins release us;
Let us find our rest in thee.

2

Israel's strength and consolation,
Hope of all the earth thou art;
Dear Desire of every nation,
Joy of every longing heart.

3

Born thy people to deliver;
Born a Child and yet a King;
Born to reign in us for ever;
Now thy gracious kingdom bring.

4

mf By thy own eternal Spirit,
Rule in all our hearts alone:
By thy all-sufficient merit,
Raise us to thy glorious throne.

C. WESLEY

Alternative Tune, Halton Holgate, 186

ADVENT

HYMN 55 Sleepers, wake

KEY D

P. Nicolai, 1556–1608
Harmony from J. S. Bach, 1685–1750

[Tonic sol-fa notation]

Wachet auf

SLEEPERS, wake! the watch-cry pealeth,
While slumber deep each eyelid sealeth:
   Awake, Jerusalem, awake!
Midnight's solemn hour is tolling,
And seraph-notes are onward rolling;
   They call on us our part to take.
     Come forth, ye virgins wise:
     The Bridegroom comes, arise!
       Alleluia!
     Each lamp be bright
     With ready light
To grace the marriage feast to-night.

2

Zion hears the voice that singeth,
With sudden joy her glad heart springeth,
   At once she wakes, she stands arrayed:
Her Light is come, her Star ascending,
Lo, girt with truth, with mercy blending,
   Her Bridegroom there, so long delayed.
     All hail! God's glorious Son,
     All hail! our joy and crown,
       Alleluia!
     The joyful call
     We answer all,
And follow to the bridal hall.

ADVENT

3

Praise to him who goes before us!
Let men and angels join in chorus,
  Let harp and cymbal add their sound.
Twelve the gates, a pearl each portal—
We haste to join the choir immortal
  Within the Holy City's bound.
    Ear ne'er heard aught like this,
    Nor heart conceived such bliss.
      Alleluia!
    We raise the song,
    We swell the throng,
    To praise thee ages all along.

P. NICOLAI *Tr.* Frances E. Cox†

HYMN 56 Walsall   Anchor's *A Choice Collection, c.* 1721

KEY **B♭**

[sol-fa notation]

WHEN came in flesh the incarnate Word,
  The heedless world slept on,
And only simple shepherds heard
  That God had sent his Son.

2

When comes the Saviour at the last,
  From east to west shall shine
The aweful pomp, and earth aghast
  Shall tremble at the sign.

3

Lord, who could dare see thee descend
  In state, unless he knew
Thou art the sorrowing sinner's friend,
  The gracious and the true?

4

Dwell in our hearts, O Saviour blest:
  So shall thine advent's dawn
'Twixt us and thee, our bosom-guest,
  Be but the veil withdrawn.

J. ANSTICE

CHRISTMAS

HYMN 57

KEY **G** Sedulius

FIRST TUNE

Nürnbergisches Gesangbuch, 1676

SECOND TUNE

KEY **E** Trinity College

J. B. Dykes, 1823-76

A solis ortus cardine

f FROM east to west, from shore to shore,
   Let every heart awake and sing
The holy Child whom Mary bore,
The Christ, the everlasting King.

2
mf Behold, the world's Creator wears
   The form and fashion of a slave;
Our very flesh our Maker shares,
   His fallen creature, man, to save.

3
For this how wondrously he wrought!
   A maiden, in her lowly place,
Became, in ways beyond all thought,
   The chosen vessel of his grace.

4
She bowed her to the angel's word
   Declaring what the Father willed,
And suddenly the promised Lord
   That pure and hallowed temple filled.

5
p   He shrank not from the oxen's stall,
    He lay within the manger bed,
  And he whose bounty feedeth all
    At Mary's breast himself was fed.

CHRISTMAS

6

mf And while the angels in the sky
　　Sang praise above the silent field,
To shepherds poor the Lord most high,
　　The one great Shepherd, was revealed.

[UNISON] **7**

f All glory for this blessèd morn
　　To God the Father ever be;
All praise to thee, O Virgin-born,
　　All praise, O Holy Ghost, to thee.

SEDULIUS
Tr. J. Ellerton

Alternative Tune, Erfurt, 151

HYMN **58**　Divinum mysterium　　　　Nyland, *Piæ Cantiones*, 1582
KEY **E**

UNISON

{| d :—:r | m :—:f | m :—:r | m :—:r | d :—:— || m :—:f | s :—:l |}

{| s :m :f | s :—:— || l :—:t | d¹:—:s | s :—:f | m :—:r | d :—:— ||}

{| l₁ :—:t₁ | d :—:r | d :l₁:t₁ | d :—:— || d :—:r | m :—:f |}

{| m :—:r | s :—:l | s :m :f | s :—:— || d :—:t₁ | l₁ :—:t₁ | d :—:l₁ |}

{| s₁ :—:— || d :—:r | m :—:s | m :—:d | r :—:— | d :—:— ||}

Corde natus ex Parentis

mf OF the Father's love begotten
　　Ere the worlds began to be,
He is Alpha and Omega,
　　He the source, the ending he,
Of the things that are, that have been,
　　And that future years shall see,
　　　Evermore and evermore.

2

O that birth for ever blessèd!
　　When the Virgin, full of grace,
By the Holy Ghost conceiving,
　　Bare the Saviour of our race,
And the Babe, the world's Redeemer,
　　First revealed his sacred face,
　　　Evermore and evermore.

3

f O ye heights of heaven, adore him;
　　Angel hosts, his praises sing;
Powers, dominions bow before him,
　　And extol our God and King;
Let no tongue on earth be silent,
　　Every voice in concert ring,
　　　Evermore and evermore.

PRUDENTIUS　*Tr.* J. M. Neale‡

NOTE. *A longer version of this hymn will be found in the 'Processional' section* (591)

CHRISTMAS

HYMN 59　Adeste fideles　　　Probably by J. F. Wade, c. 1711–86

KEY A♭

Adeste fideles

Eb.t.

DESCANT	s..f : m.f.s	r : s	d¹.s : s.l	m..f : s.
:	Yea, Lord, we	greet thee,	Born this hap-py	morn-ing;
: .d	d : s₁.d	r : s₁	m.r : m.f	m : r.d f
: .s₁	s₁ : s₁.s₁	s₁ : s₁	s₁.s₁ : s₁.l₁	s₁ : s₁.ᵐl₁
1 O	come, all ye	faith-ful,	Joy-ful and tri-	um-phant, O
2 God	of	God, ...	Light . . of	Light, . . .
3 Sing,	choirs of	an-gels,	Sing in ex-ul-	ta-tion,
4 Yea,	Lord, we	greet thee,	Born this hap-py	morn-ing;
: .m	m : m.m	r : r	d.r : d.d	d : t₁.d f
: .d	d : d.d	t₁ : t₁	d.t₁ : d.f₁	s₁ : s₁.¹r

Eb. t.

	ᵐl.s : l.t	d¹ : m¹.r¹	d¹ : t..d¹	d¹ : —.
	Je-su to	thee be	glo-ry	given;
	f : m.r	m.f : s.l	m : r..d	d : —.
	l₁.t₁ : d.t₁	d : d.d	d : t..d	d : —.
1	come, ye, O	come ye to	Beth-le-hem;	
2	Lo, he ab-	hors not the	Vir-gin's womb;	
3	Sing, all ye	ci-ti-zens of	heaven a-bove;	
4	Je-su, to	thee . . be . . .	glo-ry given;	
	f : s.s	s.f : m.d	s : f..m	m : —
	r : d.s₁	d.l₁ : m₁.f₁	s₁ : —..d	d : —

f. A♭.

¹m : f.s	d.r : m	s.m : m.l	s : r.s
Word of the	Fa-ther,	Now in flesh ap-	pear-ing; O
d¹s : f .m	f : m	r.m : d.r	t₁ : s₁.d
ᵈs₁ : l₁,t₁.d	d.t₁ : d	s₁.s₁ : l₁.l₁	s₁ : s₁.
1 Come and be-	hold him,	Born, the King of	An-gels: O
2 Ve-ry . . .	God, Be-	got-ten not cre-	a-ted:
3 'Glo-ry to	God . . .	In . . . the . . .	high-est:'
4 Word of the	Fa-ther,	Now in flesh ap-	pear-ing,
¹m : f . s	f : s	s.d : m.f	r : t₁
¹m : r . d	r : d	t₁.d : l₁.f₁	s₁ : s₁

s : —	— : —.s	s : —	— : —.m
come,	O	come,	O
d.t₁ : d.r	d : s₁.m	m.r : m.f	m : r.m
:	: .s₁	s₁.s₁ : s₁.s₁	s₁ : s₁.d
come, let us a-	dore him, O	come, let us a-	dore him, O
:	:	:	:
:	: .d	d.t₁ : d.r	d : t₁.s
:	:	:	: .d

56

CHRISTMAS

come, let us adore him, Christ the Lord.
come, let us adore him, Christ the Lord.

18th cent. *Tr.* F. OAKELEY‡

The Descant may be sung for verse 4

NOTE. *A longer version of this hymn will be found in the 'Processional' section* (593)

HYMN 60 Mendelssohn

F. Mendelssohn-Bartholdy, 1809–47

KEY **G** UNISON

HARMONY   UNISON

HARK! the herald-angels sing
Glory to the new-born King,
Peace on earth, and mercy mild,
God and sinners reconciled.
Joyful, all ye nations, rise,
Join the triumph of the skies;
With the angelic host proclaim,
'Christ is born in Bethlehem.'
    Hark! the herald-angels sing
    Glory to the new-born King.

2

Christ, by highest heaven adored,
Christ, the everlasting Lord,
Late in time behold him come,
Offspring of a Virgin's womb.
Veiled in flesh the Godhead see!
Hail, the incarnate Deity!
Pleased as Man with man to dwell,
Jesus, our Emmanuel.
    Hark, etc.

3

Hail, the heaven-born Prince of Peace!
Hail, the Sun of Righteousness!
Light and life to all he brings,
Risen with healing in his wings.
Mild he lays his glory by,
Born that man no more may die,
Born to raise the sons of earth,
Born to give them second birth.
    Hark, etc.

C. WESLEY and others

CHRISTMAS

HYMN **61** Yorkshire

J. Wainwright, 1723–68

KEY **C**

PART 1

f   CHRISTIANS, awake! salute the happy morn,
Whereon the Saviour of the world was born;
Rise to adore the mystery of love,
Which hosts of angels chanted from above:
With them the joyful tidings first begun
Of God incarnate and the Virgin's Son.

2

Then to the watchful shepherds it was told,
Who heard the angelic herald's voice, 'Behold,
I bring good tidings of a Saviour's birth
To you and all the nations upon earth:
This day hath God fulfilled his promised word,
This day is born a Saviour, Christ the Lord.'

3

He spake; and straightway the celestial choir
In hymns of joy, unknown before, conspire;
The praises of redeeming love they sang,
And heaven's whole orb with Alleluias rang:
God's highest glory was their anthem still,
Peace upon earth, and unto men good will.

4

To Bethlehem straight the enlightened shepherds ran,
To see the wonder God had wrought for man,
And found, with Joseph and the blessèd Maid,
Her Son, the Saviour, in a manger laid:
Then to their flocks, still praising God, return,
And their glad hearts with holy rapture burn.

PART 2

5

mf   O may we keep and ponder in our mind
God's wondrous love in saving lost mankind;
Trace we the Babe, who hath retrieved our loss,
From his poor manger to his bitter Cross;
Tread in his steps, assisted by his grace,
Till man's first heavenly state again takes place.

CHRISTMAS

6

f Then may we hope, the angelic hosts among,
To sing, redeemed, a glad triumphal song:
He that was born upon this joyful day
Around us all his glory shall display;
Saved by his love, incessant we shall sing
Eternal praise to heaven's almighty King.

J. BYROM‡

HYMN 62 Winchester Old

Este, *Psalms*, 1592

KEY **F**

:d	m :-.m	r :d	f :.f	m		r	m :s	s :fe	s :—	—	
:s₁	d :-.d	t₁ :l₁	l₁ :d	d		t₁	d :r	r :r	t₁ :—	—	
:m	s :-.s	s :m	f :l	s		s	s :s	l :l	s :—	—	
:d	d :-.d	s₁ :l₁	f₁ :f₁	d		s₁	d :t₁	r :r	s₁ :—	—	

:m	l :-.s	f :m	r :d	t₁		m	r :d	d :t₁	d :—	—	
:d	d :-.d	d :d	t₁ :l₁	se₁		s₁	t₁ :l	l₁ :s₁	s₁ :—	—	
:s	f :-.m	f :s	s :m	m		m	s :m	f :r	m :—	—	
:d	f :-.d	l₁ :d	s₁ :l₁	m₁		d	s₁ :l₁	f₁ :s₁	d :—	—	

ALTERNATIVE VERSION
(Melody in the Tenor part)

KEY **F**

Harmonized by T. Ravenscroft (1621)

:m	s :-.s	s :m	l :l	s		s	s :t₁	r :r	r :—	—	
:s₁	d :-.d	t₁ :d	d :d	d		t₁	d :s₁	l₁ :l₁	t₁ :—	—	
:d	m :-.m	r :d	f :f	m		r	m :s	s :fe	s :—	—	
:d	d :-.d	s₁ :l₁	f₁ :f₁	d		s₁	d :m	r :r	s₁ :—	—	

:d	f :-.m	r :d	t₁ :d	r		d	s :m	f :r	m :—	—	
:s₁	d :-.ta₁	ta₁ :s₁	s₁ :m₁	s₁		s₁	s₁ :s₁	l₁ :s₁	s₁ :—	—	
:m	l :-.s	f :m	r :d	t₁		m	r :d	d :t₁	d :—	—	
:d	f₁ :-.s₁	ta₁ :d	s₁ :l₁	s₁		d	t₁ :d	f₁ :s₁	d₁ :—	—	

The Alternative Version may be used for verses 2, 3 and 4

mf WHILE shepherds watched their flocks by night,
All seated on the ground,
The angel of the Lord came down,
And glory shone around.

2

'Fear not,' said he (for mighty dread
Had seized their troubled mind);
'Glad tidings of great joy I bring
To you and all mankind.

3

'To you in David's town this day
Is born of David's line
A Saviour, who is Christ the Lord;
And this shall be the sign:

4

'The heavenly Babe you there shall
To human view displayed, [find
All meanly wrapped in swathing
And in a manger laid.' [bands,

5

Thus spake the seraph; and forth-
with
Appeared a shining throng
Of angels praising God, who thus
Addressed their joyful song:

6

f 'All glory be to God on high,
And to the earth be peace; [to men
Good will henceforth from heaven
Begin and never cease.'

N. TATE

CHRISTMAS

HYMN 63 St. George   H. J. Gauntlett, 1805–76

KEY **C**

Jam desinant suspiria

f   GOD from on high hath heard!
      Let sighs and sorrows cease!
   Lo, from the opening heaven descends
      To man the promised peace.

2

Hark! through the silent night,
Angelic voices swell;
Their joyful songs proclaim that God
Is born on earth to dwell.

3

mf   See how the shepherd-band
      Speed on with eager feet;
   Come to the hallowed cave with them
      The holy Babe to greet.

4

p   But O what sight appears
      Within that lowly door!
   A manger, stall, and swaddling clothes,
      A child, and mother poor!

5

mf   Art thou the Christ? the Son?
      The Father's Image bright?
   And see we him whose arm upholds
      Earth and the starry height?

6

f   Yea, faith can pierce the cloud
      Which veils thy glory now;
   We hail thee God, before whose throne
      The angels prostrate bow.

7

mf   Our sinful pride to cure
      With that pure love of thine,
   O be thou born within our hearts,
      Most holy Child divine.

C. COFFIN
Tr. Bp. J. R. Woodford and Compilers

CHRISTMAS

HYMN 64 Lewes   J. Randall, 1715–99

KEY **G**

mf ANGELS, from the realms of glory,   *mf* Shepherds, in the field abiding,
      Wing your flight o'er all the earth;   Watching o'er your flocks by night,
      Ye who sang creation's story.   God with man is now residing,
      Now proclaim Messiah's birth: Yonder shines the infant Light:
f   Come and worship,   *f*   Come and worship,
Worship Christ, the new-born King.   Worship Christ, the new-born King.

3
    mf Sages, leave your contemplations;
         Brighter visions beam afar:
         Seek the great Desire of Nations;
         Ye have seen his natal star:
    f   Come and worship,
    Worship Christ, the new-born King.

4
    mf Saints before the altar bending,
         Watching long in hope and fear,
         Suddenly the Lord, descending,
         In his temple shall appear:
    f   Come and worship,
    Worship Christ, the new-born King.

5
    mf Though an infant now we view him,
         He shall fill his Father's throne,
         Gather all the nations to him;
         Every knee shall then bow down:
    f   Come and worship,
    Worship Christ, the new-born King.

                                                                           J. MONTGOMERY

CHRISTMAS

HYMN 65

FIRST TUNE

KEY **G** Forest Green

English Traditional Melody

{:s₁	d :d	d :r	m.r:m.f	s	m	f :m.d	r :r	d :—	—
:s₁	s₁ :l₁	s₁ :l₁.t₁	d :d	t₁	l₁	l₁ :d	d :t₁	d :—	—
:r	m :f	s :f	s :d	r	d	f :s	l :s.f	m :—	—
:t₁	d :f	m :r	d :l₁	s₁	l₁	r₁ :m₁	f₁ :s₁	d :—	—

{:s₁	d :d	d :r	m.r:m.f	s	m	f :m.d	r :r	d :—	—
:s₁	s₁ :l₁	s₁ :l₁.t₁	d :d	t₁	l₁	l₁ :d	d :t₁	d :—	—
:r	m :f	s :f	s :d	r	d	f :s	l :s.f	m :—	—
:t₁	d :f	m :r	d :l₁	s₁	l₁	r₁ :m₁	f₁ :s₁	d :—	—

{:d.m	s :—.l	s.f:m.r	d.r:m.f	s	s₁	d :m	r :d	s₁ :—
:d	t₁ :—.l₁	t₁ :s₁	s₁ :d	t₁	s₁	s₁ :s₁	f₁ :m₁.f₁	s₁ :—
:m	m :—.d	s :s.f	m :d	r	t₁	d :d	l₁.t₁:d	t₁ :—
:l₁	m₁ :—.f₁	s₁ :l₁.t₁	d :l₁	s₁	s₁.f₁	m₁ :d₁	f₁ :l₁	s₁ :—

{	s₁ :—	d :d	d :r	m.r:m.f	s	m	f :m.d	r :r	d :—	—
	s₁ :—	s₁ :l₁	s₁ :l₁.t₁	d :d	t₁	l₁	l₁ :d	d :t₁	d :—	—
	d :r	m :f	s :f	s :d	r	d	f :s.m	s :s.f	m :—	—
	l₁ :t₁	d :f	m :r	d :l₁	s₁	l₁	r₁ :m₁.l₁	s₁ :s₁	d :—	—

By permission of the English Hymnal Company, Ltd.

SECOND TUNE

KEY **G** Wengen

Sir H. Walford Davies, 1869–1941

{:s₁	l₁ :—.t₁	d :f	m.f :m.r	d	s₁	l₁ :d	s₁ :d	l₁ :—	—
:m₁	f₁ :—.s₁	l₁ :l₁	s₁.l₁:s₁.f₁	m₁	m₁	f₁ :l₁	s₁ :s₁	f₁ :—	—
:d	d :—.d	d :r.d	t₁ :l₁.t₁	d	d	d :r.d	s :m	d :—	—
:d₁	f₁ :—.f₁	f₁ :r₁	s₁ :s₁	d₁	d₁	f₁ :f₁	m₁ :d₁	f₁ :—	—

{:s₁	l₁ :—.t₁	d :f	m.f :m.r	d	t₁.d	r :r	r :m.r	r :—	—
:m₁	f₁ :—.s₁	l₁ :l₁	s₁.l₁:s₁.f₁	m₁	s₁.l₁	t₁ :l₁.t₁	d :t₁.l₁	t₁ :—	—
:d	d :—.d	d :r.d	t₁ :l₁.t₁	d	s	s :fe.s	l :s.fe	s :—	—
:d₁	f₁ :—.f₁	f₁ :r₁	s₁ :s₁	d	m	r :r	r :r	s₁ :—	—

{:m	f :m.r	m :f	s :m	f	s	l.s :f.m	r.m :r.d	t₁ :—	—
:t₁	t₁ :t₁	t₁ :t₁	d :r	d	ta₁	l₁ :r	l₁ :l₁	s₁ :—	—
:s	s :s	s :f	m :ta	l	m	f :l.s	f.s :f.m	r.m:s.f	m.f
:m	r :m.f	m :r	d :—	d	d	f :r.m	f :r	s₁ :—	—

CHRISTMAS

The last line of each verse is repeated in Second Tune

    p   O LITTLE town of Bethlehem,
        How still we see thee lie!
        Above thy deep and dreamless sleep
        The silent stars go by:
mf   Yet in thy dark streets shineth
        The everlasting Light;
f   The hopes and fears of all the years
        Are met in thee to-night.

2

        For Christ is born of Mary;
        And, gathered all above,
p   While mortals sleep, the angels keep
        Their watch of wondering love.
f   O morning stars, together
        Proclaim the holy birth,
        And praises sing to God the King,
        And peace to men on earth.

3

p   How silently, how silently,
        The wondrous gift is given!
        So God imparts to human hearts
        The blessings of his heaven.
        No ear may hear his coming;
        But in this world of sin,
        Where meek souls will receive him, still
        The dear Christ enters in.

4

mf   O holy Child of Bethlehem,
        Descend to us, we pray;
        Cast out our sin, and enter in:
        Be born in us to-day.
f   We hear the Christmas angels
        The great glad tidings tell:
        O come to us, abide with us,
        Our Lord Emmanuel.

BISHOP PHILLIPS BROOKS

CHRISTMAS

HYMN 66 Noel Traditional Air, adapted by Sir A. Sullivan,
KEY **F** 1842–1900

[tonic sol-fa notation]

mf IT came upon the midnight clear,
   That glorious song of old,
From angels bending near the earth
   To touch their harps of gold:
'Peace on the earth, good will to men,
   From heavens' all-gracious King!'
The world in solemn stillness lay
   To hear the angels sing.

2
Still through the cloven skies they come,
   With peaceful wings unfurled;
And still their heavenly music floats
   O'er all the weary world:
Above its sad and lowly plains
   They bend on hovering wing;
And ever o'er its Babel-sounds
   The blessèd angels sing.

3
p Yet with the woes of sin and strife
   The world has suffered long;
Beneath the angel-strain have rolled
   Two thousand years of wrong;
And man, at war with man, hears not
   The love-song which they bring:
O hush the noise, ye men of strife,
   And hear the angels sing.

4*
And ye, beneath life's crushing load,
   Whose forms are bending low,
Who toil along the climbing way
   With painful steps and slow,
Look, now! for glad and golden hours
   Come swiftly on the wing;
O rest beside the weary road,
   And hear the angels sing.

5
mf For lo, the days are hastening on,
   By prophet-bards foretold,
When, with the ever-circling years,
   Comes round the age of gold;
f When peace shall over all the earth
   Its ancient splendours fling,
And the whole world give back the song
   Which now the angels sing.

E. H. SEARS

CHRISTMAS

Hymn 67 Cranham

G. T. Holst, 1874–1934

KEY **F**

1. In the bleak mid-winter Frosty wind made moan, Earth stood hard as iron Water like a stone: Snow had fallen, snow on snow, Snow on snow, In the bleak mid-winter Long ago.

2. Our God, heaven cannot hold him Nor earth sustain; Heaven and earth shall flee away When he comes to reign: In the bleak mid-winter A stable place sufficed The Lord God Almighty, Jesus Christ.

3. Enough for him whom cherubim Worship night and day, A breast-ful of milk, And a manger-ful of hay: Enough for him, whom angels Fall down before, The ox and ass and camel Which adore.

4. Angels and archangels May have gathered there, Cherubim and seraphim Thronged the air—But only his mother In her maiden bliss Worshipped the Beloved With a kiss.

5. What can I give him, Poor as I am? If I were a shepherd I would bring a lamb; If I were a wise man I would do my part; Yet what I can I give him— Give my heart.

CHRISTINA ROSSETTI

CHRISTMAS

HYMN 68 Es ist ein' Ros' *Old German*

KEY **G**

[sol-fa notation]

μέγα καὶ παράδοξον θαῦμα

mf A GREAT and mighty wonder,
    A full and holy cure!
  The Virgin bears the Infant
    With virgin-honour pure:
f   Repeat the hymn again!
  'To God on high be glory,
    And peace on earth to men.'

2

mf The Word becomes incarnate,
    And yet remains on high;
  And cherubim sing anthems
    To shepherds from the sky:
f   Repeat, etc.

3

While thus they sing your Monarch,
    Those bright angelic bands,
Rejoice, ye vales and mountains,
    Ye oceans, clap your hands:
  Repeat, etc.

CHRISTMAS

4

mf Since all he comes to ransom,
　　By all be he adored,
　　The infant born in Bethlem,
　　　The Saviour and the Lord:
f　　Repeat, etc.

St. Germanus　*Tr.* J. M. Neale†

Hymn **69**　Kilmarnock　　　　　　　　N. Dougall, 1776–1862
key **E♭**

```
{ :d  |m  :s  |l  :s.m |m  :r  |d   ||  l  |s  :d'.l|s  :d.r|m  :r  |—  ||
{ :s₁ |d  :d  |d  :d   |d  :t₁ |d   ||  d  |d  :d   |d  :d  |d  :t₁ |—  ||
{ :m  |s  :s  |f  :s   |s  :s.f|m   ||  f  |s  :m.f |m  :fe |s  :—  |—  ||
{ :d  |d  :m  |f  :m.d |s  :s₁ |d   ||  f  |m  :l₁  |d  :l₁ |s₁ :—  |—  ||

{ :s  |l  :s  |d' :m.r |d  :r  |m   ||  l  |s  :d.r |m  :r  |d  :—  |—  ||
{ :d  |f  :m.r|d  :t₁  |l₁ :t₁ |d   ||  d  |d  :d   |d  :t₁ |d  :—  |—  ||
{ :s  |d' :t  |m.ba:se |l  :f  |s   ||  f  |s  :l   |s  :s.f|m  :—  |—  ||
{ :m₁ |f₁ :s₁ |l₁ :m   |f  :r  |d   ||  f₁ |m₁ :f₁  |s₁ :s₁ |d  :—  |—  ||
```

BEHOLD, the great Creator makes
　Himself a house of clay,
A robe of virgin flesh he takes
　Which he will wear for ay.

2

Hark, hark! the wise eternal Word
　Like a weak infant cries;
In form of servant is the Lord,
　And God in cradle lies.

3

This wonder struck the world amazed,
　It shook the starry frame;
Squadrons of spirits stood and gazed,
　Then down in troops they came.

4

Glad shepherds ran to view this sight;
　A choir of angels sings,
And eastern sages with delight
　Adore this King of Kings.

5

Join then, all hearts that are not stone,
　And all our voices prove,
To celebrate this Holy One,
　The God of peace and love.

T. Pestel

CHRISTMAS

HYMN 70 Ach Herr   Melody from M. Praetorius, 1571–1621

KEY **G**

1

I SING the birth was born to-night,
The Author both of life and light:
  The angels so did sound it;
And like the ravished shepherds said,
Who saw the light and were afraid,
  Yet searched, and true they found it.

2

The Son of God, the eternal King,
That did us all salvation bring,
  And freed the world from danger,
He whom the whole world could not take,
The Lord which heaven and earth did make,
  Was now laid in a manger.

3

The Father's wisdom willed it so,
The Son's obedience knew no 'No,'
  Both wills were in one stature;
And, as that wisdom hath decreed,
The Word was now made flesh indeed,
  And took on him our nature.

CHRISTMAS

4
What comfort by him do we win,
  Who made himself the price of sin,
    To make us heirs of glory!
To see this Babe, all innocence,
And martyr born in our defence—
    Can man forget this story?

                                BEN JONSON

HYMN 71   Devonshire   J. F. Lampe, 1703–51

KEY E♭

[Tonic sol-fa musical notation]

TO us a Child of royal birth,
  Heir of the promises, is given;
The invisible appears on earth,
  The Son of Man, the God of heaven.

2
A Saviour born, in love supreme,
  He comes our fallen souls to raise;
He comes his people to redeem,
  With all the fulness of his grace.

3
The Christ, by raptured seers foretold,
  Filled with the eternal Spirit's power,
Prophet, and Priest, and King behold,
  And Lord of all the worlds adore.

4
The Lord of Hosts, the God most high,
  Who quits his throne on earth to live,
With joy we welcome from the sky,
  With faith into our hearts receive.

                                C. WESLEY†

NEW YEAR

HYMN 72   FIRST TUNE

KEY A♭   Perranporth   A. W. Wilson

E♭. t.

{|s₁ :l₁.t₁|d :m₁ |s₁ :-.s₁|s₁ :— ||d :m |m :f |s :— ||ˢ¹d :r |m :-.m\
|m₁ :f₁ |s₁ :d₁ |r₁ :r₁ |m₁ :— ||m₁:t₁ |l₁ :l₁ |d :— ||ᵐ¹l₁:l₁ |t₁ :t₁\
|d :d |d :d |d :t₁ |d :— ||m :m.r|d :d.r|m :— ||ᵐ l :l |se :se\
|d₁ :f₁ |m₁ :l₁ |s₁ :s₁ |d :t₁ ||l₁ :se₁|l₁ :f₁ |d :— ||ᵈ f :f |m :r }

{|m :ba |se :— ||l :-.t |l :se |l :— ||l₁ :-.t₁|d :m |l :-.l|s :f\
|l₁ :m |m :— ||d :r |d :t₁ |d :— ||l₁ :-.l₁|l₁ :t₁|l₁ :d |t₁ :d.r\
|l :d¹ |t :— ||l :f |m :m |m :— ||f :-.f |m :m |f :m |r :s\
|d :l₁ |m :— ||f :r |m :m |l₁ :— ||r :-.r |l₁ :s₁ |f₁ :f₁ |s₁ :l₁.t₁ }

f. A♭.

{|m :s .f |m :r |ᵐt₁ :— ||d :s₁ |d :r |m :-.m|s :— ||s :d |f.m :r |d :— |— :— ||\
|d :d .r |d :t₁|ᵈs₁ :— ||s₁ :m₁ |l₁ :l₁|t₁ :d |d :t₁||d :d.t₁|l₁ :t₁|d :— |— :— ||\
|s :s .l |s :s |ˢr :— ||m :d |m :l |se :l |s :f ||m :s |d :f |m :— |— :— ||\
|d :m₁.f₁|s₁:s₁|ᵈs₁ :— ||d :d.t₁|l₁:f₁|m₁:l₁ |m :r ||d :m₁ |f₁ :s₁|d :— |— :— ||}

SECOND TUNE

KEY D   Father, let me dedicate   Sir G. A. Macfarren, 1813–87

{|s :m |f :s |l :-.l|l :— ||t :l |s :-.f|m :— |— :— ||\
|m :d |d :m |m :-.r|r :— ||f :m |r :t₁ |d :— |— :— ||\
|d¹ :s |d¹ :t |l :-.l|l :s ||f :l |r¹ :s |s :— |— :— ||\
|d :-.t₁|l₁:s₁|f₁ :f |f :m ||r :d |t₁ :s₁|d :— |— :— ||}

A. t.   f. D.

{|f :l |r¹ :d¹|ᵗm :-.r |d :— ||r :-.l₁|l₁ :t₁ ||ᵈs :— |— :— ||\
|d :f |s :s |ˢd :s₁ |s₁ :— ||l₁ :-.f₁|f₁ :f₁ ||ᵐt₁:— |— :— ||\
|f :d¹ |t :d¹|ʳs :t₁ |d :r.m||f :-.r |r :r ||ᵈs :— |— :— ||\
|l₁ :f₁ |f :m |ʳs₁ :f₁ |m₁ :— ||r₁ :-.s₁|s₁ :s₁ ||ᵈs₁ :— |— :— ||}

{|f :-.f |m :m |l :-.l |s :— ||d¹ :-.s|f :m |m :— |r :— ||\
|d :-.d |t₁ :t₁|l₁ :t₁ |d :r ||d :d |t₁ :d |d :— |t₁ :— ||\
|l :-.l |s :s |f :-.f |m :r ||s :s |s :s |s :— |— :— ||\
|s₁:-.s₁|s₁:s₁ |s₁ :s₁ |s₁ :f₁||m₁ :m |r :d |s :— |— :f ||}

{|d :-.r |m :f |s :l |t :— ||d¹ :-.l|l :r¹|d¹ :— |— :— ||\
|d :-.t₁|d :d |m :d |m :— ||m :-.f|f :f |m :— |— :— ||\
|s :-.f |m :d¹|d¹ :l |se :— ||l :-.l |l :t |d¹ :— |— :— ||\
|m :-.r |d :l |s :f |m :— ||l₁ :-.r|r :s₁|d :— |— :— ||}

NEW YEAR

mf FATHER, let me dedicate,
    All this year to thee,
In whatever worldly state
    Thou wilt have me be:
Not from sorrow, pain, or care
    Freedom dare I claim;
This alone shall be my prayer,
    'Glorify thy name.'

2

Can a child presume to choose
    Where or how to live?
Can a Father's love refuse
    All the best to give?
More thou givest every day
    Than the best can claim,
Nor withholdest aught that may
    Glorify thy name.

3

p If thou callest to the cross,
    And its shadow come,
Turning all my gain to loss,
    Shrouding heart and home;
mf Let me think how thy dear Son
    To his glory came,
And in deepest woe pray on,
    'Glorify thy name.'

4

If in mercy thou wilt spare
    Joys that yet are mine;
If on life, serene and fair,
    Brighter rays may shine;
f Let my glad heart, while it sings,
    Thee in all proclaim,
And, whate'er the future brings,
    Glorify thy name.

L. TUTTIETT

HYMN 73   Culbach   J. Scheffler, *Heilige Seelenlust*, 1657

KEY E♭

mf FOR thy mercy and thy grace,
    Faithful through another year,
Hear our songs of thankfulness;
    Jesu, our Redeemer, hear.

2

In our weakness and distress,
    Rock of strength, be thou our stay;
In the pathless wilderness
    Be our true and living Way.

3

p Who of us death's awful road
    In the coming year shall tread,
With thy rod and staff, O God,
    Comfort thou his dying bed.

4

mf Keep us faithful, keep us pure,
    Keep us evermore thine own,
Help, O help us to endure,
    Fit us for thy promised crown.

5

f So within thy palace gate
    We shall praise on golden strings
Thee the only potentate,
    Lord of Lords and King of Kings.

H. DOWNTON†

EPIPHANY

HYMN 74   FIRST TUNE

KEY C Hostis Herodes impie   Mode iii

Hostis Herodes impie

```
{|   s    s l t d' l    s      f m  r    r f m   f s   s  —  }
```

1. How vain the thought of Herod's fear,
2. The east - ern sa - ges saw from far
3. With - in the Jor - dan's sa - cred flood
4. And O what mi - ra - cle di - vine,
5. All glo - ry, Je - su, be to thee

```
{|   s    l d'   d'     d' t    l s l t   t    t  —  }
```

1. When told that Christ the King is near!
2. And fol - lowed on his guid - ing star;
3. The heaven - ly Lamb in meek - ness stood;
4. When wa - ter red - dened in - to wine!
5. For this thy glad E - piph - an - y;

```
{|   l    l t d' r' d'  d' t   l s l d' t l   s f   m f s l — }
```

1. He takes not earth - ly realms a - way,
2. By light their way to Light they trod,
3. That he who knew no sin that day
4. He spake the word, and forth it flowed
5. Whom with the Fa - ther we a - dore

```
{|   r   m    f   l    l d' t l   s m f s  f m   m  — ||
```

1. Who gives the realms that ne'er de - cay.
2. And by their gifts con - fessed their God.
3. His peo - ple's sin might wash a - way.
4. In streams that na - ture ne'er be - stowed.
5. And Ho - ly Ghost for ev - er - more.

EPIPHANY

HYMN 74   SECOND TUNE

KEY **G**   Ely   Bishop T. Turton, 1780–1864

Hostis Herodes impie

mf   HOW vain the cruel Herod's fear,
When told that Christ the King is near!
He takes not earthly realms away,
Who gives the realms that ne'er decay.

2

The eastern sages saw from far
And followed on his guiding star;
By light their way to Light they trod,
And by their gifts confessed their God.

3

Within the Jordan's sacred flood
The heavenly Lamb in meekness stood;
That he who knew no sin that day
His people's sin might wash away.

4

And O what miracle divine,
When water reddened into wine!
He spake the word, and forth it flowed
In streams that nature ne'er bestowed.

[UNISON]

f   All glory, Jesu, be to thee
For this thy glad Epiphany;
Whom with the Father we adore
And Holy Ghost for evermore.

SEDULIUS *Tr.* Compilers

EPIPHANY

HYMN 75

FIRST TUNE

KEY A♭ Bede

Adapted from Handel's *Athalia*
by Sir J. Goss, 1800–80

[musical notation in tonic sol-fa]

SECOND TUNE

KEY E♭ Epiphany

E. J. Hopkins, 1818–1901

[musical notation in tonic sol-fa]

f   BRIGHTEST and best of the sons of the morning,
    Dawn on our darkness, and lend us thine aid;
  Star of the east, the horizon adorning,
    Guide where our infant Redeemer is laid.

2

mf Cold on his cradle the dew-drops are shining;
    Low lies his head with the beasts of the stall;
  Angels adore him in slumber reclining,
    Maker and Monarch and Saviour of all.

EPIPHANY

3
Say, shall we yield him, in costly devotion,
  Odours of Edom, and offerings divine,
Gems of the mountain, and pearls of the ocean,
  Myrrh from the forest, or gold from the mine?

4
Vainly we offer each ample oblation,
  Vainly with gifts would his favour secure:
Richer by far is the heart's adoration,
  Dearer to God are the prayers of the poor.

BISHOP R. HEBER

The first verse may be repeated at the end

HYMN **76** Stuttgart   C. F. Witt, 1660–1716

KEY **G**

{|s₁ :s₁ |d :d |r :r |m :d ‖ s :s |l :f |r :s |m :— ‖
 |s₁ :s₁ |s₁ :s₁ |t₁ :t₁ |d :d ‖ r :d |d :d |d :t₁ |d :— ‖
 |s₁ :s₁ |m :m |s :s |s :m ‖ s :m |f :l |s :s |s :— ‖
 |s₁ :s₁ |m₁ :d₁ |s₁ :s₁ |d :d ‖ t₁ :d |f₁ :f₁ |s₁ :s₁ |d :— ‖}

{|m :m |r :m |d :r |d :t₁ ‖ d :l₁ |s₁ :d |d :t₁ |d :— ‖
 |d :d |t₁ :t₁ |l₁ :l₁ |s₁ :s₁ ‖ s₁ :f₁ |m₁ :s₁ |s₁ :s₁ |s₁ :— ‖
 |l :m |f :m |m :r |r :r ‖ d :d |d :d |r :r |m :— ‖
 |l₁ :l₁ |l₁ :se₁ |l₁ :fe₁ |s₁ :s₁ ‖ m₁ :f₁ |d₁ :m₁ |s₁ :s₁ |d₁ :— ‖}

O sola magnarum urbium

mf EARTH has many a noble city;
  Bethlem, thou dost all excel:
Out of thee the Lord from heaven
  Came to rule his Israel.

2
Fairer than the sun at morning
  Was the star that told his birth,
To the world its God announcing
  Seen in fleshly form on earth.

3
Eastern sages at his cradle
  Make oblations rich and rare;
See them give in deep devotion
  Gold and frankincense and myrrh.

4
Sacred gifts of mystic meaning:
  Incense doth their God disclose,
Gold the King of Kings proclaimeth,
  Myrrh his sepulchre foreshows.

5
f Jesu, whom the Gentiles worshipped
  At thy glad Epiphany,
Unto thee with God the Father
  And the Spirit glory be.

PRUDENTIUS *Tr.* E. CASWALL and Compilers

EPIPHANY

Hymn 77 Was lebet

Rheinhardt MS., Üttingen, 1754

KEY **D**

*For first verse only

1

O WORSHIP the Lord in the beauty of holiness!
Bow down before him, his glory proclaim;
With gold of obedience, and incense of lowliness,
Kneel and adore him: the Lord is his name.

2

Low at his feet lay thy burden of carefulness:
High on his heart he will bear it for thee,
Comfort thy sorrows, and answer thy prayerfulness,
Guiding thy steps as may best for thee be.

3

Fear not to enter his courts in the slenderness
Of the poor wealth thou wouldst reckon as thine:
Truth in its beauty, and love in its tenderness,
These are the offerings to lay on his shrine.

4

These, though we bring them in trembling and fearfulness,
He will accept for the name that is dear;
Mornings of joy give for evenings of tearfulness,
Trust for our trembling and hope for our fear.

J. S. B. MONSELL

The first verse may be repeated at the end

EPIPHANY

HYMN 78 Tallis   T. Tallis, c. 1505–85

KEY E♭

Divine crescebas puer

mf THE heavenly Child in stature grows,
   And, growing, learns to die;
   And still his early training shows
   His coming agony.

2

The Son of God his glory hides
   To dwell with parents poor;
And he who made the heavens abides
   In dwelling-place obscure.

3

Those mighty hands that rule the sky
   No earthly toil refuse;
The Maker of the stars on high
   An humble trade pursues.

4

He whom the choirs of angels praise,
   Bearing each dread decree,
His earthly parents now obeys
   In glad humility.

[UNISON]
5
f For this thy lowliness revealed,
   Jesu, we thee adore,
And praise to God the Father yield
   And Spirit evermore.

J. B. DE SANTEUIL
Tr. J. Chandler and Compilers

EPIPHANY

HYMN 79 Dix   C. Kocher, 1786–1872

KEY A♭

DESCANT

```
{ s :s  |s :m |l :s |s :—  || f :r  |s :f |m :r |m :—  }

{ d :t.d|r :d |f :f |m :—  || l₁:t₁ |d :l₁|s₁:s₁|s₁:—  }
{ s₁:s₁ |s₁:s₁|f₁:s₁|s₁:—  || l₁:s₁ |s₁:f₁|m₁:r₁|m₁:—  }
{ m :f.m|r :m |d :r |d :—  || d :r  |d :d |d :t₁|d :—  }
{ d :r.d|t₁:d |l₁:t₁|d :—  || f₁:f₁ |m₁:f₁|s₁:s₁|d₁:—  }

{ m :r.m|f :s |l :t.l|l :se || l :r  |s :f |m.s:f.m|r :— }

{ d :t.d|r :d |f :f |m :—    || l₁:t₁ |d :l₁|s₁:s₁|s₁:— }
{ m₁:l₁ |l₁:s₁|l₁:t₁.l₁|l₁:se₁|| l₁:s₁|s₁:f₁|s₁:f₁.m₁|r₁:—}
{ m :r.m|f :d |r :r.d|t₁:m   || m :r  |d :d |d :d  |d :t₁}
{ l₁:l₁ |f₁:m₁|r₁:r₁|m₁:—    || f₁:f₁ |m₁:r₁|m₁:r₁.d₁|s₁:—}

{ m :s.f|m :s |s :l.t|d':—   || l :s  |s :d |s :—.f|m :— }

{ m :r  |d :m |s :—.f|m :—   || l₁:t₁ |d :f |m :r |d :— }
{ s₁:s₁ |s₁:s₁|s₁:s₁|s₁:—    || l₁:s₁ |s₁:l₁|s₁:—.f₁|m₁:—}
{ d :s.f|m :d |r :t₁|d :—    || d :r  |d :d |d :t₁|d :— }
{ d :t₁ |d :d |t₁:s₁|d :—    || f₁:f₁ |m₁:f₁|s₁:s₁|d₁:— }
```

The Descant may be sung for verses 3 and 5

f   AS with gladness men of old
     Did the guiding star behold,
     As with joy they hailed its light,
     Leading onward, beaming bright;
     So, most gracious Lord, may we
     Evermore be led to thee.

3
As they offered gifts most rare
At thy cradle rude and bare,
So may we with holy joy,
Pure and free from sin's alloy,
All our costliest treasures bring,
Christ, to thee our heavenly King.

2
mf   As with joyful steps they sped,
     Saviour, to thy lowly bed,
     There to bend the knee before,
     Thee whom heaven and earth adore;
     So may we with willing feet
     Ever seek thy mercy-seat.

4
p   Holy Jesus, every day
    Keep us in the narrow way,
mf And, when earthly things are past,
    Bring our ransomed souls at last
f   Where they need no star to guide,
    Where no clouds thy glory hide.

5
In the heavenly country bright
Need they no created light;
Thou its light, its joy, its crown,
Thou its sun which goes not down;
There for ever may we sing
Alleluias to our King.

                      W. CHATTERTON DIX

EPIPHANY

HYMN 80 Dundee *Psalms* (Edinburgh, 1615)

KEY **F**

[sol-fa notation music score]

ALTERNATIVE VERSION
(Melody in the Tenor part)

KEY **F** Harmonized by T. Ravenscroft (1621)

[sol-fa notation music score]

The Alternative Version may be used for verses 3 and 6

mf THE people that in darkness sat
  A glorious light have seen; [long‿
The light has shined on them who
  In shades of death have been.

2
To hail thee, Sun of Righteousness,
  The gathering nations come;
They joy as when the reapers bear‿
  Their harvest treasures home.

3
For thou their burden dost remove,
  And break the tyrant's rod,
As in the day when Midian fell
  Before the sword of God.

4
f For unto us a Child is born,
  To us a Son is given,
And on his shoulder ever rests‿
  All power in earth and heaven.

5
His name shall be the Prince of Peace,
  The everlasting Lord,
The Wonderful, the Counsellor,
  The God by all adored.

6
His righteous government and
  Shall over all extend; [power‿
On judgement and on justice based,
  His reign shall have no end.

7
mf Lord Jesus, reign in us, we pray,
  And make us thine alone,
Who with the Father ever art
  And Holy Spirit One.

J. MORRISON and Compilers

EPIPHANY

Hymn 81 St. Edmund   C. Steggall, 1826–1905

KEY **G**

mf SONGS of thankfulness and praise
Jesu, Lord, to thee we raise,
Manifested by the star
To the sages from afar;
Branch of royal David's stem
In thy birth at Bethlehem:
f Anthems be to thee addrest,
God in Man made manifest.

EPIPHANY

2

mf Manifest at Jordan's stream,
    Prophet, Priest, and King supreme;
    And at Cana wedding-guest
    In thy Godhead manifest;
    Manifest in power divine,
    Changing water into wine:
f Anthems be to thee addrest,
    God in Man made manifest.

3

mf Manifest in making whole
    Palsied limbs and fainting soul;
    Manifest in valiant fight,
    Quelling all the devil's might;
    Manifest in gracious will,
    Ever bringing good from ill:
f Anthems be to thee addrest,
    God in Man made manifest.

4*

mf Sun and moon shall darkened be,
    Stars shall fall, the heavens shall flee;
f Christ will then like lightning shine,
    All will see his glorious sign;
    All will then the trumpet hear,
    All will see the Judge appear:
    Thou by all wilt be confest,
    God in Man made manifest.

5

mf Grant us grace to see thee, Lord,
    Mirrored in thy holy word;
    May we imitate thee now,
    And be pure, as pure art thou;
    That we like to thee may be
    At thy great Epiphany;
f And may praise thee, ever blest,
    God in Man made manifest.

                            BISHOP CHR. WORDSWORTH

THE WEEK BEFORE SEPTUAGESIMA

HYMN 82 FIRST TUNE

KEY E♭ Alleluia, dulce carmen
Melody from La Feillée
Méthode de Plain Chant, 1808

Alleluia, dulce carmen

{| m m̱ ṟ f ṟ ḏ r f f̱ ṟ m — | r f l s }

1 Al - le - lu - ia, song of sweet-ness, Voice of joy that
2 Al - le - lu - ia thou re - sound-est, True Je - ru - sa -
3 Al - le - lu - ia can - not al - ways_ Be our song while
4 There-fore in our hymns we pray thee, Grant us, bless - ed

{| f̱ m̱ r m — | m s l s l d' s l s f m }

1 can - not die; Al - le - lu - ia is the an - them
2 lem and free; Al - le - lu - ia, joy - ful mo - ther,
3 here be - low; Al - le - lu - ia our trans - gres - sions_
4 Tri - ni - ty, At the last to keep thine Eas - ter

{| r f l s f̱ m̱ r m — | m m̱ ṟ f ṟ ḏ }

1 Ev - er dear to choirs on high: In the house of
2 All thy chil-dren sing with thee; But by Bab - y -
3 Make us for a - while for - go; For the so - lemn
4 In our home be - yond the sky; There to thee for

{| r f f̱ ṟ m — | r f l s f̱ m̱ r m — ||

1 God a - bi - ding Thus they sing e - ter - nal - ly.
2 lon's sad wa - ters Mourn-ing ex - iles now are we.
3 time is com - ing When our tears for sin must flow.
4 ev - er sing - ing Al - le - lu - ia joy - ful - ly.

SECOND TUNE

KEY G Alleluia, dulce carmen
Essay on the Church Plain Chant,
1782

{| d :r | m :f | s :f | m :r ‖ d :d | d :f | m :r | d :— ‖
 | s₁ :s₁ | s₁ :d | t₁ :l₁.s₁| s₁ :s₁ | m₁ :s₁ | l₁ :l₁ | s₁ :-.f₁| m₁ :— ‖
 | m :t₁ | d :d | r :ḏ.ṟ | d :t₁ | d :d | d :d | d :t₁ | d :— ‖
 | d :s₁ | d :l₁ | s₁ :l₁.t₁| d :s₁ | l₁ :m₁ | f₁ :r₁ | s₁ :s₁ | d₁ :— ‖

THE WEEK BEFORE SEPTUAGESIMA

```
{|l₁:1₁ |s₁ :s₁  |d  :d    |d :t₁ ‖r  :s  |m :d    |t₁ :l₁ |s₁ :—‖
 |f₁:f₁ |m₁:m₁  |m₁ :s₁   |s₁:s₁ ‖s₁ :s₁ |s₁:s₁.l₁|s₁:fe₁|s₁ :—‖
 |d :d  |d.r:m.f |s  :m   |m :r  ‖t₁ :r  |m :m   |r :—.d|t₁:—‖
 |f₁:f₁ |d₁:d₁  |d₁.r₁:m₁.f₁|s₁:s₁ ‖s₁:t₁ |d :d₁  |r₁:r₁ |s₁:—‖}

{|t₁:t₁ |d :s₁  |l₁:t₁  |d :r  ‖m.r:d.t₁|l₁:f  |m  :r  |d :—‖
 |s₁:s₁ |s₁:d₁  |l₁:se₁ |l₁:t₁ ‖d :s₁  |f₁:l₁ |s₁:—.f₁|m₁:—‖
 |r :r  |d :d   |d :m   |m :s  ‖s :d   |d :d  |d :t₁  |d :—‖
 |s₁:—.f₁|m₁:m₁ |f₁:m₁  |l₁:s₁ ‖d :m₁  |f₁:r₁ |m₁.f₁:s₁|d₁:—‖}
```

Alleluia, dulce carmen

f   ALLELUIA, song of sweetness,
    Voice of joy that cannot die;
Alleluia is the anthem
    Ever dear to choirs on high:
In the house of God abiding
    Thus they sing eternally.

2
Alleluia thou resoundest,
    True Jerusalem and free;
Alleluia, joyful mother,
    All thy children sing with thee;
p   But by Babylon's sad waters
    Mourning exiles now are we.

3
Alleluia cannot always
    Be our song while here below;
Alleluia our transgressions
    Make us for awhile forgo;
For the solemn time is coming
    When our tears for sin must flow.

4
mf   Therefore in our hymns we pray thee,
    Grant us, blessèd Trinity,
At the last to keep thine Easter
    In our home beyond the sky,
f   There to thee for ever singing
    Alleluia joyfully.
                    Tr. J. M. NEALE and Compilers

SEPTUAGESIMA

Hymn 83 St. Gregory *Darmstadt Gesangbuch, 1698*
KEY E♭

{|: s | m :s | l :d' | s :-.f|m | s | d :m | f :m | r :d | r :— ‖
 |: r | d :d | f :m | r :t₁ | d | r | d :d | d :d | t₁:l₁| t₁:— ‖
 |: s | s :m | f :s | s :s | s | s | m :l | l :s | s :m | s :— ‖
 |: t₁ | d :m | r :d | t₁:s₁ | d | t₁| l₁:-.s₁|f₁:d| s₁:l₁| s₁:— ‖}

{|: s | m :s | l :d' | s :-.f|m | s | d :m | f :m | r :r | d :— ‖
 |: t₁ | d :d | d :d | r :t₁ | d | r | d :d | d :d | d :t₁| d :— ‖
 |: r | d :s | f :m | r :s | s | s | m :l | l :s | l :s | m :— ‖
 |: s₁ | l₁:m₁ | f₁:l₁ | t₁:s₁ | d | t₁| l₁:-.s₁|f₁:d| f₁:s₁| d :— ‖}

Te laeta, mundi Conditor

mf CREATOR of the world, to thee
   An endless rest of joy belongs;
And heavenly choirs are ever free
   To sing on high their festal songs.

2
p But we are fallen creatures here,
   Where pain and sorrow daily come;
And how can we in exile drear
   Sing out, as they, sweet songs of home?

3
mf O Father, who dost promise still
   That they who mourn shall blessèd be,
p Help us to grieve for deeds of ill
   That banish us so long from thee:

4
And, while we grieve, give faith to rest
   In hope upon thy loving care;
mf Till thou restore us, with the blest,
   Their songs of praise in heaven to share.

C. COFFIN *Tr.* Compilers

LENT

Hymn 84 FIRST TUNE

KEY F Audi, benigne Conditor Mode ii

Audi, benigne Conditor

{| **r d** r **f m** f **r m** **m r** **d r** r — | **f m** **f s** **s f m** }
1 O Ma - ker of the world, give ear; In pi - tying
2 All hearts are o - pen un - to thee; Thou know - est
3 Help us to grow in self - con - trol, To make the

LENT

{| r f m r m r d d — | d r m f m r }

1. love vouch-safe to hear The prayers our con-trite
2. each in-fir-mi-ty; Now, as we turn to
3. bo-dy serve the soul: So may thy lov-ing-

{| f m f s s — | d r f s m f m r m r d r r — ||

1. spi-rits raise In this our fast of for-ty days.
2. seek thy face, Pour down on us thy par-doning grace.
3. kind-ness bless Our fast with fruits of ho-li-ness.

SECOND TUNE

KEY A♭ Cannons G. F. Handel, 1685–1759

{| l₁ :m₁.,se₁| l₁ :t₁ | d :-.r|t₁ :— ‖ d :s₁.,t₁|d :r | m :-.f|r :— |
   m₁ :m₁.,r₁| m₁ :m₁ | l₁ :l₁ | se₁:— ‖ l₁ :s₁.,f₁|s₁ :s₁ | s₁ :l₁ | s₁ :— |
   d :d.,r | d :m | m :f | m :— ‖ m :d.,r|m :r | d :d | t₁ :— |
   l₁ :d.,t₁| l₁ :se₁| l₁ :r₁| m₁ :— ‖ l₁ :m₁.,r₁|d₁ :t₂ | d₁ :f₁| s₁ :— ||

{|:m | f :-.m|r :-.d| t₁ :l₁ | se₁ ‖ t₁ | m :l₁ | r.m:d.t₁| t₁ :-.l₁|l₁ :— |
  :s₁ | f₁ :s₁ | l₁ :s₁ | f₁ :r₁ | m₁ ‖ se₁| l₁ :l₁ | se₁:l₁ | l₁ :se₁| l₁ :— |
  :t₁ | d :t₁ | l₁ :d | r :l₁ | t₁ ‖ m | m :f.m|r :m | m :r | d :— |
  :s₁ | l₁ :s₁ | f₁ :m₁| r₁ :f₁| m₁ ‖ r₁ | d₁ :r₁.d|t₂ :l₂ | m₁ :m₁| l₂ :— ||

Audi, benigne Conditor

O MAKER of the world, give ear;
In pitying love vouchsafe to hear
The prayers our contrite spirits raise
In this our fast of forty days.

2

All hearts are open unto thee;
Thou knowest each infirmity;
Now, as we turn to seek thy face,
Pour down on us thy pardoning grace.

3

Help us to grow in self-control,
To make the body serve the soul:
So may thy loving-kindness bless
Our fast with fruits of holiness.

Tr. COMPILERS

LENT

HYMN 85 Keble
KEY G J. B. Dykes, 1823-76

[Tonic sol-fa notation]

Jesu quadragenariae

JESU, who this our Lenten-tide
Of abstinence hast sanctified,
Be with thy Church in saving power
In this her penitential hour.

2
And, as thou dost forgive the past,
Thy sheltering arms around us cast,
That we may in thy grace remain
And fall not back to sins again.

3
Make, Lord, this Lenten discipline
An expiation for our sin;
And through these days ourselves prepare
The joys of Eastertide to share.

Tr. BISHOP W. H. FRERE

Alternative Plainsong Tune, Audi, benigne Conditor, 84

HYMN 86 Aberystwyth
KEY G J. Parry, 1841-1903

[Tonic sol-fa notation]

LENT

p SAVIOUR, when in dust to thee
Low we bow the adoring knee;
When, repentant, to the skies
Scarce we lift our weeping eyes;
O by all thy pains and woe
Suffered once for man below,
Bending from thy throne on high,
Hear our solemn litany.

2
mf By thy helpless infant years,
By thy life of want and tears,
By thy days of sore distress
In the savage wilderness;
By the dread mysterious hour
Of the insulting tempter's power:
Turn, O turn a favouring eye,
p Hear our solemn litany.

3*
mf By the sacred griefs that wept
O'er the grave where Lazarus slept;
By the boding tears that flowed
Over Salem's loved abode;
By the mournful word that told
Treachery lurked within thy fold:
From thy seat above the sky
p Hear our solemn litany.

4
By thine hour of dire despair;
By thine agony of prayer;
By the Cross, the nail, the thorn,
Piercing spear, and torturing scorn;
By the gloom that veiled the skies
O'er the dreadful Sacrifice:
Listen to our humble cry,
Hear our solemn litany.

5
By thy deep expiring groan;
By the sad sepulchral stone;
By the vault whose dark abode
Held in vain the rising God:
f O, from earth to heaven restored,
Mighty, re-ascended Lord,
mf Listen, listen to the cry
p Of our solemn litany.

SIR R. GRANT†

LENT

HYMN 87 Tunbridge   J. Clarke, c. 1659–1707

KEY B♭

p 1
SINFUL, sighing to be blest;
 Bound, and longing to be free;
Weary, waiting for my rest:
 God, be merciful to me.

2
Goodness I have none to plead,
 Sinfulness in all I see,
I can only bring my need:
 God, be merciful to me.

3*
Broken heart and downcast eyes
 Dare not lift themselves to thee;
Yet thou canst interpret sighs:
 God, be merciful to me.

4
From this sinful heart of mine
 To thy bosom I would flee;
I am not my own, but thine:
 God, be merciful to me.

5
f There is One beside the throne,
 And my only hope and plea
Are in him, and him alone:
mf God, be merciful to me.

6
He my cause will undertake,
 My interpreter will be;
He's my all; and for his sake,
 God, be merciful to me.

J. S. B. MONSELL

LENT

HYMN 88 Hereford Sir F. A. G. Ouseley, 1825–89

KEY B♭

[sol-fa notation]

p WHEN wounded sore the stricken heart
　Lies bleeding and unbound,
　One only hand, a piercèd hand,
　Can salve the sinner's wound.

2

When sorrow swells the laden breast,
　And tears of anguish flow,
One only heart, a broken heart,
　Can feel the sinner's woe.

3

When penitential grief has wept
　Over some foul dark spot,
One only stream, a stream of Blood,
　Can wash away the blot.

mf 4

'Tis Jesus' Blood that washes white,
　His hand that brings relief;
His heart is touched with all our joys,
　And feels for all our grief.

5

Lift up thy bleeding hand, O Lord,
　Unseal that cleansing tide:
We have no shelter from our sin
　But in thy wounded side.

　　　　　　　　　　MRS. C. F. ALEXANDER

Alternative Tune, St. Bernard, 104

LENT

HYMN 89 Eccles B. Luard Selby, 1853-1919

KEY **G**

[sol-fa notation]

MY spirit longs for thee
Within my troubled breast,
Though I unworthy be
Of so divine a guest.

2

Of so divine a guest
Unworthy though I be,
Yet has my heart no rest
Unless it comes from thee.

3

Unless it comes from thee,
In vain I look around;
In all that I can see
No rest is to be found.

4

No rest is to be found
But in thy blessèd love:
O let my wish be crowned,
And send it from above!

J. BYROM

HYMN 90 Colchester S. S. Wesley, 1810–76

KEY E♭

```
:m  |s  :d  |f  :r  |d  :t, |d  ||s   |d' :t    |l  :r  |s  :f.m |r  :— ||
:d  |t, :d  |l, :l, |s, :s, |s, ||r   |d  :s,   |l, :t, |d  :r.d |t, :— ||
:s  |s  :m  |l  :f  |m  :r  |m  ||s   |m  :s    |d  :s  |s  :l   |t  :— ||
:d  |s, :l, |r, :f, |s, :s, |d  ||t,  |l, :m,   |f, :f  |m  :f   |s  :— ||

:m  |d  :f  |f  :m  |r  :l  |s  ||s   |l  :d'   |t  :l  |s  :fe  |s  :— ||
:t, |d  :d  |r  :d  |d  :t, |d  ||d.t,|m  :d    |r  :m  |r  :r.d |t, :— ||
:s  |m  :l  |s  :s  |l  :r  |s  ||m   |m  :m.ba |se :l  |t  :l   |s  :— ||
:s, |l, :l, |t, :d  |f  :f, |m, ||m.r |d  :l,   |t, :d  |r  :r   |s, :— ||

:t, |d  :r  |m  :m  |f  :s  |l  ||l   |t  :d'   |r  :m.f |m  :r   |d  :— ||
:s, |s, :t, |d  :d  |d  :d  |d  ||d   |f  :m    |d  :d   |d  :t,  |d  :— ||
:s  |s  :s  |s  :s  |f  :m  |f  ||f   |f  :s    |l  :f   |s  :s.f |m  :— ||
:f  |m  :r  |d  :ta,|l, :s, |f, ||m   |r  :d    |f, :r,  |s, :s,  |d  :— ||
```

STILL nigh me, O my Saviour, stand,
And guard in fierce temptation's hour;
Hide in the hollow of thy hand,
Show forth in me thy saving power;
Still be thine arm my sure defence:
Nor earth nor hell shall pluck me thence.

2

Still let thy love point out my way:
How wondrous things thy love hath wrought!
Still lead me, lest I go astray;
Direct my work, inspire my thought;
And, if I fall, soon may I hear‿
Thy voice, and know that Love is near.

3

In suffering be thy love my peace,
In weakness be thy love my power;
And when the storms of life shall cease,
Jesus, in that tremendous hour,
In death as life be thou my guide,
And save me, who for me hast died.

C. WESLEY†

LENT

HYMN 91   FIRST TUNE
KEY E♭   St. Andrew of Crete   J. B. Dykes, 1823-76

$$\left\{\begin{array}{l}
|m:m\ |m:m\quad |m\ :m\ |\quad\ :\quad \|m\ :m\quad\ |m\ :m\quad\ |m\ :-\ |-\ :-\\
|d\ :l_1\ |d\ :\underline{t_1.l_1}|l_1\ :se_1|\quad :\quad \|se_1:\underline{se_1.l_1}|t_1:\underline{l_1.se_1}|l_1\ :-\ |t_1\ :-\\
|l\ :d\ |m\ :\underline{r.d}\ |r\ :r\ |\quad :\quad \|m\ :m\quad\ |m\ :m\quad\ |d\ :-\ |m\ :-\\
|l_1\ :l_1\ |l_1\ :l_1\ |t_1\ :t_1\ |\quad :\quad \|m_1:\underline{t_1\ .d}|r\ :\underline{d.t_1}|l_1\ :-\ |s_1\ :-
\end{array}\right.$$

$$\left\{\begin{array}{l}
|l\ :l\quad\ |s\ :s\quad\ |f\ :-\ |m\ :-\ \|m\ :m\ |d\ :r\ |m\ :-\ |\quad :\\
|l_1\ :\underline{l_1.t_1}|d\ :m\quad\ |m\ :\underline{r.d}|t_1\ :-\ \|d\ :t_1\ |l_1\ :l_1\ |l_1\ :se_1|\quad :\\
|f\ :\underline{d\ .r}|m\ :\underline{s.d'}|d'\ :\underline{t.l}|se\ :-\ \|l\ :m\ |f\ :r\ |t_1\ :-\ |\quad :\\
|f_1\ :f_1\quad |d\ :d\quad\ |r\ :-\ |m\ :-\ \|l_1\ :s_1\ |f_1\ :f_1|m_1\ :-\ |\quad :
\end{array}\right.$$

UNISON IN VERSES 1, 2, 3   HARMONY
C. 3. *f*

$$\left\{\begin{array}{l}
^m s\ :d'\ |r'\ :-.s\ |m'\ :-\ |d'\ :-\ \|m'\ :r'\ |d'\ :l\ |s\ :-\ |-\ :-\\
^1_1 d:d\ |s\ :-.s\ |s\ :-\ |m\ :-\ \|s\ :s\ |s\ :\underline{f.m}|r\ :-\ |-\ :-\\
^{de} m:s\ |t\ :-.r'|m'\ :-\ |s\ :-\ \|m'\ :t\ |d'\ :d'\ |f'\ :-\ |-\ :-\\
^1 d:m\ |s\ :-.t\ |d'\ :-\ |d\ :-\ \|d'\ :s\ |l\ :l\ |t\ :-\ |-\ :-
\end{array}\right.$$

$$\left\{\begin{array}{l}
|s\ :s\quad\ |d'\ :d'\ |f'\ :-\ |m'\ :-\ \|m'\ :\underline{r'.d'}|t\ :-.t\ |d'\ :-\ |-\ :-\\
|d\ :m\quad |m\ :\underline{f.s}|l\ :-\ |s\ :-\ \|s\ :\underline{f.m}|r\ :-.f\ |m\ :-\ |-\ :-\\
|m'\ :\underline{m'.r'}|d'\ :\underline{d'.t}|d'\ :-\ |d'\ :-\ \|d'\ :l\ |t\ :-.s\ |s\ :-\ |-\ :-\\
|d'\ :\underline{d'.t}|l\ :\underline{l.s}|f\ :-\ |d\ :-\ \|m\ :f\ |s\ :-.s\ |d\ :-\ |-\ :-
\end{array}\right.$$

SECOND TUNE
KEY **F**   Gute Bäume bringen   P. Sohren, *d. c.* 1692

$$\left\{\begin{array}{l}
|l_1\ :\underline{l_1.t_1}|d\ :r\ |m\ :-\ |m\ :-\ \|s\ :m\ |l\ :se\ |l\ :-\ |-\ :-\\
|l_1\ :l_1\ |l_1\ :l_1\ |t_1\ :-\ |t_1\ :-\ \|m\ :d\ |t_1\ :t_1\ |d\ :-\ |-\ :-\\
|d\ :\underline{d.r}|m\ :l\ |l\ :-\ |se\ :-\ \|s\ :s\ |f\ :m\ |m\ :-\ |-\ :-\\
|l_1\ :l_1\ |l_1\ :f_1\ |m_1\ :-\ |m_1\ :-\ \|d\ :m\ |r\ :m\ |l_1\ :-\ |-\ :-
\end{array}\right.$$

$$\left\{\begin{array}{l}
|l_1\ :\underline{l_1.t_1}|d\ :r\ |m\ :-\ |m\ :-\ \|s\ :m\ |l\ :se\ |l\ :-\ |-\ :-\\
|l_1\ :l_1\ |l_1\ :l_1\ |t_1\ :-\ |t_1\ :-\ \|m\ :d\ |t_1\ :t_1\ |d\ :-\ |-\ :-\\
|d\ :\underline{d.r}|m\ :l\ |l\ :-\ |se\ :-\ \|s\ :s\ |f\ :m\ |m\ :-\ |-\ :-\\
|l_1\ :l_1\ |l_1\ :f_1\ |m_1\ :-\ |m_1\ :-\ \|d\ :m\ |r\ :m\ |l_1\ :-\ |-\ :-
\end{array}\right.$$

LENT

p CHRISTIAN, dost thou see them
  On the holy ground,
 How the troops of Midian
  Prowl and prowl around?
f Christian, up and smite them,
  Counting gain but loss;
 Smite them by the merit
  Of the holy Cross.

2

p Christian, dost thou feel them,
  How they work within,
 Striving, tempting, luring,
  Goading into sin?
f Christian, never tremble;
  Never be down-cast;
 Smite them by the virtue
  Of the Lenten fast.

3

p Christian, dost thou hear them,
  How they speak thee fair?
 'Always fast and vigil?
  Always watch and prayer?'
f Christian, answer boldly,
  'While I breathe I pray:'
 Peace shall follow battle,
  Night shall end in day.

4

mf 'Well I know thy trouble,
  O my servant true;
 Thou art very weary,
  I was weary too;
f But that toil shall make thee
  Some day all mine own,
 And the end of sorrow
  Shall be near my throne.'

J. M. NEALE†

LENT

HYMN 92 Heinlein
Nürnbergisches Gesangbuch, 1676

KEY **F**

```
{ |m :m |l₁ :t₁ |d :r |m :—  ||ᵐl :l |d¹ :d¹ |t :t |l :—  ||
  |m :m |l₁ :t₁ |l₁ :l₁ |se₁ :—  ||¹r :r |m :m |m :m |de :—  ||
  |m :m |l₁ :m |m :l₁ |t₁ :—  ||ᵈf :f |l :l |l :se |l :—  ||
  |m :m |l₁ :se₁ |l₁ :f₁ |m₁ :—  ||¹r :r |l₁ :l₁ |m :m |l₁ :—  ||

f. F.
{ |¹m :m |f :f |r :r |m :—  ||m :m |r :d |t₁ :t₁ |l₁ :—  ||
  |ʳl₁ :l₁ |l₁ :l₁ |s₁ :s₁ |s₁ :—  ||s₁ :d |t₁ :l₁ |l₁ :se₁ |l₁ :—  ||
  |ᶠd :d |r :r |t₁ :t₁ |d :—  ||m :s |s :m |m :m |d :—  ||
  |ʳl₁ :l₁ |r₁ :r₁ |s₁ :s₁ |d₁ :—  ||d :d |s₁ :l₁ |m₁ :m₁ |l₁ :—  ||
```

mf FORTY days and forty nights
    Thou wast fasting in the wild;
  Forty days and forty nights
    Tempted, and yet undefiled:

2
Sunbeams scorching all the day;
  Chilly dew-drops nightly shed;
Prowling beasts about thy way;
  Stones thy pillow, earth thy bed.

3
Shall not we thy sorrows share,
  And from earthly joys abstain,
Fasting with unceasing prayer,
  Glad with thee to suffer pain?

4
And if Satan, vexing sore,
  Flesh or spirit should assail,
Thou, his vanquisher before,
  Grant we may not faint nor fail.

5
p So shall we have peace divine;
  Holier gladness ours shall be;
Round us too shall angels shine,
  Such as ministered to thee.

6
mf Keep, O keep us, Saviour dear,
  Ever constant by thy side;
f That with thee we may appear
  At the eternal Eastertide.

G. H. SMYTTAN and F. POTT

HYMN 93 St. Mary
E. Prys, *Psalms*, 1621

KEY **F**

```
{ |:l₁ |d :t₁ |l₁ :l |s :f |m  ||m |s :d |m :r |d :— |—  ||
  |:l₁ |l₁ :s₁ |f₁ :d |d :l₁ |l₁  ||s₁ |s₁ :d |d :t₁ |d :— |—  ||
  |:d |m :m |d :f |m :r |de  ||d |r :m |s :s |m :— |—  ||
  |:l₁ |l₁ :m₁ |f₁ :f₁ |d :r |l₁  ||d |t₁ :l₁ |m₁.f₁ :s₁ |d :— |—  ||

C.t.                                   f. F.
{ |:ᵐl |d¹ :r¹ |m¹ :l |s :f |d¹  ||ˢr |m :l₁ |d :t₁ |l₁ :— |—  ||
  |:ᵈf |s :f |m :f |d :f |m  ||ᵐt₁ |d :l₁ |l₁ :se₁ |l₁ :— |—  ||
  |:ˢd¹ |d¹ :t |d¹ :d¹ |s :l.t |d¹  ||ᵈs |s :r |m :—.r |d :— |—  ||
  |:ᵈf |m :r |d :f |m :r |d  ||ᵈs₁ |d₁ :f₁ |m₁ :m₁ |l₁ :— |—  ||
```

LENT

O LORD, turn not thy face from me,
　Who lie in woeful state,
Lamenting all my sinful life
　Before thy mercy-gate:

2

A gate which opens wide to those
　That do lament their sin;
Shut not that gate against me, Lord,
　But let me enter in.

3

And call me not to strict account
　How I have sojourned here;
For then my guilty conscience knows
　How vile I shall appear.

4

Mercy, good Lord, mercy I ask:
　This is my humble prayer;
For mercy, Lord, is all my suit:
　O let thy mercy spare.

　　　　　J. MARCKANT‡ (Form in *Supplement to
　　　　　　　　　　　　　the New Version*, 1708)

HYMN 94 St. Philip   W. H. Monk, 1823–89
KEY E♭

LORD, in this thy mercy's day,
Ere it pass for ay away,
On our knees we fall and pray.

2

Holy Jesu, grant us tears,
Fill us with heart-searching fears,
Ere that awful doom appears.

3

Lord, on us thy Spirit pour
Kneeling lowly at the door,
Ere it close for evermore.

4

By thy night of agony,
By thy supplicating cry,
By thy willingness to die;

5

By thy tears of bitter woe
For Jerusalem below,
Let us not thy love forgo.

6

Grant us 'neath thy wings a place,
Lest we lose this day of grace
Ere we shall behold thy face.

　　　　　　　　　　　　　I. WILLIAMS

LENT

HYMN 95 FIRST TUNE

KEY **F** Christe, qui lux Mode ii

Christe, qui lux es et dies

{| m   m   r d   r   m   f   r   r |}

1 O Christ, who art the Light and Day,
2 All-ho-ly Lord, in hum-ble prayer
3 A-sleep though wea-ried eyes may be,
4* Be-hold, O God our shield, and quell
5 All praise to God the Fa-ther be,

{| r   r f   m   d   r   f m — | f   s   f   m   r |}

1 Thou driv-est night and gloom a-way; O Light of Light, whose
2 We ask to-night thy watch-ful care; O grant us calm re-
3 Still keep the heart a-wake to thee; Let thy right hand out-
4* The crafts and sub-tle-ties of hell; Di-rect thy ser-vants
5 All praise, e-ter-nal Son, to thee, Whom with the Spi-rit

{| f   r   r | m   m   r d   r   m   f   r   r — ||

1 word doth show The light of heav'n to us be-low.
2 pose in thee, A qui-et night from per-ils free.
3 stretched a-bove Guard those who serve the Lord they love.
4* in all good, Whom thou hast pur-chased with thy Blood.
5 we a-dore, For ev-er and for ev-er-more.

SECOND TUNE

KEY **G** Alfreton *Supplement to the New Version*, 1708

LENT

Christe, qui lux es et dies
(Evening)

mf 1. O CHRIST, who art the Light and Day,
Thou drivest night and gloom away;
O Light of Light, whose word doth show
The light of heaven to us below.

2. All-holy Lord, in humble prayer
We ask to-night thy watchful care;
O grant us calm repose in thee,
A quiet night from perils free.

3. Asleep though wearied eyes may be,
Still keep the heart awake to thee;
Let thy right hand outstretched above
Guard those who serve the Lord they love.

4.* Behold, O God our Shield, and quell
The crafts and subtleties of hell;
Direct thy servants in all good,
Whom thou hast purchased with thy Blood.

[UNISON]
f 5. All praise to God the Father be,
All praise, eternal Son, to thee,
Whom with the Spirit we adore,
For ever and for evermore.

Tr. COMPILERS (1904)

PASSIONTIDE

Hymn 96 FIRST TUNE
KEY E♭ Vexilla Regis Mode i
Vexilla Regis prodeunt

{| f s ta ta l s f s   s l s f m – r – | s   s   l   }

1 The roy-al ban-ners for-ward go,   The Cross shines
2 There whilst he hung, his sa-cred side By sol-dier's
3 Ful-filled is now what Da-vid told   In true pro-
4 O Tree of glo-ry, Tree most fair,   Or-dained those
5 Up-on its arms, like bal-ance true,   He weighed the
6 To thee, e-ter-nal Three in One,   Let hom-age

{| f m r f m f r d d – r – | r   r   f   r d   f   }

1 forth in mys-tic glow;   Where he in flesh, our
2 spear was o-pened wide,   To cleanse us in the
3 phe-tic song of old,   How God the hea-then's
4 ho-ly limbs to bear,   How bright in pur-ple
5 price for sin-ners due,   The price which none but
6 meet by all be done: As by the Cross thou

{| f s l s   s – f – | f f l t a l s l f m r f m f r d d – r – ||

1 flesh who made, Our sen-tence bore, our ran-som paid.
2 pre-cious flood, Of wa-ter min-gled with his blood.
3 King should be; For God is reign-ing from the Tree.
4 robe it stood,   The pur-ple of a Sa-viour's blood!
5 he could pay,   And spoiled the spoil-er of his prey.
6 dost re-store,   So rule and guide us ev-er-more.

SECOND TUNE

KEY C St. Cecilia J. Hampton, 1834–1921

G. t.
{ :s |m¹ :r¹ |d¹f :f |m :r |d   ‖ m f :r |s :m |r :r |d :—
  :m |s :f |ˢd :s₁ |s₁ :s₁.f₁|m₁ | d d :l₁ |s₁:s₁ |l₁ :s₁.f₁|m₁ :—
  :d¹ |d¹ :t |d¹f :r |d :t₁ |d   ‖ s f :f |r :d |d :t₁ |d :—
  :d |d :r |ᵐl₁:t₁|d :s₁ |l₁ | d l₁:r |t₁:d |f₁:s₁ |d :—

f. C.
{ :s r¹|m¹ :r¹|d¹:d¹|s :l |r   ‖ s s :f |f :m |r :r |d :—
  :s r|t₁ :m |m :f |s :r |r | r de:r |r :d |d :t₁ |d :—
  :r l |se.l:t |d¹:l |d¹:d¹|t   ‖ t l :l |s :s |l :s.f |m :—
  :ta,f|m .fe:s|l :f |m :fe|s | s₁ l₁:r |t₁:d |f₁:s₁ |d :—

PASSIONTIDE

(*Passion Sunday to Wednesday before Easter*)

Vexilla Regis prodeunt

f THE royal banners forward go,
The Cross shines forth in mystic glow;
Where he in flesh, our flesh who made,
Our sentence bore, our ransom paid.

2

m, There whilst he hung, his sacred side
By soldier's spear was opened wide,
To cleanse us in the precious flood
Of water mingled with his blood.

3

Fulfilled is now what David told
In true prophetic song of old,
How God the heathen's King should be;
For God is reigning from the Tree.

4

mf O Tree of glory, Tree most fair,
Ordained those holy limbs to bear,
How bright in purple robe it stood,
The purple of a Saviour's blood!

5

Upon its arms, like balance true,
He weighed the price for sinners due,
The price which none but he could pay,
f And spoiled the spoiler of his prey.

[UNISON] 6

To thee, eternal Three in One,
Let homage meet by all be done:
As by the Cross thou dost restore,
So rule and guide us evermore.

BISHOP VENANTIUS FORTUNATUS
Tr. J. M. Neale and Compilers

PASSIONTIDE

HYMN 97
KEY **G** Pange lingua

FIRST TUNE

Mode iii

Pange lingua gloriosi praelium certaminis

{| l₁ l₁ l₁ s₁ d d r f f — | f s f }
Sing, my tongue, the glo - rious bat - tle, Sing the

{| f f r f m r d — | d r f m }
last, the dread af - fray; O'er the Cross, the

{| r d r r | r m d t₁ l₁ r r — s₁ — }
Vic - tor's tro - phy, Sound the high tri - um - phal lay,

{| d d d l₁ d r r d | r m d r d ta₁ s₁ l₁ — ||
How, the pains of death en - dur - ing, Earth's Re - deem - er won the day.

This hymn may be sung to the Mechlin Version of the tune to be found at Hymn 383 or to St. Thomas, 388

SECOND TUNE

KEY **F** French Carol Traditional French Carol
UNISON

{| l₁ :t₁ | d :r | m :— | m :r | m :— | m :— || m :m | f :s | f :— | m :r }

{| m :— | — :— || l₁ :t₁ | d :r | m :— | m :r | m :— | m :— || m :m | f :s }

{| f :— | m :r | m :— | — :— || m :m | l :m | r :— | — :d | l₁ :d | m :d }

{| t₁ :— | — :— || m :m | l :m | r :— | t₁ :d | l₁ :— | — :— ||

KEY **F** HARMONIZED VERSION FOR UNACCOMPANIED SINGING (VERSES 3, 5, 7)

{| l₁:t₁ |d:r|m:—|m :r |m :—|m :—||m :m |f :s |f :—|m :r |m :—|—:—|
l₁:t₁	d:r	m:—		l₁ :—	t₁:—	t₁:—		d :t₁	d :d	r :—	l₁ :—	l₁:—	—:—
l₁:t₁	d:r	m:—		l —	l :—	l :—	s :—		l :t	l :s	l :—	l₁:—	d :—	—:—
l₁:t₁	d:r	m:—	f :—	m :—	m :—		l₁:s₁	f₁:m₁	r₁:—	f₁:—	l₁:—	—:—	

{| l₁ :t₁ |d :r |m :—|m :r |m :—|m :—||m :m |f :s |f :—|m :r |
l₁ :t₁	d :r	m :—	d :—	t₁:—	t₁:—		d :r	d :t₁	d :—	l₁ :—
l₁ :t₁	d :r	m :—	m :fe	s :—	s :—		s :s	d :r	f :—	d :t₁
l₁ :t₁	d :r	m :—	l₁ :—	s₁:fe₁	m₁:—		d :t₁	l₁:s₁	l₁:—	f₁ :—

{| m :—|—:—||m :m |l :m |r :—|—:d |l₁ :d |m :d |t₁:—|—:—|
s₁:—	—:—		m :m	l₁:m	r :—	—:d	l₁ :d	m :d	t₁:—	—:—
d :—	—:—		m :m	l :m	r :—	—:d	l₁ :d	m :d	t₁:—	—:—
d :—	—:—		m :m	l :m	r :—	—:d	l₁ :d	m :d	t₁:—	—:—	

PASSIONTIDE

(Passion Sunday to Wednesday before Easter)

Pange lingua gloriosi praelium certaminis

PART 1

1
SING, my tongue, the glorious battle,
 Sing the last, the dread affray;
O'er the Cross, the Victor's trophy,
 Sound the high triumphal lay,
How, the pains of death enduring,
 Earth's Redeemer won the day.

2
When at length the appointed fulness
 Of the sacred time was come,
He was sent, the world's Creator,
 From the Father's heavenly home,
And was found in human fashion,
 Offspring of the Virgin's womb.

3
Now the thirty years are ended
 Which on earth he willed to see,
Willingly he meets his Passion,
 Born to set his people free;
On the Cross the Lamb is lifted,
 There the Sacrifice to be.

4
There the nails and spear he suffers,
 Vinegar and gall and reed;
From his sacred body piercèd
 Blood and water both proceed:
Precious flood, which all creation
 From the stain of sin hath freed.

PART 2

5
Faithful Cross, above all other,
 One and only noble Tree,
None in foliage, none in blossom,
 None in fruit thy peer may be;
Sweet the wood, and sweet the iron,
 And thy load, most sweet is he.

6
Bend, O lofty Tree, thy branches,
 Thy too rigid sinews bend;
And awhile the stubborn hardness,
 Which thy birth bestowed, suspend;
And the limbs of heaven's high Monarch
 Gently on thine arms extend.

7
Thou alone wast counted worthy
 This world's Ransom to sustain,
That a shipwrecked race for ever
 Might a port of refuge gain,
With the sacred Blood anointed
 Of the Lamb for sinners slain.

The following Doxology may be sung at the end of either Part:

[UNISON]
8
Praise and honour to the Father,
 Praise and honour to the Son,
Praise and honour to the Spirit,
 Ever Three and ever One:
One in might, and One in glory,
 While eternal ages run.

BISHOP VENANTIUS FORTUNATUS
Tr. J. M. NEALE and Compilers

PASSIONTIDE

Hymn 98 St. Theodulph

KEY C

M. Teschner (1615)

(Palm Sunday)

Gloria, laus et honor

f ALL glory, laud, and honour
    To thee, Redeemer, King,
    To whom the lips of children
    Made sweet Hosannas ring.

2

mf Thou art the King of Israel,
    Thou David's royal Son,
    Who in the Lord's name comest,
    The King and blessèd one.
   f All glory, etc.

3

mf The company of angels
    Are praising thee on high,
    And mortal men and all things
    Created make reply.
   f All glory, etc.

4

mf The people of the Hebrews
    With palms before thee went:
    Our praise and prayer and anthems
    Before thee we present.
   f All glory, etc.

5

mf To thee before thy Passion
    They sang their hymns of praise:
    To thee now high exalted
    Our melody we raise.
   f All glory, etc.

6

mf Thou didst accept their praises:
    Accept the prayers we bring,
    Who in all good delightest,
    Thou good and gracious King.
   f All glory, etc.

ST. THEODULPH OF ORLEANS
Tr. J. M. Neale‡

NOTE. *A longer version of this hymn will be found in the 'Processional' section (597).*

PASSIONTIDE

HYMN 99 St. Drostane J. B. Dykes, 1823–76

KEY B♭

(Palm Sunday)

RIDE on! ride on in majesty!
Hark! all the tribes Hosanna cry!
O Saviour meek, pursue thy road
With palms and scattered garments strowed.

2

Ride on! ride on in majesty!
In lowly pomp ride on to die:
O Christ, thy triumphs now begin
O'er captive death and conquered sin.

3

Ride on! ride on in majesty!
The wingèd squadrons of the sky
Look down with sad and wondering eyes
To see the approaching Sacrifice.

4

Ride on! ride on in majesty!
The last and fiercest strife is nigh:
The Father on his sapphire throne
Awaits his own anointed Son.

5

Ride on! ride on in majesty!
In lowly pomp ride on to die;
Bow thy meek head to mortal pain,
Then take, O God, thy power, and reign.

H. H. MILMAN‡

Alternative Tune, Winchester New, 50

PASSIONTIDE

HYMN 100 Genevan Psalm cx L. Bourgeois, c. 1500-61

KEY B♭

(Holy Week)

mf LORD, through this Holy Week of our salvation,
  Which thou hast won for us who went astray,
 In all the conflict of thy sore temptation
  We would continue with thee day by day.

2

We would not leave thee, though our weak endurance
 Make us unworthy here to take our part;
Yet give us strength to trust the sweet assurance
 That thou, O Lord, art greater than our heart.

3

Thou didst forgive thine own who slept for sorrow,
 Thou didst have pity: O have pity now,
And let us watch through each sad eve and morrow
 With thee, in holy prayer and solemn vow.

4

p Along that sacred way where thou art leading,
  Which thou didst take to save our souls from loss,
 Let us go also, till we see thee pleading
  In all-prevailing prayer upon thy Cross;

PASSIONTIDE

5

mf Until thou see thy bitter travail's ending,
　　The world redeemed, the will of God complete,
And, to thy Father's hands thy soul commending,
　　Thou lay the work he gave thee at his feet.

W. H. DRAPER

Alternative Tune, Strength and Stay, 17

HYMN **101**　Nun komm　　　　　　　German Medieval Melody

KEY **B**♭

SEE the destined day arise!
See, a willing sacrifice,
Jesus, to redeem our loss,
Hangs upon the shameful Cross!

2

Jesu, who but thou had borne,
Lifted on that Tree of scorn,
Every pang and bitter throe,
Finishing thy life of woe?

3

Who but thou had dared to drain,
Steeped in gall, that cup of pain,
And with tender body bear
Thorns and nails and piercing spear?

4

Thence the cleansing water flowed,
Mingled from thy side with blood:
Sign to all attesting eyes
Of the finished Sacrifice.

5

Holy Jesu, grant us grace
In that Sacrifice to place
All our trust for life renewed,
Pardoned sin, and promised good.

BISHOP R. MANT

PASSIONTIDE

HYMN 102 Love Unknown John Ireland
KEY E♭

{|m :— |s :l |m :— |r :— |d :—|— :r |m :f |s :m |l :— ||— :l \
 |d :— |d :l₁|t₁:— |t₁:— |l₁:—|— :s₁|d :d |t₁:d |d :— ||— :d \
 |s :— |s :m |s :— |— :f |f :—|m |r :s |s :l |f :— ||— :f \
 |d :— |m :d |s :— |s₁:— |l₁:—|— :t₁|d :r |m :d |f :— ||m :— }

f. A♭.

{|t :l |s :s |d':t |l :s |s :m |—:fe|s :—|— ||ˢr |f :m |d :—|— :d \
 |f :f |t₁:m |d :r |m :t₁|r :—|— :r |r :d|t₁ ||ᵈs₁|l₁:s₁|m₁:—|f₁:— \
 |f :f |s :t |l :s |m :s |l :—|— :l |s :—|— ||ᵐt₁|d :t₁|d :—|l₁:— \
 |r :r |m :m |l₁:t₁|d :m |r :—|d :— |t₁:l₁|s₁ ||ᵈs₁|f₁:s₁|l₁:—|f₁:— }

E♭. t.

{|m :r |s₁:— |— |¹r |m :f |s :m |m :— |r :— |d :— |— \
 |s₁:f₁|m₁:— |— |ʳs₁ |s₁:d |d :d |t₁:— |t₁:— |d :— |— \
 |d :t₁|r :— |d |¹r |s :f |m :l |s :— |— :f |m :— |— \
 |d₁:r₁|m₁:— |— |ᶠᵉt₁|d :l₁|m₁:f₁|s₁:— |s₁:— |d :— |— }

MY song is love unknown,
My Saviour's love to me,
Love to the loveless shown,
That they might lovely be.
O who am I,
That for my sake
My Lord should take⌣
Frail flesh, and die?

2

He came from his blest throne,
Salvation to bestow;
But men made strange, and none⌣
The longed-for Christ would know.
But O, my Friend,
My Friend indeed,
Who at my need⌣
His life did spend!

3

Sometimes they strew his way,
And his sweet praises sing;
Resounding all the day
Hosannas to their King.
Then 'Crucify!'⌣
Is all their breath,
And for his death⌣
They thirst and cry.

PASSIONTIDE

4*

Why, what hath my Lord done?
 What makes this rage and spite?
He made the lame to run,
 He gave the blind their sight.
  Sweet injuries!
   Yet they at these
   Themselves displease,
  And 'gainst him rise.

5

They rise, and needs will have
 My dear Lord made away;
A murderer they save,
 The Prince of Life they slay.
  Yet cheerful he
   To suffering goes,
   That he his foes
  From thence might free.

6*

In life, no house, no home
 My Lord on earth might have;
In death, no friendly tomb
 But what a stranger gave.
  What may I say?
   Heaven was his home;
   But mine the tomb
  Wherein he lay.

7

Here might I stay and sing.
 No story so divine;
Never was love, dear King,
 Never was grief like thine!
  This is my Friend,
   In whose sweet praise
   I all my days
  Could gladly spend.

S. CROSSMAN

PASSIONTIDE

Hymn 103
FIRST TUNE

KEY **F** Genevan Psalm xii   L. Bourgeois, c. 1500–61

{| m :— | d :r | m :— | s :— | m :d | r :d | t₁ :— | l₁ :— ||
l₁ :—	l₁ :t₁	d :—	s₁ :—	s₁ :l₁	t₁ :—.l₁	l₁ :se₁	l₁ :—	
d :—	m :s	s :—	r :—	m :m	f :m	m :—	d :—	
l₁ :—	l₁ :s₁	d :—	t₁ :—	d :l₁	r :l₁	m₁ :—	l₁ :—	

C.t.
{| m :— | m l :s | l :— | r' :— | l :r' | d' :— | t :— | l :— | — :— ||
l₁ :—	s₁d :d	f :—	f :—	m :r	m :—	m :r	d :—	— :—	
d :—	m l :d'	l :—	t :—	d' :l	l :—	se :—	l :—	— :—	
l₁ :—	d f :m	r :—	r :—	d :f	d :r	m :—	l₁ :—	— :—	

f.F.
{| r l₁ :— | d :d | t₁ :— | l₁ :— | m :m | r :t₁ | d :— | t₁ :— ||
ta₁f₁ :—	s₁ :s₁	s₁ :—	m₁ :—	m₁ :l₁	t₁ :se₁	m₁ :ba₁	se₁ :—	
f d :—	m :m	r :—	d :—	t₁ :d	f :m	m :—	m :—	
ta₁f₁ :—	d₁ :m₁	s₁ :—	l₁ :—	s₁ :d₁	r₁ :m₁	l₁ :—	m₁ :—	

{| m :— | s :m | d :— | r :— | m :l₁ | d :— | t₁ :— | l₁ :— | — :— ||
s₁ :—	s₁ :s₁	l₁ :—	t₁ :—	t₁ :l₁	l₁ :—	se₁ :—	l₁ :—	— :—	
m :—	r :d	m :—	s :—	s :d	m :—	m :—	d :—	— :—	
d :—	t₁ :d	l₁ :—	s₁ :—	m₁ :f₁	d₁ :r₁	m₁ :—	l₁ :—	— :—	

SECOND TUNE

KEY **F** St. Winifred   J. B. Dykes, 1823–76

{| d :— | d :d | d :— | — :r | m :f | s :l | s :— | m :— ||
s₁ :—	l₁ :l₁	s₁ :—	— :t₁	d :d	d :d	d :t₁	d :—	
m :—	f :f	m :—	— :s	s :f	m :f	r :s	s :—	
d :—	f₁ :f₁	d :—	— :s₁	d :l₁	s₁ :f₁	s₁ :—	d :—	

{| s :— | s :l | f :s | m :m | m :— | re :— | m :— | — :— ||
t₁ :—	l₁ :l₁	l₁ :s₁	s₁ :d	t₁ :—	t₁ :—	t₁ :—	— :—	
s :f	m :m	f :r	m :fe	fe :—	fe :—	se :—	— :—	
m :r	de :de	r :t₁	d :l₁	t₁ :—	t₁ :—	m :—	— :—	

PASSIONTIDE

```
{| m :- | m :s | l :s | f :m | r :- | m :- | f :- | f ||
 | d :- | d :d | d :d | d :d | l₁:- | d :- | d :- | d ||
 | s :- | s :s | f :m | f :s | f :- | s :- | l :- | l ||
 | d :- | d :m₁| f₁:s₁| l₁:d | r :- | d :- | f :- | f ||

{| :r | m :- | f :- | s :l | f :r | d :- | r :- | d :- |- :- ||
 | :t₁| d :- | d :- | r :l₁| l₁:l₁| s₁:- | t₁:- | d :- |- :- ||
 | :s | s :- | f :- | r :m | f :f | m :- | f :- | m :- |- :- ||
 | :s | d :- | l₁:- | t₁:de| r :f₁| s₁:- | s₁:- | d :- |- :- ||
```

Est-ce vous que je vois?

mf MY Lord, my Master, at thy feet adoring,
    I see thee bowed beneath thy load of woe;
For me, a sinner, is thy life-blood pouring:
    For thee, my Saviour, scarce my tears will flow.

2

Thine own disciple to the Jews has sold thee,
    With friendship's kiss and loyal word he came;
How oft of faithful love my lips have told thee,
    While thou hast seen my falsehood and my shame!

3

With taunts and scoffs they mock what seems thy weakness,
    With blows and outrage adding pain to pain;
Thou art unmoved and steadfast in thy meekness:
    When I am wronged how quickly I complain!

4

p My Lord, my Saviour, when I see thee wearing
    Upon thy bleeding brow the crown of thorn,
Shall I for pleasure live, or shrink from bearing
    Whate'er my lot may be of pain or scorn?

5

mf O Victim of thy love! O pangs most healing!
    O saving Death! O wounds that I adore!
O shame most glorious! Christ, before thee kneeling,
    I pray thee keep me thine for evermore.

J. BRIDAINE *Tr.* T. B. Pollock

PASSIONTIDE

HYMN 104 St. Bernard *Tochter Sion* (Cologne, 1741)
KEY D

```
{ :s   |d  :r  |m  :r.d |f  :m  |r     ‖ s   |m  :l  |fe :-.fe |s  :-  |-
{ :d   |d  :t, |d  :t,.d|t, :d  |t,    ‖ r   |d  :d  |d  :-.d  |t, :-  |-
{ :m   |s  :s  |s  :s   |f  :s  |s     ‖ s   |s  :l  |l  :-.l  |s  :-  |-
{ :d   |m  :r  |d  :f .m|r  :d  |s,    ‖ t,  |d  :l, |r  :-.r  |s, :-  |-

{ :s   |d¹ :l  |s  :l   |f  :f  |m     ‖ d   |f  :m  |r  :r    |d  :-  |-
{ :t,  |d  :d  |d  :l,  |l, :r  |d     ‖ d   |t, :d  |d  :t,   |d  :-  |-
{ :s   |s  :f  |m  :m   |f  :s  |s     ‖ s   |f  :s  |l  :s.f  |m  :-  |-
{ :s   |m  :f  |d  :de  |r  :t, |d     ‖ m   |r  :d  |f, :s,   |d  :-  |-
```

Quicumque certum quaeritis

ALL ye who seek for sure relief
 In trouble and distress,
Whatever sorrow vex the mind,
 Or guilt the soul oppress,

2
Jesus, who gave himself for you
 Upon the Cross to die,
Opens to you his sacred heart:
 O to that heart draw nigh.

3
Ye hear how kindly he invites;
 Ye hear his words so blest:
'All ye that labour come to me,
 And I will give you rest.'

4
O Jesus, joy of saints on high,
 Thou hope of sinners here,
Attracted by those loving words
 To thee we lift our prayer.

5
Wash thou our wounds in that dear Blood
 Which from thy heart doth flow;
A new and contrite heart on all
 Who cry to thee bestow.

18th cent. *Tr.* E. CASWALL.‡

HYMN 105 FIRST TUNE
KEY E♭ Song 13 Orlando Gibbons, 1583-1625
B♭. t.

```
{ :m  |-  :f  |s  :l  |r  :-.r |m  :-   ‖ :sd |- :r  |m  :f  |r  :r   |d :-
{ :d  |-  :d  |t, :d  |d  :t,  |d  :-   ‖ :d f,|- :f,|m, :l, |s,.f,:r,|m, :-
{ :s  |-  :d  |r  :f  |r  :s   |s  :-   ‖ :m l,|- :l,.t,|d :d|d :t,  |d :-
{ :d  |-  :l, |s, :f, |s, :s,  |d  :-   ‖ :d f,|- :r, |d, :f,|s, :s, |d, :-
```

110

PASSIONTIDE

f. E♭.

{ | :¹₁m|—:f | s :l |f :m |r :— ‖ s |—:f.m|r :d.r,m|r :r | d :— ‖
  | :f₁d|—:d.r|m :f |r :d | t₁:— ‖ :d |—:l₁ | t₁:d | d :t₁ | d :— ‖
  | :d s|—:f |ta:d¹|ta.l:s | s :— ‖ :s |—:d | s :m | s :-.f|m :— ‖
  | :f₁d|—:l₁|s₁:f₁|ta₁:d |s₁:— ‖ :m₁|—:f₁ |s₁:d | s₁:s₁ | d :— ‖ }

SECOND TUNE

KEY **C** St. Prisca   R. Redhead, 1820–1901

{ | m :m |r :m |f :-.f |m :— ‖ s :s |d¹:l |fe:-.fe|s :— |
  | d :d |t₁:d |d :-.d |d :— ‖ m :m |m :m |r :-.r |r :— |
  | s :s |s :s |l :-.l |s :— ‖ d¹:d¹|d¹:d¹|l :-.l |t :— |
  | d :d |s₁:d |f₁:-.f₁|d :— ‖ d :-.t₁|l₁:d |r :-.r |s :— | }

f. F.   C. t.

{ | ˢr :r |r :d | ¹₁r :-.r |m :— ‖ m :m |r :m |f :-.f |m :— |
  | ᵈᵉse₁:l₁|t₁:l₁| ᶠᵉt₁:-.t₁|d :— ‖ d :d |t₁:d |d :-.d |d :— |
  | ᵗᵃf :f |f :m | ʳs :-.s |s :— ‖ s :s |s :s |l :-.l |s :— |
  | ᵐt₁:l₁|se₁:l₁| ʳ₁s₁:-.s₁|d :— ‖ d :d |s₁:d |f₁:-.f₁|d :— | }

In passione Domini

p IN the Lord's atoning grief
    Be our rest and sweet relief;
    Store we deep in heart's recess
    All the shame and bitterness:

2
Thorns and cross and nails and lance,
Wounds, our rich inheritance,
Vinegar and gall and reed,
And the cry his soul that freed.

3
mf May these all our spirits fill,
    And with love's devotion thrill;
    In our souls plant virtue's root,
    And mature its glorious fruit.

4
Crucified, we thee adore;
Thee with all our hearts implore,
Us with all thy saints unite
In the realms of heavenly light.

5
Christ, by coward hands betrayed,
Christ, for us a captive made,
Christ, upon the bitter Tree
Slain for man, be praise to thee.

ST. BONAVENTURA
Tr. F. Oakeley‡

PASSIONTIDE

HYMN 106 FIRST TUNE
KEY A♭ First Mode Melody
T. Tallis, c. 1505-85

(Tonic sol-fa notation omitted)

SECOND TUNE
KEY E♭ St. Francis Xavier
Sir J. Stainer, 1840-1901

(Tonic sol-fa notation omitted)

O Deus, ego amo te

mf MY God, I love thee; not because
I hope for heaven thereby,
Nor yet because who love thee not
Are lost eternally.

2
Thou, O my Jesus, thou didst me
Upon the Cross embrace;
For me didst bear the nails and spear,
And manifold disgrace,

PASSIONTIDE

3
p And griefs and torments numberless,
    And sweat of agony;
Yea, death itself—and all for me
    Who was thine enemy.

4
mf Then why, O blessèd Jesu Christ,
    Should I not love thee well?
Not for the sake of winning heaven,
    Nor of escaping hell;

5
Not from the hope of gaining aught,
    Not seeking a reward;
But as thyself hast lovèd me,
    O ever-loving Lord.

6
f So would I love thee, dearest Lord,
    And in thy praise will sing;
Solely because thou art my God,
    And my most loving King.

17th cent. *Tr.* E. CASWALL†

HYMN 107 Caswall   F. Filitz, 1804–76

KEY F

Viva! Viva! Gesù

1
f GLORY be to Jesus,
    Who, in bitter pains,
Poured for me the life-blood
    From his sacred veins.

2
mf Grace and life eternal
    In that Blood I find:
Blest be his compassion
    Infinitely kind.

3
Blest through endless ages
    Be the precious stream,
Which from endless torments
    Did the world redeem.

4
Abel's blood for vengeance
    Pleaded to the skies;
But the Blood of Jesus
    For our pardon cries.

5
Oft as it is sprinkled
    On our guilty hearts,
Satan in confusion
    Terror-struck departs;

6
f Oft as earth exulting
    Wafts its praise on high,
Angel-hosts rejoicing
    Make their glad reply.

7
Lift ye then your voices;
    Swell the mighty flood;
Louder still and louder
    Praise the precious Blood.

18th cent. *Tr.* E. CASWALL†

PASSIONTIDE

HYMN 108 Rockingham Adapted by E. Miller, 1731–1807

KEY E♭

(musical notation)

DESCANT *For last verse*

Were the whole realm of na - ture mine, That were an offer - ing far too small; Love so a - maz - ing, so di - vine, De - mands my soul, my life, my all.

mf WHEN I survey the wondrous Cross
On which the Prince of Glory died,
My richest gain I count but loss,
And pour contempt on all my pride.

2
Forbid it, Lord, that I should boast
Save in the Cross of Christ my God;
All the vain things that charm me most,
I sacrifice them to his Blood.

3
p See from his head, his hands, his feet,
Sorrow and love flow mingling down;
Did e'er such love and sorrow meet,
Or thorns compose so rich a crown?

[UNISON] 4
f Were the whole realm of nature mine,
That were an offering far too small;
Love so amazing, so divine,
Demands my soul, my life, my all.

I. WATTS‡

PASSIONTIDE

HYMN 109 St. Sepulchre

G. Cooper, 1820–76

KEY E♭

```
{ :d  |s :l |s :d |f :s  |m  ‖s  |d :r.m |f :f  |f :m |r :—  ‖
  :d  |d :d |d :d |l₁:s₁ |s₁ ‖s₁ |l₁:l₁.de|r :r  |r :d |t₁:—  ‖
  :m  |s :f |s :s |f :r  |m  ‖r  |m :f₁.s|l :l  |s :s |s :—   ‖
  :d  |m :f |m :m |r :t₁ |d  ‖t₁ |l₁:f₁.m|r :d  |t₁:d |s₁:—   ‖ }

{ :t  |d':s |l :s |f :l  |s  ‖f  |m :s  |d :r  |m :r |d :—   ‖
  :m  |m :d |d :m |r :r  |r  ‖t₁ |d :t₁ |d :d  |d :t₁|d :—   ‖
  :r' |d':ta|l :l |l :f  |s  ‖s  |s :f  |s :l  |s :s.f|m :—  ‖
  :se₁|l₁:m |f :de|r :d  |t₁ ‖s₁ |d :r  |m :f  |s :s₁|d :—   ‖ }
```

LORD Jesu, when we stand afar,
    And gaze upon thy holy Cross,
In love of thee and scorn of self,
    O may we count the world as loss!

2

When we behold thy bleeding wounds,
    And the rough way that thou hast trod,
Make us to hate the load of sin
    That lay so heavy on our God.

3

O holy Lord, uplifted high,
    With outstretched arms, in mortal woe,
Embracing in thy wondrous love
    The sinful world that lies below,

4

Give us an ever-living faith,
    To gaze beyond the things we see;
And in the mystery of thy Death
    Draw us and all men unto thee.

BISHOP W. WALSHAM HOW

PASSIONTIDE

HYMN 110 FIRST TUNE
KEY **G** The Good Shepherd

P. Heinlein, 1626–86

[Tonic sol-fa notation]

SECOND TUNE

KEY **C** Gethsemane

W. H. Monk, 1823–89
From C. Tye (1553)

[Tonic sol-fa notation]

GO to dark Gethsemane,
  Ye that feel the tempter's power,
Your Redeemer's conflict see,
  Watch with him one bitter hour;
Turn not from his griefs away:
Learn of Jesus Christ to pray.

2
Follow to the judgement-hall,
  View the Lord of Life arraigned;
O the wormwood and the gall!
  O the pangs his soul sustained!
Shun not suffering, shame, or loss:
Learn of him to bear the cross.

PASSIONTIDE

3
Calvary's mournful mountain climb;
  There, adoring at his feet,
Mark that miracle of time,
  God's own Sacrifice complete;
'It is finished!' hear him cry:
Learn of Jesus Christ to die.

J. MONTGOMERY

HYMN 111 Passion Chorale
H. L. Hassler, 1564–1612

KEY **C**

[sol-fa notation]

O Haupt voll Blut und Wunden

mf O SACRED head, surrounded
  By crown of piercing thorn!
O bleeding head, so wounded,
  So shamed and put to scorn!
Death's pallid hue comes o'er thee,
  The glow of life decays;
Yet angel-hosts adore thee,
  And tremble as they gaze.

2
p Thy comeliness and vigour
  Is withered up and gone,
And in thy wasted figure
  I see death drawing on.

O agony and dying!
  O love to sinners free!
Jesu, all grace supplying,
  Turn thou thy face on me.

3
mf In this thy bitter Passion,
  Good Shepherd, think of me
With thy most sweet compassion,
  Unworthy though I be:
Beneath thy Cross abiding
  For ever would I rest,
In thy dear love confiding,
  And with thy presence blest.

P. GERHARDT Based on *Salve caput cruentatum*
Tr. Sir H. W. Baker‡

PASSIONTIDE

HYMN 112   Ades Pater supreme   *Melodiae Prudentianae*, 1533
KEY C

(Evening)   Ades Pater supreme

mf FATHER most high, be with us,
    Unseen, thy goodness showing,
    And Christ the Word incarnate,
    And Spirit grace bestowing.

2

f O Trinity, O Oneness
    Of light and power exceeding;
    O God of God eternal,
    O God, from Both proceeding!

3

mf While daylight hours are passing,
    We live and work before thee;
    Now, ere we rest in slumber,
    We gather to adore thee.

4

Our Christian name and calling
    Of our new birth remind us;
    The Spirit's gifts and sealing
    To firm obedience bind us.

[UNISON] 5

f Begone, ye powers of evil
    With snares and wiles unholy!
    Disturb not with your temptings
    The spirits of the lowly.

[UNISON] 6

Depart! for Christ is present,
    Beside us, yea, within us;
    Away! his sign (ye know it)
    The victory shall win us.

7

p Awhile the body resteth;
    The spirit, wakeful ever,
    Abideth in communion
    With Christ, who sleepeth never.

[UNISON] 8

f To God, the eternal Father,
    To Christ our sure salvation,
    To God, the Holy Spirit,
    Be endless adoration.

                           PRUDENTIUS
                           Tr. Compilers (1889)

GOOD FRIDAY

Hymn 113 St. Cross

J. B. Dykes, 1823–76

KEY **F**

p   O COME and mourn with me awhile;
      O come ye to the Saviour's side;
      O come, together let us mourn:
        Jesus, our Lord, is crucified.

2

Have we no tears to shed for him,
    While soldiers scoff and Jews deride?
Ah, look how patiently he hangs:
    Jesus, our Lord, is crucified.

3

How fast his hands and feet are nailed;
    His throat with parching thirst is dried;
His failing eyes are dimmed with blood:
    Jesus, our Lord, is crucified.

4

Seven times he spake, seven words of love;
    And all three hours his silence cried
For mercy on the souls of men:
    Jesus, our Lord, is crucified.

5

mf   O love of God! O sin of man!
      In this dread act your strength is tried;
      And victory remains with love:
        Jesus, our Lord, is crucified.

                      F. W. Faber‡

GOOD FRIDAY

HYMN 114

FIRST TUNE

KEY E♭ Vulpius

M. Vulpius, c. 1560–1616

THE FIRST WORD FROM THE CROSS

'Father, forgive them, for they know not what they do'

'FORGIVE them, O my Father,
 They know not what they do:'
The Saviour spake in anguish,
 As the sharp nails went through.

2

No word of anger spake he
 To them that shed his blood,
But prayer and tenderest pity
 Large as the love of God.

3

For me was that compassion,
 For me that tender care;
I need his wide forgiveness
 As much as any there.

SECOND TUNE

KEY G St. Margaret

W. Statham, 1832–98

GOOD FRIDAY

4
It was my pride and hardness
That hung him on the Tree;
Those cruel nails, O Saviour,
Were driven in by me.

5
And often I have slighted
Thy gentle voice that chid:
Forgive me too, Lord Jesus;
I knew not what I did.

6
O depth of sweet compassion!
O love divine and true!
Save thou the souls that slight thee,
And know not what they do.

MRS. C. F. ALEXANDER†

HYMN 115 Intercessor   Sir C. H. H. Parry, 1848–1918
KEY C

p O WORD of pity, for our pardon pleading,
   Breathed in the hour of loneliness and pain;
mf O voice, which through the ages interceding
   Calls us to fellowship with God again!

2
p O word of comfort, through the silence stealing,
   As the dread act of sacrifice began;
   O infinite compassion, still revealing
   The infinite forgiveness won for man!

3
mf O word of hope to raise us nearer heaven,
   When courage fails us and when faith is dim!
   The souls for whom Christ prays to Christ are given,
   To find their pardon and their joy in him.

4
O Intercessor, who art ever living
To plead for dying souls that they may live,
Teach us to know our sin which needs forgiving,
Teach us to know the love which can forgive.

ADA R. GREENAWAY

Alternative Tune, St. Winifred, 103

GOOD FRIDAY

HYMN 116 St. Agnes

J. Langran, 1835-1909

KEY **F**

```
{|m :— |d :r |m :— |s :— |f :m |m :r |d :— |— :— ||m :— |m :r
 |d :— |d :d |d :— |d :— |d :d |d :t₁|d :— |— :— ||d :— |l₁:l₁
 |s :— |m :f |s :— |s :— |l :s |s :f |m :— |— :— ||s :— |fe :fe
 |d :— |d :d |d :— |m₁:— |f₁:d |s₁:s₁|d :— |— :— ||d :— |d :d }

{|s :— |r :— |m :r |r :d |t₁:— |— :— ||d :— |d :d |f :— |m :— |s :—.m|r :d
 |r :— |s₁:— |s₁:s₁|s₁:l₁|s₁:— |— :— ||d :— |d :d |t₁:— |d :— |d :—.d|l₁:l₁
 |s :— |s :— |d :r |m :fe|s :— |— :— ||s :— |l :s |s :— |s :— |m :—.s|f :m
 |t₁:— |t₁:— |d :t₁|l₁:r₁|s₁:— |— :— ||m :— |f :m |r :— |d :— |d :—.d|f₁:f₁}

{|t₁:— |— :— ||d :— |r :d |d :r |m :f |m :— |r :— |d :— |— :— ||
 |s₁:— |— :— ||s₁:— |s₁:s₁|l₁:t₁|d :d |d :— |t₁:— |d :— |— :— ||
 |r :— |— :— ||s :— |ta:ta|l :la|s :l |s :— |f :— |m :— |— :— ||
 |s₁:— |— :— ||m :— |m :m |f :f |m :r |s :— |s₁:— |d :— |— :— ||}
```

THE SECOND WORD FROM THE CROSS

'Verily I say unto thee, To-day shalt thou be with me in Paradise'

'LORD, when thy Kingdom comes, remember me!'
    Thus spake the dying lips to dying ears:
O faith, which in that darkest hour could see
    The promised glory of the far-off years!

2

No kingly sign declares that glory now,
    No ray of hope lights up that awful hour;
A thorny crown surrounds the bleeding brow,
    The hands are stretched in weakness, not in power.

3

Hark! through the gloom the dying Saviour saith,
    'Thou too shalt rest in Paradise to-day:'
O words of love to answer words of faith!
    O words of hope for those who live to pray!

4

Lord, when with dying lips my prayer is said,
    Grant that in faith thy Kingdom I may see;
And, thinking on thy Cross and bleeding head,
    May breathe my parting words, 'Remember me.'

5*

Remember me, but not my shame or sin:
    Thy cleansing Blood hath washed them all away;
Thy precious Death for me did pardon win;
    Thy Blood redeemed me in that awful day.

GOOD FRIDAY

6
Remember me; and, ere I pass away,
  Speak thou the assuring word that sets us free,
And make thy promise to my heart, 'To-day,
  Thou too shalt rest in Paradise with me.'

ARCHBISHOP W. D. MACLAGAN

Alternative Tune, Ellers, 31

HYMN 117 Burford   J. Chetham, *Psalms*, 1718

KEY **B♭**

mf   O THOU from whom all goodness flows,
         I lift my heart to thee;
       In all my sorrows, conflicts, woes,
p   Good Lord, remember me.

2
mf   When on my aching burdened heart
         My sins lie heavily,
       Thy pardon grant, thy peace impart:
p   Good Lord, remember me.

3
mf   When trials sore obstruct my way,
         And ills I cannot flee,
       Then let my strength be as my day:
p   Good Lord, remember me.

4
mf   If worn with pain, disease, and grief
         This feeble spirit be,
       Grant patience, rest, and kind relief:
p   Good Lord, remember me.

5
mf   And O, when in the hour of death
         I bow to thy decree,
       Jesu, receive my parting breath:
p   Good Lord, remember me.

T. HAWEIS‡

Alternative Tune, Abridge, 300

GOOD FRIDAY

Hymn 118 Stabat Mater *Traditional Melody*
Key F

```
    |d :r |m :r |m :s |f :m ||m :r |d :t₁| l₁:t₁|l₁:s₁| r :d |r :m | r :-.d|d :-||
    |s₁:t₁|d :s₁| d :d |d :d || d :t₁|s₁:s₁|fe₁:s₁|fe₁:s₁| l₁:l₁|t₁:d | d :t₁|d :-||
    |m :s |s :s | s :s |l :s || s :s |d :r | r :r |r :t₁| r :m |s :s | s :s |m :-||
    |d :s₁|d :t₁| d :m₁|f₁:d || d :s₁|m₁:s₁| r₁:s₁|r₁:s₁| f₁:l₁|s₁:m₁| s₁:s₁|d₁:-||
```
D.C.

THE THIRD WORD FROM THE CROSS

'Woman, behold thy son . . . Behold thy mother'

Stabat Mater dolorosa

mf AT the Cross her station keeping
    Stood the mournful Mother weeping,
      Where he hung, the dying Lord;
    For her soul, of joy bereavèd,
    Bowed with anguish, deeply grievèd,
      Felt the sharp and piercing sword.

2

p O how sad and sore distressèd
    Now was she, that Mother blessèd
      Of the Sole-begotten One!
    Deep the woe of her affliction,
    When she saw the Crucifixion
      Of her ever-glorious Son.

3

mf Who, on Christ's dear Mother gazing
    Pierced by anguish so amazing,
      Born of woman, would not weep?
    Who, on Christ's dear Mother thinking
    Such a cup of sorrow drinking,
      Would not share her sorrows deep?

4

p For his people's sins chastisèd,
    She beheld her Son despisèd,
      Scourged, and crowned with thorns entwined;
    Saw him then from judgement taken,
    And in death by all forsaken,
      Till his spirit he resigned.

5

mf O good Jesu, let me borrow
    Something of thy Mother's sorrow,
      Fount of love, Redeemer kind,
    That my heart fresh ardour gaining,
    And a purer love attaining,
      May with thee acceptance find.

Ascribed to JACOPONE DA TODI
Tr. E. Caswall and Compilers

GOOD FRIDAY

HYMN 119 Cassel *Christen-schatz* (Basle, 1745)

KEY **G**

THE FOURTH WORD FROM THE CROSS

'My God, my God, why hast thou forsaken me?'

THRONED upon the awful Tree,
King of grief, I watch with thee;
Darkness veils thine anguished face,
None its lines of woe can trace,
None can tell what pangs unknown
Hold thee silent and alone:

2

Silent through those three dread hours,
Wrestling with the evil powers,
Left alone with human sin,
Gloom around thee and within,
Till the appointed time is nigh,
Till the Lamb of God may die.

3

Hark that cry that peals aloud
Upward through the whelming cloud!
Thou, the Father's only Son,
Thou, his own Anointed One,
Thou dost ask him (can it be?)
'Why hast thou forsaken me?'

4

Lord, should fear and anguish roll
Darkly o'er my sinful soul,
Thou, who once wast thus bereft
That thine own might ne'er be left,
Teach me by that bitter cry
In the gloom to know thee nigh.

J. ELLERTON

GOOD FRIDAY

Hymn 120 Saffron Walden
A. H. Brown, 1830–1926
KEY D

By permission of the Oxford University Press

THE FIFTH WORD FROM THE CROSS

'I thirst'

HIS are the thousand sparkling rills
That from a thousand fountains burst,
And fill with music all the hills;
    And yet he saith, 'I thirst.'

2
All fiery pangs on battle-fields,
On fever beds where sick men toss,
Are in that human cry he yields
    To anguish on the Cross.

3
But more than pains that racked him
Was the deep longing thirst divine [then
That thirsted for the souls of men:
    Dear Lord! and one was mine.

4
O Love most patient, give me grace;
Make all my soul athirst for thee:
That parched dry lip, that fading face,
    That thirst, were all for me.

MRS. C. F. ALEXANDER

Alternative Tune, Misericordia, 349

Hymn 121 Walmisley
T. A. Walmisley, 1814–56
KEY B♭

mf O PERFECT God, thy love
As perfect Man did share
Here upon earth each form of ill
Thy fellow-men must bear.

2
Now from the Tree of scorn
We hear thy voice again;
Thou who didst take our mortal flesh
Hast felt our mortal pain.

GOOD FRIDAY

3
p Thy body suffers thirst,
Parched are thy lips and dry:
How poor the offering man can bring
Thy thirst to satisfy!

4
mf O Saviour, by thy thirst
Borne on the Cross of shame,
Grant us in all our sufferings here
To glorify thy name;

5
That through each pain and grief
Our souls may onward move
To gain more likeness to thy life,
More knowledge of thy love.

ADA R. GREENAWAY

Alternative Tune, St. Bride, 322

HYMN 122 Southwell   W. Damon, *Psalms*, 1579
KEY A♭

{ :l₁ | d :d | t₁ :t₁ | l₁ :— | — | | l₁ | d :d | r :r | m :— | — |
  :m₁ | m₁ :l₁ | l₁ :se₁ | l₁ :— | — | | m₁ | m₁ :m₁ | l₁ :s₁ | s₁ :— | — |
  :d | d :d | f :m | d :— | — | | d | d :d | d :t₁ | d :— | — |
  :l₁ | l₁ :f₁ | r₁ :m₁ | l₁ :— | — | | l₁ | l₁ :s₁ | f₁ :s₁ | d₁ :— | — | }

{ :m | s :s | f :f | m :m | r | | m | r :d | t₁ :t₁ | l₁ :— | — |
  :d | d :t₁ | l₁ :s₁ | s₁ :s₁ | s₁ | | s₁ | f₁ :m₁ | m₁ :m₁ | d₁ :— | — |
  :m | r :r | d :r | d :d | t₁ | | d | l₁ :l₁ | l₁ :se₁ | l₁ :— | — |
  :d | s₁ :s₁ | l₁ :t₁ | d :m₁ | s₁ | | d₁ | r₁ :l₁ | m₁ :m₁ | l₂ :— | — | }

THE SIXTH WORD FROM THE CROSS

'It is finished'

1
O PERFECT life of love!
All, all is finished now;
All that he left his throne above
To do for us below.

2
No work is left undone
Of all the Father willed;
His toil, his sorrows, one by one,
The scripture have fulfilled.

3
No pain that we can share
But he has felt its smart;
All forms of human grief and care
Have pierced that tender heart.

4
And on his thorn-crowned head,
And on his sinless soul,
Our sins in all their guilt were laid,
That he might make us whole.

5
In perfect love he dies;
For me he dies, for me:
O all-atoning Sacrifice,
I cling by faith to thee.

6
In every time of need,
Before the judgement-throne,
Thy works, O Lamb of God, I'll plead,
Thy merits, not my own.

7
Yet work, O Lord, in me
As thou for me hast wrought;
And let my love the answer be
To grace thy love has brought.

SIR H. W. BAKER

Alternative Tune, St. Paul's, 200

GOOD FRIDAY

Hymn 123 Strength and Stay J. B. Dykes, 1823-76
Key D

[tonic sol-fa notation]

THE SEVENTH WORD FROM THE CROSS

'Father, into thy hands I commend my spirit'

AND now, belovèd Lord, thy soul resigning
  Into thy Father's arms with conscious will,
Calmly, with reverend grace, thy head inclining,
  The throbbing brow and labouring breast grow still.

2
Freely thy life thou yieldest, meekly bending
  E'en to the last beneath our sorrows' load,
Yet, strong in death, in perfect peace commending
  Thy spirit to thy Father and thy God.

3
Sweet Saviour, in mine hour of mortal anguish,
  When earth grows dim, and round me falls the night,
O breathe thy peace, as flesh and spirit languish;
  At that dread eventide let there be light.

4
To thy dear Cross turn thou mine eyes in dying;
  Lay but my fainting head upon thy breast;
Those outstretched arms receive my latest sighing—
  And then, O then, thine everlasting rest.

MRS. E. S. ALDERSON

GOOD FRIDAY EVENING AND EASTER EVEN

HYMN 124　　　　　　　　　FIRST TUNE
KEY E♭　Batty　　　　　　　　　*Christen-schatz* (Basle, 1745)

```
| d :r  | m :r  | m :f  | s :m  || l :s  | f :m  | r :r  | m :—  ||
| d :t₁ | d :s₁ | d :d  | t₁:d  || d :d  | d :d  | d :t₁ | d :—  ||
| m :s  | s :s  | s :d  | r :m  || f :s  | l :s  | s :s  | s :—  ||
| d :s₁ | d :t₁ | d :l₁ | s₁:d  || f₁:m₁ | f₁:d  | s₁:s₁ | d :—  ||

| s :s  | s :r  | m :f  | m :r  || d :r  | m :f  | m :r  | d :—  ||
| d :d  | t₁:r  | d :d  | d :t₁ || l₁:t₁ | d :d  | d :t₁ | d :—  ||
| m :m  | r :s  | s :l  | s :s  || m :s  | s :l  | s :s  | m :—  ||
| d :d  | s₁:t₁ | d :f₁ | s₁:s₁ || l₁:s₁ | d :f₁ | s₁:s₁ | d :—  ||
```

SECOND TUNE
KEY E♭　Portsea　　　　　　　　　W. Boyce, 1710–79

```
| l :s.f | m :f  | r :m  | d :t₁ || l₁:t₁  | d.r:m  | l :t  | se:— ||
| d :r   | d :d  | t₁:t₁ | l₁:se₁|| l₁:se₁ | l₁:l   | d :r  | t₁:— ||
| m :s   | s :l  | f :m  | m :m  || d :m   | m :m   | f :f  | m :— ||
| l₁:t₁  | d :l₁ | t₁:se₁| l₁:m₁ || f₁:m₁  | l₁:d   | f :r  | m :— ||

| l :t  | d':t.l | s :f   | m :r  || d :r  | m :l   | r.d:t₁  | l₁:— ||
| m :m  | m :r   | r :t₁  | d :t₁ || l₁:t₁ | d :d   | t₁.l₁:l₁.se₁ | l₁:— ||
| l :se | l :f   | s :s   | s :f  || m :s  | s :f   | f.l:m.r | d :— ||
| d :t₁ | l₁:r   | t₁:s₁  | d :s₁ || l₁:s₁ | d :f₁  | r₁:m₁   | l₁:— ||
```

p IT is finished! blessèd Jesus,
　Thou hast breathed thy latest sigh,
　Teaching us the sons of Adam
　　How the Son of God can die.

2
Lifeless lies the piercèd body,
　Resting in its rocky bed;
Thou hast left the Cross of anguish
　For the mansions of the dead.

mf In the hidden realms of darkness
　Shines a light unseen before,
When the Lord of dead and living
　Enters at the lowly door.

4
Lo, in spirit, rich in mercy
　Comes he from the world above,
Preaching to the souls in prison
　Tidings of his dying love.

5
Lo, the heavenly light around him,
　As he draws his people near;
All amazed they come rejoicing
　At the gracious words they hear.

6
Patriarch and priest and prophet
　Gather round him as he stands,
In adoring faith and gladness
　Hearing of the piercèd hands.

7
There in lowliest joy and wonder
　Stands the robber at his side,
Reaping now the blessèd promise
　Spoken by the Crucified.

8
p Jesus, Lord of dead and living,
　Let thy mercy rest on me;
Grant me too, when life is finished,
　Rest in Paradise with thee.

ARCHBISHOP W. D. MACLAGAN
(Revised version by the author, 1902)

GOOD FRIDAY EVENING AND EASTER EVEN

HYMN 125 Holy Sepulchre   E. H. Thorne, 1834–1916

KEY **D**

[Tonic sol-fa notation]

BY Jesus' grave on either hand,
While night is brooding o'er the land,
The sad and silent mourners stand.

2
At last the weary life is o'er,
The agony and conflict sore
Of him who all our sufferings bore.

3
Deep in the rock's sepulchral shade
The Lord by whom the worlds were made,
The Saviour of mankind, is laid.

4
O hearts bereaved and sore distressed,
Here is for you a place of rest;
Here leave your griefs on Jesus' breast.

I. GREGORY SMITH

HYMN 126 O Traurigkeit   German Melody, 1628

KEY **A♭**

[Tonic sol-fa notation]

O SORROW deep!
Who would not weep
  With heartfelt pain and sighing?
God the Father's only Son
  In the tomb is lying.

2
O Jesus blest,
My help and rest,
  With tears I pray thee, hear me:
Now, and even unto death,
  Dearest Lord, be near me.

JOHANN RIST *Tr.* W. DOUGLAS

GOOD FRIDAY EVENING AND EASTER EVEN

Hymn 127 Petra   R. Redhead, 1820–1901

KEY **D**

```
{ |d :d |r :m |f :-.f |m :- || |d :d |r :m |r :r |d :- ||
  |s, :s, |t, :d |d :-.d |d :- || |s, :l, |t, :d |d :t, |d :- ||
  |m :m |s :s |l :-.l |s :- || |m :m |s :s |l :s |m :- ||
  |d :d |s, :d |f, :-.f, |d :- || |d :l, |s, :d |f, :s, |d :- || }

{ |d :m |s :s |l :l |s :- || |d :m |s :s |l :-.l |s :- ||
  |d :d |r :m |d :r |m :- || |d :d |r :t, |m :r.d |t, :- ||
  |m :l |t :d' |d' :t |d' :- || |s :s |s :s |s :fe |s :- ||
  |d :l, |s, :d |f :f |d :- || |m :d |t, :m |d :r |s :- || }

{ |d :d |r :m |f :-.f |m :- || |d :r |m :r |d :t, |d :- ||
  |d :d |t, :d |d :-.d |d :- || |d :t, |d :l, |s, :s, |s, :- ||
  |s :s |f :s |l :-.l |s :- || |s :f |s :f |m :r |m :- ||
  |m :m |r :d |f, :-.f, |d :- || |m :r |d :f, |s, :s, |d :- || }
```

RESTING from his work to-day
In the tomb the Saviour lay;
Still he slept, from head to feet‿
Shrouded in the winding-sheet,
Lying in the rock alone,
Hidden by the sealèd stone.

2

Late at even there was seen
Watching long the Magdalene;
Early, ere the break of day,
Sorrowful she took her way
To the holy garden glade,
Where her buried Lord was laid.

3

So with thee, till life shall end,
I would solemn vigil spend;
Let me hew thee, Lord, a shrine
In this rocky heart of mine,
Where in pure embalmèd cell
None but thou may ever dwell.

4

Myrrh and spices will I bring,
True affection's offering;
Close the door from sight and sound‿
Of the busy world around;
And in patient watch remain
Till my Lord appear again.

                         T. WHYTEHEAD‡

EASTER

HYMN 128 St. Fulbert H. J. Gauntlett, 1805–76

KEY E♭

Chorus novae Jerusalem

f   YE choirs of new Jerusalem,
       Your sweetest notes employ,
     The Paschal victory to hymn
       In strains of holy joy.

2

For Judah's Lion bursts his chains,
   Crushing the serpent's head;
And cries aloud through death's domains
   To wake the imprisoned dead.

3

Devouring depths of hell their prey
   At his command restore;
His ransomed hosts pursue their way
   Where Jesus goes before.

[UNISON]   4

Triumphant in his glory now
   To him all power is given;
To him in one communion bow
   All saints in earth and heaven.

5

mf   While we his soldiers praise our King,
       His mercy we implore,
     Within his palace bright to bring
       And keep us evermore.

EASTER

[UNISON] 6

f All glory to the Father be,
All glory to the Son,
All glory, Holy Ghost, to thee,
While endless ages run.
Alleluia! Amen.

{| s : s | l :— | s :— | l :— | d¹ :— |
d : d	d :—	d :—	f :—	m :—
m : m	f :—	m :—	d¹ :—	d¹ :—
d : d	f₁:—	d :—	{f/f₁}:—	d :—	

Al - le - lu - ia!   A - men.

ST. FULBERT OF CHARTRES
Tr. R. Campbell and Compilers

NOTE. *In verse 2, lines 1–2, Christ, 'the Lion that is of the tribe of Judah' (Rev. 5. 5), is portrayed as fulfilling the promise of redemption in Gen. 3. 15.*

HYMN 129   FIRST TUNE

KEY **C** Ad cenam Agni   Mode viii

Ad cenam Agni providi

{| s   d¹   l   s   d¹   t   d¹   r¹   d¹   t   l }
 1 The Lamb's high ban - quet called to share,
 2 Up - on the al - tar of the Cross
 3 Now Christ our Pass - o - ver is slain,
 4 Christ ris - es con - queror from the grave,
 5 All praise be thine, O ris - en Lord,

{| l   l   s   m   f   s   m   s   f   m   r — }
 1 Ar - rayed in gar - ments white and fair,
 2 His bo - dy hath re - deemed our loss;
 3 The Lamb of God with - out a stain;
 4 From death re - turn - ing strong to save;
 5 From death to end - less life re - stored;

{| m   m   r   d   s   s   l   d¹   d¹   t }
 1 The Red Sea past, we fain would sing
 2 And, tast - ing of his pre - cious Blood,
 3 His flesh, the true un - leav - ened bread,
 4 With his right hand the ty - rant chains,
 5 All praise to God the Fa - ther be

{| d¹   r¹   d¹   t   l   s   t   l   t   d¹   l   s   s — ||
 1 To Je - sus our tri - um - phant King.
 2 In him we live a - new to God.
 3 For us is free - ly off - er - ed.
 4 And Par - a - dise for man re - gains.
 5 And Ho - ly Ghost e - ter - nal - ly.

133

EASTER

SECOND TUNE

HYMN 129

KEY **C**   Grenoble

Melody from J. B. Croft's *Collection*

Ad cenam Agni providi

THE Lamb's high banquet called to share,
Arrayed in garments white and fair,
The Red Sea past, we fain would sing
To Jesus our triumphant King.

2
Upon the altar of the Cross
His body hath redeemed our loss;
And, tasting of his precious Blood,
In him we live anew to God.

3
Now Christ our Passover is slain,
The Lamb of God without a stain;

His flesh, the true unleavened bread,
For us is freely offerèd.

4
Christ rises conqueror from the grave,
From death returning, strong to save;
With his right hand the tyrant chains,
And Paradise for man regains.

[UNISON]
5
All praise be thine, O risen Lord,
From death to endless life restored;
All praise to God the Father be
And Holy Ghost eternally.

Tr. J. M. NEALE and Compilers

HYMN 130   O filii et filiae

French Melody (17th cent.)

KEY **B♭**

UNISON

Al - le - lu - ia!   Al - le - lu - ia!   Al - - le - lu - ia!

EASTER

(musical notation in tonic sol-fa, with text "Al - le - lu - ia!" beneath)

O filii et filiae

f ALLELUIA! Alleluia! Alleluia!
O sons and daughters, let us sing!
The King of Heaven, the glorious King,
O'er death to-day rose triumphing.
 Alleluia!

2
mf That Easter morn, at break of day,
The faithful women went their way
To seek the tomb where Jesus lay.
 Alleluia!

3
An angel clad in white they see,
Who sat, and spake unto the three,
'Your Lord doth go to Galilee.'
 Alleluia!

4
p That night the apostles met in fear;
Amidst them came their Lord most dear,
And said, 'My peace be on all here.'
 Alleluia!

5
mf When Thomas first the tidings heard,
How they had seen the risen Lord,
He doubted the disciples' word.
 Alleluia!

6
p 'My piercèd side, O Thomas, see;
My hands, my feet I show to thee;
Not faithless, but believing be.'
 Alleluia!

7
mf No longer Thomas then denied;
He saw the feet, the hands, the side;
f 'Thou art my Lord and God,' he cried.
 Alleluia!

8
mf How blest are they who have not seen,
And yet whose faith hath constant been!
For they eternal life shall win.
 Alleluia!

9
f On this most holy day of days,
To God your hearts and voices raise
In laud and jubilee and praise.
 Alleluia!

J. TISSERAND
Tr. J. M. Neale and Compilers

EASTER

HYMN 131

FIRST TUNE

KEY **C** Sampford   John Ireland

With movement

```
{ :d'.t  | l  :d'  :s.f  | m  || m.f  :s.l   | s  :-.m :r   ||
{ :s.s   | s  :f   :m.r  | d  || m.r  :d.l₁  | d  :-.d :t₁  ||
{ :d'.d' | d' :l   :s.s  | s  || d'.t :s.d'  | s  :-.s :s   ||
{ :m.m   | f  :-.r :t₁.t₁| d  || d.r  :m.f   | m  :-.d :s₁  ||
```

G. t.
```
{ ᵐl₁.t₁:d.l₁ :d.r   | m || m.f   :s.m    | r  :-.d | d :- ||
{ ᵈf₁.s₁:s₁.m₁:l₁.t₁ | d || d.d   :d.s₁   | l₁ :s₁.m₁| m₁:- ||
{ ˢd.r  :d.d  :m.s   | s || l.l   :s.d    | d  :t₁.d | d :- ||
{ ᵈf₁.f₁:m₁.l₁:l₁.s₁ | d || l₁.l₁ :m₁.m₁  | f₁ :s₁.d₁| d₁:- ||
```

f. C.   G. t.
```
{ ᵈs.l :d' :-.t | l.se :l  | ¹r.m :s.m   | m  :-.r :m ||
{ s₁.r.f:s :f   | m.m  :m  | ¹r.d :t₁.d  | l₁ :t₁   :d ||
{ ᵐt.d':d' :r'  | d'.t :d' | r's.s:f.s   | l  :s    :s ||
{ ᵈs.f :m  :r   | m.m  :l  | ᶠᵉt₁.d:r.m  | f  :s    :d ||
```

f. C.
```
{ ᶠd'.r':m' :d'.t | l.s  :m :-. || f.s  :l :d' | r  :-.d | d :- ||
{ ᵈs.f :m  :s.s  | f.r  :de:-. || r.m  :f :r  | d  :t₁.d| d :- ||
{ ᵈs.t :d' :-.d' | d'.t :l :-.  || l.d' :d':l  | s  :-.m | m :- ||
{ ˡm.r :d  :m.m  | f.s  :l :-.  || r.d  :f :f  | s  :-.d | d :- ||
```

SECOND TUNE

KEY **G** St. George   Sir G. J. Elvey, 1816–93

```
{ m :-.m | s :m | d :r | m :-  || m :-.m | s :m  | d :r | m :-   ||
{ s₁:-.s₁| s₁:s₁| l₁:t₁| d :-  || s₁:-.s₁| s₁:s₁ | l₁:l₁| se:-   ||
{ d :-.d | r :m | m :s | s :-  || d :-.d | r :d  | m :f | t₁:-   ||
{ d :-.d | t₁:d | l₁:s₁| d :-  || d :-.d | t₁:d  | l₁:f₁| m₁:-   ||
```

D. t.
```
{ m :-.m | f :f | r :-.r| m :- || ᵐl :t | d' :f | m :r | d :-   ||
{ l₁:-.l₁| l₁:l₁| s₁:s₁ | s₁:- || ˢd :r | d  :r | d :t₁| d :-   ||
{ d :-.d | r :r | t₁:t₁ | d :- || ᵈf :f | s  :l | s :-.f| m :-  ||
{ l₁:-.l₁| r₁:r₁| s₁:s₁ | d₁:- || ᵈf :r | m  :f | s :s₁| d :-   ||
```

EASTER

(Sol-fa notation omitted)

CHRIST the Lord is risen to-day!
Christians, haste your vows to pay.
Offer ye your praises meet
At the Paschal Victim's feet.
For the sheep the Lamb hath bled,
Sinless in the sinner's stead:
'Christ is risen!' to-day we cry;
Now he lives no more to die.

2

Christ, the Victim undefiled,
Man to God hath reconciled;
Whilst in strange and awful strife
Met together death and life.
Christians, on this happy day
Haste with joy your vows to pay:
'Christ is risen!' to-day we cry;
Now he lives no more to die.

3

Christ, who once for sinners bled,
Now the First-born from the dead,
Throned in endless might and power,
Lives and reigns for evermore.
Hail, eternal hope on high!
Hail, thou King of victory!
Hail, thou Prince of Life adored!
Help and save us, gracious Lord.

JANE E. LEESON

EASTER

HYMN 132 Ellacombe   *Würtemburg Gesangbuch, 1784*

KEY B♭

ἀναστάσεως ἡμέρα

f   THE day of Resurrection!
       Earth, tell it out abroad;
   The Passover of gladness,
       The Passover of God!
   From death to life eternal,
       From earth unto the sky,
   Our God hath brought us over
       With hymns of victory.

2

mf   Our hearts be pure from evil,
       That we may see aright
   The Lord in rays eternal
       Of Resurrection-light;
   And, listening to his accents,
       May hear so calm and plain
   His own 'All hail,' and, hearing,
       May raise the victor strain.

3

f   Now let the heavens be joyful,
       And earth her song begin,
   The round world keep high triumph,
       And all that is therein;
   Let all things seen and unseen
       Their notes of gladness blend,
   For Christ the Lord is risen,
       Our joy that hath no end.

ST. JOHN OF DAMASCUS
Tr. J. M. Neale‡

EASTER

HYMN 133 St. John Damascene   A. H. Brown, 1830–1926

KEY **G**

[tonic sol-fa notation]

αἴσωμεν πάντες λαοί

1
COME, ye faithful, raise the strain
  Of triumphant gladness!
God hath brought his Israel
  Into joy from sadness;
Loosed from Pharaoh's bitter yoke
  Jacob's sons and daughters;
Led them with unmoistened foot
  Through the Red Sea waters.

2
'Tis the spring of souls to-day;
  Christ hath burst his prison,
And from three days' sleep in death
  As a sun hath risen:
All the winter of our sins,
  Long and dark, is flying
From his light, to whom we give
  Laud and praise undying.

3
Now the queen of seasons, bright
  With the day of splendour,
With the royal feast of feasts,
  Comes its joy to render;
Comes to glad Jerusalem,
  Who with true affection
Welcomes in unwearied strains
  Jesu's Resurrection.

4
Alleluia now we cry
  To our King immortal,
Who triumphant burst the bars
  Of the tomb's dark portal;
Alleluia, with the Son
  God the Father praising;
Alleluia yet again
  To the Spirit raising.

ST. JOHN OF DAMASCUS
Tr. J. M. Neale and Compilers

Alternative Tune, Ave virgo, 294

EASTER

HYMN 134 Easter Hymn *Lyra Davidica*, 1708

KEY **C**

[sheet music with Descant, G.t., and f.C. settings]

The Descant may be used for verse 3

JESUS Christ is risen to-day,   Alleluia!
Our triumphant holy day,   Alleluia!
Who did once, upon the Cross,   Alleluia!
Suffer to redeem our loss.   Alleluia!

2

Hymns of praise then let us sing,   Alleluia!
Unto Christ, our heavenly King,   Alleluia!
Who endured the Cross and grave,   Alleluia!
Sinners to redeem and save.   Alleluia!

EASTER

3
But the pains that he endured, Alleluia!
Our salvation have procured; Alleluia!
Now above the sky he's King, Alleluia!
Where the angels ever sing. Alleluia!

Lyra Davidica (1708) and the *Supplement* (1816)

HYMN **135** FIRST TUNE
KEY **C** Gelobt sei Gott M. Vulpius, *Gesangbuch*, 1609

d':d':t	d' :-.t:l	s:s :fe	s :-.f:m	r:d :t₁	d :-:-
s :s :-.f	m :- :f	r:r :-.d	t₁ :- :d	t₁:l₁:s₁	s₁:-:-
Al - le - lu-	ia! . . .	Al-le-lu-	ia! . . .	Al - le - lu-	ia!
m':m':r'	d' :- :-	t:t :l	s :- :-	s :m :f	m :-:-
d':d' :s	d'.t:l.s:f	s:s :r	s.f:m.r:d	s₁:l₁ :r	d :-:-

d' :t :l	s :- :s	l :- :t	d' :- :-	d':d' :r'	s :- :d'
s :s :m	m :- :m	f :m :s	s :- :-	m :f :f	m :- :l
m' :r' :d'	t :- :d'	d' :- :r'	m' :- :-	s :l :t	d' :-.r':m'
d :s₁:l₁	m :- :d	f :l :s	d :- :-	d :f :r	d :-.t₁:l₁

t :l :-	s :- :-	s :m :l	s :- :f	m :r :-	d :- :-
s :- :fe	s :- :-	d :d :l₁	d :-.m :r	d :- :t₁	d :- :-
r':m':r'	t :- :-	m :s :f	s :-.d':l	s :l :s	m :- :-
t₁:d :r	s₁:- :-	d :d :r	m :-.d :r	m :f :s	d :- :-

d':d':t	d' :-.t:l	s:s :fe	s :-.f:m	r:d :t₁	d :-:-
s :s :-.f	m :- :f	r:r :-.d	t₁ :- :d	t₁:l₁:s₁	s₁:-:-
Al - le - lu-	ia! . . .	Al-le-lu-	ia! . . .	Al - le - lu-	ia!
m':m':r'	d' :- :-	t:t :l	s :- :-	s :m :f	m :-:-
d':d' :s	d'.t:l.s:f	s:s :r	s.f:m.r:d	s₁:l₁ :r	d :-:-

Finita jam sunt praelia

f   ALLELUIA! Alleluia! Alleluia!
    The strife is o'er, the battle done;
    Now is the Victor's triumph won;
    O let the song of praise be sung: Alleluia!

2
Death's mightiest powers have done their worst,
And Jesus hath his foes dispersed;
Let shouts of praise and joy outburst: **Alleluia!**

3
On the third morn he rose again
Glorious in majesty to reign;
O let us swell the joyful strain: Alleluia!

4
p   Lord, by the stripes which wounded thee
    From death's dread sting thy servants free,
f   That we may live, and sing to thee   Alleluia!

? 17th cent. *Tr.* F. POTT‡

EASTER

SECOND TUNE

HYMN 135
KEY E Victory   Adapted from P. da Palestrina, 1525–94

:m :m	f :—:—	:m :s :s	l :—:—:—	:s :s :d¹	t :—:—:—	d¹ : :
:d :d	d :—:—	:d :d :d	d :—:—:—	:d :d :m	r :—:—:—	m : :
Al-le-	lu -	ia! Al-le-	lu —	ia! Al-le-	lu -	ia!
:s :s	l :—:—	:s :m :m	f :—:—:—	:m :s :s	s :—:—:—	s : :
:d :d	f₁ :—:—	:d :d :d	f₁ :—:—:—	:d :m :d	s₁ :—:—:—	d : :

Finita jam sunt praelia

f   ALLELUIA! Alleluia! Alleluia!
The strife is o'er, the battle done;
Now is the Victor's triumph won;
O let the song of praise be sung: Alleluia!

2
Death's mightiest powers have done their worst,
And Jesus hath his foes dispersed;
Let shouts of praise and joy outburst: Alleluia!

3
On the third morn he rose again
Glorious in majesty to reign;
O let us swell the joyful strain: Alleluia!

4
p   Lord, by the stripes which wounded thee
From death's dread sting thy servants free,
f   That we may live, and sing to thee   Alleluia!

                                      ? 17th cent. *Tr.* F. POTT‡

HYMN 136   Würtemburg   *Hundert Arien* (Dresden, 1694)
KEY E♭   B♭. t.

EASTER

f. E♭.

[Tonic sol-fa notation]

Al - le - lu - ia!

Christus ist erstanden

f CHRIST the Lord is risen again!
Christ hath broken every chain!
Hark! angelic voices cry,
Singing evermore on high,
　　　　　　Alleluia!

2

mf He who gave for us his life,
Who for us endured the strife,
Is our Paschal Lamb to-day;
f We too sing for joy, and say
　　　　　　Alleluia!

3

mf He who bore all pain and loss
Comfortless upon the Cross,
f Lives in glory now on high,
Pleads for us, and hears our cry:
　　　　　　Alleluia!

4*

He whose path no records tell,
Who descended into hell,
Who the strong man armed hath bound,
Now in highest heaven is crowned.
　　　　　　Alleluia!

5

mf He who slumbered in the grave
f Is exalted now to save;
Now through Christendom it rings
That the Lamb is King of Kings.
　　　　　　Alleluia!

6

mf Now he bids us tell abroad
How the lost may be restored,
How the penitent forgiven,
How we too may enter heaven.
　　　　　　Alleluia!

7

Thou, our Paschal Lamb indeed,
Christ, thy ransomed people feed;
Take our sins and guilt away:
f Let us sing by night and day
　　　　　　Alleluia!

M. WEISSE
Tr. Catherine Winkworth†

HYMN 137 Lux Eoi Sir A. Sullivan, 1842–1900

KEY D

```
s  :-.s |d'  :s   |s   :f   |f   :m   || l   :l   |s   :m    |r   :d   |r   :—  ||
d  :-.d |d   :d   |m   :r   |r   :d   || d   :r   |m   :s,   |l,  :l,  |t,  :—  ||
m  :-.m |m   :s   |d'  :t   |t   :d'  || l   :t   |d'  :m    |fe  :fe  |s   :—  ||
d  :-.d |d   :m   |s   :s,  |s,  :d   || f   :f   |m   :d    |l,  :r   |s,  :—  ||
```

A. t.

```
s  :-.s  |d'  :d'  |[t]m  :r   |s   :d   || t,  :l,  |s,  :d     |d   :t,  |d   :—  ||
t, :-.t, |d   :d   |[r]s, :s,  |s,  :s,  || s,  :f,  |m,  :l,.s, |f,  :f,  |m,  :—  ||
s  :-.s  |s   :s   |[s]d  :t,  |d   :d   || d   :r   |m   :f.m   |r   :s,  |s,  :—  ||
f  :-.f  |m   :m   |[r]s, :f,  |m,  :m,  || f,  :f,  |s,  :s,    |s,  :s,  |d,  :—  ||
```

f. D.

```
[ta,]f :f  |m   :m   |l   :-.l |l   :se  || l   :t   |d'  :t    |m   :se  |l   :—  ||
[f]d   :d  |t,  :t,  |d   :r   |m   :m   || m   :m   |m   :f    |m   :m   |m   :—  ||
[ta,]f :f  |s   :s   |l   :l   |t   :t   || l   :se  |l   :l.t  |d'  :t   |d'  :—  ||
[r,]l, :l, |s,  :s,  |f,  :f   |m   :m   || d   :t,  |l,  :r    |m   :m   |l   :—  ||
```

```
s  :d'  |m'  :r'  |d'  :t   |l   :s   || fe  :f   |m   :l    |d   :r   |d   :—  ||
f  :m   |s   :s   |s   :s   |f   :m   || ma  :r   |d   :d    |s,  :t,  |d   :—  ||
r' :d'  |d'  :t   |d'  :d'  |d'  :d'  || d'  :s   |d   :r    |m   :f   |m   :—  ||
t  :d'  |s   :f   |m   :m,  |f,  :s,  || l,  :t,  |d   :f,   |s,  :s,  |d   :—  ||
```

f ALLELUIA! Alleluia!
 Hearts to heaven and voices raise;
Sing to God a hymn of gladness,
 Sing to God a hymn of praise:
He who on the Cross a Victim
 For the world's salvation bled,
Jesus Christ, the King of Glory,
 Now is risen from the dead.

2

Christ is risen, Christ the first-fruits‿
 Of the holy harvest field,
Which will all its full abundance
 At his second coming yield;
Then the golden ears of harvest
 Will their heads before him wave,
Ripened by his glorious sunshine,
 From the furrows of the grave.

3

mf Christ is risen, we are risen;
 Shed upon us heavenly grace,
Rain, and dew, and gleams of glory‿
 From the brightness of thy face;
That we, with our hearts in heaven,
 Here on earth may fruitful be,
And by angel-hands be gathered,
 And be ever, Lord, with thee.

EASTER

4

f Alleluia! Alleluia!
  Glory be to God on high;
Alleluia to the Saviour,
  Who has gained the victory;
Alleluia to the Spirit,
  Fount of love and sanctity;
Alleluia! Alleluia!
  To the Triune Majesty.

BISHOP CHR. WORDSWORTH

Alternative Tune, Everton, 267

HYMN 138 Victimae Paschali   Mode i

KEY **D**

Victimae Paschali

{| r d r f s f m r | l s m   s   f m — r — ||

1 Chris-tians, to the Pas-chal Vic-tim Of-fer your thank-ful prais-es!

{|: l   d¹ r¹ l s   l   l — | l   s l   s f   m   r —}

MEN
2 A Lamb the sheep re-deem-eth: Christ, who on-ly is sin-less,
TREBLES
3 Death and life have con-tend-ed In that com-bat stu-pen-dous:

{| f s r m   r d   m f m — r —: ||: l₁ d r f s f m r}

Re-con-cil-eth sin-ners to the Fa-ther. 4 Speak, Ma-ry, de-clar-ing
                                        TREBLES
The Prince of Life, who died, reigns im-mor-tal. 6 Bright an-gels at-test-ing,

{| d   f   m r m   d — r — || f l s l   f s f m r —}

                              TREBLES
What thou saw-est way-far-ing; 5 'The tomb of Christ, who is liv-ing,
                              TREBLES
The shroud and nap-kin rest-ing. 7 Yea, Christ my hope is a-ris-en:

{| r s f s l s   f s   f m   r —: || : l d¹ r¹ l   l s l l}

                                    FULL
The glo-ry of Je-sus' Re-sur-rec-tion; 8*Hap-py they who hear the wit-ness,
                                       FULL
To Ga-li-lee he goes be-fore you.' 9 Christ in-deed from death is ris-en,

{| l d¹ s m f   m   r | d   m r s l   l   s m f   m — r —: ||

Ma-ry's word be-liev-ing A-bove the tales of Jew-ry de-ceiv-ing.
Our new life ob-tain-ing: Have mer-cy, Vic-tor King, ev-er reign-ing!

11th cent. *Tr. cento*

145

EASTER

HYMN 139 Salzburg J. Hintze, 1622-1702
KEY D

[Tonic sol-fa notation]

1

AT the Lamb's high feast we sing
Praise to our victorious King,
Who hath washed us in the tide
Flowing from his piercèd side;
Praise we him, whose love divine
Gives his sacred Blood for wine,
Gives his Body for the feast,
Christ the Victim, Christ the Priest.

2

Where the Paschal blood is poured,
Death's dark angel sheathes his sword;
Israel's hosts triumphant go
Through the wave that drowns the foe.
Praise we Christ, whose Blood was shed,
Paschal Victim, Paschal Bread;
With sincerity and love
Eat we manna from above.

3

Mighty Victim from the sky,
Hell's fierce powers beneath thee lie;
Thou hast conquered in the fight,
Thou hast brought us life and light.
Now no more can death appal,
Now no more the grave enthral:
Thou hast opened Paradise,
And in thee thy saints shall rise.

EASTER

4
Easter triumph, Easter joy,
Sin alone can this destroy;
From sin's power do thou set free
Souls new-born, O Lord, in thee.
Hymns of glory and of praise,
Risen Lord, to thee we raise;
Holy Father, praise to thee,
With the Spirit, ever be.

R. CAMPBELL
Based on *Ad regias Agni dapes*

HYMN 140 St. Albinus H. J. Gauntlett, 1805–76
KEY B♭

[tonic sol-fa notation]

Al-le-lu - ia!

Jesus lebt

JESUS lives! thy terrors now
　Can no more, O death, appal us;
Jesus lives! by this we know
　Thou, O grave, canst not enthral us.
　　　Alleluia!

2
Jesus lives! henceforth is death
　But the gate of life immortal:
This shall calm our trembling breath,
　When we pass its gloomy portal.
　　　Alleluia!

3
Jesus lives! for us he died;
　Then, alone to Jesus living,
Pure in heart may we abide,
　Glory to our Saviour giving.
　　　Alleluia!

4
Jesus lives! our hearts know well
　Naught from us his love shall sever;
Life nor death nor powers of hell
　Tear us from his keeping ever.
　　　Alleluia!

5
Jesus lives! to him the throne
　Over all the world is given:
May we go where he is gone,
　Rest and reign with him in heaven.
　　　Alleluia!

C. F. GELLERT
Tr. Frances E. Cox and others

EASTER

HYMN 141 Savannah   J. Wesley's *Foundery Collection*, 1742

KEY E♭

1

LOVE'S redeeming work is done;
Fought the fight, the battle won:
Lo, our Sun's eclipse is o'er!
Lo, he sets in blood no more!

2

Vain the stone, the watch, the seal!
Christ has burst the gates of hell;
Death in vain forbids his rise;
Christ has opened Paradise.

3

Lives again our glorious King;
Where, O death, is now thy sting?
Dying once, he all doth save;
Where thy victory, O grave?

4

Soar we now where Christ has led,
Following our exalted Head;
Made like him, like him we rise;
Ours the cross, the grave, the skies.

5

Hail the Lord of earth and heaven!
Praise to thee by both be given:
Thee we greet triumphant now;
Hail, the Resurrection thou!

C. WESLEY

EASTER

HYMN 142 St. Michael *Anglo-Genevan Psalms*, 1561

KEY A

```
{ :s₁ |d :m |r :r |m :— |—  ‖ s  |f :m |r :r |d :— |— ‖
  :m₁ |m₁:s₁|l₁:s₁|s₁:— |—   ‖ s₁ |d :d |d :t₁|d :— |— ‖
  :d  |d :d |d :t₁|d :— |—   ‖ r  |f :s |s :-f|m :— |— ‖
  :d  |l₁:m₁|f₁:s₁|d :— |—   ‖ t₁ |l₁:d |s₁:s₁|d₁:— |— ‖

{ :d  |t₁:l₁|s₁:d |d :r |m   ‖ m  |r :d |d :t₁|d :— |— ‖
  :s₁ |f₁:f₁|s₁:m₁|m₁:l₁|se₁ ‖ s₁ |s₁:s₁|l₁:s₁|s₁:— |— ‖
  :m  |r :d |d :d |d :l₁|t₁  ‖ d  |t₁:d |f :r |m :— |— ‖
  :d₁ |r₁:f₁|m₁:d₁|l₁:f₁|m₁  ‖ d₁ |s₁:m₁|f₁:s₁|d₁:— |— ‖
```

THE Lord is risen indeed!
  Now is his work performed;
Now is the mighty captive freed,
  And death's strong castle stormed.

2

The Lord is risen indeed!
  Then hell has lost his prey;
With him is risen the ransomed seed
  To reign in endless day.

3

The Lord is risen indeed!
  He lives, to die no more;
He lives, the sinner's cause to plead,
  Whose curse and shame he bore.

4

The Lord is risen indeed!
  Attending angels, hear!
Up to the courts of heaven with speed
  The joyful tidings bear.

5

Then take your golden lyre,
  And strike each cheerful chord;
Join, all ye bright celestial choirs,
  To sing our risen Lord.

T. KELLY‡

Alternative Tune, Narenza, 229

EASTER

HYMN 143 Aethelwold   Sir S. H. Nicholson, 1875-1947

KEY A♭

[Tonic sol-fa musical notation]

By permission of the Royal School of Church Music

HE is risen, he is risen!
  Tell it with a joyful voice;
He has burst his three days' prison;
  Let the whole wide earth rejoice.
Death is conquered, man is free,
Christ has won the victory.

2

Come, ye sad and fearful-hearted,
  With glad smile and radiant brow;
Lent's long shadows have departed,
  All his woes are over now,
And the Passion that he bore:
Sin and pain can vex no more.

3

Come, with high and holy hymning
  Chant our Lord's triumphant lay;
Not one darksome cloud is dimming
  Yonder glorious morning ray,
Breaking o'er the purple east:
Brighter far our Easter-feast.

                              MRS. C. F. ALEXANDER

Alternative Tune, All Saints, 570

ROGATIONTIDE

Hymn 144 Lincoln   T. Ravenscroft, *Psalms*, 1621

(musical notation in tonic sol-fa)

ALTERNATIVE VERSION
(Melody in the Tenor part)

(musical notation in tonic sol-fa)

The Alternative Version may be used for verses 2 and 4

1
LORD, in thy name thy servants plead,
  And thou hast sworn to hear:
Thine is the harvest, thine the seed,
  The fresh and fading year.

2
Our hope, when autumn winds blew wild,
  We trusted, Lord, with thee;
And still, now spring has on us smiled,
  We wait on thy decree.

3
The former and the latter rain,
  The summer sun and air,
The green ear, and the golden grain,
  All thine, are ours by prayer.

4
Thine too by right, and ours by grace,
  The wondrous growth unseen,
The hopes that soothe, the fears that [brace,
  The love that shines serene.

5
So grant the precious things brought forth
  By sun and moon below,
That thee in thy new heaven and earth
  We never may forgo.

J. KEBLE

ASCENSIONTIDE

Hymn 145 FIRST TUNE

KEY **A** Paule, doctor egregie Mode vii

Aeterne Rex altissime

{| s, s, s, l, d t, d r | r r r m m r }
1 O thou e- ter- nal King most high, Whose Blood has brought sal-
2 As-cend- ing to the Fa- ther's throne Thou tak'st the king-dom
3 Be thou our joy, O migh- ty Lord, As thou wilt be our

{| d t, d r — | r r d t, l, d r d t, l, }
1 va- tion nigh, The bonds of death are burst by thee,
2 as thine own; While awe-struck an- gels con- tem- plate
3 great re- ward; Let all our glo- ry be in thee

{| f, l, d d d t, l, s, l, t, l, s, s, — ||
1 And love has won the vic- to- ry.
2 The won- drous change of man's es- tate.
3 Both now and through e- ter- ni- ty.

SECOND TUNE

KEY **G** A Morning Hymn Melody by J. Clarke, *c.* 1659–1707

D. t.
{ :d |m :—.f|r :t, |d :r |t, | r s l :—.d¹|t :d¹|r¹ :t |d¹ :—||
  :s, |t, :d |s, :s, |s, :l, |s, | s d d :f |s :s |f :r |m :—
  :m |s :d |r :r |d :f |r | r s d¹:r¹|r¹ :d¹|l :s |s :—
  :d |s, :l, |t, :s,.f,|m, :r, |s, | t m f :r |s.f:m|f :s |d :—

f. G.
{ :d's |f :m |r :m |f.m:r.d|t, ||s, |d.,r:d.r |m :f |r :—.d|d :—||
  :m t, |d :d |t, :s, |f,.s,:l, |s, ||s, |s, :—.t,|d :d |d :t, |s, :—
  :¹m |d.r:m.f|s :d |r :f.m|r ||t, |d :—.f |s :f |l :s |m :—
  :¹m, |l,.t,:d |s, :f,.m,|r, :r, |s, ||s,.f,|m, :—.r,|d,:l,|f, :s, |d, :—

Aeterne Rex altissime

O THOU eternal King most high,
Whose Blood has brought salvation nigh,
The bonds of death are burst by thee,
And love has won the victory.

152

ASCENSIONTIDE

2
Ascending to the Father's throne
Thou tak'st the kingdom as thine own;
While awestruck angels contemplate
The wondrous change of man's estate.

3
Be thou our joy, O mighty Lord,
As thou wilt be our great reward;
Let all our glory be in thee
Both now and through eternity.

Tr. COMPILERS† (1904)

HYMN 146 Metzler's Redhead   R. Redhead, 1820–1901

KEY **D**

Jesu, nostra redemptio

JESU, our hope, our heart's desire,
  Thy work of grace we sing;
Redeemer of the world art thou,
  Its Maker and its King.

2
How vast the mercy and the love
  Which laid our sins on thee,
And led thee to a cruel death,
  To set thy people free!

3
But now the bonds of death are burst,
  The ransom has been paid;
And thou art on thy Father's throne,
  In glorious robes arrayed.

4
O may thy mighty love prevail
  Our sinful souls to spare!
O may we stand around thy throne,
  And see thy glory there!

5
Jesu, our only joy be thou,
  As thou our prize wilt be;
In thee be all our glory now
  And through eternity.

[UNISON] **6**
All praise to thee who art gone up
  Triumphantly to heaven;
All praise to God the Father's name
  And Holy Ghost be given.

Tr. J. CHANDLER and Compilers

ASCENSIONTIDE

HYMN 147 FIRST TUNE
KEY **G** Ascension   W. H. Monk, 1823-89

DESCANT
```
{ |m :s  |d :d  |r :f |m :—  ||m :s.l |t :d' |s :—  |m :—  ||
                              ||Al  -   le - lu  -  ia!        ||

  |m :s  |d :d  |r :f |m :—  ||m :—   |s :d  |r :—  |d :—  ||
  |d :t₁ |l₁:s₁ |l₁:s₁|s₁:—  ||s₁:—   |— :d  |d :t₁ |d :—  ||
  |s :s  |m :d  |d :t₁|d :—  ||d :—   |r :m  |f :—  |m :—  ||
  |d :s₁ |l₁:m₁ |f₁:s₁|d₁:—  ||d :—   |t₁:l₁ |s₁:—  |d :—  ||
```

```
{ |m :s  |d :d  |r :f |m :—  ||m :s.l |t :d' |s :—  |m :—  ||
                              ||Al  -   le - lu  -  ia!        ||

  |m :s  |d :d  |r :f |m :—  ||m :—   |s :d  |r :—  |d :—  ||
  |d :t₁ |l₁:s₁ |l₁:s₁|s₁:—  ||s₁:—   |— :d  |d :t₁ |d :—  ||
  |s :s  |m :d  |d :t₁|d :—  ||d :—   |r :m  |s :—  |s :—  ||
  |d :s₁ |l₁:m₁ |f₁:s₁|d₁:—  ||d :—   |t₁:l₁ |s₁:—  |d :—  ||
```

D.t.
```
{ |r :m₁ |ᵈf :s |m :s  |r :—  ||d' :s |m' :r'.d' |l :t |d' :—  ||
                                ||Al  -  le  -  lu  -  ia!      ||

  |r :m  |ᵈf :s |m :s  |r :—  ||m :—  |s :d  |r :—  |d :—  ||
  |s₁:se₁|¹r:t₁ |d :d  |t₁:—  ||d :—  |— :d  |d :t₁ |d :—  ||
  |t₁:m  |ᵐl :s |s :s  |s :—  ||s :—  |m :m  |f :—  |m :—  ||
  |s₁:m₁ |¹r:s₁ |d :m₁ |s₁:—  ||d :—  |m :l₁ |s₁:—  |d :—  ||
```

f.G.
```
{ |ᵈs₁:l₁.t₁|d :r  |m :f |s :—  ||m :s.l |t :d' { |d' :t  |d' :—  ||
                                                  |l :s.f |m :—   ||
                                  ||Al  -  le - lu  -  ia!         ||

  |ᵈs₁:l₁.t₁|d :r  |m :f |s :—  ||m :—   |s :d  |r :—  |d :—  ||
  |ᵈs₁:f₁ |m₁:s₁ |s₁:d |t₁:—  ||s₁:—   |— :d  |d :t₁ |d :—  ||
  |ᶠd :f  |d :t₁ |d :d |r :—  ||d :—   |r :m  |f :—  |m :—  ||
  |¹m₁:r₁ |l₁:s₁ |d :l₁|s₁:—  ||d :—   |t₁:l₁ |s₁:—  |d :—  ||
```

The Descant may be sung for verses 3 and 6

SECOND TUNE
KEY **G** Llanfair   Welsh Hymn Melody

```
{ |d :d  |m :m  |s :f.m|r :—  ||s :—.f |m :f.m |r :—  |d :—  ||
  |s₁:s₁ |d :d  |d :r.d|t₁:—  ||s₁:—.l₁.t₁ :d :d  |d :t₁ |d :—  ||
  |m :m  |d :d  |s :l  |r :—  ||m :—.f |s :f.s |l :s  |m :—  ||
  |d :d  |l₁:l₁ |m₁:f₁ |s₁:—  ||m :—.r |d :l₁.s₁ |f₁:s₁ |d :—  ||
                                ||Al  -  le  -  lu  -  ia!   ||
```

ASCENSIONTIDE

[Tonic sol-fa notation]

Al - le - lu - ia!

Al - le - lu - ia!

UNISON
Al - le - lu - ia!

f HAIL the day that sees him rise,
   Alleluia!
To his throne above the skies;
   Alleluia!
Christ, the Lamb for sinners given,
   Alleluia!
Enters now the highest heaven.
   Alleluia!

2
There for him high triumph waits;
   Alleluia!
Lift your heads, eternal gates!
   Alleluia!
He hath conquered death and sin;
   Alleluia!
Take the King of Glory in!
   Alleluia!

3
Lo, the heaven its Lord receives,
   Alleluia!
Yet he loves the earth he leaves;
   Alleluia!
Though returning to his throne,
   Alleluia!
Still he calls mankind his own.
   Alleluia!

4
mf See! he lifts his hands above;
   Alleluia!
See! he shews the prints of love;
   Alleluia!
Hark! his gracious lips bestow,
   Alleluia!
Blessings on his Church below.
   Alleluia!

5
Still for us he intercedes,
   Alleluia!
His prevailing Death he pleads;
   Alleluia!
Near himself prepares our place,
   Alleluia!
He the first-fruits of our race.
   Alleluia!

6
Lord, though parted from our sight,
   Alleluia!
Far above the starry height,
   Alleluia!
f Grant our hearts may thither rise,
   Alleluia!
Seeking thee above the skies.
   Alleluia!

C. WESLEY, T. COTTERILL,
and Compilers

NOTE—*A longer version of this hymn will be found in the 'Processional' section (610).*

Alternative Tune, Chislehurst, 610

ASCENSIONTIDE

Hymn 148 Rex gloriae

H. Smart, 1813–79

key A♭

[Tonic sol-fa notation]

f SEE the Conqueror mounts in tri-
See the King in royal state [umph,
Riding on the clouds his chariot
 To his heavenly palace gate;
Hark! the choirs of angel voices
 Joyful Alleluias sing,
And the portals high are lifted
 To receive their heavenly King.

2
mf Who is this that comes in glory,
 With the trump of jubilee?
Lord of battles, God of armies,
 He has gained the victory;
He who on the Cross did suffer,
f He who from the grave arose,
He has vanquished sin and Satan,
 He by death has spoiled his foes.

3
He has raised our human nature
 On the clouds to God's right hand;
There we sit in heavenly places,
 There with him in glory stand:
Jesus reigns, adored by angels;
 Man with God is on the throne;
Mighty Lord, in thine Ascension
 We by faith behold our own.

4*
mf See him who is gone before us
 Heavenly mansions to prepare,
See him who is ever pleading
 For us with prevailing prayer,
See him who with sound of trumpet
 And with his angelic train,
Summoning the world to judgement,
 On the clouds will come again.

5
f Glory be to God the Father;
 Glory be to God the Son,
Dying, risen, ascending for us,
 Who the heavenly realm has won;
Glory to the Holy Spirit:
 To One God in Persons Three
Glory both in earth and heaven,
 Glory, endless glory be.

BISHOP CHR. WORDSWORTH

ASCENSIONTIDE

Hymn 149 Old 25th *Anglo-Genevan Psalms*, 1558

KEY **G**

THOU art gone up on high,
  To mansions in the skies;
And round thy throne unceasingly
  The songs of praise arise:
p But we are lingering here,
  With sin and care oppressed;
Lord, send thy promised Comforter,
  And lead us to thy rest.

2
mf Thou art gone up on high;
  But thou didst first come down,
Through earth's most bitter misery
  To pass unto thy crown;
And girt with griefs and fears
  Our onward course must be;
But only let this path of tears
  Lead us at last to thee.

3
f Thou art gone up on high;
  But thou shalt come again,
With all the bright ones of the sky
  Attendant in thy train.
Lord, by thy saving power
  So make us live and die,
That we may stand in that dread hour
  At thy right hand on high.

Mrs. E. TOKE

ASCENSIONTIDE

HYMN 150 Nun freut euch *Etlich Christliche Lyeder*, 1524

KEY **G**

1

LET all the multitudes of light,
 Their songs in concert raising,
With earth's triumphal hymns unite,
 The risen Saviour praising.
Ye heavens, his festival proclaim!
Our King returneth whence he came,
 With victory amazing.

2

For us he bore the bitter Tree,
 To death's dark realm descending;
Our foe he slew, and set us free,
 Man's ancient bondage ending.
No more the tyrant's chains oppress;
O conquering Love, thy name we bless,
 With thee to heaven ascending.

3

Jesus, to thee be endless praise,
 For this thy great salvation;
O holy Father, thine always
 Be thanks and adoration;
Spirit of life and light, to thee
Eternal praise and glory be:
 One God of all creation!

F. B. MACNUTT

Alternative Tune, Laus Deo (Bach), 422

WHITSUNTIDE

Hymn 151

FIRST TUNE

KEY A♭   Felix dies   Mode ii

Beata nobis gaudia

{| d   d   r   m   r   r   d   t₁ |}

1. O joy, be-cause the circ-ling year
2. Like un-to quiver-ing tongues of flame
3. Thus un-to all was spread a-broad
4. Of old in eve-ry hal-lowed breast

{| r   t₁   d   l   s₁   d   d   d— | d   d   r   m   r |}

1. Hath brought our day of bless-ing here! The day when first
2. Up-on each one the Spi-rit came: Tongues, that the earth might
3. The won-der of the works of God; They knew the pro-phet's
4. Thou ca-mest in thy grace to rest: O grant us now from

{| r   d   t₁ | r   t₁   d   l₁   s₁   d   l₁   l₁— ||}

1. light di-vine Up-on the Church be-gan to shine.
2. hear their call, And fire, that love might burn in all.
3. word ful-filled, And owned the work which God had willed.
4. sin re-lease, And in our time, good Lord, give peace.

SECOND TUNE

KEY C   Erfurt   *Geistliche Leider* (Leipzig, 1539)

:d'	t :l	t :s	l :t	d'	d'	d' :s	s :m	s :f	m :—
:m	r :r	r :d	d :f	m	m	d :m	r :d	d :d	d :—
:s	s :fe	s :m	f :s	s	s	s :s	s :s	s :l	s :—
:d	s :r	s₁ :d	f :r	d	d	m :d	t₁ :d	m :f	d :—

:m	l :l	s :t	d' :l	s	d'	t :l	s :l	f.m :r	d :—
:d	d :f	m :s	s :fe	s	m	m :d.r	m :d	l₁ :t₁	d :—
:l	l :d'	d' :r'	d' :d'	t	l	s :l.t	d' :m	f :s	m :—
:l	f :l	d' :t	l :r	s	l	m :f	d :l₁	r :s₁	d :—

Beata nobis gaudia

O JOY, because the circling year
Hath brought our day of blessing here!
The day when first the light divine
Upon the Church began to shine.

2

Like unto quivering tongues of flame
Upon each one the Spirit came:
Tongues, that the earth might hear their call,
And fire, that love might burn in all.

3

Thus unto all was spread abroad
The wonder of the works of God;
They knew the prophet's word fulfilled,
And owned the work which God had willed.

4

Of old in every hallowed breast
Thou camest in thy grace to rest:
O grant us now from sin release,
And in our time, good Lord, give peace.

Tr. J. ELLERTON and Compilers† (1904)

WHITSUNTIDE

Hymn 152 Veni creator No. 2   J. B. Dykes, 1823–76

KEY **C**

[Sol-fa notation]

Veni, creator Spiritus

COME, O Creator Spirit, come,
And make within our hearts thy home;
To us thy grace celestial give,
Who of thy breathing move and live.

2

O Paraclete, that name is thine,
Of God most high the gift divine;
The well of life, the fire of love,
Our soul's anointing from above.

3

Thou dost appear in sevenfold dower
The sign of God's almighty power;
The Father's promise, making rich
With saving truth our earthly speech.

4

Our senses with thy light inflame,
Our hearts to heavenly love reclaim;
Our bodies' poor infirmity
With strength perpetual fortify.

5

Our mortal foe afar repel,
Grant us henceforth in peace to dwell;
And so to us, with thee for guide,
No ill shall come, no harm betide.

WHITSUNTIDE

6
May we by thee the Father learn,
And know the Son, and thee discern,
Who art of Both; and thus adore
In perfect faith for evermore.

? ARCHBISHOP RABANUS MAURUS
Tr. Yattendon Hymnal

NOTE. '*Paraclete*' in verse 2, line 1, is the English form of '*Parakletos*,' a title of the Holy Spirit used by St. John and translated '*Comforter*' (or '*Advocate*').

HYMN **153** Warrington   R. Harrison, 1748–1810

KEY B♭

SPIRIT of mercy, truth, and love,
O shed thine influence from above,
And still from age to age convey
The wonders of this sacred day.

2

In every clime, by every tongue,
Be God's surpassing glory sung;
Let all the listening earth be taught
The acts our great Redeemer wrought.

3

Unfailing comfort, heavenly guide,
Still o'er thy holy Church preside;
Still let mankind thy blessings prove,
Spirit of mercy, truth, and love.

Foundling Hospital Collection† (1774)

Alternative Tune, Melcombe, 4

WHITSUNTIDE

HYMN 154　　　　　FIRST TUNE

KEY E♭　Sudeley　　　　　　　　　　　Sir J. Stainer, 1840–1901

KEY G　Winchester Old　　SECOND TUNE　　　Este, *Psalms*, 1592

f WHEN God of old came down from heaven,
　In power and wrath he came;
　Before his feet the clouds were riven,
　　Half darkness and half flame:

2
p But, when he came the second time,
　He came in power and love;
　Softer than gale at morning prime
　　Hovered his holy Dove.

3
f The fires, that rushed on Sinai down
　In sudden torrents dread,
　Now gently light, a glorious crown,
　　On every sainted head.

4
And as on Israel's awestruck ear
　The voice exceeding loud,
The trump that angels quake to hear,
　Thrilled from the deep, dark cloud;

5
So, when the Spirit of our God
　Came down his flock to find,
A voice from heaven was heard abroad,
　A rushing, mighty wind.

6
mf It fills the Church of God; it fills
　The sinful world around:
Only in stubborn hearts and wills
　No place for it is found.

7
p　Come, Lord, come Wisdom, Love, and Power,
　　Open our ears to hear;
　　Save, Lord, by love or fear.

J. KEBLE

WHITSUNTIDE

HYMN 155 Naphill   H. E. Darke

KEY **G**

[sol-fa musical notation]

1
OUR Lord, his Passion ended,
Hath gloriously ascended,
Yet though from him divided,
He leaves us not unguided;
  All his benefits to crown
  He hath sent his Spirit down,
  Burning like a flame of fire
  His disciples to inspire.

2
God's Spirit is directing;
No more they sit expecting;
But forth to all the nation
They go with exultation;
  That which God in them hath wrought
  Fills their life and soul and thought;
  So their witness now can do
  Work as great in others too.

3
The centuries go gliding,
But still we have abiding
With us that Spirit Holy
To make us brave and lowly—
  Lowly, for we feel our need:
  God alone is strong indeed;
  Brave, for with the Spirit's aid
  We can venture unafraid.

4
O Lord of every nation,
Fill us with inspiration!
We know our own unfitness,
Yet for thee would bear witness.
  By thy Spirit now we raise
  To the heavenly Father praise:
  Holy Spirit, Father, Son,
  Make us know thee, ever One.

F. C. BURKITT

WHITSUNTIDE

HYMN 156 Veni, Sancte Spiritus S. Webbe, 1740–1816

KEY **F**

[music notation]

Veni, Sancte Spiritus

1
COME, thou Holy Spirit, come,
And from thy celestial home
  Shed a ray of light divine;
Come, thou Father of the poor,
Come, thou source of all our store,
  Come, within our bosoms shine:

2
Thou of comforters the best,
Thou the soul's most welcome guest,
  Sweet refreshment here below;
In our labour rest most sweet,
Grateful coolness in the heat,
  Solace in the midst of woe.

3
O most blessèd Light divine,
Shine within these hearts of thine,
  And our inmost being fill;
Where thou art not, man hath naught,
Nothing good in deed or thought,
  Nothing free from taint of ill.

4
Heal our wounds; our strength renew;
On our dryness pour thy dew;
  Wash the stains of guilt away;
Bend the stubborn heart and will;
Melt the frozen, warm the chill;
  Guide the steps that go astray.

5
On the faithful, who adore
And confess thee, evermore
  In thy sevenfold gifts descend:
Give them virtue's sure reward,
Give them thy salvation, Lord,
  Give them joys that never end.

ARCHBISHOP STEPHEN LANGTON
Tr. E. Caswall and Compilers

WHITSUNTIDE

Hymn 157 Veni, creator Spiritus   Mode viii

KEY B♭

{| s₁ l₁ s₁ f₁   s₁ l₁   s₁   d r r   d }

1 Come, Ho - ly Ghost, our souls in - spire,
2 Thy bless - èd unc - tion from a - bove,
3 A - noint and cheer our soil - èd face
4 Teach us to know the Fa - ther, Son,

{| d   s₁   l₁   d r   d   r m   m   r — }

1 And light - en with ce - les - tial fire;
2 Is com - fort, life, and fire of love;
3 With the a - bun - dance of thy grace:
4 And thee, of Both, to be but One;

{| d   r m   d   t₁ l₁   s₁   r l₁   t₁   d }

1 Thou the a - noint - ing Spi - rit art,
2 En - a - ble with per - pet - ual light
3 Keep far our foes, give peace at home;
4 That through the a - ges all a - long

{| t₁   d   l₁   s₁ f₁   l₁   d t₁   l₁   s₁ — ||

1 Who dost thy seven - fold gifts im - part.
2 The dul - ness of our blind - ed sight.
3 Where thou art guide no ill can come.
4 This . . . . . may be our end - less song.

CONCLUSION

{| d r m   d   t₁ l₁   s₁   r l₁   t₁   d   d }

'Praise to thy e - ter - nal mer - it,

{| t₁   d   l₁   s₁ f₁   l₁   d t₁   l₁   s₁   s₁ — ||

Fa - ther, Son, and Ho - ly Spi - rit.'

Bishop J. Cosin
Based on *Veni, creator Spiritus*

TRINITY SUNDAY

Hymn 158 FIRST TUNE

KEY E♭ O Pater sancte Mode iv

O Pater sancte

{| f r m m m m m s l l s }
1. Fa - ther most ho - ly, mer - ci - ful and lo - ving,
2. Three in a won - drous U - ni - ty un - bro - ken,
3. All thy cre - a - tion ser - veth its Cre - a - tor,
4. Lord God Al - migh - ty, un - to thee be glo - ry,

{| l ta l s s l s f r m — m — | f r }
1. Je - su, Re-deem - er, ev - er to be wor-shipped, Life - giv -
2. One per - fect God-head, love that ne - ver fail - eth, Light of
3. Thee eve - ry crea - ture prais-eth with-out ceas - ing; We too
4. One in three Per - sons, ov - er all ex - alt - ed. Thine, as

{| d r r f s l s s f | l s f m — m — ||
1. ing Spi - rit, Com - for - ter most gra-cious, God ev - er - last - ing;
2. the an - gels, suc - cour of the need - y, Hope of all liv - ing;
3. would sing thee psalms of true de - vo - tion: Hear, we be-seech thee.
4. is meet, be hon - our, praise and bless - ing. Now and for ev - er.

SECOND TUNE

KEY G Angers Melody from J. B. Croft's *Collection*

May be sung in Unison

{| s₁ :— | d :t₁ | l₁ :— | s₁ :— | d :—.t₁ | d :r | m :— | m :— ||
   m₁ :— | s₁ :s₁ | s₁ :f₁ | r₁ :— | s₁ :—.s₁ | l₁ :t₁ | d :t₁ | l₁ :— |
   d :— | d :d | d :— | — :t₁ | d :r | m :f | s :— | m :— |
   d₁ :r₁ | m₁ :m₁ | f₁ :— | s₁ :— | m₁ :f₁ | m₁ :r₁ | d₁ :— | d :— |}

{| s :— | s :m | f :— | m :— | d :—.r | m :f | s :— | s :— || s₁ :— | l₁ :t₁ |
   s₁ :— | t₁ :t₁ | d :— | t₁ :— | l₁ :d | t₁ :d | d :— | t₁ :— | s₁ :— | s₁ :f₁ |
   r :— | r :s | l :— | s :— | m :f | s :l | s :— | r :— | d :— | d :r |
   t₁ :l₁ | s₁ :s₁ | f₁ :— | s₁ :— | l₁ :l₁ | s₁ :f₁ | m₁ :f₁ | s₁ :— | m₁ :— | m₁ :r₁ |}

{| d :— | d :— | m :—.f | s :f | m :— | r :— | m :— | f :m | r :— | d :— ||
   s₁ :— | l₁ :— | t₁ :l₁ | s₁ :d | t₁ :d | r :— | d :— | d :d | d :t₁ | d :— |
   m :— | m :— | m :d | d :l | s :— | s :— | s :— | f :s | s :— | m :— |
   d₁ :— | l₁ :— | s₁ :f₁ | m₁ :f₁ | s₁ :l₁ | t₁ :— | d :t₁ | l₁ :d | s₁ :— | d :— |}

O Pater sancte

FATHER most holy, merciful and loving,
Jesu, Redeemer, ever to be worshipped,
Life-giving Spirit, Comforter most gracious,
  God everlasting;

2
Three in a wondrous Unity unbroken,
One perfect Godhead, love that never faileth,
Light of the angels, succour of the needy,
  Hope of all living;

TRINITY SUNDAY

3
All thy creation serveth its Creator,
Thee every creature praiseth without ceasing;
We too would sing thee psalms of true devotion:
　　Hear, we beseech thee.

4
Lord God Almighty, unto thee be glory,
One in three Persons, over all exalted.
Thine, as is meet, be honour, praise and blessing
　　Now and for ever.

Before 10th cent. *Tr.* A. E. ALSTON

HYMN **159**　St. Flavian　　　　Psalm cxxxii, adapted from *Psalms*, 1562
KEY **F**

```
:d  |d  :t, |d  :m  |r  :r  |d  ‖ d  |f  :m  |d  :r  |m  :—  |—  ‖
:s, |s, :s, |s, :d  |d  :t, |d  ‖ d  |d  :d  |d  :l, |t, :—  |—  ‖
:m  |r  :r  |m  :m  |l  :s  |m  ‖ m  |f  :s  |l  :l  |se :—  |—  ‖
:d  |s, :s, |d  :l, |f, :s, |d  ‖ d  |l, :d  |f  :f  |m  :—  |—  ‖
```

```
:m  |m  :f  |s  :m  |d  :r  |m  ‖ m  |r  :d  |d  :t, |d  :—  |—  ‖
:d  |d  :d  |t, :t, |l, :t, |d  ‖ d  |t, :l, |l, :s, |s, :—  |—  ‖
:s  |s  :f  |r  :m  |m  :s  |s  ‖ s  |s  :m  |r  :r  |m  :—  |—  ‖
:d  |d  :l, |s, :l, |l, :s, |d  ‖ d  |s, :l, |f, :s, |d  :—  |—  ‖
```

ALTERNATIVE VERSION
(Melody in the Tenor part)

KEY **F**　　　　　　　　　　　　　　　　Harmonized by T. Ravenscroft (1621)

```
:m  |f  :r  |m  :—.s |f  :r  |m  ‖ l  |f  :s  |l  :—.l |se :—  |—  ‖
:s, |l, :s, |s, :s, |l, :s, |s, ‖ l, |r  :d  |l, :r  |t, :—  |—  ‖
:d  |d  :t, |d  :m  |r  :r  |d  ‖ d  |f  :m  |d  :r  |m  :—  |—  ‖
:d  |f, :s,.f,|m, :d, |f, :s, |d, ‖ f, |r, :m, |f, :f, |m, :— |—  ‖
```

```
:s  |s  :l  |r  :m  |f  :—.s |l  ‖ s  |s  :m  |f  :m.r |m  :— |—  ‖
:d  |d  :d  |t, :s, |l, :r  |de ‖ d  |t, :l, |l, :s, |s, :— |—  ‖
:m  |m  :f  |s  :m  |d  :r  |m  ‖ m  |r  :d  |d  :t, |d  :— |—  ‖
:d, |d  :l, |t, :d  |l, :ta,|l, ‖ d  |s, :l, |f, :s, |d, :— |—  ‖
```

The Alternative Version may be used for verses 2 and 4

1
MOST ancient of all mysteries,
　Before thy throne we lie;
Have mercy now, most merciful,
　Most holy Trinity.

2
When heaven and earth were yet unmade,
　When time was yet unknown,
Thou in thy bliss and majesty
　Didst live and love alone.

3
Thou wast not born; there was no fount
　From which thy being flowed;
There is no end which thou canst reach:
　But thou art simply God.

4
How wonderful creation is,
　The work which thou didst bless!
And O what then must thou be like,
　Eternal loveliness!

5
Most ancient of all mysteries,
　Low at thy throne we lie;
Have mercy now, most merciful,
　Most holy Trinity.

F. W. FABER

GENERAL HYMNS

Hymn 160 Nicaea   J. B. Dykes, 1823–76
Key E

```
{| d  :d   |m  :m   | s  :—  | s  :—   | l  :—  | l  :l   | s  :—  |m  :— ||
 | s₁ :s₁  |d  :d   | t₁ :r  | d  :t₁  | l₁ :t₁ | d  :r   | m  :—  |d  :— ||
 | m  :m   |d  :d   | r  :f  | m  :s   | f  :s  | l  :t   | d' :s  |s  :— ||
 | d  :d   |l₁ :l₁  | s₁ :—  | d  :—   | f₁ :—  | f  :f   | d  :—  |d  :— ||}

B.t.
{|ᶠd :—.d |d  :d   | f  :—  |m  :d   | s₁ :d  |r  :—.d  | d  :—  |— :— ||
 |ʳs₁:s₁  |l₁ :s₁  | f₁ :s₁ |s₁ :l₁  | s₁ :m₁ |f₁ :—.m₁ | n₁ :—  |— :— ||
 |ˢd :d   |d  :d   | l₁ :t₁ |d  :d   | m  :d  |t₁ :—.d  | d  :—  |ta₁:—||
 |ᵗm₁:m₁  |f₁ :m₁  | r₁ :—  |m₁ :f₁  | s₁ :s₁ |s₁ :—.d₁ | d₁ :—  |— :— ||}

f. E.
{|ᶠd :d  |m  :m   | s  :—  |s  :—   | l  :—.l |l  :l   | s  :—  |s  :— ||
 |ᵈs₁:s₁ |d  :d   | t₁ :r  |d  :t₁  | l₁ :t₁  |d  :r   | m  :—  |d  :— ||
 |ˡm :m  |d  :d   | r  :f  |m  :s   | f  :s   |l  :t   | d' :s  |m  :— ||
 |ᶠd :d  |l₁ :l₁  | s₁ :—  |d  :—   | f₁ :—.f₁|f  :f   | d  :—  |d  :— ||}

{| d' :—  |s  :s   | l  :—  |m  :—   | f  :r  |r  :—.d | d  :—  |— :— ||
 | d  :—  |d  :d   | d  :—  |d  :ta₁ | l₁ :l₁ |t₁ :—.d | d  :—  |— :— ||
 | m  :f  |s  :ta  | l  :—  |s  :—   | f  :f  |f  :—.m | m  :—  |— :— ||
 | l₁ :—  |m₁ :m₁  | f₁ :—  |d  :—   | f₁ :f₁ |s₁ :—.d | d  :—  |— :— ||}
```

mf HOLY, Holy, Holy! Lord God Almighty!
    Early in the morning our song shall rise to thee;
    Holy, Holy, Holy! merciful and mighty!
    God in three Persons, blessèd Trinity!

2

    Holy, Holy, Holy! all the saints adore thee,
    Casting down their golden crowns around the glassy sea;
    Cherubim and seraphim falling down before thee,
    Which wert and art and evermore shalt be.

3

p Holy, Holy, Holy! though the darkness hide thee,
    Though the eye of sinful man thy glory may not see,
mf Only thou art holy, there is none beside thee
    Perfect in power, in love, and purity.

4

    Holy, Holy, Holy! Lord God Almighty!
f All thy works shall praise thy name in earth and sky and sea;
    Holy, Holy, Holy! merciful and mighty!
    God in three Persons, blessèd Trinity!

                                    BISHOP R. HEBER

GENERAL

HYMN 161 Laus Deo R. Redhead, 1820–1901
KEY A♭

The Descant may be sung for verses 3 and 6

mf BRIGHT the vision that delighted
    Once the sight of Judah's seer;
Sweet the countless tongues united
    To entrance the prophet's ear.

2
Round the Lord in glory seated
    Cherubim and seraphim
Filled his temple, and repeated
    Each to each the alternate hymn:

[UNISON]
3
f 'Lord, thy glory fills the heaven;
    Earth is with its fulness stored;
Unto thee be glory given,
    Holy, Holy, Holy, Lord.'

4
Heaven is still with glory ringing,
    Earth takes up the angels' cry,
'Holy, Holy, Holy', singing,
    'Lord of Hosts, the Lord most high.'

mf With his seraph train before him,
    With his holy Church below,
Thus unite we to adore him,
    Bid we thus our anthem flow:

[UNISON]
6
f 'Lord, thy glory fills the heaven;
    Earth is with its fulness stored;
Unto thee be glory given,
    Holy, Holy, Holy, Lord.'

BISHOP R. MANT†

NOTE. *This hymn is based on the account of Isaiah's vision in Is. 6*

GENERAL

Hymn 162 St. Patrick's Breastplate
KEY B♭

Old Irish Melodies
Arranged by Sir C. V. Stanford, 1852–1924

Átomriur inoiu

VOICES. *Full Unison. Rather quickly and with strong rhythm*

: m₁	l₁ :— :l₁	s₁ :m₁ :s₁	d :m :r.d	d :t₁ :t₁	r :t₁ : s₁
1 *f* I	bind un- to	my - self	to - day	The	strong name

s₁ :t₁ :r	d :— : d	t₁ :— :m	l₁ :—.t₁:d.l₁	s₁ :m₁ : d₁	d :— : s₁
of the	Trin - i - ty,	By in -	vo - ca - tion	of the

l₁ :t₁ :d.r	m :— :r.m	d :l₁ : t₁	l₁ :— : l₁	l₁ :— :—	— :
same, The	Three in	One, and	One in	Three.	

: m₁	l₁ :— : l₁	s₁ :m₁ :s₁	d :m : r.d	d :t₁ :t₁	r :t₁ :s₁
MEN 2 *mf* I	bind this day	to me	for ev - er,	By	power of
TREBLES 4* *mf* I	bind un - to	my - self	to - day	The	vir - tues
FULL 7* A-	gainst all Sa-	tan's spells	and wiles,	A-	gainst false

s₁ :t₁ : r	d :— : d	t₁ :t₁ : m	l₁ :—.t₁ :d.l₁	s₁ :m₁ : d₁	d :— :s₁
2 faith, Christ's	In - car -	na - tion, His	Bap - tism	in the	Jor - dan
4*of the	star - lit	hea - ven, The	glo - rious	sun's life -	giv - ing
7*words of	her - e -	sy, A-	gainst the	know - ledge	that de-

l₁ :t₁ :d.r	m :— :r.m	d :l₁ : t₁	l₁ :— :l₁	l₁ :l₁ :— :	: s₁
2 riv - er, His	death on	Cross for	my sal -	va - tion:	(FULL) *f* His
4*ray, The	white - ness	of the	moon at	ev - en,	(FULL) *f* The
7*files, A-	gainst the	heart's i-	dol - a -	try,	A-

d :— : d	d :— : r.m	r :— :de	r :— :m	l₁ :— : l₁
2 burst - ing	from the	spic - èd	tomb, His	rid - ing
4* flash - ing	of the	light - ning	free, The	whirl - ing
7* gainst the	wiz - ard's	e - vil	craft, A-	gainst the

s₁ :t₁ : r	d :— : d	t₁ :t₁ : m₁	l₁ :—.t₁ :d.l₁	s₁ :m₁ : d₁
2 up the	heaven - ly	way, His	com - ing	at the
4*winds' tem-	pest - uous	shocks, The	sta - ble	earth, the
7*death-wound	and the	burn - ing, The	chok - ing	wave, the

d :— :s₁	l₁ :t₁ :d.r	m :— : r.m	d :l₁ : t₁	l₁ :— :l₁	l₁ : l₁
2 day of	doom, I	bind un-	to my-	self to -	day.
4* deep salt	sea A-	round the	old e-	ter - nal	rocks.
7* poi - soned	shaft, Pro-	tect me,	Christ, till	thy re -	turn - ing.

170

GENERAL

VOICES *in Harmony with Organ*

: m₁	l₁ :— :l₁	s₁ :m₁ : s₁	d :m : r.d	d :t₁ : t₁	r :t₁ : s₁	
: m₁	m₁ :— :m₁	r₁ :d₁ : r₁	m₁ :— : l₁	s₁ :— : s₁	s₁ :— : s₁	
3* *mf* I	bind un-to	my-self	the power		Of the great	
5 *mf* I	bind un-to	my-self	to-day	The	power of	
6* *mf* A-	gainst the	de-mon	snares of	sin,	The vice that	
: m	d :— :d	r :m :r	d :— :l₁	m :r :r	r :— :r	
: m₁	l₁ :— :l₁	t₁ :d :t₁	l₁ :— :f₁	s₁ :— : s₁	t₁ :s₁ : t₁	

s₁ :t₁ : r	d :— :d	t₁ :— :m	l₁ :—.t₁ :d.l₁	s₁ :m₁ :d₁	d :— : s₁
s₁ :— :s₁	s₁ :m₁ :fe₁	s₁ :— :s₁	f₁ :—.f₁ : r₁	r₁ :m₁ :d₁	d₁ :r₁ :m₁
3* love of	cher-u-	bim; The	sweet 'Well	done!' in	judge-ment
5 God to	hold and	lead, His	eye to	watch, His	might to
6* gives temp-	ta-tion	force, The	na-tur-al	lusts that	war with-
m :r :t₁	d :— :d	r :— :d	d :—.t₁ :l₁.d	t₁ :— :d	f :— :ta₁
d :t₁ :s₁.f₁	m₁ :l₁ :l₁	s₁ :— :d₁	f₁ :—.f₁ :f₁	s₁ :— :l₁	l₁ :ta₁ :s₁

Org.

l₁ :t₁ :d.r	m :— :r.m	d :l₁ :t₁	l₁ :— :l₁	l₁ :— :l₁	
f₁ :— :d	d :t₁ :l₁.t₁	m₁ :f₁ :s₁	m₁ :r₁ :f₁	f₁ :m₁ :	
3* hour; The	ser-vice	of the	ser-a	phim;	
5 stay, His	ear to	heark-en	to my	need;	
6* in, The	hos-tile	men that	mar my	course—	
d :r :m.f	s :— :f.s	d :r :r	l₁ :— :r	r :d :	
f₁ :r₁ :l₁	s₁ :— : s₁	l₁ :r₁ :s₁	s₁ :f₁ :r₁	l₁ :— :	

Org.

t₁ :d :s₁	d :— :d	d :— :r.m	r :— :de	r :— :m	l₁ :— :l₁
: :s₁	s₁ :l₁ :f₁	s₁ :— :l₁.s₁	f₁ :l₁ :l₁	l₁ :— :s₁	f₁ :— :f₁
3* *mf* Con-	fess-ors'	faith, a-	pos-tles'	word, The	pa-triarchs'
5 *mp* The	wis-dom	of my	God to	teach, His	hand to
6* *p* Or	few or	ma-ny,	far or	nigh, In	ev-e-ry
: :s₁	s₁ :— :s₁	s₁ :d :l₁.ta₁	l₁ :f :m	r :d :t₁	d :r :r
: :s₁	m₁ :f₁ :r₁	m₁ :— :f₁.s₁	l₁ :— :s₁	f₁ :— :s₁	l₁ :r :d

s₁ :t₁ :r	d :— :d	t₁ :— :m	l₁ :—.t₁ :d.l₁	s₁ :m₁ :d₁	
f₁ :— :f₁	m₁ :l₁ :fe₁	se₁ :— :m₁	m₁ :— :m₁	r₁ :d₁ :d₁	
3* prayers, the	pro-phets'	scrolls, *p* All	good deeds	done un-	
5 guide, his	shield to-	ward, The	word of	God to	
6* place, and in	all hours, A-	gainst their	fierce hos-		
r :— :t₁	d :— :d	m :— :r	d :—.r :m.d	r :m : s₁	
t₁ :s₁ : se₁	l₁ :— :l₁	m₁ :— : se₁	l₁ :— :l₁	t₁ :d :m₁	

171

GENERAL

Hymn 162 (*continued*)

```
{ | d :— :s, | l, :t, :d.r | m :— :r.m | d :l, :t, | l, :— :l, | l, :— |
  | m, :— :d, | f, :— :d  | d :t, :l,.t, | m, :f, :r, | f, :m, :r, | m, :— | }

3* to    the  Lord,     And  pu - ri - ty       of   vir - gin souls.
5  give  me   speech,   His  heaven-ly host    to   be  my   guard.
6* til - i -  ty   I    bind to     me   these ho - ly  powers.

  | d :— :d | d :r :m.f | s :— :f.s | d :r :t, | r :d :t, | d :— |
  | l, :— :m, | f, :r, :l, | s, :— :s, | l, :f, :s, | l, :— :f, | l, :— |
```

PART II

In moderate time

G. 3.

```
{ |¹,d :—.r | m :l  | s :—.s | s :m  | s :—.s | s.m :r.m |
  |¹,d :—.d | d :d  | t, :—.t, | t, :t, | t, :—.t, | d :d |
  8 Christ be with me, Christ with-in me, Christ be-hind me,
  de m :—.f | s :f  | r :—.r | m :s  | s :—.f | m.s :f.s |
  |¹,d :—.d | d :f, | s, :—.s, | m, :m | r :—.r | d :d | }

{ | s :—.s | s.m :r.m | d :—.r | m :l  | s :—.s | s :m |
  | r :—.r | d :t,   | d :—.t, | d :l, | t, :—.t, | t, :t, |
  Christ be-fore me, Christ be-side me, Christ to win me,
  | s :—.f | m.s :f.s | m :—.l | m :f  | r :—.r | m :s |
  | t, :—.t, | d :s, | l, :—.l, | l, :r, | f, :—.f, | m, :m | }

{ | s :—.s | s.m :r.m | d :— | m :—  || d :—.r | m :l |
  | t, :—.t, | d.d :t,.t, | l, :— | d :— || d :—.d | d :d |
  Christ to com-fort and re - store  me, Christ be-neath me,
  | f :—.f | m.s :f.s | m :f | s :— || m :—.f | s :f |
  | r :—.r | d.d :s,.s, | l, :f, | d :— || d :—.d | d :f, | }

{ | s :—.s | s :m  | s :—.s | s.m :r.m | s :—.s | s.m :r.m |
  | t, :—.t, | t, :t, | t, :—.t, | d :d   | r :—.r | d :t, |
  Christ a-bove me, Christ in qui-et, Christ in dan-ger,
  | r :—.r | m :s  | s :—.f | m.s :f.s | s :—.f | m.s :f.s |
  | s, :—.s, | m, :m | r :—.r | d :d    | t, :—.t, | d :s, | }

{ | d :—.r | m :l | s :—.s | s :m  | s :—.s | s.m :r.m | d :— | m :— |
  | d :—.t, | d :l, | t, :—.t, | t, :t, | t, :—.t, | d.d :t,.t, | l, :— | d :— |
  Christ in hearts of all that love me, Christ in mouth of friend and stran - ger.
  | m :—.l | m :f | r :—.r | m :s | f :—.f | m.s :f.s | m :f | s :— |
  | l, :—.l, | l, :r, | f, :—.f, | m, :m | r :—.r | d.d :s,.s, | l, :f, | d :— | }
```

GENERAL

DOXOLOGY

FULL. *A little slower*
3. B♭.

9 I bind unto myself the name, The strong name of the Trinity, By invocation of the same, The Three in One, and One in Three, Of whom all nature hath creation, Eternal Father, Spirit, Word. Praise to the Lord of my salvation: Salvation is of Christ the Lord.

A - - men.

By permission of Stainer & Bell, Ltd.

Ascribed to ST. PATRICK
Tr. Mrs. C. F. Alexander

HYMN **163** Capetown   F. Filitz, 1804–76
KEY **D**

  THREE in One, and One in Three,
  Ruler of the earth and sea,
  Hear us, while we lift to thee
    Holy chant and psalm.

  2
  Light of lights! with morning shine;
  Lift on us thy light divine;
  And let charity benign
    Breathe on us her balm.

  3
  Light of lights! when falls the even,
  Let it close on sin forgiven;
  Fold us in the peace of heaven;
    Shed a holy calm.

  4
  Three in One and One in Three,
  Dimly here we worship thee;
  With the saints hereafter we
    Hope to bear the palm.

G. RORISON†

GENERAL

HYMN 164

FIRST TUNE

KEY A♭   Song 5

Orlando Gibbons, 1583-1625

SECOND TUNE

KEY D   Rivaulx

J. B. Dykes, 1823-76

FATHER of heaven, whose love profound
A ransom for our souls hath found,
Before thy throne we sinners bend,
To us thy pardoning love extend.

2
Almighty Son, incarnate Word,
Our Prophet, Priest, Redeemer, Lord,
Before thy throne we sinners bend,
To us thy saving grace extend.

3
Eternal Spirit, by whose breath
The soul is raised from sin and death,
Before thy throne we sinners bend,
To us thy quickening power extend.

4
Thrice Holy! Father, Spirit, Son;
Mysterious Godhead, Three in One,
Before thy throne we sinners bend,
Grace, pardon, life to us extend.

E. COOPER.†

GENERAL

HYMN 165 St. Anne   *Supplement to the New Version*, 1708

KEY **C**

The Descant may be sung for verse 6

Psalm 90

f O GOD, our help in ages past,
  Our hope for years to come,
Our shelter from the stormy blast,
  And our eternal home;

mf Beneath the shadow of thy throne
  Thy saints have dwelt secure;
Sufficient is thine arm alone,
  And our defence is sure.

3

Before the hills in order stood,
  Or earth received her frame,
From everlasting thou art God,
  To endless years the same.

4

p A thousand ages in thy sight
  Are like an evening gone;
Short as the watch that ends the night
  Before the rising sun.

5*

Time, like an ever-rolling stream,
  Bears all its sons away;
They fly forgotten, as a dream
  Dies at the opening day.

[UNISON] 6

f O God, our help in ages past,
  Our hope for years to come,
Be thou our guard while troubles last,
  And our eternal home.

I. WATTS†

GENERAL

HYMN 166 Old 100th L. Bourgeois, *c.* 1500–61
KEY A♭

{ |d : —	d : t₁	l₁ : s₁	d : —	r : —	m : — ‖
|s₁ : —	s₁ : s₁	m₁ : m₁	m₁ : —	s₁ : —	s₁ : — ‖
|m : —	m : r	d : t₁	d : —	t₁ : —	d : — ‖
|d₁ : —	d₁ : s₁	l₁ : m₁	l₁ : —	s₁ : —	d₁ : — }‖

{ |m : —	m : m	r : d	f : —	m : —	r : — ‖
|s₁ : —	s₁ : s₁	s₁ : m₁	l₁ : —	s₁ : —	s₁ : — ‖
|d : —	d : d	t₁ : d	d : —	d : —	t₁ : — ‖
|d₁ : —	d₁ : d	s₁ : l₁	f₁ : —	d₁ : —	s₁ : — }‖

{ |d : —	r : m	r : d	l₁ : —	t₁ : —	d : — ‖
|s₁ : —	s₁ : s₁	s₁ : m₁	f₁ : —	f₁ : —	s₁ : — ‖
|m : —	t₁ : d	t₁ : d	d : —	r : —	m : — ‖
|d₁ : —	s₁ : d	s₁ : l₁	f₁ : —	r₁ : —	d₁ : — }‖

{ |s : —	m : d	r : f	m : —	r : —	d : — ‖
|m₁ : —	m₁ : l₁	l₁ : f₁	s₁ : d	— : t₁	d : — ‖
|t₁ : —	d : m	f : l	s : —	— : :.f	m : — ‖
|m₁ : —	l₁ : —.s₁	f₁.m₁: r₁	m₁ : —.f₁	s₁ : —	d₁ : — }‖

ALTERNATIVE VERSION
(Melody in the Tenor part)

KEY A♭ Harmonized by J. Dowland, 1563–1626

{ |m : —	m : r	f : m	m : —	s : —	s : — ‖
|s₁ : —	s₁ : s₁	l₁.t₁: d	d : —	t₁ : —	d : — ‖
|d : —	d : t₁	l₁ : s₁	d : —	r : —	m : — ‖
|d₁ : —	d₁ : s₁	r₁ : m₁	l₁ : —	s₁ : —	d₁ : — }‖

{ |s : —	s : s	s : m	l : —	s : —	s : — ‖
|d : —	d : d	t₁ : l₁	d : —	d : —	t₁ : — ‖
|m : —	m : m	r : d	f : —	m : —	r : — ‖
|d : —	d : d	s₁ : l₁	f₁ : —	d : —	s₁ : — }‖

{ |m : —	r : d	t₁ : s	f : —	r : —	m : — ‖
|s₁ : —	t₁ : s₁	s₁ : —.s₁	l₁ : —	s₁ : —	s₁ : — ‖
|d : —	r : m	r : d	l₁ : —	t₁ : —	d : — ‖
|d₁ : —	s₁ : d₁	s₁ : m₁	f₁ : —	s₁ : —	d₁ : — }‖

GENERAL

```
|m  : —  |d  :-.d |s  : l   |s  : —  |s  :-.f |m  : —  ||
|d  : —  |s₁ : d  |t₁ : d   |d  : —  |t₁ : —  |d  : —  ||
|s  : —  |m  : d  |r  : f   |m  : —  |r  : —  |d  : —  ||
|d  : —  |d  : l₁ |s₁ : f₁  |d  : —  |s₁ : —  |d₁ : — ||
```

The Alternative Version may be used for verses 2 and 4

Psalm 100

f   ALL people that on earth do dwell,
       Sing to the Lord with cheerful voice;
    Him serve with fear, his praise forth tell,
       Come ye before him, and rejoice.

2

mf   The Lord, ye know, is God indeed;
       Without our aid he did us make;
    We are his folk, he doth us feed,
       And for his sheep he doth us take.

3

f   O enter then his gates with praise,
       Approach with joy his courts unto;
    Praise, laud, and bless his name always,
       For it is seemly so to do.

4

mf   For why? the Lord our God is good;
       His mercy is for ever sure;
    His truth at all times firmly stood,
       And shall from age to age endure.

[UNISON] **5**

f   To Father, Son, and Holy Ghost,
       The God whom heaven and earth adore,
    From men and from the angel-host
       Be praise and glory evermore.

W. KETHE, *Day's Psalter* (1561)

GENERAL

HYMN 167

FIRST TUNE

KEY **G** Old 104th

T. Ravenscroft, *Psalms*, 1621
Descant by Alan Gray, 1855–1935

DESCANT

{ :m | m :m :l | se :— :l | t :l.t :d' | t :— ‖

  :l, | d :t, :l, | m :— :d | r :f :m | r :—
  :m, | m, :m, :l, | se, :— :l, | t, :d :d | t, :—
  :d | l, :t, :d | m :— :m | s :l :s | s :—
  :l, | l, :s, :f, | m, :— :l, | s, :f, :d | s, :— }

{ :t | d' :s :l | t :— :d' | s :l.s :f | m :— ‖

  :r | m :s :fe | s :— :d | m :r :r | d :—
  :t, | s, :s, :l, | t, :— :l, | s, :l, :s, | m, :—
  :s | m :r :d | r :— :d | d :d :t, | d :—
  :s, | d :t, :l, | s, :— :l, | m, :f, :s, | d, :— }

{ :m | l :s.l :s.f | m.s :f :m.f | s :l.t :d' | t :— ‖

  :d | d :d :r | m :d :d | r :f :m | r :—
  :s, | l, :s, :f, | m, :f, :m, | s, :l, :s, | s, :—
  :m | f :d :t, | d :l, :d | t, :d :d | t, :—
  :d, | f, :m, :r, | d, :f, :l, | s, :f, :d, | s, :— }

{ :d' | t :l.t :l.s | f :m :f.s | m :l :se | l :— ‖

  :l | s :d :f.m | r :d :r | m :t, :t, | l, :—
  :l, | t, :d :d | s, :s, :l, | l, :l, :se, | l, :—
  :f | r :d :d | r :m :l,.t, | d ·f :m | d :—
  :f, | s, :l, :l, | t, :d :f, | d, :r, :m, | l, :— }

SECOND TUNE

KEY **A♭** Hanover

Supplement to the New Version, 1708
Descant by Alan Gray, 1855–1935

DESCANT   E♭. t.

{ :s, | s :s :f | m :— :r | d :l :s.f | m :— ‖ s d' | d' :d' :r'

  :s, | d :d :r | m :— :s | d :r :t, | d :—   ‖ r s | l :s :f
  :m, | m, :s, :s, | s, :· :s, | l, :l, :s, | s, :—   ‖ s,d | d :d :—.t,
  :d | d :d :t, | d .— :r | m :f :r | m :—   ‖ t,m | f :s :l.s
  :d, | d, :m, :s, | d :— :t, | l, :f, :s, | d, :—   ‖ s,d | f :m :r }

178

GENERAL

f. Ab.

Descants by permission of the Cambridge University Press

The Descants may be sung for verse 6

Psalm 104

f O WORSHIP the King all glorious above;
O gratefully sing his power and his love;
Our Shield and Defender, the Ancient of Days,
Pavilioned in splendour and girded with praise.

2
O tell of his might, O sing of his grace,
Whose robe is the light, whose canopy space;
His chariots of wrath the deep thunder clouds form,
And dark is his path on the wings of the storm.

3*
mf The earth with its store of wonders untold,
Almighty, thy power hath founded of old;
Hath stablished it fast by a changeless decree,
And round it hath cast, like a mantle, the sea.

4
Thy bountiful care what tongue can recite?
It breathes in the air, it shines in the light;
It streams from the hills, it descends to the plain,
And sweetly distils in the dew and the rain.

5
p Frail children of dust and feeble as frail,
In thee do we trust, nor find thee to fail;
Thy mercies how tender, how firm to the end!
Our Maker, Defender, Redeemer, and Friend.

[UNISON]
6
f O measureless Might, ineffable Love,
While angels delight to hymn thee above,
Thy ransomed creation, though feeble their lays,
With true adoration shall sing to thy praise.

SIR R. GRANT†
Based on W. Kethe (1561)

GENERAL

HYMN 168 Tranmere   W. Hayes, 1706–77
KEY F

mf THERE is a book, who runs may read,
   Which heavenly truth imparts,
And all the lore its scholars need,
   Pure eyes and Christian hearts.
The works of God above, below,
   Within us and around,
Are pages in that book, to show
   How God himself is found.

2
The glorious sky, embracing all,
   Is like the Maker's love,
Wherewith encompassed, great and small,
   In peace and order move. [small
The moon above, the Church below,
   A wondrous race they run;
But all their radiance, all their glow,
   Each borrows of its sun.

3*
The Saviour lends the light and heat
   That crown his holy hill;
The saints, like stars, around his seat
   Perform their courses still.
The dew of heaven is like thy grace,
   It steals in silence down;
But where it lights, the favoured place
   By richest fruits is known.

4
f One name, above all glorious names,
   With its ten thousand tongues
The everlasting sea proclaims,
   Echoing angelic songs.
The raging fire, the roaring wind,
   Thy boundless power display;
But in the gentler breeze we find
   Thy Spirit's viewless way.

5
mf Two worlds are ours: 'tis only sin
   Forbids us to descry
The mystic heaven and earth within,
   Plain as the sea and sky.
Thou who hast given me eyes to see
And love this sight so fair,
Give me a heart to find out thee,
   And read thee everywhere.

J. KEBLE

Alternative Tune, St. Matthew, 478

GENERAL

HYMN 169 Westminster J. Turle, 1802–82

KEY **C**

[musical notation]

mf MY God, how wonderful thou art,
　　Thy majesty how bright,
　　How beautiful thy mercy-seat,
　　　In depths of burning light!

2

p How dread are thine eternal years,
　　O everlasting Lord,
　　By prostrate spirits day and night
　　　Incessantly adored!

3

mf How wonderful, how beautiful,
　　The sight of thee must be,
　　Thine endless wisdom, boundless power,
　　　And aweful purity!

4

p O how I fear thee, living God,
　　With deepest, tenderest fears,
　　And worship thee with trembling hope,
　　　And penitential tears!

5

mf Yet I may love thee too, O Lord,
　　Almighty as thou art,
　　For thou hast stooped to ask of me⌣
　　　The love of my poor heart.

6

　　No earthly father loves like thee,
　　　No mother, e'er so mild,
　　Bears and forbears as thou hast done⌣
　　　With me thy sinful child.

7

　　Father of Jesus, love's reward,
　　　What rapture will it be,
　　Prostrate before thy throne to lie,
　　　And gaze and gaze on thee!

F. W. FABER

GENERAL

Hymn 170 Addison's

J. Sheeles, 1688–1761

KEY G

[tonic sol-fa notation]

1
THE spacious firmament on high,
With all the blue ethereal sky,
And spangled heavens, a shining frame,
Their great Original proclaim.
The unwearied sun from day to day
Does his Creator's power display,
And publishes to every land
The works of an almighty hand.

2
Soon as the evening shades prevail
The moon takes up the wondrous tale,
And nightly to the listening earth
Repeats the story of her birth;
Whilst all the stars that round her burn,
And all the planets in their turn,
Confirm the tidings, as they roll,
And spread the truth from pole to pole.

3
What though in solemn silence all
Move round the dark terrestrial ball;
What though nor real voice nor sound
Amid their radiant orbs be found;
In reason's ear they all rejoice,
And utter forth a glorious voice,
For ever singing as they shine,
'The hand that made us is divine.'

J. ADDISON

The last line of each verse is repeated

HYMN 171 Dix

C. Kocher, 1786–1872

KEY A♭

DESCANT

```
| s  :s     | s  :m  | l  :s     | s  :—  || f  :r  | s  :f  | m   :r     | m  :—  ||
| d  :t,.d  | r  :d  | f  :f     | m  :—  || l, :t, | d  :l, | s,  :s,    | s, :—  ||
| s, :s,    | s, :s, | f, :s,    | s, :—  || l, :s, | s, :f, | m,  :r,    | m, :—  ||
| m  :f.m   | r  :m  | d  :r     | d  :—  || d  :r  | d  :d  | d   :t,    | d  :—  ||
| d  :r.d   | t, :d  | l, :t,    | d  :—  || f, :f, | m, :f, | s,  :s,    | d, :—  ||

| m  :r.m   | f  :s  | l  :t.l   | l  :se || l  :r  | s  :f  | m.s :f.m   | r  :—  ||
| d  :t,.d  | r  :d  | f  :f     | m  :—  || l, :t, | d  :l, | s,  :s,    | s, :—  ||
| m, :l,    | l, :s, | l, :t,.l, | l, :se,|| l, :s, | s, :f, | s,  :f,.m, | r, :—  ||
| m  :r.m   | f  :d  | d  :r.d   | t, :m  || m  :r  | d  :d  | d   :d     | d  :t, ||
| l, :l,    | f, :m, | r, :r,    | m, :—  || f, :f, | m, :r, | m,  :r,.d, | s, :—  ||

| m  :s.f   | m  :s  | s  :l.t   | d' :—  || l  :s  | s  :d  | s   :—.f   | m  :—  ||
| m  :r     | d  :m  | s  :—.f   | m  :—  || l, :t, | d  :f  | m   :r     | d  :—  ||
| s, :s,    | s, :s, | s, :s,    | s, :—  || l, :s, | s, :l, | s,  :—.f,  | m, :—  ||
| d  :s.f   | m  :d  | r  :t,    | d  :—  || d  :r  | d  :d  | d   :t,    | d  :—  ||
| d  :t,    | d  :d  | t, :s,    | d  :—  || f, :f, | m, :f, | s,  :s,    | d, :—  ||
```

The Descant may be sung for verse 5

mf FOR the beauty of the earth,
For the beauty of the skies,
For the love which from our birth
Over and around us lies,
f Lord of all, to thee we raise‿
This our grateful hymn of praise.

2

mf For the beauty of each hour‿
Of the day and of the night,
Hill and vale, and tree and flower,
Sun and moon and stars of light,
f Lord of all, etc.

3

mf For the joy of human love,
Brother, sister, parent, child,
Friends on earth, and friends above,
Pleasures pure and undefiled,
f Lord of all, etc.

4

mf For each perfect gift of thine,
To our race so freely given,
Graces human and divine,
Flowers of earth and buds of heaven,
f Lord of all, etc.

[UNISON] 5

For thy Church which evermore‿
Lifteth holy hands above,
Offering up on every shore
Her pure sacrifice of love,
Lord of all, etc.

F. S. PIERPOINT†

GENERAL

HYMN 172 Easter Song   *Catholische Kirchengesänge* (Cologne, 1623)
KEY E♭

[sol-fa notation musical score]

f ALL creatures of our God and King,
Lift up your voice and with us sing
    Alleluia, alleluia!
Thou burning sun with golden beam,
Thou silver moon with softer gleam.
    O praise him, O praise him,
    Alleluia, alleluia, alleluia!

2
Thou rushing wind that art so strong,
Ye clouds that sail in heaven along,
    O praise him, alleluia!
Thou rising morn, in praise rejoice,
Ye lights of evening, find a voice;
    O praise him, O praise him,
    Alleluia, alleluia, alleluia!

GENERAL

3

mf Thou flowing water, pure and clear,
Make music for thy Lord to hear,
  Alleluia, alleluia!
Thou fire so masterful and bright,
That givest man both warmth and light,
  O praise him, O praise him,
  Alleluia, alleluia, alleluia!

4*

Dear mother earth, who day by day
Unfoldest blessings on our way,
  O praise him, alleluia!
The flowers and fruits that in thee grow,
Let them his glory also show;
  O praise him, O praise him,
  Alleluia, alleluia, alleluia!

5

And all ye men of tender heart,
Forgiving others, take your part,
  O sing ye alleluia!
Ye who long pain and sorrow bear,
Praise God and on him cast your care;
  O praise him, O praise him!
  Alleluia, alleluia, alleluia!

6*

p And thou, most kind and gentle death,
Waiting to hush our latest breath,
  O praise him, alleluia!
Thou leadest home the child of God,
And Christ our Lord the way hath trod;
  O praise him, O praise him,
  Alleluia, alleluia, alleluia!

7

f Let all things their Creator bless,
And worship him in humbleness;
  O praise him, alleluia!
Praise, praise the Father, praise the Son,
And praise the Spirit, Three in One;
  O praise him, O praise him,
  Alleluia, alleluia, alleluia!

W. H. DRAPER Based on St. Francis
of Assisi's *Canticle of the Sun*

GENERAL

HYMN 173 Nature   Sir C. H. H. Parry, 1848–1918

KEY D

```
{ :d  | m :-.f | s :s   | l :f | d' :-. || l  | s :m   | m :-.r  | d :f  | r :- ||
{ :d  | d :-.r | m :d   | d :f | f  :-. || f  | s :d   | t, :t,  | d :d  | t, :- ||
{ :m  | l :-.l | s :d'  | d' :l| d' :-. || d' | d' :s  | s :f    | m :l  | s :- ||
{ :d  | l, :f, | d :m   | f :f | l  :-. || f  | m :d   | s, :-.s,| l, :f,| s, :- ||
```

A.t.

```
{ :m l,| d :-.r | m :d   | m :f | s       || s  | s :f   | f :m    | r :-.r | d :- ||
{ :d f,| s, :-.t,| d :d  | d :l,| s,      || s, | l, :l, | t, :d   | 1, :s,.f,|m, :- ||
{ :s d | d :-.f | m :m   | d :d | d       || d  | m :r   | r :d    | d :t,  | d :- ||
{ :d f,| m, :-.r,| d, :d | l, :f,| m,     || m, | f, :f, | s, :l,  | f, :s, | d, :- ||
```

f. D.

```
{ :d s | d' :-.t| l :f   | l :-.s | f     || l  | l :s   | s :f    | m :-.r | d :- ||
{ :d s | s :-.s | f :d   | de :m  | r     || f  | f :m   | m :r    | t, :-.t,| d :- ||
{ :m t | d' :d' | d' :l  | l :l   | l     || l  | l :t   | d' :l :l| s :-.f | m :- ||
{ :d s | m :-.m | f :f   | l, :de | r     || r  | r :m   | f :f,   | s, :-.s,| d :- ||
```

1

I PRAISED the earth, in beauty seen,
With garlands gay of various green;
I praised the sea, whose ample field
Shone glorious as a silver shield—
And earth and ocean seemed to say,
'Our beauties are but for a day.'

2

I praised the sun, whose chariot rolled
On wheels of amber and of gold;
I praised the moon, whose softer eye
Gleamed sweetly through the summer sky—
And moon and sun in answer said,
'Our days of light are numberèd.'

3

O God, O good beyond compare,
If thus thy meaner works are fair,
If thus thy beauties gild the span
Of ruined earth and sinful man,
How glorious must the mansion be
Where thy redeemed shall dwell with thee!

BISHOP R. HEBER

Alternative Tune, Surrey, 179

GENERAL

HYMN 174 St. Audrey

B. Harwood, 1859–1949

KEY E♭

[Tonic sol-fa notation]

Bb. t.   f. E♭

[Tonic sol-fa notation continues]

LORD of beauty, thine the splendour
   Shewn in earth and sky and sea,
Burning sun and moonlight tender,
   Hill and river, flower and tree:
Lest we fail our praise to render
   Touch our eyes that they may see.

2
Lord of wisdom, whom obeying
   Mighty waters ebb and flow,
While unhasting, undelaying,
   Planets on their courses go:
In thy laws thyself displaying,
   Teach our minds thyself to know.

3
Lord of life, alone sustaining
   All below and all above,
Lord of love, by whose ordaining
   Sun and stars sublimely move:
In our earthly spirits reigning,
   Lift our hearts that we may love.

4
Lord of beauty, bid us own thee,
   Lord of truth, our footsteps guide,
Till as Love our hearts enthrone thee,
   And, with vision purified,
Lord of all, when all have known thee,
   Thou in all art glorified.

C. A. ALINGTON

Alternative Tune, Regent Square, 279

GENERAL

Hymn 175 Ivyhatch
B. Luard Selby, 1853-1919

KEY A♭

[sol-fa notation]

d. f. D♭.   E♭. t. m.   f. A♭.

[sol-fa notation]

THE Lord is King! lift up thy voice,
O earth, and all ye heavens, rejoice;
From world to world the joy shall ring,
'The Lord omnipotent is King!'

2
The Lord is King! who then shall dare
Resist his will, distrust his care,
Or murmur at his wise decrees,
Or doubt his royal promises?

3
He reigns! ye saints, exalt your strains;
Your God is King, your Father reigns;
And he is at the Father's side,
The Man of love, the Crucified.

4*
Alike pervaded by his eye
All parts of his dominion lie:
This world of ours and worlds unseen,
And thin the boundary between.

5
One Lord one empire all secures;
He reigns, and life and death are yours;
Through earth and heaven one song shall ring,
'The Lord omnipotent is King!'

J. CONDER

Hymn 176 Offertorium
M. Haydn, 1737-1806

KEY D

[sol-fa notation]

GENERAL

SOMETIMES a light surprises
  The Christian while he sings:
It is the Lord who rises
  With healing in his wings;
When comforts are declining,
  He grants the soul again
A season of clear shining
  To cheer it after rain.

2

In holy contemplation
  We sweetly then pursue
The theme of God's salvation,
  And find it ever new:
Set free from present sorrow,
  We cheerfully can say,
E'en let the unknown morrow
  Bring with it what it may,

3

It can bring with it nothing
  But he will bear us through;
Who gives the lilies clothing
  Will clothe his people too:
Beneath the spreading heavens
  No creature but is fed;
And he who feeds the ravens
  Will give his children bread.

4

Though vine nor fig-tree neither
  Their wonted fruit should bear,
Though all the fields should wither,
  Nor flocks nor herds be there;
Yet, God the same abiding,
  His praise shall tune my voice;
For, while in him confiding,
  I cannot but rejoice.

W. COWPER

HYMN 177 Contemplation Sir F. A. G. Ouseley, 1825-89

KEY E

mf WHEN all thy mercies, O my God,
  My rising soul surveys,
Transported with the view, I'm lost
  In wonder, love, and praise.

2

Unnumbered comforts to my soul
  Thy tender care bestowed,
Before my infant heart conceived
  From whom those comforts flowed.

3

p When in the slippery paths of youth
  With heedless steps I ran,
mf Thine arm unseen conveyed me safe,
  And led me up to man.

4*

Ten thousand thousand precious gifts
  My daily thanks employ,
And not the least a cheerful heart
  Which tastes those gifts with joy.

5

f Through every period of my life
  Thy goodness I'll pursue,
And after death in distant worlds
  The glorious theme renew.

6

Through all eternity to thee,
  A joyful song I'll raise;
For O, eternity's too short
  To utter all thy praise.

J. ADDISON

GENERAL

HYMN 178 University   C. Collignon, 1725–85
KEY C

Psalm 23

mf THE God of love my Shepherd is,
    And he that doth me feed;
While he is mine and I am his,
    What can I want or need?

2
He leads me to the tender grass,
    Where I both feed and rest;
Then to the streams that gently pass:
    In both I have the best.

3
Or if I stray, he doth convert,
    And bring my mind in frame,
And all this not for my desert,
    But for his holy name.

4
p Yea, in death's shady black abode
    Well may I walk, not fear;
For thou art with me, and thy rod
    To guide, thy staff to bear.

5
mf Surely thy sweet and wondrous love
    Shall measure all my days;
f And, as it never shall remove,
    So neither shall my praise.

GEORGE HERBERT

HYMN 179 Surrey   H. Carey, *c.* 1690–1743
KEY G

GENERAL

{ | f :— :m.r | m :— ‖ m | r :— :f | m :r :d | r :d :t, | d :— |
  | l, :d :t, | d :— ‖ d | t, :— :d | d :t, :l, | l, :s, :s, | s, :— |
  | f :— :s | s :— ‖ s | s :— :l | s :—.f:m | f :m :r | m :— |
  | r :— :s, | d :— ‖ d | s, :— :f, | d :s, :l, | f, :s, :s, | d, :— | }

Psalm 23

mf THE Lord my pasture shall prepare,
And feed me with a shepherd's care;
His presence shall my wants supply;
And guard me with a watchful eye;
My noonday walks he shall attend,
And all my midnight hours defend.

2

p When in the sultry glebe I faint,
Or on the thirsty mountain pant,
To fertile vales and dewy meads
My weary wandering steps he leads,
Where peaceful rivers, soft and slow,
Amid the verdant landscape flow.

3

mf Though in a bare and rugged way
Through devious lonely wilds I stray,
Thy bounty shall my pains beguile;
The barren wilderness shall smile
With sudden greens and herbage crowned,
And streams shall murmur all around.

4

p Though in the paths of death I tread,
With gloomy horrors overspread,
mf My steadfast heart shall fear no ill,
For thou, O Lord, art with me still:
Thy friendly crook shall give me aid,
And guide me through the dreadful shade.

J. ADDISON

HYMN **180** Collingwood   H. A. Bate

KEY **G**

{ | d :s,.m | r :s, | d.r :m.f | s | —.f | f.m :r.d | f :m | r :— | — |
  | m, :s,.s, | s, :s, | s, :d | s, | t, | d :s, | f, :s, | s, :l, | t, |
  | d :d.d | t, :t, | d :d | r | r | d :d | t, :d | t, :d | r |
  | d, :m,.d, | s, :f, | m, :l, | t, | s, | d :m, | r, :d, | s, :— | — | }

{ | :s, | d.r :d.t, | l, | :t,.d | r.m :r.d | t, | s, | s :d | m.r :d.t, | d :— |
  | :s, | m, :se, | l, | :s, | l, :l, | s, | s, | s, :l, | l, :s,.f, | m, :— |
  | :r | d :m.r | d | :r.m | f.s :f.m | r | t, | d :m | s.f :m.r | d :— |
  | :t, | l, :m, | f,.s, :f,.m, | r, :f, | s,.l, | s,.f, | m, :l, | f, :s, | d, :— | }

FATHER, whate'er of earthly bliss
  Thy sovereign will denies,
Accepted at thy throne of grace
  Let this petition rise:

2

Give me a calm and thankful heart,
  From every murmur free;
The blessings of thy grace impart,
  And let me live to thee.

3

Let the sweet hope that thou art mine
  My path of life attend;
Thy presence through my journey shine,
  And crown my journey's end.

ANNE STEELE†

GENERAL

HYMN 181 London New
Psalms (Edinburgh, 1635)

KEY E♭

[sol-fa notation]

1
GOD moves in a mysterious way
 His wonders to perform;
He plants his footsteps in the sea,
 And rides upon the storm.

2
Deep in unfathomable mines
 Of never-failing skill
He treasures up his bright designs,
 And works his sovereign will.

3
Ye fearful saints, fresh courage take;
 The clouds ye so much dread
Are big with mercy, and shall break
 In blessings on your head.

4
Judge not the Lord by feeble sense,
 But trust him for his grace;
Behind a frowning providence
 He hides a smiling face.

5
His purposes will ripen fast,
 Unfolding every hour;
The bud may have a bitter taste,
 But sweet will be the flower.

6
Blind unbelief is sure to err,
 And scan his work in vain;
God is his own interpreter,
 And he will make it plain.

W. COWPER

HYMN 182 Marching
Martin Shaw

KEY A

[sol-fa notation]

By permission of J. Curwen & Sons, Ltd., from Curwen edition No. 80631

1
FATHER, hear the prayer we offer:
 Not for ease that prayer shall be,
But for strength that we may ever
 Live our lives courageously.

2
Not for ever in green pastures
 Do we ask our way to be;
But the steep and rugged pathway
 May we tread rejoicingly.

192

GENERAL

3
Not for ever by still waters
  Would we idly rest and stay;
But would smite the living fountains
  From the rocks along our way.

4
Be our strength in hours of weakness,
  In our wanderings be our guide;
Through endeavour, failure, danger,
  Father, be thou at our side.

MRS. L. M. WILLIS (1864)

HYMN 183   A stronghold sure   M. Luther, 1483–1546
KEY C

Ein' feste Burg

A SAFE stronghold our God is still,
  A trusty shield and weapon;
He'll keep us clear from all the ill
  That hath us now o'ertaken.
    The ancient prince of hell
    Hath risen with purpose fell;
  Strong mail of craft and power
  He weareth in this hour;
On earth is not his fellow.

2
With force of arms we nothing can,
  Full soon were we down-ridden;
But for us fights the proper Man,
  Whom God himself hath bidden.
    Ask ye, Who is this same?
    Christ Jesus is his name,
  The Lord Sabaoth's Son;
  He, and no other one,
Shall conquer in the battle.

3
And were this world all devils o'er,
  And watching to devour us,
We lay it not to heart so sore;
  Not they can overpower us.
    And let the prince of ill
    Look grim as e'er he will,
  He harms us not a whit;
  For why?—his doom is writ;
A word shall quickly slay him.

4
God's word, for all their craft and force,
  One moment will not linger,
But, spite of hell, shall have its course;
  'Tis written by his finger.
    And though they take our life,
    Goods, honour, children, wife,
  Yet is their profit small;
  These things shall vanish all:
The City of God remaineth!

M. LUTHER *Tr.* T. Carlyle

GENERAL

HYMN 184　　　　　　　　　　FIRST TUNE

KEY E♭　Repton　　　　　　Sir C. H. H. Parry, 1848–1918 (from *Judith*)

UNISON

{ :d | s :-.s | l.s : m.f | s :-.s | d:d | f :m | t, :d | s, :—|—: s, }

{ | l, :m | r :d | t, :f | m :r | d :-.d | l :f | r : m.f | s : l.t }

://:

{ | d' :s | l.s : m.f | s :—|—: s | f : l, | d :-.t, | d :—|— ||

When the above tune is used the last line of the words must be repeated

SECOND TUNE

KEY F　Engedi　　　　　　　　　　　S. S. Wesley, 1810–76

:d	r :s	m :r	d :r.d	t,	d	r :s	m	:r.d	s :—	—		t,	d :r	m:f
:s,	l, :s,	s, :t,	d :l,	s,	m,	s, :t,	d	:d	t, :—	—		s,	d :s,	d:d
:m	f :r	m :s	m :f.m	r	d	s :s	s	:fe	s :—	—		s	m :s	s:l
:d	d :t,	d :s,	l, :f,	s,	l,	t, :s,	d.t,	:l,	s, :—	—		s,	l, :t,	d:l,

f :m	r		r	m :f	s :l	l	:se	l		l	r :s	s :-.f	m :—	—
r :d	t,		t,	d :t,	d :l,	t,	:t,	d		d	t, :d	d :t,	d :—	—
s :s	s		s	s :s	s :m	m	:m	m		f	f :m	r :-.s	s :—	—
t,:d	s,		s,	d :r	m :d	m	:m	l,		f,	s, :s,	s, :-.s,	d, :—	—

|
1

DEAR Lord and Father of mankind,
　Forgive our foolish ways!
Re-clothe us in our rightful mind,
In purer lives thy service find,
　In deeper reverence praise.

2

In simple trust like theirs who heard,
　Beside the Syrian sea,
The gracious calling of the Lord,
Let us, like them, without a word
　Rise up and follow thee.

3*

O Sabbath rest by Galilee!
　O calm of hills above,
Where Jesus knelt to share with thee
The silence of eternity,
　Interpreted by love!

4

Drop thy still dews of quietness,
　Till all our strivings cease;
Take from our souls the strain and stress,
And let our ordered lives confess
　The beauty of thy peace.

5

Breathe through the heats of our desire
　Thy coolness and thy balm;
Let sense be dumb, let flesh retire;
Speak through the earthquake, wind, and fire,
　O still small voice of calm!

J. G. WHITTIER

GENERAL

HYMN 185 FIRST TUNE
KEY **A** Gerontius   J. B. Dykes, 1823–76

(musical notation – tonic sol-fa)

SECOND TUNE
KEY **E♭** Somervell   Sir A. Somervell, 1863–1937

(musical notation – tonic sol-fa)

f PRAISE to the Holiest in the height,
   And in the depth be praise:
   In all his words most wonderful,
   Most sure in all his ways.

   2
mf O loving wisdom of our God!
   When all was sin and shame,
   A second Adam to the fight
   And to the rescue came.

   3
   O wisest love! that flesh and blood,
   Which did in Adam fail,
   Should strive afresh against the foe,
   Should strive and should prevail;

   4
   And that a higher gift than grace
   Should flesh and blood refine,
   God's presence and his very self,
   And essence all-divine.

   5
   O generous love! that he, who
   In Man for man the foe, [smote
   The double agony in Man
   For man should undergo;

   6
p And in the garden secretly,
   And on the Cross on high,
   Should teach his brethren, and in-
   To suffer and to die.   spire

   7
f Praise to the Holiest in the height,
   And in the depth be praise:
   In all his words most wonderful,
   Most sure in all his ways.

CARDINAL J. H. NEWMAN

Alternative Tune, Richmond, 258

GENERAL

Hymn 186 Halton Holgate   W. Boyce, 1710–79

KEY E♭

```
{| m :d | s :d | r.m :f | f :m | l :s | t :d' | f :m | m :r  ||
 | s₁:d | t₁:d | d  :t₁ | t₁:d | d :d | s.f:m  | r :d | d :t₁ ||
 | s :m | r :d | l  :s  | s :s | f :s | s  :s  | s :s | s :—  ||
 | d :d | s₁:l₁| f₁ :s₁ | d :d | f :m | r  :d  | t₁:d | s₁:—  ||

{| f.m:r.d| s :t | l.t:d' | d':t | d':l | f :m | f.m:r | d :—    ||
 | s₁:s₁  | s₁:r | m :r   | r :r | d :d | d.t₁:d| d :d.t₁| s₁:—  ||
 | s :f.m | r :s | s :fe  | s :s | s :f | s  :s | l.s:f | m :—   ||
 | d :d   | t₁:s₁| d :r   | s :s.f| m :f | r :d | f₁:s₁ | d :—   ||
```

       FIRMLY I believe and truly
         God is Three and God is One;
       And I next acknowledge duly
         Manhood taken by the Son.

2

       And I trust and hope most fully
         In that Manhood crucified;
       And each thought and deed unruly
         Do to death, as he has died.

3

       Simply to his grace and wholly
         Light and life and strength belong,
       And I love supremely, solely,
         Him the Holy, him the Strong.

4

       And I hold in veneration,
         For the love of him alone,
       Holy Church as his creation,
         And her teachings as his own.

5

       Adoration ay be given,
         With and through the angelic host,
       To the God of earth and heaven,
         Father, Son, and Holy Ghost.

                               CARDINAL J. H. NEWMAN

Alternative Tune, Stuttgart, 76

GENERAL

Hymn 187 Eisenach J. H. Schein, 1586–1630

KEY E♭

[tonic sol-fa notation omitted]

O amor quam ecstaticus

mf O LOVE, how deep, how broad, how high!
It fills the heart with ecstasy,
That God, the Son of God, should take
Our mortal form for mortals' sake.

2
He sent no angel to our race
Of higher or of lower place,
But wore the robe of human frame
Himself, and to this lost world came.

3
For us he was baptized, and bore
His holy fast, and hungered sore;
For us temptations sharp he knew;
For us the tempter overthrew.

4
p For us to wicked men betrayed,
Scourged, mocked, in purple robe arrayed,
He bore the shameful Cross and death;
For us at length gave up his breath.

5
f For us he rose from death again,
For us he went on high to reign,
For us he sent his Spirit here
To guide, to strengthen, and to cheer.

6
To him whose boundless love has won
Salvation for us through his Son,
To God the Father, glory be
Both now and through eternity.

Ascribed to THOMAS À KEMPIS
Tr. B. WEBB‡

GENERAL

Hymn 188 — FIRST TUNE

KEY **D** Jesu dulcis memoria Mode i

Jesu dulcis memoria

{| d   r   m s   s f   m r   f   m r d   r — | d m   s   s l }

1 Je-su! the ve-ry thought is sweet; In that dear
2 No word is sung more sweet than this, No sound is
3 Je-su, the hope of souls for-lorn, How good to
4 No tongue of mor-tal can ex-press, No pen can
5* O Je-su, King of won-drous might! O Vic-tor,
6 A-bide with us, O Lord, to-day, Ful-fil us

{| l   l s   s d'   t l s   l — | l d'   s   s f   m   r d }

1 name all heart-joys meet; But O, than hon-ey
2 heard more full of bliss, No thought brings sweet-er
3 them for sin that mourn! To them that seek thee,
4 write, the bless-ed-ness: He on-ly who hath
5* glo-rious from the fight! Sweet-ness that may not
6 with thy grace, we pray; And with thine own true

{| r   r m   m — | d   r   m s   s f   m r   f   m r d   r — ||

1 sweet-er far The glimp-ses of his pre-sence are.
2 com-fort nigh, Than Je-sus, Son of God most high.
3 O how kind! But what art thou to them that find?
4 proved it knows What bliss from love of Je-sus flows.
5* be ex-prest, And al-to-geth-er love-li-est!
6 sweet-ness feed Our souls from sin and dark-ness freed.

SECOND TUNE

KEY **E♭** St. Bernard W. H. Monk, 1823–89

B♭. t.

{ :s | m :s | d':l | s :r | m | m l₁ | s₁:t₁ | d :r.m | f :t₁ | d :— ||
  :d | d :r | d :d | d :—.t₁| d | d f₁ | s₁:f₁ | m₁:l₁.s₁ | f₁:f₁ | m₁:— ||
  :m | s :s | m :f | m.f:s | s | s d | d :r | d :d | r :r | d :— ||
  :d | d :t₁ | l₁:f₁ | s₁:s₁ | d | d f₁ | m₁:r₁ | l₁:f₁.m₁ | r₁:s₁ | d₁:— ||

f. E♭.

{ :ᵈs | s :s.f | m :m | l :t | d' | t.l | s :d | d :r.m | f :r | d :— ||
  :ᵐt₁ | d :t₁ | d :m.r| d :m | m | r | m :d.ta₁| l₁:l₁ | l₁:t₁ | d :— ||
  :ᵈs | s :s | s :se | l :se | l | f | m :s | f :l.s | f :f | m :— ||
  :ᵈ s.f| m :r | d :t₁ | l₁:m₁ | l₁ | t₁ | d :m | f :f.m | r :s₁ | d :— ||

GENERAL

Jesu dulcis memoria

JESU! the very thought is sweet,
In that dear name all heart-joys meet;
But O, than honey sweeter far
The glimpses of his presence are.

2

No word is sung more sweet than this,
No sound is heard more full of bliss,
No thought brings sweeter comfort nigh,
Than Jesus, Son of God most high.

3

Jesu, the hope of souls forlorn,
How good to them for sin that mourn!
To them that seek thee, O how kind!
But what art thou to them that find?

4

No tongue of mortal can express,
No pen can write, the blessedness:
He only who hath proved it knows
What bliss from love of Jesus flows.

5*

O Jesu, King of wondrous might!
O Victor, glorious from the fight!
Sweetness that may not be exprest,
And altogether loveliest!

6

Abide with us, O Lord, to-day,
Fulfil us with thy grace, we pray;
And with thine own true sweetness feed
Our souls from sin and darkness freed.

c. 12th cent.
Tr. J. M. NEALE and Compilers

GENERAL

HYMN 189　　FIRST TUNE

KEY **D**　Metzler's Redhead　　　　R. Redhead, 1820–1901

{:m |r :d |d¹ :s |l :l |s　　s |l :t |d¹ :t |l :— |— ||
 :d |t₁ :d |d :d |d :r |m　　m |d :f |m :–.r |d :— |— ||
 :s |s :m |s :d¹ |l :t |d¹　　d¹|d¹:t.l |l :se |l :— |— ||
 :d |s₁ :l₁|m₁:m |f :f |d　　d |f :r |m :m₁|l₁:— |— ||

{:l |l :s |l :s.f |m :r |s　　d |f :m |r :r |d :— |— ||
 :d |d :d |d :r |d :t₁|d　　l₁|l₁.t₁:d|d :t₁|d :— |— ||
 :f |f :m |f :l |s :s |s　　l |f :s |s :–.f|m :— |— ||
 :f |f :d |f :r |s :–.f|m　　f |r :d |s₁:s₁|d :— |— ||

SECOND TUNE

KEY **G**　Belmont　　　　　　Adapted from W. Gardiner's
Sacred Melodies, 1812

{:s₁|m :— :r |d :— :t₁|t₁:l₁:d |s₁:—　　s |s :f :m |m :r :d |d :t₁||
 :s₁|d :— :t₁|d :— :s₁|f₁:— :f₁|m₁:—　　s₁|d :t₁:d |l₁:— :l₁|s₁:— ||
 :m |s :— :f |m :— :m |d :— :d |d :—　　m |m :f :s |f :— :r |m :r ||
 :d |d :— :s₁|l₁:— :m₁|f₁:— :l₁|d :—　　d |d₁:r₁:m₁|f₁:— :f₁|s₁:— ||

{:s₁|m :— :r |d :— :t₁|t₁:l₁:d |s₁:—　　s |s :f :r |d :m :r |d :— ||
 :s₁|s₁:— :f₁|m₁:— :s₁|f₁:— :f₁|s₁:—　　ta₁|l₁:— :l₁|s₁:d :t₁|d :— ||
 :r |d :— :t₁|d :— :d |d :— :d |m :—　　d |d :r :f |m :s :f |m :— ||
 :t₁|d :m₁:s₁|l₁:— :m₁|f₁:— :l₁|d :—　　m₁|f₁:— :f₁|s₁:— :s₁|d :— ||

Jesu dulcis memoria

PART 1

JESU, the very thought of thee
　With sweetness fills the breast;
But sweeter far thy face to see,
　And in thy presence rest.

2

No voice can sing, no heart can frame,
　Nor can the memory find,
A sweeter sound than Jesu's name,
　The Saviour of mankind.

GENERAL

3

O hope of every contrite heart,
    O joy of all the meek,
To those who ask how kind thou art,
    How good to those who seek!

4

But what to those who find? Ah, this
    Nor tongue nor pen can show;
The love of Jesus, what it is
    None but his loved ones know.

5

Jesu, our only joy be thou,
    As thou our prize wilt be;
In thee be all our glory now,
    And through eternity.

PART 2

6

O Jesu, King most wonderful,
    Thou Conqueror renowned,
Thou sweetness most ineffable,
    In whom all joys are found!

7

When once thou visitest the heart,
    Then truth begins to shine,
Then earthly vanities depart,
    Then kindles love divine.

8

Thee, Jesu, may our voices bless,
    Thee may we love alone,
And ever in our lives express
    The image of thine own.

9

Abide with us, and let thy light
    Shine, Lord, on every heart;
Dispel the darkness of our night,
    And joy to all impart.

10

Jesu, our love and joy, to thee,
    The Virgin's holy Son,
All might and praise and glory be
    While endless ages run.

c. 12th cent.   *Tr.* E. CASWALL†

GENERAL

HYMN 190

FIRST TUNE

KEY **G** Oriel

C. Ett, *Cantica Sacra*, 1840

DESCANT — Descant by Alan Gray, 1855–1935

Descant by permission of the Cambridge University Press

The Descant may be sung for verses 3 and 6

SECOND TUNE

KEY **G** St. Nicholas

W. Ellis, 1868–1947

By permission of the Royal School of Church Music

GENERAL

Gloriosi Salvatoris

TO the name of our salvation
  Laud and honour let us pay,
Which for many a generation
  Hid in God's foreknowledge lay,
But with holy exultation
  We may sing aloud to-day.

2

Jesus is the name we treasure,
  Name beyond what words can tell;
Name of gladness, name of pleasure,
  Ear and heart delighting well;
Name of sweetness passing measure,
  Saving us from sin and hell.

3*

'Tis the name for adoration,
  Name for songs of victory,
Name for holy meditation
  In this vale of misery,
Name for joyful veneration
  By the citizens on high.

4

'Tis the name that whoso preacheth
  Speaks like music to the ear;
Who in prayer this name beseecheth
  Sweetest comfort findeth near;
Who its perfect wisdom reacheth
  Heavenly joy possesseth here.

5

Jesus is the name exalted
  Over every other name;
In this name, whene'er assaulted,
  We can put our foes to shame;
Strength to them who else had halted,
  Eyes to blind, and feet to lame.

6

Therefore we in love adoring
  This most blessèd name revere,
Holy Jesu, thee imploring
  So to write it in us here,
That hereafter heavenward soaring
  We may sing with angels there.

c. 15th cent.
Tr. J. M. NEALE and Compilers

GENERAL

Hymn 191 FIRST TUNE

KEY A Hartford

B. Milgrove, 1731–1810

[Tonic sol-fa notation]

SECOND TUNE

KEY E Innocents

The Parish Choir, 1850

[Tonic sol-fa notation]

Victis sibi cognomina

1
CONQUERING kings their titles take
From the foes they captive make:
Jesus, by a nobler deed,
From the thousands he hath freed.

2
Yes, none other name is given
Unto mortals under heaven,
Which can make the dead arise,
And exalt them to the skies.

3
That which Christ so hardly wrought,
That which he so dearly bought,
That salvation, brethren, say,
Shall we madly cast away?

4
Rather gladly for that name
Bear the cross, endure the shame:
Joyfully for him to die
Is not death but victory.

5
Jesu, who dost condescend
To be called the sinner's friend,
Hear us, as to thee we pray,
Glorying in thy name to-day.

[UNISON] 6
Glory to the Father be,
Glory, holy Son, to thee,
Glory to the Holy Ghost,
From the saints and angel-host.

18th cent. *Tr.* J. CHANDLER and Compilers

GENERAL

Hymn 192 St. Peter

A. R. Reinagle, 1799–1877

KEY E♭

HOW sweet the name of Jesus sounds
 In a believer's ear!
It soothes his sorrows, heals his wounds,
 And drives away his fear.

2

It makes the wounded spirit whole,
 And calms the troubled breast;
'Tis manna to the hungry soul,
 And to the weary rest.

3

Dear name! the rock on which I build,
 My shield and hiding-place,
My never-failing treasury filled
 With boundless stores of grace.

4

Jesus! my Shepherd, Brother, Friend,
 My Prophet, Priest, and King,
My Lord, my Life, my Way, my End,
 Accept the praise I bring.

5

Weak is the effort of my heart,
 And cold my warmest thought;
But when I see thee as thou art,
 I'll praise thee as I ought.

6

Till then I would thy love proclaim
 With every fleeting breath;
And may the music of thy name
 Refresh my soul in death.

J. NEWTON†

GENERAL

HYMN 193 Hollingside   J. B. Dykes, 1823-76

KEY E♭

```
{ m :s |l :s  |s :-.f|m :-  || d' :t |l :s  |m :d |r :-  |
  d :d |l₁:d  |d :t₁ |d :-  || d  :d |d :t₁ |d :d |t₁:-  |
  s :s |d':s  |l :s  |s :-  || s  :s |f :f  |s :fe|s :-  |
  d :m |f :m  |r :s₁ |d :-  || m  :m |f :r  |d :l₁|s₁:-  }

{ m :s |l :s    |s :-.f|m :- || m :f |m :r |m :-.r|d :- |
  d :d |d.f:m   |r :d  |t₁:- || d :d |d :d |d :t₁ |d :- |
  s :m |f.l:d'  |t :l  |se:- || l :f |s :l |s :f  |m :- |
  d :d |d :d    |r :r  |m :- || l₁:l₁|s₁:f₁|s₁:s₁ |d :- }
```

f. A♭.   E♭. t.

```
{ ᵈs₁:d |t₁:d  |f :m  |r :-  || ᵐl:l |t :d' |f :m  |r :-  |
  ¹m₁:s₁|s₁:s₁ |s₁:s₁ |t₁:-  || ˢd:d |d :f  |r :d  |t₁:-  |
  ᶠd :m |r :m  |r :m  |s :-  || ᵐl:s |s :s  |s :s  |s :-  |
  ᵈs₁:s₁|s₁:d  |t₁:d  |s₁:-  || ᵈf:m |r :d  |t₁:d  |s₁:-  }

{ m :s |l :s    |s :-.f|m :- || m :f |m :r |m :-.r|d :- |
  d :d |d.f:m   |r :d  |t₁:- || d :d |d :d |d :t₁ |d :- |
  s :m |f.l:d'  |t :l  |se:- || l :f |s :l |s :f  |m :- |
  d :d |d :d    |r :r  |m :- || l₁:l₁|s₁:f₁|s₁:s₁ |d :- }
```

mf JESU, lover of my soul,
    Let me to thy bosom fly,
While the gathering waters roll,
    While the tempest still is high:
Hide me, O my Saviour, hide,
    Till the storm of life is past;
Safe into the haven guide,
    O receive my soul at last.

2
p Other refuge have I none;
    Hangs my helpless soul on thee;
Leave, ah, leave me not alone,
    Still support and comfort me.
All my trust on thee is stayed,
    All my help from thee I bring;
Cover my defenceless head
    With the shadow of thy wing.

3
f Plenteous grace with thee is found,
    Grace to cleanse from every sin;
Let the healing streams abound;
    Make and keep me pure within:
Thou of life the fountain art;
    Freely let me take of thee;
Spring thou up within my heart,
    Rise to all eternity.

C. WESLEY†

Alternative Tune, Aberystwyth, 86

GENERAL

HYMN 194 St. Constantine   W. H. Monk, 1823-89

KEY **D**

[Music notation in tonic sol-fa]

    p JESU, meek and gentle,
        Son of God most high,
        Pitying, loving Saviour,
        Hear thy children's cry.

2

Pardon our offences,
Loose our captive chains,
Break down every idol
Which our soul detains.

3

  mf Give us holy freedom,
      Fill our hearts with love,
      Draw us, holy Jesus,
      To the realms above.

4

Lead us on our journey,
Be thyself the Way
Through terrestrial darkness
To celestial day.

5

  p Jesu, meek and gentle,
     Son of God most high,
     Pitying, loving Saviour,
     Hear thy children's cry.

Hear thy chil-dren's cry.

G. R. PRYNNE

GENERAL

HYMN 195 Cornwall   S. S. Wesley, 1810–76
KEY **D**

[Tonic sol-fa notation]

O LOVE divine, how sweet thou art!
When shall I find my longing heart
    All taken up by thee?
I thirst, I faint and die to prove
The greatness of redeeming love,
    The love of Christ to me.

2
Stronger his love than death or hell!
Its riches are unsearchable:
    The first-born sons of light,
Desire in vain its depth to see;
They cannot reach the mystery,
    The length and breath and height.

3*
God only knows the love of God;
O that it now were shed abroad
    In this poor stony heart!
For love I sigh, for love I pine;
This only portion, Lord, be mine,
    Be mine this better part.

4
For ever would I take my seat
With Mary at the Master's feet:
    Be this my happy choice;
My only care, delight, and bliss,
My joy, my heaven on earth, be this,
    To hear the Bridegroom's voice.

C. WESLEY†

HYMN 196   FIRST TUNE
KEY **C** Oxford New   Isaac Smith's *Collection*, c. 1770

[Tonic sol-fa notation]

GENERAL

SECOND TUNE

KEY **F** Selby   A. J. Eyre, 1853–1919

IN SECOND TUNE VERSES 3 AND 5 TO BEGIN THUS

3 He speaks; and, listen - ing
5 My gra - cious Mas - ter

1

O FOR a thousand tongues to sing
  My dear Redeemer's praise,
The glories of my God and King,
  The triumphs of his grace!

2

Jesus! the name that charms our fears,
  That bids our sorrows cease;
'Tis music in the sinner's ears,
  'Tis life and health and peace.

3

He speaks; and, listening to his voice,
  New life the dead receive,
The mournful broken hearts rejoice,
  The humble poor believe.

4

Hear him, ye deaf; his praise, ye dumb,
  Your loosened tongues employ;
Ye blind, behold your Saviour come;
  And leap, ye lame, for joy!

5

My gracious Master and my God,
  Assist me to proclaim
And spread through all the earth abroad
  The honours of thy name.

C. WESLEY

GENERAL

HYMN 197 Dominus regit me
J. B. Dykes, 1823–76
KEY G

[Sol-fa notation staves]

Psalm 23   *The Descant may be sung for verse 6*

mf THE King of love my Shepherd is,
    Whose goodness faileth never;
I nothing lack if I am his
    And he is mine for ever.

2
Where streams of living water flow
    My ransomed soul he leadeth,
And where the verdant pastures grow
    With food celestial feedeth.

3
Perverse and foolish oft I strayed,
    But yet in love he sought me,
And on his shoulder gently laid,
    And home rejoicing brought me.

4
p In death's dark vale I fear no ill
    With thee, dear Lord, beside me;
Thy rod and staff my comfort still,
    Thy Cross before to guide me.

5
mf Thou spread'st a table in my sight;
    Thy unction grace bestoweth;
And O what transport of delight
    From thy pure chalice floweth!

[UNISON] 6
f And so through all the length of days
    Thy goodness faileth never:
Good Shepherd, may I sing thy praise
    Within thy house for ever.

SIR H. W. BAKER

HYMN 198 St. George
H. J. Gauntlett, 1805–76
KEY C

[Sol-fa notation staves]

GENERAL

Summi Parentis Filio

mf 1. TO Christ, the Prince of Peace,
And Son of God most high,
The Father of the world to come,
We lift our joyful cry.

p 2. Deep in his heart for us
The wound of love he bore,
That love which he enkindles still
In hearts that him adore.

mf 3. O Jesu, Victim blest,
What else but love divine
Could thee constrain to open thus
That sacred heart of thine?

4. O wondrous fount of love,
O well of waters free,
O heavenly flame, refining fire,
O burning charity!

p 5. Hide us in thy dear heart,
Jesu, our Saviour blest,
mf So shall we find thy plenteous grace,
And heaven's eternal rest.

18th cent. *Tr.* E. CASWALL and Compilers

HYMN 199 St. James   R. Courteville (1697)

KEY **A**

mf 1. THOU art the Way: by thee alone
From sin and death we flee;
And he who would the Father seek
Must seek him, Lord, by thee.

2. Thou art the Truth: thy word alone
True wisdom can impart;
Thou only canst inform the mind
And purify the heart.

f 3. Thou art the Life: the rending tomb
Proclaims thy conquering arm;
And those who put their trust in thee
Nor death nor hell shall harm.

mf 4. Thou art the Way, the Truth, the Life:
Grant us that Way to know,
That Truth to keep, that Life to win,
Whose joys eternal flow.

BISHOP G. W. DOANE

GENERAL

HYMN 200 St. Paul's
Sir J. Stainer, 1840–1901

KEY **D**

μνώεο Χριστέ

1
LORD Jesus, think on me,
And purge away my sin;
From earthborn passions set me free,
And make me pure within.

2
Lord Jesus, think on me
With many a care opprest,
Let me thy loving servant be,
And taste thy promised rest.

3
Lord Jesus, think on me,
Nor let me go astray;
Through darkness and perplexity
Point thou the heavenly way.

4
Lord Jesus, think on me,
That, when the flood is past,
I may the eternal brightness see,
And share thy joy at last.

BISHOP SYNESIUS OF CYRENE
Tr. A. W. Chatfield†

HYMN 201 Eatington
W. Croft, 1678–1727

KEY **G**

Amor, Jesu dulcissime

1
JESU, thy mercies are untold
Through each returning day;
Thy love exceeds a thousandfold
Whatever we can say:

2
That love which in thy Passion drained
For us thy precious Blood;
That love whereby the saints have gained
The vision of their God.

212

GENERAL

3

'Tis thou hast loved us from the womb,
Pure source of all our bliss,
Our only hope of life to come,
Our happiness in this.

4

Lord, grant us, while on earth we stay,
Thy love to feel and know;
And, when from hence we pass away,
To us thy glory show.

Cento from Jesu, dulcis memoria
Tr. E. CASWALL

Alternative Tune, St. Fulbert, 128

HYMN 202 St. Chrysostom   Sir J. Barnby, 1838-96
KEY E♭

mf JESU, my Lord, my God, my all,
Hear me, blest Saviour, when I call;
Hear me, and from thy dwelling-place
Pour down the riches of thy grace.
    Jesu, my Lord, I thee adore,
    O make me love thee more and more.

2

p Jesu, too late I thee have sought:
mf How can I love thee as I ought?
And how extol thy matchless fame,
The glorious beauty of thy name?
    Jesu, my Lord, etc.

3

p Jesu, what didst thou find in me,
That thou hast dealt so lovingly?
f How great the joy that thou hast brought,
So far exceeding hope or thought!
mf   Jesu, my Lord, etc.

4

f Jesu, of thee shall be my song,
To thee my heart and soul belong;
All that I have or am is thine,
And thou, blest Saviour, thou art mine.
mf   Jesu, my Lord, etc.

H. COLLINS†

Alternative Tune, St. Matthias, 203

213

GENERAL

HYMN 203

FIRST TUNE

KEY **G** St. Matthias

W. H. Monk, 1823–1889

SECOND TUNE

KEY **E♭** Stella

Easy Hymns for Catholic Schools, 1851

Liebe, die du mich zum Bilde

mf O LOVE, who formedst me to wear
   The image of thy Godhead here;
Who soughtest me with tender care
   Through all my wanderings wild and drear:
O Love, I give myself to thee,
Thine ever, only thine to be.

GENERAL

2

O Love, who ere life's earliest dawn
On me thy choice hast gently laid;
O Love, who here as Man wast born,
And wholly like to us wast made:
O Love, I give myself to thee,
Thine ever, only thine to be.

3

p O Love, who once in time wast slain,
Pierced through and through with bitter woe;
O Love, who wrestling thus didst gain
That we eternal joy might know:
mf O Love, I give myself to thee,
Thine ever, only thine to be.

4

f O Love, who once shalt bid me rise
From out this dying life of ours;
O Love, who once o'er yonder skies
Shalt set me in the fadeless bowers:
O Love, I give myself to thee,
Thine ever, only thine to be.

J. SCHEFFLER. *Tr.* Catherine Winkworth†

HYMN 204 Almsgiving   S. S. Wesley, 1810–76
KEY E

mf WHERE high the heavenly temple stands,
The house of God not made with hands,
A great High Priest our nature wears,
The guardian of mankind appears.

2

He who for men their surety stood,
And poured on earth his precious Blood,
Pursues in heaven his mighty plan,
The Saviour and the Friend of man.

3

Though now ascended up on high,
He bends on earth a brother's eye;
Partaker of the human name,
He knows the frailty of our frame.

4

p In every pang that rends the heart
The Man of Sorrows had a part;
He sympathizes with our grief,
And to the sufferer sends relief.

5

mf With boldness therefore at the throne
Let us make all our sorrows known;
And ask the aid of heavenly power
To help us in the evil hour.

M. BRUCE

GENERAL

HYMN 205

FIRST TUNE

KEY B♭ Airedale

Sir C. V. Stanford, 1852-1924

mf LOVE divine, all loves excelling,
　　Joy of heaven, to earth come down,
Fix in us thy humble dwelling,
　　All thy faithful mercies crown.
Jesu, thou art all compassion,
　　Pure unbounded love thou art;
Visit us with thy salvation,
　　Enter every trembling heart.

2

Come, almighty to deliver,
　　Let us all thy grace receive;
Suddenly return, and never,
　　Never more thy temples leave.
Thee we would be always blessing,
　　Serve thee as thy hosts above;
Pray, and praise thee, without ceasing,
　　Glory in thy perfect love.

3

f Finish then thy new creation:
　　Pure and spotless let us be;
Let us see thy great salvation,
　　Perfectly restored in thee;
Changed from glory into glory,
　　Till in heaven we take our place,
Till we cast our crowns before thee,
　　Lost in wonder, love, and praise.

C. WESLEY†

GENERAL

HYMN 205 SECOND TUNE

KEY **G** Love Divine   Sir J. Stainer, 1840-1901

mf LOVE divine, all loves excelling,
　　Joy of heaven, to earth come down,
　Fix in us thy humble dwelling,
　　All thy faithful mercies crown.

2

Jesus, thou art all compassion,
　Pure unbounded love thou art;
Visit us with thy salvation,
　Enter every trembling heart.

3

Come, almighty to deliver,
　Let us all thy grace receive;
Suddenly return, and never,
　Never more thy temples leave.

4

Thee we would be always blessing,
　Serve thee as thy hosts above;
Pray, and praise thee, without ceasing,
　Glory in thy perfect love.

5

f Finish then thy new creation:
　Pure and spotless let us be;
Let us see thy great salvation,
　Perfectly restored in thee;

6

Changed from glory into glory,
　Till in heaven we take our place,
Till we cast our crowns before thee,
　Lost in wonder, love, and praise.

C. WESLEY †

GENERAL

HYMN 206 Bow Church G. Bullivant, 1883–1937
KEY F

|d :r	|m :—	|s :—	|d :—	|d :r	|m :—	|s :—	|d :— ||
|s₁:t₁	|d :s₁	|s₁:—	|s₁:f₁	|d :d	|d :s₁	|s₁:—	|l₁:— ||
|s :f	|s :—	|r :—	|m :f	|m :l	|s :—	|r :—	|m :— ||
|m :r	|d :—	|t₁:—	|t₁:l₁	|s₁:f₁	|d :—	|— :t₁	|l₁:s₁ ||

|r :m	|f :l	|s :—.f	|f :m	|r :m	|f :d'	|t :—.l	|l :s ||
|l₁:l₁	|l₁:l₁	|r :d	|t₁:d	|l₁.t₁:d	|d :l	|t₁:d	|r :m ||
|l :s	|f :m	|r :m.f	|s :s	|l :s	|l :f	|s :l	|t :d' ||
|f₁:l₁	|r :d	|t₁:—.l₁	|s₁:d	|f :m	|m :r	|s :s	|f :m ||

|d :r	|m :—	|s :—	|l₁:—	|t₁:d	|d :—	|r :—	|d :— ||
|d :t₁	|d :—	|— :s₁	|s₁:f₁	|f₁:m₁.f₁	|s₁:l₁	|— :t₁	|d :— ||
|l :f	|s :—	|d :—	|m :r	|r :d	|m :—	|f :—	|m :— ||
|f :r	|d :—	|m₁:—	|f₁:—	|s₁:l₁	|s₁:—	|s₁:—	|d :— ||

Jesu, geh' voran

mf JESUS, still lead on,
Till our rest be won,
And, although the way be cheerless,
We will follow calm and fearless;
Guide us by thy hand
To our fatherland.

2

p If the way be drear,
If the foe be near,
Let not faithless fears o'ertake us,
Let not faith and hope forsake us;
For, through many a foe,
To our home we go.

3

mf Jesus, still lead on,
Till our rest be won;
Heavenly leader, still direct us,
Still support, console, protect us,
Till we safely stand
In our fatherland.

COUNT N. L. ZINZENDORF *Tr.* Jane L. Borthwick

HYMN 207 Everton H. Smart, 1813–79
KEY E♭ *D.C.*

|m :f	|s :d'	|l :t	|d' :s	|f :s	|m :d	|r :r	|r :— ||
|d :t₁	|d :m	|d :f	|m :d	|d :r	|d :s₁	|l₁:t₁.d	|t₁:— ||
|s :s	|s :s	|l :f	|s :s	|l :r	|s :s	|s :fe	|s :— ||
|d :r	|m :d	|f :r	|d :m	|l₁:t₁	|d :m	|r :r₁	|s₁:— ||

218

GENERAL

Bb. t.

```
{ r  s₁ :s₁ |l₁ :d    d :t₁  |d :m     m :m  |r  :l₁.t₁   d :t₁ |l₁ :—
  t₁m₁:s₁ |f₁ :f₁   s₁ :s₁  |s₁ :s₁   l₁ :l₁ |l₁ :l₁     l₁ :se₁|l₁ :—
  s d :d  |d  :d    r  :r   |d  :d    d  :m  |f  :r      m  :r  |d  :—
  s d₁:m₁ |f₁ :l₁   s₁ :s₁.f₁|m₁ :d₁  d  :d₁ |r₁ :f₁     m₁ :m₁ |l₁ :— }
```

f. Eb.

```
{ d s :s  |s  :d¹   f :l   |l :s      d :r   |m :s       f :r  |d :—
  m t₁:t₁ |d  :d    d :d   |d :d      d :t₁  |d :d       d :t₁ |d :—
  d s :f  |m  :m    f :f   |f :m      m :s   |s :s       l :s.f|m :—
  l m :r  |d  :ta₁  l₁:f₁  |d :d      l₁:s₁  |d :m₁      f₁:s₁ |d :— }
```

SON of God, eternal Saviour,
    Source of life and truth and grace,
Son of Man, whose birth incarnate
    Hallows all our human race,
Thou, our Head, who, throned in glory,
    For thine own dost ever plead,
Fill us with thy love and pity;
    Heal our wrongs, and help our need.

2

As thou, Lord, hast lived for others,
    So may we for others live;
Freely have thy gifts been granted,
    Freely may thy servants give:
Thine the gold and thine the silver,
    Thine the wealth of land and sea,
We but stewards of thy bounty,
    Held in solemn trust for thee.

3

Come, O Christ, and reign among us,
    King of love, and Prince of Peace;
Hush the storm of strife and passion,
    Bid its cruel discords cease;
By thy patient years of toiling,
    By thy silent hours of pain,
Quench our fevered thirst of pleasure,
    Shame our selfish greed of gain.

4

Son of God, eternal Saviour,
    Source of life and truth and grace,
Son of Man, whose birth incarnate
    Hallows all our human race,
Thou who prayedst, thou who willest,
    That thy people should be one,
Grant, O grant our hope's fruition:
    Here on earth thy will be done.

S. C. LOWRY

Alternative Tune, Rex gloriae, 148

GENERAL

Hymn 208 Bishopthorpe   J. Clarke, *c.* 1659–1707
KEY **G**

IMMORTAL love for ever full,
  For ever flowing free,
For ever shared, for ever whole,
  A never-ebbing sea!

2

Our outward lips confess the name
  All other names above;
Love only knoweth whence it came
  And comprehendeth love.

3

We may not climb the heavenly steeps
  To bring the Lord Christ down;
In vain we search the lowest deeps,
  For him no depths can drown:

4

But warm, sweet, tender, even yet
  A present help is he;
And faith has still its Olivet,
  And love its Galilee.

5

The healing of his seamless dress
  Is by our beds of pain;
We touch him in life's throng and press,
  And we are whole again.

6*

Through him the first fond prayers are said
  Our lips of childhood frame;
The last low whispers of our dead
  Are burdened with his name.

7

Alone, O Love ineffable,
  Thy saving name is given;
To turn aside from thee is hell,
  To walk with thee is heaven.

J. G. WHITTIER

GENERAL

HYMN 209 Dunfermline *Scottish Psalter*, 1615

KEY **F**

mf LIGHT of the lonely pilgrim's heart,
Star of the coming day,
Arise, and with thy morning beams
Chase all our griefs away.

2

f Come, blessèd Lord, bid every shore
And answering island sing
The praises of thy royal name,
And own thee as their King.

3

Bid the whole world, responsive now
To the bright world above,
Break forth in rapturous strains of joy
In answer to thy love.

4

mf Jesus, thy fair creation groans—
The air, the earth, the sea—
In unison with all our hearts,
And calls aloud for thee.

5

Thine was the Cross, with all its fruits
Of grace and peace divine:
f Be thine the crown of glory now,
The palm of victory thine.

SIR E. DENNY†

GENERAL

HYMN 210 Petra
KEY D

R. Redhead, 1820-1901

[tonic sol-fa notation]

mf ROCK of ages, cleft for me,
Let me hide myself in thee;
Let the water and the blood,
From thy riven side which flowed,
Be of sin the double cure:
Cleanse me from its guilt and power.

2
Not the labours of my hands
Can fulfil thy law's demands;
Could my zeal no respite know,
Could my tears for ever flow,
All for sin could not atone:
Thou must save, and thou alone.

3
p Nothing in my hand I bring,
Simply to thy Cross I cling;
Naked, come to thee for dress;
Helpless, look to thee for grace;
Foul, I to the fountain fly;
Wash me, Saviour, or I die.

4
While I draw this fleeting breath,
When my eyelids close in death,
When I soar through tracts unknown,
See thee on thy judgement throne;
mf Rock of ages, cleft for me,
Let me hide myself in thee.

A. M. TOPLADY†

HYMN 211 Song 13
KEY E♭

Orlando Gibbons, 1583-1625

[tonic sol-fa notation]

222

GENERAL

Dignare me, O Jesu, rogo te

1
JESU, grant me this, I pray,
Ever in thy heart to stay;
Let me evermore abide
Hidden in thy wounded side.

2
If the world or Satan lay
Tempting snares about my way,
I am safe when I abide
In thy heart and wounded side.

3
If the flesh, more dangerous still,
Tempt my soul to deeds of ill,
Naught I fear when I abide
In thy heart and wounded side.

4
Death will come one day to me;
Jesu, cast me not from thee:
Dying let me still abide
In thy heart and wounded side.

17th cent. *Tr.* SIR H. W. BAKER†

HYMN **212** Wigan S. S. Wesley, 1810–76
KEY **B♭**

1
mf   BEHOLD the Lamb of God!
p   O thou for sinners slain,
       Let it not be in vain
          That thou hast died:
mf Thee for my Saviour let me take,
     My only refuge let me make
          Thy piercèd side.

2
Behold the Lamb of God!
All hail, incarnate Word,
Thou everlasting Lord,
    Saviour most blest!
Fill us with love that never faints,
Grant us with all thy blessèd saints
    Eternal rest.

3
Behold the Lamb of God!
f Worthy is he alone
     To sit upon the throne
        Of God above;
     One with the Ancient of all Days,
     One with the Comforter in praise,
        All Light and Love.

M. BRIDGES and Compilers

GENERAL

HYMN 213   FIRST TUNE

KEY E♭   Ave radix   *Sens Processional*, 1728

SECOND TUNE

KEY E♭   St. Martin   C. Ett, *Cantica Sacra*, 1840

mf   JESU, meek and lowly,
      Saviour, pure and holy,
      On thy love relying
      Hear me humbly crying.

2

      Prince of life and power,
      My salvation's tower,
p   On the Cross I view thee
      Calling sinners to thee.

3

mf   There behold me gazing
      At the sight amazing;
      Bending low before thee,
      Helpless I adore thee.

4

p   By thy red wounds streaming
      With thy life-blood gleaming,
      Blood for sinners flowing,
      Pardon free bestowing;

GENERAL

5

mf By thy fount of blessing,
Thy dear love expressing,
All my aching sadness
Turn thou into gladness.

6

— Lord, in mercy guide me,
Be thou e'er beside me;
In thy ways direct me,
'Neath thy wings protect me.

H. COLLINS

HYMN 214 Horsley   W. Horsley, 1774–1858

KEY E♭

:d	r :m	f :m	s :f.m	r	s	m :d¹	t :l	s :—	—
:d	t₁:d	d :d	d :d̄	t₁	s₁	d :d	r :r	t₁:—	—
:m	s :s	f :s	s :l	r	r	s :l	s :fe	s :—	—
:d	s₁:d	l₁:d	m₁:f₁	s₁	t₁	d :l₁	r :r	s₁:—	—

:r.m	f :f	f :m	l :l	se	se	l :f	m :r	d :—	—
:t₁	d :d	r :m	m :r	m	m	d :r	d :t₁	d :—	—
:s	f :l	s :s	l :l	t	t	l :l	s :-.f	m :—	—
:s₁	l₁:l₁	t₁:d	f :f	m	m	f :f₁	s₁:s₁	d :—	—

mf   THERE is a green hill far away,
     Without a city wall,
p   Where the dear Lord was crucified,
     Who died to save us all.

2

mf We may not know, we cannot tell,
     What pains he had to bear,
But we believe it was for us
     He hung and suffered there.

3

He died that we might be forgiven,
     He died to make us good,
That we might go at last to heaven,
     Saved by his precious Blood.

4

There was no other good enough
     To pay the price of sin;
He only could unlock the gate
     Of heaven, and let us in.

5

O dearly, dearly has he loved,
     And we must love him too,
And trust in his redeeming Blood,
     And try his works to do.

MRS. C. F. ALEXANDER

GENERAL

HYMN 215 Bow Brickhill   Sir S. H. Nicholson, 1875–1947

KEY **C**

[UNISON]
WE sing the praise of him who died,
   Of him who died upon the Cross;
The sinner's hope let men deride,
   For this we count the world but loss.

2
Inscribed upon the Cross we see,
   In shining letters, 'God is love;'
He bears our sins upon the Tree;
   He brings us mercy from above.

3
The Cross! it takes our guilt away;
   It holds the fainting spirit up;
It cheers with hope the gloomy day,
   And sweetens every bitter cup.

4
It makes the coward spirit brave,
   And nerves the feeble arm for fight;
It takes its terror from the grave,
   And gilds the bed of death with light:

[UNISON] 5
The balm of life, the cure of woe,
   The measure and the pledge of love,
The sinner's refuge here below,
   The angels' theme in heaven above.

                                           T. KELLY

Alternative Tune, Breslau, 333

Hymn 216 Gopsal G. F. Handel, 1685–1759

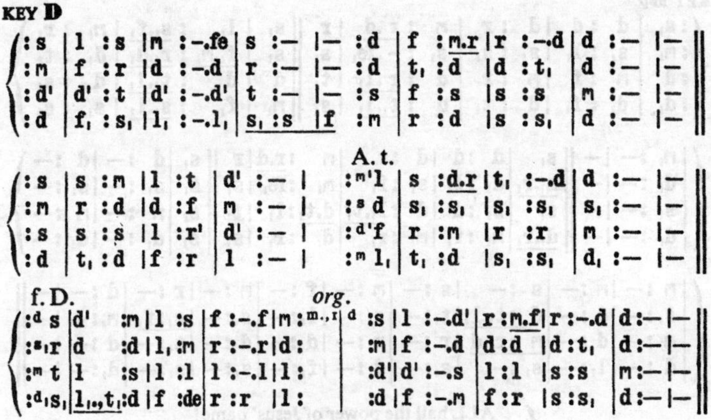

f REJOICE! the Lord is King!
Your Lord and King adore;
Mortals, give thanks and sing,
And triumph evermore:
Lift up your heart, lift up your voice;
Rejoice, again I say, rejoice.

2

mf Jesus, the Saviour, reigns,
The God of truth and love;
When he had purged our stains,
He took his seat above:
f Lift up your heart, lift up your voice;
Rejoice, again I say, rejoice.

3

mf His kingdom cannot fail;
He rules o'er earth and heaven;
The keys of death and hell
Are to our Jesus given:
f Lift up your heart, lift up your voice;
Rejoice, again I say, rejoice.

4

mf He sits at God's right hand
Till all his foes submit,
And bow to his command,
And fall beneath his feet:
f Lift up your heart, lift up your voice;
Rejoice, again I say, rejoice.

C. Wesley

GENERAL

HYMN 217   Miles Lane   W. Shrubsole, 1760–1806
KEY B♭

f   ALL hail the power of Jesus' name!
      Let angels prostrate fall;
      Bring forth the royal diadem
      And crown him Lord of all.

2

mf Crown him, ye morning stars of light,
      Who fixed this floating ball;
      Now hail the Strength of Israel's might,
f   And crown him Lord of all.

3

mf Crown him, ye martyrs of your God,
      Who from his altar call;
      Extol the Stem-of-Jesse's Rod,
f   And crown him Lord of all.

4

mf Ye seed of Israel's chosen race,
      Ye ransomed of the fall,
      Hail him who saves you by his grace,
f   And crown him Lord of all.

5

p   Sinners, whose love can ne'er forget
      The wormwood and the gall,
mf Go spread your trophies at his feet,
f   And crown him Lord of all.

6

      Let every tribe and every tongue
      Before him prostrate fall,
      And shout in universal song
      The crownèd Lord of all.

                                                  E. PERRONET‡

Alternative Tune, Ladywell, 297

GENERAL

HYMN 218 St. Magnus   J. Clarke, c. 1659–1707

KEY A

f   THE head that once was crowned with thorns
      Is crowned with glory now:
   A royal diadem adorns
      The mighty Victor's brow.

2
The highest place that heaven affords
   Is his, is his by right,
The King of Kings, and Lord of Lords,
   And heaven's eternal Light;

3
mf The joy of all who dwell above,
     The joy of all below,
   To whom he manifests his love,
     And grants his name to know.

4
p   To them the Cross, with all its shame,
     With all its grace, is given:
f   Their name an everlasting name,
     Their joy the joy of heaven.

5
p   They suffer with their Lord below,
f   They reign with him above;
   Their profit and their joy to know
     The mystery of his love.

6
mf The Cross he bore is life and health,
     Though shame and death to him;
f   His people's hope, his people's wealth,
     Their everlasting theme.

                              T. KELLY

GENERAL

HYMN 219 Crüger J. Crüger, 1598–1662
KEY F

f HAIL to the Lord's Anointed,
  Great David's greater Son!
Hail, in the time appointed,
  His reign on earth begun!
He comes to break oppression,
  To set the captive free,
To take away transgression,
  And rule in equity.

2*
He comes with succour speedy
  To those who suffer wrong;
To help the poor and needy,
  And bid the weak be strong;
To give them songs for sighing,
  Their darkness turn to light,
Whose souls, condemned and dying,
  Were precious in his sight.

3
mf He shall come down like showers
  Upon the fruitful earth,
And love, joy, hope, like flowers,
  Spring in his path to birth:
Before him on the mountains
  Shall peace, the herald, go;
And righteousness in fountains
  From hill to valley flow.

4*
Arabia's desert-ranger
  To him shall bow the knee;
The Ethiopian stranger
  His glory come to see;
With offerings of devotion
  Ships from the isles shall meet,
To pour the wealth of ocean
  In tribute at his feet.

5
Kings shall bow down before him,
  And gold and incense bring;
All nations shall adore him,
  His praise all people sing:
To him shall prayer unceasing
  And daily vows ascend;
His kingdom still increasing,
  A kingdom without end.

6
f O'er every foe victorious,
  He on his throne shall rest;
From age to age more glorious,
  All-blessing and all-blest:
The tide of time shall never
  His covenant remove;
His name shall stand for ever,
  His changeless name of Love.

J. MONTGOMERY

GENERAL

HYMN 220 FIRST TUNE
KEY **D** Truro *Psalmodia Evangelica*, 1789

SECOND TUNE
KEY **E** Galilee P. Armes, 1836–1908

1. JESUS shall reign where'er the sun
Does his successive journeys run;
His kingdom stretch from shore to shore,
Till moons shall wax and wane no more.

2. People and realms of every tongue
Dwell on his love with sweetest song,
And infant voices shall proclaim
Their early blessings on his name.

3. Blessings abound where'er he reigns;
The prisoner leaps to lose his chains;
The weary find eternal rest,
And all the sons of want are blest.

4.* To him shall endless prayer be made,
And praises throng to crown his head;
His name like incense shall arise
With every morning sacrifice.

5. Let every creature rise and bring
Peculiar honours to our King;
Angels descend with songs again,
And earth repeat the loud Amen.

I. WATTS†

GENERAL

HYMN 221 Nativity H. Lahee, 1826–1912
KEY B♭

[Tonic sol-fa notation]

f COME, let us join our cheerful songs
  With angels round the throne;
 Ten thousand thousand are their tongues,
  But all their joys are one.

2
'Worthy the Lamb that died,' they [cry,
 'To be exalted thus;'
'Worthy the Lamb,' our lips reply,
 'For he was slain for us.'

3
mf Jesus is worthy to receive
  Honour and power divine;
 And blessings, more than we can give,
  Be, Lord, for ever thine.

4
f Let all creation join in one
  To bless the sacred name
 Of him that sits upon the throne,
  And to adore the Lamb.

I. WATTS†

HYMN 222 Unser Herrscher J. Neander, 1640–80
KEY C

DESCANT

[Tonic sol-fa notation]

GENERAL

The Descant may be sung for verse 6

f COME, ye faithful, raise the anthem,
　Cleave the skies with shouts of praise;
Sing to him who found the ransom,
　Ancient of eternal Days,
God of God, the Word incarnate,
　Whom the heaven of heaven obeys.

2

mf Ere he raised the lofty mountains,
　Formed the seas, or built the sky,
Love eternal, free, and boundless,
　Moved the Lord of Life to die,
Fore-ordained the Prince of Princes
　For the throne of Calvary.

3*

p There, for us and our redemption,
　See him all his life-blood pour!
mf There he wins our full salvation,
　Dies that we may die no more;
f Then, arising, lives for ever,
　Reigning where he was before.

4

High on yon celestial mountains
　Stands his sapphire throne, all bright,
Midst unending Alleluias
　Bursting from the sons of light;
Sion's people tell his praises,
　Victor after hard-won fight.

5

mf Bring your harps, and bring your incense,
　Sweep the string and pour the lay;
f Let the earth proclaim his wonders,
　King of that celestial day;
He the Lamb once slain is worthy,
　Who was dead, and lives for ay.

[UNISON] 6

Laud and honour to the Father,
　Laud and honour to the Son,
Laud and honour to the Spirit,
　Ever Three and ever One,
Consubstantial, co-eternal,
　While unending ages run.

J. HUPTON and J. M. NEALE†

GENERAL

Hymn 223 — FIRST TUNE

KEY F Barnet R. H. Jesson

```
{ :s₁  | d :r  | m :s  | l   || s  | m :d  | r :m  | s :—
{ :s₁  | l₁:t₁ | d :r  | d   || r  | d :d  | l₁:d  | d :t₁
{ :m   | m :s  | s :s  | m   || s  | s :s  | l :s  | f :—
{ :d   | l₁:s₁ | d :t₁ | l₁  || t₁ | d :m  | f :m  | r :—

{ |s :— | l :m  |m :t₁ |r :— |— || s₁ | d :r  |m :s  |l
{ |d :— | d :d  |t₁:s₁ |f₁:— |s₁|| s₁ | s₁:t₁ |d :r  |d
{ |m :— | m :fe |s :m  |r :d |t₁|| t₁ | d :s  |s :s  |m
{ |d :t₁| l₁:l₁ |s₁:s₁ |r₁:— |s₁|| f₁ | m₁:s₁ |d :t₁ |l₁

{ :s  |m :d |r :m |d :— || d':l |s :f |r :r |d :— |— :—
{ :r  |d :d |l₁:t₁|l₁:— || l₁:t₁|d :d |d :t₁|d :— |— :—
{ :s  |s :s |l :se|m :— || f :— |s :l |s :—.f|m :— |— :—
{ :t₁ |d :m |f :m |l₁:s₁|| f₁:— |m₁:r₁|s₁:s₁ |d :— |— :—
```

By permission of the Royal School of Church Music

SECOND TUNE

KEY C Laudes Domini Sir J. Barnby, 1838–96

G.t.
```
{ :m  |f :s  |l :d' |t :— |l  || s  |l :t  |d' :m'l |s :— |—
{ :d  |d :d  |d :f  |f :— |—  || f  |m :s  |s :ˢd  |t₁:— |d
{ :s  |s :s  |f :l  |t :— |d' || r' |d' :r' |d' :d'f |f :— |m
{ :d  |r :m  |f :r  |s :— |l  || t  |d' :t  |l :¹r  |s₁:— |l₁
```

f.C.
```
{ :f  |m :f  |r :—.d |ᵈs :— |—  || s  |s :d' |t :d' |s :— |—
{ :s₁ |s₁:l₁ |f₁:—.f₁|ᵐt₁:— |—  || r  |d :d  |f :f  |f :— |m
{ :r  |d :d  |d :t₁ |ᵈs :— |—  || t  |d' :s |t :l  |r' :d' |t
{ :t₁ |d :f₁ |s₁:s₁ |ᵈs₁:— |—  || f  |m :m  |r :d  |t₁:l₁ |s₁

{ :s |s :d'|t :d'|s :— |— || s |s :— |d' :— |d' :— |r' :— |d' :— |—
{ :r |d :m |fe:fe|s :r |m || f |m :f |s :— |f :— |f :— |m :— |—
{ :t |d':s |r':d'|t :— |— || t |d':r'|m' :— |d' :— |— :t |d' :— |—
{ :f |m :d |r :r |s :f |m || r |d :— |ta:— |l :— |s :— |d :— |—
```

234

GENERAL

Beim frühen Morgenlicht

WHEN morning gilds the skies,
My heart awaking cries,
    May Jesus Christ be praised:
Alike at work and prayer
To Jesus I repair;
    May Jesus Christ be praised.

2

Whene'er the sweet church bell
Peals over hill and dell,
    May Jesus Christ be praised:
O hark to what it sings,
As joyously it rings,
    May Jesus Christ be praised.

3

My tongue shall never tire
Of chanting with the choir,
    May Jesus Christ be praised:
This song of sacred joy,
It never seems to cloy,
    May Jesus Christ be praised.

4

Does sadness fill my mind?
A solace here I find,
    May Jesus Christ be praised:
Or fades my earthly bliss?
My comfort still is this,
    May Jesus Christ be praised.

5*

The night becomes as day,
When from the heart we say,
    May Jesus Christ be praised:
The powers of darkness fear,
When this sweet chant they hear,
    May Jesus Christ be praised.

6

Be this, while life is mine,
My canticle divine,
    May Jesus Christ be praised:
Be this the eternal song
Through ages all along,
    May Jesus Christ be praised.

19th cent. *Tr.* E. CASWALL

GENERAL

HYMN 224

FIRST TUNE

KEY **C**   Corona

C. Hylton Stewart, 1884–1932

d' :—	s :s	l :s.f	s :—		d :—	f :s	m :f	r :—	
m :—	d :d	d :d	r :—		d :—	d :r	d :d	t₁ :—	
s :—	d' :s	f :l	s :—		s :—	l :s	s :l	s :—	
d :—	m :m	f :r	t₁ :—		m :—	r :t₁	d :f₁	s₁ :—	

G. t.

r :—	m :d	m :s	d' :t	l :—		¹r :—	s :m	f :m.r	d :—	
t₁ :—	d :s₁	d :r	m :m	m :—		ᶠᵉt₁ :—	t₁ :d	d :t₁	s₁ :—	
s :—	s :s	s :s	m' :r'	d' :—		¹r :—	r :d	l :s.f	m :—	
s :—	d :m	d :t₁	l₁ :t₁	d :—		ʳs₁ :—	m₁ :l₁	r₁ :s₁	d₁ :—	

d. f. F.   C. t.

ᵈr :—	s :r	f :m.r	m		ᵐl :t	d :d'	r' :—	— :d'	t :—	
s₁l₁ :—	r :t₁	d :s₁	d		ᵗᵐm :s	s :s	f :—	s :l	r :—	
ᵐfe :—	s :s	f :s	s		ˢd'¹r' :d'	l :—	r' :—	r' :—	
ᵈr :—	t₁ :s₁	l₁ :t₁	d		ᵐl :s	m :m	r :—	m :f	s :—	

s :—	m' :r'	d' :s	l :s.f	s		s :l	d' :s	— :m :r	d :— :— :—	
r :—	s :f	m :s	d :r	r		m :d	f :s	— :t₁ :—	d :— :— :—	
f' :—	m' :t	d' :d'	l :l	s		d' :l	l :d'	— :s :f	m :— :— :—	
t :—	d' :s	l :m	f :r	t₁		d :f :r	m :—	s₁ :—	d :— :— :—	

By permission of the Oxford University Press

SECOND TUNE

KEY **E♭**   Diademata

Sir G. J. Elvey, 1816–93

d :d.d	m :m	l :—	—		l	s :d	f :m	r :—	—	
s₁ :s₁.s₁	d :d	d :—	—		d	d :d	t₁ :d	t₁ :—	—	
m :m.m	m :m	f :—	—		f	s :l	f :s	s :—	—	
d :d.d	l₁ :l₁	f₁ :—	—		f	m :f	r :d	s₁ :—	—	

B♭. t.

:ʳs₁	l₁ :d	r :d	t₁ :l₁.s₁	d		f	m :f	r :r	d :—	—	
:ᵗm₁	f₁ :s₁	f₁ :f₁	r₁ :r₁	s₁		f₁	s₁ :l₁	r₁ :s₁	m₁ :—	—	
:ˢd	d :d	l₁ :l₁	t₁ :t₁	d		t₁	d :d	d :t₁	d :—	—	
:ˢd₁	f₁ :m₁	r₁ :f₁	s₁ :f₁	m₁		r₁	d₁ :f₁	s₁ :s₁	d₁ :—	—	

f. E♭.   B♭. t.

:ᵈs	s :m	r :d	l :—	—		¹r	r :t₁	l₁ :s₁	d :—	—	
:ᵐt₁	d :d	t₁ :d	d :—	—		ᵈᵉfe₁	s₁ :s₁	f₁ :f₁	m₁ :—	—	
:ᵈs	s :s	f :s	l :—	—		ˢd	t₁ :r	d :r	d :—	—	
:ᵗᵃf	m :d	r :m	f :—	—		ᵐl₁	s₁ :s₁	l₁ :t₁	d :—	—	

GENERAL

```
f. Eb.
{ :ⁿ t  |d':-.t|l :s  |f :r |m   ‖ s  |f :m |r :r  |d :— |— :— 
  :s₁r |d :d |d :d  |d :t₁|d     ‖ d  |d :d |d :t₁ |d :— |— :—
  :ᵈs  |s :s |f :s  |l :s |s     ‖ s  |l :s |s :-.f|m :— |— :—
  :t₂,|f  |m :m |f :m  |r :s |d   ‖ m₁ |f₁:d |s₁:s₁ |d :— |— :— }
```

f   CROWN him with many crowns,
      The Lamb upon his throne;
Hark! how the heavenly anthem drowns
      All music but its own:
      Awake, my soul, and sing
      Of him who died for thee,
And hail him as thy matchless King
      Through all eternity.

2

mf   Crown him the Virgin's Son,
      The God incarnate born,
p   Whose arm those crimson trophies won
      Which now his brow adorn:
      Fruit of the mystic Rose,
      As of that Rose the Stem;
The Root whence mercy ever flows,
      The Babe of Bethlehem.

3

mf   Crown him the Lord of love;
p   Behold his hands and side,
Those wounds yet visible above
      In beauty glorified:
      No angel in the sky
      Can fully bear that sight,
But downward bends his burning eye
      At mysteries so bright.

4

mf   Crown him the Lord of peace,
f   Whose power a sceptre sways
From pole to pole, that wars may cease,
      And all be prayer and praise:
      His reign shall know no end,
mf   And round his piercèd feet
Fair flowers of Paradise extend
      Their fragrance ever sweet.

[UNISON] 5

f   Crown him the Lord of years,
      The Potentate of time,
Creator of the rolling spheres,
      Ineffably sublime:
      All hail, Redeemer, hail!
      For thou hast died for me;
Thy praise shall never, never fail
      Throughout eternity.

M. BRIDGES‡

NOTE. *The expression 'mystic Rose' in verse 2, line 5, is a medieval title for the Blessed Virgin, and is combined here with a reference to Isaiah 11. 1*

GENERAL

HYMN 225 Evelyns W. H. Monk, 1823–89

KEY E♭

[sol-fa notation musical score]

* *In verse 5 sing this chord to the first word of line 2, and divide the note of the melody to the same*

mf AT the name of Jesus
  Every knee shall bow,
Every tongue confess him
  King of glory now:
'Tis the Father's pleasure
  We should call him Lord,
Who from the beginning
  Was the mighty Word.

2*

f At his voice creation
  Sprang at once to sight,
All the angel faces,
  All the hosts of light,
Thrones and Dominations,
  Stars upon their way,
All the heavenly orders,
  In their great array.

3

p Humbled for a season,
  To receive a name
From the lips of sinners
  Unto whom he came,
mf Faithfully he bore it
  Spotless to the last,
Brought it back victorious,
  When from death he passed:

4

f Bore it up triumphant
  With its human light,
Through all ranks of creatures,
  To the central height,
To the throne of Godhead,
  To the Father's breast;
Filled it with the glory
  Of that perfect rest.

5

Name him, brothers, name him,
  With love as strong as death,
p But with awe and wonder
  And with bated breath:
mf He is God the Saviour,
  He is Christ the Lord,
Ever to be worshipped,
  Trusted, and adored.

GENERAL

6*
In your hearts enthrone him;
  There let him subdue
All that is not holy,
  All that is not true:
Crown him as your Captain
  In temptation's hour;
Let his will enfold you
  In its light and power.

7
f Brothers, this Lord Jesus
  Shall return again,
With his Father's glory,
  With his angel train;
For all wreaths of empire
  Meet upon his brow,
And our hearts confess him
  King of glory now.

CAROLINE M. NOEL

HYMN 226 Paderborn
Paderborn Gesangbuch, 1765

KEY **G**

1
YE servants of God, your Master proclaim,
And publish abroad his wonderful name;
The name all-victorious of Jesus extol:
His Kingdom is glorious, and rules over all.

2
God ruleth on high, almighty to save;
And still he is nigh: his presence we have.
The great congregation his triumph shall sing,
Ascribing salvation to Jesus our King.

3
Salvation to God who sits on the throne!
Let all cry aloud, and honour the Son.
The praises of Jesus the angels proclaim,
Fall down on their faces, and worship the Lamb.

[UNISON]
4
Then let us adore, and give him his right:
All glory and power, all wisdom and might,
And honour and blessing, with angels above,
And thanks never-ceasing, and infinite love.

C. WESLEY

GENERAL

HYMN 227   Old 112th   *Psalms*, 1560
KEY E♭

[sol-fa notation]

1
O QUICKLY come, dread Judge of all;
  For, aweful though thine advent be,
All shadows from the truth will fall,
  And falsehood die, in sight of thee:
O quickly come! for doubt and fear
Like clouds dissolve when thou art near.

2
O quickly come, great King of all;
  Reign all around us, and within;
Let sin no more our souls enthral,
  Let pain and sorrow die with sin:
O quickly come! for thou alone
Canst make thy scattered people one.

3
O quickly come, true Life of all;
  For death is mighty all around;
On every home his shadows fall,
  On every heart his mark is found:
O quickly come! for grief and pain
Can never cloud thy glorious reign.

4
O quickly come, sure Light of all,
  For gloomy night broods o'er our way;
And weakly souls begin to fall
  With weary watching for the day:
O quickly come! for round thy throne
No eye is blind, no night is known.

L. TUTTIETT

HYMN 228   Babylon's Streams   T. Campion, *c.* 1575-1619
KEY G

[sol-fa notation]

GENERAL

mf THAT day of wrath, that dreadful day,
When heaven and earth shall pass away,
What power shall be the sinner's stay?
How shall he meet that dreadful day?

2

f When, shrivelling like a parchèd scroll,
The flaming heavens together roll;
When louder yet, and yet more dread,
Swells the high trump that wakes the dead:

3

p O on that day, that wrathful day,
When man to judgement wakes from clay,
Be thou, O Christ, the sinner's stay,
Though heaven and earth shall pass away.

SIR WALTER SCOTT Based on *Dies irae*

HYMN 229 Narenza   J. Leisentrit, *Catholicum Hymnologium*, 1587

KEY B♭

3

YE servants of the Lord,
Each in his office wait,
Observant of his heavenly word,
And watchful at his gate.

2

Let all your lamps be bright,
And trim the golden flame;
Gird up your loins as in his sight,
For aweful is his name.

3

Watch! 'tis your Lord's command,
And while we speak, he's near;
Mark the first signal of his hand,
And ready all appear.

4

O happy servant he
In such a posture found!
He shall his Lord with rapture see,
And be with honour crowned.

5

Christ shall the banquet spread
With his own royal hand,
And raise that faithful servant's head
Amid the angelic band.

P. DODDRIDGE†

GENERAL

HYMN 230
FIRST TUNE

KEY E♭ St. Cuthbert J. B. Dykes, 1823–76

[Tonic sol-fa notation]

SECOND TUNE

KEY A♭ Shrewsbury J. E. Hunt

[Tonic sol-fa notation]

---

p OUR blest Redeemer, ere he breath-
    His tender last farewell, [ed
A guide, a Comforter, bequeathed
    With us to dwell.

3

p And his that gentle voice we hear,
    Soft as the breath of even,
That checks each fault, that calms each
    And speaks of heaven. [fear,

2

mf He came sweet influence to impart,
    A gracious willing guest,
While he can find one humble heart
    Wherein to rest.

4

mf And every virtue we possess,
    And every conquest won,
And every thought of holiness.
    Are his alone.

5

Spirit of purity and grace,
    Our weakness, pitying, see:
O make our hearts thy dwelling-place,
    And worthier thee.

HARRIET AUBER

GENERAL

Hymn 231 Tallis
T. Tallis, c. 1505–85

KEY **D**

[sol-fa notation]

O fons amoris, Spiritus

mf O HOLY Spirit, Lord of grace,
  Eternal fount of love,
Inflame, we pray, our inmost hearts
  With fire from heaven above.

2

As thou in bond of love dost join
  The Father and the Son,
So fill us all with mutual love,
  And knit our hearts in one.

[UNISON]
3
f All glory to the Father be,
  All glory to the Son,
All glory, Holy Ghost, to thee,
  While endless ages run.

C. COFFIN *Tr.* J. Chandler‡

Hymn 232 Hawkhurst
H. J. Gauntlett, 1805–76

KEY **A♭**

[sol-fa notation]

f. A♭.

[sol-fa notation]

COME, gracious Spirit, heavenly Dove,
With light and comfort from above;
Be thou our guardian, thou our guide,
O'er every thought and step preside.

2

The light of truth to us display,
And make us know and choose thy way;
Plant holy fear in every heart,
That we from God may ne'er depart.

3

Lead us to Christ, the living Way,
Nor let us from his pastures stray;
Lead us to holiness, the road,
That we must take to dwell with God.

4

Lead us to heaven, that we may share
Fulness of joy for ever there;
Lead us to God, our final rest,
To be with him for ever blest.

S. BROWNE and others

GENERAL

Hymn 233 Charity   Sir J. Stainer, 1840–1901

KEY A♭

mf **GRACIOUS** Spirit, Holy Ghost,
Taught by thee, we covet most
Of thy gifts at Pentecost,
   Holy, heavenly love.

2

Love is kind, and suffers long,
Love is meek, and thinks no wrong,
Love than death itself more strong;
   Therefore give us love.

3

Prophecy will fade away,
Melting in the light of day;
Love will ever with us stay;
   Therefore give us love.

4

Faith will vanish into sight;
Hope be emptied in delight;
Love in heaven will shine more bright;
   Therefore give us love.

5

Faith and hope and love we see
Joining hand in hand agree;
But the greatest of the three,
   And the best, is love.

6

p From the overshadowing
Of thy gold and silver wing
Shed on us, who to thee sing,
   Holy, heavenly love.

                                BISHOP CHR. WORDSWORTH

Alternative Tune, Capetown, 163

GENERAL

Hymn 234 St. Timothy
Sir H. W. Baker, 1821-77

KEY A

[tonic sol-fa notation]

f.A.
[tonic sol-fa notation]

mf O HOLY Ghost, thy people bless
    Who long to feel thy might,
And fain would grow in holiness
    As children of the light.

2

To thee we bring, who art the Lord,
    Our selves to be thy throne;
Let every thought and deed and word
    Thy pure dominion own.

3

Life-giving Spirit, o'er us move,
    As on the formless deep;
Give life and order, light and love,
    Where now is death or sleep.

4

f Great gift of our ascended King,
    His saving truth reveal;
Our tongues inspire his praise to sing,
    Our hearts his love to feel.

5

mf True wind of heaven, from south or north,
    For joy or chastening, blow;
The garden-spices shall spring forth
    If thou wilt bid them flow.

6

f O Holy Ghost, of sevenfold might,
    All graces come from thee;
Grant us to know and serve aright
    One God in Persons Three.

Sir H. W. Baker

HYMN 235 North Petherton — W. H. Harris

KEY A

E. t.

```
s,:l,:s, | d :—:t, | d :—:— || ^m l :r :m | f:—:f | m:— || d  | r :m | f :m
m,:f,:r, | s,:l,:s, | s,:—:— || ^s d :t,:d | d:l,:t, | d:— || s, | s,:d | d :d
d :d :t, | d :f :r | m :—:—  || ^d f :s :s | l:—:f | s:— || m  | s :s | f :s
d,:f,:f, | m,:f,:s, | d,:—:— || ^d f,:f :m | r:—:r | d:— || d  | t,:d | l,:d
```

d. f. D. — A. t.

```
s :f | m :d | r :— | d:—    || ^d r :r':d' | t:—:t | l :—:— || ^l r :f :m
d :r | t,:l, | d :t, | d:—  || ^d r :r :m | f:l :se | m :—:— || ^m l,:t,:d
s :l | s :m | s :— | m:—    || ^m ba:se:l | t:—:m'.r' | d':—:— || ^d' f :f :s
m,:f, | s,:l, | s,:— | d:—  || ^d r :t,:d | r:—:m | l :—:— || ^l r :r,:m,
```

```
r :— :d      | t, :— || s, | l, :t, | d :m   | r :d   | l, :d  | r :—   | d :—
l, :— :m,.f, | s, :— || s, | s, :f, | m, :s, | l, :s, | f, :m, | s, :—  | m, :—
f :— :d      | r :—  || t, | d :r   | d :t,  | l, :d  | d :d   | d :t,  | d :—
f, :s, :l,   | s, :— || s, | f, :r, | l, :s, | f, :m, | f, :l, | s, :—  | d, :—
```

Discendi, Amor santo

mf COME down, O Love divine,
Seek thou this soul of mine,
And visit it with thine own ardour glowing;
O Comforter, draw near,
Within my heart appear,
And kindle it, thy holy flame bestowing.

2

O let it freely burn,
Till earthly passions turn
To dust and ashes in its heat consuming;
f And let thy glorious light
Shine ever on my sight,
And clothe me round, the while my path illuming.

3

mf Let holy charity
Mine outward vesture be,
And lowliness become mine inner clothing:
True lowliness of heart,
Which takes the humbler part,
And o'er its own shortcomings weeps with loathing.

4

f And so the yearning strong,
With which the soul will long,
Shall far outpass the power of human telling;
For none can guess its grace,
Till he become the place
Wherein the Holy Spirit makes his dwelling.

BIANCO DA SIENA *Tr.* R. F. Littledale

HYMN 236 Aylesbury — J. Chetham, *Psalms*, 1718

KEY A♭

```
l, :— | m :r   | d :t,   | l, :— || m :—  | s :f   | m :r   | m :—
m, :— | l, :t, | l, :se, | l, :— || s, :— | s, :l, | s, :s, | s, :—
d :—  | m :f   | m :m    | d :—  || d :—  | d :d   | d :t,  | d :—
l, :— | d, :r, | m, :m,  | l, :— || d, :— | m, :f, | s, :s, | d, :—
```

GENERAL

mf BREATHE on me, Breath of God,
　Fill me with life anew,
That I may love what thou dost love,
　And do what thou wouldst do.

2
Breathe on me, Breath of God,
　Until my heart is pure;
Until with thee I will one will,
　To do and to endure.

3
Breathe on me, Breath of God,
　Till I am wholly thine;
Until this earthly part of me
　Glows with thy fire divine.

4
Breathe on me, Breath of God:
f　So shall I never die,
But live with thee the perfect life
　Of thine eternity.

E. HATCH

Alternative Tune, Carlisle, 362

HYMN 237　Amen Court　　　　　　J. Dykes Bower

βασιλεῦ οὐράνιε, Παράκλητε

O KING enthroned on high,
　Thou Comforter divine,
Blest Spirit of all truth, be nigh
　And make us thine.

2
Thou art the source of life,
　Thou art our treasure-store;
Give us thy peace, and end our strife
　For evermore.

3
Descend, O heavenly Dove,
　Abide with us alway;
And in the fulness of thy love
　Cleanse us, we pray.

Pentecostarion, c. 8th cent.
Tr. J. BROWNLIE

Alternative Tune, Totteridge, 302

247

GENERAL

HYMN 238 Song 22   Orlando Gibbons, 1583–1625
KEY **G**

1
LOVE of the Father, Love of God the Son,
From whom all came, in whom was all begun;
Who formest heavenly beauty out of strife,
Creation's whole desire and breath of life:

2
Thou the all-holy, thou supreme in might,
Thou dost give peace, thy presence maketh right;
Thou with thy favour all things dost enfold,
With thine all-kindness free from harm wilt hold.

3*
Hope of all comfort, splendour of all aid,
That dost not fail nor leave the heart afraid;
To all that cry thou dost all help accord,
The angels' armour, and the saint's reward.

4
Purest and highest, wisest and most just,
There is no truth save only in thy trust;
Thou dost the mind from earthly dreams recall,
And bring, through Christ, to him for whom are all.

5
Eternal glory, all men thee adore,
Who art and shalt be worshipped evermore:
Us whom thou madest, comfort with thy might,
And lead us to enjoy thy heavenly light.

Yattendon Hymnal Based on
Amor Patris et Filii, 12th cent.

GENERAL

HYMN 239 Störl J. G. C. Störl, 1675-1719

KEY E♭

SPIRIT divine, attend our prayers,
And make this house thy home;
Descend with all thy gracious powers;
O come, great Spirit, come!

2
Come as the light: to us reveal
Our emptiness and woe;
And lead us in those paths of life
Where all the righteous go.

3
Come as the fire: and purge our hearts
Like sacrificial flame;
Let our whole soul an offering be
To our Redeemer's name.

4
Come as the dew: and sweetly bless
This consecrated hour;
May barrenness rejoice to own
Thy fertilizing power.

5
Come as the dove: and spread thy wings,
The wings of peaceful love;
And let thy Church on earth become
Blest as the Church above.

6
Come as the wind, with rushing sound
And Pentecostal grace,
That all of woman born may see
The glory of thy face.

7
Spirit divine, attend our prayers;
Make a lost world thy home;
Descend with all thy gracious powers;
O come, great Spirit, come!

A. REED

GENERAL

Hymn 240

FIRST TUNE

KEY **D** Salzburg

J. Hintze, 1622–1702

{| s :d' | s :1 | s :-.f | m :— ‖ s :s | f :m | r :r | d :— ‖
 | d :d | d :d | d :t₁ | d :— ‖ d :d.t₁| l₁.t₁:d | d :t₁ | d :— ‖
 | m :m.f| s :f.m| r.d :r | d :— ‖ m :m | f :s | l :s | m :— ‖
 | d :l₁ | m₁:f₁ | s₁:s₁ | d :— ‖ d :d | r :m | f :s | d :— ‖}

{| s :d' | s :1 | s :-.f | m :— ‖ s :s | f :m | r :r | d :— ‖
 | d :d | d :d | d :t₁ | d :— ‖ d :d.t₁| l₁.t₁:d | d :t₁ | d :— ‖
 | m :m.f| s :f.m| r.d :r | d :— ‖ m :m | f :s | l :s | m :— ‖
 | d :l₁ | m₁:f₁ | s₁:s₁ | d :— ‖ d :d | r :m | f :s | d :— ‖}

A.t.

f.D.

{| r s₁:s₁| l₁.t₁:d | d :t₁ | d :— ‖ r l :-.t| d' :d' | t :t | l :— ‖
 | t m₁:m₁| f₁ :m₁| l₁:s₁.f₁|m₁:— ‖ s r.m :f | m :m | m :m.r| d :— ‖
 | s d :d | d :d | r :r | d :— ‖ ta₁f :-.s| l :l | l :se | l :— ‖
 | s d₁:d₁| f₁ : l₁.s₁|f₁:s₁ | d₁:— ‖ s r :r | l₁.t₁:d.r| m :m | l₁:— ‖}

{| m :m | l :s | s :fe | s :— ‖ l :s | f :m | r :r | d :— ‖
 | d :d | d :t₁ | d :d | t₁:— ‖ d :d.t₁| l₁.t₁:d | d :t₁ | d :— ‖
 | s :s | f.m:r | d.m:r.d| r :— ‖ f :m | f :s | l :s | m :— ‖
 | d :d | f₁:s₁ | l₁ :l₁ | s₁:— ‖ f₁:d | r :m | f :s | d :— ‖}

SECOND TUNE

KEY **G** Maidstone

W. B. Gilbert, 1829–1910

D.C.

{| s₁:l₁:t | d :r :m | f₁:m :r | m₁:—:— ‖ s :f :m | r :m :f | d :—:t₁| d :—:— ‖
 | m₁:—:f₁| m₁:l₁:s₁| l₁:s₁:s₁| s₁:—:— ‖ d :t₁:d | l₁:—:l₁| s₁:—:s₁| s₁:—:— ‖
 | d :—:r | d :—:d | d :—:t₁| d :—:— ‖ m :f :s | l :s :f | m :—:r | m :—:— ‖
 | d :—:s₁| l₁:f₁:m₁| r₁:s₁:s₁| d₁:—:— ‖ m :r :d | f₁:m₁:r₁| s₁:—:s₁| d₁:—:— ‖}

{| r :—:m | f :—:m | r :—:d | t₁:—:— ‖ m :—:f | s :—:f | m :—:r | m :—:— ‖
 | s₁:—:s₁| f₁:—:s₁| l₁:—:l₁| s₁:—:— ‖ s₁:—:l₁| s₁:—:l₁| s₁:—:s₁| s₁:—:— ‖
 | t₁:—:de| r :—:de| r :—:r | r :—:— ‖ d :—:d | d :—:d | d :—:t₁| d :—:— ‖
 | s₁:—:m₁| r₁:—:m₁| f₁:—:fe₁| s₁:—:— ‖ d :—:l₁| m₁:—:f₁| s₁:—:s₁| d :—:— ‖}

GENERAL

Psalm 84

mf PLEASANT are thy courts above
In the land of light and love;
Pleasant are thy courts below
In this land of sin and woe:
O, my spirit longs and faints
For the converse of thy saints,
For the brightness of thy face,
For thy fulness, God of grace.

2

Happy birds that sing and fly
Round thy altars, O Most High;
Happier souls that find a rest
In a heavenly Father's breast!
Like the wandering dove that found
No repose on earth around,
They can to their ark repair,
And enjoy it ever there.

3

Happy souls, their praises flow
Even in this vale of woe;
Waters in the desert rise,
Manna feeds them from the skies;
f On they go from strength to strength,
Till they reach thy throne at length,
At thy feet adoring fall,
Who hast led them safe through all.

4

p Lord, be mine this prize to win,
Guide me through a world of sin,
Keep me by thy saving grace,
Give me at thy side a place.
mf Sun and Shield alike thou art;
Guide and guard my erring heart:
f Grace and glory flow from thee;
Shower, O shower them, Lord, on me.

H. F. LYTE

GENERAL

HYMN 241 FIRST TUNE
KEY C Praises

B. Luard Selby, 1853–1919

(Tonic sol-fa notation)

SECOND TUNE

KEY E Hosanna

J. W. Elliott, 1833–1915

(Tonic sol-fa notation)

HOSANNA to the living Lord!
Hosanna to the incarnate Word!
To Christ, Creator, Saviour, King,
Let earth, let heaven Hosanna sing,
        Hosanna in the highest!

2

O Saviour, with protecting care
Abide in this thy house of prayer,
Where we thy parting promise claim,
Assembled in thy sacred name:
        Hosanna in the highest!

GENERAL

3

But, chiefest, in our cleansèd breast,
Eternal, bid thy Spirit rest;
And make our secret soul to be
A temple pure and worthy thee:
    Hosanna in the highest!

4

To God the Father, God the Son,
And God the Spirit, Three in One,
Be honour, praise, and glory given
By all on earth and all in heaven:
    Hosanna in the highest!

BISHOP R. HEBER†

HYMN **242**   Quam dilecta   Bishop H. L. Jenner, 1820–98

KEY **F**

mf We love the place, O God,
    Wherein thine honour dwells;
The joy of thine abode
    All earthly joy excels.

2

It is the house of prayer,
    Wherein thy servants meet;
And thou, O Lord, art there
    Thy chosen flock to greet.

3

We love the sacred font;
    For there the holy Dove
To pour is ever wont
    His blessing from above.

4

We love thine altar, Lord;
    O what on earth so dear?
For there, in faith adored,
    We find thy presence near.

5

We love the word of life,
    The word that tells of peace,
Of comfort in the strife,
    And joys that never cease.

6

f We love to sing below
    For mercies freely given;
But O, we long to know
    The triumph-song of heaven.

7

mf Lord Jesus, give us grace
    On earth to love thee more,
f In heaven to see thy face,
    And with thy saints adore.

W. BULLOCK and SIR H. W. BAKER

GENERAL

Hymn 243 Harewood
S. S. Wesley, 1810–76

KEY A

[sol-fa notation staves]

Angularis fundamentum

mf CHRIST is our Corner-stone,
    On him alone we build;
    With his true saints alone
    The courts of heaven are filled:
      On his great love
      Our hopes we place
      Of present grace
    And joys above.

2

f O then with hymns of praise
    These hallowed courts shall ring;
    Our voices we will raise
    The Three in One to sing;
      And thus proclaim
      In joyful song,
      Both loud and long,
    That glorious name.

3

mf Here, gracious God, do thou
    For evermore draw nigh;
    Accept each faithful vow,
    And mark each suppliant sigh;
      In copious shower
      On all who pray
      Each holy day
    Thy blessings pour.

4

p Here may we gain from heaven
    The grace which we implore;
    And may that grace, once given,
    Be with us evermore,
      Until that day
      When all the blest
      To endless rest
    Are called away.

Tr. J. CHANDLER†

GENERAL

HYMN 244 Canon viii

G. C. E. Ryley, 1866–1947

KEY **F**

[sol-fa notation]

By permission of the Royal School of Church Music

O quam juvat fratres, Deus

O LORD, how joyful 'tis to see
The brethren join in love to thee!
On thee alone their heart relies,
Their only strength thy grace supplies.

2

How sweet within thy holy place
With one accord to sing thy grace,
Besieging thine attentive ear
With all the force of fervent prayer!

3

O may we love the house of God,
Of peace and joy the blest abode;
O may no angry strife destroy
That sacred peace, that holy joy.

4

The world without may rage, but we
Will only cling more close to thee,
With hearts to thee more wholly given,
More weaned from earth, more fixed on heaven.

5

Lord, shower upon us from above
The sacred gift of mutual love;
Each other's wants may we supply,
And reign together in the sky.

C. COFFIN *Tr.* J. Chandler

Alternative Tune, Melcombe, 4

GENERAL

HYMN **245** Wareham   W. Knapp, 1698–1768

KEY **B♭**

[Sheet music omitted]

The Descant may be sung for verses 3 and 5

mf JESUS, where'er thy people meet,
There they behold thy mercy-seat;
Where'er they seek thee thou art found,
And every place is hallowed ground.

2

For thou, within no walls confined,
Inhabitest the humble mind;
Such ever bring thee when they come,
And, going, take thee to their home.

[UNISON] 3

f Dear Shepherd of thy chosen few,
Thy former mercies here renew;
Here to our waiting hearts proclaim
The sweetness of thy saving name.

4

mf Here may we prove the power of prayer
To strengthen faith and sweeten care,
To teach our faint desires to rise,
And bring all heaven before our eyes.

[UNISON] 5

Lord, we are few, but thou art near;
Nor short thine arm, nor deaf thine ear:
f O rend the heavens, come quickly down,
And make a thousand hearts thine own.

W. COWPER

GENERAL

Hymn 246 Angel voices   E. G. Monk, 1819–1900

KEY **D**

[sol-fa notation]

mf ANGEL-VOICES ever singing
    Round thy throne of light,
Angel-harps for ever ringing,
    Rest not day nor night;
f Thousands only live to bless thee
    And confess thee
      Lord of might.

2

mf Thou who art beyond the farthest
    Mortal eye can scan,
Can it be that thou regardest
    Songs of sinful man?
Can we know that thou art near us,
    And wilt hear us?
f   Yea, we can.

3

mf Yea, we know that thou rejoicest
    O'er each work of thine;
Thou didst ears and hands and voices
    For thy praise design;
Craftsman's art and music's measure
    For thy pleasure
      All combine.

4

In thy house, great God, we offer
    Of thine own to thee;
And for thine acceptance proffer
    All unworthily
Hearts and minds and hands and [voices
    In our choicest
      Psalmody.

5

f Honour, glory, might, and merit
    Thine shall ever be,
Father, Son, and Holy Spirit,
    Blessèd Trinity!
Of the best that thou hast given
    Earth and heaven
      Render thee.

F. POTT‡

GENERAL

HYMN 247 Oswald's Tree   Sir H. Walford Davies, 1869–1941

KEY D

f
GREAT Shepherd of thy people, hear,
Thy presence now display;
As thou hast given a place for prayer,
So give us hearts to pray.

2
mf Within these walls let holy peace
And love and concord dwell;
Here give the troubled conscience ease,
The wounded spirit heal.

3
May we in faith receive thy word,
In faith present our prayers,
And in the presence of our Lord
Unbosom all our cares.

4
The hearing ear, the seeing eye,
The contrite heart, bestow;
f And shine upon us from on high,
That we in grace may grow.

J. NEWTON†

HYMN 248 Croft's 148th   W. Croft, 1678–1727

KEY D

A. t.

GENERAL

f.D.

[Sol-fa notation staves]

Psalm 84

LORD of the worlds above,
  How pleasant and how fair
The dwellings of thy love,
  Thy earthly temples, are!
    To thine abode
    My heart aspires,
      With warm desires
    To see my God.

2

O happy souls that pray
  Where God appoints to hear!
O happy men that pay
  Their constant service there!
    They praise thee still;
    And happy they
      That love the way
    To Zion's hill.

3

They go from strength to strength
  Through this dark vale of tears,
Till each arrives at length,
  Till each in heaven appears:
    O glorious seat!
    When God our King
      Shall thither bring
    Our willing feet.

I. WATTS

Alternative Tune, Darwall's 148th, 371

GENERAL

HYMN 249 Althorp   James Green's *Psalmody*, 1744

KEY A♭

Gott ist gegenwärtig!

mf LO, God is here! let us adore,
    And own how dreadful is this place!
Let all within us feel his power,
    And silent bow before his face;
Who know his power, his grace who prove,
p   Serve him with awe, with reverence love.

2

mf Lo, God is here! him day and night
    Rejoicing choirs of angels sing;
To him, enthroned above all height,
    The hosts of heaven their praises bring:
p   Disdain not, Lord, our meaner song,
Who praise thee with a faltering tongue.

3

Being of beings! may our praise
    Thy courts with grateful fragrance fill;
Still may we stand before thy face,
    Still hear and do thy sovereign will;
To thee may all our thoughts arise
A true and ceaseless sacrifice.

                              G. TERSTEEGEN   *Tr.* J. Wesley†

Alternative Tune, Colchester, 90

GENERAL

HYMN 250 Ravenshaw   German Medieval Melody

KEY F

```
{| d :d  | m :f  | s :—  | s :—   || l  :t  | d' :s | m :fe | s :—   ||
 | s₁:s₁ | d :d  | d :t₁ | d :—   || d  :r  | m  :r | d :—  | t₁:—   |
 | m :m  | s :f  | r :—  | m :—   || f  :f  | s  :s | s :d  | r :—   |
 | d :d  | d :l₁ | s₁:—  | d :—   || f₁ :r  | d  :t₁| d :l₁ | s₁:—   |}

{| f :r  | m :f  | m :r  | d :—   || t₁ :d  | r  :m | r :—  | d :—   ||
 | l₁:s₁ | s₁:l₁ | s₁:—  | m₁:—   || s₁ :s₁ | t₁ :d | d :t₁ | d :—   |
 | d :r  | d :d  | d :t₁ | d :—   || r  :m  | f  :s | s :—  | m :—   |
 | l₁:t₁ | d :f₁ | s₁:—  | l₁:—   || s₁ :m₁ | r₁ :d₁| s₁:—  | d₁:—   |}
```

        LORD, thy word abideth,
        And our footsteps guideth;
        Who its truth believeth
        Light and joy receiveth.

            2
        When our foes are near us,
        Then thy word doth cheer us,
        Word of consolation,
        Message of salvation.

            3
        When the storms are o'er us,
        And dark clouds before us,
        Then its light directeth,
        And our way protecteth.

            4
        Who can tell the pleasure,
        Who recount the treasure,
        By thy word imparted
        To the simple-hearted?

            5
        Word of mercy, giving
        Succour to the living;
        Word of life, supplying
        Comfort to the dying!

            6
        O that we discerning
        Its most holy learning,
        Lord, may love and fear thee,
        Evermore be near thee.

                            SIR H. W. BAKER

GENERAL

Hymn 251 Angmering   Sir C. H. H. Parry, 1848–1918

[Tonic sol-fa notation]

FATHER of mercies, in thy word
  What endless glory shines!
For ever be thy name adored
  For these celestial lines.

2
Here may the blind and hungry come,
  And light and food receive;
Here shall the lowliest guest have room,
  And taste and see and live.

3
Here springs of consolation rise
  To cheer the fainting mind,
And thirsting souls receive supplies,
  And sweet refreshment find.

4
Here the Redeemer's welcome voice
  Spreads heavenly peace around,
And life and everlasting joys
  Attend the blissful sound.

5
O may these heavenly pages be
  My ever dear delight,
And still new beauties may I see,
  And still increasing light.

6
Divine instructor, gracious Lord,
  Be thou for ever near;
Teach me to love thy sacred word,
  And view my Saviour here.

ANNE STEELE

Alternative Tune, Southwell (Irons), 282

GENERAL

HYMN 252 Alfreton *Supplement to the New Version, 1708*

KEY A♭

Eb. t.

```
{ :d  |m  :f  |r  :m  |d  :r  |t₁ ‖ʳs |l  :t  |d' :s  |l  :s.f|m :—
  :s₁ |s₁ :f₁ |s₁ :m₁ |m₁ :l₁ |s₁ ‖ˢd |d  :r  |d  :d  |d  :t₁ |d :—
  :m  |d  :d  |r  :t₁ |d  :f  |r  ‖ᵗm |l  :s  |s  :s  |f.m:r  |d :—
  :d  |d  :l₁ |t₁ :s₁ |l₁ :f₁ |s₁ ‖ᵗm |f  :f  |m  :m₁ |f₁ :s₁ |d :— ‖
```

f. A♭.

```
{ :ʳr |s  :m  |f  :m  |r  :d  |t₁ ‖r  |m  :f  |s  :d  |d :—.t₁|d :—
  :ᵈs₁|s₁ :l₁ |l₁.t₁:d|l₁ :m₁.f₁|s₁‖s₁ |s₁ :s₁ |s₁ :l₁ |s₁ :s₁ |s₁:—
  :ᵐt₁|t₁ :de |r  :s  |f  :d  |r  ‖t₁ |d  :—.t₁|d  :f  |m  :r  |m :—
  :ᵈs₁|m₁ :l₁ |r₁ :m₁ |f₁ :l₁ |s₁ ‖s₁ |d₁ :r₁ |m₁ :f₁ |s₁ :s₁ |d₁:— ‖
```

Psalm 19

THE heavens declare thy glory, Lord;
  In every star thy wisdom shines;
But when our eyes behold thy word,
  We read thy name in fairer lines.

2

Sun, moon, and stars convey thy praise
  Round the whole earth, and never stand;
So, when thy truth began its race,
  It touched and glanced on every land.

3

Nor shall thy spreading Gospel rest
  Till through the world thy truth has run;
Till Christ has all the nations blest
  That see the light or feel the sun.

4

Great Sun of Righteousness, arise;
  Bless the dark world with heavenly light;
Thy Gospel makes the simple wise,
  Thy laws are pure, thy judgements right.

5

Thy noblest wonders here we view,
  In souls renewed and sins forgiven:
Lord, cleanse my sins, my soul renew,
  And make thy word my guide to heaven.

I. WATTS

GENERAL

Hymn 253 FIRST TUNE

KEY G   Iste Confessor   French Melody

mf LORD of our life, and God of our salvation,
   Star of our night, and hope of every nation,
   Hear and receive thy Church's supplication,
f   Lord God Almighty.

2

mf See round thine ark the hungry billows curling;
   See how thy foes their banners are unfurling;
   Lord, while their darts envenomed they are hurling,
f   Thou canst preserve us.

3

f Lord, thou canst help when earthly armour faileth,
   Lord, thou canst save when deadly sin assaileth;
   Lord, o'er thy Church nor death nor hell prevaileth:
p   Grant us thy peace, Lord.

4

mf Grant us thy help till foes are backward driven,
   Grant them thy truth, that they may be forgiven,
p   Grant peace on earth, and, after we have striven,
      Peace in thy heaven.

P. PUSEY† Based on *Christe du Beistand*, M. von Löwenstern

GENERAL

SECOND TUNE

KEY E♭ Cloisters Sir J. Barnby, 1838–96

[Sol-fa musical notation]

mf LORD of our life, and God of our salvation,
  Star of our night, and hope of every nation,
  Hear and receive thy Church's supplication,
    f Lord God Almighty.

2

mf See round thine ark the hungry billows curling;
  See how thy foes their banners are unfurling;
  Lord, while their darts envenomed they are hurling,
    f Thou canst preserve us.

3

f Lord, thou canst help when earthly armour faileth,
  Lord, thou canst save when deadly sin assaileth;
  Lord, o'er thy Church nor death nor hell prevaileth:
    p Grant us thy peace, Lord.

4

mf Grant us thy help till foes are backward driven,
  Grant them thy truth, that they may be forgiven,
  p Grant peace on earth, and, after we have striven,
    Peace in thy heaven.

P. PUSEY† Based on *Christe du
Beistand*, M. von Löwenstern

GENERAL

HYMN 254 University   C. Collignon, 1725-85
KEY **C**

[sol-fa notation music score]

f   THE Church of God a kingdom is,
       Where Christ in power doth reign;
mf Where spirits yearn till, seen in bliss,
       Their Lord shall come again.

2

f   Glad companies of saints possess
       This Church below, above;
   And God's perpetual calm doth bless
       Their paradise of love.

3

An altar stands within the shrine
   Whereon, once sacrificed,
Is set, immaculate, divine,
   The Lamb of God, the Christ.

4

There rich and poor, from countless lands,
   Praise Christ on mystic Rood;
There nations reach forth holy hands
   To take God's holy food.

5

mf There pure life-giving streams o'erflow
      The sower's garden-ground;
   And faith and hope fair blossoms show,
      And fruits of love abound.

6

O King, O Christ, this endless grace
   To us and all men bring,
f   To see the vision of thy face
   In joy, O Christ, our King.

                                       L. B. C. L. MUIRHEAD

GENERAL

Hymn 255 Aurelia　　　　　　　　　　　　　　S. S. Wesley, 1810–76

KEY E♭

mf THE Church's one foundation
　Is Jesus Christ her Lord;
She is his new creation
　By water and the word:
From heaven he came and sought
　To be his holy Bride;
With his own Blood he bought her, [her
　And for her life he died.

2

Elect from every nation,
　Yet one o'er all the earth,
Her charter of salvation
　One Lord, one faith, one birth;
One holy name she blesses,
　Partakes one holy food,
And to one hope she presses
　With every grace endued.

3*

p Though with a scornful wonder
　Men see her sore opprest,
By schisms rent asunder,
　By heresies distrest,
mf Yet saints their watch are keeping,
　Their cry goes up, 'How long?'
f And soon the night of weeping
　Shall be the morn of song.

4

mf Mid toil and tribulation,
　And tumult of her war,
She waits the consummation
　Of peace for evermore;
Till with the vision glorious
　Her longing eyes are blest,
f And the great Church victorious
　Shall be the Church at rest.

5

mf Yet she on earth hath union
　With God the Three in One,
And mystic sweet communion
　With those whose rest is won:
O happy ones and holy!
　Lord, give us grace that we,
Like them the meek and lowly,
　On high may dwell with thee.

S. J. STONE

GENERAL

Hymn 256 Thornbury   B. Harwood, 1859–1949

KEY **D**

VERSES 1, 2, 4 AND 6, UNISON

{: s | m : t₁ | d : l | d :— | t₁ : r | s : l | <u>f.m</u> : r }

1 Thy hand, O God, has guid - ed⌣ Thy flock, from age to
2 Thy her - alds brought glad tid - ings To great - est, as to
4 Through many a day of dark - ness, Through many a scene of
6 Thy mer - cy will not fail us, Nor leave thy work un -

{| m :— | — || s | m : t₁ | d : l | d :— | t₁ : r }

1 age; The won - drous tale is writ - ten, Full
2 least; They bade men rise, and hast - en To
4 strife. The faith - ful few fought brave - ly, To
6 done; With thy right hand to help us, The

A.t.

{| s : l | <u>f.m</u> : r | d :— | — || ᵐl₁ | l₁.t₁ : d | t₁ : l₁ }

1 clear, on ev - ery page; Our fa - thers owned thy
2 share the great King's feast; And this was all their
4 guard the na - tion's life. Their Gos - pel of re -
6 vic - tory shall be won; And then, by men and

f.D.

{| <u>l₁ : se₁</u> | l₁ : t₁ | <u>d.r</u> : m | l₁ : se₁ | l₁ :— | — || ᵈs }

1 good - ness, And we their deeds re - cord: And
2 teach - ing, In ev - ery deed and word, To
4 demp - tion, Sin par - doned, man re - stored, Was
6 an - gels, Thy name shall be a - dored, And

{| s :<u>l.t</u>|d¹: m|<u>f : s</u>| l : s |d¹:—|—: s| d :—|l:—|s:—|—:—|—: | ||

1 both of this bear wit - ness:
2 all a - like pro - claim - ing } One Church, one faith, one Lord.
4 all in this en - fold - ed:
6 this shall be their an - them:

268

GENERAL

KEY **D**

VERSES 3 AND 5, HARMONY

(Musical notation in tonic sol-fa)

Lyrics:

3* When shadows thick were falling, And all seemed sunk in night, Thou, Lord, didst send the servants, Thy chosen sons of light. On them and on thy people Thy plenteous grace was poured, And this was still their message: One Church, one faith, one Lord, one faith, one Lord.

5* And we, shall we be faithless? Shall hearts fail, hands hang down? Shall we evade thy conflict, And cast away our crown? Not so: in God's deep counsels Some better thing is stored; We will maintain unflinching, One Church, one faith, one Lord, one faith, one Lord.

E. H. PLUMPTRE

GENERAL

HYMN 257   FIRST TUNE

KEY D   Abbot's Leigh   C. V. Taylor

[Sol-fa notation musical score omitted]

Reprinted by permission of the Oxford University Press

SECOND TUNE

KEY E♭   Austria   F. J. Haydn, 1732-1809

[Sol-fa notation musical score omitted]

GENERAL

```
{|r  :m   |r.t₁:s₁ |f  :m   |r.t₁:s₁ |s  :f   |m :-.m |fe :-.fe|s  :—  ||
 |s₁ :s₁  |s₁ :s₁ |s₁ :s₁  |s₁ :s₁  |s₁ :l₁.t₁|d :-.d |d  :-.d |t₁ :—  ||
 |t₁ :d   |t₁ :t₁ |r  :d   |t₁ :t₁  |m  :r    |d :-.d |r  :-.l |s  :—  ||
 |s₁ :s₁  |s₁ :s₁ |t₁ :d   |s₁ :s₁  |m₁ :f₁.s₁|l₁:-.l₁|r  :-.r |s₁ :—  ||

{|d' :-.t |l  :s  |l  :-.s |s.f:m   |r  :m.f |s.l:f.r |d  :m.r |d  :—  ||
 |d  :-.d |d  :d  |d  :-.d |t₁ :d   |t₁ :t₁  |d  :l₁  |s₁ :t₁  |d  :—  ||
 |s  :-.s |f  :m  |f  :-.s |s  :s   |s  :s   |s.d:l.f |m  :f   |m  :—  ||
 |m  :-.m |f  :d  |f  :-.m |r  :d   |s₁ :f₁  |m₁ :f₁  |s₁ :-.s₁|d  :—  ||
```

GLORIOUS things of thee are spoken
   Zion, city of our God;
He whose word cannot be broken
   Formed thee for his own abode.
On the Rock of ages founded,
   What can shake thy sure repose?
With salvation's walls surrounded,
   Thou may'st smile at all thy foes.

2

See, the streams of living waters,
   Springing from eternal love,
Well supply thy sons and daughters,
   And all fear of want remove.
Who can faint while such a river
   Ever flows their thirst to assuage:
Grace which, like the Lord the giver,
   Never fails from age to age?

3*

Round each habitation hovering,
   See the cloud and fire appear
For a glory and a covering,
   Showing that the Lord is near.
Thus they march, the pillar leading,
   Light by night and shade by day;
Daily on the manna feeding
   Which he gives them when they pray.

4

Saviour, since of Zion's city
   I through grace a member am,
Let the world deride or pity,
   I will glory in thy name.
Fading is the worldling's pleasure,
   All his boasted pomp and show;
Solid joys and lasting treasure
   None but Zion's children know.

J. NEWTON‡

GENERAL

HYMN 258 Richmond   T. Haweis, 1734–1820

KEY **G**

[sol-fa notation]

1
CITY of God, how broad and far
  Outspread thy walls sublime!
The true thy chartered freemen are
  Of every age and clime:

2
One holy Church, one army strong,
  One steadfast, high intent;
One working band, one harvest-song,
  One King omnipotent.

3
How purely hath thy speech come down
  From man's primeval youth!
How grandly hath thine empire grown
  Of freedom, love, and truth!

4
How gleam thy watch-fires through the night
  With never-fainting ray!
How rise thy towers, serene and bright,
  To meet the dawning day!

[UNISON]
5
In vain the surge's angry shock,
  In vain the drifting sands:
Unharmed upon the eternal Rock
  The eternal city stands.

                                        S. JOHNSON

HYMN 259 Old 120th *Psalms*, 1570

KEY E♭

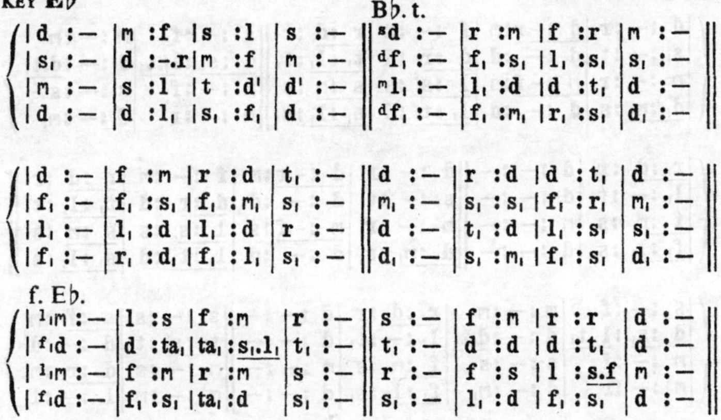

O THOU not made with hands,
  Not throned above the skies,
Nor walled with shining walls,
  Nor framed with stones of price,
More bright than gold or gem,
God's own Jerusalem!

2

Where'er the gentle heart
  Finds courage from above;
Where'er the heart forsook
  Warms with the breath of love;
Where faith bids fear depart,
City of God, thou art.

3

Thou art where'er the proud‿
  In humbleness melts down;
Where self itself yields up;
  Where martyrs win their crown;
Where faithful souls possess‿
Themselves in perfect peace;

4

Where in life's common ways
  With cheerful feet we go;
Where in his steps we tread,
  Who trod the way of woe;
Where he is in the heart,
City of God, thou art.

5

Not throned above the skies,
  Nor golden-walled afar,
But where Christ's two or three‿
  In his name gathered are,
Be in the midst of them,
God's own Jerusalem!

F. T. PALGRAVE

GENERAL

HYMN 260 Hyfrydol R. H. Prichard, 1811–87
KEY **F**

[Tonic sol-fa notation]

YE that know the Lord is gracious,
Ye for whom a Corner stone
Stands, of God elect and precious,
Laid that ye may build thereon,
See that on that sure foundation
Ye a living temple raise,
Towers that may tell forth salvation,
Walls that may re-echo praise.

2

Living stones, by God appointed
Each to his allotted place,
Kings and priests, by God anointed,
Shall ye not declare his grace?
Ye, a royal generation,
Tell the tidings of your birth,
Tidings of a new creation
To an old and weary earth.

GENERAL

3
Tell the praise of him who called you
   Out of darkness into light,
Broke the fetters that enthralled you,
   Gave you freedom, peace and sight:
Tell the tale of sins forgiven,
   Strength renewed and hope restored,
Till the earth, in tune with heaven,
   Praise and magnify the Lord!

C. A. ALINGTON

HYMN **261** Binchester   W. Croft, 1678–1727

1
HAPPY are they, they that love God,
   Whose hearts have Christ confest,
Who by his Cross have found their life,
   And 'neath his yoke their rest.

2
Glad is the praise, sweet are the songs,
   When they together sing;
And strong the prayers that bow the ear
   Of heaven's eternal King.

3
Christ to their homes giveth his peace,
   And makes their loves his own:
But ah, what tares the evil one
   Hath in his garden sown!

4
Sad were our lot, evil this earth,
   Did not its sorrows prove
The path whereby the sheep may find
   The fold of Jesus' love.

5
Then shall they know, they that love him,
   How all their pain is good;
And death itself cannot unbind
   Their happy brotherhood.

Yattendon Hymnal
Based on *O quam juvat*, C. COFFIN

GENERAL

HYMN 262 St. Cecilia   L. G. Hayne, 1836–83

KEY **G**

mf THY Kingdom come, O God,
    Thy rule, O Christ, begin;
    Break with thine iron rod·
    The tyrannies of sin.

2
p Where is thy reign of peace
    And purity and love?
    When shall all hatred cease,
    As in the realms above?

3
When comes the promised time
That war shall be no more,
And lust, oppression, crime
Shall flee thy face before?

4
mf We pray thee, Lord, arise,
    And come in thy great might;
    Revive our longing eyes,
    Which languish for thy sight.

5
p Men scorn thy sacred name,
    And wolves devour thy fold;
    By many deeds of shame
    We learn that love grows cold.

6
O'er heathen lands afar
Thick darkness broodeth yet:
f Arise, O morning star,
   Arise, and never set!

L. HENSLEY

HYMN 263 Irish   *Hymns and Sacred Poems* (Dublin, 1749)

KEY **E**

GENERAL

1. THY Kingdom come! on bended knee
   The passing ages pray;
   And faithful souls have yearned to see
   On earth that Kingdom's day:

2. But the slow watches of the night
   Not less to God belong;
   And for the everlasting right
   The silent stars are strong.

3. And lo, already on the hills
   The flags of dawn appear;
   Gird up your loins, ye prophet souls,
   Proclaim the day is near:

4. The day in whose clear-shining light
   All wrong shall stand revealed,
   When justice shall be throned in might,
   And every hurt be healed;

5. When knowledge, hand in hand with peace,
   Shall walk the earth abroad:
   The day of perfect righteousness,
   The promised day of God.

F. L. HOSMER

HYMN 264 Heathlands   H. Smart, 1813–79
KEY D

s :d'	t :s	l :l	s :—	f :r	m :f	s :f.m	r :—
d :m	r :m.r	d :d	d :—	d :r	d :d	d :r.d	t₁ :—
s :s	s :d'.t	l :f	m :—	l :s	s :f	m :l	r :—
m :d	s :m	f :l₁	d :—	l₁:t₁	d :l₁	m₁:f₁	s₁ :—

A. t.

s d :d	l₁ :d	f :m	r :—	s :r	m :r.d	r :t₁	d :—
r s₁:m₁	l₁ :s₁	f₁ :s₁	s₁ :—	s₁:s₁	s₁:l₁	l₁ :s₁	s₁ :—
r s₁:d	d :s₁	l₁.t₁:d	t₁ :—	r :t₁	d :f.m	f :r	m :—
t m₁:d₁	f₁ :m₁	r₁ :m₁.f₁	s₁ :—	t₁ :s₁	d :l₁	f₁ :s₁	d₁ :—

f. D.

d s :s	l :l	t :t	d' :—	l :s	f :m	r :r	d :—
l m :t₁	d :d	f :m.r	d :—	d :d	d :d	d :t₁	d :—
m t :s	m :l.s	f :s.f	m :—	f :s	d :d.m	l :s.f	m :—
l m :m	d :f.m	r :s₁	l₁ :—	f₁:m₁	l₁:s₁	f₁ :s₁	d :—

Psalm 67

mf 1. GOD of mercy, God of grace,
   Show the brightness of thy face;
   Shine upon us, Saviour, shine,
   Fill thy Church with light divine;
   And thy saving health extend
   Unto earth's remotest end.

f 2. Let the people praise thee, Lord!
   Be by all that live adored;
   Let the nations shout and sing
   Glory to their Saviour King;
mf At thy feet their tribute pay,
   And thy holy will obey.

f 3. Let the people praise thee, Lord!
   Earth shall then her fruits afford;
   God to man his blessing give,
   Man to God devoted live;
   All below, and all above,
   One in joy and light and love.

H. F. LYTE

GENERAL

HYMN 265 Aurelia   S. S. Wesley, 1810–76
KEY E♭

mf FROM Greenland's icy mountains,
    From India's coral strand,
Where Afric's sunny fountains
    Roll down their golden sand,
From many an ancient river,
    From many a palmy plain,
They call us to deliver
    Their land from error's chain.

2
What though the spicy breezes
    Blow soft o'er Java's isle,
Though every prospect pleases
    And only man is vile:
In vain with lavish kindness
    The gifts of God are strown;
The heathen in his blindness
    Bows down to wood and stone.

3
Can we, whose souls are lighted
    With wisdom from on high,
Can we to men benighted
    The lamp of life deny?
f Salvation! O salvation!
    The joyful sound proclaim,
Till each remotest nation
    Has learned Messiah's name.

4
Waft, waft, ye winds, his story,
    And you, ye waters, roll,
Till, like a sea of glory,
    It spreads from pole to pole;
Till o'er our ransomed nature
    The Lamb for sinners slain,
Redeemer, King, Creator,
    In bliss returns to reign.

                        BISHOP R. HEBER

GENERAL

HYMN 266 MOSCOW F. Giardini, 1716–96
KEY **G**

f THOU, whose almighty word
Chaos and darkness heard,
  And took their flight;
mf Hear us, we humbly pray,
And where the Gospel-day
Sheds not its glorious ray,
  f Let there be light!

2

mf Thou, who didst come to bring
On thy redeeming wing
  Healing and sight,
Health to the sick in mind,
Sight to the inly blind,
O now to all mankind
  f Let there be light!

3

mf Spirit of truth and love,
Life-giving, holy Dove,
  Speed forth thy flight;
Move on the water's face,
Bearing the lamp of grace,
And in earth's darkest place
  f Let there be light!

4

Holy and blessèd Three,
Glorious Trinity,
  Wisdom, Love, Might;
Boundless as ocean's tide
Rolling in fullest pride,
Through the earth far and wide
  Let there be light!

J. MARRIOTT†

GENERAL

HYMN 267 Everton   H. Smart, 1813–79
KEY E♭

[Sol-fa notation, D.C.]

Bb. t.

f. E♭.

mf LORD, her watch thy Church is keeping;
   When shall earth thy rule obey?
   When shall end the night of weeping?
   When shall break the promised day?
p See the whitening harvest languish,
   Waiting still the labourers' toil;
mf Was it vain, thy Son's deep anguish?
   Shall the strong retain the spoil?

2
p Tidings, sent to every creature,
   Millions yet have never heard;
   Can they hear without a preacher?
mf Lord almighty, give the word:
f Give the word; in every nation
   Let the Gospel-trumpet sound,
   Witnessing a world's salvation
   To the earth's remotest bound.

3
Then the end: thy Church completed,
   All thy chosen gathered in,
With their King in glory seated,
   Satan bound, and banished sin;
Gone for ever parting, weeping,
   Hunger, sorrow, death, and pain:
Lo, her watch thy Church is keeping;
   Come, Lord Jesus, come to reign!

H. DOWNTON

HYMN 268 Duke Street   Attributed to J. Hatton, *d.* 1793
KEY D

[Sol-fa notation]

GENERAL

FLING out the banner! let it float
    Skyward and seaward, high and wide:
Our glory only in the Cross,
    Our only hope the Crucified.

2

Fling out the banner! angels bend
    In anxious silence o'er the sign,
And vainly seek to comprehend
    The wonders of the love divine.

3

Fling out the banner! heathen lands
    Shall see from far the glorious sight,
And nations, crowding to be born,
    Baptize their spirits in its light.

4

Fling out the banner! wide and high,
    Seaward and skyward let it shine;
Nor skill nor might nor merit ours:
    We conquer only in that sign.

BISHOP G. W. DOANE

HYMN 269   Little Cornard   Martin Shaw

By permission of J. Curwen & Sons, Ltd., from Curwen edition No. 80634

HILLS of the north, rejoice,
    River and mountain-spring,
Hark to the advent voice;
    Valley and lowland, sing:
Though absent long, your Lord is nigh;
He judgement brings and victory.

2

Isles of the southern seas,
    Deep in your coral caves
Pent be each warring breeze,
    Lulled be your restless waves:
He comes to reign with boundless sway,
And makes your wastes his great highway.

3

Lands of the east, awake,
    Soon shall your sons be free;
The sleep of ages break,
    And rise to liberty.
On your far hills, long cold and grey,
Has dawned the everlasting day.

4

Shores of the utmost west,
    Ye that have waited long,
Unvisited, unblest,
    Break forth to swelling song;
High raise the note, that Jesus died,
Yet lives and reigns, the Crucified.

[UNISON]
5

Shout, while ye journey home;
    Songs be in every mouth;
Lo, from the north we come,
    From east and west and south.
City of God, the bond are free,
We come to live and reign in thee!

C. E. OAKLEY

GENERAL

HYMN 270 Rangoon
KEY **D**
C. Wood, 1866-1926

(Tonic sol-fa notation)

TRUMPET of God, sound high,
  Till the hearts of the heathen shake,
And the souls that in slumber lie
  At the voice of the Lord awake.
    Till the fencèd cities fall
    At the blast of the Gospel call,
  Trumpet of God, sound high!

2
Hosts of the Lord, go forth:
  Go, strong in the power of his rest,
Till the south be at one with the north,
  And peace upon east and west;
    Till the far-off lands shall thrill
    With the gladness of God's good
  Hosts of the Lord, go forth! [will,

3
Come, as of old, like fire;
  O force of the Lord, descend,
Till with love of the world's Desire
  Earth burn to its utmost end;
    Till the ransomed people sing
    To the glory of Christ the King,
  Come, as of old, like fire!

A. BROOKS

HYMN 271 Benson
KEY **G**
Millicent D. Kingham (1894)

(Vss. 2, 3, 4)

GENERAL

(Vss. 2, 5)

[Tonic sol-fa notation staves]

mf GOD is working his | purpose out as | year succeeds to | year,
God is working his | purpose out and the | time is drawing | near;
Nearer and nearer | draws the time, the | time that shall surely | be,
f When the | earth shall be filled with the | glory of God as the | waters cover the | sea.

2

mf From | utmost east to | utmost west wher- | e'er man's foot hath | trod,
By the | mouth of many | messengers goes | forth the voice of | God,
f 'Give | ear to me, ye | continents, ye | isles, give ear to | me,
That the | earth may be filled with the | glory of God as the | waters cover the | sea.'

3

p What can we do to | work God's work, to | prosper and in- | crease
The | brotherhood of | all mankind, the | reign of the Prince of | Peace?
What can we do to | hasten the time, the | time that shall surely | be,
f When the | earth shall be filled with the | glory of God as the | waters cover the | sea?

4

March we forth in the | strength of God with the | banner of Christ un- | furled,
That the | light of the glorious | Gospel of truth may | shine throughout the | world.
Fight we the fight with | sorrow and sin, to | set their captives | free,
That the | earth may be filled with the | glory of God as the | waters cover the | sea.

5

p All we can do is | nothing worth un- | less God blesses the | deed;
Vainly we hope for the | harvest-tide till | God gives life to the | seed;
mf Yet | nearer and nearer | draws the time, the | time that shall surely | be,
f When the | earth shall be filled with the | glory of God as the | waters cover the | sea.

A. C. AINGER

GENERAL

HYMN 272 Dundee   *Psalms* (Edinburgh, 1615)

KEY E♭

```
{ :d   | m :f  | s :d   | r :m  | f      || m | r :d     | d :t,   | d :— | — ||
{ :s,  | d :d  | s, :s, | ta, :ta, | d    || d | t, :l,   | l, :s,  | s, :— | — ||
{ :m   | s :l  | r :m   | f :s  | l      || s | s :m     | f :r    | m :— | — ||
{ :d   | d :l, | t, :d  | ta, :s, | f,   || d | s, :l,   | f, :s,  | d :— | — ||


{ :s   | d¹ :t | l :s   | s :fe | s      || m | r :d     | d :t,   | d :— | — ||
{ :d   | m :r  | d :r   | m :r  | t,     || d | l, :m,.f,| s, :s,  | s, :— | — ||
{ :m   | s :s  | m :r   | l :l  | s      || s | f :d     | r :r    | m :— | — ||
{ :d   | d :s, | l, :t, | d :r  | s,     || d | f, :l,   | s, :s,  | d :— | — ||
```

ALTERNATIVE VERSION
(Melody in the Tenor part)

KEY E♭   Harmonized by T. Ravenscroft (1621)

```
{ :m   | s :l  | r :m   | f :s  | l      || s | s :m     | f :r    | m :— | — ||
{ :s,  | d :d  | t, :s, | ta, :ta, | d   || d | t, :l,   | l, :s,  | s, :— | — ||
{ :d   | m :f  | s :d   | r :m  | f      || m | r :d     | d :t,   | d :— | — ||
{ :d   | d :l, | t, :d  | ta, :s, | f,   || d | s, :l,   | f, :s,  | d :— | — ||


{ :m   | m :s  | f :r   | m :r  | r      || m | f :m.f   | s :r    | m :— | — ||
{ :s,  | s, :r | d :t,  | l, :l,| t,     || s,| l, :d    | s, :s,  | s, :— | — ||
{ :s   | d¹ :t | l :s   | s :fe | s      || m | r :d     | d :t,   | d :— | — ||
{ :d   | d :s, | l, :t, | d :r  | s,     || d | f, :l,   | s, :s,  | d :— | — ||
```

The Alternative Version may be used for verses 2 and 4

1

mf LET saints on earth in concert sing
    With those whose work is done;
  For all the servants of our King
    In heaven and earth are one.

2

One family, we dwell in him,
    One Church, above, beneath;
p Though now divided by the stream,
    The narrow stream of death.

3

mf One army of the living God,
    To his command we bow:
  Part of the host have crossed the flood,
p   And part are crossing now.

4

E'en now to their eternal home
    There pass some spirits blest;
While others to the margin come,
    Waiting their call to rest.

5

mf Jesu, be thou our constant guide;
f   Then, when the word is given,
  Bid Jordan's narrow stream divide,
    And bring us safe to heaven.

                                        C. WESLEY and others

GENERAL

HYMN 273 Vienna   J. H. Knecht, 1752–1817

KEY **G**

```
{| m :r  |d :m   | s  :f    |m :—  || l₁ :t₁ |d :r   |t₁ :l₁  |s₁ :— |
 | d :t₁ |l₁ :d  | d.s₁:l₁.t₁|d :— || f₁ :f₁ |m₁ :l₁ |s₁ :fe₁|s₁ :— |
 | s :—.f|m :m   | d  :f    |s :—  || d  :r  |m :r   |r :—.d|t₁ :— |
 | d :s₁ |l₁ :l₁ | m₁ :r₁   |d₁ :— || f₁ :r₁ |l₁ :fe₁|s₁ :r₁ |s₁ :— |}

{| d :t₁ |l₁ :d  | f  :m   |r :—   || s :f  |m :r  |d :t₁  |d :— |
 | m₁:s₁ |f₁ :s₁ | l₁.t₁:d |t₁ :—  || d :r  |d :l₁ |s₁ :s₁ |s₁ :—|
 | d :m  |d :m   | f  :s   |s :—   || s :s  |s :f  |m :r   |m :— |
 | l₁:m₁.|f₁ :m₁ | r₁ :m₁.f₁|s₁ :— || m :t₁ |d :f₁ |s₁ :s₁ |d₁ :—|}
```

    p   THEY whose course on earth is o'er,
           Think they of their brethren more?
           They before the throne who bow,
           Feel they for their brethren now?

2

We by enemies distrest,
They in Paradise at rest;
We the captives, they the freed—
We and they are one indeed.

3

Those whom many a land divides,
Many mountains, many tides,
Have they with each other part,
Fellowship of heart with heart?

4

Each to each may be unknown,
Wide apart their lots be thrown;
Differing tongues their lips may speak,
One be strong, and one be weak:

5

mf   Yet in Sacrament and prayer
     Each with other hath a share;
     Hath a share in tear and sigh,
     Watch and fast and litany.

6

Saints departed even thus
Hold communion still with us;
Still with us, beyond the veil
Praising, pleading, without fail.

7

f   With them still our hearts we raise,
    Share their work and join their praise,
    Rendering worship, thanks, and love
    To the Trinity above.
                             J. M. NEALE and Compilers

GENERAL

HYMN 274 Uffingham

KEY **A**

J. Clarke, *c.* 1659–1707

[sol-fa notation staves]

1. HE wants not friends that hath thy love,
   And may converse and walk with thee,
   And with thy saints here and above,
   With whom for ever I must be.

2. In the blest fellowship of saints
   Is wisdom, safety, and delight;
   And when my heart declines and faints,
   It's raised by their heat and light.

3. As for my friends, they are not lost;
   The several vessels of thy fleet,
   Though parted now, by tempests tost,
   Shall safely in the haven meet.

4. Still we are centred all in thee,
   Members, though distant, of one [Head;
   In the same family we be,
   By the same faith and spirit led.

5. Before thy throne we daily meet
   As joint-petitioners to thee;
   In spirit we each other greet,
   And shall again each other see.

6. The heavenly hosts, world without end,
   Shall be my company above;
   And thou, my best and surest Friend,
   Who shall divide me from thy love?

R. BAXTER†

HYMN 275 FIRST TUNE

KEY **G** Werde munter

J. Schop, *d.* 1644

[sol-fa notation staves]

286

GENERAL

(Sol-fa notation, first tune in f.C. and G.t.)

SECOND TUNE

KEY **G** St. Alphege H. J. Gauntlett, 1805–76

(Sol-fa notation)

Hic breve vivitur

p BRIEF life is here our portion,
    Brief sorrow, short-lived care:
mf The life that knows no ending,
    The tearless life, is there.
O happy retribution:
    Short toil, eternal rest;
For mortals and for sinners
    A mansion with the blest!

2
And now we fight the battle,
f   But then shall wear the crown
Of full and everlasting
    And passionless renown.
mf And now we watch and struggle,
    And now we live in hope,
And Sion in her anguish
    With Babylon must cope.

3
f But he whom now we trust in
    Shall then be seen and known,
And they that know and see him
    Shall have him for their own.
The morning shall awaken,
    The shadows shall decay,
And each true-hearted servant
    Shall shine as doth the day.

4
There God, our King and portion,
    In fulness of his grace,
Shall we behold for ever,
    And worship face to face.
Then all the halls of Sion
    For ay shall be complete,
And in the Land of Beauty
    All things of beauty meet.

BERNARD OF CLUNY
Tr. J. M. Neale†

GENERAL

Hymn 276 Pearsall   R. L. Pearsall, 1795-1856

KEY **D**

[sol-fa notation music, 4 systems]

Hora novissima

mf THE world is very evil,
  The times are waxing late;
Be sober and keep vigil,
  The Judge is at the gate:
The Judge who comes in mercy,
  The Judge who comes with might,
Who comes to end the evil,
  Who comes to crown the right.

2
Arise, arise, good Christian,
  Let right to wrong succeed;
Let penitential sorrow
  To heavenly gladness lead,
To light that has no evening,
  That knows no moon nor sun,
The light so new and golden,
  The light that is but one.

3
O home of fadeless splendour,
  Of flowers that bear no thorn,
Where they shall dwell as children
p Who here as exiles mourn!
mf 'Midst power that knows no limit,
  Where wisdom has no bound,
The beatific vision
  Shall glad the saints around.

4
O happy, holy portion,
  Refection for the blest,
True vision of true beauty,
  True cure of the distrest!
f Strive, man, to win that glory;
  Toil, man, to gain that light;
Send hope before to grasp it,
  Till hope be lost in sight.

BERNARD OF CLUNY
Tr. J. M. Neale†

GENERAL

HYMN 277 Holy Well   Traditional Carol
KEY F

O bona patria

mf FOR thee, O dear, dear country,
　Mine eyes their vigils keep;
For very love, beholding
　Thy happy name, they weep.
The mention of thy glory
　Is unction to the breast,
And medicine in sickness,
　And love and life and rest.

2
O one, O only mansion!
　O Paradise of joy!
Where tears are ever banished,
　And smiles have no alloy;
The Lamb is all thy splendour,
　The Crucified thy praise;
His laud and benediction
　Thy ransomed people raise.

3
With jasper glow thy bulwarks,
　Thy streets with emeralds blaze;
The sardius and the topaz
　Unite in thee their rays;
Thine ageless walls are bonded
　With amethyst unpriced;
The saints build up thy fabric,
　Thy Corner-stone is Christ.

4
Thou hast no shore, fair ocean!
　Thou hast no time, bright day!
Dear fountain of refreshment
　To pilgrims far away!
f Upon the Rock of ages
　They raise thy holy tower;
Thine is the victor's laurel,
　And thine the golden dower.

BERNARD OF CLUNY
Tr. J. M. Neale†

GENERAL

HYMN 278 Ewing
KEY D
A. Ewing, 1830–95

Urbs Sion aurea

mf JERUSALEM the golden,
  With milk and honey blest,
Beneath thy contemplation
  Sink heart and voice opprest.
I know not, O, I know not
  What joys await us there,
What radiancy of glory,
  What bliss beyond compare.

2

f They stand, those halls of Sion,
  All jubilant with song,
And bright with many an angel,
  And all the martyr throng;
The Prince is ever with them,
  The daylight is serene,
The pastures of the blessèd
  Are decked in glorious sheen.

3

mf There is the throne of David;
  And there, from care released,
The shout of them that triumph,
  The song of them that feast;
f And they, who with their Leader
  Have conquered in the fight,
For ever and for ever
  Are clad in robes of white.

4

mf O sweet and blessèd country,
  The home of God's elect!
O sweet and blessèd country
  That eager hearts expect!
p Jesu, in mercy bring us
  To that dear land of rest;
mf Who art, with God the Father
  And Spirit, ever blest.

BERNARD OF CLUNY
Tr. J. M. Neale and Compiler

GENERAL

HYMN 279 Regent Square   H. Smart, 1813–79

KEY **C**

```
{ s :m  |d':s  | m':-.r'|d':s  || l :l  |s :d'  | s :f  |m :—  ||
{ m :d  |s :m  | s :-.s |s :s  || d :d  |d :d   | r :t₁ |d :—  ||
{ d':s  |s :d' | d':-.t |d':d' || l :d' |s :l   | s :s  |s :—  ||
{ d :d  |m :d  | s :-.f |m :m  || f :f  |m :l₁  | t₁:s₁ |d :—  ||


{ s :m  |d':s  | m':-.r'|d':t  || d':t  |l :t.d'| t :l  |s :—  ||
{ m :d  |s :s.f| m :-.f |m :m  || m :m  |m :m   | s :fe |s :—  ||
{ d':d' |s :s  | d':-.t |l :se || l :s  |m':r'.d'| r':d'|t :—  ||
{ d':s  |m :m.r| d :-.r |m :m  || l :m  |d :l₁  | r :r  |s₁:—  ||


{ r':-.r'|t :s | m':-.r'|d':l  || f':m' |r' :d' | d':t  |d':—  ||
{ s :-.s |s :s | s :-.m |f :f  || l :s  |f  :m.f| s :-.f|m :—  ||
{ t :-.t |r':t | d':-.ta|l :d' || r':s  |l.t:d' | r':r' |d':—  ||
{ s :-.s |s :s | d :-.d |f :f  || r :m  |f.s:l  | s :s₁ |d :—  ||
```

Jerusalem luminosa

1

LIGHT'S abode, celestial Salem,
  Vision whence true peace doth spring,
Brighter than the heart can fancy,
  Mansion of the highest King;
O how glorious are the praises
  Which of thee the prophets sing!

2

There for ever and for ever
  Alleluia is outpoured;
For unending, for unbroken
  Is the feast-day of the Lord;
All is pure and all is holy
  That within thy walls is stored.

3

There no cloud or passing vapour
  Dims the brightness of the air;
Endless noon-day, glorious noon-day,
  From the Sun of suns is there;
There no night brings rest from labour,
  For unknown are toil and care.

4*

O how glorious and resplendent,
  Fragile body, shalt thou be,
When endued with so much beauty,
  Full of health and strong and free,
Full of vigour, full of pleasure
  That shall last eternally!

5*

Now with gladness, now with courage,
  Bear the burden on thee laid,
That hereafter these thy labours
  May with endless gifts be paid;
And in everlasting glory
  Thou with brightness be arrayed.

[UNISON]   6

Laud and honour to the Father,
  Laud and honour to the Son,
Laud and honour to the Spirit,
  Ever Three and ever One,
Consubstantial, co-eternal,
  While unending ages run.

Ascribed to THOMAS à KEMPIS
Tr. J. M. Neale†

GENERAL

HYMN 280 Christchurch
C. Steggall, 1826–1905

KEY C

[sol-fa notation]

G.t.

[sol-fa notation]

f.C.

[sol-fa notation]

mf JERUSALEM on high
　My song and city is,
My home whene'er I die,
　The centre of my bliss:
f　O happy place!
　　When shall I be,
　My God, with thee,
　　To see thy face?

2

mf There dwells my Lord, my King,
　Judged here unfit to live;
There angels to him sing,
　And lowly homage give:
f　O happy, etc.

3

mf The patriarchs of old
　There from their travels cease;
The prophets there behold
　Their longed-for Prince of Peace:
f　O happy, etc.

4

mf The Lamb's apostles there
　I might with joy behold,
The harpers I might hear
　Harping on harps of gold:
f　O happy, etc.

5

mf The bleeding martyrs, they
　Within those courts are found,
Clothèd in pure array,
　Their scars with glory crowned:
f　O happy, etc.

6

p Ah me! ah me! that I
　In Kedar's tents here stay:
No place like that on high;
　Lord, thither guide my way;
f　O happy, etc.

S. CROSSMAN

HYMN 281 O quanta qualia
La Feillée, *Méthode*, 1808

KEY G

[sol-fa notation]

292

GENERAL

O quanta qualia sunt illa sabbata

mf O WHAT their joy and their glory must be,
Those endless sabbaths the blessèd ones see!
Crown for the valiant, to weary ones rest;
God shall be all, and in all ever blest.

2*

What are the Monarch, his court, and his throne?
What are the peace and the joy that they own?
O that the blest ones, who in it have share,
All that they feel could as fully declare!

3

Truly Jerusalem name we that shore,
'Vision of peace,' that brings joy evermore!
Wish and fulfilment can severed be ne'er,
Nor the thing prayed for come short of the prayer.

4

There, where no troubles distraction can bring,
We the sweet anthems of Sion shall sing,
While for thy grace, Lord, their voices of praise
Thy blessèd people eternally raise.

5*

There dawns no sabbath, no sabbath is o'er,
Those sabbath-keepers have one evermore;
f One and unending is that triumph-song
Which to the angels and us shall belong.

p 6
Now in the meanwhile, with hearts raised on high,
We for that country must yearn and must sigh;
Seeking Jerusalem, dear native land,
Through our long exile on Babylon's strand.

mf 7
Low before him with our praises we fall,
Of whom, and in whom, and through whom are all:
f Of whom, the Father; and in whom, the Son;
Through whom, the Spirit, with them ever One.

PETER ABELARD *Tr.* J. M. NEALE‡

GENERAL

HYMN 282 Southwell   H. S. Irons, 1834–1905

KEY E

mf JERUSALEM, my happy home,
    Name ever dear to me,
When shall my labours have an end?
    Thy joys when shall I see?

2

When shall these eyes thy heaven-built walls
    And pearly gates behold?
Thy bulwarks with salvation strong,
    And streets of shining gold?

3

f Apostles, martyrs, prophets, there
    Around my Saviour stand;
And all I love in Christ below
    Will join the glorious band.

4

mf Jerusalem, my happy home,
    When shall I come to thee?
When shall my labours have an end?
    Thy joys when shall I see?

5

O Christ, do thou my soul prepare
    For that bright home of love;
That I may see thee and adore,
    With all thy saints above.

'F.B.P.' (*c.* 1600) and Compilers

NOTE. *The poem on which this hymn is based will be found (abbreviated) in the 'Processional' section (623)*

GENERAL

HYMN 283 St. Sebastian Sir P. C. Buck, 1871–1947

KEY **C**

UNISON

{ :s | l :s.f | s :d¹ | t :l | s :m | d :— | — :r | m :—.r | m :fe | s :l }

{ | t :r¹ | s : s | d¹ :—.t | l :s.f | s :d | r :— | d :— | — || }

By permission of Stainer & Bell, Ltd.

Alleluia piis edite laudibus

[FULL]

SING Alleluia forth in duteous praise,
Ye citizens of heaven; O sweetly raise
                An endless Alleluia.

[MEN] 2

Ye powers who stand before the eternal Light,
In hymning choirs re-echo to the height
                An endless Alleluia.

[TREBLES] 3

The holy city shall take up your strain,
And with glad songs resounding wake again
                An endless Alleluia.

[MEN] 4

In blissful antiphons ye thus rejoice
To render to the Lord with thankful voice
                An endless Alleluia.

[TREBLES] 5

Ye who have gained at length your palms in bliss,
Victorious ones, your chant shall still be this:
                An endless Alleluia.

[MEN] 6

There, in one grand acclaim, for ever ring
The strains which tell the honour of your King:
                An endless Alleluia.

[TREBLES] 7

This is sweet rest for weary ones brought back,
This is glad food and drink which ne'er shall lack:
                An endless Alleluia.

[MEN] 8

While thee, by whom were all things made, we praise
For ever, and tell out in sweetest lays
                An endless Alleluia.

[FULL] 9

Almighty Christ, to thee our voices sing,
Glory for evermore; to thee we bring
                An endless Alleluia.

MOZARABIC (5th–8th cent.)
Tr. J. Ellerton

GENERAL

HYMN **284** Alford J. B. Dykes, 1823–76

KEY **B♭**

[sol-fa notation]

1. *f* TEN thousand times ten thousand,
   In sparkling raiment bright,
   The armies of the ransomed saints
   Throng up the steeps of light:
   mf 'Tis finished! all is finished,
   Their fight with death and sin;
   f Fling open wide the golden gates,
   And let the victors in.

2. What rush of Alleluias
   Fills all the earth and sky!
   What ringing of a thousand harps
   Bespeaks the triumph nigh!
   O day, for which creation
   And all its tribes were made!
   O joy, for all its former woes
   A thousand-fold repaid!

3. *mf* O then what raptured greetings
   On Canaan's happy shore,
   What knitting severed friendships up,
   Where partings are no more!
   Then eyes with joy shall sparkle
   That brimmed with tears of late:
   Orphans no longer fatherless,
   Nor widows desolate.

4. Bring near thy great salvation,
   Thou Lamb for sinners slain,
   f Fill up the roll of thine elect,
   Then take thy power and reign:
   mf Appear, Desire of Nations;
   Thine exiles long for home; [sign;
   f Show in the heavens thy promised
   Thou Prince and Saviour, come.

H. ALFORD

296

GENERAL

HYMN 285 Beulah G. M. Garrett, 1834–97

KEY **E**

f THERE is a land of pure delight,
Where saints immortal reign;
Infinite day excludes the night,
And pleasures banish pain.

2

There everlasting spring abides,
And never-withering flowers;
p Death, like a narrow sea, divides
That heavenly land from ours.

3

mf Sweet fields beyond the swelling flood
Stand dressed in living green;
So to the Jews old Canaan stood,
While Jordan rolled between.

4

p But timorous mortals start and shrink
To cross the narrow sea,
And linger shivering on the brink,
And fear to launch away.

5

mf O could we make our doubts remove,
Those gloomy doubts that rise,
And see the Canaan that we love
With unbeclouded eyes;

6

f Could we but climb where Moses stood,
And view the landscape o'er;
Nor Jordan's stream, nor death's cold flood,
Should fright us from the shore.

I. WATTS

GENERAL

HYMN 286 Vulpius   Melody by M. Vulpius, *c.* 1560–1616

KEY E♭

1. My soul, there is a country Far beyond the stars, Where stands a wingèd sentry All skilful in the wars:
2. There above noise, and danger, Sweet peace sits crowned with smiles, And One born in a manger Commands the beauteous files.
3. He is thy gracious Friend, And — O my soul, awake! — Did in pure love descend, To die here for thy sake.
4. If thou canst get but thither, There grows the flower of peace, The Rose that cannot wither, Thy fortress and thy ease.
5. Leave then thy foolish ranges, For none can thee secure But one who never changes, Thy God, thy life, thy cure.

HENRY VAUGHAN

GENERAL

HYMN 287 Woolmer's   Sir F. A. G. Ouseley, 1825–89

KEY **F**

mf THEY come, God's messengers of love,
They come from realms of peace above,
From homes of never-fading light,
From blissful mansions ever bright.

2

They come to watch around us here,
To soothe our sorrow, calm our fear:
Ye heavenly guides, speed not away;
God willeth you with us to stay.

3

p But chiefly at its journey's end
'Tis yours the spirit to befriend,
And whisper to the faithful heart,
'O Christian soul, in peace depart.'

4

Blest Jesu, thou whose groans and tears
Have sanctified frail nature's fears,
To earth in bitter sorrow weighed,
Thou didst not scorn thine angel's aid:

5

mf An angel guard to us supply,
When on the bed of death we lie;
And by thine own almighty power
p O shield us in the last dread hour.

6

f To God the Father, God the Son,
And God the Spirit, Three in One,
From all above and all below
Let joyful praise unceasing flow.

R. CAMPBELL and others

GENERAL

Hymn 288 Trisagion

H. Smart, 1813-79

KEY **G**

f STARS of the morning, so gloriously bright,
Filled with celestial virtue and light,
These that, where night never followeth day,
Praise the Thrice-Holy for ever and ay:

2

mf These are thy ministers, these dost thou own,
Lord God of Sabaoth, nearest thy throne;
These are thy messengers, these dost thou send,
Help of the helpless ones, man to defend.

3

These keep the guard amidst Salem's dear bowers,
Thrones, Principalities, Virtues, and Powers,
Where, with the Living Ones, mystical four,
Cherubim, Seraphim, bow and adore.

4

Then, when the earth was first poised in mid space,
Then, when the planets first sped on their race,
Then, when was ended the six days' employ,
f Then all the sons of God shouted for joy.

5

mf Still let them succour us; still let them fight,
Lord of angelic hosts, battling for right;
f Till, where their anthems they ceaselessly pour,
We with the angels may bow and adore.

J. M. NEALE† Based on φωστῆρες τῆς ἀΰλου,
St. Joseph the Hymnographer

GENERAL

HYMN 289 Kocher J. H. Knecht, 1752–1817

KEY F

mf O HAPPY band of pilgrims,
　　If onward ye will tread
　With Jesus as your fellow
　　To Jesus as your Head!

2

O happy if ye labour
　As Jesus did for men!
O happy if ye hunger
　As Jesus hungered then!

3

p　The Cross that Jesus carried
　　　He carried as your due:
f　The Crown that Jesus weareth
　　　He weareth it for you.

4

mf　The faith by which ye see him,
　　　The hope in which ye yearn,
　　The love that through all troubles
　　　To him alone will turn.

5

p　The trials that beset you,
　　　The sorrows ye endure,
　　The manifold temptations
　　　That death alone can cure.

6

mf　What are they but his jewels
　　　Of right celestial worth?
　　What are they but the ladder
　　　Set up to heaven on earth?

7

f　O happy band of pilgrims,
　　　Look upward to the skies,
　　Where such a light affliction
　　　Shall win so great a prize.

J. M. NEALE

GENERAL

HYMN 290 Wiltshire   Sir G. Smart, 1776–1867
KEY **A**

Psalm 34

mf THROUGH all the changing scenes of life,
   In trouble and in joy,
The praises of my God shall still
   My heart and tongue employ.

2

O magnify the Lord with me,
   With me exalt his name;
When in distress to him I called,
   He to my rescue came.

3

The hosts of God encamp around
   The dwellings of the just;
Deliverance he affords to all
   Who on his succour trust.

4

O make but trial of his love:
   Experience will decide
How blest are they, and only they,
   Who in his truth confide.

5

Fear him, ye saints, and you will then
   Have nothing else to fear;
Make you his service your delight,
   Your wants shall be his care.

6

f To Father, Son, and Holy Ghost,
   The God whom we adore,
Be glory, as it was, is now,
   And shall be evermore.

N. TATE and N. BRADY (*New Version*)

GENERAL

HYMN 291 University College   H. J. Gauntlett, 1805–76
KEY **F**

{| m :d |l :s | f :m |r :— ‖ m :d |s :s | s :fe |s :— ‖
 | d :d |d :d | r :d |t₁:— ‖ d :d |m :r | d :d |t₁:— ‖
 | s :m |f :s | s :s |s :— ‖ s :s |s :s | l :l |r :— ‖
 | d :d |f :m | t₁:d |s₁:— ‖ d :m |d :t₁ | l₁:l₁ |s₁:— ‖

{| m :r |d :l | s :f |m :—   ‖ m :m |s :m | m :r |d :— ‖
 | d :t₁ |d :d | d :d.t₁ |d :—   ‖ t₁:d |t₁:d | d :t₁ |d :— ‖
 | m :s.f |m :f.m | r :s |s :—   ‖ m :d |r :m.f | s :s.f |m :— ‖
 | d :s₁ |l₁:f₁ | s₁:s₁ |d :—   ‖ se₁:l₁|s₁:d | s₁:s₁ |d :— ‖

   mf OFT in danger, oft in woe,
        Onward, Christians, onward go;
        Bear the toil, maintain the strife,
        Strengthened with the Bread of Life.

2
Onward, Christians, onward go,
Join the war, and face the foe;
Will ye flee in danger's hour?
Know ye not your Captain's power?

3
Let not sorrow dim your eye;
Soon shall every tear be dry:
Let not fears your course impede;
  f Great your strength, if great your need.

4
  mf Let your drooping hearts be glad;
March in heavenly armour clad;
Fight, nor think the battle long:
  f Soon shall victory wake your song.

5
Onward then in battle move;
More than conquerors ye shall prove:
Though opposed by many a foe,
Christian soldiers, onward go.

H. KIRK WHITE and others

303

GENERAL

Hymn 292   FIRST TUNE

KEY **G**   Rustington   Sir C. H. H. Parry, 1848–1918

[Sol-fa notation musical score]

D.t.

[Sol-fa notation musical score]

f. G.

[Sol-fa notation musical score]

[Sol-fa notation musical score]

KEY **D**   St. Oswald   SECOND TUNE   J. B. Dykes, 1823–76

DESCANT

[Sol-fa notation musical score]

[Sol-fa notation musical score]

When Second Tune is used the Descant may be sung for the last four lines of verses 2 and 4

GENERAL

Igjennem Nat og Trængsel

mf THROUGH the night of doubt and sorrow
    Onward goes the pilgrim band,
Singing songs of expectation,
    Marching to the Promised Land.
Clear before us through the darkness
    Gleams and burns the guiding light;
Brother clasps the hand of brother,
    Stepping fearless through the night.

2

One the light of God's own presence
    O'er his ransomed people shed,
Chasing far the gloom and terror,
    Brightening all the path we tread:
One the object of our journey,
    One the faith which never tires,
One the earnest looking forward,
    One the hope our God inspires:

3*

f One the strain that lips of thousands
    Lift as from the heart of one:
One the conflict, one the peril,
    One the march in God begun:
One the gladness of rejoicing
    On the far eternal shore,
Where the one almighty Father
    Reigns in love for evermore.

4

nf Onward, therefore, pilgrim brothers,
    Onward with the Cross our aid;
Bear its shame, and fight its battle,
    Till we rest beneath its shade.
f Soon shall come the great awaking,
    Soon the rending of the tomb;
Then the scattering of all shadows,
    And the end of toil and gloom.

                        B. S. INGEMANN *Tr.* S. Baring-Gould

Alternative Tune, Marching, 182

GENERAL

HYMN 293 Bunyan *Christen-schatz* (Basle, 1745)

KEY B♭

[sol-fa notation]

1

WHO would true valour see,
  Let him come hither;
One here will constant be,
  Come wind, come weather;
There's no discouragement
Shall make him once relent
His first avowed intent
  To be a pilgrim.

2

Whoso beset him round
  With dismal stories,
Do but themselves confound;
  His strength the more is.
No lion can him fright;
He'll with a giant fight,
But he will have the right
  To be a pilgrim.

3

No goblin nor foul fiend
  Can daunt his spirit;
He knows he at the end
  Shall life inherit.
Then, fancies, fly away;
He'll not fear what men say;
He'll labour night and day
  To be a pilgrim.

JOHN BUNYAN†

GENERAL

HYMN 294 Ave virgo

KEY **G**

Medieval melody as given by
J. Horn (1544)

{ | d :d | s₁ :s₁ | d :r | m :— || l :— | s :— | f :m | r :— | d :— ||
  | s₁ :l₁ | r :m₁ | m₁ :s₁ | s₁ :— || l₁ :— | t₁ :— | d :d | d :t₁ | d :— ||
  | m :f | t₁ :t₁ | d :t₁ | d :— || f :m | r :— | l :s | s :— | m :— ||
  | d :f₁ | s₁ :m₁ | l₁ :s₁ | d :— || f₁ :— | s₁ :— | l₁ :d | s₁ :— | d :— || }

{ | d :d | s₁ :s₁ | d :r | m :— || l :— | s :— | f :m | r :— | d :— ||
  | m₁ :f₁ | s₁ :s₁ | l₁ :l₁ | l₁ :se₁ || l₁ :— | ta₁ :l₁ | l₁ :d | d :t₁ | d :— ||
  | d :d | r :m | m :l₁ | t₁ :— || f :m | r :de | r :s | l :s | m :— ||
  | l₁ :l₁ | t₁ :d | l₁ :f₁ | m₁ :— || f₁ :— | s₁ :l₁ | r₁ :m₁ | f₁ :s₁ | d₁ :— || }

{ | s :— | l :— | s :f | m :m | r :— || m :— :r | d :— :t₁ | l₁ :— | s₁ :— ||
  | d :— | d :— | t₁ :l₁ | s₁ :s₁ | s₁ :— || m₁ :fe₁ :s₁ | s :fe₁ :s₁ | s₁ :fe₁ | s₁ :— ||
  | m :— | f :m | r :d | d :d | t₁ :— || d :— :r | m :d | m | m :r | t₁ :— ||
  | d :— | f₁ :— | s₁ :l₁ | d :m₁ | s₁ :— || d :— :t₁ | l₁ :— :m₁ | d₁ :r₁ | s₁ :— || }

{ | d :d | s₁ :s₁ | d :r | m :— || l :— | s :— | f :m | r :— | d :— ||
  | m₁ :f₁ | r₁ :s₁ | l₁ :t₁ | d :— || l₁ :— | ta₁ :l₁ | l₁ :d | d :t₁ | d :— ||
  | d :l₁ | t₁ :t₁ | s :f | m :— || f :m | r :de | r :s | l :s | m :— ||
  | l₁ :f₁ | s₁ :m₁ | m :r | l₁ :s₁ || f₁ :— | s₁ :l₁ | r₁ :m₁ | f₁ :s₁ | d₁ :— || }

BROTHERS, joining hand to hand
  In one bond united,
Pressing onward to that land
  Where all wrongs are righted:
Let your words and actions be
  Worthy your vocation;
Chosen of the Lord, and free,
  Heirs of Christ's salvation.

2
Christ, the Way, the Truth, the Life,
  Who hath gone before you
Through the turmoil and the strife,
  Holds his banner o'er you:
All who see the sacred sign
  Press towards heaven's portal,
Fired by hope that is divine,
  Love that is immortal.

3
They who follow fear no foe,
  Care not who assail them;
Where the Master leads they go,
  He will never fail them.
Courage, brothers! we are one,
  In the love that sought us;
Soon the warfare shall be done,
  Through the grace he brought us.

J. A. WARNER

GENERAL

HYMN 295 Bewdley
Sir F. A. G. Ouseley, 1825–89

KEY **A**

[sol-fa notation]

f.D.   A.t.

[sol-fa notation]

mf CHILDREN of the heavenly King,
As ye journey, sweetly sing;
Sing your Saviour's worthy praise,
Glorious in his works and ways.

2
We are travelling home to God
In the way the fathers trod;
They are happy now, and we
Soon their happiness shall see.

3
f Lift your eyes, ye sons of light!
Sion's city is in sight;
There our endless home shall be,
There our Lord we soon shall see.

4
Fear not, brethren! joyful stand
On the borders of your land;
Jesus Christ, your Father's Son
Bids you undismayed go on.

5
p Lord, obedient we would go,
Gladly leaving all below;
mf Only thou our leader be,
f And we still will follow thee.

J. CENNICK†

Alternative Tune, Innocents, 191

HYMN 296   FIRST TUNE
KEY **E** Pilgrimage
Sir G. J. Elvey, 1816–93

[sol-fa notation]

308

GENERAL

SECOND TUNE

KEY A♭ Cwm Rhondda   J. Hughes, 1873–1932

Arglwydd arwain trwy'r anialwch

mf GUIDE me, O thou great Redeemer,
   Pilgrim through this barren land;
I am weak, but thou art mighty;
   Hold me with thy powerful hand:
      Bread of heaven,
   Feed me now and evermore.

2

Open now the crystal fountain
   Whence the healing stream doth flow;
Let the fiery cloudy pillar
   Lead me all my journey through:
      Strong deliverer,
f Be thou still my strength and shield.

3

p When I tread the verge of Jordan,
   Bid my anxious fears subside;
f Death of death, and hell's destruction,
   Land me safe on Canaan's side:
      Songs and praises
   I will ever give to thee.

W. WILLIAMS
Tr. P. and W. Williams‡

GENERAL

HYMN 297 Ladywell   W. H. Ferguson, 1872-1950
KEY A♭

By permission of the Royal School of Church Music

f LIFT up your voice, ye Christian folk,
   To praise the Holy One,
Who ransoms us from Satan's yoke
   Through Christ, his blessed Son.
mf Lo, we who were in grievous state
   By reason of our sin,
f Our heads look up, our fears abate,
   Our triumphs now begin.

2
p The mists hung cold, the night was black,
   About the way we trod;
Our feet were stumbling from the track
   Which leads the soul to God.
mf But Christ, who broke from death's dark shroud,
   Hath sent his quickening ray:
f The sun breaks through the drifting cloud,
   And now 'tis glorious day.

3
Lift up your voice! with shout and song
   Extol his majesty,
Whose power hath made the feeble strong
   And caused the blind to see.
And when the sound of praise grows dim
   Still may our lives forth tell,
In all we do, our love of him
   Who doeth all things well.

P. H. B. LYON

GENERAL

HYMN 298 — FIRST TUNE

KEY **C** Alberta
IN UNISON
W. H. Harris

(Tonic sol-fa notation)

By permission of the Oxford University Press

KEY **A♭** Lux benigna — SECOND TUNE
J. B. Dykes, 1823–76

(Tonic sol-fa notation)

mf LEAD, kindly Light, amid the encircling gloom,
   Lead thou me on;
p The night is dark, and I am far from home;
   Lead thou me on.
mf Keep thou my feet; I do not ask to see
   The distant scene; one step enough for me.

2

I was not ever thus, nor prayed that thou
   Shouldst lead me on;
I loved to choose and see my path; but now
   Lead thou me on.
I loved the garish day, and, spite of fears,
Pride ruled my will: remember not past years.

3

So long thy power hath blest me, sure it still
   Will lead me on,
O'er moor and fen, o'er crag and torrent, till
   The night is gone,
And with the morn those angel faces smile,
Which I have loved long since, and lost a while.

CARDINAL J. H. NEWMAN

GENERAL

HYMN 298

THIRD TUNE

KEY **G** Sandon

C. H. Purday, 1799–1885

mf LEAD, kindly Light, amid the encircling gloom.
　　Lead thou me on;
p The night is dark, and I am far from home;
　　Lead thou me on.
mf Keep thou my feet; I do not ask to see
　The distant scene; one step enough for me.

2

I was not ever thus, nor prayed that thou
　　Shouldst lead me on;
I loved to choose and see my path; but now
　　Lead thou me on.
I loved the garish day, and, spite of fears,
Pride ruled my will: remember not past years.

3

So long thy power hath blest me, sure it still
　　Will lead me on,
O'er moor and fen, o'er crag and torrent, till
　　The night is gone,
And with the morn those angel faces smile,
Which I have loved long since, and lost a while.

CARDINAL J. H. NEWMAN

GENERAL

HYMN 299
KEY **D** Stracathro

FIRST TUNE

Melody by C. Hutcheson, 1792–1860
from *Christian Vespers*, Glasgow, 1832

From *Enlarged Songs of Praise* by permission of the Oxford University Press

SECOND TUNE

KEY **G** Martyrdom   H. Wilson, 1766–1824

mf O GOD of Bethel, by whose hand
    Thy people still are fed,
Who through this weary pilgrimage
    Hast all our fathers led;

2
Our vows, our prayers, we now present
    Before thy throne of grace;
God of our fathers, be the God
    Of their succeeding race.

3
p Through each perplexing path of life
    Our wandering footsteps guide;
Give us each day our daily bread,
    And raiment fit provide.

4
mf O spread thy covering wings around,
    Till all our wanderings cease,
And at our Father's loved abode
    Our souls arrive in peace.

                                            P. DODDRIDGE

GENERAL

Hymn 300 Abridge
I. Smith, c. 1735–1800

KEY D

[sol-fa notation music staves]

mf BE thou my guardian and my guide,
    And hear me when I call;
Let not my slippery footsteps slide,
    And holds me lest I fall.

2
p The world, the flesh, and Satan dwell
    Around the path I tread;
O save me from the snares of hell,
    Thou quickener of the dead.

3
And if I tempted am to sin,
    And outward things are strong,
Do thou, O Lord, keep watch within,
    And save my soul from wrong.

4
mf Still let me ever watch and pray,
    And feel that I am frail;
That if the tempter cross my way,
    Yet he may not prevail.

I. WILLIAMS

Hymn 301 York
Psalms (Edinburgh, 1615)

KEY F

[sol-fa notation music staves]

GENERAL

HE that is down need fear no fall,
　　He that is low no pride;
He that is humble ever shall
　　Have God to be his guide.

2

I am content with what I have,
　　Little be it of much;
And, Lord, contentment still I crave,
　　Because thou savest such.

3

Fullness to such a burden is
　　That go on pilgrimage;
Here little, and herafter bliss,
　　Is best from age to age.

JOHN BUNYAN

HYMN 302　Totteridge　　　　Sir S. H. Nicholson, 1875–1947

KEY C

{ | m :f :s | l :— :d¹ | r¹ :— | s | d¹ :— :s | l :s :f | s :— ||
  | d :d :s | s :f :s | s :— | s | s :f :m | d :m :f | r :— ||
  | s :s :d¹ | d¹ :— :d¹ | t :— | t | d¹ :— :d¹.t | l :t :d¹ | d¹ :t ||
  | d :r :m | f :— :m | s :— | f | m :r :d | f :s :l | s :— || }

{ | :d¹ | r¹ :s | m¹ :t | d¹ :l | s :— | l :r¹ :—.t | d¹ :— :— ||
  | :s | l :s | se :m | m :f.m | r :d | d :f :—.f | m :— :— ||
  | :d¹ | d¹ :t | t :r¹ | d¹ :d¹ | t :d¹ | l :l :—.s | s :— :— ||
  | :m | f :s.f | m :se | l :r | f :m | f :r :—.s | d :— :— || }

RISE in the strength of God,
　　And face life's uphill way:
The steps which other feet have trod
　　You tread to-day.

2

Press onward, upward still,
　　To win your way at last,
With better hope and stronger will
　　Than in the past:

3

Life's work more nobly wrought,
　　Life's race more bravely run,
Life's daily conflict faced and fought,
　　Life's duty done.

ADA R. GREENAWAY

315

GENERAL

HYMN 303 St. Ethelwald
KEY **G**
W. H. Monk, 1823–89

{ :s | f :m | r :m.f | m :— | — | m | r :s₁ | l₁ :l₁ | s₁ :— | — ||
:d | l₁.t₁:d | d :t₁ | d :— | — | s₁ | s₁ :s₁ | s₁ :fe₁ | s₁ :— | — ||
:m | f :s | l :s | s :— | — | d | r :m.r | m :r | t₁ :— | — ||
:d | r :m | f :s | d :— | — | d | t₁ :d.t₁| d :r | s₁ :— | — ||

{ :s₁ | l₁ :t₁ | d :m | r :r | m | m | f :m | r :r | d :— | — ||
:s₁ | s₁ :f₁ | m₁ :d.t₁ | l₁ :l₁ | se₁ | l₁ | l₁.t₁:d | d :t₁ | d :— | — ||
:t₁ | d :r | d :d | r.d:t₁.l₁| t₁ | de | r :d | d.r:m.f | m :— | — ||
:s₁ | f₁ :r₁ | l₁ :l₁.s₁| f₁ :f₁ | m₁ | l₁ | r₁ :m₁.f₁| s₁ :s₁ | d₁ :— | — ||

SOLDIERS of Christ, arise,
And put your armour on,
Strong in the strength which God supplies,
Through his eternal Son;

2
Strong in the Lord of Hosts,
And in his mighty power:
Who in the strength of Jesus trusts
Is more than conqueror.

3
Stand then in his great might,
With all his strength endued;
And take, to arm you for the fight,
The panoply of God.

4
From strength to strength go on,
Wrestle and fight and pray;
Tread all the powers of darkness down,
And win the well-fought day;

5
That, having all things done,
And all your conflicts past,
Ye may o'ercome, through Christ alone,
And stand entire at last.

C. WESLEY

HYMN 304
KEY **D** Duke Street
FIRST TUNE
Attributed to J. Hatton, *d.* 1793

{ d :m.f | s :l.t | d' :t.l | s :— | s :s.s | l :—.s | f :m | r :— ||
d :d.t₁ | d :m | d.m:r.d | t₁ :— | d :t₁.d | d :d | l₁.t₁:d | t₁ :— ||
m :s.f | m :m | l :fe | s :— | m :f.s | f :d' | f :s | s :— ||
d :d.r | m :d.t₁ | l₁ :r | s₁ :— | d :r.m | f :m | r :d | s₁ :— ||

GENERAL

```
{| m :m .r  | d.m :s .d' | l.s :f.m | r :—  || s :l .t    | d' :—.f   | m :r    | d :—  ||
 | d :t,.t, | d :d       | d :r.d   | r :—  || d :f .f    | m.f:s.d   | d :t,   | s, :— ||
 | s :s .f  | m.l :s     | f :l     | t :—  || d' :d'.f   | s :—.l    | s :—.f  | m :—  ||
 | d :s,.s, | l, :m      | f :r     | s :f  || m :f .r    | d.r:m.f   | s :s,   | d :—  ||}
```

SECOND TUNE

KEY **G** Pentecost   W. Boyd, 1847–1928

```
{| m :m :m  | m :— :m  | r :— :d  | f :— :—  || m :m :m  | m :— :r   | r :— :d   | r :— :—  ||
 | s,:s,:s, | s,:— :d  | t,:— :d  | t,:— :—  || s,:s,:d  | l, :—:l,  | l, :—:fe, | s, :— :— ||
 | d :d :d  | d.m :s   | s :— :s  | s :— :—  || d :m :s  | s :— :f   | r :— :r   | t,:— :—  ||
 | d :d :d  | d :— :d  | f :— :m, | r :— :—  || d :d :d  | f, :—:f,  | fe,:—:l,  | s,:— :— ||}

{| m :m :m  | m :— :m  | r :— :m  | f :— :—  || r :r :r  | m :— :d   | d :— :t,  | d :— :—  ||
 | s,:s,:se,| l,:— :l, | l,:— :l, | l,:— :—  || s,:s,:s, | s,:— :l,  | s,:— :s,  | m,:— :—  ||
 | m :m :r  | d :— :de | r :— :de | r :— :—  || t,:t,:t, | d :s :f   | f :m :r   | d :— :—  ||
 | d :d :t, | l,:— :s, | f,:—:m,  | r, :— :— || s,:s,:s, | m,:—:f,   | s,:— :s,  | d,:— :— ||}
```

By permission of Novello & Co., Ltd.

f   FIGHT the good fight with all thy might!
    Christ is thy strength, and Christ thy right;
    Lay hold on life, and it shall be
    Thy joy and crown eternally.

2

    Run the straight race through God's good grace,
    Lift up thine eyes, and seek his face;
    Life with its way before us lies;
    Christ is the path, and Christ the prize.

3

mf   Cast care aside, lean on thy guide;
    His boundless mercy will provide;
    Trust, and thy trusting soul shall prove
    Christ is its life, and Christ its love.

4

f   Faint not nor fear, his arms are near;
    He changeth not, and thou are dear;
    Only believe, and thou shalt see
    That Christ is all in all to thee.

J. S. B. MONSELL†

GENERAL

HYMN 305 Crucis milites　　　　　　　　　M. B. Foster, 1851-1922
KEY E

```
{| s  :m  |r  :d   |f  :l   |s  :-   || d' :s  |l  :s   |m  :r.d |r  :-  ||
 | d  :d  |t, :d   |d  :-.r |m  :-   || d  :d  |d  :d   |d  :d   |d  :t, ||
 | m  :s  |s  :m   |l  :-.t |d' :-   || s  :s  |f  :s    |s  :fe |s  :-  ||
 | d  :d  |s, :l,  |f, :f   |d  :-   || m  :m  |f  :m    |d  :l, |s, :-  ||
```

f. A.　　　　　　　　　　　　　　　　　　E. t.
```
{| r l,:-.l,|d  :d   |t, :t, |d  :-   ||ʳs  :-.f |m  :d   |r  :r   |d  :-  ||
 | r l,:-.l,|l, :l,  |l, :se,|l, :-   ||¹r  :-.r |d  :d    |d  :t, |d  :-  ||
 | ¹m :-.m  |d  :m   |f  :m  |m  :-   ||ʳs  :-.s |s  :s   |s  :-.f|m  :-  ||
 |ᶠd,:-.d,|l̄₂:d,   |r, :m, |l,:s,  ||ᶠᵉt,:-.t,|d  :m    |s  :s, |d  :-  ||
```

f   SOLDIERS of the Cross, arise!
     Gird you with your armour bright:
   Mighty are your enemies,
     Hard the battle ye must fight.

2

mf O'er a faithless fallen world
     Raise your banner in the sky;
   Let it float there wide unfurled;
     Bear it onward, lift it high.

3

   'Mid the homes of want and woe,
     Strangers to the living word,
f   Let the Saviour's herald go,
     Let the voice of hope be heard.

4

mf Where the shadows deepest lie,
     Carry truth's unsullied ray;
   Where are crimes of blackest dye,
     There the saving sign display.

5

p   To the weary and the worn
     Tell of realms where sorrows cease;
   To the outcast and forlorn
     Speak of mercy and of peace.

6

mf Guard the helpless, seek the strayed;
     Comfort troubles, banish grief;
   In the might of God arrayed,
     Scatter sin and unbelief.

7

f   Be the banner still unfurled,
     Still unsheathed the Spirit's sword,
   Till the kingdoms of the world
     Are the Kingdom of the Lord.

BISHOP W. WALSHAM HOW

GENERAL

Hymn 306 Crucis victoria
M. B. Foster, 1851-1922

KEY **E**

```
{ :d  | m :f  | s :m  | f :s   | l   || s  | s :l   | f  :m    | r :— | — ||
  :d  | d :d  | t₁:d  | d :ta₁ | l₁  || t₁ | d :d   | l₁.t₁:d  | t₁:— | — ||
  :m  | s :d  | r :m  | d :r.m | f   || s  | s :m   | f  :s.l  | t :— | — ||
  :d  | d :l₁ | s₁:d  | l₁:s₁  | f₁  || f  | m :d   | r  :m.f  | s :— | — ||
```

B. t.   f. E.

```
{ :ʳs₁ | l₁:r  | t₁:d  | r :f   | m   || ᵈs  | d¹:s.f | m :r    | d :— | — ||
  :ᵗm₁ | f₁:l₁ | s₁:s₁ | l₁:s₁  | s₁  || ᵐt₁ | d :d   | d :t₁   | d :— | — ||
  :ˢd  | d :f  | r :d  | d :t₁  | d   || ᵈs  | s :s.l | s :-.f  | m :— | — ||
  :ˢᵢd₁| f₁:r₁ | s₁:m₁ | f₁:s₁  | d   || ᵈs.f| m :m₁.f₁| s₁:s₁ | d :— | — ||
```

f LIFT up your heads, ye gates of brass;
   Ye bars of iron, yield!
   And let the King of Glory pass:
   The Cross is in the field.

2
That banner, brighter than the star
   That leads the train of night,
Shines on the march, and guides from
   His servants to the fight. [far

3
mf A holy war those servants wage:
   In that mysterious strife
The powers of heaven and hell engage,
   For more than death or life.

4
Ye armies of the living God,
   Sworn warriors of Christ's host,
Where hallowed footsteps never trod
   Take your appointed post.

5
Though few and small and weak your bands,
   Strong in your Captain's strength,
Go to the conquest of all lands:
   All must be his at length.

6
The spoils at his victorious feet
   You shall rejoice to lay,
And lay yourselves as trophies meet,
   In his great judgement day.

7
f Then fear not, faint not, halt not now;
   In Jesus' name be strong!
To him shall all the nations bow,
   And sing the triumph song:

8
Uplifted are the gates of brass,
   The bars of iron yield;
Behold the King of Glory pass:
   The Cross hath won the field!

J. MONTGOMERY†

GENERAL

HYMN 307   FIRST TUNE

KEY D   Golden Grove   Greville Cooke

SECOND TUNE

KEY A   Morning Light   G. J. Webb, 1803–87

GENERAL

```
{ :s,   |d :-.d |m :d   |d :—  |l,  ||d   |s, :d  |m :r   |d :— |—
  :s,   |s, :-.s,|s, :s,|l, :— |f,  ||f,  |s, :m, |s, :f, |m, :— |—
  :t,   |d :-.d |d :d   |d :—  |d   ||l,  |d :s,  |d :t,  |d :— |—
  :s,.f,|m, :-.m,|d, :m,|f, :— |f,  ||f,  |m, :d, |s, :s, |d, :— |— }
```

f   STAND up, stand up for Jesus,
        Ye soldiers of the Cross!
    Lift high his royal banner,
        It must not suffer loss.
    From victory unto victory
        His army he shall lead,
    Till every foe is vanquished,
        And Christ is Lord indeed.

2*

mf   Stand up, stand up for Jesus!
        The solemn watchword hear;
    If while ye sleep he suffers,
        Away with shame and fear.
    Where'er ye meet with evil,
        Within you or without,
f   Charge for the God of battles,
        And put the foe to rout.

3

mf   Stand up, stand up for Jesus!
        The trumpet call obey;
    Forth to the mighty conflict
        In this his glorious day.
    Ye that are men now serve him
        Against unnumbered foes;
    Let courage rise with danger
        And strength to strength oppose.

4

    Stand up, stand up for Jesus!
        Stand in his strength alone;
    The arm of flesh will fail you,
        Ye dare not trust your own.
f   Put on the Gospel armour,
        Each piece put on with prayer;
    When duty calls or danger
        Be never wanting there.

5

mf   Stand up, stand up for Jesus!
        The strife will not be long;
    This day the noise of battle,
        The next the victor's song.
f   To him that overcometh
        A crown of life shall be;
    He with the King of Glory
        Shall reign eternally.

                    G. DUFFIELD

GENERAL

HYMN 308 FIRST TUNE

KEY **F** Sentinel Greville Cooke

[musical notation]

C.t. f. F.

[musical notation]

SECOND TUNE

KEY **E♭** Vigilate W. H. Monk, 1823–89

[musical notation]

> *mf* 'CHRISTIAN, seek not yet repose,'
> Hear thy guardian angel say;
> 'Thou art in the midst of foes:
> Watch and pray!'
>
> 2
> Principalities and powers,
> Mustering their unseen array,
> Wait for thine unguarded hours:
> Watch and pray!
>
> 3
> *f* Gird thy heavenly armour on,
> Wear it ever night and day;
> Ambushed lurks the evil one:
> Watch and pray!

GENERAL

4

Hear the victors who o'ercame;
Still they mark each warrior's way;
All with one sweet voice exclaim:
'Watch and pray!'

5

mf Hear, above all, hear thy Lord,
Him thou lovest to obey;
Hide within thy heart his word:
'Watch and pray!'

6

Watch, as if on that alone
Hung the issue of the day;
Pray, that help may be sent down:
Watch and pray!

CHARLOTTE ELLIOTT

HYMN 309 Old Martyrs   *Psalms* (Edinburgh, 1615)
KEY **F**

{ | l₁ :— | d :l₁ | m :d | t₁ :l₁ | m :— || m :— | s :m | fe.s :l | m :— ||
  | l₁ :— | l₁ :l₁ | s₁ :m₁ | s₁ :fe₁ | s₁ :— || l₁ :— | t₁ :d | r :r | t₁ :— ||
  | d :— | m :d | t₁ :d | r :r | t₁ :— || d :— | r :l | l :fe | se :— ||
  | l₁ :— | l₁ :l₁ | m₁ :l₁ | s₁ :r₁ | m₁ :— || l₁ :— | s₁ :l₁ | r :r₁ | m₁ :— || }

{ | m :— | s :r | m :d | t₁ :l₁ | m :— || s :— | fe :r | fe :m | l₁ :— ||
  | d :— | r :t₁ | s₁ :l₁ | m₁ :l₁ | s₁ :— || t₁ :— | r :t₁ | r.d :t₁ | l₁ :— ||
  | s :— | s :s | m :m | t₁ :d.r | m :— || m :— | l :s | l :s | d :— ||
  | d :— | t₁ :s₁ | d :l₁ | s₁ :f₁ | m₁ :— || m :— | r :s₁ | r₁ :m₁ | l₁ :— || }

mf O GOD of truth, whose living word
    Upholds whate'er hath breath,
Look down on thy creation, Lord,
    Enslaved by sin and death.

2

f Set up thy standard, Lord, that we
    Who claim a heavenly birth
May march with thee to smite the lies
    That vex thy ransomed earth.

3

mf Ah, would we join that blest array,
    And follow in the might
Of him, the Faithful and the True,
    In raiment clean and white?

4

We fight for truth? we fight for God?
    Poor slaves of lies and sin!
He who would fight for thee on earth
    Must first be true within.

5

f Then, God of truth, for whom we long,
    Thou who wilt hear our prayer,
Do thine own battle in our hearts,
    And slay the falsehood there.

6

Yea, come! Then, tried as in the fire,
    From every lie set free,
Thy perfect truth shall dwell in us,
    And we shall live in thee.

T. HUGHES

GENERAL

HYMN 310 Doncaster

S. Wesley, 1766–1837

KEY **D**

[sol-fa notation]

f   PUT thou thy trust in God,
      In duty's path go on;
    Walk in his strength with faith and hope,
      So shall thy work be done.

2

mf   Commit thy ways to him,
      Thy works into his hands,
    And rest on his unchanging word,
      Who heaven and earth commands.

3

    Though years on years roll on,
      His covenant shall endure;
f   Though clouds and darkness hide his path,
      The promised grace is sure.

4

mf   Give to the winds thy fears;
      Hope, and be undismayed:
    God hears thy sighs and counts thy tears;
f   God shall lift up thy head.

5

mf   Through waves and clouds and storms
      His power will clear thy way:
f   Wait thou his time; the darkest night
      Shall end in brightest day.

GENERAL

6

mf Leave to his sovereign sway
To choose and to command;
So shalt thou, wondering, own his way,
How wise, how strong his hand.

J. WESLEY and others
Cento from *Befiehl du deine Wege*, P. Gerhardt

HYMN **311** Mannheim　　　　　　　　　　　　F. Filitz, 1804–76
KEY **E**

{|d :m |s :s |l :s |f :m ‖m :f |s :d |m :r |d :— ‖
 |s, :d |r :d |d :t, |d :d |d :r |r :d |d :t, |d :— ‖
 |m :s |s :m |f :r |d :d |l :l |s :m |s :f |m :— ‖
 |d :d |t, :d |f, :s, |l, :d |l, :r |t, :d |s, :s, |d :— ‖}

{|s :s |l :s |ta :l |l :s ‖s :r |m :l |s :fe |s :— ‖
 |d :d |d :d |d :d |d :d |r :t, |d :m |r :d |t, :— ‖
 |m :m |f :m |s :f |f :m |s :s |s :d¹|t :l |s :— ‖
 |d :d |d :d |m :f |d :d |t, :s, |d :l, |r :r |s, :— ‖}

{|d :m |s :s |l :s |f :r. ‖m :f |s :d |m :r |d :— ‖
 |s, :d |r :d |d :t, |d :d |d :r |r :d |d :t, |d :— ‖
 |m :s |s :m |f :r |d :d |l :l |s :m |s :f |m :— ‖
 |d :d |t, :d |f, :s, |l, :d |l, :r |t, :d |s, :s, |d :— ‖}

mf LEAD us, heavenly Father, lead us
O'er the world's tempestuous sea;
Guard us, guide us, keep us, feed us,
For we have no help but thee;
Yet possessing every blessing,
If our God our Father be.

2

p Saviour, breathe forgiveness o'er us:
All our weakness thou dost know;
Thou didst tread this earth before us,
Thou didst feel its keenest woe;
Lone and dreary, faint and weary,
Through the desert thou didst go.

3

mf Spirit of our God, descending,
Fill our hearts with heavenly joy,
Love with every passion blending,
Pleasure that can never cloy;
Thus provided, pardoned, guided,
Nothing can our peace destroy.

J. EDMESTON

GENERAL

HYMN 312 Tempest   J. B. König, 1691–1758
KEY B♭

[Tonic sol-fa musical notation]

By permission of Schott & Co., Ltd.

ζοφερᾶς τρικυμίας

f FIERCE was the wild billow,
    Dark was the night;
  Oars laboured heavily,
    Foam glimmered white;
  Trembled the mariners,
    Peril was nigh:
  Then said the God of God,
p   'Peace! It is I.'

f Ridge of the mountain-wave,
    Lower thy crest!
  Wail of the hurricane,
    Be thou at rest!
  Sorrow can never be,
    Darkness must fly,
  Where saith the Light of Light,
p   'Peace! It is I.'

3
mf Jesus, deliverer,
    Nigh to us be;
  Soothe thou my voyaging
    Over life's sea:
f Thou, when the storm of death
    Roars, sweeping by,
p Whisper, O Truth of Truth,
  'Peace! It is I.'

ST. ANATOLIUS *Tr.* J. M. Neale†

HYMN 313 St. Aëlred   J. B. Dykes, 1823–76
KEY E♭

[Tonic sol-fa musical notation]

GENERAL

mf FIERCE raged the tempest o'er the deep,
  Watch did thine anxious servants keep,
p But thou wast wrapped in guileless sleep,
      Calm and still.

2
mf 'Save, Lord, we perish,' was their cry,
  'O save us in our agony!'
Thy word above the storm rose high,
      'Peace, be still.'

3
The wild winds hushed; the angry deep
Sank, like a little child, to sleep;
The sullen billows ceased to leap,
      At thy will.

4
So, when our life is clouded o'er,
And storm-winds drift us from the shore,
Say, lest we sink to rise no more,
    p 'Peace, be still.'

G. THRING

HYMN **314** Martyrdom   H. Wilson, 1766–1824

KEY **A**

Psalm 42

mf AS pants the hart for cooling streams
  When heated in the chase,
So longs my soul, O God, for thee,
  And thy refreshing grace.

2
For thee, my God, the living God,
  My thirsty soul doth pine:
O when shall I behold thy face,
  Thou majesty divine?

3
p Why restless, why cast down, my soul?
f Hope still, and thou shalt sing
The praise of him who is thy God,
  Thy health's eternal spring.

4
To Father, Son, and Holy Ghost,
  The God whom we adore,
Be glory, as it was, is now,
  And shall be evermore.

N. TATE and N. BRADY
(*New Version*)

GENERAL

HYMN 315 Belstead   C. V. Taylor

KEY D

[musical notation]

f   UP to the throne on high,
       In loyal love and trust,
     We, children of an hour,
       Lift voices from the dust.

2

mf   Suffer us not to stray
       From thee, our God, our guide,
     Whatever trials come,
       Whatever ills betide.

3

Grant us in mercy, Lord,
   The gifts thou deemest best,
Help for the daily task,
   And for our spirits rest.

4

f   Strong in the power of faith,
     From doubt and care set free,
   We tread the appointed path
     That brings us home to thee.

5

Bid empty terror cease;
   Neath thy o'ershadowing might
Uphold our hearts in hope,
   And lead us into light.

                             E. H. BLAKENEY

Alternative Tune, Eden, 327

GENERAL

HYMN 316 Chapel Royal W. Boyce, 1710–79

KEY **G**

[sol-fa notation]

Supreme motor cordium

mf GREAT mover of all hearts, whose hand
Doth all the secret springs command
  Of human thought and will,
Thou, since the world was made, dost bless
Thy saints with fruits of holiness,
  Their order to fulfil.

2

Faith, hope, and love here weave one chain;
But love alone shall then remain
  When this short day is gone;
f O Love, O Truth, O endless Light,
When shall we see thy sabbath bright
  With all our labours done?

3

p We sow 'mid perils here and tears;
There the glad hand the harvest bears,
  Which here in grief hath sown:
mf Great Three in One, the increase give;
Thy gifts of grace, by which we live,
  With heavenly glory crown.

C. COFFIN *Tr.* I. Williams

GENERAL

HYMN 317 St. Hugh   E. J. Hopkins, 1818–1901

KEY E♭

```
{ :d  | d :r  |m :d    | s :r   |m    || m  | f :l  |s :d    | r :—  |—
{ :s₁ | l₁:s₁ |s₁:d    | d :—.t₁|d    || d  | d :t₁ |d :d    | t₁:—  |—
{ :m  | f :f  |m :m    | m :f   |m    || s  | f :f  |s :—.fe | s :—  |—
{ :d  | l₁:t₁ |d :l₁   | s₁:s₁  |d    || ta₁| l₁:r  |m :l₁   | s₁:—  |—

{ :s  | d¹:t  |l :s    | f :m   |r    || l  | s :d  |r :—.r  | d :—  |—
{ :t₁ | d :m  |m :d    | d :d   |d    || t₁ | d :d  |d :t₁   | d :—  |—
{ :f  | m :se |l :m    | f :s   |l    || r  | s :m  |r :f    | m :—  |—
{ :s₁ | l₁:t₁ |d :ta₁  | l₁:s₁  |fe₁  || f₁ | m₁:l₁ |f₁:s₁   | d :—  |—
```

LORD, teach us how to pray aright
  With reverence and with fear;
Though dust and ashes in thy sight,
  We may, we must, draw near.

2

We perish if we cease from prayer:
  O grant us power to pray;
And, when to meet thee we prepare,
  Lord, meet us by the way.

3

God of all grace, we bring to thee
  A broken, contrite heart;
Give what thine eye delights to see,
  Truth in the inward part;

4

Faith in the only Sacrifice
  That can for sin atone,
To cast our hopes, to fix our eyes,
  On Christ, on Christ alone;

5

Patience to watch and wait and weep.
  Though mercy long delay;
Courage our fainting souls to keep,
  And trust thee though thou slay.

6

Give these, and then thy will be done;
  Thus, strengthened with all might,
We, through thy Spirit and thy Son,
  Shall pray, and pray aright.

                        J. MONTGOMERY†

GENERAL

HYMN 318 St. Etheldreda   Bishop T. Turton, 1780–1864

KEY **F**

```
{ :d  | d :r  | m :r  | d :t, | d  || r  | m :s  | f  :m   | r :— | — ||
{ :s, | d :t, | d :l, | s,:s, | s, || t, | d :d  | l,.t,:d | t,:— | — ||
{ :m  | m :s  | s :f  | m :r  | m  || s  | s :m  | f  :s   | s :— | — ||
{ :d  | l,:s, | d :f, | s,:s, | d  || s, | d :m  | r  :d   | s,:— | — ||

{ :m  | f :l  | s :t, | d :f  | m  || s  | l :f  | m :r    | d :— | — ||
{ :d  | d :d  | d :s,.f,| m,:s,| s,|| d  | d :d  | d :t,   | d :— | — ||
{ :s  | f :f  | s :m.r| d :r  | d  || s  | f :f  | s :—.f  | m :— | — ||
{ :d  | l,:f, | m,:s, | l,:t,| d  || m, | f,:l, | s,:s,   | d :— | — ||
```

    mf SHEPHERD divine, our wants relieve
          In this our evil day;
        To all thy tempted followers give
          The power to watch and pray.

2

Long as our fiery trials last,
    Long as the cross we bear,
O let our souls on thee be cast
    In never-ceasing prayer.

3

The Spirit's interceding grace
    Give us in faith to claim;
To wrestle till we see thy face,
    And know thy hidden Name.

4

Till thou thy perfect love impart,
    Till thou thyself bestow,
Be this the cry of every heart,
    'I will not let thee go.'

5

I will not let thee go, unless
    Thou tell thy Name to me;
With all thy great salvation bless,
    And make me all like thee.

6

    f Then let me on the mountain-top
          Behold thy open face;
        Where faith in sight is swallowed up,
          And prayer in endless praise.
                                  C. WESLEY†

NOTE. *The latter part of this hymn makes reference to Jacob's encounter with the angel* (Gen. 32. 24–30)

GENERAL

HYMN 319 FIRST TUNE

KEY E♭   Song 13   Orlando Gibbons, 1583-1625

[Tonic sol-fa notation]

SECOND TUNE

KEY F   East Peckham   G. C. E. Ryley, 1866-1947

UNISON

[Tonic sol-fa notation]

By permission of the Royal School of Church Music

mf COME, my soul, thy suit prepare:
Jesus loves to answer prayer;
He himself has bid thee pray,
Therefore will not say thee nay.

2

Thou art coming to a King:
Large petitions with thee bring;
For his grace and power are such
None can ever ask too much.

3

p With my burden I begin:
Lord, remove this load of sin;
Let thy Blood, for sinners spilt,
Set my conscience free from guilt.

4

Lord, I come to thee for rest;
Take possession of my breast;
There thy blood-bought right maintain,
And without a rival reign.

GENERAL

5

mf While I am a pilgrim here,
Let thy love my spirit cheer;
Be my guide, my guard, my friend,
Lead me to my journey's end.

J. NEWTON†

HYMN **320** Bedford   W. Wheale, 1690–1727

KEY E♭

O HELP us, Lord! each hour of need
Thy heavenly succour give;
Help us in thought and word and deed
Each hour on earth we live.

2

O help us, when our spirits bleed
With contrite anguish sore;
And when our hearts are cold and dead,
O help us, Lord, the more.

3

O help us, through the prayer of faith
More firmly to believe;
For still the more the servant hath,
The more shall he receive.

4

O help us, Jesus, from on high;
We know no help but thee:
O help us so to live and die
As thine in heaven to be.

H. H. MILMAN

Alternative Tune, Nun danket all, 347

333

GENERAL

HYMN 321 St. Raphael
KEY G
E. J. Hopkins, 1818–1901

[Tonic sol-fa notation]

D.t.

f. G.

mf JESUS, Lord of life and glory,
 Bend from heaven thy gracious ear;
 While our waiting souls adore thee,
 Friend of helpless sinners, hear:
p By thy mercy,
 O deliver us, good Lord.

2
mf From the depths of nature's blindness,
 From the hardening power of sin,
 From all malice and unkindness,
 From the pride that lurks within:
p By thy mercy, etc.

3
When temptation sorely presses,
 In the day of Satan's power,
 In our times of deep distresses,
 In each dark and trying hour:
 By thy mercy, etc.

4
mf When the world around is smiling,
 In the time of wealth and ease,
 Earthly joys our hearts beguiling,
 In the day of health and peace:
p By thy mercy, etc.

5
In the weary hours of sickness,
 In the times of grief and pain,
 When we feel our mortal weakness,
 When all human help is vain:
 By thy mercy, etc.

6
In the solemn hour of dying,
 In the aweful judgement day,
mf May our souls, on thee relying,
 Find thee still our Rock and stay:
p By thy mercy, etc.

J. J. CUMMINS†

HYMN 322 St. Bride
KEY B♭
S. Howard, 1710–82

[Tonic sol-fa notation]

GENERAL

Psalm 130

p OUT of the deep I call
To thee, O Lord, to thee;
Before thy throne of grace I fall:
Be merciful to me.

2

Out of the deep I cry,
The woeful deep of sin,
Of evil done in days gone by,
Of evil now within.

3

Out of the deep of fear,
And dread of coming shame,
From morning watch till night is near
I plead the precious name.

4

mf Lord, there is mercy now,
As ever was, with thee;
Before thy throne of grace I bow:
p Be merciful to me.

SIR H. W. BAKER

HYMN **323** Derry   J. B. Dykes, 1823–76

KEY **G**

FORSAKEN once, and thrice denied,
The risen Lord gave pardon free,
Stood once again at Peter's side,
And asked him, 'Lov'st thou me?'

2

How many times with faithless word
Have we denied his holy name,
How oft forsaken our dear Lord,
And shrunk when trial came!

3

Saint Peter, when the cock crew clear,
Went out, and wept his broken faith:
Strong as a rock through strife and fear,
He served his Lord till death.

4

How oft his cowardice of heart
We have without his love sincere,
The sin without the sorrow's smart,
The shame without the tear!

5

O oft forsaken, oft denied,
Forgive our shame, wash out our sin;
Look on us from thy Father's side
And let that sweet look win.

6

Hear when we call thee from the deep,
Still walk beside us on the shore,
Give hands to work, and eyes to weep,
And hearts to love thee more.

MRS. C. F. ALEXANDER

GENERA

HYMN 324 FIRST TUN.

KEY A♭ Remission L. J. Blake

{: l₁ | l₁ : t₁ | d : m | r : — : d | t₁ : l₁ | s₁ : s₁ | l₁ : — | — ||
 : m₁ | m₁ : l₁ | l₁ : m₁ | f₁ : — : s₁ | s₁ : f₁ | m₁ : m₁ | f₁ : — | — ||
 : d | d : r | m : l₁ | l₁ : t₁ : d | r : —d | t₁ : d | d : — | — ||
 : l₁ | s₁ : f₁ | m₁,r₁: d₁| r₁ : — : m₁ | s₁ : r₁ | m₁ : d₁ | f₁ : — | — ||

{: t₁ | d : r | m : s | f : — : m | r : t₁ | d : l₁ | s₁ : — | — ||
 : f₁ | m₁ : s₁ | s₁ : s₁ | d : r : d.t₁ | l₁ : s₁ | s : f₁,m₁ | r₁ : — | — ||
 : r | d : t₁ | d : r.m | f : r : s | f : r | d : d | d : t₁ | — ||
 : r₁ | l₁ : s₁ | d : t₁ | l₁ : t₁ : d | f₁ : s₁ | m₁ : f₁ | s₁ : — | — ||

{: s₁ | l₁ : d | ta₁ : s₁ | l₁ : d | f : m : r | m : — | — : t₁ | de : — | — ||
 : m₁ | f₁ : f₁ | f₁ : m₁ | f₁ : s₁ | f₁ : — : l₁ | l₁ : fe₁ | se₁ : — | l₁ : — | — ||
 : d | d : d | r : d | d : d | l₁ : — : r | t₁ : — | m : — | m : — | — ||
 : d₁ | f₁ : l₂ | ta₂ : d₁ | f₁ : m₁ | r₁ : — : f₁ | m₁ : — | m₁ : — | l₁ : — | — ||

SECOND TUNE

KEY F Waltham W. H. Monk, 1823–89

{: m | m : r.m | f : s | m : — | — : s | s : f.m | f : f | m : — | — ||
 : d | d : d | d : r | d : — | — : r | d : d | t₁: r | d : — | — ||
 : s | s : f.s | l : s | s : — | — : s | l : l | s : s | s : — | — ||
 : d | d : d | d : t₁| d : — | — : t₁| l₁: r | s₁: t₁| d : — | — ||

C. t.

{: ᵐl | t : d¹ | r¹ : f | m : s | l : d¹ | d¹ : — | t : — | d¹ : — | — ||
 : ᵈf | f : f | f : t₁ | d : s | f : f | s : — | — : f | m : — | — ||
 : ˢd¹| f : l | s : s | s : d¹| d¹: d¹ | m¹ : — | r¹ : — | d¹ : — | — ||
 : ᵈf | r : d | t₁: r | d : m | f : l | s : — | s : — | d : — | — ||

f. F.

{: ᵈs | l : l | s : t₁ | d : d | d : f | r : — | m : r | d : — | — ||
 : ᵐᵃ ta₁ | l₁: d | d : t₁ | l₁: l₁| d : d | d : t₁ | — : t₁ | d : — | — ||
 : ˡ m | f : f.m | r : f | m : l | s : l | s : — | — : f | m : — | — ||
 : ᶠ d | f₁: f₁ | s₁: s₁ | l₁: f₁ | m₁: r₁ | s₁: — | — : s₁ { d : — | — ||
                                                           { d₁: — | — ||

GENERAL

p   NOT for our sins alone
     Thy mercy, Lord, we sue;
  Let fall thy pitying glance
     On our devotions too,
  What we have done for thee,
     And what we think to do.

2

mf   The holiest hours we spend
     In prayer upon our knees,
  The times when most we deem
     Our songs of praise will please,
  Thou searcher of all hearts,
p   Forgiveness pour on these.

3

mf   And all the gifts we bring,
     And all the vows we make,
  And all the acts of love
     We plan for thy dear sake,
p   Into thy pardoning thought,
     O God of mercy, take.

4

mf   And most, when we, thy flock,
     Before thine altar bend,
  And strange, bewildering thoughts
     With those sweet moments blend,
p   By him whose Death we plead,
     Good Lord, thy help extend.

5

mf   Bow down thine ear and hear!
     Open thine eyes and see!
  Our very love is shame,
     And we must come to thee
  To make it of thy grace
     What thou wouldst have it be.

H. TWELLS

GENERAL

HYMN 325

FIRST TUNE

KEY E♭ Song 67

Melody from E. Prys, *Psalms*, 1621

SECOND TUNE

KEY E♭ Stockton

T. Wright, 1763–1829

1
O FOR a heart to praise my God,
  A heart from sin set free;
A heart that's sprinkled with the Blood
  So freely shed for me:

2
A heart resigned, submissive, meek,
  My great Redeemer's throne;
Where only Christ is heard to speak,
  Where Jesus reigns alone:

3
A humble, lowly, contrite heart,
  Believing, true, and clean,
Which neither life nor death can part
  From him that dwells within:

4
A heart in every thought renewed,
  And full of love divine;
Perfect and right and pure and good—
  A copy, Lord, of thine!

5
Thy nature, gracious Lord, impart,
  Come quickly from above;
Write thy new name upon my heart,
  Thy new best name of Love.

C. WESLEY†

GENERAL

HYMN 326 Caithness   *Scottish Psalter*, 1635

KEY E♭

```
{|d :— |m :f |s :d |t₁:d |r :— |m :— |f :s |l :l |s :—||
 |s₁:— |d :d |t₁:s₁|f₁:s₁.l₁|t₁:— |d :— |d :ta₁|l₁:l₁.t₁|d :—||
 |m :— |s :f |r :m |f :m |s :— |s :— |f :m |f :d.r |m :—||
 |d :— |d :l₁|s₁:m |r :d |s₁:— |d :— |l₁:s₁|f₁:f₁ |d :—||

{|s :— |l :t |d':m |f :s |l :— |s :— |f :m |r :r |d :—||
 |m :— |m :r |d :t₁|d :d |d :— |t₁:— |d :d |d :t₁|d :—||
 |m :— |m :s |l :m |l :s |f :— |r :— |f :s |l :s.f|m :—||
 |d :— |d :t₁|l₁:s₁|f₁:m₁|f₁:— |s₁:— |l₁:d |f₁:s₁|d :—||
```

By permission of the English Hymnal Company, Ltd.

O FOR a closer walk with God,
    A calm and heavenly frame;
A light to shine upon the road
    That leads me to the Lamb!

2

What peaceful hours I once enjoyed!
    How sweet their memory still!
But they have left an aching void
    The world can never fill.

3

Return, O holy Dove, return,
    Sweet messenger of rest;
I hate the sins that made thee mourn,
    And drove thee from my breast.

4

The dearest idol I have known,
    Whate'er that idol be,
Help me to tear it from thy throne,
    And worship only thee.

5

So shall my walk be close with God,
    Calm and serene my frame;
So purer light shall mark the road
    That leads me to the Lamb.

W. COWPER

GENERAL

HYMN 327 Eden
O. M. Feilden, 1837-1924

KEY E♭

[sol-fa notation]

1
LORD, be thy word my rule,
In it may I rejoice;
Thy glory be my aim,
Thy holy will my choice;

2
Thy promises my hope,
Thy providence my guard,
Thine arm my strong support,
Thyself my great reward.

BISHOP CHR. WORDSWORTH

HYMN 328 Galway
E. Miller, 1731-1807

KEY F

[sol-fa notation]

1
A CHARGE to keep I have,
A God to glorify,
A never-dying soul to save,
And fit it for the sky.

2
To serve the present age,
My calling to fulfil,
O may it all my powers engage
To do my Master's will.

3
Arm me with jealous care,
As in thy sight to live;
And O, thy servant, Lord, prepare
A good account to give.

4
Help me to watch and pray,
And on thyself rely;
And let me ne'er my trust betray,
But press to realms on high.

C. WESLEY

GENERAL

Hymn 329 **FIRST TUNE**

KEY **F** Hereford S. S. Wesley, 1810–76

[tonic sol-fa notation]

SECOND TUNE

KEY **D** St. Gregory *Darmstadt Gesangbuch*, 1698

[tonic sol-fa notation]

O THOU who camest from above
    The fire celestial to impart,
Kindle a flame of sacred love
    On the mean altar of my heart.

2

There let it for thy glory burn
    With inextinguishable blaze,
And trembling to its source return
    In humble prayer and fervent praise.

3

Jesus, confirm my heart's desire
    To work and speak and think for thee;
Still let me guard the holy fire
    And still stir up the gift in me.

4

Still let me prove thy perfect will,
    My acts of faith and love repeat;
Till death thy endless mercies seal,
    And make the sacrifice complete.

C. WESLEY†

GENERAL

HYMN 330 Newington   Archbishop W. D. Maclagan, 1826–1910
KEY A♭   E♭. t.

```
 m :-.m |f :r   l₁:t₁ |d :-     ‖ r s :-.s |l :s    s :f |m :-
 s₁:-.s₁|f₁:l₁  f₁:f₁ |m₁:-     ‖ s₁d :-.d |d :t₁   d :r |d :-
 d :-.d |d :r   r :r  |d :-     ‖ t₁m :-.m |f :r    l :s |s :-
 d :-.d |l₁:f₁  r₁:s₁ |d₁:-     ‖ s₁d :-.d |f₁:s₁   l₁:t₁|d :-
```

f. A♭.

```
 s r :-.m |f :r   s :d   |d :t₁    d :-.d |r :m     f :r |d :-
 r l₁:-.s₁|f₁:s₁  s₁:fe₁ |s₁:-     m₁:-.m₁|l₁:s₁    f₁:f₁|m₁:-
 s r :-.de|r :t₁  d :r   |r :-     l₁:-.l₁|l₁:de    r :t₁|d :-
 ta₁f₁:-.m₁|r₁:s₁ m₁:l₁  |s₁:-     l₁:-.s₁|f₁:m₁    r₁:s₁|d₁:-
```

THINE for ever! God of love,
Hear us from thy throne above;
Thine for ever may we be
Here and in eternity.

3
Thine for ever! O how blest
They who find in thee their rest!
Saviour, guardian, heavenly friend,
O defend us to the end.

2
Thine for ever! Lord of life,
Shield us through our earthly strife;
Thou the Life, the Truth, the Way,
Guide us to the realms of day.

4*
Thine for ever! Shepherd, keep
Us thy frail and trembling sheep;
Safe alone beneath thy care,
Let us all thy goodness share.

5
Thine for ever! thou our guide,
All our wants by thee supplied,
All our sins by thee forgiven,
Lead us, Lord, from earth to heaven.

MRS. M. F. MAUDE

HYMN 331 Wolvercote   W. H. Ferguson, 1872–1950
KEY A

UNISON
```
{: s₁ | d : f | m : r.m | d :l₁ | s₁: m₁.f₁ | s₁: m | r.d: r | d :- | - ‖
```
E. t.
```
{: s₁ | d : f | m : r.m | d :l₁ | s₁:  ᵐl₁.t₁ | d : r | m.f: r | d :- | - ‖
```
4. C.
```
{: ᵈm | d¹: t | l : m.f | s :-.l | s : m.r | d : d¹| t : t | t :- | - ‖
```
A. 3.
```
{: ᵐs₁ | d : f | m : r.m | d :l₁ | s₁: m₁.f₁ | s₁: m | r.d: r | d :- | - ‖
```

342

GENERAL

O JESUS, I have promised
  To serve thee to the end;
Be thou for ever near me,
  My Master and my Friend;
I shall not fear the battle
  If thou art by my side,
Nor wander from the pathway
  If thou wilt be my guide.

2*

O let me feel thee near me:
  The world is ever near;
I see the sights that dazzle,
  The tempting sounds I hear;
My foes are ever near me,
  Around me and within;
But, Jesus, draw thou nearer,
  And shield my soul from sin.

3

O let me hear thee speaking
  In accents clear and still,
Above the storms of passion,
  The murmurs of self-will;
O speak to reassure me,
  To hasten or control;
O speak, and make me listen,
  Thou guardian of my soul.

4

O Jesus, thou hast promised
  To all who follow thee,
That where thou art in glory
  There shall thy servant be;
And, Jesus, I have promised
  To serve thee to the end:
O give me grace to follow,
  My Master and my Friend.

5

O let me see thy foot-marks,
  And in them plant mine own;
My hope to follow duly
  Is in thy strength alone;
O guide me, call me, draw me,
  Uphold me to the end;
And then in heaven receive me,
  My Saviour and my Friend.

J. E. BODE

Alternative Tune, Thornbury, 256

GENERAL

HYMN 332

FIRST TUNE

KEY **C** Poplar

Bishop T. B. Strong, 1861–1944

[Sol-fa notation, 5 verses]

1 God be in my head, And in my under-stand-ing;

2 God be in my eyes, And in my look-ing;

3 God be in my mouth, And in my speak-ing;

4 God be in my heart, And in my think-ing;

5 God be at my end, And at my de-part-ing.

By permission of the Oxford University Press

GENERAL

SECOND TUNE

KEY D Lytlington   Sir S. H. Nicholson, 1875–1947

Slow

```
{| m : -.r : d.m | s.,d : f.m : r.d | r : d : |
 | d : -.t₁: d.d | r.,d : d.t₁: l₁.l₁| t₁: d : |
 1 God   be  in my head,  And in my  un-der- stand-ing;
 | s : -.f : s.s | s.,m : l.s : f.m | s : m : |
 | d : -.r : m.d | t₁.,d: f₁.s₁: l₁.l₁| s₁: d : |}
```

```
{| s : -.m : r.d | d' : -.t : l.s | l : s : |
 | d : -.d : t₁.d | d : -.r : d.t₁| r : t₁: |
 2 God   be  in my eyes,   And in my  look-ing;
 | m : -.s : f.m | s : -.s : m.s | fe: s : |
 | d : -.d : s₁.l₁| m₁: -.s₁: l₁.m | r : s₁: |}
```

```
{| m : -.r : d.m | s.,d : f.m : r.d | r : d : |
 | d : -.t₁: d.d | r.,d : d.t₁: l₁ | t₁: d : |
 3 God   be  in my mouth, And in   my  speak-ing;
 | s : -.f : s.s | s.,m : l.s : f.m | s : m : |
 | d : -.r : m.d | t₁.,d: f₁.s₁: l₁ | s₁: d : |}
```

```
{| s : -.m : r.d | d' : -.t : l.s | l : s : |
 | d : -.d : t₁.d | d : -.r : d.t₁| r : t₁: |
 4 God   be  in my heart,  And in my  think-ing;
 | m : -.s : f.m | s : -.s : m.s | fe: s : |
 | d : -.d : s₁.l₁| m₁: -.s₁: l₁.m | r : s₁: |}
```

```
{| m : -.r : d.m | s.,d : f.m : r.d | r : d ; |
 | d : -.t₁: d.d | r.,d : d : ta₁.s₁| d.t₁: d : |
 5 God   be  at my end,   And  at  my de- part-ing.
 | s : -.f : s.s | s.,m : l : f.m | s : m : |
 | d : -.r : m.d | t₁.,d: f₁.l₁: ta₁.d| s₁: d : |}
```

By permission of the Royal School of Church Music

Pynson's *Horae*, 1514

GENERAL

HYMN 333 Breslau   *Geistliche Gesänge* (Leipzig, 1625)

KEY **A**

TAKE up thy cross, the Saviour said,
   If thou wouldst my disciple be;
Deny thyself, the world forsake,
   And humbly follow after me.

2

Take up thy cross! let not its weight
   Fill thy weak spirit with alarm:
His strength shall bear thy spirit up,
   And brace thy heart, and nerve thine arm.

3

Take up thy cross, nor heed the shame,
   Nor let thy foolish pride rebel:
Thy Lord for thee the Cross endured,
   To save thy soul from death and hell.

4

Take up thy cross then in his strength,
   And calmly every danger brave;
'Twill guide thee to a better home,
   And lead to victory o'er the grave.

5

Take up thy cross, and follow Christ,
   Nor think till death to lay it down;
For only he who bears the cross
   May hope to wear the glorious crown.

6

To thee, great Lord, the One in Three,
   All praise for evermore ascend:
O grant us in our home to see
   The heavenly life that knows no end.

C. W. EVEREST ‡

GENERAL

HYMN 334　　　　　　　　　　　FIRST TUNE

KEY B♭　Windsor　　　　　　　　　　W. Damon, *Psalms*, 1591

SECOND TUNE

KEY G　Westminster New　　　　　　J. Nares, 1715–83

Slow

LORD, as to thy dear Cross we flee,
　And plead to be forgiven,
So let thy life our pattern be,
　And form our souls for heaven.

2
Help us, through good report and ill,
　Our daily cross to bear;
Like thee, to do our Father's will,
　Our brethren's griefs to share.

3
Let grace our selfishness expel,
　Our earthliness refine,
And kindness in our bosoms dwell
　As free and true as thine.

4
If joy shall at thy bidding fly,
　And grief's dark day come on,
We in our turn would meekly cry,
　'Father, thy will be done.'

5
Kept peaceful in the midst of strife,
　Forgiving and forgiven,
O may we lead the pilgrim's life,
　And follow thee to heaven.

J. H. GURNEY

GENERAL

HYMN 335 Franconia *Harmonischer Liederschatz*, 1738
KEY E♭

BLEST are the pure in heart,
For they shall see our God;
The secret of the Lord is theirs,
Their soul is Christ's abode.

2
The Lord, who left the heavens
Our life and peace to bring,
To dwell in lowliness with men,
Their pattern and their King;

3
Still to the lowly soul
He doth himself impart,
And for his dwelling and his throne
Chooseth the pure in heart.

4
Lord, we thy presence seek;
May ours this blessing be;
Give us a pure and lowly heart,
A temple meet for thee.

J. KEBLE and others

HYMN 336 Song 34 Orlando Gibbons, 1583–1625
KEY F

FORTH in thy name, O Lord, I go,
My daily labour to pursue;
Thee, only thee, resolved to know,
In all I think or speak or do.

2
The task thy wisdom hath assigned
O let me cheerfully fulfil;
In all my works thy presence find,
And prove thy good and perfect will.

GENERAL

3
Thee may I set at my right hand,
  Whose eyes my inmost substance see,
And labour on at thy command,
  And offer all my works to thee.

4
Give me to bear thy easy yoke,
  And every moment watch and pray,
And still to things eternal look,
  And hasten to thy glorious day;

5
For thee delightfully employ
  Whate'er thy bounteous grace hath given,
And run my course with even joy,
  And closely walk with thee to heaven.

C. WESLEY†

HYMN 337 Sandys   *Sandys' Christmas Carols*, 1833
KEY **D**

[Sol-fa notation]

3
TEACH me, my God and King,
In all things thee to see;
And what I do in anything
To do it as for thee.

2
A man that looks on glass,
On it may stay his eye;
Or, if he pleaseth, through it pass,
And then the heaven espy.

3
All may of thee partake;
Nothing can be so mean
Which, with this tincture, *For thy sake*,
Will not grow bright and clean.

4
A servant with this clause
Makes drudgery divine;
Who sweeps a room, as for thy laws,
Makes that and the action fine.

5
This is the famous stone
That turneth all to gold;
For that which God doth touch and own
Cannot for less be told.

GEORGE HERBERT

GENERAL

HYMN 338 Holyrood

J. Watson, 1816–80

KEY E♭

{ tonic sol-fa notation }

mf 1. FAIR waved the golden corn
In Canaan's pleasant land,
When full of joy, some shining morn,
Went forth the reaper-band.

f 2. To God so good and great
Their cheerful thanks they pour;
Then carry to his Temple-gate
The choicest of their store.

mf 3. Like Israel, Lord, we give
Our earliest fruits to thee,
And pray that, long as we shall live,
We may thy children be.

4. Thine is our youthful prime,
And life and all its powers:
Be with us in our morning time,
And bless our evening hours.

5. In wisdom let us grow,
As years and strength are given.
f That we may serve thy Church below,
And join thy saints in heaven.

J. H. GURNEY

Alternative Tune, St. Helena, 531

HYMN 339 Qui laborat orat

Sir H. P. Allen, 1869–1946

KEY F

UNISON

{ tonic sol-fa notation }

1. COME, labour on!
Who dares stand idle on the harvest plain,
While all around him waves of golden grain?
And to each servant does the Master say,
'Go, work to-day!'

2. Come, labour on!
Away with gloomy doubts and faithless fear!
No arm so weak but may do service here;
My feeblest agents can our God fulfil
His righteous will.

GENERAL

3
Come, labour on!
No time for rest, till glows the western sky,
Till the long shadows o'er our pathway lie,
And a glad sound comes with the setting sun,
'Servants, well done!'

4
Come, labour on!
The toil is pleasant, the reward is sure;
Blessèd are those who to the end endure:
How full their joy, how deep their rest shall be,
O Lord, with thee!

JANE L. BORTHWICK

HYMN 340 Hamburg
J. W. Franck, *c.* 1641–88

KEY E♭

[musical notation in tonic sol-fa]

1
O GOD, before whose altar
 The stars like tapers burn,
At whose inscrutable decree
 The planets wheel and turn,
Though earth and sea and heaven
 Unite thy praise to sing,
Man in his weakness yet may give
 A worthier offering.

2
Those who give up life's bounty
 To serve a race to be,
Whose bones lie white along the trail
 Which leads the world to thee;
Those who when fears beset them
 Stand fast and fight and die,
Their unconsidered lives go up
 Like incense to the sky.

3
All those oppressed or lonely
 Or long at strife with pain,
Who face the darkness undismayed
 And turn their loss to gain,
Those who with love and meekness
 Outlast the years of wrong,
Their silent courage pleads to heaven
 More eloquent than song.

4
O Lord, be ours the glory
 Beyond all earthly fame,
Like those to conquer for thy sake
 Despair and doubt and shame;
Till through a world made noble,
 Through lands from sin set free,
The armies of the living God
 Shall march to victory.

P. H. B. LYON

GENERAL

HYMN 341 Magda — R. Vaughan Williams

KEY D

By permission of the Oxford University Press

'LIFT up your hearts!' We lift them, Lord, to thee;
Here at thy feet none other may we see:
'Lift up your hearts!' E'en so, with one accord,
We lift them up, we lift them to the Lord.

2

Above the level of the former years,
The mire of sin, the slough of guilty fears,
The mist of doubt, the blight of love's decay,
O Lord of Light, lift all our hearts to-day!

3*

Above the swamps of subterfuge and shame,
The deeds, the thoughts, that honour may not name,
The halting tongue that dares not tell the whole,
O Lord of Truth, lift every Christian soul!

4

Lift every gift that thou thyself hast given:
Low lies the best till lifted up to heaven;
Low lie the bounding heart, the teeming brain,
Till, sent from God, they mount to God again.

GENERAL

5

Then, as the trumpet-call in after years,
'Lift up your hearts!' rings pealing in our ears,
Still shall those hearts respond with full accord,
'We lift them up, we lift them to the Lord!'

H. MONTAGU BUTLER

HYMNS OF PERSONAL DEVOTION

HYMN 342 Cheshire   Este, *Psalms*, 1592

KEY A♭

LORD, it belongs not to my care
　Whether I die or live:
To love and serve thee is my share,
　And this thy grace must give.

2

Christ leads me through no darker rooms
　Than he went through before;
He that unto God's Kingdom comes
　Must enter by this door.

3

Come, Lord, when grace hath made me meet
　Thy blessèd face to see;
For if thy work on earth be sweet,
　What will thy glory be!

4

Then I shall end my sad complaints
　And weary, sinful days,
And join with the triumphant saints
　That sing my Saviour's praise.

5

My knowledge of that life is small,
　The eye of faith is dim;
But 'tis enough that Christ knows all,
　And I shall be with him.

R. BAXTER†

Alternative Tune, St. Hugh, 317

353

GENERAL

HYMN 343 Wrestling Jacob   S. S. Wesley, 1810–76

KEY **G**

[Tonic sol-fa notation]

D.t.

f.G.

mf COME, O thou Traveller unknown,
    Whom still I hold, but cannot see;
My company before is gone,
    And I am left alone with thee;
With thee all night I mean to stay,
And wrestle till the break of day.

2

p I need not tell thee who I am,
    My misery or sin declare;
Thyself hast called me by my name;
    Look on thy hands, and read it there!
But who, I ask thee, who art thou?
Tell me thy Name, and tell me now.

3

mf In vain thou strugglest to get free;
    I never will unloose my hold.
Art thou the Man that died for me?
    The secret of thy love unfold:
Wrestling, I will not let thee go,
Till I thy Name, thy nature know.

4

Yield to me now, for I am weak,
    But confident in self-despair;
Speak to my heart, in blessings speak,
    Be conquered by my instant [prayer.
Speak, or thou never hence shalt move,
And tell me if thy Name is Love?

5

f   'Tis Love! 'tis Love! thou diedst for me!
    I hear thy whisper in my heart!
The morning breaks, the shadows flee;
    Pure universal Love thou art:
To me, to all, thy mercies move;
Thy nature and thy Name is Love.

C. WESLEY†

NOTE. *This hymn is based on the story of Jacob's encounter with the angel in Gen. 32. 24–30*

Alternative Tune, EMMAUS, 585

GENERAL

HYMN 344

FIRST TUNE

KEY B♭ Tunbridge

J. Clarke, c. 1659–1707

SECOND TUNE

KEY A♭ St. Bees

J. B. Dykes, 1823–76

mf HARK, my soul! it is the Lord;
'Tis thy Saviour, hear his word;
Jesus speaks, and speaks to thee,
p 'Say, poor sinner, lov'st thou me?

2

mf 'I delivered thee when bound,
And, when wounded, healed thy wound;
Sought thee wandering, set thee right,
Turned thy darkness into light.

3

'Can a woman's tender care
Cease towards the child she bare?
Yes, she may forgetful be,
Yet will I remember thee.

4

f Mine is an unchanging love,
Higher than the heights above,
Deeper than the depths beneath,
Free and faithful, strong as death.

5

'Thou shalt see my glory soon,
When the work of grace is done;
Partner of my throne shalt be:
p Say, poor sinner, lov'st thou me?'

6

mf Lord, it is my chief complaint
That my love is weak and faint;
f Yet I love thee, and adore;
O for grace to love thee more!

W. COWPER

GENERAL

HYMN 345 Bangor   W. Tans'ur, *Harmony of Zion*, 1735
KEY E♭

mf APPROACH, my soul, the mercy-seat,
Where Jesus answers prayer;
There humbly fall before his feet,
For none can perish there.

2
p Thy promise is my only plea,
With this I venture nigh:
Thou callest burdened souls to thee,
And such, O Lord, am I.

3
Bowed down beneath a load of sin,
By Satan sorely pressed,
By war without and fears within,
I come to thee for rest.

4
Be thou my shield and hiding-place,
That, sheltered near thy side,
I may my fierce accuser face,
And tell him thou hast died.

5
mf O wondrous love, to bleed and die,
To bear the Cross and shame,
That guilty sinners, such as I,
Might plead thy gracious name!

J. NEWTON

Alternative Tune, Bedford, 320

HYMN 346 Nearer Home   I. B. Woodbury, 1819–58
KEY A

GENERAL

[Tonic sol-fa notation]

VERSE 2, LINES 5 AND 6

† Ah! then my spi-rit faints | To reach the land I love,

'FOR ever with the Lord!'
  Amen; so let it be:
Life from the dead is in that word,
  'Tis immortality.
Here in the body pent,
  Absent from him I roam,
Yet nightly pitch my moving tent
  A day's march nearer home.

2

My Father's house on high,
  Home of my soul, how near
At times to faith's foreseeing eye
  Thy golden gates appear!
†Ah, then my spirit faints
  To reach the land I love,
The bright inheritance of saints,
  Jerusalem above.

3

'For ever with the Lord!'
  Father, if 'tis thy will,
The promise of that faithful word
  Even here to me fulfil.
Be thou at my right hand,
  Then can I never fail;
Uphold thou me, and I shall stand,
  Fight, and I must prevail.

4

So when my latest breath
  Shall rend the veil in twain,
By death I shall escape from death,
  And life eternal gain.
Knowing as I am known,
  How shall I love that word,
And oft repeat before the throne,
  'For ever with the Lord!'

J. MONTGOMERY

GENERAL

HYMN 347 Nun danket all   *Praxis pietatis melica*, 1653

KEY **G**

{| :d | l₁.s₁ :d :r | m.m :r :— ‖ .m | s.f :m   :r | d :— |
 | :s₁ | f₁.s₁ :l₁ :t₁ | t₁.d :t₁ :— | .t₁ | d.l :d   :t₁ | d :— |
 | :m | d.d :m :s | s.s :s :— | .s | m.f :s   :s | m :— |
 | :d | f₁.m₁ :l₁ :s₁ | m₁.d₁ :s₁ :— ‖ .m₁ | d₁.r₁ :m₁.f₁ :s₁ | d :— |}

{| :s | m.s :l :s | f.m :r :— ‖ .s | d.f :m   :r | d :— |
 | :r | d.r :d :t₁ | l₁.s₁ :s₁ :— | .t₁ | l₁.l₁ :d :t₁ | d :— |
 | :s | s.r :m :—.r | d.d :t₁ :— | .m | m.f :s   :—.f | m :— |
 | :t₁ | d.t₁ :l₁ :m₁ | f₁.d :s₁ :— ‖ .m₁ | l₁.r₁ :m₁.f₁ :s₁ | d₁ :— |}

JESUS, these eyes have never seen
   That radiant form of thine;
The veil of sense hangs dark between
   Thy blessèd face and mine.

2

I see thee not, I hear thee not,
   Yet art thou oft with me;
And earth hath ne'er so dear a spot
   As where I meet with thee.

3

Yet, though I have not seen, and still
   Must rest in faith alone,
I love thee, dearest Lord, and will,
   Unseen, but not unknown.

4

When death these mortal eyes shall seal
   And still this throbbing heart,
The rending veil shall thee reveal
   All glorious as thou art.

R. PALMER

HYMN 348 Stephanos   Sir H. W. Baker, 1821–77

KEY **G**

{| m :m | m :r | m :s | s :f | m :m | r :d | r :— | :— |
 | s₁:s₁ | s₁:s₁ | s₁:s₁ | d :s₁ | s₁:s₁ | s₁:s₁ | s₁:— | :— |
 | d :d | d :t₁ | d :r | m :r | d :m | f :m | t₁:— | :— |
 | d₁:m₁ | s₁:s₁ | d :t₁ | l₁:t₁ | d :d | t₁:d | s₁:— | :— |}

358

GENERAL

```
{ s₁ :l₁.t₁|d :t₁  |d :r.m|f :m  |r :—  |r :—  |d :—  |— :—
  s₁ :s₁ |s₁ :s₁ |s₁ :s₁|f₁ :s₁|l₁ :— |s₁ :— |m₁ :— |— :—
  s  :f  |m  :r  |m  :r |d  :d |d  :— |t₁ :— |d  :— |— :—
  m  :r  |d  :s₁ |d  :t₁|l₁ :s₁|f₁ :— |s₁ :— |d₁ :— |— :—  }
```

p ART thou weary, art thou languid,
    Art thou sore distrest?
mf 'Come to me,' saith One, 'and coming
p   Be at rest!'

2

Hath he marks to lead me to him,
    If he be my guide?
'In his feet and hands are wound-prints,
    And his side.'

3

mf Hath he diadem as Monarch
    That his brow adorns?
p 'Yea, a crown, in very surety,
    But of thorns.'

4

mf If I find him, if I follow,
    What his guerdon here?
p 'Many a sorrow, many a labour,
    Many a tear.'

5

mf If I still hold closely to him,
    What hath he at last?
f 'Sorrow vanquished, labour ended,
    Jordan past.'

6

mf If I ask him to receive me,
    Will he say me nay?
f 'Not till earth, and not till heaven,
    Pass away.'

7

mf Finding, following, keeping, struggling,
    Is he sure to bless?
f 'Angels, martyrs, prophets, virgins,
    Answer, Yes!'

J. M. NEALE†

GENERAL

Hymn 349 Misericordia H. Smart, 1813–79

KEY E♭

(tonic sol-fa notation)

p JUST as I am, without one plea
But that thy Blood was shed for me,
And that thou bidst me come to thee,
　　O Lamb of God, I come.

2

Just as I am, though tossed about
With many a conflict, many a doubt,
Fightings and fears within, without,
　　O Lamb of God, I come.

3

Just as I am, poor, wretched, blind;
Sight, riches, healing of the mind,
Yea, all I need, in thee to find,
　　O Lamb of God, I come.

4

mf Just as I am, thou wilt receive,
Wilt welcome, pardon, cleanse, relieve:
Because thy promise I believe,
　　O Lamb of God, I come.

5

Just as I am (thy love unknown
Has broken every barrier down),
f Now to be thine, yea, thine alone,
　　O Lamb of God, I come.

6

mf Just as I am, of that free love
The breadth, length, depth, and height to prove,
f Here for a season, then above,
　　O Lamb of God, I come.

CHARLOTTE ELLIOTT

Alternative Tune, Saffron Walden, 120

GENERAL

Hymn 350   Come unto Me   J. B. Dykes, 1823–76

KEY **G**

[sol-fa notation]

1
mf 'COME unto me, ye weary,
  And I will give you rest.'
O blessèd voice of Jesus,
  Which comes to hearts opprest!
It tells of benediction,
  Of pardon, grace, and peace,
Of joy that hath no ending,
  Of love which cannot cease.

2
'Come unto me, ye wanderers,
  And I will give you light.'
O loving voice of Jesus,
  Which comes to cheer the night!
p Our hearts were filled with sadness,
  And we had lost our way;
f But he has brought us gladness
  And songs at break of day.

3
mf 'Come unto me, ye fainting,
  And I will give you life.'
O cheering voice of Jesus,
  Which comes to aid our strife!
The foe is stern and eager,
  The fight is fierce and long;
f But he has made us mighty,
  And stronger than the strong.

4
mf 'And whosoever cometh,
  I will not cast him out.'
f O welcome voice of Jesus,
  Which drives away our doubt!
Which calls us very sinners,
  Unworthy though we be,
Of love so free and boundless,
  To come, dear Lord, to thee.

W. CHATTERTON DIX

GENERAL

Hymn 351 Vox dilecti J. B. Dykes, 1823–76

KEY B♭

[tonic sol-fa notation]

G. 3.

[tonic sol-fa notation]

* VERSES 2 AND 3, LINES 5 AND 6

[tonic sol-fa notation]

2 I came to Je-sus, and I drank Of that life-giv-ing stream.
3 I looked to Je-sus, and I found In him my Star, my Sun.

mf I HEARD the voice of Jesus say,
　'Come unto me and rest;
　Lay down, thou weary one, lay down
　　Thy head upon my breast:'
f I came to Jesus as I was,
　Weary and worn and sad;
　I found in him a resting-place,
　　And he has made me glad.

GENERAL

2
mf I heard the voice of Jesus say,
  'Behold, I freely give
The living water, thirsty one;
  Stoop down and drink and live:'
f *I came to Jesus, and I drank
  Of that life-giving stream;
My thirst was quenched, my soul re-
And now I live in him. [vived,

3
mf I heard the voice of Jesus say,
  'I am this dark world's Light;
Look unto me, thy morn shall rise,
  And all thy day be bright:'
f *I looked to Jesus, and I found
  In him my Star, my Sun;
And in that Light of life I'll walk
  Till travelling days are done.

H. BONAR

HYMN 352   Horbury   J. B. Dykes, 1823–76
KEY E♭

[sol-fa notation music score]

mf NEARER, my God, to thee,
    Nearer to thee!
  E'en though it be a cross
    That raiseth me;
  Still all my song shall be,
  'Nearer, my God, to thee,
    Nearer to thee!'

2
p Though, like the wanderer,
      The sun gone down,
    Darkness comes over me,
      My rest a stone;
    Yet in my dreams I'd be
    Nearer, my God, to thee,
      Nearer to thee.

3
mf There let my way appear
      Steps unto heaven.
    All that thou sendest me
      In mercy given;
    Angels to beckon me
    Nearer, my God, to thee,
      Nearer to thee.

4
f Then, with my waking thoughts
      Bright with thy praise,
    Out of my stony griefs
      Beth-el I'll raise;
    So by my woes to be
    Nearer, my God, to thee,
      Nearer to thee.

MRS. S. F. ADAMS†

NOTE. *This hymn is based on the story of Jacob's dream in Gen. 28. 11-19.*

GENERAL

Hymn 353 Pearsall
R. L. Pearsall, 1795-1856

KEY **D**

```
{ :s   | d' :t  | d' :m  | l :—  | s    || s    | f :m   | r :r     | m :— | — ||
{ :m   | d  :f  | m  :m  | f :—  | m    || m    | r :d   | d :t₁    | d :— | — ||
{ :d'  | s  :f  | l  :t  | d':—  | d'   || d'.t | l :s   | l :s     | s :— | — ||
{ :d   | m  :r  | l  :s  | f :—  | d    || d    | r :m   | f :s     | d :— | — ||

{ :d   | m :f   | s :s   | l :—  | s    || s    | l :t   | d' :r'.d'| t :— | — ||
{ :s₁  | d :d   | r :m   | f :—  | m    || m    | f :f   | m :fe    | s :— | — ||
{ :s   | s :l   | t :d'  | d':—  | d'   || d'   | d' :r' | d' :d'   | r':— | — ||
{ :m   | d :l₁  | s₁:d   | f₁:—  | d    || d    | f :r   | l :l     | s :— | — ||

{ :d'  | l :s   | f :m   | f :—  | r    || l    | s :f   | m :r     | s :— | — ||
{ :s   | f :m   | r :de  | r :—  | r    || m    | r :l₁.t₁| d :r    | d :— | — ||
{ :d'  | d':d'  | l :l   | l :—  | l    || m.f  | s :l .f| s :l     | s :— | — ||
{ :m   | f :d   | r :l₁  | r :—  | f    || d    | t₁:r   | d :f     | m :— | — ||

{ :l.t | d':t   | d' :m  | l :—  | s    || s    | f :m   | r :r     | d :— | — ||
{ :f   | m :f   | m :m   | f :—  | m    || d    | d :d   | d :t₁    | d :— | — ||
{ :f   | s :r'  | d' :t  | d':—  | d'   || d'   | l :s   | l :s.f   | m :— | — ||
{ :r   | d :r   | l :s   | f :—  | d    || m    | f :d   | f₁:s₁    | d :— | — ||
```

I COULD not do without thee,
  O Saviour of the lost,
Whose precious Blood redeemed me
  At such tremendous cost:
Thy righteousness, thy pardon,
  Thy precious Blood, must be—
My only hope and comfort,
  My glory and my plea.

2
I could not do without thee,
  I cannot stand alone,
I have no strength or goodness,
  No wisdom of my own;
But thou, belovèd Saviour,
  Art all in all to me,
And weakness will be power
  If leaning hard on thee.

3
I could not do without thee,
  O Jesus, Saviour dear;
E'en when my eyes are holden,
  I know that thou art near:
How dreary and how lonely
  This changeful life would be
Without the sweet communion,
  The secret rest, with thee!

4
I could not do without thee,
  For years are fleeting fast,
And soon in solemn loneness
  The river must be passed;
But thou wilt never leave me,
  And, though the waves roll high,
I know thou wilt be near me,
  And whisper, 'It is I.'

FRANCES R. HAVERGAL

Hymn 354 Pilgrims
H. Smart, 1813-79

KEY **E**

```
{ | m :s.f  | m :—.r | d .r :m .f | m :r   || s :d'.t  | l :—.s | f .r :m.f | r :—   ||
{ | d :r .r | d :t₁  | d .t₁:d .r | d :t₁  || d :d .d  | d :—.d | t₁.r :d.r | t₁:—   ||
{ | s :s .s | s :—.f | m .m :l .l | s :s   || s :m.s   | f :—.s | s .s :s.l | s :—   ||
{ | d :t₁.t₁| d :s₁  | l₁.l₁:l₁.f₁| s₁:s₁  || m :d .m  | f :—.m | r .t₁:d.f₁| s₁:—   ||
```

GENERAL

B. t.

mf HARK! hark, my soul! angelic songs are swelling
　O'er earth's green fields and ocean's wave-beat shore:
How sweet the truth those blessèd strains are telling
　Of that new life when sin shall be no more!
p　Angels of Jesus, angels of light,
　Singing to welcome the pilgrims of the night!

2

mf Onward we go, for still we hear them singing,
p　'Come, weary souls, for Jesus bids you come;'
mf And through the dark, its echoes sweetly ringing,
　The music of the Gospel leads us home.
p　Angels of Jesus, angels of light,
　Singing to welcome the pilgrims of the night!

3*

Far, far away, like bells at evening pealing,
　The voice of Jesus sounds o'er land and sea,
And laden souls, by thousands meekly stealing,
　Kind Shepherd, turn their weary steps to thee.
p　Angels of Jesus, angels of light,
　Singing to welcome the pilgrims of the night!

4

mf Rest comes at length: though life be long and dreary,
　The day must dawn, and darksome night be past;
Faith's journey ends in welcome to the weary,
　And heaven, the heart's true home, will come at last.
p　Angels of Jesus, angels of light,
　Singing to welcome the pilgrims of the night!

5

f Angels, sing on, your faithful watches keeping,
　Sing us sweet fragments of the songs above;
Till morning's joy shall end the night of weeping,
　And life's long shadows break in cloudless love.
p　Angels of Jesus, angels of light,
　Singing to welcome the pilgrims of the night!

F. W. Faber†

GENERAL

Hymn 355 St. Catherine
R. F. Dale, 1845–1919

KEY D

[Sol-fa notation]

1
p O JESU, thou art standing
 Outside the fast-closed door,
 In lowly patience waiting
 To pass the threshold o'er:
mf Shame on us, Christian brethren,
 His name and sign who bear,
 O shame, thrice shame upon us
p To keep him standing there!

2
O Jesu, thou art knocking;
 And lo, that hand is scarred,
And thorns thy brow encircle,
 And tears thy face have marred:
mf O love that passeth knowledge,
 So patiently to wait!
O sin that hath no equal
 So fast to bar the gate!

3
p O Jesu, thou art pleading
 In accents meek and low,
'I died for you, my children,
 And will ye treat me so?'
mf O Lord, with shame and sorrow
 We open now the door:
Dear Saviour, enter, enter,
 And leave us nevermore.

BISHOP W. WALSHAM HOW

GENERAL

HYMN 356 Ibstone   Maria Tiddeman, 1837–1911
KEY D

mf THY way, not mine, O Lord,
However dark it be;
Lead me by thine own hand,
Choose out the path for me.

2
Smooth let it be or rough,
It will be still the best;
Winding or straight, it leads
Right onward to thy rest.

3
I dare not choose my lot;
I would not if I might:
Choose thou for me, my God,
So shall I walk aright.

4
The Kingdom that I seek
Is thine; so let the way
That leads to it be thine,
Else I must surely stray.

5
p Take thou my cup, and it
With joy or sorrow fill,
As best to thee may seem;
Choose thou my good and ill.

6
Choose thou for me my friends,
My sickness or my health;
Choose thou my cares for me,
My poverty or wealth.

7
mf Not mine, not mine, the choice
In things or great or small;
Be thou my guide, my strength,
My wisdom, and my all.

H. BONAR

GENERAL

HYMN 357 FIRST TUNE

KEY **G** Ins Feld geh *Geistliche Volkslieder* (Paderborn, 1856)

[Sol-fa notation]

SECOND TUNE

KEY **E♭** Troyte's Chant No. 1 A. H. Dyke Troyte, 1811–57

[Sol-fa notation]

MY God, my Father, while I stray,
Far from my home, on life's rough way,
O teach me from my héart to say,
        'Thy will be done!'

2

Though dark my path, and sád my lot,
Let me be still and múrmur not,
Or breathe the prayer divínely taught,
        'Thy will be done!'

3

What though in lonely gríef I sigh
For friends beloved no lónger nigh,
Submissive would I stíll reply,
        'Thy will be done!'

4

If thou shouldst call me tó resign
What most I prize, it ne'ér was mine;
I only yield thee whát is thine:
        Thy will be done!

5

Let but my fainting héart be blest
With thy sweet Spirit fór its guest,
My God, to thee I léave the rest:
        Thy will be done!

6

Renew my will from dáy to day,
Blend it with thine, and táke away
All that now makes it hárd to say,
        'Thy will be done!'

CHARLOTTE ELLIOTT

GENERAL

HYMN 358   FIRST TUNE
KEY **F**   Song 46   Orlando Gibbons, 1583–1625

SECOND TUNE
KEY **C**   Pax tecum   G. T. Caldbeck (1877)

mf   PEACE, perfect peace, in this dark world of sin?
p   The Blood of Jesus whispers peace within.

2
mf   Peace, perfect peace, by thronging duties pressed?
p   To do the will of Jesus, this is rest.

3
mf   Peace, perfect peace, with sorrows surging round?
p   On Jesus' bosom naught but calm is found.

4
mf   Peace, perfect peace, with loved ones far away?
p   In Jesus' keeping we are safe and they.

5
mf   Peace, perfect peace, our future all unknown?
f   Jesus we know, and he is on the throne.

6
p   Peace, perfect peace, death shadowing us and ours?
f   Jesus has vanquished death and all its powers.

7
mf   It is enough: earth's struggles soon shall cease,
       And Jesus call us to heaven's perfect peace.

BISHOP E. H. BICKERSTETH

GENERAL

HYMN 359 Wyke
L. H. Heward, 1897-1943

KEY **D**

A.t.

[sol-fa notation musical score]

f.D.

[sol-fa notation musical score]

mf O LOVE that wilt not let me go,
    I rest my weary soul in thee:
    I give thee back the life I owe,
    That in thine ocean depths its flow
    May richer, fuller, be.

2
p O Light that followest all my way,
    I yield my flickering torch to thee:
mf My heart restores its borrowed ray,
    That in thy sunshine's blaze its day
    May brighter, fairer be.

3
p O Joy that seekest me through pain,
    I cannot close my heart to thee:
mf I trace the rainbow through the rain,
    And feel the promise is not vain
    That morn shall tearless be.

4
O Cross that liftest up my head,
    I dare not ask to fly from thee:
    I lay in dust life's glory dead,
f And from the ground there blossoms red
    Life that shall endless be.

G. MATHESON

HYMN 360 North Coates
T. R. Matthews, 1826-1910

KEY **G**

[sol-fa notation musical score]

370

GENERAL

p O MY Saviour, lifted
From the earth for me,
Draw me, in thy mercy,
Nearer unto thee.

2

Lift my earth-bound longings,
Fix them, Lord, above;
Draw me with the magnet
Of thy mighty love.

3

mf Lord, thine arms are stretching
Ever far and wide,
To enfold thy children
To thy loving side.

4

And I come, O Jesus:
Dare I turn away?
f No, thy love hath conquered,
And I come to-day;

5

mf Bringing all my burdens,
Sorrow, sin, and care,
At thy feet I lay them,
And I leave them there.

BISHOP W. WALSHAM HOW

HYMN 361 Consecration   W. H. Havergal, 1793–1870

KEY D

TAKE my life, and let it be
Consecrated, Lord, to thee;
Take my moments and my days,
Let them flow in ceaseless praise.

2

Take my hands, and let them move
At the impulse of thy love.
Take my feet, and let them be
Swift and beautiful for thee.

3

Take my voice, and let me sing
Always, only, for my King;
Take my lips, and let them be
Filled with messages from thee.

4

Take my silver and my gold;
Not a mite would I withhold
Take my intellect, and use
Every power as thou shalt choose.

5

Take my will, and make it thine:
It shall be no longer mine.
Take my heart: it is thine own;
It shall be thy royal throne.

6

Take my love; my Lord, I pour
At thy feet its treasure-store.
Take myself, and I will be
Ever, only, all for thee.

FRANCES R. HAVERGAL

GENERAL

HYMN 362 Carlisle C. Lockhart, 1745–1815

KEY E♭

Slow

REVIVE thy work, O Lord!
Thy mighty arm make bare;
Speak with the voice that wakes the dead,
And make thy people hear.

2
Revive thy work, O Lord!
Disturb this sleep of death;
Quicken the smouldering embers now
By thine almighty breath.

3
Revive thy work, O Lord!
Create soul-thirst for thee:
And hungering for the Bread of Life
O may our spirits be.

4
Revive thy work, O Lord!
Exalt thy precious name;
And by the Holy Ghost our love
For thee and thine inflame.

5
Revive thy work, O Lord!
Give Pentecostal showers;
The glory shall be all thine own,
The blessing, Lord, be ours.

A. MIDLANE

HYMN 363 Margaret T. R. Matthews, 1826–1910

KEY D

GENERAL

(tonic sol-fa notation omitted)

mf THOU didst | leave thy throne and thy | kingly crown,
When thou | camest to earth for me;
But in | Bethlehem's home was there | found no room
For thy | holy Nativity:
O come to my heart, Lord Jesus;
There is room in my heart for thee.

2

f Heaven's | arches rang when the | angels sang,
Pro- | claiming thy royal degree;
p But in | lowly birth didst thou | come to earth,
And in | great humility:
O come to my heart, Lord Jesus;
There is room in my heart for thee.

3

mf The | foxes found rest, and the | bird had its nest
In the | shade of the cedar tree;
p But thy couch | was the sod, O thou | Son of God,
In the | desert of Galilee:
O come to my heart, Lord Jesus;
There is room in my heart for thee.

4

mf Thou | camest, O Lord, with the | living word
That should | set thy people free;
p But with | mocking scorn and with | crown of thorn
They | bore thee to Calvary:
O come to my heart, Lord Jesus;
There is room in my heart for thee.

5

f When the | heavens shall ring, and the | angels sing,
At thy | coming to victory,
Let thy | voice call me home, saying, | 'Yet there is room,
There is | room at my side for thee:'
O come to my heart, Lord Jesus;
There is room in my heart for thee.

EMILY E. S. ELLIOTT

GENERAL

Hymn 364 Gott will's machen
J. L. Steiner, 1688–1761

KEY G

1. SOULS of men! why will ye scatter
Like a crowd of frightened sheep?
Foolish hearts! why will ye wander
From a love so true and deep?

2. Was there ever kindest shepherd
Half so gentle, half so sweet,
As the Saviour who would have us
Come and gather round his feet?

3. There's a wideness in God's mercy
Like the wideness of the sea;
There's a kindness in his justice
Which is more than liberty.

4. There is no place where earth's sorrows
Are more felt than up in heaven;
There is no place where earth's failings
Have such kindly judgement given.

5. There is plentiful redemption
In the Blood that has been shed;
There is joy for all the members
In the sorrows of the Head.

6. For the love of God is broader
Than the measures of man's mind;
And the heart of the Eternal
Is most wonderfully kind.

7. Pining souls! come nearer Jesus,
And oh, come not doubting thus,
But with faith that trusts more bravely
His huge tenderness for us.

8. If our love were but more simple,
We should take him at his word;
And our lives would be all sunshine
In the sweetness of our Lord.

F. W. Faber

Hymn 365 Praise, my soul
Sir J. Goss, 1800–80

KEY D

UNISON

1 Praise, my soul, the King of hea - ven, To his feet thy tri - bute bring;
Ran-somed, healed, re - stored, for - giv - en, Who like me his praise should sing?
Al - le - lu - ia! Al - le - lu - ia! Praise the ev - er - last - ing King.

GENERAL

HARMONY

[Tonic sol-fa notation]

2. Praise him for his grace and favour
To our fathers in distress;
Praise him still the same as ever,
Slow to chide, and swift to bless:
Alleluia! Alleluia! Glorious in his faithfulness.

TREBLES

3. Father-like, he tends and spares us,
Well our feeble frame he knows,
In his hands he gently bears us.
Rescues us from all our foes:
Alleluia! Alleluia! Widely as his mercy flows.

UNISON

4. Angels, help us to adore him;
Ye behold him face to face;
Sun and moon, bow down before him,
Dwellers all in time and space:
Alleluia! Alleluia! Praise with us the God of grace.

H. F. LYTE†

GENERAL

HYMN 366 FIRST TUNE

KEY E♭ Saving health   *Etlich Christliche Lyeder*, 1524

```
       f. A♭.                    E♭. t.
{:s   |s  :s   |ˢr  :f   |m    :r    |d   ||ʳs   |m  :d.r |m  :fe  
 :t₁  |d  :d.t₁|ᵈs₁ :l₁  |s₁   :l₁.s₁|m₁  ||¹ʳr  |d  :d   |d  :d   
 :r   |m  :f   |ˢr  :d.r |m.d  :d.t₁ |d   ||¹ʳr  |s  :s.f |s  :l   
 :s₁  |d  :r   |ᵐt₁ :l₁.t₁|d.m₁:f₁.s₁|d₁  ||feₒt₁|d  :m.r |d  :l₁ }
```

```
                          f. A♭.                        E♭. t.
{ |s :l   |s  :—  ||s   |s  :s   |ˢr :f   |m      :r    |d   ||ʳs
  |t₁:r   |t₁ :—  ||r   |d  :d.t₁|ᵈs₁:l₁  |t₁.se₁ :l₁.t₁|d   ||¹ʳr
  |s :-.fe|s  :—  ||s.f |m  :f   |ˢr :d   |t₁     :m    |m   ||ʳs
  |m :r   |s₁ :—  ||t₁  |d  :r   |ᵐt₁:l₁  |se₁.m₁ :ba₁.se₁|l₁||feₒt₁ }
```

```
{ |m :d.r |m  :fe  |s  :l   |s  :—  ||s  |d' :t  |l  :t  |d'.t:l |s
  |d :l₁.t₁|d :d   |t₁ :r.d |t₁ :—  ||r  |d  :m.r|d  :r  |d  :r.d|t₁
  |s :s.f |m.r:d   |r  :fe  |s  :—  ||s  |l  :s  |l.s:f  |l.s:fe |s
  |d :m.r |d.t₁:l₁ |s₁ :r₁  |s₁ :—  ||t₁ |l₁ :m  |f.m:r  |l₁ :r  |s₁ }
```

```
{ :s  |d' :s  |l  |m.f |s  :f   |m   ||d   |r  :f   |m  :r   |l₁:t₁|d :—
  :r  |d  :m.r|d  |m   |m  :r   |de  ||d   |t₁ :r.d |t₁ :l₁  |m₁:s₁|s₁:—
  :t  |l  :d'.t|l |:s.l|l  :l.se|l   ||m.fe|s  :l   |s  :—.f |d :r |m :—
  :s  |l  :m  |f  :d   |de :r   |l₁  ||l₁  |s₁ :r₁  |m₁ :f₁  |l₁:s₁|d :— }
```

SECOND TUNE

KEY G Luther   M. Luther, 1483–1546

```
{ :d   |d  :m  |r  :d  |r  :r  |m   ||d  |m  :f  |s  :m   |r  :—  |d :—
  :s₁  |s₁ :d  |t₁ :d  |d  :t₁ |d   ||s₁ |s₁ :d  |t₁ :d   |d  :t₁ |d :—
  :m   |d  :s  |s  :m  |l  :s  |s   ||m  |s  :d  |r  :d   |l  :s.f|m :—
  :d₁  |m₁ :d₁ |s₁ :l₁ |f₁ :s₁ |d₁  ||d  |d  :l₁ |s₁ :l₁  |f₁ :s₁ |d₁:— }
```

```
{ :d   |d  :m  |r  :d  |r  :r  |m   ||d  |m  :f  |s  :m   |r  :—  |d :—
  :s₁  |s₁ :d  |t₁ :d  |d  :t₁ |d   ||s₁ |s₁ :d  |t₁ :d   |d  :t₁ |d :—
  :m   |d  :s  |s  :m  |l  :s  |s   ||s.f|m.r:d  |r  :d   |l  :s.f|m :—
  :d₁  |m₁ :d₁ |s₁ :l₁ |f₁ :s₁ |d   ||m.r|d.t₁:l₁|s₁ :l₁   |f₁ :s₁ |d :— }
```

376

GENERAL

(musical notation in tonic sol-fa)

Sei Lob und Ehr' dem höchsten Gut

SING praise to God who reigns above,
 The God of all creation,
The God of power, the God of love,
 The God of our salvation;
With healing balm my soul he fills,
And every faithless murmur stills:
 To God all praise and glory.

2

The Lord is never far away,
 But, through all grief distressing,
An ever-present help and stay,
 Our peace and joy and blessing;
As with a mother's tender hand,
He leads his own, his chosen band:
 To God all praise and glory.

3

Thus all my gladsome way along
 I sing aloud thy praises,
That men may hear the grateful song
 My voice unwearied raises.
Be joyful in the Lord, my heart;
Both soul and body bear your part:
 To God all praise and glory.

J. J. SCHÜTZ *Tr.* FRANCES E. COX

Alternative Tune, Laus Deo (Bach), 422

GENERAL

HYMN 367 FIRST TUNE
KEY A♭ Salve cordis gaudium J. R. Ahle, 1625-73

[Tonic sol-fa notation musical score]

D.C. E♭ t.

f. A♭.

Al - le - lu - ia.

SECOND TUNE
KEY G Gwalchmai J. D. Jones, 1827-70

[Tonic sol-fa notation musical score]

GENERAL

f KING of glory, King of peace,
   I will love thee;
And, that love may never cease,
   I will move thee.
Thou hast granted my request,
   Thou hast heard me;
Thou didst note my working breast,
   Thou hast spared me. [Alleluia!]

2

Wherefore with my utmost art
   I will sing thee,
And the cream of all my heart
   I will bring thee.
mf Though my sins against me cried,
   Thou didst clear me,
And alone, when they replied,
   Thou didst hear me. [Alleluia!]

3

f Seven whole days, not one in seven,
   I will praise thee;
In my heart, though not in heaven,
   I can raise thee.
mf Small it is, in this poor sort
   To enrol thee:
f E'en eternity's too short
   To extol thee. [Alleluia!]

GEORGE HERBERT

HYMN **368** Austria   F. J. Haydn, 1732–1809

KEY **F**

Psalm 148

PRAISE the Lord! ye heavens, adore
   Praise him, angels, in the height; [him;
Sun and moon, rejoice before him,
   Praise him, all ye stars and light.
Praise the Lord! for he hath spoken;
   Worlds his mighty voice obeyed:
Laws, which never shall be broken,
   For their guidance he hath made.

2

Praise the Lord! for he is glorious;
   Never shall his promise fail:
God hath made his saints victorious;
   Sin and death shall not prevail.
Praise the God of our salvation;
   Hosts on high, his power proclaim;
Heaven and earth and all creation,
   Laud and magnify his name!

Foundling Hospital Collection, 1796

GENERAL

HYMN 369 Northampton   C. J. KING, 1859–1934

KEY **A**

mf SONGS of praise the angels sang,
Heaven with Alleluias rang,
When creation was begun,
When God spake and it was done.

2

Songs of praise awoke the morn
When the Prince of Peace was born;
Songs of praise arose when he
Captive led captivity.

3

p Heaven and earth must pass away;
Songs of praise shall crown that day:
God will make new heavens and earth;
Songs of praise shall hail their birth.

4

p And will man alone be dumb
Till that glorious Kingdom come?
f No, the Church delights to raise
Psalms and hymns and songs of praise.

5

mf Saints below, with heart and voice,
Still in songs of praise rejoice;
Learning here, by faith and love,
Songs of praise to sing above.

[UNISON]
6
f Hymns of glory, songs of praise,
Father, unto thee we raise,
Jesu, glory unto thee,
With the Spirit, ever be.

J. MONTGOMERY and Compilers

Alternative Tune, Culbach, 73

GENERAL

Hymn 370 Old 100th   L. Bourgeois, *c.* 1500–61

KEY A♭

Psalm 100

mf BEFORE Jehovah's awful throne,
   Ye nations, bow with sacred joy;
   Know that the Lord is God alone:
   He can create, and he destroy.

2

His sovereign power, without our aid,
   Made us of clay, and formed us men;
And, when like wandering sheep we strayed,
   He brought us to his fold again.

3

f We'll crowd thy gates with thankful songs,
   High as the heavens our voices raise;
And earth, with her ten thousand tongues,
   Shall fill thy courts with sounding praise.

4

Wide as the world is thy command,
   Vast as eternity thy love;
Firm as a rock thy truth shall stand,
   When rolling years shall cease to move.

I. WATTS‡

GENERAL

Hymn 371 Darwall's 148th J. Darwall, 1731-89

Key D

The Descant may be sung for verse 4

1. *f* YE holy angels bright,
   Who wait at God's right hand,
   Or through the realms of light
   Fly at your Lord's command,
   Assist our song,
   For else the theme
   Too high doth seem
   For mortal tongue.

2. *mf* Ye blessèd souls at rest,
   Who ran this earthly race,
   And now, from sin released,
   Behold the Saviour's face,
   His praises sound,
   As in his light
   With sweet delight
   Ye do abound.

GENERAL

3
Ye saints, who toil below,
Adore your heavenly King,
And onward as ye go
Some joyful anthem sing;
Take what he gives
And praise him still,
Through good and ill,
Who ever lives.

[UNISON] **4**
f My soul, bear thou thy part,
Triumph in God above,
And with a well-tuned heart
Sing thou the songs of love.
Let all thy days
Till life shall end,
Whate'er he send,
Be filled with praise.

R. BAXTER and J. H. GURNEY

HYMN **372** St. Denio   Welsh Hymn Melody
KEY A♭

IMMORTAL, invisible, God only wise,
In light inaccessible hid from our eyes,
Most blessèd, most glorious, the Ancient of Days,
Almighty, victorious, thy great name we praise.

2
Unresting, unhasting, and silent as light,
Nor wanting, nor wasting, thou rulest in might;
Thy justice like mountains high soaring above
Thy clouds which are fountains of goodness and love.

3
To all life thou givest, to both great and small;
In all life thou livest, the true life of all;
We blossom and flourish as leaves on the tree,
And wither and perish; but naught changeth thee.

4
Great Father of glory, pure Father of light,
Thine angels adore thee, all veiling their sight;
All laud we would render: O help us to see
'Tis only the splendour of light hideth thee.

W. CHALMERS SMITH

GENERAL

HYMN 373 Richmond   T. Haweis, 1734–1820

KEY G

[musical notation]

FILL thou my life, O Lord my God,
   In every part with praise,
That my whole being may proclaim
   Thy being and thy ways.

2

Not for the lip of praise alone,
   Nor e'en the praising heart,
I ask, but for a life made up
   Of praise in every part:

3

Praise in the common things of life,
   Its goings out and in;
Praise in each duty and each deed,
   However small and mean.

4

Fill every part of me with praise:
   Let all my being speak
Of thee and of thy love, O Lord,
   Poor though I be and weak.

5*

So shalt thou, Lord, receive from me
   The praise and glory due;
And so shall I begin on earth
   The song for ever new.

6*

So shall each fear, each fret, each care,
   Be turnèd into song;
And every winding of the way
   The echo shall prolong.

GENERAL

[UNISON] 7
So shall no part of day or night
Unblest or common be;
But all my life, in every step,
Be fellowship with thee.

H. BONAR†

HYMN 374 Carlisle
C. Lockhart, 1745-1815

KEY F

[Tonic sol-fa notation]

1
STAND up, and bless the Lord,
Ye people of his choice;
Stand up, and bless the Lord your God
With heart and soul and voice.

2
Though high above all praise,
Above all blessing high,
Who would not fear his holy name,
And laud and magnify?

3
O for the living flame
From his own altar brought,
To touch our lips, our mind inspire,
And wing to heaven our thought!

4
God is our strength and song,
And his salvation ours;
Then be his love in Christ proclaimed
With all our ransomed powers.

5
Stand up, and bless the Lord,
The Lord your God adore;
Stand up, and bless his glorious name
Henceforth for evermore.

J. MONTGOMERY

GENERAL

HYMN 375 Luckington   B. Harwood, 1859-1949

KEY E♭

Cheerfully

{ :d |m :— |s :— |d¹:— |— :d |r :l |s :f |m :— ||s :— |l :— |r :— \
  :s₁ |d :— |r :— |m :— |— :d |d :d |d :t₁|d :— ||r :— |m :— |r :— \
  :m |s :— |t :— |d¹:— |— :s |l :f |r¹:s |s :— ||s :— |s :— |fe:— \
  :d |d :— |t₁:— |l₁:— |— :m |f :r |s :s |d :— ||t₁:— |d :— |r :— / }

{ |t :— |— |d¹:l :f |r :t |d¹:— ||d¹:— |l :f |r :t |d¹:— ||s :— \
  |r :— |— |d d :d |d :r |d :— ||d :— |d :d |d :r |d :— ||r :— \
  |s :— |— |s f :l |s :f |m :— ||s :— |f :l |s :f |m :— ||s :— \
  |s₁:— |— |m f :r |s :s₁|d :— ||m :— |f :r |s :s₁|d :— ||t₁:— / }

{ |m :d |l₁:r |t₁:— |s :— |m :d |l₁:r |t₁:— || :d |m :— |s :— \
  |d :s₁|l₁:l₁|s₁:— |r :— |d :s₁|l₁:l₁|s₁:— || :s₁|l₁:— |t₁:— \
  |s :s |s :fe|r :— |s :— |s :s |s :fe|r :— || :m |d :— |r :— \
  |d :m |r :r |s₁:— |t₁:— |d :m |r :r |s₁:— || :d |l₁:— |s₁:— / }

{ |d¹:— |— :d |r :l |s :f |m :— ||d¹:— |r¹:— |s :— |d¹:— |— || \
  |d :— |— :d |d :d |t₁:r |d :— ||s :— |l :— |s :f |m :— |— || \
  |s :— |— :m |l :f |r :s |s :— ||d¹:— |d¹:— |t :— |d¹:— |— || \
  |m₁:— |— :d |f :r |s₁:t₁|d :— ||m :— |f :— |s :— |d :— |— || }

                                                        2

LET all the world in every corner sing,   Let all the world in every corner sing,
  My God and King!   My God and King!
The heavens are not too high,   The Church with psalms must shout,
His praise may thither fly: No door can keep them out;
The earth is not too low,   But above all the heart
His praises there may grow.   Must bear the longest part.
Let all the world in every corner sing,   Let all the world in every corner sing,
  My God and King!   My God and King!

                                                                                                  GEORGE HERBERT

HYMN 376   FIRST TUNE
KEY B♭   Laudate Dominum   Sir C. H. H. Parry, 1848-1918

Vigorously

{ :s₁ |m :d :r |s₁:— ||d |l₁:s₁:f₁|m₁:— ||s₁ |m :r :s₁ \
  :s₁ |s₁:s₁:l₁|s₁:— ||s₁ |d₁:m₁:r₁|d₁:— ||s₁ |d :t₁:s₁ \
  :s₁ |d :m :r.d|t₁:— ||s₁ |l₁:l₁:t₁|d :— ||m |fe:s :r \
  :s₁ |d :m₁:f₁|s₁:— ||m₁ |f₁:r₁:s₁|d₁:— ||d |l₁:t₁:t₂ / }

GENERAL

Based on Psalm 150

f   O PRAISE ye the Lord! praise him in the height;
Rejoice in his word, ye angels of light;
Ye heavens adore him by whom ye were made,
And worship before him, in brightness arrayed.

2

mf   O praise ye the Lord! praise him upon earth,
In tuneful accord, ye sons of new birth;
f   Praise him who hath brought you his grace from above,
Praise him who hath taught you to sing of his love.

3

O praise ye the Lord, all things that give sound;
Each jubilant chord re-echo around;
Loud organs, his glory forth tell in deep tone,
mf   And, sweet harp, the story of what he hath done.

[UNISON]
4

f   O praise ye the Lord! thanksgiving and song
To him be outpoured all ages along:
For love in creation, for heaven restored,
For grace of salvation, O praise ye the Lord!

SIR H. W. BAKER

GENERAL

Hymn 376 SECOND TUNE

KEY **G** Gauntlett H. J. Gauntlett, 1805–76

[Sol-fa notation music]

Based on Psalm 150

f O PRAISE ye the Lord! praise him in the height;
Rejoice in his word, ye angels of light;
Ye heavens adore him by whom ye were made,
And worship before him, in brightness arrayed.

2

mf O praise ye the Lord! praise him upon earth,
In tuneful accord, ye sons of new birth;
f Praise him who hath brought you his grace from above,
Praise him who hath taught you to sing of his love.

3

O praise ye the Lord, all things that give sound;
Each jubilant chord re-echo around;
Loud organs, his glory forth tell in deep tone,
mf And, sweet harp, the story of what he hath done.

4

f O praise ye the Lord! thanksgiving and song
To him be outpoured all ages along:
For love in creation, for heaven restored,
For grace of salvation, O praise ye the Lord!

SIR H. W. BAKER

GENERAL

Hymn 377 Monkland   J. Wilkes, 1785–1869, adapted from J. Lee's
Hymn Tunes of the United Brethren, 1824

KEY **C**

Psalm 136

f   LET us, with a gladsome mind,
Praise the Lord, for he is kind:
    For his mercies ay endure,
    Ever faithful, ever sure.

2

Let us blaze his name abroad,
For of gods he is the God:
    For his mercies, etc.

3

He with all-commanding might
Filled the new-made world with light:
    For his mercies, etc.

4

mf He the golden-tressèd sun
Caused all day his course to run:
f   For his mercies, etc.

5

p And the hornèd moon at night
'Mid her spangled sisters bright:
f   For his mercies, etc.

6

mf All things living he doth feed,
His full hand supplies their need:
f   For his mercies, etc.

7

Let us, with a gladsome mind,
Praise the Lord, for he is kind:
    For his mercies, etc.

JOHN MILTON‡

GENERAL

HYMN 378 Harvest   C. J. Frost, 1843-1922

KEY **G**

Thanksgiving for the Church's work overseas

mf LORD of the Harvest, it is right and meet
That we should lay our first-fruits at thy feet
                      With joyful Alleluia.

2
Sweet is the soul's thanksgiving after prayer;
Sweet is the worship that with heaven we share,
                      Who sing the Alleluia.

3
Lowly we prayed, and thou didst hear on high,
Didst lift our hearts and change our suppliant cry
                      To festal Alleluia.

4
Sing we now in tune with that great song,
That all the age of ages shall prolong,
                      The endless Alleluia.

5*
To thee, O Lord of Harvest, who hast heard,
And to thy white-robed reapers given the word,
                      We sing our Alleluia.

6*
O Christ, who in the wide world's ghostly sea
Hast bid the net be cast anew, to thee
                      We sing our Alleluia.

7*
To thee, eternal Spirit, who again
Hast moved with life upon the slumbrous main,
                      We sing our Alleluia.

8
Yea, for sweet hope new-born, blest work begun,
Sing Alleluia to the Three in One,
                      Adoring Alleluia.

GENERAL

9

f 'Glory to God!' the Church in patience cries;
'Glory to God!' the Church at rest replies,
   With endless Alleluia.

S. J. STONE

Alternative Tune, St. Sebastian, 283

HYMN 379   Nun danket   J. Crüger, 1598–1662
KEY **F**

Nun danket alle Gott

f   NOW thank we all our God,
    With heart and hands and voices,
      Who wondrous things hath done,
    In whom his world rejoices;
      Who from our mother's arms
        Hath blessed us on our way
      With countless gifts of love,
      And still is ours to-day.

2

mf O may this bounteous God
    Through all our life be near us,
      With ever joyful hearts
    And blessèd peace to cheer us;
      And keep us in his grace,
        And guide us when perplexed,
      And free us from all ills
      In this world and the next.

[UNISON] 3

f   All praise and thanks to God
    The Father now be given,
      The Son, and him who reigns
    With them in highest heaven,
      The one eternal God,
        Whom earth and heaven adore,
      For thus it was, is now,
      And shall be evermore.

M. RINKART *Tr.* Catherine Winkworth

GENERAL

Hymn 380 Old 124th   Melody in *Genevan Psalter*, 1551

KEY G

By permission of the English Hymnal Co., Ltd.

Psalm 145

WE would extol thee, ever-blessèd Lord;
Thy holy name for ever be adored;
Each day we live to thee our psalm we raise:
Thou, God and King, art worthy of our praise,
Great and unsearchable in all thy ways.

2

Age shall to age pass on the endless song,
Telling the wonders which to thee belong,
Thy mighty acts with joy and fear relate;
Laud we thy glory while on thee we wait,
Glad in the knowledge of thy love so great.

GENERAL

3

Thou, Lord, art gracious, merciful to all,
Nigh to thy children when on thee they call;
Slow unto anger, pitiful and kind,
Thou to compassion ever art inclined:
We love thee with our heart and strength and mind.

Verse 1 may be repeated at the end NICHOL GRIEVE

HYMN **381** Arncliffe H. D. Statham

KEY **C**

[sol-fa notation]

Psalm 148

PRAISE the Lord of heaven, praise him in the height;
Praise him, all ye angels, praise him, stars and light;
Praise him, skies and waters, which above the skies,
When his word commanded, stablished did arise.

2

Praise the Lord, ye fountains of the deeps and seas,
Rocks and hills and mountains, cedars and all trees;
Praise him, clouds and vapours, snow and hail and fire,
Stormy wind fulfilling only his desire.

3

Praise him, fowls and cattle, princes and all kings;
Praise him, men and maidens, all created things;
For the name of God is excellent alone:
On the earth his footstool, over heaven his throne.

T. B. BROWNE

GENERAL

HYMN 382 Praxis pietatis   P. Sohren's edition of *Praxis pietatis melica*, 1668

KEY G

{ | d :d :s | m :-.r :d | t₁ :l₁ :s₁ | l₁ :t₁ :d | r :- :- |
  | s₁ :l₁ :s₁ | s₁ :-.t₁:l₁ | s₁ :f₁ :m₁ | f₁ :f₁ :m₁ | l₁ :s₁ :f₁ |
  | m :m :r | s :-.s :m | m :d :d | d :r :d | d :t₁ :- |
  | d :l₁ :t₁ | d :-.s₁:l₁ | m₁ :f₁ :d₁ | f₁ :r₁ :l₁ | f₁ :s₁ :- | }

D.C.

{ | d :- :- || s :s :s | l :- :- || m :f :s | s :f :m |
  | m₁ :- :- || d :r :d | d :- :- || d :d :r | d :l₁.t₁:d |
  | d :- :- || m :r :m | f :- :- || s :f :r | m :f :s |
  | d₁ :- :- || d :t₁ :d | f₁ :- :- || d :l₁ :t₁ | d :r :m.d | }

{ | r :- :- || s₁ :l₁ :t₁ | d :r :m | r :- :- | d :- :- ||
  | t₁ :- :- || s₁ :f₁ :f₁ | m₁ :l₁ :se₁ | l₁ :- :s₁ | m₁ :- :- ||
  | s :- :- || s :d :r | d :l₁ :t₁ | l₁ :r.d:t₁ | d :- :- ||
  | s₁ :- :- || m₁ :f₁ :r₁ | l₁ :f₁ :m₁ | f₁ :- :s₁ | d₁ :- :- || }

Lobe den Herrn

f   PRAISE to the Lord, the Almighty, the King of creation;
O my soul, praise him, for he is thy health and salvation:
     All ye who hear,
     Now to his temple draw near,
Joining in glad adoration.

2

Praise to the Lord, who o'er all things so wondrously reigneth,
mf   Shieldeth thee gently from harm, or when fainting sustaineth:
     Hast thou not seen◡
     How thy heart's wishes have been◡
Granted in what he ordaineth?

3

f   Praise to the Lord, who doth prosper thy work and defend thee;
Surely his goodness and mercy shall daily attend thee:
     Ponder anew
     What the Almighty can do,
If to the end he befriend thee.

4

Praise to the Lord! O let all that is in me adore him!
All that hath life and breath, come now with praises before him!
     Let the Amen
     Sound from his people again:
Gladly for ay we adore him.

                                      J. NEANDER   *Tr.* Catherine Winkworth‡

HOLY COMMUNION

Hymn 383
Key C Pange lingua

FIRST TUNE

Mode iii

PART 1

Pange, lingua, gloriosi Corporis mysterium

{| m m m r s s l t d' d' — | d' r' d' t l d' t l s — }

1. Now, my tongue, the mys-tery tell - ing   Of the glo - rious Bo - dy sing,
2. Given for us, and con-de-scend-ing   To be born for us be-low,
3. That last night, at sup-per ly - ing,   'Mid the Twelve, his cho-sen band,
4. Word made flesh, true bread he mak - eth   By his word his Flesh to be,

{| s l d' t l s s l l — | l d' l s f m l s m r — }

1. And the Blood, all price ex - cell - ing,   Which the Gen-tiles' Lord and King,
2. He, with men in con-verse blend-ing,   Dwelt the seed of truth to sow,
3. Je-sus, with the law com-ply - ing,   Keeps the feast its rites de-mand;
4. Wine his Blood; which who - so tak - eth   Must from car - nal thoughts be free:

{| s s s m f s s l l — | l d' l s l s f m r m — ||

1. In a Vir - gin's womb once dwell-ing,   Shed for this world's ran-som-ing.
2. Till he closed with won-drous end - ing,   His most pa - tient life of woe.
3. Then, more pre-cious food sup-ply - ing,   Gives him-self with his own hand.
4. Faith a - lone, though sight for-sak - eth,   Shows true hearts the mys-ter - y.

PART 2

Tantum ergo

{| m m m r s s l t d' d' — | d' r' d' t l d' t l s — }

5. There-fore we, be-fore him bend - ing,   This great Sa - cra - ment re - vere:
6. Glo - ry let us give and bless - ing   To the Fa - ther and the Son,

{| s l d' t l s s l l — | l d' l s f m l s m r — }

5. Types and sha - dows have their end - ing,   For the new - er rite is here;
6. Hon-our, might, and praise ad - dress-ing,   While e - ter - nal a - ges run;

{| s s s m f s s l l — | l d' l s l s f m r m — ||

5. Faith, our out-ward sense be - friend - ing,   Makes our in - ward vi - sion clear.
6. Ev - er too his love con - fess - ing,   Who, from Both, with Both is One.

The Sarum form of this melody will be found at Hymn 97

HOLY COMMUNION

HYMN 383   SECOND TUNE

KEY E♭   Tantum ergo   French Melody

Slow

{ | d : r | m : d | m.r : m.f | s : m || s : s | f : f |
  | s₁ : t₁ | d : d | d.r : d | t₁ : d || s₁ : d | d : t₁ |
  | m : s | s : s | s   : s.f | r : m || d¹ : s | l : s |
  | d : s.f| m.f: m.r| d.t₁: l₁ | s₁ : d || m : m | r : s₁ | }

{ | m.r : m.d | r : — || r : m | f : —.m || f.m : r.d | r : s₁ ||
  | d.r : d | t₁ : — || s₁ : d | d : —.d || d   : l₁ | t₁ : s₁ ||
  | s.f : s.m | r : — || s : s | f : —.s || l.s : f.m | s : s ||
  | d   : m₁ | s₁ : — || t₁ : d | l₁ : —.s₁|| f₁ : l₁ | s₁ : t₁ || }

{ | d : d | r : r | m.r : m.f | s : — || s.l : s.f | m : m |
  | l₁ : s₁ | l₁ : t₁ | d   : d | d : t₁ || d   : t₁ | d : s₁ |
  | m : s | f : s | s   : —.f | r : — || s   : s | s : s |
  | l₁ : m | r : s₁ | d.t₁: l₁ | s₁ : — || m   : r | d.r: d.t₁| }

{ | f.s : f.m | r : r || s.l : s.f | m.s : d¹.f | m : r | d : — ||
  | d   : r.d | d : t₁ || d   : d.r | m.r : d.r | r.d: d.t₁| d : — ||
  | f   : l | l : s || s   : l.t | d¹.s: l.l | s : f | m : — ||
  | l₁ : f₁ | s₁ : s.f|| m   : r | d.t₁: l₁.f₁| s₁ : s₁ | d : — || }

PART 1

Pange, lingua, gloriosi Corporis mysterium

mf NOW, my tongue, the mystery telling
    Of the glorious Body sing,
  And the Blood, all price excelling,
    Which the Gentiles' Lord and King,
p In a Virgin's womb once dwelling,
    Shed for this world's ransoming.

2

mf Given for us, and condescending
    To be born for us below,
  He, with men in converse blending,
    Dwelt the seed of truth to sow,
p Till he closed with wondrous ending
    His most patient life of woe.

HOLY COMMUNION

3

mf That last night, at supper lying
    'Mid the Twelve, his chosen band,
Jesus, with the law complying,
    Keeps the feast its rites demand;
Then, more precious food supplying,
    Gives himself with his own hand.

4

p Word made flesh, true bread he maketh
    By his word his Flesh to be,
Wine his Blood; which whoso taketh
    Must from carnal thoughts be free:
mf Faith alone, though sight forsaketh,
    Shows true hearts the mystery.

PART 2

Tantum ergo

5

f Therefore we, before him bending,
    This great Sacrament revere:
Types and shadows have their ending,
    For the newer rite is here;
mf Faith, our outward sense befriending,
    Makes our inward vision clear.

6

f Glory let us give and blessing
    To the Father and the Son,
Honour, might, and praise addressing,
    While eternal ages run;
Ever too his love confessing,
    Who, from Both, with Both is One.

ST. THOMAS AQUINAS
Tr. E. Caswall, J. M. Neale and others

HOLY COMMUNION

Hymn 384 FIRST TUNE

KEY **C** Verbum supernum prodiens Mode viii

PART 1 — Verbum supernum prodiens   PART 2 — O salutaris

{| s l̲ s̲ l d¹ t l s̲ m̲ f s | s t d¹ }

1 The heaven-ly Word, pro-ceed-ing forth Yet leav-ing
2 By false dis-ci-ple to be given To foe-men
3 He gave him-self in eith-er kind, His pre-cious
4 By birth their fel-low-man was he, Their meat, when

PART 2

5 O sav-ing Vic-tim, ope-ning wide The gate of
6 All praise and thanks to thee as-cend For ev-er-

{| r¹ d¹ t s l d¹ — | l d¹ t d¹ s l̲ s̲ }

1 not the Fa-ther's side, Ac-com-plish-ing his work
2 for his life a-thirst, Him-self, the ve-ry Bread
3 Flesh, his pre-cious Blood; In love's own ful-ness thus
4 sit-ting at the board; He died, their ran-som-er

PART 2

5 heaven to man be-low, Our foes press on from ev-
6 more, blest One in Three; O grant us life that shall

{| f s | s l̲ s̲ l d¹ t l s̲ m̲ f s — ||

1 on earth Had reached at length life's e-ven-tide.
2 of heaven, He gave to his dis-ci-ples first.
3 de-signed Of the whole man to be the food.
4 to be; He ev-er reigns, their great re-ward.

PART 2

5 ery side: Thine aid sup-ply, thy strength be-stow.
6 not end In our true na-tive land with thee.

SECOND TUNE

KEY **E♭** Das walt' Gott D. Vetter (1713)

Slow B♭. t.

{| :d | m:s | s:m | d :r |m | ᵈf₁| d:d | r :m | f.m:r | d :— |
:s₁	d:d	t₁:t₁	t₁.l₁:s₁	s₁		ˢd₁	f₁:s₁	l₁.t₁:d	l₁ :—.s₁.f₁	m₁:—
:m	s:s	r:m	m :r	d		ᵐl₁	l₁:d	f :s	d :—t₁	s₁:—
:d	d:m₁.f₁	s₁:se₁	l₁ :t₁	d		ᵈf₁	f₁:—.m₁	r₁ :d₁	f₁ :s₁	d₁:—	

398

HOLY COMMUNION

f. E♭.

```
{ :d s  | m :s  | l :s  | f :m  | r    || s  m.f:s | f :m.r | d  :r  | d  :—
  :s,r  | r.d:d | d :d  | l,.r:de | l, || r  d :d  | d :t,  | t,.l,:t,| s, :—
  :d s  | s :s  | f :f.m| r.f:l.s | f  || s  s :s  | l :s.f | m  :s.f|m  :—
  :m t, | d :m  | f :d  | r :l,   | r  || t, d :m, | f, :s, | l, :s, | d  :— }
```

PART 1 — Verbum supernum prodiens

mf THE heavenly Word, proceeding forth
      Yet leaving not the Father's side,
      Accomplishing his work on earth
p   Had reached at length life's eventide.

2

mf By false disciple to be given
      To foemen for his life athirst,
      Himself, the very Bread of heaven,
      He gave to his disciples first.

3

He gave himself in either kind,
  His precious Flesh, his precious Blood;
In love's own fulness thus designed
  Of the whole man to be the food.

4

p By birth their fellow-man was he,
      Their meat, when sitting at the board;
      He died, their ransomer to be;
f   He ever reigns, their great reward.

PART 2 — O salutaris

5

p O saving Victim, opening wide
      The gate of heaven to man below,
      Our foes press on from every side:
      Thine aid supply, thy strength bestow.

6

f All praise and thanks to thee ascend
      For evermore, blest One in Three;
      O grant us life that shall not end
      In our true native land with thee.

ST. THOMAS AQUINAS
Tr. J. M. Neale, E. Caswall, and others

HOLY COMMUNION

Hymn 385 FIRST TUNE

KEY **D** Adoro te devote Mode v

Adoro te devote, latens Deitas

{| <u>d m</u> s s <u>s l</u> s f m r d d — | <u>d m</u> s s }

1 Thee we a - dore, O hid - den Sa - viour, thee, Who in thy
2 O blest mem - or - ial of our dy - ing Lord, Who liv - ing
3 Foun - tain of good - ness, Je - su, Lord and God, Cleanse us, un -
4 O Christ, whom now be - neath a veil we see, May what we

{| <u>s l</u> s f m r d d — | s <u>l t</u> d' d' t s l }

1 Sa - cra - ment dost deign to be; Both flesh and spi - rit at
2 Bread to men doth here af - ford! O may our souls for ev -
3 clean, with thy most clean - sing Blood; In - crease our faith and love,
4 thirst for soon our por - tion be: To gaze on thee un - veiled,

{| s f m r — | <u>m s</u> f m <u>r d</u> r m d r d d — ||

1 thy Pre - sence fail, Yet here thy Pre - sence we de - vout - ly hail.
2 er feed on thee, And thou, O Christ, for ev - er pre - cious be.
3 that we may know, The hope and peace which from thy Pre - sence flow.
4 and see thy face, The vi - sion of thy glo - ry and thy grace.

SECOND TUNE

KEY **D** Leamington Sir S. H. Nicholson, 1875–1947

{| m :— | r :—.d | d :— | — :d | r :m | s :f :m | r :— | — ||
d :—	l₁ :—.l₁	l₁ :—	— :l₁	t₁ :d	r :— :d	l₁ :—	—	
s :—	f :—.m	m :—	— :m	s :s	s :— :s	f :—	—	
d :—	r :—.l₁	l₁ :—	— :l₁	s₁ :d	t₁ :— :d	r :—	—	

{| r :r :m | f :—.m | r :m | l :— :m | s :— ||
ta₁ :ta₁ :d	d :—.d	r :d	m :— :d	t₁ :—	
f :s :s	l :—.s	s :s	d' :— :l	s :—	
ta₁ :s₁ :d	f₁ :—.d	t₁ :d	l₁ :t₁ :d	m :—	

400

HOLY COMMUNION

```
{ :s   d':—  |t :r':t  |s :l  |m :— :r  |d :— |— ||
  :t₁  m:f   |s :f :f  |m :r  |d :l₁:t₁ |t₁:l₁|—
  :f   s :—  |s :l :t  |d':l  |s :— :f  |m :— |—
  :r   d :r  |m :r :r  |m :f  |s :— :s₁ |l₁:— |— }

{ :d   f :—  :m |l :— :s  |m :d  |f :m :r  |d :— |— ||
  :s₁  d :—  :t₁|l₁:t₁:d  |t₁:d  |d :— :t₁ |d :— |—
  :m   f :—  :s |d :r :m  |s :m  |l :s :f  |m :— |—
  :ta₁ l₁:—  :s₁|f₁:— :d  |s₁:l₁ |f₁:— :s₁ |d :— |— }
```

By permission of the Faith Press, Ltd.

Adoro te devote, latens Deitas

THEE we adore, O hidden Saviour, thee,
Who in thy Sacrament dost deign to be;
Both flesh and spirit at thy Presence fail,
Yet here thy Presence we devoutly hail.

2

O blest memorial of our dying Lord,
Who living Bread to men doth here afford!
O may our souls for ever feed on thee,
And thou, O Christ, for ever precious be.

3

Fountain of goodness, Jesu, Lord and God,
Cleanse us, unclean, with thy most cleansing Blood;
Increase our faith and love, that we may know
The hope and peace which from thy Presence flow.

4

O Christ, whom now beneath a veil we see,
May what we thirst for soon our portion be:
To gaze on thee unveiled, and see thy face,
The vision of thy glory and thy grace.

ST. THOMAS AQUINAS.
Tr. Bishop J. R. Woodford†

HOLY COMMUNION

Hymn 386   FIRST TUNE

KEY **C**   St. Sechnall   Irish Traditional Melody

Slowly. May be sung in Unison

SECOND TUNE

KEY **G**   Elberton   B. Harwood, 1859–1949

Sancti, venite, Christi Corpus sumite

  p   DRAW nigh and take the Body of the Lord,
       And drink the holy Blood for you outpoured.

2

Saved by that Body and that holy Blood,
With souls refreshed, we render thanks to God.

HOLY COMMUNION

3
Salvation's giver, Christ the only Son,
By his dear Cross and Blood the victory won.

4
Offered was he for greatest and for least,
Himself the Victim, and himself the Priest.

5*
Victims were offered by the law of old,
Which in a type this heavenly mystery told.

6*
mf He, Lord of life, and Saviour of our race,
Hath given to his saints a wondrous grace.

7
p Approach ye then with faithful hearts sincere,
And take the safeguard of salvation here.

8
mf He that his saints in this world rules and shields
To all believers life eternal yields;

9
He feeds the hungry with the Bread of heaven,
And living streams to those who thirst are given.

10*
p Alpha and Omega, to whom shall bow
All nations at the Doom, is with us now.

7th cent. *Tr.* J. M. NEALE and Compilers (1904)

NOTE. Alpha and Omega, *the first and last letters of the Greek alphabet, are used in the book of Revelation as a title of Jesus Christ, who, as the Word of God, is the beginning and the end of all creation*

Alternative Tune, Song 46, 358

HYMN 387   FIRST TUNE
KEY **B♭**   Jesu, dulcedo cordium   Mode ii

Jesu, dulcedo cordium

1. Jesu, thou joy of loving hearts!
2. Thy truth unchanged hath ever stood;
3. We taste thee, O thou living Bread,
4. Our restless spirits yearn for thee,
5. O Jesu, ever with us stay;

1. Thou fount of life, thou Light of men! From the best bliss
2. Thou savest those that on thee call; To them that seek
3. And long to feast upon thee still; We drink of thee,
4. Where-'er our changeful lot is cast, Glad when thy gra-
5. Make all our moments calm and bright; Chase the dark night

1. that earth imparts We turn unfilled to thee again.
2. thee thou art good, To them that find thee all in all.
3. the fountain-head, And thirst our souls from thee to fill.
4. cious smile we see, Blest when our faith can hold thee fast.
5. of sin away; Shed o'er the world thy holy light.

403

HOLY COMMUNION

Hymn 387 SECOND TUNE

KEY **F** Ealing   Sir H. Oakeley, 1830–1903

[Tonic sol-fa musical notation]

Jesu, dulcedo cordium

JESU, thou joy of loving hearts!
  Thou fount of life, thou Light of men!
From the best bliss that earth imparts
  We turn unfilled to thee again.

2
Thy truth unchanged hath ever stood;
  Thou savest those that on thee call;
To them that seek thee thou art good,
  To them that find thee all in all.

3
We taste thee, O thou living Bread,
  And long to feast upon thee still;
We drink of thee, the fountain-head,
  And thirst our souls from thee to fill.

4
Our restless spirits yearn for thee,
  Where'er our changeful lot is cast,
Glad when thy gracious smile we see,
  Blest when our faith can hold thee fast.

5
O Jesu, ever with us stay;
  Make all our moments calm and bright;
Chase the dark night of sin away;
  Shed o'er the world thy holy light.

Cento from Jesu dulcis memoria
Tr. R. PALMER

Alternative Tune, St. Bernard (Monk), 188

Hymn 388 FIRST TUNE

KEY **D** Eia, Jesu adorande   Mode iii

Eia, Jesu adorande

{| f r m f s l s f | s l s f m r m —}

1 O Lord Je-sus, I a-dore thee For the bread of worth un-told
2 Make thou of my soul an or-chard Quick-ened in-to fruit-ful-ness;
PART 2
3 Ah, Lord Je-sus, go not from me, Stay, ah, stay with me, my Lord;
4 Would that I could keep thee al-ways In mine in-most heart to be,

HOLY COMMUNION

{| m r s s | l t d' : t s | l t a l s f s m —}

1. Free-ly given in thy Com-mun-ion, Won-der-ful a thou-sand-fold,
2. Come, O come, life-giv-ing Man-na, Mak-ing glad my wil-der-ness:

PART 2

3. Make me shrink from what-so-ev-er_ Will not with thy name ac-cord;
4. Thou and on-ly thou sug-gest-ing Ev-ery thought and wish in me;

{| f r m f s l s f | s l s f m r m — ||

1. Given to-day in lov-ing boun-ty More than my poor heart can hold.
2. Sweet-er far than an-y sweet-ness Tongue can taste, or words ex-press.

PART 2

3. Act through me in ev-ery ac-tion, Speak through me in ev-ery word.
4. All my soul, with sing-ing, of-fered For a sa-cri-fice to thee.

SECOND TUNE

KEY E♭ St. Thomas Traditional Melody (18th cent.)

d :r	m :d	r :m	f :m	l :s	f :m	r :r	d :—
s₁ :t₁	d :d	s₁ :d	t₁ :d	d :d	d.t₁:d	d :t₁	d :—
m :s	s :s	s :s	s :s	f :s	l.f :s	s :—.f	m :—
d :s₁	d :m	t₁ :d	r :d	f :m	r :d	s₁ :s₁	d :—

d' :t	d' :s	l :s	f :m	l :t	d' :t	l :l	s :—
m :r	d :d	d :d	t₁ :d	m :—.r	d :r	r :—.d	t₁ :—
s :f	m :m	f :s	s :s	d' :t	l :s	s :fe	s :—
d :r	m :d	f :m	r :d	l₁ :se₁	l₁ :t₁.d	r :r₁	s₁ :—

s :s	m :d	r :m	f :m	s :m	l :s.f	m :r	d :—
d :r	d :d	t₁ :d	d.t₁:d	d :—.t₁	l₁.t₁:d	d :t₁	d :—
s :s	s :s	s :s	f :s	s :s	f :s.l	s :—.f	m :—
m :t₁	d :m	f :m	r :d	m :d	f :m.f	s :s₁	d :—

Eia, Jesu adorande

PART 1

O LORD Jesus, I adore thee
 For the bread of worth untold
Freely given in thy Communion,
 Wonderful a thousandfold,
Given to-day in loving bounty
 More than my poor heart can hold.

2

Make thou of my soul an orchard
 Quickened into fruitfulness;
Come, O come, life-giving Manna,
 Making glad my wilderness:
Sweeter far than any sweetness
 Tongue can taste, or words express.

PART 2

3

Ah, Lord Jesus, go not from me,
 Stay, ah, stay with me, my Lord;
Make me shrink from whatsoever_
 Will not with thy name accord;
Act through me in every action,
 Speak through me in every word.

4

Would that I could keep thee always
 In mine inmost heart to be,
Thou and only thou suggesting
 Every thought and wish in me;
All my soul, with singing, offered
 For a sacrifice to thee.

JOHN MAUBURN *Tr.* J. M. C. Crum

HOLY COMMUNION

HYMN 389

FIRST TUNE

KEY **D** Magdalen College

W. Hayes, 1706-77

O esca viatorum

1
O FOOD that weary pilgrims love,
O Bread of angel-hosts above,
  O Manna of the saints,
The hungry soul would feed on thee;
Ne'er may the heart unsolaced be
  Which for thy sweetness faints.

2
O fount of love, O cleansing tide,
Which from the Saviour's piercèd side
  And sacred heart dost flow,
Be ours to drink of thy pure rill,
Which only can our spirits fill,
  And all our need bestow.

SECOND TUNE — KEY **A♭** Manna — J. G. Schicht, 1753-1823

HOLY COMMUNION

3

Lord Jesu, whom, by power divine
Now hidden 'neath the outward sign,
   We worship and adore,
Grant, when the veil away is rolled,
With open face we may behold
   Thyself for evermore.

17th cent. *Tr.* COMPILERS

HYMN 390   French Carol   Traditional

KEY **F**   UNISON

KEY **F**   HARMONIZED VERSION FOR UNACCOMPANIED SINGING

σιγησάτω πᾶσα σάρξ

p LET all mortal flesh keep silence
    And with fear and trembling stand;
    Ponder nothing earthly-minded,
    For with blessing in his hand
mf Christ our God to earth descendeth,
    Our full homage to demand.

2

King of Kings, yet born of Mary,
As of old on earth he stood,
Lord of Lords, in human vesture—
In the Body and the Blood—
He will give to all the faithful
His own self for heavenly food.

3

f Rank on rank the host of heaven
    Spreads its vanguard on the way,
    As the Light of Light descendeth
    From the realms of endless day,
    That the powers of hell may vanish
    As the darkness clears away.

4

mf At his feet the six-winged seraphs,
    Cherubim with sleepless eye,
    Veil their faces to the Presence,
    As with ceaseless voice they cry,
f Alleluia, Alleluia,
    Alleluia! Lord most high.

Liturgy of St. James   *Tr.* G. MOULTRIE

HOLY COMMUNION

Hymn 391 Cherubic Hymn French Melody
KEY E♭

UNISON οἱ τὰ χερουβὶμ μυστικῶς εἰκονίζοντες

{| s m d r m f m r d l, t, d — | d m f s }
1 Here, while the cher - u - bim with - in the veil A - dore the blest,
2 So let all earth - ly cares be cast a - side, That we may wel -

{| l s fe s l t l s — | s l t d¹ s   m d }
1 life - giv - ing Trin - i - ty, We, in earth's wor - ship
2 come him who draw - eth nigh, The King of Glo - ry

{| f m r m r d — | r l d d d t, r m f m r d d — ||
1 ech-o - ing their part, Hymn the Thrice Ho - ly in their com-pa-ny.
2 en-ter-ing his courts, Girt by the hid-den arm - ies of the sky.

AFTER THE SECOND VERSE ONLY

HARMONY
{ s :m :d | r :— | d :— ‖ d¹:t :s | l :— :s ‖ m :f | s :d | r :d | d :— ‖
  d :— :d | l, :t,| d :— ‖ d :— :t,| m :r : r ‖ d :— | r :d | l,:— | s,:— ‖
  Al -   le - lu - ia!   Al - le - lu - ia!   Al -   le - lu - ia!
  m :— :m | f :— | m :— ‖ m :— :s | m :f : s ‖ l :— | s :m | d :— | m :— ‖
  d :— :l,| f, :— | d :— ‖ l,:— :m | d :r : t, ‖ l,:— | t,:d | f,:— | d :— ‖

6th cent. *Tr.* C. S. Phillips

Hymn 392 Feniton Sir S. H. Nicholson, 1875–1947
KEY F

Slow
{ d :l,| d :r | m :s | s :— ‖ l :s | m :d | r :d | l,:— | s,:— ‖
  s,:l,| s,:l,.t,| d :t,| d :— ‖ d :d | t,:l,| l,:s,| f,:m,| r,:— ‖
  m :f | s :f | s :f | s :— ‖ f :s | s :m | f :m | d :— | — :t, ‖
  d :f | m :r | d :r | m :— ‖ f :m | s,:l,| r,:m,| f,:— | s,:— ‖

{ d :l,| d :r | m :s | l :— ‖ fe :m.r | s :t.l | s :m | fe:— | s :— ‖
  l,:f,| s,:l,.t,| d :d | de:— ‖ l,:l, | r :m | r :m | r :d | t,:— ‖
  m :f | m :l | s.f:m| m :— ‖ r :m.fe| s :s.l | t :d¹| t :l | s :— ‖
  l,:r | d :f | m.r:d.t,| l,:— ‖ r :d | t,:d | r :r | r :— | s,:— ‖

AFTER THE LAST VERSE ONLY
{ s :s | l :— | s : | s :l | ta :— | l : | d.r:m.f| s :— | s :— ‖
  r :r | f :m | r : | d :d | r :— | d : | d.r:m.f| s :— | s :— ‖
  Al - le - lu - ia,   Al - le - lu -   ia,   Al - le - lu - ia.
  t :t | d¹:— | t : | m :f | f :— .s| l : | d.r:m.f| s :— | s :— ‖
  s :s | f :— | s : | d :f | ta,.d:r.m| f : | d.r:m.f| s :— | s :— ‖

408

HOLY COMMUNION

σιγησάτω πᾶσα σάρξ

mf NOT a thought of earthly things!
　　Every head in awe be bended:
f 　Christ our God, the King of Kings,
　　Comes by angel troops attended.

2

mf Forth he comes, a Victim he
　　For the wide world's need availing,
　　And his people's food to be,
　　With himself their souls regaling.

3

　　Cherubim with watchful eyes,
　　Seraphim their brows concealing,
f 　Powers and Principalities,
　　Cry aloud, like thunder pealing,
　　　　　　　Alleluia!

Liturgy of St. James   Tr. A. J. MASON

HYMN 393   Schmücke dich   J. Crüger, 1598-1662
KEY E♭   *D.C.*

Schmücke dich

PART 1

f DECK thyself, my soul, with gladness,
　Leave the gloomy haunts of sadness;
　Come into the daylight's splendour,
　There with joy thy praises render
　Unto him whose grace unbounded
　Hath this wondrous banquet founded:
　High o'er all the heavens he reigneth,
　Yet to dwell with thee he deigneth.

2

p Now I sink before thee lowly,
　Filled with joy most deep and holy,
　As with trembling awe and wonder
　On thy mighty works I ponder:
　How, by mystery surrounded,
　Depth no man hath ever sounded,
　None may dare to pierce unbidden
　Secrets that with thee are hidden.

PART 2

3

mf Sun, who all my life dost brighten,
　Light, who dost my soul enlighten,
　Joy, the sweetest man e'er knoweth,
　Fount, whence all my being floweth,
　At thy feet I cry, my Maker,
　Let me be a fit partaker
　Of this blessèd food from heaven,
　For our good, thy glory, given.

4

　Jesus, Bread of Life, I pray thee,
　Let me gladly here obey thee;
　Never to my hurt invited,
　Be thy love with love requited:
　From this banquet let me measure,
　Lord, how vast and deep its treasure;
　Through the gifts thou here dost give
　As thy guest in heaven receive me.

J. FRANCK   *Tr.* Catherine Winkworth

HOLY COMMUNION

Hymn 394　　　　　　　　FIRST TUNE

KEY D　Gweedore　　　　　　　　　　　　　S. S. Wesley, 1810–76

{ sheet music }

G. t.

{ sheet music }

f. D.

{ sheet music }

SECOND TUNE

KEY A♭　Author of Life　　　　　　　　　　Sir J. Stainer, 1840–1901

E♭. t.　　　　　　　　　　d. f. D♭.

{ sheet music }

A♭. t.

{ sheet music }

{ sheet music }

HOLY COMMUNION

p AUTHOR of life divine,
    Who hast a table spread,
    Furnished with mystic Wine
    And everlasting Bread,
mf Preserve the life thyself hast given,
    And feed and train us up for heaven.

2

p Our needy souls sustain
    With fresh supplies of love,
    Till all thy life we gain,
    And all thy fulness prove,
mf And, strengthened by thy perfect grace,
    Behold without a veil thy face.

J. WESLEY

HYMN 395 Das neugeborne Kindelein M. Vulpius, *c.* 1560–1616
KEY G D. t.

O THOU, before the world began
Ordained a Sacrifice for man,
And by the eternal Spirit made
An Offering in the sinner's stead;
Our everlasting Priest art thou,
Pleading thy Death for sinners now.

2

Thy Offering still continues new
Before the righteous Father's view;
Thyself the Lamb for ever slain,
Thy Priesthood doth unchanged remain;
Thy years, O God, can never fail,
Nor thy blest work within the veil.

3

O that our faith may never move,
But stand unshaken as thy love!
Sure evidence of things unseen,
Now let it pass the years between,
And view thee bleeding on the Tree,
My Lord, my God, who dies for me.

C. WESLEY and others

Alternative Tune, Surrey, 179

HOLY COMMUNION

HYMN 396 — FIRST TUNE

KEY **G** Swanmore

A. K. Blackall

(sol-fa notation)

SECOND TUNE

KEY **E♭** Rockingham

Adapted by E. Miller, 1731–1807

(sol-fa notation)

mf MY God, and is thy table spread,
   And doth thy cup with love o'erflow?
   Thither be all thy children led,
   And let them all thy sweetness know.

2

Hail, sacred feast which Jesus makes,
   Rich banquet of his Flesh and Blood!
   Thrice happy he who here partakes
   That sacred stream, that heavenly food.

3

p Why are its bounties all in vain
   Before unwilling hearts displayed?
   Was not for them the Victim slain?
   Are they forbid the children's Bread?

HOLY COMMUNION

4

mf O let thy table honoured be,
  And furnished well with joyful guests;
 And may each soul salvation see,
  That here its sacred pledges tastes.

         P. DODDRIDGE†

HYMN 397   FIRST TUNE

KEY E♭   Song 24   Orlando Gibbons, 1583–1625

```
{ :f |f :s |l :-.l |s :f |m :m  |r :—||  :l |l :t  |d':-.d'|t :l |1 :se|l :—||
  :l |l,:d |d :-.f |m :r |r :de |r :—||  :r |m:r   |d :-.m |m :d |m:m  |de:—||
  :r |r :m |f :-.d'|d':l |l :-.s|fe:—||  :f |l :se |l :-.l |se:l |t :t |l :—||
  :r |r :d |f,:-.f,|d :r |l,:l, |r,:—||  :r |d:t,  |l,:-.l,|m :f |m:m, |l,:—||

  :m |m :f |s :-.m |f :f |s :ta |l :—||  :s |d':t  |l :-.s |f :f |m :m |r :—||
  :d |d :r |m :-.d |r :d |ta,:ta,|d :—||  :d |m :m |d :-.ta,|d :r |r :de|r :—||
  :l |l :l |d':-.s |ta:f |f :m  |f :—||  :m |l :s  |f :-.m |f :l |l :l |f :—||
  :l,|l,:r |d :-.d |ta,:l,|s, :s,|f,:—||  :d |l,:m,|f,:-.s,|l,:r,|l,:l,|r,:—||

  :m |m :f |s :-.m |f :f |s :ta |l :—||  :s |d':t  |l :-.s |f :f |m :m |r :—||
  :d |d :r |m :-.d |r :d |ta,:ta,|d :—||  :d |m :m |d :-.ta,|d :r |r :de|r :—||
  :l |l :l |d':-.s |ta:f |f :m  |f :—||  :m |l :s  |f :-.m |f :l |l :-.s|fe:—||
  :l,|l,:r |d :d   |ta,:l,|s, :s,|f,:—||  :d |l,:m,|f,:-.s,|l,:r,|l,:l, |r,:—||
```

p AND now, O Father, mindful of the love
 That bought us, once for all, on Calvary's Tree,
And having with us him that pleads above,
 We here present, we here spread forth to thee
mf That only Offering perfect in thine eyes,
 The one true, pure, immortal Sacrifice.

2

p Look, Father, look on his anointed face,
 And only look on us as found in him;
Look not on our misusings of thy grace,
 Our prayer so languid, and our faith so dim:
mf For lo, between our sins and their reward
We set the Passion of thy Son our Lord.

3

p And then for those, our dearest and our best,
 By this prevailing Presence we appeal;
mf O fold them closer to thy mercy's breast,
 O do thine utmost for their souls' true weal;
From tainting mischief keep them white and clear,
And crown thy gifts with strength to persevere.

4

p And so we come: O draw us to thy feet,
 Most patient Saviour, who canst love us still;
mf And by this food, so awful and so sweet,
 Deliver us from every touch of ill:
f In thine own service make us glad and free,
And grant us never more to part with thee.

         W. BRIGHT

HOLY COMMUNION

HYMN 397　　　　　SECOND TUNE

KEY D　Unde et memores

W. H. Monk, 1823–89

[Tonic sol-fa notation]

p   AND now, O Father, mindful of the love
    That bought us, once for all, on Calvary's Tree,
  And having with us him that pleads above,
    We here present, we here spread forth to thee
mf That only Offering perfect in thine eyes,
    The one true, pure, immortal Sacrifice.

2

p   Look, Father, look on his anointed face,
    And only look on us as found in him;
  Look not on our misusings of thy grace,
    Our prayer so languid, and our faith so dim:
mf For lo, between our sins and their reward
    We set the Passion of thy Son our Lord.

3

p   And then for those, our dearest and our best,
    By this prevailing Presence we appeal:
mf O fold them closer to thy mercy's breast,
    O do thine utmost for their souls' true weal;
  From tainting mischief keep them white and clear,
    And crown thy gifts with strength to persevere.

4

p   And so we come: O draw us to thy feet,
    Most patient Saviour, who canst love us still;
mf And by this food, so awful and so sweet,
    Deliver us from every touch of ill:
f   In thine own service make us glad and free,
    And grant us never more to part with thee.

W. BRIGHT

HOLY COMMUNION

HYMN 398 Albano V. Novéllo, 1781–1861
KEY F

mf ONCE, only once, and once for all,
His precious life he gave;
Before the Cross our spirits fall,
And own it strong to save.

2
'One Offering, single and complete,'
With lips and heart we say;
But what he never can repeat
He shows forth day by day.

3
For, as the priest of Aaron's line
Within the Holiest stood,
And sprinkled all the mercy-shrine
With sacrificial blood;

4
p So he who once atonement wrought,
Our Priest of endless power,
Presents himself for those he bought
In that dark noontide hour.

5
mf His Manhood pleads where now it lives
On heaven's eternal throne,
And where in mystic rite he gives
Its Presence to his own.

6
And so we show thy Death, O Lord,
Till thou again appear;
And feel, when we approach thy board,
We have an altar here.

7
f All glory to the Father be,
All glory to the Son,
All glory, Holy Ghost, to thee
While endless ages run.

W. BRIGHT

HOLY COMMUNION

Hymn 399 FIRST TUNE

KEY **F** Alleluia S. S. Wesley, 1810–76

```
{ |d :d  |t, :d  |l, :s, |l, :t, |d  :r  |m :s  |l :l  |s :— ||
  |s, :s, |r, :s, |f, :s, |fe, :f, |m, :s, |d :d  |d :d  |d :— ||
  |m :m  |f :m  |d :d  |d :s, |d :s  |s :s  |s :f  |m :— ||
  |d :d  |d :d  |f, :m, |r, :s, |l, :t, |d :m, |f, :l, |d :— ||
```

C.t.
```
{ |s :m.r |d :r  |m :f  |m :r  |ᵗm :s  |d' :r' |m' :r' |d' :— ||
  |d :t,  |d :s, |d :d  |d :t, |ᵗm :r  |s :fe  |s :s.f |m :— ||
  |s :s.f |m :s  |s :l  |s :s  |ˢd' :t |d' :d' |d' :t  |s :— ||
  |m, :s, |l, :t, |d :f  |s :s  |ˢd' :s.f |m :l |s :s, |d :— ||
```

f. F.
```
{ |ᶠd :d  |t, :d  |l, :s, |l, :t, |d :r  |m :t, |t, :t, |t, :— ||
  |ᵈs, :s, |s, :m, |f, :s, |fe, :f, |m, :l, |se, :m, |ba, :ba, |se, :— ||
  |ˡm :m  |r :d  |d :d  |d :s, |d :t,.l, |t, :m |m :re |m :— ||
  |ᶠd :d  |s, :l, |f, :m, |r, :s, |l, :f, |m :se, |t, :t, |m, :— ||
```

```
{ |s :m  |r :m  |f :f.m |m :r  |s :l  |f :m  |r :r  |d :— ||
  |s, :t, |l, :l, |l, :r.d |d :t, |d :l, |l,.t, :d |d :t, |d :— ||
  |t, :m |f :de  |r :l  |s :s  |s :m  |l :l  |l :s.f |m :— ||
  |m, :s, |l, :l, |r :f  |s :s  |m :d  |r :l,.s, |f, :s, |d :— ||
```

SECOND TUNE

KEY **F** Hyfrydol R. H. Prichard, 1811–87

```
{ |d :— :r |d :—.r :m |f :— :m |r :d :r  ||s :— :f |m :— :m
  |s, :— :t, |d :— :d |d :r :d |t,:l, :t, |d :s, :l,.t, |d :— :d.t,
  |m :— :r |m :—.f :s |l :s :s |s :m :s  |m :— :f |s :— :s
  |d, :m, :s, |d :— :d |l,:t, :d |s,:l, :s, |m :— :r |d :— :m,  }

  |r :d :r  |d :— :— ||d :— :r |d :—.r :m |f :— :m |r :d :r
  |l, :— :t, |d :— :— |s, :— :t, |d :— :d |d :r :d |t, :l, :t,
  |f :m :s |m :— :— |m :— :r |m :—.f :s |l :s :s |s :m :s
  |f, :l, :s, |d :— :— |d, :m, :s, |d :— :d |l, :t, :d |s, :l, :s,  }

  |s :— :f |m :— :m |r :d :r |d :— :— ||s :— :s |s :f :m
  |d :s, :l,.t, |d :— :d.t, |l, :— :t, |d :— :— |t,:s, :t, |d :— :d
  |m :— :f |s :— :s |f :m :s |m :— :— |m :— :s |d :r :m
  |m :— :r |d :— :m, |f, :l, :s, |d :— :— |m :— :m |l, :— :l,  }
```

HOLY COMMUNION

f ALLELUIA! sing to Jesus!
    His the sceptre, his the throne;
Alleluia! his the triumph,
    His the victory alone:
Hark! the songs of peaceful Sion
    Thunder like a mighty flood;
Jesus out of every nation
    Hath redeemed us by his Blood.

2

mf Alleluia! not as orphans
    Are we left in sorrow now;
Alleluia! he is near us,
    Faith believes, nor questions how:
Though the cloud from sight received him,
    When the forty days were o'er,
Shall our hearts forget his promise,
    'I am with you evermore'?

3

Alleluia! Bread of angels,
    Thou on earth our food, our stay;
Alleluia! here the sinful
    Flee to thee from day to day:
Intercessor, Friend of sinners,
    Earth's Redeemer, plead for me,
Where the songs of all the sinless
    Sweep across the crystal sea.

4

Alleluia! King eternal,
    Thee the Lord of Lords we own;
Alleluia! born of Mary,
    Earth thy footstool, heaven thy throne:
Thou within the veil hast entered,
    Robed in flesh, our great High Priest;
Thou on earth both Priest and Victim
    In the Eucharistic feast.

W. CHATTERTON DIX

The first verse may be repeated at the end

HOLY COMMUNION

Hymn 400 St. Helen   Sir G. C. Martin, 1844–1916
Key C

1
f LORD, enthroned in heavenly splendour,
   First-begotten from the dead,
Thou alone, our strong defender,
   Liftest up thy people's head.
      Alleluia!
   Jesu, true and living Bread.

2
mf Here our humblest homage pay we,
   Here in loving reverence bow;
Here for faith's discernment pray we,
   Lest we fail to know thee now.
f   Alleluia!
   Thou art here, we ask not how.

3
p Though the lowliest form doth veil thee
   As of old in Bethlehem,
Here as there thine angels hail thee,
   Branch and Flower of Jesse's Stem.
f   Alleluia!
   We in worship join with them.

4
mf Paschal Lamb, thine Offering, finished
   Once for all when thou wast slain,
In its fulness undiminished
   Shall for evermore remain,
f   Alleluia!
   Cleansing souls from every stain.

5
Life-imparting heavenly Manna,
   Stricken Rock with streaming side,
Heaven and earth with loud Hosanna
   Worship thee, the Lamb who died,
      Alleluia!
   Risen, ascended, glorified!

G. H. BOURNE

HOLY COMMUNION

HYMN 401 Dies Dominica   J. B. Dykes, 1823-76

KEY E♭

[sol-fa notation]

1

WE pray thee, heavenly Father,
  To hear us in thy love,
And pour upon thy children
  The unction from above;
That so in love abiding,
  From all defilement free,
We may in pureness offer
  Our Eucharist to thee.

2

Be thou our guide and helper,
  O Jesu Christ, we pray;
So may we well approach thee,
  If thou wilt be the Way:
Thou, very Truth, hast promised
  To help us in our strife,
Food of the weary pilgrim,
  Eternal source of Life.

3

And thou, Creator Spirit,
  Look on us, we are thine;
Renew in us thy graces,
  Upon our darkness shine;
That, with thy benediction
  Upon our souls outpoured.
We may receive in gladness
  The Body of the Lord.

4

O Trinity of Persons!
  O Unity most high!
On thee alone relying
  Thy servants would draw nigh:
Unworthy in our weakness,
  On thee our hope is stayed,
And blessed by thy forgiveness
  We will not be afraid.

V. S. S. COLES

HOLY COMMUNION

HYMN 402 Song 1 Orlando Gibbons, 1583-1625
KEY **G**

mf O THOU, who at thy Eucharist didst pray
   That all thy Church might be for ever one,
p Grant us at every Eucharist to say
   With longing heart and soul, 'Thy will be done:'
  O may we all one Bread, one Body be,
  Through this blest Sacrament of unity.

2

mf For all thy Church, O Lord, we intercede;
   Make thou our sad divisions soon to cease:
  Draw us the nearer each to each, we plead,
   By drawing all to thee, O Prince of Peace:
  Thus may we all one Bread, one Body be,
p Through this blest Sacrament of unity.

3

  We pray thee too for wanderers from thy fold;
   O bring them back, Good Shepherd of the sheep,
  Back to the faith which saints believed of old,
   Back to the Church which still that faith doth keep:
  Soon may we all one Bread, one Body be,
  Through this blest Sacrament of unity.

4

mf So, Lord, at length when sacraments shall cease,
   May we be one with all thy Church above,
  One with thy saints in one unbroken peace,
   One with thy saints in one unbounded love:
  More blessèd still, in peace and love to be
p One with the Trinity in Unity.

W. H. TURTON

HOLY COMMUNION

HYMN 403 Offertorium M. Haydn, 1737–1806
KEY D

[tonic sol-fa notation]

f 1. WE hail thy Presence glorious,
O Christ our great High Priest,
O'er sin and death victorious,
At thy thanksgiving feast:
As thou art interceding
For us in heaven above,
Thy Church on earth is pleading
Thy perfect work of love.

mf 2. Through thee in every nation
Thine own their hearts upraise,
Offering one pure Oblation,
One Sacrifice of praise:
With thee in blest communion
The living and the dead
Are joined in closest union,
One Body with one Head.

3. O Living Bread from heaven,
Jesu, our Saviour good,
Who thine own self hast given
To be our souls' true food;
For us thy body broken
Hung on the Cross of shame:
This Bread its hallowed token
We break in thy dear name.

4. O stream of love unending,
Poured from the one true Vine,
With our weak nature blending
The strength of life divine;
Our thankful faith confessing
In thy life-blood outpoured,
We drink this Cup of blessing
And praise thy name, O Lord.

5. May we thy word believing
Thee through thy gifts receive,
That, thou within us living,
We all to God may live;
Draw us from earth to heaven
Till sin and sorrow cease,
Forgiving and forgiven,
In love and joy and peace.

BISHOP R. G. PARSONS

HOLY COMMUNION

Hymn 404 Stonor · S. Watson

KEY D

(Tonic sol-fa notation)

A.t.

f.D.

1

O JOY of God, that comest in the morning,
    For thee, unsunned, we wait and eastward gaze,
Lift on our dark the splendours of thy dawning,
    Flood all our being in the feast of praise.

2

O life of God, for whom our spirits hunger,
    Except we eat and drink indeed of thee,
With love and faith renewed and hope grown younger
    Send us out hence thy saving health to see.

3

O peace of God, that passest understanding,
    Guard thou our heart through every fretting day:
In him who is our Peace, our wills commanding,
    Direct our path and perfect all our way.

BISHOP C. H. BOUTFLOWER

HOLY COMMUNION

Hymn 405 St. Mark W. Crowfoot, 1724–83, from Crisp's
Divine Harmony, 1755

KEY **E**

At the Offertory

f ALMIGHTY Father, Lord most high,
Who madest all, who fillest all,
Thy name we praise and magnify,
For all our needs on thee we call.

2

mf We offer to thee of thine own
Ourselves and all that we can bring,
In Bread and Cup before thee shown,
Our universal offering.

3

All that we have we bring to thee,
Yet all is naught when all is done,
Save that in it thy love can see
The Sacrifice of thy dear Son.

4

By his command in Bread and Cup
His Body and his Blood we plead:
p What on the Cross he offered up
Is here our Sacrifice indeed.

5

mf For all thy gifts of life and grace,
Here we thy servants humbly pray
That thou would'st look upon the face
Of thine anointed Son to-day.

V. S. S. COLES

HOLY COMMUNION

HYMN 406   Gott des Himmels   H. Albert, 1604–51

KEY **G**

At the Offertory

LORD, accept the alms we offer,
   Tokens of our love to thee;
Out of grateful hearts we render
   This our act of charity;
Even though full well we know
All we have to thee we owe.

2

Use them, Father, to thy glory,
   Teach us fully how to give,
For his sake who leaving heaven
   Gave us all that we might live:
All we have could not suffice
To repay his Sacrifice.

3

Now the priest upon the altar
   Doth present the bread and wine,
To become, in wondrous manner,
   For our souls the food divine:
Soul and body by thee fed,
Praise we give for daily bread.

4

With our alms and our oblations
   Take, O Lord, our prayers of love;
Make thy Church in fullest concord
   Serve as one, below, above;
And in fellowship complete
Reach at last thy mercy-seat.

S. N. SEDGWICK

HYMN 407   FIRST TUNE

KEY **F**   Ave verum Corpus natum   Mode v

Ave verum Corpus natum

1. Hail, true Bo-dy, born of Ma-ry, By a won-drous Vir-gin-birth!
Thou who on the Cross wast of-fered To re-deem the sons of earth;

HOLY COMMUNION

{| m s l s f m r d r m — | f f m r m r d t₁ r m r r — d — :||

2. Thou whose side became a fountain Pouring forth thy precious Blood,
Give us now, and at our dying, Thine own self to be our food.

{| d r m d f f m r m — | d r m d f f m r m — }
O sweetest Jesu, O gracious Jesu,

{| m s l s f m r m d r m f m r r — d — ||
O Jesu, blessèd Mary's Son.

SECOND TUNE

KEY B♭ Standish   J. Dykes Bower

Slow and sustained   May be sung in Unison

AFTER THE SECOND VERSE

At the Communion

Ave verum Corpus natum

HAIL, true Body, born of Mary,
    By a wondrous Virgin-birth!
Thou who on the Cross wast offered
    To redeem the sons of earth;

2
Thou whose side became a fountain
    Pouring forth thy precious Blood,
Give us now, and at our dying,
    Thine own self to be our food.

    O sweetest Jesu, O gracious Jesu,
    O Jesu, blessèd Mary's Son.

14th cent.   *Tr.* H. N. OXENHAM‡

HOLY COMMUNION

HYMN 408 Liebster Jesu   J. R. Ahle, 1625-73

KEY **G**

[Tonic sol-fa notation]

At the Communion

Liebster Jesu, wir sind hier

mf DEAREST Jesu, we are here,
   At thy call, thy Presence owning;
   Pleading now in holy fear
   That great Sacrifice atoning:
p Word incarnate, much in wonder
   On this mystery deep we ponder.

mf Jesu, strong to save—the same
   Yesterday, to-day, for ever—
   Make us fear and love thy name,
   Serving thee with best endeavour:
f In this life, O ne'er forsake us,
   But to bliss hereafter take us.

T. CLAUSNITZER
Tr. G. R. Woodward

HYMN 409   FIRST TUNE

KEY **G** Genevan Psalm cxviii   L. Bourgeois, *Genevan Psalter*, 1543

[Tonic sol-fa notation]

1 *p* Bread of the world in mercy broken, Wine of the soul in mercy shed, *mf* By whom the words of life were spoken, And in whose Death our sins are dead;

HOLY COMMUNION

[Sol-fa notation for first tune]

2 *p* Look on the heart by sorrow broken, Look
on the tears by sinners shed; *mf* And be thy feast
to us the token That by thy grace our souls are fed.

SECOND TUNE

KEY **D** Emmanuel   German 'Courante,' c. 1675

[Sol-fa notation for second tune]

At the Communion

p BREAD of the world in mercy broken,
    Wine of the soul in mercy shed,
mf By whom the words of life were spoken,
    And in whose Death our sins are dead;

2
p Look on the heart by sorrow broken,
    Look on the tears by sinners shed;
mf And be thy feast to us the token
    That by thy grace our souls are fed.

BISHOP R. HEBER

HOLY COMMUNION

HYMN 410 Sicily   Sicilian Melody

KEY E♭

At the Communion
Slow

{ s :— | l :— | s :-.f | m :f | s :— | l :— | s :-.f | m :f ||
  d :— | d :— | r :-.r | d :— | d :— | f :m | r :-.r | d :— ||
  O   most   mer-ci-ful!   O   most   boun-ti-ful!
  m :— | m :— | s :-.s | s :— | d' :t | l :— | t :-.t | d' :— ||
  d :— | l₁ :— | t₁ :-.t₁ | d :r | m :— | f :— | s :-.s | l :— || }

{ s :— | s :— | l :— | t : d' | t :— | l :— | s :— | — :— ||
  r :— | m :— | m :— | m : m | r :— | — :d | t₁ :— | — :— ||
  God   the   Fa-ther Al-migh - ty,
  t :— | t :— | l :— | s : s | s :— | fe :— | s :— | — :— ||
  s :f | m :r | d :— | t₁ : l₁ | r :— | — :— | s₁ :— | — :— || }

{ r :-.m | r : m | f :— | f :— | m :-.f | m : f | s :— | s :— ||
  t₁ :— | t₁ : t₁ | l₁ :d | t₁ :l₁ | d :— | d : d | t₁ :— | d :r ||
  By   the Re-deem-er's   Sweet in-ter-ces - sion,
  s :— | s : s | f :— | f :— | l :— | l : l | s :— | s :— ||
  s₁ :— | s₁ : s₁ | r :— | r :— | l₁ :— | l₁ : l₁ | m :f | m :r || }

{ d' :t | l :s | d' :l | s :f | m :— | r :— | d :— | — :— ||
  m :— | m :r | d :— | d :r | r :d | — :t₁ | d :— | — :— ||
  Hear   us,   help   us,   when   we   cry.
  s :— | l :t | s :d' | t :l | s :— | s :— | m :— | — :— ||
  d :— | d :f | m :— | m :f | s :— | s₁ :— | d :— | — :— || }

BISHOP R. HEBER

HYMN 411   FIRST TUNE

KEY **C**   Nicht so traurig   J. S. Bach, 1685–1750

{ d' :t.l | m' :r'.d' | t :d'.r' | se :— || l.t :d' | f :m | r :s | m :— ||
  m :r | d.r:m | f :m .r | m :— || m :m | r :d | d :t₁ | d :— ||
  l :se | l :l | l :se.l | t :— || l :l | l.t:d' | s :s | s :— ||
  l₁ :t₁ | d :l₁ | r :m .f | m :— || d.t₁:l₁ | r :m.f | s :s₁ | d :— || }

{ d' :t.l | m' :r'.d' | t :d'.r' | se :— || l.t :d' | f :m | r :s | m :— ||
  m :r | d.r:m | f :m .r | m :— || m :m | r :d | d.l₁:t₁ | d :— ||
  l :se | l :l | l :se.l | t :— || l :l | l.t:d' | s :s | s :— ||
  l₁ :t₁ | d :l₁ | r :m .f | m :— || d.t₁:l₁ | r :m.f | s :s₁ | d :— || }

428

HOLY COMMUNION

(Tonic sol-fa notation, G.t. / f.C.)

SECOND TUNE

KEY E♭   Bread of Heaven   Archbishop W. D. Maclagan, 1826–1910

(Tonic sol-fa notation in keys E♭, B♭.t., f.E♭.)

At the Communion

mf BREAD of heaven, on thee we feed,
    For thy Flesh is meat indeed;
    Ever may our souls be fed
    With this true and living Bread;
    Day by day with strength supplied
    Through the life of him who died.

2
    Vine of heaven, thy Blood supplies
    This blest Cup of Sacrifice;
p Lord, thy wounds our healing give,
    To thy Cross we look and live:
mf Jesus, may we ever be
    Grafted, rooted, built in thee.

                                J. CONDER‡

HOLY COMMUNION

HYMN 412 St. Flavian   Psalm cxxxii adapted from *Psalms*, 1562

KEY **F**

[music notation]

ALTERNATIVE VERSION
(Melody in the Tenor part)

KEY **F**   Harmonized by T. Ravenscroft (1621)

[music notation]

The Alternative Version may be used for verses 2 and 4

At the Communion

p   O GOD, unseen yet ever near,
    Thy Presence may we feel;
  And, thus inspired with holy fear,
    Before thine altar kneel.

2

mf Here may thy faithful people know
    The blessings of thy love,
  The streams that through the desert flow,
    The manna from above.

3

We come, obedient to thy word,
    To feast on heavenly food;
Our meat the Body of the Lord,
    Our drink his precious Blood.

HOLY COMMUNION

4

Thus may we all thy word obey,
For we, O God, are thine;
f And go rejoicing on our way,
Renewed with strength divine.

E. OSLER

Alternative Tune, Irish, 263

HYMN **413** Eccles   B. Luard Selby, 1853–1919
KEY A♭

At the Communion

p I HUNGER and I thirst:
Jesu, my manna be;
Ye living waters, burst
Out of the rock for me.

2

Thou bruised and broken Bread,
My life-long wants supply;
As living souls are fed,
O feed me, or I die.

3

mf Thou true life-giving Vine,
Let me thy sweetness prove;
Renew my life with thine,
Refresh my soul with love.

4

p Rough paths my feet have trod
Since first their course began:
Feed me, thou Bread of God;
Help me, thou Son of Man.

5

For still the desert lies
My thirsting soul before:
mf O living waters, rise
Within me evermore.

J. S. B. MONSELL

HOLY COMMUNION

Hymn 414 Farley Castle H. Lawes, 1596–1662
KEY **D**

At the Communion

mf HERE, O my Lord, I see thee face to face;
   Here faith would touch and handle things unseen;
   Here grasp with firmer hand the eternal grace,
   And all my weariness upon thee lean.

2

   Here would I feed upon the Bread of God;
   Here drink with thee the royal Wine of heaven;
   Here would I lay aside each earthly load;
   Here taste afresh the calm of sin forgiven.

3

p   I have no help but thine; nor do I need
   Another arm save thine to lean upon:
mf It is enough, my Lord, enough indeed,
   My strength is in thy might, thy might alone.

H. BONAR

Hymn 415 Pastor pastorum F. Silcher, 1789–1860
KEY **D**

At the Communion

FAITHFUL Shepherd, feed me
 In the pastures green;
Faithful Shepherd, lead me
 Where thy steps are seen.

2

Hold me fast, and guide me
 In the narrow way;
So, with thee beside me,
 I shall never stray.

432

HOLY COMMUNION

3
Daily bring me nearer
To the heavenly shore;
Make my faith grow clearer,
May I love thee more.

4
Hallow every pleasure,
Every gift and pain;
Be thyself my treasure,
Though none else I gain.

5
Day by day prepare me
As thou seest best,
Then let angels bear me
To thy promised rest.

T. B. POLLOCK

HYMN 416   Christe fons jugis   Rouen Church Melody
KEY E♭

By permission of the English Hymnal Co., Ltd.

At the Communion

WHEREFORE, O Father, we thy humble servants
Here bring before thee Christ thy well-belovèd,
All perfect Offering, Sacrifice immortal,
    Spotless Oblation.

2
See now thy children, making intercession
Through him our Saviour, Son of God incarnate,
For all thy people, living and departed,
    Pleading before thee.

W. H. H. JERVOIS

HOLY COMMUNION

HYMN 417 Sheen

G. Holst, 1874–1934

KEY **G**

[Tonic sol-fa musical notation]

After Communion

ἀπὸ δόξης εἰς δόξαν πορευόμενοι

FROM glory to glory advancing, we praise thee, O Lord;
Thy name with the Father and Spirit be ever adored.

2

From strength unto strength we go forward on Sion's highway,
To appear before God in the city of infinite day.

3

Thanksgiving, and glory and worship, and blessing and love,
One heart and one song have the saints upon earth and above.

4

Evermore, O Lord, to thy servants thy presence be nigh;
Ever fit us by service on earth for thy service on high.

Liturgy of St. James
Tr. C. W. HUMPHREYS

HOLY COMMUNION

Hymn 418 FIRST TUNE

KEY G Bournemouth Sir C. H. H. Parry, 1848–1918

{|m :f |s :r |f :— |m :— ||r :m |d :l₁ |t₁ :— |— :—||
|d :d |d :t₁ |l₁ :— |s₁ :— ||t₁ :t₁ |l₁ :fe₁ |s₁ :— |— :—||
|s :f |r :s |d :r |m :— ||s :s |m :r |r :— |— :—||
|d :l₁ |s₁ :s₁ |l₁:t₁ |d :— ||s₁ :m₁ |l₁ :r₁ |s₁ :— |— :—||}

{|t₁ :t₁ |d :m |r :d |t₁ :— ||d :m |r :r |d :— |— :—||
|se₁ :se₁ |l₁ :l₁ |l₁ :— |s₁ :— ||s₁ :s₁ |l₁ :t₁ |d :— |— :—||
|m :m |m :d |r :— |r :— ||d :s |f :f |m :— |— :—||
|m₁ :m₁ |l₁ :s₁ |fe₁:— |s₁ :— ||m₁ :m₁ |f₁ :s₁ |d :— |— :—||}

SECOND TUNE

KEY E♭ Eucharisticus Sir J. Stainer, 1840–1901

{|m :m |r :m |f :— |r :— ||s :d |r :m |f :— |— :—||
|d :d |t₁ :de |r :— |t₁ :— ||d :d |d :t₁ |d :— |— :—||
|s :s |s :s |l :— |s :— ||s :d¹ |s :s |f :— |— :—||
|d :d |f :m |r :— |s :— ||m :l |s :s₁ |l₁ :— |— :—||}

f. A♭. E♭. t.

{|ᵈ¹s :m |r :d |d :— |t₁ :— ||¹r :m |f :t₁ |d :— |— :—||
|ᵈs₁ :s₁ |se₁ :l₁ |l₁ :— |se₁ :— ||¹r :d |l₁ :s₁ |s₁ :— |— :—||
|ᶠd :d |r :m |f :— |f :— ||ᵐl :s |f :f |m :— |— :—||
|¹m₁ :d |t₁ :l₁ |r :— |r :— ||ᵈf :m |r :s₁ |d :— |— :—||}

After Communion

p JESU, gentlest Saviour,
  Thou art in us now:
mf Fill us with thy goodness,
  Till our hearts o'erflow.

2
p Multiply our graces,
  Chiefly love and fear,
mf And, dear Lord, the chiefest,
  Grace to persevere.

3*
Nature cannot hold thee,
  Heaven is all too strait
For thine endless glory
  And thy royal state.

4*
Yet the hearts of children
  Hold what worlds cannot,
And the God of wonders
  Loves the lowly spot.

5
O how can we thank thee
  For a gift like this,
Gift that truly maketh
  Heaven's eternal bliss?

6
p Ah, when wilt thou always
  Make our hearts thy home?
mf We must wait for heaven;
  Then the day will come.

F. W. FABER

HOLY COMMUNION

Hymn 419 O Jesu Christ
P. Reinigius (1587)
KEY B♭

After Communion   O Jesu, sode Jesu, dig

mf O JESU, blessèd Lord, to thee
   My heartfelt thanks for ever be,
Who hast so lovingly bestowed
   On me thy Body and thy Blood.

2

f Break forth, my soul, for joy, and say,
   'What wealth is come to me to-day!
mf My Saviour dwells within me now;
   How blest am I! how good art thou!'

T. Kingo   *Tr.* A. J. Mason

Hymn 420 Brockham
J. Clarke, *c.* 1659–1707
KEY G

f HOW glorious is the life above
   Which in this ordinance we taste,
That fulness of celestial love,
   That joy which shall for ever last!

2

mf That heavenly life in Christ concealed
   These earthen vessels could not [bear;
The part which now we find revealed
   No tongue of angels can declare.

3

f The light of life eternal darts
   Into our souls a dazzling ray;
A drop of heaven o'erflows our hearts,
   And floods with joy the house of clay.

4

Sure pledge of ecstasies unknown
   Shall this divine Communion be:
The ray shall rise into a sun,
   The drop shall swell into a sea.

C. Wesley†

HOLY COMMUNION

Hymn 421 Hosanna in excelsis Sir S. H. Nicholson, 1875–1947

KEY **C**

[Tonic sol-fa notation]

VERSES 2 AND 3 SHOULD BEGIN THUS:

[Tonic sol-fa notation]

f HOSANNA in the highest
To our exalted Saviour,
  Who left behind
  For all mankind
These tokens of his favour:
mf His bleeding love and mercy,
His all-redeeming Passion;
f Who here displays,
  And gives the grace
Which brings us our salvation.

2
Louder than gathered waters,
Or bursting peals of thunder,
  We lift our voice
  And speak our joys,
And shout our loving wonder.
Shout, all our elder brethren,
While we record the story
  Of him that came
  And suffered shame,
To carry us to glory.

3
mf Angels in fixed amazement
Around our altars hover,
  With eager gaze
  Adore the grace
Of our eternal Lover:
Himself and all his fulness
Who gives to the believer;
f And by this Bread
  Whoe'er are fed
Shall live with God for ever.

C. WESLEY

HOLY COMMUNION

HYMN 422 Laus Deo
KEY **F**

J. S. Bach, 1685–1750
From G. C. Schemelli's *Gesang-Buch*, 1736

UNISON

{| d | s :l.s | f.m :r.d | t₁.d : r | s₁ : l₁.t₁ | d : r.m | f.r : s }

D.C.
{| m :-.r | r ||:r | s :f.m | l :r | de.r :m | l₁ : t₁.d | r : m.f | s.m :r.d }

{| l : -.ta | s : s₁ | l₁ : t₁.d | r.f : m.r | r : -.d | d : — ||

THEE, living Christ, our eyes behold
  Amid thy Church appearing,
All girt about thy breast with gold
  And bright apparel wearing;
Thy countenance is burning light,
A sun that shineth in his might:
  Lord Christ, we see thy glory.

2
Thy glorious feet have sought and found
  Thy sons of every nation;
Thine everlasting voice doth sound
  The call of our salvation;

Thine eyes of flame do search and scan
The whole outspreading realm of man:
  Lord Christ, we see thy glory.

3
O risen Christ, who art alive,
  Amid thy Church abiding,
Who dost thy Blood and Body give
  New life and strength providing,
We join in heavenly company
To sing thy praise triumphantly:
  For we have seen thy glory.

BISHOP E. R. MORGAN

NOTE. *This hymn is based on the vision of the Glorified Christ in Rev. 1. 12–16*

HYMN 423 Mit Freuden zart
KEY **E♭**

Hymn Melody of the Bohemian Brethren, 1566

{| d :— | m :f | s :— | d' :— | t :l | s :— | l :-.s | f :m | r :— | m :f |
| s₁:— | d :d | r :— | m :— | s :f | r :— | r :de | r :l₁ | l₁:t₁ | d :— |
| m :— | l :l | s :— | s :— | s :d'| d':t | l :— | l :-.s | f :— | s :f |
| d :— | l₁:l₁| t₁:— | d :— | m :f | s :— | f :m | r :de | r :— | d :l₁ }

D.C.
{| r :— | d :— | d':— | t :l | s :d' | t :— | l :— | s :— | — |
| d :t₁| s₁:— | m :— | m :d | d :d | r :— | r :— | t₁:— | — |
| s :— | m :— | s :— | s :f | m :l | l :s | s :fe | s :— | — |
| s₁:— | d :— | d :— | m :f | d :l₁| t₁:— | r :— | s :— | f }

{:s | d :r | m :d | m :f | s :— | s :— | l :f | r :— | m :f | r :— | d :— |
:d | l₁:t₁| d :d | d :d | d :t₁| d :r | d :d | d :ta₁| ta₁:d | d :t₁| d :— |
:s | f :f | s :d'| t :l | s :f | m :r | m :f | f :— | s :l | s :— | m :— |
:m | f :r | d :l | s :f | m :r | d :t₁| l₁:l₁| ta₁:-.l₁| s₁:f₁| s₁:— | d :— }

438

HOLY COMMUNION

LET us employ all notes of joy
   And praise that never endeth
To God above, whose mighty love
   Our hearts and minds defendeth;
Who by his grace, in every place,
To all who need and duly plead
   His power and presence lendeth.

2
For, ere he died, the Crucified
   Wrought things eternal for us
By bread and wine, which Love divine
   Hath given to assure us:
O taste and see; find him to be
Our great reward, our living Lord
   Most willing to restore us.

3
The word he spoke, the bread he broke
   Shall fill our lives with glory,
If we are true and loving too
   And for our sins are sorry:
O do his will, and praise him still,
And still proclaim his glorious name
   And deathless Gospel story.

ADAM FOX

HOLY BAPTISM

HYMN 424 St. Stephen   W. Jones, 1726–1800

KEY **G**

mf IN token that thou shalt not fear
   Christ crucified to own,
We print the cross upon thee here,
   And stamp thee his alone.

2
In token that thou shalt not blush
   To glory in his name,
We blazon here upon thy front
   His glory and his shame.

3
In token that thou shalt not flinch
   Christ's quarrel to maintain,
But 'neath his banner manfully
   Firm at thy post remain;

4
In token that thou too shalt tread
   The path he travelled by,
Endure the cross, despise the shame,
   And sit thee down on high;

5
f   Thus outwardly and visibly
      We seal thee for his own;
   And may the brow that wears his Cross
      Hereafter share his crown.

H. ALFORD

HOLY BAPTISM

HYMN 425 The Child Jesus   Melody by S. Scheidt, 1587–1654

KEY **A**

[tonic sol-fa notation]

Ach lieber Herre, Jesu Christ

LORD Jesu Christ, our Lord most dear,
As thou wast once an infant here,
So give this child of thine, we pray,
Thy grace and blessing day by day:
    O holy Jesu, Lord divine.

2
As in thy heavenly kingdom, Lord,
All things obey thy sacred word,
Do thou thy mighty succour give,
And shield this child by morn and eve:
    O holy Jesu, Lord divine.

3
Their watch let angels round *him* keep
Where'er *he* be, awake, asleep;
Thy holy Cross now let *him* bear,
That *he* thy crown with saints may wear:
    O holy Jesu, Lord divine.

H. VON LAUFENBERG
Tr. Catherine Winkworth ‡

HYMN 426 St. Hugh   E. J. Hopkins, 1818–1901

KEY **D**

[tonic sol-fa notation]

HOLY BAPTISM

O FATHER, for this little life
  Entrusted from above,
Ere yet *he* face earth's sin and strife,
  We supplicate thy love.

2
As Hannah to the Temple gate
  Her dearest treasure bore,
So, Lord, to thee we consecrate
  This child for evermore.

3
Thy faithful soldier, may *he* fight
  With falsehood, sin, and shame,
And losing all to win the right
  Confess thy holy name.

4
Thy faithful servant, may *he* learn
  To love and labour still,
And with a flaming spirit burn
  To know and do thy will.

5
O Saviour, all *he* is is thine,
  And all *he* yet may be:
O shelter *him* with love divine,
  And draw *him* near to thee.

6
For thou, O Lord, art all our life,
  In thee all struggles end:
Through all the sorrow and the strife
  Our Maker and our Friend.

BISHOP GILBERT WHITE

HYMN 427 Hawkhurst

H. J. Gauntlett, 1805–76

KEY G

O LOVING Father, to thy care
  We give again this child of thine,
Baptized and blessed with faithful prayer
  And sealed with Love's victorious sign.

2
As Christ, thy Son, did not refuse
  The homage of the children's cry,
So teach *him* childhood's gifts to use
  Thy name to praise and magnify.

3
Through youth and age, through shine and shade,
  Grant *him* to run *his* earthly race,
Forgetting not that man was made
  To show thy glory and thy grace:

4
A loving child, a faithful friend,
  A light in doubt and darkness given
To point the path that knows no end
  Save in the fuller light of heaven;

5
Till, at the last, before thy throne
  He lays *his* earthly armour down,
His task of loving service done,
  And, in thy mercy, takes *his* crown.

C. A. ALINGTON

HOLY BAPTISM

HYMN 428 Christe sanctorum   La Feillée, *Méthode*, 1782

KEY **D**

May be sung in Unison

[sol-fa notation]

1

TO thee, O Father, lamp of all the living,
We offer now this life of thine own giving:
Humbly we pray thee, through this earth's endeavour
    Light *his* steps ever.

2

Jesus, thyself a baby once from heaven,
To thee this little pilgrim here is given:
Within the mercy of thy fold befriend *him*;
    Thy love attend *him*.

3

Spirit of Comfort, fountain ever welling,
This infant's heart take now to be thy dwelling;
So may *he* live, grace, pity, truth confessing,
    Thy peace possessing.

4

Gather *him*, Holy Trinity, for ever
Into the wisdom of thy strength, that never
In life's dark shadow-lands thy love may leave *him*:
    Thine own receive *him*.

RONALD, LORD GORELL

FOR THE YOUNG

HYMN 429 Keine Schönheit hat die Welt Melody in G. Joseph's
KEY **D** *Seelenlust*, 1657

By permission of Schott & Co., Ltd.

Morning

THROUGH the night thy angels kept
Watch beside me while I slept;
Now the dark has passed away,
Thank thee, Lord, for this new day.

2
North and south and east and west
May thy holy name be blest;
Everywhere beneath the sun,
As in heaven, thy will be done.

3
Give me food that I may live;
Every naughtiness forgive;
Keep all evil things away
From thy little child this day. W. CANTON

HYMN 430 Puer nobis M. Praetorius, 1571–1621
KEY **D**

Morning

A WORK hath Christ for thee to do:
He bore the Cross, he laboured too.
He marks thine every deed and word:
Be true this day to Christ thy Lord.

2
A way hath Christ for thee to go,
The royal way he trod below:
Fear not, for he is at thy side,
Thy heart to cheer, thy steps to guide.

3
Then bravely forth his praise to tell,
With song on lip, to serve him well.
Life this new dawn begins anew:
For Jesus' sake be true, be true. E. D. SEDDING

FOR THE YOUNG

HYMN 431 Eudoxia S. Baring-Gould, 1834-1924
KEY G

```
{ |m :m |f :f |s :- |m :- || |f :f |m :m |r :- | :    ||
  |s₁:s₁|l₁:d |t₁:- |s₁:- || |l₁:l₁|s₁:s₁|s₁:- | :    ||
  |d :d |d :d |r :- |m :- || |d :d |d :d |t₁:- | :    ||
  |d :d |l₁:l₁|s₁:- |d :- || |f₁:f₁|d :d₁|s₁:- | :    ||

{ |m :m |r :d |f :- |m :- || |m :m |r :r |d :- |- :   ||
  |s₁:s₁|s₁:m₁|l₁:- |s₁:- || |l₁:s₁|l₁:s₁.f₁|m₁:- |- : ||
  |t₁:t₁|t₁:d |d :- |d :- || |d :d |d :t₁|d :- |- :   ||
  |m₁:m₁|s₁:l₁|f₁:- |d :- || |l₁:m₁|f₁:s₁|d₁:- |- :   ||
```

By permission of J. Curwen & Sons, Ltd.

Evening

p NOW the day is over,
    Night is drawing nigh,
    Shadows of the evening
    Steal across the sky.

2
Now the darkness gathers,
    Stars begin to peep,
    Birds and beasts and flowers
    Soon will be asleep.

3
mf Jesu, give the weary
    Calm and sweet repose;
p With thy tenderest blessing
    May mine eyelids close.

4
mf Grant to little children
    Visions bright of thee;
    Guard the sailors tossing
    On the deep blue sea.

5
p Comfort every sufferer
    Watching late in pain;
    Those who plan some evil
    From their sin restrain.

6
Through the long night watches
    May thine angels spread
    Their white wings above me,
    Watching round my bed.

7
mf When the morning wakens,
    Then may I arise
    Pure and fresh and sinless
    In thy holy eyes.

8
f Glory to the Father,
    Glory to the Son,
    And to thee, blest Spirit,
    Whilst all ages run.

S. BARING-GOULD

HYMN 432 Irby H. J. Gauntlett, 1805-76
KEY G

```
{ |s₁:t₁|d :-.d|d.t₁:d.r|r :d || |d :m |s :-.m|m.r:d.t₁|d :- ||
  |s₁:f₁|s₁:-.s₁|s₁:s₁.t₁|t₁:d || |s₁:d |d :-.d|l₁:s₁|s₁:- ||
  |m :r |d :-.m|m.r:m.f|f :m || |m :d |d :-.s|s.f:m.r|m :- ||
  |d₁:r₁|m₁:-.d₁|s₁:s₁|s₁:d || |d :l₁|m₁:-.d₁|f₁:s₁|d₁:- ||

{ |s₁:t₁|d :-.d|d.t₁:d.r|r :d || |d :m |s :-.m|m.r:d.t₁|d :- ||
  |s₁:f₁|s₁:-.s₁|fe₁:fe₁|s₁.f₁:m₁|s₁:d || |d :-.d|l₁:s₁|s₁:- ||
  |m :r |d :-.m|d :d |t₁:d || |m :d |d :-.s|s.f:m.r|m :- ||
  |d₁:r₁|m₁:-.d₁|l₁:r₁|s₁:d || |d :l₁|m₁:-.d₁|f₁:s₁|d₁:- ||
```

FOR THE YOUNG

l :l	s :-.d	f :f	m :—	l :l	s :-.m	m.r:d.t,	d :—
d :d	d.t,:d.d	d :t,	d :—	l,.t,:d .r	s,.t,:d.s,	l, :s,	s, :—
f :f	m.f :s.m	r :s	s :—	f :f	f .r:m.s	s.f :m.r	m :—
f,.s,:l,.t,	d.r :m.d	s, :s,	d :—	f,.s,:l,.t,	d :-.d	f, :s,	d, :—

In verses 2 and 4 these notes are sung as one-pulse notes

Suitable for Christmas

mf ONCE in royal David's city
    Stood a lowly cattle shed,
Where a mother laid her baby
    In a manger for his bed:
Mary was that Mother mild,
Jesus Christ her little Child.

2

He came down to earth from heaven
    Who is God and Lord of all,
p And his shelter was a stable,
    And his cradle was a stall;
With the poor and mean and lowly
Lived on earth our Saviour holy.

3

mf And through all his wondrous childhood
    He would honour and obey,
Love and watch the lowly Maiden,
    In whose gentle arms he lay:
Christian children all must be
Mild, obedient, good as he.

4

For he is our childhood's pattern,
    Day by day like us he grew,
p He was little, weak, and helpless,
    Tears and smiles like us he knew;
mf And he feeleth for our sadness,
And he shareth in our gladness.

5

f And our eyes at last shall see him,
    Through his own redeeming love,
For that Child so dear and gentle
    Is our Lord in heaven above;
And he leads his children on
To the place where he is gone.

6

mf Not in that poor lowly stable,
    With the oxen standing by,
We shall see him; but in heaven,
f   Set at God's right hand on high;
Where like stars his children crowned
All in white shall wait around.

MRS. C. F. ALEXANDER

FOR THE YOUNG

HYMN 433

FIRST TUNE

KEY **G** Glenfinlas

K. G. Finlay

KEY **D** Newland

SECOND TUNE

J. Armstrong, 1840–1928

Suitable for Lent

mf DO no sinful action,
  Speak no angry word:
  Ye belong to Jesus,
  Children of the Lord.

2
Christ is kind and gentle,
  Christ is pure and true;
And his little children
  Must be holy too.

3
p There's a wicked spirit
  Watching round you still,
And he tries to tempt you
  To all harm and ill.

4
mf But ye must not hear him,
  Though 'tis hard for you
To resist the evil,
  And the good to do.

5
For ye promised truly,
  In your infant days,
To renounce him wholly,
  And forsake his ways.

6
Ye are new-born Christians,
  Ye must learn to fight
With the bad within you,
  And to do the right.

FOR THE YOUNG

7
Christ is your own Master,
He is good and true,
And his little children
Must be holy too.

MRS. C. F. ALEXANDER

HYMN 434 Dayspring   C. H. Lloyd, 1845–1919

KEY E♭   B♭. t.

[tonic sol-fa notation]

f. E♭.

[tonic sol-fa notation]

Suitable for Lent

WE have a King who came to earth
  To win the world for God,
And we, the children of the King,
  Must follow where he trod.

2
The banner that our King unfurled
  Was love to every man,
So we must try to show that love
  In all the ways we can.

3
The enemies he came to fight
  Are selfishness and sin:
Then who would be a traitor now
  And let his foemen in?

4
He bids us keep our bodies pure,
  For 'tis the pure and clean
Can see the glory of the King,
  And tell what they have seen.

5
We are a little company,
  But we are pledged to bring
Pure holy lives, kind joyful hearts,
  And bring them to the King.

MARGARET CROPPER

FOR THE YOUNG

HYMN 435 Alstone C. E. Willing, 1830–1904
KEY C

```
{ :s  |s :-.l |s :d' |m :r  |d   ||r  |m :-.f |s :l  |s :m  |r :— |
  :d  |d :-.d |d :d  |d :t, |d   ||t, |d :-.t,|d :d  |d :d  |t, :—|
  :m  |m :-.f |m :s  |s :f  |m   ||s  |s :-.s |s :f  |s :s  |s :— |
  :d  |d :-.d |d :m  |s :s, |l,  ||s, |d :-.r |m :f  |m :d  |s, :—}

{ :s  |s :-.l |s :d' |m':r' |d'  ||l  |s :-.l |t :d' |m :r  |d :— |
  :t, |d :-.d |d :m  |s :f  |m   ||f  |s :-.f |f :m  |d :t, |d :— |
  :s  |s :-.f |s :l  |d':t  |d'  ||d' |d':-.d'|f :s  |s :f  |m :— |
  :s  |m :-.f |m :l  |s :s  |l   ||f  |m :-.f |r :d  |s :s, |d :—}
```

Suitable for Passiontide

mf IT is a thing most wonderful,
  Almost too wonderful to be,
That God's own Son should come from heaven,
  And die to save a child like me.

2

And yet I know that it is true:
  He chose a poor and humble lot,
p And wept and toiled and mourned and died
  For love of those who loved him not.

3

mf I cannot tell how he could love
  A child so weak and full of sin;
His love must be most wonderful,
  If he could die my love to win.

4

p I sometimes think about the Cross,
  And shut my eyes, and try to see
The cruel nails and crown of thorns,
  And Jesus crucified for me.

5

But even could I see him die,
  I could but see a little part
mf Of that great love which, like a fire,
  Is always burning in his heart.

6

It is most wonderful to know
  His love for me so free and sure;
p But 'tis more wonderful to see
  My love for him so faint and poor.

FOR THE YOUNG

7

mf And yet I want to love thee, Lord!
O light the flame within my heart,
f And I will love thee more and more,
Until I see thee as thou art.

BISHOP W. WALSHAM HOW

HYMN **436** Albano   V. Novello, 1781–1861
KEY **F**

Suitable for Passiontide

O DEAREST Lord, thy sacred head
  With thorns was pierced for me;
O pour thy blessing on my head
  That I may think for thee.

2

O dearest Lord, thy sacred hands
  With nails were pierced for me;
O shed thy blessing on my hands
  That they may work for thee.

3

O dearest Lord, thy sacred feet
  With nails were pierced for me;
O pour thy blessing on my feet
  That they may follow thee.

4

O dearest Lord, thy sacred heart
  With spear was pierced for me;
O pour thy Spirit in my heart
  That I may live for thee.

H. E. HARDY (Father Andrew)

FOR THE YOUNG

HYMN **437** Infantium laudes   Sir C. H. H. Parry, 1848–1918

KEY E♭

Suitable for Palm Sunday

WHEN, his salvation bringing,
  To Zion Jesus came,
The children all stood singing
  Hosanna to his name;
Nor did their zeal offend him,
  But, as he rode along,
He let them still attend him,
  And listened to their song:
    Hosanna to Jesus they sang.

2

And since the Lord retaineth
  His love for children still,
Though now as King he reigneth
  On Zion's heavenly hill,
We'll flock around his banner,
  Who sits upon the throne,
And cry aloud 'Hosanna'
  To David's royal Son:
    Hosanna to Jesus we'll sing.

FOR THE YOUNG

3
For should we fail proclaiming
Our great Redeemer's praise,
The stones, our silence shaming,
Would their Hosannas raise.
But shall we only render
The tribute of our words?
No, while our hearts are tender,
They, too, shall be the Lord's:
Hosanna to Jesus, our King!

J. KING

HYMN **438** Jerusalem   J. B. Dykes, 1823–76

KEY **D**

[sol-fa notation]

Easter

1
GOOD Joseph had a garden,
Close by that sad green hill
Where Jesus died a bitter death
To save mankind from ill.

2
One evening in that garden,
Their faces dark with gloom,
They laid the Saviour's body
Within good Joseph's tomb.

3
There came the holy women
With spices and with tears;
The angels tried to comfort them,
But could not calm their fears.

4
Came Mary to that garden
And sobbed with heart forlorn;
She thought she heard the gardener ask
'Whom seekest thou this morn?'

5
She heard her own name spoken,
And then she lost her care:
All in his strength and beauty
The risen Lord stood fair!

6
Good Joseph had a garden;
Amid its trees so tall
The Lord Christ stood on Easter Day:
He lives to save us all.

7
And as he rose at Easter
He is alive for ay,
The very same Lord Jesus Christ
Who hears us sing to-day.

8
Go tell the Lord Christ's message,
The Easter triumph sing,
Till all his waiting children know
That Jesus is their King.

ALDA M. MILNER-BARRY

FOR THE YOUNG

HYMN 439 St. James   R. Courteville (1697)

KEY **A**

[sol-fa notation]

Ascension

THE golden gates are lifted up,
  The doors are opened wide,
The King of Glory is gone up
  Unto his Father's side.

2

And ever on our earthly path
  A gleam of glory lies,
A light still breaks behind the cloud
  That veils thee from our eyes.

3

Lift up our hearts, lift up our minds,
  And let thy grace be given,
That, while we linger yet below,
  Our treasure be in heaven;

4

That, where thou art at God's right hand,
  Our hope, our love may be:
Dwell in us now, that we may dwell
  For evermore in thee.

MRS. C. F. ALEXANDER

HYMN 440 London New   *Psalms* (Edinburgh, 1635)

KEY **E♭**

[sol-fa notation]

Suitable for Whitsuntide

mf THOU Wind of God, whose coming
  A world as yet unmade, [stirred
And things, which were not, woke
    and heard
  And answered and obeyed;

2

By thee the lives that live and move
  In earth and sea began,
And human thought and human
    love
  Lit up the heart of man;

FOR THE YOUNG

3
p Until thou camest, Holy One,
　In Jesus' heart to dwell,
That man, in him, might be a son
And please the Father well.

4
mf O thou, who from the Father art,
　Upon our spirits move,
f Until the children's thankful heart
Reflects the Father's love.

J. M. C. CRUM

HYMN 441 Radwell   H. P. Chadwyck-Healey
KEY C

By permission of the Royal School of Church Music

Suitable for Dedication

O FATHER, we thank thee for Jesus thy Son,
For all that for us by his death he hath won,
His rising at Easter, his reign on thy throne,
His gift of the Spirit to make us thine own.

2
All praise to thee, Lord, for evangelists brave,
The witness by word and by life that they gave,
The Church of our fathers, the home of us all,
Her sturdy grey towers and steeples so tall.

3
All praise for the masons who built them so true
With axe and with chisel, the best that they knew;
All praise for the craftsmen who carved with a will,
The nave and the chancel with glory to fill.

4
How surely they painted, those guildsmen of old,
The screen with its martyrs aglimmer with gold!
How fair shone their windows which let the sun through,
And flecked the white pillars with crimson and blue!

5
Then ring out, ye belfries, from hill and from plain,
And thunder, ye organs, in deep-toned refrain:
Praise God, priest and people, for blessings outpoured
On Britain, our homeland. Yes, praise ye the Lord!

E. D. SEDDING

NOTE. *Most of the above hymns, while being specially suitable for the seasons indicated, may be sung throughout the year*

FOR THE YOUNG

Hymn 442 — FIRST TUNE

Key A♭ Royal Oak
Adapted from an English traditional melody by Martin Shaw

VOICES IN UNISON Fast

{| s : m | f : m | r.d : t₁.l₁ | s₁ : m | f : l₁ | t₁ : l₁.t₁ | d :—|—:— ‖

1 All things bright and beau-ti-ful, All crea-tures great and small,

⌢ *Fine.*

{| s : m | f : m | r.d : t₁.l₁ | s₁ : m | f : l₁ | t₁ : l₁.t₁ | d :—|— ‖

All things wise and won-der-ful, The Lord God made them all.

{: s₁ | m₁ : s₁ | s₁ : f₁.m₁ | f₁ : l₁ |—: l₁ | t₁.d : r | t₁.d : r | s₁ :—|—:d.r }

2 Each lit-tle flower that o-pens, Each lit-tle bird that sings, He

D.C.

{| m : r | d : r.m | f :—.m | r : m.f | s : l₁ | t₁ : l₁.t₁ | d :—|—:— ‖

made their glow-ing col-ours, He made their ti-ny wings.

By permission of J. Curwen & Sons, Ltd., from Curwen edition No. 80629

NOTE. *The pause (⌢) is for the last time only*

SECOND TUNE

Key D All things bright and beautiful
W. H. Monk, 1823–89

VERSE 1, AND THE REFRAIN AFTER VERSES 2, 3, 4, 5, 6

{| d′: m | f : l | s :—.m | d : m | r : t | t : l | s :—|—:— |
| m : d | d : f | m :—.d | d : d | r : t₁ | d : d | t₁:—|—:— ‖
| 1 All things bright and | beau-ti-ful, All | crea-tures great and | small,
| s : s | f : t | d′:—.s | m : m.fe | s : s | m : fe | s :—|—:— |
| d : d | l₁ : r | m :—.m | l₁ : l₁ | t₁.d : r | r : r | s :—|—:f |

Fine.

{| d′: m | f : l | s :—.m | d : l | s : d′ | m :—.r | d :—|— |
| d : d | t₁ : t₁ | d :—.t₁ | d : d.t₁ | d : d.r | m.d : t₁ | d :—|— ‖
| All things wise and | won-der-ful, The | Lord God made them | all.
| s : s | s : s | s :—.s | m : f | s : m.f | s :—.f | m :—|— |
| m : d | r : f | m :—.m | l₁ : r | m : l₁ | s₁ : s₁ | d :—|— |

A.t. VERSES 2, 3, 4, 5, 6

{:ᵐl₁ | s₁ : d | d :—.t₁ | d :— | d : l₁ | s₁ : d | d :—.t₁ | d :— |— |
:ᵈf₁ | s₁ : m₁ | f₁ :—.f₁ | m₁ : s₁.f₁ | m₁ : f₁ | s₁ : m₁.f₁ | s₁ :—.f₁ | m₁ : s₁.f₁ | m₁ |
:ˢd | d : d | l₁ :—.s₁ | d :m.r | d : d | d : d.r | m :—.r | d : m.r | d |
:ᵈf₁ | m₁ : d₁ | r₁ :—.s₁ | d₁ :— | d₁ : f₁ | m₁ : l₁ | s₁ :—.s₁ | d₁ :— |— ‖

FOR THE YOUNG

```
                                                   f.D.      D.C.
:de |r :-.m |f :r    |t₁ :-   |d :l₁ |s₁ :-.l₁|t₁ :r  |ᵈs :- |- :-
:s₁ |l₁ :-.s₁|f₁ :l₁ |l₁ :s₁.f₁|m₁ :f₁|m₁ :-.m₁|f₁ :f₁ |ᵐt₁:- |- :-
:m  |f  :-.de|r  :r  |r.f:m.r|d  :d  |d  :-.d |r  :t₁ |ᵈs :- |- :-
:l₁ |l₁ :-.l₁|r₁ :f₁ |s₁ :-  |l₁ :f₁ |s₁ :-.s₁|s₁ :s₁ |ᵈs :- |- :-
```

    f   ALL things bright and beautiful,
         All creatures great and small,
         All things wise and wonderful,
         The Lord God made them all.

2

   mf   Each little flower that opens,
         Each little bird that sings,
         He made their glowing colours,
         He made their tiny wings.
    f   All things bright, etc.

3

   mf   The purple-headed mountain,
         The river running by,
         The sunset, and the morning
         That brightens up the sky:
    f   All things bright, etc.

4

   mf   The cold wind in the winter,
         The pleasant summer sun,
         The ripe fruits in the garden,
         He made them every one.
    f   All things bright, etc.

5*

   mf   The tall trees in the greenwood,
         The meadows where we play,
         The rushes by the water
         We gather every day:
    f   All things bright, etc.

6

   mf   He gave us eyes to see them,
         And lips that we might tell
         How great is God Almighty,
         Who has made all things well.
    f   All things bright, etc.

Mrs. C. F. Alexander

FOR THE YOUNG

HYMN **443** St. Leonard H. Smart, 1813–79

KEY B♭

[sol-fa notation]

LORD, I would own thy tender care,
  And all thy love to me;
The food I eat, the clothes I wear,
  Are all bestowed by thee.

2

'Tis thou preservest me from death
  And dangers every hour;
I cannot draw another breath
  Unless thou give me power.

3

Kind angels guard me every night,
  As round my bed they stay;
Nor am I absent from thy sight
  In darkness or by day.

4

My health and friends and parents dear
  To me by God are given;
I have not any blessing here
  But what is sent from heaven.

5

Such goodness, Lord, and constant care
  I never can repay;
But may it be my daily prayer,
  To love thee and obey.

JANE TAYLOR

Alternative Tune, Stracathro, 299

FOR THE YOUNG

HYMN **444** Buckland   L. G. Hayne, 1836–83

KEY **D**

A.t.

(sol-fa notation)

f.D.

(sol-fa notation)

   mf LOVING Shepherd of thy sheep,
        Keep thy lamb, in safety keep;
        Nothing can thy power withstand,
        None can pluck me from thy hand.

2

   p Loving Saviour, thou didst give
       Thine own life that we might live,
       And the hands outstretched to bless
       Bear the cruel nails' impress.

3

   f I would praise thee every day,
       Gladly all thy will obey,
       Like thy blessèd ones above
       Happy in thy precious love.

4

   mf Loving Shepherd, ever near,
        Teach thy lamb thy voice to hear;
        Suffer not my steps to stray
        From the straight and narrow way.

5

    Where thou leadest I would go,
    Walking in thy steps below,
   f Till before my Father's throne
    I shall know as I am known.

                                             JANE E. LEESON

FOR THE YOUNG

Hymn 445 — FIRST TUNE

KEY **F** Mernle   D. P. Symonds

{: s | m :-.r | d :r | d :l₁ | s₁ ‖ s | d' :s | m :r | s :— |— ‖
 : r | d :-.t₁ | l₁ :l₁ | s₁ :f₁.m₁ | r₁ ‖ t₁ | d :d | d :t₁ | d :t₁ | l₁ ‖
 : s | s :-.f | m :f | m :d | t₁ ‖ s | s :m | s :s | s :f | m ‖
 : t₁ | d :-.s₁ | l₁ :r₁ | m₁ :f₁ | s₁ ‖ f | m :d | s :f | m :r | d ‖ }

Fine.

{: s | m :-.r | d :r | d :l₁ | s₁ ‖ d | l :s | m :r | d :— |— ‖
 : s₁ | d :t₁ | d :l₁ | s₁ :-.fe₁ | s₁ ‖ s₁ | l₁ :d | d :t₁ | d :— |— ‖
 : r | s :-.f | m :f | m :d | r ‖ m | d :s | s :-.f | m :— |— ‖
 : t₁ | d :s₁ | l₁ :f₁ | s₁ :l₁ | t₁ ‖ f₁ | m₁ :s₁ | s₁ | d :— |— ‖ }

{: d | f :m | r :m | d :-.t₁ | l₁ ‖ r | s :m | l :-.s | f :— |— ‖
 : d | l₁ :se₁ | l₁ :t₁ | l₁ :se₁ | s₁ ‖ l₁ | t₁ :t₁ | l₁ :de | r :— |— ‖
 : m | r :t₁ | l₁ :m | r :m | m ‖ f | s :s | m :l | l :— | s ‖
 : l₁ | r₁ :m₁ | ba₁ :se₁ | l₁ :t₁ | d ‖ f | m :r | de :l₁ | r :d | t₁ ‖ }

C.t.   f.F. *D.C.*

{: ʳs | l :d' | t :r' | m' :-.r' | d' ‖ r' | s :d' | l :t | d's :— |— ‖
 : ᵗm | f :s | f :l | se:m | m ‖ r | r :s | s :-.f | ᵐt₁ :— | d ‖
 : ˢd' | d' :d' | r' :l | t :— | l ‖ l | t :d' | m' :r' | d's :— |— ‖
 : ˢd | f :m | r :f | m :se | l ‖ f | m :r | s ‖ ᵈs₁ :— | l₁ ‖ }

By permission of the Royal School of Church Music

SECOND TUNE

KEY **G** I love to hear the story   H. J. Gauntlett, 1805–76

{: m | m :-.m | m.r :m.f | m :r |— ‖ l | s :f.m | r :m.f | m :—|— ‖
I love to hear the sto-ry   Which an-gel voi-ces tell,

Fine.

{: m | f :-.m | m.r :r.d | t₁.l₁ :s₁ |— ‖ l | s :f.m | m :r | d :—|— ‖
How once the King of Glo-ry   Came down on earth to dwell.

{: l₁.t₁ | d :t₁.l₁ | r :m.f | f :m |— ‖ m | m :r.d | t₁ :l₁ | m :—|— ‖
I am both weak and sin-ful,   But this I sure-ly know,

D.t.   f.G. *D.C.*

{: ᵐl | r' : d' | d'.t :d'.r' | s :-.f | m ‖ d' | d'.t :d'.r' | t :t | d's :—|— ‖
The Lord came down to save me, Be-cause he loved me so.

FOR THE YOUNG

1. I LOVE to hear the story
   Which angel voices tell,
  How once the King of Glory
   Came down on earth to dwell.
  I am both weak and sinful,
   But this I surely know,
  The Lord came down to save me,
    Because he loved me so.
     I love to hear the story, etc.

2. I'm glad my blessèd Saviour
    Was once a child like me,
   To show how pure and holy
    His little ones might be;
   And if I try to follow
    His footsteps here below,
   He never will forget me,
    Because he loves me so.
     I love to hear the story, etc.

3. To tell his love and mercy
    My sweetest songs I'll raise;
   And though I cannot see him,
    I know he hears my praise;
   For he himself has promised
    That even I may go
   To sing among his angels,
    Because he loves me so.
     I love to hear the story, etc.

MRS. E. MILLER†

HYMN 446 Valley   G. H. Knight

KEY D

[tonic sol-fa notation]

mf 1. SING to the Lord the children's hymn,
     His gentle love declare,
    Who bends amid the seraphim
     To hear the children's prayer.

p 2. He at a mother's breast was fed,
      Though God's own Son was he;
     He learnt the first small words he said
      At a meek mother's knee.

3. Close to his loving heart he pressed
    The children of the earth;
   He lifted up his hands and blessed
    The babes of human birth.

mf 4. Lo, from the stars his face will turn
      On us with glances mild;
     The angels of his presence yearn
      To bless the little child.

5. Keep us, O Jesus, Lord, for thee,
    That so, by thy dear grace,
   We, children of the font, may see
    Our heavenly Father's face.

R. S. HAWKER

FOR THE YOUNG

Hymn 447 Pastor bonus

Sir J. Stainer, 1840–1901

KEY **G**

[sol-fa notation staves]

f.C.

G.t.

---

f CHRIST, who once amongst us
    As a child did dwell,
Is the children's Saviour,
    And he loves us well;
mf If we keep our promise
    Made him at the font,
f He will be our Shepherd,
    And we shall not want.

2

mf There it was they laid us
    In those tender arms,
Where the lambs are carried
    Safe from all alarms;
If we trust his promise,
    He will let us rest
In his arms for ever,
    Leaning on his breast.

3

Though we may not see him
    For a little while,
We shall know he holds us,
    Often feel his smile;
p Death will be to slumber
    In that sweet embrace,
f And we shall awaken
    To behold his face.

4

mf He will be our Shepherd
    After as before,
By still heavenly waters
    Lead us evermore;
Make us lie in pastures
    Beautiful and green,
Where none thirst or hunger,
    And no tears are seen.

FOR THE YOUNG

5

p Jesus, our Good Shepherd,
　　Laying down thy life,
　　Lest thy sheep should perish
　　　In the cruel strife,
mf Help us to remember
　　All thy love and care,
f Trust in thee, and love thee
　　Always, everywhere.

W. ST. HILL BOURNE

HYMN **448** Solothurn　　　　　　　Swiss Traditional Melody

KEY E♭

[sol-fa notation]

mf AROUND the throne of God a band
　　Of glorious angels ever stand;
f Bright things they see, sweet harps they hold,
　　And on their heads are crowns of gold.

2

mf Some wait around him, ready still
　　To sing his praise and do his will;
　　And some, when he commands them, go
　　To guard his servants here below.

3

Lord, give thy angels every day
Command to guide us on our way,
And bid them every evening keep
Their watch around us while we sleep.

4

So shall no wicked thing draw near,
To do us harm or cause us fear;
f And we shall dwell, when life is past,
　　With angels round thy throne at last.

J. M. NEALE†

FOR THE YOUNG

Hymn 449 David

D. W. Dearle (1926)

KEY D

[tonic sol-fa notation]

By permission of the Proprietors of the Church and School Hymnal

O, DAVID was a shepherd lad,
    And guarded well the sheep;
By night and day, good times or bad,
    His watch he used to keep.
But David's less than David's Son,
    Though a Shepherd too is he;
Through all the world his pastures run,
    And of his flock are we.

2

O, David was a shepherd lad,
    And more he dared to do:
Goliath all in armour clad
    With sling and stone he slew.
But David's Son, more daring yet,
    Put weapons all away;
All evil things with goodness met,
    And stronger was than they.

FOR THE YOUNG

3

O, David was a shepherd lad,
  And a kingdom he attained;
And gold and glory great he had,
  And forty years he reigned.
But David's Son is rich in love,
  And reigns eternally;
For King he is in heaven above,
  And on the earth shall be.

C. ERSKINE CLARKE

HYMN 450 St. Botolph — G. Slater

KEY E♭

[Tonic sol-fa notation]

By permission of the Oxford University Press

mf O CHRIST, whom we may love and know
  And follow to the end,
We who are friends together come
  To thee our heavenly Friend.

2

Thou who didst share our daily toil
  To make us good and free,
Help us to share thy fiery love
  And shining purity.

3

Give us thy love, that loves us all
  And dared the glorious Cross,
That we may love to share and know
  Each other's joy and loss.

4

Give us thy purity to shield
  Our souls in each dark place,
f To give us wings to raise to thee,
  And power to see thy face.

MARGARET CROPPER

FOR THE YOUNG

HYMN 451 Simplicity ... Sir J. Stainer, 1840–1901
KEY E♭

For young children

PART 1

1
GENTLE Jesus, meek and mild,
Look upon a little child;
Pity my simplicity,
Suffer me to come to thee.

2
Fain I would to thee be brought:
Dearest God, forbid it not;
Give me, blessed Lord, a place
In the kingdom of thy grace.

3
Hide me, from all evil hide,
Self and stubbornness and pride;
Hold me fast in thine embrace,
Let me see thy smiling face.

PART 2

4
Lamb of God, I look to thee;
Thou shalt my example be:
Thou art gentle, meek, and mild,
Thou wast once a little child.

5
Fain I would be as thou art;
Give me thy obedient heart.
Thou art pitiful and kind;
Let me have thy loving mind.

6
Let me, above all, fulfil
God my heavenly Father's will,
Never his good Spirit grieve,
Only to his glory live.

PART 3

7
Thou didst live to God alone;
Thou didst never seek thine own;
Thou thyself didst never please:
God was all thy happiness.

8
Loving Jesus, gentle Lamb,
In thy gracious hands I am:
Make me, Saviour, what thou art;
Live thyself within my heart.

9
I shall then show forth thy praise,
Serve thee all my happy days;
Then the world shall always see
Christ, the holy Child, in me.

C. WESLEY

FOR THE YOUNG

Hymn 452 In memoriam   Sir J. Stainer, 1840–1901

KEY E♭

{| m :—: m | f :—: m | r :—: m | d :—: —| d :—: r | m :—: f |s :m : l |}
There's a Friend for lit - tle chil - dren A - bove the bright blue

{| s :—:—| : : s | d¹:—: t | l :—: t | d¹ :—:—| s :—: s |}
sky, A Friend who ne - ver chan - ges, Whose

{| l :—: s | s :f : m | r :—:—| r :—:—| r :—: de | r :—: m |}
love will ne - ver die: Our earth - ly friends may

{| f :—:—| f :—: d | d :—: t₁ | d :—: r | m :—:—| s :—:—|}
fail us, And change with chang - ing years; This

| d¹:—: d¹| t :—: t | l :—:—| s :—: f |m :f : s | m :—: r | d :—:—||
Friend is al - ways wor - thy Of that dear name he bears.

For young children

mf THERE'S a Friend for little children
    Above the bright blue sky,
  A Friend who never changes,
    Whose love will never die:
p Our earthly friends may fail us,
    And change with changing years;
f This Friend is always worthy
    Of that dear name he bears.

2*

mf There's a rest for little children
    Above the bright blue sky,
  Who love the blessèd Saviour,
    And to the Father cry:
p A rest from every turmoil,
    From sin and sorrow free,
  Where every little pilgrim
    Shall rest eternally.

3

mf There's a home for little children
    Above the bright blue sky,
f Where Jesus reigns in glory,
    A home of peace and joy;
mf No home on earth is like it,
    Nor can with it compare;
f For every one is happy,
    Nor could be happier, there.

4*

There's a crown for little children
    Above the bright blue sky,
mf And all who look for Jesus
    Shall wear it by and by:
f A crown of brightest glory,
    Which he will then bestow
mf On those who found his favour
    And loved his name below.

5

f There's a song for little children
    Above the bright blue sky,
  A song that will not weary,
    Though sung continually:
mf A song which even angels
    Can never, never sing;
  They know not Christ as Saviour,
    But worship him as King.

6

f There's a robe for little children
    Above the bright blue sky;
  And a harp of sweetest music,
    And palms of victory.
  All, all above is treasured,
    And found in Christ alone:
p Lord, grant thy little children
    To know thee as their own

A. MIDLANE

FOR THE YOUNG

HYMN 453 Airlie — Sir S. H. Nicholson, 1875–1947
KEY E♭

UNISON

{ :s.s | d':t:l | s :—:d.r | m:f:r | s :— ‖ m.m | f:s:l | s:m:r | d :—:m | r :— ‖

{ :r.m | f:s:r | f:m:m.f | s:l:m | s:f ‖ l.t | d':t:l | s:m:d.r | m:f:r | d :— ‖

    f   HOSANNA we sing, like the children dear,
         In the olden days when the Lord lived here;
   mf He blessed little children, and smiled on them,
         While they chanted his praise in Jerusalem.

2

    f   Alleluia we sing, like the children bright
         With their harps of gold and their raiment white,
         As they follow their Shepherd with loving eyes
         Through the beautiful valleys of Paradise.

3

         Hosanna we sing, for he bends his ear,
         And rejoices the hymns of his own to hear;
   mf We know that his heart will never wax cold
         To the lambs that he feeds in his earthly fold.

4

    f   Alleluia we sing in the church we love,
         Alleluia resounds in the Church above;
         To thy little ones, Lord, may such grace be given,
         That we lose not our part in the song of heaven.

                                              G. S. HODGES

HYMN 454 Lyne — *Magdalen Hospital Hymns, c. 1762*
KEY E♭

{ | d :—:r | m :—.r:d | m:—:fe | s :—:— ‖ s :—:l | s :—:f | m:—.f:r | d :—:— ‖
  | d :—:s₁ | s₁:— :d | d :—:d | t₁:—:— ‖ d :—:d | d :—:d | d :— :t₁ | d :—:— ‖
  | m:—:s | s :— :s | s :—:l | t :—:— ‖ s :—:f | s :—:l | s :— :f | m:—:— ‖
  | d :—:t₁ | d :— :m | d:t₁:l₁ | s:s :f ‖ m:—:f | m :—:f | s :— :s₁ | d :—:— ‖

{ | s :—.f:m | s :—:d | m:—.f:m | r :—:— ‖ m:—.f:s | d':s :f | m:f :r | d :—:— ‖
  | r :— :d | d:—:d | d:—.r:d | t₁:—:— ‖ d :— :t₁ | d :—:d | d:r :t₁ | d :—:— ‖
  | s :— :s | s:—:s | s :— :s | s :—:— ‖ s :— :f | m:s :l | s :—:f | m:—:— ‖
  | t₁:— :d | m:—:m | d :— :m₁ | s₁:—:— ‖ d :— :r | m :—:f | s :—:s₁ | d :—:— ‖

    IN our work and in our play,
    Jesus, be thou ever near,
    Guarding, guiding, all the day,
    Keeping in thy holy fear.

2

    Thou didst toil, O royal Child,
    In the far-off Holy Land,
    Blessing labour undefiled,
    Pure and honest, of the hand.

FOR THE YOUNG

3
Thou wilt bless our play-hour too,
  If we ask thy succour strong;
Watch o'er all we say and do,
  Hold us back from guilt and wrong.

4
O, how happy thus to spend
  Work and play-time in his sight,
Till the rest which shall not end,
  Till the day which knows not night!

W. CHATTERTON DIX

HYMN 455 Buffham   D. E. Hopkins
KEY E♭

National

LET us thank the Christ for all who did their duty,
  Famous men of old and great of heart in fight;
Who fought their way and laboured for their day,
    And strove to make our England
    A happy, lovely England,
  Happy in his praise and lovely in his light.

2
Now they thank the Christ who called them to be captains;
  Now they sing his praise in everlasting light;
And still they pray, they pray the Lord to-day
    That he would make our England
    A happy, lovely England,
  Happy in his praise and lovely in his light.

3
Let us pray the Christ that he would make us soldiers
  Truer in his ways and braver in his fight;
That we, as they, may loyally obey,
    And help to make our England
    A happy, lovely England,
  Happy in his praise and lovely in his light.

J. M. C. CRUM

467

FOR THE YOUNG

HYMN 456 Quem pastores   German Medieval Melody

KEY F

[sol-fa notation музыка]

By permission of the Oxford University Press

A closing prayer

JESUS, kind above all other,
Gentle Child of gentle Mother,
In the stable born our Brother,
  Whom the angel hosts adore:

2
Jesus, cradled in a manger,
Keep us free from sin and danger,
And to all, both friend and stranger,
  Give thy blessing evermore.

J. M. NEALE†
Based on Adam of St. Victor

FOR SCHOOL AND COLLEGE USE

HYMN 457 Pilgrimage   Sir G. J. Elvey, 1816–93

KEY D

[sol-fa notation]

FOR SCHOOL AND COLLEGE USE

Beginning of Term

1
LORD, behold us with thy blessing
  Once again assembled here:
Onward be our footsteps pressing
  In thy love and faith and fear;
    Still protect us‿
  By thy presence ever near.

2
For thy mercy we adore thee,
  For this rest upon our way;
Lord, again we bow before thee,
  Speed our labours day by day;
    Mind and spirit‿
  With thy choicest gifts array.

3
Keep the spell of home affection
  Still alive in every heart;
May its power, with mild direction,
  Draw our love from self apart,
    Till thy children‿
  Feel that thou their Father art.

4
Break temptation's fatal power,
  Shielding all with guardian care,
Safe in every careless hour,
  Safe from sloth and sensual snare;
    Thou, our Saviour,‿
  Still our failing strength repair.

H. J. BUCKOLL

HYMN **458** St. Raphael   E. J. Hopkins, 1818–1901

KEY **G**

End of Term

1
LORD, dismiss us with thy blessing,
  Thanks for mercies past receive;
Pardon all, their faults confessing;
  Time that's lost may all retrieve;
    May thy children‿
  Ne'er again thy Spirit grieve.

2
Bless thou all our days of leisure,
  Help us selfish lures to flee;
Sanctify our every pleasure;
  Pure and blameless may it be;
    May our gladness‿
  Draw us evermore to thee.

3
By thy kindly influence cherish
  All the good we here have gained;
May all taint of evil perish
  By thy mightier power restrained;
    Seek we ever‿
  Knowledge pure and love unfeigned.

4
Let thy Father-hand be shielding
  All who here shall meet no more;
May their seed-time past be yielding
  Year by year a richer store;
    Those returning‿
  Make more faithful than before.

H. J. BUCKOLL

CONFIRMATION

HYMN 459 St. Peter

A. R. Reinagle, 1799–1877

KEY E♭

mf MY God, accept my heart this day,
    And make it always thine,
That I from thee no more may stray,
    No more from thee decline.

2
p Before the Cross of him who died,
    Behold, I prostrate fall;
Let every sin be crucified,
    And Christ be all in all.

3
mf Anoint me with thy heavenly grace,
    And seal me for thine own;
f That I may see thy glorious face,
    And worship near thy throne.

4
mf Let every thought and work and word
    To thee be ever given:
Then life shall be thy service, Lord,
    And death the gate of heaven.

[UNISON]
5
f All glory to the Father be,
    All glory to the Son,
All glory, Holy Ghost, to thee,
    While endless ages run.

M. BRIDGES

HYMN 460 Breslau

Geistliche Gesänge (Leipzig, 1625)

KEY A♭

O GOD, in this thine hour of grace,
    With needy heart and empty hand,
Yet bidden of thee to seek thy face,
    For blessing at thy feet we stand.

2
Ours are the vows, the frail desires,
    The high resolve to dare and do;
Our flickering faith to thee aspires,
    And passes like the morning dew.

CONFIRMATION

3

Ours is the mighty need of thee—
　How great, thy love alone can know;
Ours but the hunger and the plea
　That strives and will not let thee go.

4

Thy word we clasp, thy touch we wait;
　Our eyes, O God, are unto thee,
Whose lovingkindness makes us great,
　Whose strength shall seal our victory.

BISHOP C. H. BOUTFLOWER

HYMN **461**　St. Magnus　　　　　　　　　J. Clarke, *c.* 1659–1707

KEY A♭

STRONG Captain, in thy holy ranks
　We take our places now:
Give us the mood befitting those
　Who make so great a vow.

2

For foolishness it were to come
　In hardihood of pride,
And cowardice it were to come
　And wish to be untried.

3

We'll not mistrust our want of strength
　Nor trust our strength of will;
Our only confidence, that thou
　Believest in us still.

4

Make, then, our task to match our strength,
　Our strength to match our task,
And make us unafraid to do
　Whatever thou wilt ask.

J. M. C. CRUM

CONFIRMATION

Hymn 462 Paderborn *Paderborn Gesangbuch*, 1765
KEY G

After the Confirmation

ONCE pledged by the Cross, as children of God,
To tread in the steps your Captain has trod,
Now, sealed by the Spirit of wisdom and might,
Go forward, Christ's soldiers, go forward and fight!

2

Your weapons of war are sent from above:
The Spirit's good sword, the breastplate of love;
Your feet with the Gospel of peace be well shod;
Put on the whole armour, the armour of God.

3

Full well do ye know the foe must be met,
Full well do ye feel that Satan has set
His powèrs of darkness in battle array;
But those who are for you are stronger than they.

4

The fight may be long, but triumph is sure,
And rest comes at last to those who endure:
The rest that remaineth, the victory won,
And (dearer than all things) your Captain's 'Well done!'

5

Then, on to the fight 'gainst sin and the world!
Stand fast in his strength, his banner unfurled;
And, sealed by the Spirit of wisdom and might,
Go forward, Christ's soldiers, go forward and fight!

ALICE M. BODE

Alternative Tune, Hanover, 167

HOLY MATRIMONY

Hymn 463 Felix F. Mendelssohn-Bartholdy, 1809–47

KEY E

mf O PERFECT Love, all human thought transcending,
Lowly we kneel in prayer before thy throne,
That theirs may be the love which knows no ending,
Whom thou for evermore dost join in one.

2

O perfect Life, be thou their full assurance
Of tender charity and steadfast faith,
Of patient hope, and quiet brave endurance,
With childlike trust that fears nor pain nor death.

3

Grant them the joy which brightens earthly sorrow,
p Grant them the peace which calms all earthly strife;
mf And to life's day the glorious unknown morrow
That dawns upon eternal love and life.

MRS. D. F. GURNEY

Alternative Tune, Strength and Stay, 17

HOLY MATRIMONY

HYMN 464 Melcombe S. Webbe, 1740-1816
KEY E♭

[Tonic sol-fa musical notation]

1
O THOU who gavest power to love
 That we might fix our hearts on thee,
Preparing us for joys above
 By that which here on earth we see;

2
Thy Spirit trains our souls to know
 The growing purpose of thy will,
And gives to love the power to show
 That purpose growing larger still:

3
Larger, as love to reverent eyes
 Makes manifest another soul,
And shows to life a richer prize,
 A clearer course, a nobler goal.

4
Lord, grant thy servants who implore
 Thy blessing on the hearts they blend,
That from that union evermore
 New joys may blossom to the end.

5
Make what is best in each combine
 To purge all earthly dross away,
To strengthen, purify, refine,
 To beautify each coming day.

6
So may they hand in hand advance
 Along life's paths from troubles free;
Brave to meet adverse circumstance
 Because their love points up to thee.

BISHOP MANDELL CREIGHTON

HYMN 465 Wareham W. Knapp, 1698-1768
KEY B♭

[Tonic sol-fa musical notation]

474

HOLY MATRIMONY

O FATHER, by whose sovereign sway
  The sun and stars in order move,
Yet who hast made us bold to say
  Thy nature and thy name is love:

2
O royal Son, whose every deed
  Showed love and love's divinity,
Yet didst not scorn the humblest need
  At Cana's feast in Galilee:

3
O Holy Spirit, who dost speak
  In saint and sage since time began,
Yet givest courage to the weak
  And teachest love to selfish man:

4
Be present in our hearts to-day,
  All powerful to bless, and give
To these thy children grace that they
  May love, and through their loving live.

C. A. ALINGTON

THE DEPARTED

HYMN 466   Dies irae, dies illa   Modes i and ii
KEY E♭
              Dies irae, dies illa

1 Day of wrath! O day of mourning! See fulfilled the
2 O what fear man's bosom rendeth, When from heaven the
7 What shall I, frail man, be pleading, Who for me be
8 King of majesty tremendous, Who dost free sal-

1 prophets' warning! Heaven and earth to ashes turning!
2 Judge descendeth, On whose sentence all dependeth!
7 interceding, When the just are mercy needing?
8 vation send us, Fount of pity, then befriend us.

3 Wondrous sound the trumpet flingeth, Through earth's sepul-
4 Death amazed and nature quaking, See all creatures
9 Think, good Jesu, my salvation Caused the wondrous
10 Faint and weary thou hast sought me, On the Cross of

3 chres it ringeth, All before the throne it bringeth.
4 now awaking, To the Judge their answer making.
9 Incarnation; Leave me not to reprobation.
10 suffering bought me; Shall such grace be vainly brought me?

475

THE DEPARTED

Hymn 466 (*continued*)

```
{|: l  sfs  s  lrrd  l,  dr  r — | fm  r  d   l, }
```
5 Lo, the book ex-act-ly word-ed, Where-in all hath
6 When the Judge his seat at-tain-eth, And each hid-den
11 Right-eous Judge! for sin's pol-lu-tion Grant thy gift of
12 Guil-ty, now I pour my moan-ing, All my shame with

```
{|  d  r  f  mdr — |  l  f  s  r  d  r  f  mdr — :||
```
5 been re-cord-ed; Thence shall judge-ment be a-ward-ed.
6 deed ar-raign-eth, Not a sin un-judged re-main-eth.
11 ab-so-lu-tion, Ere that day of re-tri-bu-tion.
12 an-guish own-ing; Spare, O God, thy sup-pliant groan-ing.

```
{|:  f  m  f  r  m  d  r — r — | f  fs  fm  rd  }
```
13 By the sin-ful wo-man shri-ven, By the dy-ing
14 Worth-less are my prayers and sigh-ing; Yet, thy mer-cy

```
{|  m  f  m — r — | l,  dr r  rd  m  f  m — r — :||
```
13 thief for-giv-en, Thou to me a hope hast giv-en.
14 not de-ny-ing, Save me from the wrath un-dy-ing.

```
{|:  l  d¹  d¹  tsl  lsfs  l  l — r — | f  m  f  r }
```
15 With the sheep vouch-safe to place me; Do not with the
16 While the wick-ed are con-found-ed, Doomed to grief and

```
{|  m d r — r — | f  sl lsf mrd  m  f  m — r — :||
```
15 goats a-base me; But to thy right hand up-raise me.
16 loss un-bound-ed, Call me with thy saints sur-round-ed.

```
{|  l  sfs  s  lr  rd  l,  dr  r — | fm  r  d  l, }
```
17 Low I kneel, with heart-sub-mis-sion, Bowed to dust in

```
{|  d  r  f  mdr — | l  f  s  r  d  r  f  mdr — ||
```
sore con-tri-tion: Shield me, dy-ing, from per-di-tion.

```
{|  r  l ltals f  ms — l — | f  m  s lrfmrd fm — r —}
```
18 Ah, that day of tears and mourn-ing! From the dust of earth re-turn-ing

```
{| l  d¹  d¹  tsllsfs  l  l — r — | f  m  s lrfmrd fm — r — ||
```
Man for judge-ment must pre-pare him: Spare, O God, in mer-cy spare him!

```
{|  l  sf m ss l — | f  m  s mrm  f  m  r — ||
```
19 Lord, all pity-ing, Je-su blest, Grant them thine e-ter-nal rest.

Thomas of Celano
Tr. W. J. Irons and Compilers

THE DEPARTED

Hymn 467 Requiescat

J. B. Dykes, 1823–76

[Tonic sol-fa notation]

* *These notes may be sung if there is no accompaniment*

p NOW the labourer's task is o'er,
 Now the battle day is past;
mf Now upon the farther shore
 Lands the voyager at last:
p Father, in thy gracious keeping
 Leave we now thy servant sleeping.

2

 There the tears of earth are dried,
  There its hidden things are clear;
mf There the work of life is tried
  By a juster Judge than here:
p Father, in thy, etc.

3

 There the sinful souls, that turn
  To the Cross their dying eyes,
mf All the love of Christ shall learn
  At his feet in Paradise:
p Father, in thy, etc.

4

mf There no more the powers of hell
  Can prevail to mar their peace;
 Christ the Lord shall guard them well,
  He who died for their release:
p Father, in thy, etc.

5

 'Earth to earth, and dust to dust,'
  Calmly now the words we say,
 Leaving *him* to sleep in trust
  Till the resurrection-day:
 Father, in thy, etc.

J. ELLERTON

THE DEPARTED

HYMN 468 Brecknock   S. S. Wesley, 1810–76
KEY E♭

1
p O LORD, to whom the spirits live
      Of all the faithful passed away,
mf Unto their path that brightness give
      Which shineth to the perfect day:
p   O Lamb of God, Redeemer blest,
      Grant them eternal light and rest.

2
mf Bless thou the dead that die in thee;
      As thou hast given them release,
      So quicken them thy face to see,
      And give them everlasting peace:
p   O Lamb of God, etc.

3
mf Direct us with thine arm of might,
      And bring us, perfected with them,
f To dwell within thy city bright,
      The heavenly Jerusalem:
p   O Lamb of God, etc.

R. F. LITTLEDALE and Compilers

HYMN 469 Swahili   J. A. P. Schulz, 1747–1800
KEY A♭

THE DEPARTED

Yesu Bin Mariamu

PART 1

mf JESU, Son of Mary,
　　Fount of life alone,
　Here we hail thee present
　　On thine altar-throne:
　Humbly we adore thee,
　　Lord of endless might,
　In thy mystic symbols
　　Veiled from earthly sight.

PART 2

2

p Think, O Lord, in mercy
　　On the souls of those
　Who, in faith gone from us,
　　Now in death repose.
　Here 'mid stress and conflict
　　Toils can never cease;
　There, the warfare ended,
　　Bid them rest in peace.

3

　Often were they wounded
　　In the deadly strife;
　Heal them, Good Physician,
　　With the balm of life.
　Every taint of evil,
　　Frailty, and decay,
　Good and gracious Saviour,
　　Cleanse and purge away.

4

　Rest eternal grant them,
　　After weary fight;
　Shed on them the radiance
　　Of thy heavenly light.
mf Lead them onward, upward,
　　To the holy place,
　Where thy saints made perfect
　　Gaze upon thy face.

From the Swahili Tr. E. S. PALMER

EMBER DAYS

HYMN **470** St. David   T. Ravenscroft, *Psalms*, 1621

KEY E♭

mf CHRIST is gone up; yet ere he
    passed
From earth, in heaven to reign,
He formed one holy Church to last
    Till he should come again.

2

His twelve apostles first he made
    His ministers of grace;
And they their hands on others laid,
    To fill in turn their place.

3

So age by age, and year by year,
    His grace was handed on;
And still the holy Church is here,
    Although her Lord is gone.

4

p Let those find pardon, Lord, from
    thee,
    Whose love to her is cold:
mf Bring wanderers in, and let there be
    One Shepherd and one fold.

J. M. NEALE

HYMN **471** St. Laurence   L. G. Hayne, 1836–83

KEY A♭

mf O THOU who makest souls to shine
    With light from lighter worlds above,
And droppest glistening dew divine
    On all who seek a Saviour's love;

2

Do thou thy benediction give
    On all who teach, on all who learn,
That so thy Church may holier live,
    And every lamp more brightly burn.

EMBER DAYS

3
Give those who teach pure hearts and wise,
   Faith, hope, and love, all warmed by prayer:
Themselves first training for the skies,
   They best will raise their people there.

4
Give those who learn the willing ear,
   The spirit meek, the guileless mind:
Such gifts will make the lowliest here
   Far better than a kingdom find.

5
O bless the shepherd, bless the sheep,
   That guide and guided both be one:
One in the faithful watch they keep,
   Until this hurrying life be done.

6
f   If thus, good Lord, thy grace be given,
   In thee to live, in thee to die,
Before we upward pass to heaven
   We taste our immortality.

BISHOP J. ARMSTRONG

HYMN **472**   Manchester New   R. Wainwright, 1748–82
KEY **E♭**

THE earth, O Lord, is one wide field
   Of all thy chosen seed;
The crop prepared its fruit to yield,
   The labourers few indeed.

2
We therefore come before thee now
   With fasting and with prayer,
Beseeching of thy love that thou
   Wouldst send more labourers there.

3
Not for our land alone we pray,
   Though that above the rest;
The realms and islands far away,
   O let them all be blest.

4
Endue the bishops of thy flock
   With wisdom and with grace,
Against false doctrine like a rock
   To set the heart and face.

5
To all thy priests thy truth reveal,
   And make thy judgements clear;
Make thou thy deacons full of zeal,
   And humble and sincere:

6
And give their flocks a lowly mind
   To hear—and not in vain;
That each and all may mercy find
   When thou shalt come again.

J. M. NEALE

EMBER DAYS

Hymn 473 Ludborough T. R. Matthews, 1826–1910
KEY E♭

mf LORD, pour thy Spirit from on high,
And thine ordainèd servants bless;
Graces and gifts to each supply,
And clothe thy priests with righteousness.

2
Within thy temple when they stand,
To teach the truth as taught by thee,
Saviour, like stars in thy right hand
Let all thy Church's pastors be.

3
Wisdom and zeal and faith impart,
Firmness with meekness, from above,
To bear thy people in their heart,
And love the souls whom thou dost love;

4
p To watch and pray and never faint,
By day and night their guard to keep,
To warn the sinner, cheer the saint,
To feed thy lambs and tend thy sheep.

5
mf So, when their work is finished here,
May they in hope their charge resign;
f When the Chief Shepherd shall appear,
O God, may they and we be thine.

J. MONTGOMERY‡

DEDICATION OF A CHURCH

Hymn 474 FIRST TUNE
KEY E♭ Urbs beata Mode ii

Urbs beata Jerusalem

1 Bless-èd ci-ty, heaven-ly Sa-lem, Vi-sion dear of peace and love,
2 Christ is made the sure Foun-da-tion, Christ the Head and Cor-ner-stone,
3 To this tem-ple, where we call thee, Come, O Lord of hosts, to-day;
4 *Here vouch-safe to all thy ser-vants What they ask of thee to gain,

482

THE DEDICATION OF A CHURCH

{| f r m f s l s f m r — | m f m r m r d — }

1 Who of liv-ing stones art build-ed   In the height of heaven a-bove,
2 Cho-sen of the Lord, and pre-cious,   Bind-ing all the Church in one,
3 With thy wont-ed lov-ing kind-ness   Hear thy ser-vants as they pray;
4 What they gain from thee for ev - er   With the bless-èd to re-tain,

{| l₁ d r r rd f s s f | l s f m f s f m r d r — ||

1 And by an-gel hosts en-cir-cled   As a bride dost earth-ward move!
2 Ho-ly Si-on's help for ev-er,   And her con-fi-dence a-lone.
3 And thy full-est ben-e-dic-tion   Shed with-in its walls al-way.
4 And here-af-ter in thy glo-ry   Ev-er-more with thee to reign.

SECOND TUNE

KEY **A** Oriel   C. Ett, *Cantica Sacra*, 1840

E. t.

{| d :d | d :d | r :m | f :m   m l :l | s :f | m :r | d :— ||
   s₁:l₁| s₁:m₁| s₁:s₁| l₁,s₁:s₁   s d :r | m :r | d :t₁| d :—
   m :d | d :d | t₁:d | d.t₁:d   m l :t | d¹:l | s :—.f| m :—
   d₁:f₁| m₁:l₁| s₁:m₁| r₁:d₁   d f :f | m :f | s :s₁| d :— ||

f. A.   E. t.

{| f d :d | d :d | r :m | f :m   m l :l | s :f | m :r | d :— ||
   d s₁:l₁| s₁:m₁| s₁:s₁| l₁:s₁   s d :d.r| m :r | d :t₁| d :—
   l m :d | d :d | t₁:d | d :d   d f.s:l.t| d¹:l | s :—.f| m :—
   f d₁:f₁| m₁:l₁| s₁:d | f₁:d₁   d f :f | m :f | s :s₁| d :— ||

                                f. A.

{| m :m | l :m | m :f | s :f   ta f :f | m :r | d :t₁| d :— ||
   d :r | d :t₁| d :l₁| d :l₁   r l₁:l₁| s₁:l₁| s₁:s₁| m₁:—
   s :se| l :t | l :f | m :f   f d.t₁:d.r| m :f | m :r | d :—
   d :t₁| l₁:se₁| l₁:r | d :r   ta f₁.s₁:l₁.t₁| d :f₁| s₁:s₁| d₁:— ||

Urbs beata Jerusalem

BLESSÈD city, heavenly Salem,
  Vision dear of peace and love,
Who of living stones art builded
  In the height of heaven above,
And by angel hosts encircled
  As a bride dost earthward move!

2
Christ is made the sure Foundation,
  Christ the Head and Corner-stone,
Chosen of the Lord, and precious,
  Binding all the Church in one,
Holy Sion's help for ever,
  And her confidence alone.

3
To this temple, where we call thee,
  Come, O Lord of hosts, to-day;
With thy wonted loving-kindness
  Hear thy servants as they pray;
And thy fullest benediction
  Shed within its walls alway.

4*
Here vouchsafe to all thy servants
  What they ask of thee to gain,
What they gain from thee for ever
  With the blessèd to retain,
And hereafter in thy glory
  Evermore with thee to reign.

Alternative Tune, Westminster Abbey, 620

Tr. J. M. NEALE‡

NOTE. *The complete version of the above hymn (the several parts of which may be sung separately) will be found in the 'Processional' section (620)*

THE DEDICATION OF A CHURCH

Hymn 475 St. Helena (Mt. Ephraim) Adapted from B. Milgrove,
Key E 1731–1810

```
{ :d  | m :d | r :r | d :— |— || s  | t  :s  | l  :l  | s  :— |— ||
{ :s, | d :d | d :t,| d :— |— || r  | r  :r  | m  :r  | t, :— |— ||
{ :m  | s :s | l :s | m :— |— || s  | s  :s  | s  :fe | s  :— |— ||
{ :d  | d :m | f :s | d :— |— || t, | s, :t, | d  :r  | s, :— |— ||

{ :f  | m :d | l :s | l :t | d' || l   | s :f  | m :r  | d :— |— ||
{ :d  | d :d | d :d | d :f | m  || d.r | m :r  | d :t, | d :— |— ||
{ :d  | s :s | f :s | f :f | s  || l.t | d':l  | s :-.f| m :— |— ||
{ :l, | d :m | f :m | f :r | d  || f,  | m,:f, | s,:s, | d :— |— ||
```

Patris aeterni Suboles coaeva

f O WORD of God above,
Who fillest all in all,
Hallow this house with thy sure love,
And bless our festival.

2

mf Here from the font is poured
The grace to cleanse from sin;
Here the anointing of the Lord
Confirms the soul within.

3

Here Christ to faithful hearts
His Body gives for food;
The Lamb of God himself imparts
The chalice of his Blood.

4

Here guilty souls that pine
May health and pardon win;
The Judge acquits, and grace divine
Restores the dead in sin.

5

Yea, God enthroned on high
Here also dwells to bless;
Here trains adoring souls that sigh
His mansions to possess.

6

f Against this holy home
Rude tempests harmless beat,
And Satan's angels fiercely come
But to endure defeat.

[UNISON]

7

All might, all praise be thine,
Father, co-equal Son,
And Spirit, bond of love divine,
While endless ages run.

C. GUIET *Tr.* I. Williams and Compilers

THE DEDICATION OF A CHURCH

Hymn 476 St. Catherine's Court   R. Strutt, 1848–1927

KEY D♭

[tonic sol-fa notation]

IN REMEMBRANCE OF PAST WORSHIPPERS

f IN our day of thanksgiving one psalm let us offer
    For the saints who before us have found their reward;
p When the shadow of death fell upon them, we sorrowed,
f   But now we rejoice that they rest in the Lord.

2

mf In the morning of life, and at noon, and at even,
    He called them away from our worship below;
But not till his love, at the font and the altar,
    Had girt them with grace for the way they should go.

3

These stones that have echoed their praises are holy,
    And dear is the ground where their feet have once trod;
Yet here they confessed they were strangers and pilgrims,
    And still they were seeking the city of God.

4

f Sing praise, then, for all who here sought and here found him,
    Whose journey is ended, whose perils are past:
They believed in the Light; and its glory is round them,
    Where the clouds of earth's sorrow are lifted at last.

W. H. DRAPER

HOSPITALS: THE SICK

HYMN 477　　　　　　　　FIRST TUNE

KEY **G**　Gott des Himmels　　　　　　　　H. Albert, 1604–51

HOSPITALS : THE SICK

[Music notation in tonic sol-fa: f.D♭. and A♭.t.]

mf THOU to whom the sick and dying
Ever came, nor came in vain,
Still with healing word replying
To the wearied cry of pain,
p   Hear us, Jesu, as we meet
    Suppliants at thy mercy-seat.

2

Still the weary, sick, and dying
Need a brother's, sister's, care,
mf On thy higher help relying
May we now their burden share,
    Bringing all our offerings meet
    Suppliants at thy mercy-seat.

3

May each child of thine be willing,
Willing both in hand and heart,
All the law of love fulfilling,
Ever comfort to impart;
    Ever bringing offerings meet
    Suppliant to thy mercy-seat.

4

So may sickness, sin, and sadness
To thy healing virtue yield,
f Till the sick and sad, in gladness,
Rescued, ransomed, cleansèd, healed,
    One in thee together meet
    Pardoned at thy judgement-seat.

G. THRING

HOSPITALS: THE SICK

Hymn 478 St. Matthew

W. Croft, 1678-1727

KEY **C**

[sol-fa notation]

f THINE arm, O Lord, in days of old
    Was strong to heal and save;
  It triumphed o'er disease and death,
    O'er darkness and the grave:
p To thee they went, the blind, the dumb,
    The palsied and the lame,
  The leper with his tainted life,
    The sick with fevered frame.

2

f And lo, thy touch brought life and health,
    Gave speech and strength and sight;
  And youth renewed and frenzy calmed
    Owned thee, the Lord of light:
  And now, O Lord, be near to bless,
    Almighty as of yore,
  In crowded street, by restless couch,
    As by Gennesareth's shore.

HOSPITALS: THE SICK

3

mf Be thou our great deliverer still,
　　Thou Lord of life and death;
　Restore and quicken, soothe and bless,
　　With thine almighty breath:
　To hands that work, and eyes that see,
　　Give wisdom's heavenly lore,
　That whole and sick, and weak and strong,
　　May praise thee evermore.

　　　　　　　　　　　　E. H. PLUMPTRE

HYMN **479** Belgrave　　　　　　W. Horsley, 1774–1858

KEY D

mf FROM thee all skill and science flow,
　　All pity, care, and love,
　All calm and courage, faith and hope:
　　O pour them from above!

2

And part them, Lord, to each and all,
　As each and all shall need,
To rise, like incense, each to thee,
　In noble thought and deed.

3

　And hasten, Lord, that perfect day
　　When pain and death shall cease,
f　And thy just rule shall fill the earth
　　With health and light and peace;

4

When ever blue the sky shall gleam,
　And ever green the sod,
And man's rude work deface no more
　The paradise of God.

　　　　　　　　　　　　CHARLES KINGSLEY

ALMSGIVING

HYMN 480 Almsgiving   J. B. Dykes, 1823-76

KEY **G**

[sol-fa notation]

f O LORD of heaven and earth and sea,
    To thee all praise and glory be!
    How shall we show our love to thee,
        Who givest all?

2
mf The golden sunshine, vernal air,
    Sweet flowers and fruit, thy love declare;
    When harvests ripen, thou art there,
        Who givest all.

3
For peaceful homes, and healthful days,
For all the blessings earth displays,
We owe thee thankfulness and praise,
    Who givest all.

4
p Thou didst not spare thine only Son,
But gav'st him for a world undone,
And freely with that blessèd One
    Thou givest all.

5
mf Thou giv'st the Holy Spirit's dower,
Spirit of life and love and power,
And dost his sevenfold graces shower
    Upon us all.

6
For souls redeemed, for sins forgiven,
For means of grace and hopes of heaven,
Father, what can to thee be given,
    Who givest all?

7
We lose what on ourselves we spend,
f We have as treasure without end
Whatever, Lord, to thee we lend,
    Who givest all;

8
To thee, from whom we all derive
Our life, our gifts, our power to give:
O may we ever with thee live,
    Who givest all.

BISHOP CHR. WORDSWORTH

Alternative Tune, Es ist kein Tag, 589

HARVEST

HYMN **481** Monkland
KEY **C**

J. Wilkes, 1785–1869, adapted from J. Lee's *Hymn Tunes of the United Brethren*, 1824

[Tonic sol-fa notation]

PRAISE, O praise our God and King;
Hymns of adoration sing:
   For his mercies still endure
   Ever faithful, ever sure.

2
Praise him that he made the sun
Day by day his course to run:
   For his mercies, etc.

3
And the silver moon by night,
Shining with his gentle light:
   For his mercies, etc.

4
Praise him that he gave the rain
To mature the swelling grain:
   For his mercies, etc.

5
And hath bid the fruitful field
Crops of precious increase yield:
   For his mercies, etc.

6
Praise him for our harvest-store;
He hath filled the garner-floor:
   For his mercies, etc.

7
And for richer food than this,
Pledge of everlasting bliss:
   For his mercies, etc.

[UNISON] 8
Glory to our bounteous King;
Glory let creation sing:
   Glory to the Father, Son,
   And blest Spirit, Three in One.

SIR H. W. BAKER

HARVEST

HYMN 482 St. George Sir G. J. Elvey, 1816–93
KEY **G**

1.
f COME, ye thankful people, come,
   Raise the song of harvest-home:
   All is safely gathered in,
   Ere the winter storms begin;
mf God, our Maker, doth provide
   For our wants to be supplied:
f Come to God's own temple, come;
   Raise the song of harvest-home.

2
mf All this world is God's own field,
   Fruit unto his praise to yield;
   Wheat and tares therein are sown,
   Unto joy or sorrow grown;
   Ripening with a wondrous power
   Till the final harvest-hour:
p Grant, O Lord of life, that we
   Holy grain and pure may be.

3
mf For we know that thou wilt come,
   And wilt take thy people home;
   From thy field wilt purge away
   All that doth offend, that day;
p And thine angels charge at last
   In the fire the tares to cast,
f But the fruitful ears to store
   In thy garner evermore.

4
mf Come then, Lord of mercy, come,
   Bid us sing thy harvest-home:
   Let thy saints be gathered in,
   Free from sorrow, free from sin;
f All upon the golden floor
   Praising thee for evermore:
   Come, with all thine angels come,
   Bid us sing thy harvest-home.

H. ALFORD and Compilers

HARVEST

HYMN 483 Wir pflügen   J. A. P. Schulz, 1747–1800

KEY B♭

Wir pflügen und wir streuen

mf WE plough the fields, and scatter
    The good seed on the land,
But it is fed and watered
    By God's almighty hand:
He sends the snow in winter,
    The warmth to swell the grain,
The breezes, and the sunshine,
    And soft, refreshing rain.
f   All good gifts around us
      Are sent from heaven above;
    Then thank the Lord, O thank
      For all his love. [the Lord,

2
mf He only is the Maker
    Of all things near and far;
He paints the wayside flower,
    He lights the evening star;
The winds and waves obey him,
    By him the birds are fed;
Much more to us, his children,
    He gives our daily bread.
f   All good gifts, etc.

3
mf   We thank thee then, O Father,
      For all things bright and good,
    The seed-time and the harvest,
      Our life, our health, our food.
    Accept the gifts we offer
      For all thy love imparts,
    And, what thou most desirest,
      Our humble, thankful hearts.
f   All good gifts, etc.

                                    M. CLAUDIUS *Tr.* Jane M. Campbell

HYMN 484 Golden Sheaves

Sir A. Sullivan, 1842–1900

KEY G

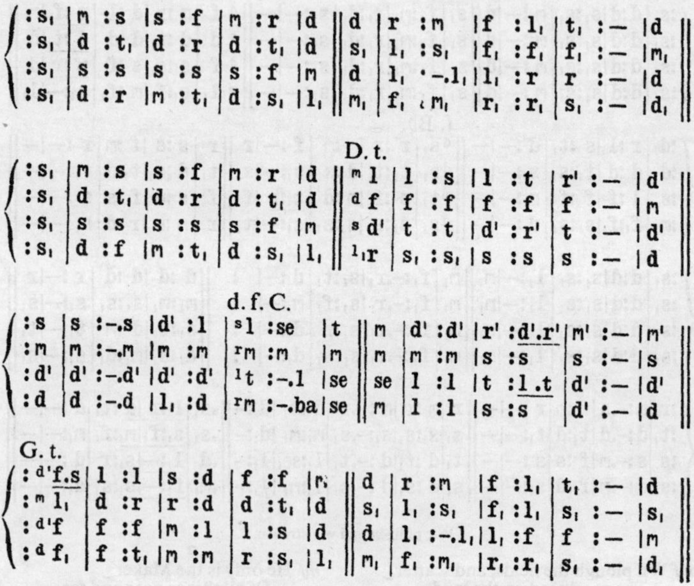

f TO thee, O Lord, our hearts we raise
In hymns of adoration,
To thee bring sacrifice of praise
With shouts of exultation:
Bright robes of gold the fields adorn,
The hills with joy are ringing,
The valleys stand so thick with corn
That even they are singing.

2

mf And now, on this our festal day,
Thy bounteous hand confessing,
Upon thine altar, Lord, we lay‿
The first-fruits of thy blessing:
p By thee the souls of men are fed
With gifts of grace supernal;
Thou who dost give us earthly bread,
Give us the Bread eternal.

HARVEST

3

mf We bear the burden of the day,
  And often toil seems dreary;
But labour ends with sunset ray,
  And rest comes for the weary:
May we, the angel-reaping o'er,
  Stand at the last accepted,
Christ's golden sheaves for evermore
  To garners bright elected.

4

f O blessèd is that land of God,
  Where saints abide for ever;
Where golden fields spread far and broad,
  Where flows the crystal river:
The strains of all its holy throng
  With ours to-day are blending;
Thrice blessèd is that harvest-song
  Which never hath an ending.

W. CHATTERTON DIX

HYMN **485** Xavier   Sir F. Champneys, 1848-1930

KEY **B♭**

[sol-fa notation]

3

PRAISE to God, immortal praise,
For the love that crowns our days!
Bounteous source of every joy,
Let thy praise our tongues employ:

2

For the blessings of the field,
For the stores the gardens yield,
Flocks that whiten all the plain,
Yellow sheaves of ripened grain:

All that spring with bounteous hand
Scatters o'er the smiling land;
All that liberal autumn pours
From her rich o'erflowing stores.

4

These to thee, my God, we owe,
Source whence all our blessings flow;
And for these my soul shall raise
Grateful vows and solemn praise.

MRS. A. L. BARBAULD

Alternative Tune, Culbach, 73

HYMN 486 St. Beatrice — Sir J. F. Bridge, 1844–1924

KEY C

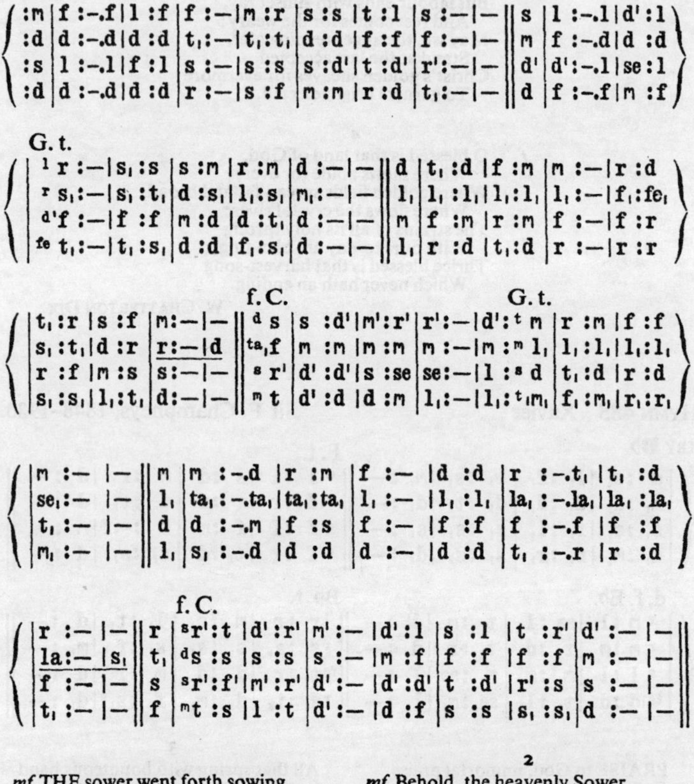

mf THE sower went forth sowing,
The seed in secret slept
Through weeks of faith and patience,
Till out the green blade crept;
And warmed by golden sunshine
And fed by silver rain,
At last the fields were whitened
To harvest once again.
f O praise the heavenly Sower,
Who gave the fruitful seed,
And watched and watered duly,
And ripened for our need.

2

mf Behold, the heavenly Sower
Goes forth with better seed,
The word of sure salvation,
With feet and hands that bleed;
Here in his Church 'tis scattered,
Our spirits are the soil;
Then let an ample fruitage
Repay his pain and toil.
O beauteous is the harvest
Wherein all goodness thrives!
And this the true thanksgiving—
The first-fruits of our lives.

HARVEST

3

p Within a hallowed acre
 He sows yet other grain,
When peaceful earth receiveth
 The dead he died to gain;
For though the growth be hidden,
mf We know that they shall rise;
Yea, even now they ripen
 In sunny Paradise.
f O summer land of harvest,
 O fields for ever white
With souls that wear Christ's raiment,
 With crowns of golden light!

4

mf One day the heavenly Sower
 Shall reap where he hath sown,
And come again rejoicing,
 And with him bring his own;
p And then the fan of judgement
 Shall winnow from his floor
The chaff into the furnace
 That flameth evermore.
O holy, aweful Reaper,
 Have mercy in the day
Thou puttest in thy sickle,
 And cast us not away.

W. St. Hill Bourne

FOR THOSE AT SEA

Hymn **487** Melita   J. B. Dykes, 1823–76

ETERNAL Father, strong to save,
Whose arm hath bound the restless wave,
Who bidd'st the mighty ocean deep
Its own appointed limits keep:
 O hear us when we cry to thee
 For those in peril on the sea.

2

O Christ, whose voice the waters heard
And hushed their raging at thy word,
Who walkedst on the foaming deep,
And calm amid the storm didst sleep:
 O hear us when we cry to thee
 For those in peril on the sea.

3

O Holy Spirit, who didst brood
Upon the waters dark and rude,
And bid their angry tumult cease,
And give, for wild confusion, peace:
 O hear us when we cry to thee
 For those in peril on the sea.

4

O Trinity of love and power,
Our brethren shield in danger's hour;
From rock and tempest, fire and foe,
Protect them wheresoe'er they go:
 Thus evermore shall rise to thee
 Glad hymns of praise from land and sea.

W. Whiting

FOR ABSENT FRIENDS

HYMN 488 Cairnbrook
KEY **G**
E. Prout, 1835–1909

mf HOLY Father, in thy mercy
Hear our anxious prayer:
Keep our loved ones, now far distant,
'Neath thy care.

2

Jesus, Saviour, let thy presence
Be their light and guide;
p Keep, O keep them, in their weakness,
At thy side.

3

When in sorrow, when in danger,
When in loneliness,
In thy love look down and comfort
Their distress.

4

mf May the joy of thy salvation
Be their strength and stay;
May they love and may they praise thee
Day by day.

5

p Holy Spirit, let thy teaching
Sanctify their life;
mf Send thy grace, that they may conquer
In the strife.

6

Father, Son, and Holy Spirit,
God the One in Three,
Bless them, guide them, save them, keep them
Near to thee.

ISABEL S. STEVENSON

FAREWELL SERVICES

HYMN 489 Dominus vobiscum   Sir A. Somervell, 1863–1937
KEY D

GOD be with you till we meet again;
 By his counsels guide, uphold you,
 With his sheep securely fold you:
God be with you till we meet again.

2
God be with you till we meet again;
 'Neath his wings protecting hide you,
 Daily manna still provide you:
God be with you till we meet again.

3
God be with you till we meet again;
 When life's perils thick confound you,
 Put his arm unfailing round you:
God be with you till we meet again.

4
God be with you till we meet again;
 Keep love's banner floating o'er you,
 Smite death's threatening wave before you:
God be with you till we meet again.

J. E. RANKIN

IN TIME OF WAR

HYMN 490 Rockingham   Adapted by E. Miller, 1731–1807
KEY D

mf O GOD of love, O King of peace,
 Make wars throughout the world to cease;
 The wrath of sinful man restrain:
p Give peace, O God, give peace again.

2
mf Remember, Lord, thy works of old,
 The wonders that our fathers told;
 Remember not our sin's dark stain:
p Give peace, O God, give peace again.

3
mf Whom shall we trust but thee, O Lord?
 Where rest but on thy faithful word?
 None ever called on thee in vain:
p Give peace, O God, give peace again.

4
f Where saints and angels dwell above,
 All hearts are knit in holy love;
 O bind us in that heavenly chain:
p Give peace, O God, give peace again.

SIR H. W. BAKER

IN TIME OF WAR

Hymn 491 Russian Anthem A. Lvov, 1799–1870
KEY D

f GOD the all-terrible! King, who ordainest
  Great winds thy clarions, the lightnings thy sword,
mf Show forth thy pity on high where thou reignest:
  Grant to us peace, O most merciful Lord.

2
p God the omnipotent! mighty avenger,
  Watching invisible, judging unheard,
  Doom us not now in the day of our danger:
  Grant to us peace, O most merciful Lord.

3
God the all-merciful! earth has forsaken
  Thy ways of blessedness, slighted thy word;
Bid not thy wrath in its terrors awaken:
  Grant to us peace, O most merciful Lord.

4
f So shall thy children in thankful devotion
  Praise him who saved them from peril and sword,
Singing in chorus from ocean to ocean,
  'Peace to the nations, and praise to the Lord.'

H. F. CHORLEY

IN TIME OF WAR

HYMN 492 Ad Astra H. G. Ley

KEY **C**

[Tonic sol-fa notation]

By permission of the S.P.C.K.

For Airmen

mf LORD of the worlds, unseen or seen,
  Whose eyes behold all things that are,
Who rulest earth and sea and air
  And guid'st the course of every star,
Look pitying from thy throne, nor cease
  To draw the nations to thy peace.

2
And if, at duty's trumpet call,
  Our manhood now be summoned hence
To battle for the right, the just,
  O shield them by thy providence.
f How confident are those that stand
Beneath the shelter of thy hand!

3
mf To all who, spurning earthly joys,
  Seek undismayed the trackless way
High in the wide expanse of heaven,
  Be thou their help, by night and day;
Through fire, through cloud, o'er land, o'er wave,
Still be thy presence strong to save.

4
p But should, O God, thy sovran will
  Allow the final sacrifice,
To thee their lives are dedicate:
  Not theirs to falter at the price.
O Lord of earth and sea and air
For those in peril hear our prayer.

5
mf Not given in vain, these gallant lives!
  The silent passing of the years
Shall touch them not, who fought—and fell:
  They ask no tribute of our tears.
f O loyal hearts, from death set free!
Not lost, but living unto thee.

E. H. BLAKENEY

Alternative Tune, Melita, 487

SOCIETIES AND MEETINGS

HYMN 493 Harewood   S. S. Wesley, 1810–76
KEY A

CHOIRS

f   HOW joyful 'tis to sing
    To God enthroned on high,
    To raise the ancient strain
    Of tuneful psalmody
      As choristers, who thus delight
      To chant his praise by day and night!

2

mf Yet art is not enough,
    Nor voice that charms the ear,
    Unless the heart be tuned
    And worship be sincere:
      Help us to fix our minds on thee,
      And lead us to simplicity.

3

Should we with wandering thoughts
  Our minds allow to stray,
Nor heed God's holy word,
  And, kneeling, fail to pray,
    Help us to serve with godly fear,
    Lest we forget thy presence near

4

We seek to perfect praise
  On earth, in hope that we
Some glimpses here may gain
  Of heavenly harmony,
    Where discord ne'er shall mar the tone
    Of those that sing around the throne.

SOCIETIES AND MEETINGS

5

f Then in the praise of God
Let boys and men unite,
And, mindful of our trust,
Gird on our robes of white,
As symbol of the purity
That all must seek, who seek for thee.

SIR S. H. NICHOLSON

HYMN **494** Glenfinlas   K. G. Finlay
KEY **G**

SERVERS

1

HANDS that have been handling
Holy things and high
Still, Lord, in thy service
Bless and fortify.

2

Ears which heard the message
Of the words of life
Keep thou closed and guarded
From the noise of strife.

3

Eyes whose contemplation
Looked upon thy love,
Let them gaze expectant
On the world above.

4

'Holy, Holy, Holy',
Thee our lips confessed:
On those lips for ever
Let no falsehood rest.

5

Feet which trod the pavement
Round about God's board,
Let them walk in glory
Where God's light is poured.

6

Bodies that have tasted
Of the living Bread,
Be they re-created
In their living Head.

7*

Be we all one Body,
All our members one,
Measured by the stature
Of God's full-grown Son.

ADAM FOX
Based on *Liturgy of Malabar*

SOCIETIES AND MEETINGS

HYMN 495 Marching   Martin Shaw
KEY **A**

By permission of J. Curwen & Sons, Ltd., from Curwen edition No. 80631

TEACHERS

LORD and Master, who hast called us
  All our days to follow thee,
We have heard thy clear commandment,
  'Bring the children unto me.'

2
So we come to thee, the Teacher,
  At thy feet we kneel to pray:
We can only lead the children
  When thyself shalt show the way.

3
Teach us thy most wondrous method,
  As of old in Galilee
Thou didst show thy chosen servants
  How to bring men unto thee.

4
Give us store of wit and wisdom,
Give us love which never tires,
Give us thine abiding patience,
Give us hope which ay inspires.

5
Mighty Wisdom of the Godhead,
Thou the one eternal Word,
Thou the Counsellor, the Teacher,
Fill us with thy fullness, Lord.

                                                    FLORENCE SMITH

HYMN 496 Belfry Praise   J. H. Matthews
KEY **C**

SOCIETIES AND MEETINGS

```
{ :s  |s  :s  |s  :l.t  |d' :—  |d'   ||d' |r' :r' |d' :t.l  |s  :—  |—
{ :m  |r  :f  |m  :r    |d  :—  |d    ||s  |s  :s.f|m  :fe   |s  :—  |—
{ :d' |r' :d' |t  :l    |s  :f  |m    ||d' |t  :s  |s  :r'.d'|t  :—  |—
{ :d' |t  :l  |s  :f    |m  :r  |d    ||m  |r  :t₁ |d  :r    |s  :—  |—
```

```
{ :s  |d' :l  |f  :s  |s  :—  |s    ||l  |t  :d' |m  :r   |d  :—  |—
{ :m  |m  :f  |f  :f  |m  :—  |m    ||f  |f  :m  |d  :t₁  |d  :—  |—
{ :d' |d' :d' |r' :r' |d' :—  |d'   ||d' |s  :s  |s  :f   |m  :—  |—
{ :d' |l  :f  |r  :t  |s  :m  |d    ||f  |r  :d  |s₁ :s₁  |d  :—  |—
```

BELL-RINGERS

UNCHANGING God, who livest
    Enthroned in realms on high,
To men the power thou givest
    Thy name to magnify.
We raise the bells for ringing
    With ready mind and will,
And come before thee, bringing
    Our hearts, our strength, our skill.

2

We call, from tower and steeple,
    Upon the day of days,
All faithful Christian people
    To worship, prayer, and praise;
We ring with joyous gladness
    When man and wife are blessed;
We peal in muffled sadness
    For loved ones laid to rest.

3

By union free and willing
    The work of God is done;
Our Master's prayer fulfilling,
    We would in him be one:
One, as the Church our Mother
    Would have her children stand,
Befriending one another,
    And strong and steadfast band.

4

Our lives, like bells, while changing,
    An ordered course pursue;
Through joys and sorrows ranging,
    May all those lives ring true.
May we, through Christ forgiven,
    Our faults and failures past,
Attain our place in heaven,
    Called home to rest at last.

H. C. WILDER

SOCIETIES AND MEETINGS

Hymn 497 Battle cry
A. Gray, 1855–1935

KEY **A**

UNISON — MEN'S SERVICES

{| l₁ : l₁ : l₁ | d :—: d | t₁ :—:— | l₁ :—:— | d : s₁ : l₁ }

1 Rise at the cry of bat - tle, Arm for the
2 Fie - ry and fierce the con - flict, Dar - ing and
3 Strive till the strife is o - ver, Fight till the

{| s₁ :—: f₁ | m₁ :—: s₁ | d :—: d | t₁ : s₁ : m₁ | m :—: m }

1 com - ing strife; By night and day you must fight your
2 swift the foe; His hosts are found on the bat - tle
3 fight is won; Though sore op - prest, seek not for

{| r :—: t₁ . t₁ | s₁ :—: d | t₁ :—: l₁ | s₁ :—:— | l₁ : l₁ : l₁ | d :—: d }

1 way Till you pass through death to life; Rea - dy to face the
2 ground, Where they wait to lay you low. Sharp are his darts and
3 rest Un - til the day is done. Af - ter the well-fought

{| r :—:— | m :—:— | l₁ : l₁ : l₁ | d :—: r | r :—: r . r | f :—.f : f }

1 dan - ger, Rea - dy to right the wrong. There is ma - ny a
2 dead - ly, Keen is the strife and long; Then arm for the
3 bat - tle Join in the vic - tor's song; Your tro - phies

{| m . d : l, {| r :— : r / r :—.r : r |} d :—:— | m :—.r : d | d :—: t₁ | l₁ :—:— ||

1 foe on the way you go: Quit you like men, be strong!
2 fight in the ar - mour of light: Quit you like men, be strong!
3 bring to Christ your King: Quit you like men, be strong!

ADA R. GREENAWAY

Hymn 498 Alleluia, dulce carmen
Essay on the Church Plain Chant,
1782

KEY **G**

{| d : r | m : f | s : f | m : r | d : d | d : f | m : r | d :— |
s₁ : s₁ | s₁ : d | t₁ : l₁.s₁ | s₁ : s₁ | m₁ : s₁ | l₁ : l₁ | s₁ :—.f₁ | m₁ :— |
m : t₁ | d : d | r : d.r | d : t₁ | d : d | d : d | d : t₁ | d :— |
d : s₁ | d : l₁ | s₁ : l₁.t₁ | d : s₁ | l₁ : m₁ | f₁ : r₁ | s₁ : s₁ | d₁ :— ||

SOCIETIES AND MEETINGS

MOTHERS' SERVICES

LORD of life and King of Glory,
　　Who didst deign a child to be,
Cradled on a mother's bosom,
　　Throned upon a mother's knee;
For the children thou hast given
　　We must answer unto thee.

2

Since the day the blessèd Mother
　　Thee, the world's Redeemer, bore,
Thou hast crowned us with an honour
　　Women never knew before;
And that we may bear it meetly
　　We must seek thine aid the more.

3

Grant us then pure hearts and patient,
　　That in all we do or say
Little souls our deeds may copy,
　　And be never led astray;
Little feet our steps may follow
　　In a safe and narrow way.

4

When our growing sons and daughters
　　Look on life with eager eyes,
Grant us then a deeper insight
　　And new powers of sacrifice;
Hope to trust them, faith to guide them,
　　Love that nothing good denies.

5

May we keep our holy calling
　　Stainless in its fair renown,
That, when all the work is over
　　And we lay the burden down,
Then the children thou hast given
　　Still may be our joy and crown.

CHRISTIAN BURKE

SOCIETIES AND MEETINGS

HYMN 499 Palms of glory Archbishop W. D. Maclagan, 1826–1910
KEY A♭

1

'HAIL, O Mary, full of grace,
Daughter true of David's race!
Thou, of women first and best,
Art beyond all others blest.

2

Fear not, thou shalt bear a Son,
Aided by the Holy One;
Greater than the greatest, he
Son of God most high shall be.'

3

Thus the holy angel said.
Blessèd Mary bowed her head:
'Lo, the handmaid of the Lord;
With his word may all accord.'

4

So to hearts still undefiled
Comes the promise of a child,
Full of joy, akin to tears,
Full of hope, yet full of fears.

5

Happy she who answers still,
'Be it, Lord, as thy sweet will;
All I am to thee I owe,
All thy purpose thou dost know.

6

What thou givest to be mine,
May it ne'er be aught but thine
Be it good or be it ill,
Still be all at thy sweet will.'

7

Holy Mary, taught by thee
Let us vain forebodings flee.
God is giving; fears must cease:
In his will is perfect peace.

BISHOP GILBERT WHITE

SOCIETIES AND MEETINGS

HYMN 500 Toc H   Martin Shaw
KEY D

In March Time

[sol-fa notation]

By permission of the Oxford University Press

YOUTH SERVICES

GO forth with God! the day is now
    That thou must meet the test of youth:
Salvation's helm upon thy brow,
    Go, girded with the living truth.
        In ways thine elder brethren trod
        Thy feet are set. Go forth with God!

2

Think fair of all, and all men love,
    And with the builder bear thy part:
Let every day and duty prove
    The humble witness of thy heart.
        Go forth! tis God bids thee increase
        The bounds of love and joy and peace.

3

Behold with thine uplifted eyes
    Beauty through all that sorrow seems,
And make of earth a paradise,
    The substance of thy dearest dreams.
        Bring laughter to thy great employ:
        Go forth with God and find his joy.

4

Go forth with God! the world awaits
    The coming of the pure and strong;
Strike for the faith and storm the gates
    That keep the citadel of wrong.
        Glory shall shine about thy road,
        Great heart, if thou go forth with God!

B. BARON

SOCIETIES AND MEETINGS

HYMN 501 Agincourt   English Melody (15th cent.)
KEY C

[Tonic sol-fa notation]

National

O GOD, whose mighty works of old
Our fathers to their sons have told,
Be with us still from age to age,
Our children's children's heritage.

2
Thine are the kingdoms: at thy feet
All peoples of the earth do meet
In equal lowliness of prayer
To find thine equal pity there.

3
Thy strength made strong our fathers' hands,
A people great on seas and lands,
To win, till earth shall pass away,
Such honour as the earth can pay.

4
Be with their children: give us grace
To know, nor fear to hold, their place,
Nor meanly shrink, nor boast at ease—
A people great on lands and seas.

5
Keep now our boyhood free and fair
And quick to help and brave to dare:
From greed and selfishness and shame
Guard thou, O Lord, the English name.

6
Keep thou our girlhood fair and free
In mirth and love and modesty:
From ugly thought and deed and word
Guard thou our English homes, O Lord.

7
O God, whose mighty works of old
Our fathers to their sons have told,
Be thou our strength from age to age,
Our children's children's heritage.

J. M. C. CRUM

Alternative Tune, Canon, 23

SOCIETIES AND MEETINGS

HYMN 502 Wareham   W. Knapp, 1698–1768

KEY A♭

REUNION GATHERINGS

THOU gracious God, whose mercy lends
The light of home, the smile of friends,
Our gathered flock thine arms enfold
As in the peaceful days of old.

2

Wilt thou not hear us while we raise
In sweet accord of solemn praise
The voices that have mingled long
In joyous flow of mirth and song?

3

For all the blessings life has brought,
For all its sorrowing hours have taught,
For all we mourn, for all we keep,
The hands we clasp, the loved that sleep,

4

The noon-tide sunshine of the past,
These brief, bright moments fading fast,
The stars that gild our darkening years,
The twilight ray from holier spheres,

5

We thank thee, Father; let thy grace
Our loving circle still embrace,
Thy mercy shed its heavenly store,
Thy peace be with us evermore.

O. W. HOLMES

SAINTS' DAYS: GENERAL
FESTIVALS OF APOSTLES

Hymn 503 FIRST TUNE
KEY B♭ Aeterna Christi munera Mode vii

Aeterna Christi munera

{| s₁ s₁ l₁t₁ t₁ s₁   l₁t₁dt₁ l₁s₁ s₁ | s₁ t₁ d }
1 The e - ter - nal gifts of Christ the King, The a - pos - tles'
2 For they the Church-'s prin - ces are, Tri - umph - ant
3 Theirs is the stead-fast faith of saints, And hope that
4 In them the Fa-ther's glo - ry shone, In them the
5 To thee, Re - deem - er, now we cry, That thou wouldst

{| r rmr dt₁ d r — | t₁ r m   m   r dt₁ }
1 glo - ry, let us sing; And all, with hearts of glad -
2 lead - ers in the war, In heaven - ly courts a war -
3 nev - er yields nor faints, And love of Christ in per -
4 will of God the Son, In them ex - ults the Ho -
5 join to them on high Thy ser - vants, who this grace

{| l₁s₁ l₁t₁dt₁ | s₁ s₁ l₁t₁ t₁ s₁ l₁t₁dt₁ l₁s₁ s₁ — ||
1 ness, raise ⌣ Due hymns of thank - ful love and praise.
2 rior band, True lights to light - en ev - ery land.
3 fect glow That lays the prince of this world low.
4 ly Ghost, Through them re - joice the heaven - ly host.
5 im - plore, For ev - er and for ev - er - more.

SECOND TUNE

KEY **G** Illsley (*or* Bishop) J. Bishop, 1665–1737

{| :d |d :s₁ |d.r:m |f.m:r |d || d :s₁ |d.r:m.fe|s :fe|s :— ||
 :s₁|s₁:m₁|m₁.f₁:s₁|l₁.s₁:f₁.s₁|m₁|s₁:s₁|l₁ :l₁ |t₁:l₁|t₁:— |
 :m |m :m.r|d :—.t₁|l₁ :t₁ |d || m m :m.r|d :d |r :r |r :— |
 :d |d :d.t₁|l₁ :—.s₁|f₁ :s₁|d₁|| d d :d.t₁|l₁ :l₁ |s₁:r₁|s₁:— ||

{| :s |f :m |l :—.s |f :m |r || r m :—.f|s :r |m :r |d :— ||
 :t₁|d :t₁|l₁ :—.d|d :d |t₁|s₁|s₁:—.t₁|d :d |d :t₁|d :— |
 :r |f :s |d :—.s|l :s |s || t₁ d :—.r|m :l |s :—.f|m :— |
 :s₁|l₁:s₁|f₁ :—.m₁|f₁:d |s₁|| s₁ m₁:—.r₁|d₁:f₁|s₁:s₁|d :— ||

Aeterna Christi munera

f THE eternal gifts of Christ the King,
The apostles' glory, let us sing;
And all, with hearts of gladness, raise ⌣
Due hymns of thankful love and praise.

FESTIVALS OF APOSTLES

2
For they the Church's princes are,
Triumphant leaders in the war,
In heavenly courts a warrior band,
True lights to lighten every land.

mf 3
Theirs is the steadfast faith of saints,
And hope that never yields nor faints,
And love of Christ in perfect glow
That lays the prince of this world low.

f 4
In them the Father's glory shone,
In them the will of God the Son,
In them exults the Holy Ghost,
Through them rejoice the heavenly host.

p 5
To thee, Redeemer, now we cry,
That thou wouldst join to them on high
Thy servants, who this grace implore,
mf For ever and for evermore.

? St. Ambrose
Tr. J. M. Neale and Compilers

HYMN 504 — FIRST TUNE

KEY **E** Exultet caelum laudibus   Mode iv

Exultet caelum laudibus

1. Let all on earth their voices raise, Re-echoing heaven's triumphant praise, To him who gave the apostles grace To run on earth their glorious race.
2. Thou at whose word they bore the light Of Gospel truth o'er heathen night, To us that heavenly light impart, To glad our eyes and cheer our heart.
3. Thou at whose will to them was given To bind and loose in earth and heaven, Our chains unbind, our sins undo, And in our hearts thy grace renew.
4. Thou in whose might they spake the word Which cured disease and health restored, To us its healing power prolong, Support the weak, confirm the strong.
5. And when the thrones are set on high, And judgement's awful hour draws nigh, Then, Lord, with them pronounce us blest, And take us to thine endless rest.

FESTIVALS OF APOSTLES

HYMN 504   SECOND TUNE

KEY **E**   Rex gloriose martyrum   *Catholische Geistliche Gesänge*
(Andernach, 1608)

B. t.

```
{ :d   |m  :f  |s  :s   |l  :t  |d' ‖ sd |f :-.m|r  :d  |r  :t₁ |d     ‖
{ :d   |d  :d  |t₁ :d   |d  :f  |m    ‖ ᵐl₁|f₁ :s₁ |l₁ :s₁  |l₁ :s₁.f₁|m₁ ‖
{ :m   |s  :f  |r  :s   |f  :f  |s    ‖ ˢd |d  :d  |l₁.t₁:d |f  :r   |d     ‖
{ :d   |d.t₁:l₁|s₁ :m   |f.m:r  |d    ‖ ᵈf₁|l₁ :s₁ |f₁ :m₁  |r₁ :s₁  |d₁    ‖
```

f. E.

```
{ :ᵈs  |l  :f  |s  :m   |f  :r  |d     ‖ d' |t :l  |s  :m   |f.m:r  |d :— ‖
{ :ᶠ¹d |d' :d  |t₁ :d   |d  :t₁ |d     ‖ d  |r :r  |m  :m   |r.d:t₁ |d :— ‖
{ :ᵈs  |f.s:l  |s  :l   |l  :s.f|m     ‖ l  |s :-.f|m  :l.s |f  :-.s|m :— ‖
{ :¹m  |f.m:r  |m  :d   |r  :s₁ |l₁    ‖ l₁ |t₁:t₁ |d  :de  |r  :s₁ |d :— ‖
```

Exultet caelum laudibus

LET all on earth their voices raise,
Re-echoing heaven's triumphant praise,
To him who gave the apostles grace
To run on earth their glorious race.

2

Thou at whose word they bore the light
Of Gospel truth o'er heathen night,
To us that heavenly light impart,
To glad our eyes and cheer our heart.

3

Thou at whose will to them was given
To bind and loose in earth and heaven,
Our chains unbind, our sins undo,
And in our hearts thy grace renew.

4

Thou in whose might they spake the word
Which cured disease and health restored,
To us its healing power prolong,
Support the weak, confirm the strong.

5

And when the thrones are set on high,
And judgement's aweful hour draws nigh,
Then, Lord, with them pronounce us blest,
And take us to thine endless rest.

Tr. BISHOP R. MANT and Compilers

FESTIVALS OF APOSTLES

HYMN 505 Annue Christe

Melody from La Feillée,
Méthode, 1808

KEY **G**

Annue, Christe

O CHRIST, thou Lord of worlds, thine ear to hear us bow
On this the festival of thine apostle now,
Who taught to men thy power to free from sin's offence
The souls of those that tread the way of penitence.

2

Redeemer, save thy work, thy noble work of grace,
Sealed with the holy light that beameth from thy face;
Nor suffer them to fall to Satan's wiles a prey
For whom thou didst on earth death's costly ransom pay.

3

Pity thy flock, enthralled by sin's captivity,
Forgive each guilty soul and set the bondmen free,
And those thou hast redeemed by thine own Passion sore
Grant to rejoice with thee, O King, for evermore.

Tr. J. M. NEALE‡

FESTIVALS OF APOSTLES

HYMN 506 Hanover *Supplement to the New Version*, 1708
KEY G Descant by Alan Gray, 1855–1935

The Descant may be sung for verse 6

Supreme, quales, Arbiter

mf DISPOSER supreme, and Judge of the earth,
  Who choosest for thine the meek and the poor;
 To frail earthen vessels, and things of no worth,
  Entrusting thy riches which ay shall endure;

2
 Those vessels soon fail, though full of thy light,
  And at thy decree are broken and gone;
f Thence brightly appeareth thy truth in its might,
  As through the clouds riven the lightnings have shone.

3
 Like clouds are they borne to do thy great will,
  And swift as the winds about the world go:
 The Word with his wisdom their spirits doth fill;
  They thunder, they lighten, the waters o'erflow.

[UNISON] 4
 Their sound goeth forth, 'Christ Jesus the Lord!'
  Then Satan doth fear, his citadels fall;
 As when the dread trumpets went forth at thy word,
  And one long blast shattered the Canaanite's wall.

5
mf O loud be their trump, and stirring their sound,
  To rouse us, O Lord, from slumber of sin!
 The lights thou hast kindled in darkness around
  O may they awaken our spirits within!

FESTIVALS OF APOSTLES

[UNISON]
6
f All honour and praise, dominion and might,
To God, Three in One, eternally be,
Who round us hath shed his own marvellous light,
And called us from darkness his glory to see.

J. B. DE SANTEUIL *Tr.* I. Williams‡

HYMN **507**   FIRST TUNE
KEY E♭ Corbeil   Office of P. de Corbeil (*d.* 1222)

SECOND TUNE
KEY F University College   H. J. Gauntlett, 1805–76

Caelestis aulae principes

f CAPTAINS of the saintly band,
Lights who lighten every land,
Princes who with Jesus dwell,
Judges of his Israel;

2
On the nations sunk in night
Ye have shed the Gospel light;
Sin and error flee away,
Truth reveals the promised day.

mf **3**
Not by warrior's spear and sword,
Not by art of human word,
Preaching but the Cross of shame,
Rebel hearts for Christ ye tame.

4
p Earth, that long in sin and pain
Groaned in Satan's deadly chain,
f Now to serve its God is free
In the law of liberty.

5
Distant lands with one acclaim
Tell the honour of your name,
Who, wherever man has trod,
Teach the mysteries of God.

[UNISON]
6
Glory to the Three in One
While eternal ages run,
Who from deepest shades of night
Called us to his glorious light.

J. B. DE SANTEUIL *Tr.* Sir H. W. Baker

See also hymn 529 and accompanying note

NOTE. *Hymn 602, parts 2 and 3, may be used on the Festivals of Apostles or Evangelists between Easter Day and Trinity Sunday*

FESTIVALS OF EVANGELISTS

HYMN 508 Evangelists   Melody by J. B. König (?), 1691-1758
KEY **G**

mf COME, pure hearts, in sweetest measures
Sing of those who spread the treasures
　In the holy gospels shrined:
Blessèd tidings of salvation,
Peace on earth, their proclamation,
　Love from God to lost mankind.

2
Thou, by whom the words were given
For our light and guide to heaven,
　Spirit, on our darkness shine;
Graft them in our hearts, increasing
Faith, hope, love, and joy unceasing,
　Till our hearts are wholly thine.

3
O that we, thy truth confessing
And thy holy word possessing,
　Jesu, may thy love adore;
f　Unto thee our voices raising,
Thee with all thy ransomed praising
　Ever and for evermore.

R. CAMPBELL and others. Based on Adam of St. Victor

HYMN 509 Ach Gott vom Himmelreiche   M. Praetorius, 1571-1621
KEY **A**

FESTIVALS OF EVANGELISTS

Plausu chorus laetabundo

f COME sing, ye choirs exultant,
  Those messengers of God,
Through whom the living gospels
  Came sounding all abroad;
Whose voice proclaimed salvation,
  That poured upon the night,
And drove away the shadows,
  And flushed the world with light.

2

mf He chose them, our Good Shepherd,
  And, tending evermore
His flock through earth's four quarters,
  In wisdom made them four:
In one harmonious witness
  The chosen four combine,
While each his own commission
  Fulfils in every line.

3

f Four-square on this foundation
  The Church of Christ remains,
A house to stand unshaken
  By floods or winds or rains.
O glorious happy portion
  In this safe home to be,
By God, true Man, united
  With God eternally!

ADAM OF ST. VICTOR *Tr.* Jackson Mason

Alternative Tune, Erfreut euch, 625

FESTIVALS OF EVANGELISTS

HYMN 510 Venice   W. Amps, 1824–1910

KEY E♭

mf HOW beauteous are their feet,
    Who stand on Sion's hill,
    Who bring salvation on their tongues
    And words of peace instil!

2
How happy are our ears
That hear this happy sound, [for,
Which kings and prophets waited
And sought, but never found!

3
How blessèd are our eyes
That see this heavenly light!
Prophets and kings desired it long,
But died without the sight.

4
f The Lord makes bare his arm
    Through all the earth abroad:
    Let every nation now behold
    Their Saviour and their God.

I. WATTS

HYMN 511 Song 34   Orlando Gibbons, 1583–1625

KEY F

SPIRIT of Jesus, who didst move
    The hearts and pens of men to write
    The story of the world's true Light,
His words of power and deeds of love;

FESTIVALS OF EVANGELISTS

2
We thank thee for those scribes of old
 Who, while apostles journeyed still
 Their worldwide witness to fulfil,
Set down the glorious tale they told;

3
We thank thee for the writers three,
 Who from such fleeting records wrought
 The first three gospels, and so taught
The truth for every age to see.

4
Then, as faith ripened, thou didst call
 A fourth evangelist, to show
 The Christ whom souls had come to know
As Way, as Truth, as Life, for all.

5
Spirit of Jesus, give thy grace
 To us who read, that so we may
 Know him more fully day by day
Until we see him face to face.

C. S. PHILLIPS

FESTIVALS OF THE BLESSED VIRGIN MARY

HYMN 512   **FIRST TUNE**

KEY F   Quem terra, pontus, aethera   **Mode ii**

Quem terra, pontus, aethera

1. The God whom earth and sea and sky
  Adore and laud and magnify,
  Whose might they own, whose praise they tell,
  In Mary's body deigned to dwell.

2. O Mother blest! the chosen shrine
  Wherein the Architect divine,
  Whose hand contains the earth and sky,
  Vouchsafed in hidden guise to lie:

3. Blest in the message Gabriel brought;
  Blest in the work the Spirit wrought;
  Most blest, to bring to human birth
  The long Desired of all the earth.

4. O Lord, the Virgin born, to thee
  Eternal praise and glory be,
  Whom with the Father we adore
  And Holy Ghost for evermore.

FESTIVALS OF THE BLESSED VIRGIN MARY

HYMN 512 SECOND TUNE
KEY **F** St. Ambrose   La Feillée, *Méthode*, 1808

[sol-fa notation]

Quem terra, pontus, aethera

mf THE God whom earth and sea and
    Adore and laud and magnify, [sky
    Whose might they own, whose praise
      they tell,
p In Mary's body deigned to dwell.

2
mf O Mother blest! the chosen shrine
    Wherein the Architect divine, [sky,
    Whose hand contains the earth and
p Vouchsafed in hidden guise to lie:

3
mf Blest in the message Gabriel
    brought;
    Blest in the work the Spirit wrought;
f Most blest, to bring to human birth
    The long Desired of all the earth.

[UNISON] 4
O Lord, the Virgin-born, to thee
Eternal praise and glory be,
Whom with the Father we adore
And Holy Ghost for evermore.

BISHOP VENANTIUS FORTUNATUS
Tr. J. M. Neale and Compilers

HYMN 513 Farley Castle   H. Lawes, 1596–1662
KEY **D**

[sol-fa notation]

mf HER Virgin eyes saw God incarnate born,
    When she to Bethlem came that happy morn:
    How high her raptures then began to swell,
    None but her own omniscient Son can tell.

FESTIVALS OF THE BLESSED VIRGIN MARY

    p   As Eve, when she her fontal sin reviewed,
        Wept for herself and all she should include,
    f   Blest Mary, with man's Saviour in embrace,
        Joyed for herself and for all human race.

3
  mf All saints are by her Son's dear influence blest:
        She kept the very fountain at her breast:
        The Son adored and nursed by the sweet Maid
        A thousandfold of love for love repaid.

4
    f   Heaven with transcendent joys her entrance graced,
        Near to his throne her Son his Mother placed;
        And here below, now she's of heaven possest,
        All generations are to call her blest.

                                  BISHOP T. KEN†

HYMN 514   Genevan Psalm lxxxvi   L. Bourgeois, *Genevan Psalter*, 1543
KEY F

1 Virgin born, we bow before thee: Blessèd was the womb that bore thee;
3 Blessèd she by all creation, Who brought forth the world's Salvation, And

1 Mary, Maid and Mother mild, Blessèd was she in her Child.
3 blessèd they—for ever blest—Who love thee most and serve thee best.

2 Blessèd was the breast that fed thee; Blessèd was the hand that led thee;
4 Virgin born, we bow before thee: Blessèd was the womb that bore thee;

2 Blessèd was the parent's eye That watched thy slumbering infancy.
4 Mary, Maid and Mother mild, Blessèd was she in her Child.

                                  BISHOP R. HEBER

FESTIVALS OF THE BLESSED VIRGIN MARY

HYMN 515 FIRST TUNE

KEY **G** Belmont Adapted from W. Gardiner's *Sacred Melodies*, 1812

SECOND TUNE

KEY **G** St. Agnes J. B. Dykes, 1823–76

mf SHALL we not love thee, Mother dear,
Whom Jesus loves so well?
And to his glory year by year
Thy joy and honour tell?

2

p Bound with the curse of sin and shame
We helpless sinners lay,
mf Until in tender love he came
To bear the curse away.

3

mf And thee he chose from whom to take
True flesh his flesh to be;
p In it to suffer for our sake,
f By it to make us free.

4

p Thy Babe he lay upon thy breast,
To thee he cried for food;
Thy gentle nursing soothed to rest
The incarnate Son of God.

FESTIVALS OF THE BLESSED VIRGIN MARY

5

mf O wondrous depth of grace divine
 That he should bend so low!
 And, Mary, O what joy 'twas thine
 In his dear love to know!

6

f Joy to be Mother of the Lord,
 And thine the truer bliss,
 In every thought and deed and word
 To be for ever his.

7

mf And as he loves thee, Mother dear,
 We too will love thee well;
 And to his glory year by year
 Thy joy and honour tell.

[UNISON] **8**

f Jesu, the Virgin's holy Son,
 We praise thee and adore,
 Who art with God the Father One
 And Spirit evermore.

SIR H. W. BAKER

FESTIVALS OF MARTYRS AND OTHERS

HYMN 516   FIRST TUNE

KEY C Deus, tuorum militum   Mode viii

Deus, tuorum militum

{| s l t d¹ t l s | l f s — | t r¹ d¹ }

1 O God, thy sol-diers' great re-ward, Their por-tion,
2 By wis-dom taught he learned to know The van-i-
3 Right man-ful-ly his cross he bore, And ran his
4 We there-fore pray thee, Lord of love, Re-gard us
5 All praise to God the Fa-ther be, All praise, e-

{| t r¹ d¹ t l s — | s l f s m f }

1 crown, and faith-ful Lord, From all trans-gres-sions set
2 ty of all be-low, The fleet-ing joys of earth
3 race of tor-ments sore; For thee he poured his life
4 from thy throne a-bove; On this thy mar-tyr's tri-
5 ter-nal Son, to thee, Whom with the Spi-rit we

{| m r d — | s l t d¹ t l s l f s — ||

1 us free Who sing thy mar-tyr's vic-to-ry.
2 dis-dained, And ev-er-last-ing glo-ry gained.
3 a-way, With thee he lives in end-less day.
4 umph-day, Wash ev-ery stain of sin a-way.
5 a-dore For ev-er and for ev-er-more.

FESTIVALS OF MARTYRS AND OTHERS

HYMN 516   SECOND TUNE

KEY **C**   Agincourt   English Melody (15th cent.)

[Sol-fa notation]

FOR A MARTYR

Deus, tuorum militum

O GOD, thy soldiers' great reward,
Their portion, crown, and faithful Lord,
From all transgressions set us free
Who sing thy martyr's victory.

2

By wisdom taught he learned to know
The vanity of all below,
The fleeting joys of earth disdained,
And everlasting glory gained.

3

Right manfully his cross he bore,
And ran his race of torments sore;
For thee he poured his life away,
With thee he lives in endless day.

4

We therefore pray thee, Lord of love,
Regard us from thy throne above;
On this thy martyr's triumph-day
Wash every stain of sin away.

[UNISON]   5

All praise to God the Father be,
All praise, eternal Son, to thee,
Whom with the Spirit we adore
For ever and for evermore.

Tr. J. M. NEALE and Compilers

Alternative Tune, Grenoble, 129

FESTIVALS OF MARTYRS AND OTHERS

Hymn 517 Salus mortalium *Gesangbuch* (Erfurt, 1663)

KEY **G**

FOR A MARTYR

Ex quo salus mortalium

mf OUR Lord the path of suffering trod;
    And, since his Blood for man hath flowed,
'Tis meet that man should yield to God
    The life he owed. Alleluia!

2

No shame to own the Crucified!
    Nay, 'tis our immortality
That we confess our God who died,
    And for him die. Alleluia!

3

p Beholding his predestined crown,
    Into death's arms the martyr goes:
f Dying, he conquers death; o'erthrown,
    O'erthrows his foes. Alleluia!

4

mf Lord, make us thine own soldiers true;
    Grant us brave faith, a spirit pure,
That for thy name, thy Cross in view,
    We may endure. Alleluia!

[UNISON] 5

f Eternal Father of the World,
    Eternal Word, we thee adore,
Eternal Spirit, God and Lord
    For evermore. Alleluia!

J. B. DE SANTEUIL *Tr.* I. Williams†

FESTIVALS OF MARTYRS AND OTHERS

HYMN **518** Schwing dich   Peter Franck (1657)

KEY **D**

$$
\begin{cases}
\begin{array}{|l|l||l|l||l|l|}
\hline
d':s & d':s & l:s & m:- & m:r & m:s & l:- & s:- \\
d:t_1 & d:m & f:r & d:- & d:t_1 & d:-.t_1 & r:- & t_1:- \\
m:f & s:d' & d':t & d':- & s:s & s:s & s:fe & s:- \\
d:r & m:d & f:s & d:- & d:s_1 & d:m & r:- & s_1:- \\
\hline
\end{array}
\end{cases}
$$

$$
\begin{cases}
\begin{array}{|l|l||l|l||l|l|}
\hline
d':s & d':s & l:s & m:- & m:r & m:s & l:- & s:- \\
d:t_1 & d:m & f:r & d:- & d:t_1 & d:-.t_1 & r:- & t_1:- \\
m:f & s:d' & d':t & d':- & s:s & s:s & s:fe & s:- \\
d:r & m:d & f:s & d:- & d:s_1 & d:m & r:- & s_1:- \\
\hline
\end{array}
\end{cases}
$$

$$
\begin{cases}
\begin{array}{|l|l||l|l||l|l|}
\hline
l:t & d':d' & t:t & l:- & r':t & d':t & l:- & s:- \\
m:r & d:f & f:m & d:- & r:r & m:r & r:- & t_1:- \\
m:se & l:l & l:se & l:- & l:s & s:s & s:fe & s:- \\
d:t_1 & l_1:f & r:m & l_1:- & fe:s & d:s_1 & r:- & s_1:- \\
\hline
\end{array}
\end{cases}
$$

$$
\begin{cases}
\begin{array}{|l|l||l|l||l|l|}
\hline
d':s & d':s & l:s & m:- & s:s & l:d' & t:- & d':- \\
d:t_1 & d:m & f:r & d:- & d:m & f:m & s:- & m:- \\
m:f & s:d' & d':t & d':- & s:d' & d':d' & r':- & d':- \\
d:r & m:d & f:s & d:- & m:d & f:l & s:- & d:- \\
\hline
\end{array}
\end{cases}
$$

FOR MARTYRS

τῶν ἱερῶν ἀθλοφόρων

LET our choir new anthems raise,
  Wake the song of gladness:
God himself to joy and praise
  Turns the martyrs' sadness.
Bright the day that won their crown,
Opened heaven's bright portal,
As they laid the mortal down
  To put on the immortal.

2
Never flinched they from the flame,
  From the torture never;
Vain the foeman's sharpest aim,
  Satan's best endeavour:
For by faith they saw the land
Decked in all its glory,
Where triumphant now they stand
  With the victor's story.

3
Up and follow, Christian men!
  Press through toil and sorrow;
Spurn the night of fear, and then,
  O the glorious morrow!
Who will venture on the strife?
Blest who first begin it!
Who will grasp the land of life?
  Warriors, up and win it!

ST. JOSEPH THE HYMNOGRAPHER
Tr. J. M. Neale†

FESTIVALS OF MARTYRS AND OTHERS

HYMN 519 Diva servatrix

French Melody

KEY **G**

```
{ |m :— |m :f |m :— |d :— |r :-.d|r :m |r :— |d :— ||
  |d :— |d :d |t₁:— |l₁:— |l₁:l₁ |s₁:s₁ |s₁:— |m₁:— 
  |s :— |l :l |m :— |m :— |f :m  |r :d  |d :t₁ |d :— 
  |d :t₁|l₁:f₁|s₁:— |l₁:— |f₁:l₁ |t₁:d  |s₁:— |d₁:— ||

{ |m :— |m :s |f :— |m :— |r :-.d|t₁:d |l₁:— |s₁:— ||
  |l₁:— |t₁:d |d :— |d :— |l₁:l₁ |s₁:s₁ |s₁:fe₁|s₁:— 
  |d :— |m :d |l :— |s :— |f :m  |m :m  |r :— |t₁:— 
  |l₁:— |s₁:m₁|f₁:l₁|d :— |f₁:l₁ |m₁:d₁ |r₁:— |s₁:— ||

{ |m :— |r :d |f :—|m :— |d :—.r|m:f |s :— |s :— ||m :— |r :d |r :— |d :— ||
  |t₁:d |s₁:s₁|r :d|t₁:— |l₁:—.t₁|d:d |d :— |t₁:— ||t₁:s₁|l₁:d |d :t₁|d :— 
  |t₁:m |s :m |l :—|l :se|l :s.f|s:d |r :— |r :— ||t₁:d |f :m |s :— |m :— 
  |s₁:l₁|t₁:d |r :—|m :— |f :m.r|d:l₁|s₁:— |s₁:— ||s₁:m₁|f₁:l₁|s₁:— |d₁:— ||
```

FOR A CONFESSOR OR BISHOP

Iste confessor

HE who to Jesus manfully bore witness,
He whom God's people join to-day to honour,
Now in the hidden mansions of the blessèd
    Bideth for ever.

2

With store of virtues God adorned his spirit,
Guiding his willing feet in paths of goodness,
Through all the earthly years while in his body
    Mortal breath tarried.

3

Wherefore with voices linked in happy chorus
Hymn we his praises on this holy feast-day,
Praying for grace to follow in his footsteps
    Now and hereafter.

4

Glory and honour, powèr and salvation
Be unto him, who, thronèd in the highest,
Ordereth meetly earth and sky and ocean,
    Triune, eternal.

Tr. COMPILERS

FESTIVALS OF MARTYRS AND OTHERS

HYMN 520 Diva servatrix   French Melody

KEY **G**

```
{|m :— |m :f |m :— |d :— |r :-.d |r :m |r :— |d :—  ||
 |d :— |d :d |t, :— |l, :— |l, :l, |s, :s, |s, :— |m, :— |
 |s :— |l :l |m :— |m :— |f :m |r :d |d :t, |d :—  |
 |d :t, |l, :f, |s, :— |l, :— |f, :l, |t, :d |s, :— |d, :— ||

 |m :— |m :s |f :— |m :— |r :-.d|t, :d |l, :— |s, :— ||
 |l, :— |t, :d |d :— |d :— |l, :l, |s, :s, |s, :fe, |s, :— |
 |d :— |m :d |l :— |s :— |f :m |m :m |r :— |t, :— |
 |l, :— |s, :m, |f,:l, |d :— |f, :l, |m, :d, |r, :— |s, :— ||

 |m :—|r :d |f :—|m :— |d :-.r |m :f |s :—|s :— ||m :—|r :d |r :—|d :—||
 |t,:d |s,:s,|r :d |t,:— |l,:-.t, |d :d |d :—|t,:— |t,:s,|l,:d |d :t,|d :—|
 |t,:m |s :m |l :—|l :se |l :s.f |s :d |r :—|r :— |t,:d |f :m |s :—|m :—|
 |s,:l,|t,:d |r :—|m :— |f :m.r |d :l, |s,:—|s,:— |s,:m,|f,:l,|s,:—|d,:—||
```

FOR DOCTORS OF THE CHURCH

STALWART as pillars bearing high their burden,
So do the Church's doctors stay the temple
Where truth abideth, on the one Foundation
    Grounded for ever.

2

O faithful stewards in God's holy household,
Out of your treasure new and old things bringing,
Still do your writings to the Light of ages
    Steadfastly witness.

3

Souls wise and loyal to the Spirit's leading,
Bravely ye battled for the faith delivered,
While of its ageless mysteries ye furnished
    New understanding.

4

Now with unclouded gaze ye are beholding
Him of whose face ye strained to catch the vision;
To whom be glory, Father, Son, and Spirit,
    Through endless ages.

                        C. S. PHILLIPS

HYMN 521 Ealing   Sir H. S. Oakeley, 1830–1903

KEY **F**

```
{ :d  |t, :d |r :r  |d :r |m  |m |f :m    |r :m  |d  :l, |s, :— ||
  :s, |s,:s,|s,:t, |d :s,|s, |d |d.t,:l,.se,|l, :m, |l,.s,:fe,.r,|r, :— |
  :m  |f :m |r :s  |s :f |m  |m |m.r:d.t, |l, :t, |m  :r .d |t, :— |
  :d  |r :d |t,:f  |m :t,|d  |l,|r, :m,   |ba,:se,|l, :r, |s, :— ||
```

530

FESTIVALS OF MARTYRS AND OTHERS

FOR VIRGINS
Jesu, corona virginum

1. O JESU, thou the virgins' crown,
Thy gracious ear to us bow down,
Born of that Virgin whom alone
The Mother and the Maid we own.

2. In thee, their Bridegroom and their Lord,
The virgins find their bright reward,
And wheresoe'er thy footsteps wend
With hymns and praises thee attend.

3. O gracious Lord, we thee implore
Thy grace into our minds to pour;
From all defilement keep us free,
And make us pure in heart for thee.

[UNISON]
4. All praise to God the Father be,
All praise, eternal Son, to thee,
Whom with the Spirit we adore,
For ever and for evermore.

? ST. AMBROSE *Tr.* Compilers† (1904)

Alternative Plainsong Tune, Deus, tuorum militum, 516

HYMN 522 Vernham Dean
A. Alleyne, 1867–1949
KEY C

FOR MISSIONARY SAINTS

1. THE saints who toiled from place to place,
Spreading the Gospel of God's grace,
Now in their heavenly homeland dwell
With Christ, whom here they served so well.

2. Alert at thy command to go,
And everywhere thy word to sow,
They went, O Master, far and wide,
Eager, but yet unsatisfied.

3. Thine was the task they took in hand,
Thine their good news for every land,
Thine was their power, and thine again
Their passion for the souls of men.

4. That task of thine, by them begun,
Must now by our weak hands be done:
Strengthen, O Lord, to work for thee
These hands, at home and over sea.

BISHOP W. H. FRERE†

FOR ANY SAINT'S DAY

HYMN 523 Genevan Psalm xlii

KEY **G**

Melody by L. Bourgeois, *Genevan Psalter*, 1515

Supernae matris gaudia

JOY and triumph everlasting
   Hath the heavenly Church on high;
For that pure immortal gladness
   All our feast-days mourn and sigh;
Yet in death's dark desert wild
Doth the mother aid her child;
Guards celestial thence attend us,
Stand in combat to defend us.

2
Here the world's perpetual warfare
   Holds from heaven the soul apart;
Legioned foes in shadowy terror
   Vex the Sabbath of the heart.
O how happy that estate
Where delight doth not abate!
For that home the spirit yearneth,
Where none languisheth nor mourneth.

3
There the body hath no torment,
   There the mind is free from care,
There is every voice rejoicing,
   Every heart is loving there.
Angels in that city dwell;
Them their King delighteth well:
Still they joy and weary never,
More and more desiring ever.

FOR ANY SAINT'S DAY

4
There the seers and fathers holy,
There the prophets glorified,
All their doubts and darkness ended,
In the Light of Light abide.
There the saints, whose memories old
We in faithful hymns uphold,
Have forgot their bitter story
In the joy of Jesus' glory.

ADAM OF ST. VICTOR
Tr. Yattendon Hymnal

HYMN 524 Orientis partibus   Office of P. de Corbeil (*d.* 1222)

KEY **G**

| d :-.r\|m :d | r :t,\|d :— ‖ s :s \|l :m.f | s :s \|m :— ‖
| s₁:-.s₁\|s₁: s₁ | l₁:s₁ \|s₁:— ‖ d :d \|d :d | d :t₁ \|d :— ‖
| m :-.f\|s :s | f :r \|m :— ‖ m :m \|f :d | r :r \|m :— ‖
| d :-.d\|d :m₁ | f₁:s₁ \|d₁:— ‖ d :d \|f₁:l₁ | s₁:s₁ \|d :— ‖

| m :r \|f :m | r :d.r\|m :— ‖ s :-.f\|m :d | r :t,\|d :— ‖
| d :s₁\|d :d | l₁:l₁ \|t₁:— ‖ d :-.d\|t₁:l₁ | l₁:s₁ \|s₁:— ‖
| s :s \|f :s | l :l \|se:— ‖ s :-.l\|s :m | f :r \|m :— ‖
| d :t₁\|l₁:s₁ | f₁:f₁ \|m₁:— ‖ m₁:-.f₁\|s₁:l₁ | f₁:s₁ \|d₁:— ‖

Pugnate, Christi milites

f SOLDIERS, who are Christ's below,
Strong in faith resist the foe:
Boundless is the pledged reward
Unto them who serve the Lord.

2
mf 'Tis no palm of fading leaves
That the conqueror's hand receives;
Joys are his, serene and pure,
Light that ever shall endure.

3
For the souls that overcome
Waits the beauteous heavenly home,
Where the blessèd evermore
Tread on high the starry floor.

4
p Passing soon and little worth
Are the things that tempt on earth;
mf Heavenward lift thy soul's regard:
God himself is thy reward.

5
f Father, who the crown dost give,
Saviour, by whose Death we live,
Spirit, who our hearts dost raise,
Three in One, thy name we praise.

18th cent. *Tr.* J. H. CLARK

FOR ANY SAINT'S DAY

HYMN 525 Sandys Psalm viii   H. Lawes, 1596–1662
KEY **A**

{ |d :—|t₁:l₁ |d :m₁|f₁:l₁ |s₁:— ‖ |s₁:—|l₁:t₁|d:t₁|l₁:m|r :— ‖
  |s₁:—|m₁:l₁|s₁:m₁|d₁:f₁.m₁|r₁:— ‖ |s₁:—|f₁:r₁|d₁:s₁|f₁:s₁|s₁:— ‖
  |m :—|t₁:d |d :d |d :r.d |t₁:— ‖ |d :—|d :s |m:m |d :d |t₁:— ‖
  |d :—|s₁:f₁|m₁:d₁|l₁:f₁ |s₁:— ‖ |m₁:—|f₁:s₁|l₁:m₁|f₁:d₁|s₁:— ‖ }

{ |r :f :m |l₁:t₁ |d :r |m :— ‖ |m |s :r |f:m |r :r |d :— ‖
  |t₁:t₁:d.t₁|l₁:s₁.f₁|m₁:r₁|s₁:— ‖ |d |ta₁:s₁|d:d |d :t₁|d :— ‖
  |s :f :s |s.f:m.r|d :s |s :— ‖ |m |r :s |f:s |s :—.f|m :— ‖
  |s₁:r₁:m₁|f₁:s₁ |l₁:t₁|d :— ‖ |d |s₁:ta₁|l₁:d|s₁:s₁|d₁:— ‖ }

mf LO, round the throne, a glorious band, [stand,
The saints in countless myriads
Of every tongue redeemed to God,
Arrayed in garments washed in Blood.

2
p Through tribulation great they came;
They bore the cross, despised the shame;
From all their labours now they rest,
In God's eternal glory blest.

3
mf They see their Saviour face to face,
And sing the triumphs of his grace;
f Him day and night they ceaseless praise,
To him the loud thanksgiving raise:

4
'Worthy the Lamb, for sinners slain,
Through endless years to live and reign!
Thou hast redeemed us by thy Blood,
And made us kings and priests to God.'

5
mf O may we tread the sacred road
That saints and holy martyrs trod;
Wage to the end the glorious strife,
f And win, like them, a crown of life.

R. HILL and others

Alternative Tune, Old 100th, 166

HYMN 526 Deerhurst   J. Langran, 1835–1909
KEY **F**

{ |m :s |m :d |t₁:d |r :m |f :m |r :s |t :l |s :— ‖
  |d :r |d :s₁|s₁:s₁|s₁:s₁|d :d.t₁|l₁:r |r :d |t₁:— ‖
  |s :s |s :s |f :m |r :d |l :s |fe:s |r :fe|s :— ‖
  |d :t₁|d :m |r :d |t₁:d |d :d |d :t₁|r :r |s₁:— ‖ }

{ |m :s |m :d |t₁:d |r :m |f :m |l :s |m :r |d :— ‖
  |d :r |d :s₁|s₁:s₁|s₁:s₁|d :d |d :d |d :t₁|d :— ‖
  |s :s |s :s |f :m |r :d |d :m |f :s |s :f |m :— ‖
  |d :t₁|d :m |r :d |t₁:d |l₁:s₁|f₁:m₁|s₁:s₁|d :— ‖ }

FOR ANY SAINT'S DAY

f HARK! the sound of holy voices,
  Chanting at the crystal sea
  Alleluia, Alleluia,
    Alleluia, Lord, to thee:
Multitude, which none can number,
  Like the stars in glory stands,
Clothed in white apparel, holding
  Palms of victory in their hands.

2

mf Patriarch, and holy prophet,
  Who prepared the way of Christ,
King, apostle, saint, confessor,
  Martyr, and evangelist,
Saintly maiden, godly matron,
  Widows who have watched to prayer,
f Joined in holy concert, singing
  To the Lord of all, are there.

3*

p They have come from tribulation,
  And have washed their robes in Blood,
Washed them in the Blood of Jesus;
  Tried they were, and firm they stood:
Mocked, imprisoned, stoned, tormented,
  Sawn asunder, slain with sword,
f They have conquered death and Satan
  By the might of Christ the Lord.

[UNISON] 4

Marching with thy Cross their banner,
  They have triumphed following
Thee, the Captain of Salvation,
  Thee their Saviour and their King:
[HARMONY]
mf Gladly, Lord, with thee they suffered;
  Gladly, Lord, with thee they died,
f And by death to life immortal
  They were born, and glorified.

[UNISON] 5

Now they reign in heavenly glory,
  Now they walk in golden light,
Now they drink, as from a river,
  Holy bliss and infinite;
[HARMONY]
p Love and peace they taste for ever,
  And all truth and knowledge see
mf In the beatific vision
  Of the blessèd Trinity.

6

f God of God, the One-begotten,
  Light of Light, Emmanuel,
In whose Body joined together
  All the saints for ever dwell;
Pour upon us of thy fulness,
  That we may for evermore
God the Father, God the Son, and
  God the Holy Ghost adore.

BISHOP CHR. WORDSWORTH

FOR ANY SAINT'S DAY

HYMN 527   FIRST TUNE

KEY **G**   Engelberg   Sir C. V. Stanford, 1852–1924

1. For all the saints who from their labours rest,
Who thee by faith before the world confessed,
Thy name, O Jesu, be for ever blest.
Alleluia!

2. Thou wast their rock, their fortress, and their might;
Thou, Lord, their Captain in the well-fought fight;
Thou, in the darkness, still their one true Light.
Alleluia!

3. O may thy soldiers, faithful, true, and bold,
Fight as the saints who nobly fought of old,
And win, with them, the victor's crown of gold.
Alleluia!

4. O blest communion! fellowship divine!
We feebly struggle, they in glory shine;
Yet all are one in thee, for all are thine.
Alleluia!

5. And when the strife is fierce, the warfare long,

FOR ANY SAINT'S DAY

mf
{| −: s₁ | s : f | m :−.r | d : m | r : l₁ | s₁ :− || −: r | m : s }
Steals on the ear the dis-tant tri-umph-song, And hearts are

{| s :−.d | r : f | m : r | m :− || −: f.m | f.m : r | m:f | s :− ||
brave a-gain and arms are strong. Al - le-lu - ia!

TREBLES ONLY
mf
{| : s₁ | d : m | r :−.s₁ | l₁ : t₁ | d : l₁ | s₁ :− ||
6 The gold-en eve-ning bright-ens in the west;

{| −: s₁ | s : f | m :−.r | d : m | r : l₁ | s₁ :− || −: r | m : s }
Soon, soon to faith-ful war-riors comes their rest: *p* Sweet is the

{| s : d | r :−.f | m : r | m :− || −: f.m | f.m : r | m : f | s :− ||
calm of Par - a-dise the blest. Al - le-lu - ia!

TENORS AND BASSES ONLY
f
{| : s₁ | d : m | r :−.s₁ | l₁ : t₁ | d : l₁ | s₁ :− ||
7 But lo! there breaks a yet more glo-rious day;

{| −: s₁ | s : f | m :−.r | d : m | r : l₁ | s₁ :− || −: r | m : s }
The saints tri-umph-ant rise in bright ar-ray: The King of

{| s : d | r :−.f | m : r | m :− || −: f.m | f.m : r | m : f | s :− ||
Glo-ry pass-es on his way. Al - le-lu - ia!

UNISON
ff
{| : s₁ | d : m | r :−.s₁ | l₁ : t₁ | d : l₁ | s₁ :− ||
8 From earth's wide bounds, from o-cean's far-thest coast,

{| −: s₁ | s : f | m :−.r | d : m | r : l₁ | s₁ :− ||
Through gates of pearl streams in the count-less host,

{| −: r | m : s | s : d | r :−.f | m : r | m :− ||
Sing-ing to Fa-ther, Son, and Ho-ly Ghost.

HARMONY
{| −: f.m | f.m : r | m:f | s :− || {| l :− |−.− | s :− |−:− ||
Al - le-lu - ia!   d :− |−:− | d :− |−:− ||
                                          A -   men.
                                          f :− |−:− | m :− |−:− ||
                                          f₁:− |−:− | d₁:− |−:− ||

By permission of Stainer & Bell, Ltd.

FOR ANY SAINT'S DAY

HYMN 527 SECOND TUNE

KEY E♭ For all the Saints Sir J. Barnby, 1838–96

[UNISON]
f FOR all the saints who from their labours rest,
Who thee by faith before the world confessed,
Thy name, O Jesus, be for ever blest. Alleluia!

[HARMONY]
2
Thou wast their rock, their fortress, and their might;
Thou, Lord, their Captain in the well-fought fight,
Thou, in the darkness, still their one true Light. Alleluia!

[HARMONY]
3
O may thy soldiers, faithful, true, and bold,
Fight as the saints who nobly fought of old,
And win, with them, the victor's crown of gold. Alleluia!

[UNISON]
4
mf O blest communion, fellowship divine!
We feebly struggle, they in glory shine;
Yet all are one in thee, for all are thine. Alleluia!

[HARMONY]
5
p And when the strife is fierce, the warfare long,
Steals on the ear the distant triumph-song,
mf And hearts are brave again and arms are strong. Alleluia!

[HARMONY]
6
The golden evening brightens in the west;
Soon, soon to faithful warriors comes their rest:
p Sweet is the calm of Paradise the blest. Alleluia!

[HARMONY]
7
But lo, there breaks a yet more glorious day;
The saints triumphant rise in bright array:
The King of Glory passes on his way. Alleluia!

FOR ANY SAINT'S DAY

[UNISON]

8
From earth's wide bounds, from ocean's farthest coast,
Through gates of pearl streams in the countless host,
Singing to Father, Son, and Holy Ghost.   Alleluia!

BISHOP W. WALSHAM HOW

Alternative Tune, Woodchurch, 532

HYMN 528   FIRST TUNE

KEY **G**   Sennen Cove   D. t.   W. H. Harris

f HOW bright these glorious spirits shine!
Whence all their white array?
How came they to the blissful seats
Of everlasting day?

2
p Lo, these are they from sufferings great
Who came to realms of light;
And in the Blood of Christ have washed
Those robes that shine so bright.

3
f Now with triumphal palms they stand
Before the throne on high,
And serve the God they love amidst
The glories of the sky.

4
mf Hunger and thirst are felt no more,
Nor suns with scorching ray;
God is their Sun, whose cheering beams
Diffuse eternal day.

5
The Lamb, which dwells amidst the throne,
Shall o'er them still preside,
Feed them with nourishment divine,
And all their footsteps guide.

6
p Midst pastures green he'll lead his flock,
Where living streams appear;
mf And God the Lord from every eye
Shall wipe off every tear.

[UNISON]
7
f To Father, Son, and Holy Ghost,
The God whom we adore,
Be glory, as it was, is now,
And shall be evermore.

I. WATTS and others

FOR ANY SAINT'S DAY

HYMN 528 SECOND TUNE

KEY A♭ Beatitudo   J. B. Dykes, 1823-76

[music notation]

 f   HOW bright these glorious spirits shine!
    Whence all their white array?
   How came they to the blissful seats
    Of everlasting day?

       2
 p   Lo, these are they from sufferings great
    Who came to realms of light;
   And in the Blood of Christ have washed
    Those robes that shines so bright.

       3
 f   Now with triumphal palms they stand
    Before the throne on high,
   And serve the God they love amidst
    The glories of the sky.

       4
 mf   Hunger and thirst are felt no more,
    Nor suns with scorching ray;
   God is their Sun, whose cheering beams
    Diffuse eternal day.

       5
    The Lamb, which dwells amidst the throne,
    Shall o'er them still preside,
   Feed them with nourishment divine,
    And all their footsteps guide.

       6
 p   Midst pastures green he'll lead his flock,
    Where living streams appear;
 mf   And God the Lord from every eye
    Shall wipe off every tear.

    [UNISON]   7
 f   To Father, Son, and Holy Ghost,
    To God whom we adore,
   Be glory, as it was, is now,
    And shall be evermore.

           I. WATTS and others

FOR ANY SAINT'S DAY

Hymn 529 Old 81st

Day's *Psalms*, 1562

KEY E♭

[sol-fa notation]

f THE Son of God goes forth to war
A kingly crown to gain;
His blood-red banner streams afar:
Who follows in his train?
Who best can drink his cup of woe,
Triumphant over pain,
Who patient bears his cross below,
He follows in his train.

2

mf The martyr first, whose eagle eye
Could pierce beyond the grave;
Who saw his Master in the sky,
And called on him to save.
Like him, with pardon on his tongue
In midst of mortal pain,
He prayed for them that did the wrong:
Who follows in his train?

3

A glorious band, the chosen few
On whom the Spirit came, [knew,
Twelve valiant saints, their hope they
And mocked the cross and flame.
They met the tyrant's brandished
The lion's gory mane; [steel,
They bowed their necks, the death to feel:
Who follows in their train?

4

f A noble army, men and boys,
The matron and the maid,
Around the Saviour's throne rejoice
In robes of light arrayed.
They climbed the steep ascent of heaven
Through peril, toil, and pain:
O God, to us may grace be given
To follow in their train.

BISHOP R. HEBER

Alternative Tune, St. Anne, 165

NOTE. Verses 1 and 4 are suitable for any saint's day. Verse 2 refers to St. Stephen, verse 3 to the apostles, and may be used with verses 1 and 4 on the festivals for which they are respectively appropriate. The whole hymn is suitable for All Saints' Day.

FOR ANY SAINT'S DAY

HYMN 530 Palms of glory

Archbishop W. D. Maclagan,
1826–1910

KEY A♭

[sol-fa notation]

PALMS of glory, raiment bright,
Crowns that never fade away,
Gird and deck the saints in light:
Priests and kings and conquerors they.

2
mf Yet the conquerors bring their palms
To the Lamb amidst the throne,
f And proclaim in joyful psalms
Victory through his Cross alone.

3
mf Kings for harps their crowns resign,
Crying, as they strike the chords,
f 'Take the Kingdom, it is thine,
King of Kings and Lord of Lords.'

4
p Round the altar priests confess,
If their robes are white as snow,
'Twas the Saviour's righteousness,
And his Blood, that made them so.

5
mf They were mortal too like us:
O, when we like them must die,
f May our souls translated thus
Triumph, reign, and shine on high.

J. MONTGOMERY

HYMN 531 FIRST TUNE

KEY **D** Mount Ephraim

B. Milgrove, 1731–1810

[sol-fa notation]

FOR ANY SAINT'S DAY

{ | m,.r:d :l | s,.f :m :s | l,.s:l :t | d¹:— | l | s .,f :m .r | :d .f | m :—:r | d:— |
  | s₁ :—:l₁ | d.,t₁:d :d | d :—:f | m:— | l₁ | d :—.t₁:d .r | d:—:t₁ | d:— |
  | s.,f:m :f | s :—:d¹ | d¹ :—:t | l :— | d¹ | s .,l :s .f | :m .l | s :—:f | m:— |
  | d :—:f | m,.r:d :m | f,.m:f :r | l₁:— | f₁ | m,.,f₁:s,.se:l,.f, | s₁:—:s, | d:— | }

SECOND TUNE

KEY E♭   St. Helena (Mount Ephraim)   Adapted from B. Milgrove, 1731-1810

{ | :d | m :d | r :r | d :— | :— | s | t :s | l :l | s :— | :— |
  | :s₁ | d :'d | d :t₁ | d :— | :— | r | r :r | m :r | t₁ :— | :— |
  | :m | s :s | l :s | m :— | :— | s | s :s | s :fe | s :— | :— |
  | :d | d :m | f :s | d :— | :— | t₁ | s₁,:t₁ | d :r | s₁ :— | :— | }

{ | :f | m :d | l :s | l :t | d¹ :— | l | s :f | m :r | d :— | :— |
  | :d | d :d | d :d | d :f | m | d.r | m :r | d :t₁ | d :— | :— |
  | :d | s :s | f :s | f :f | s | l.t | d¹ :l | s :—.f | m :— | :— |
  | :l₁ | d :m | f :m | f :r | d | f₁, | m₁:f₁ | s₁,:s, | d :— | :— | }

mf   FOR all thy saints, O Lord,
Who strove in thee to live,
Who followed thee, obeyed, adored,
Our grateful hymn receive.

2
For all thy saints, O Lord,
Who strove in thee to die,
And found in thee a full reward,
Accept our thankful cry.

3
Thine earthly members fit
To join thy saints above,
In one communion ever knit,
One fellowship of love.

4
Jesu, thy name we bless,
And humbly pray that we
May follow them in holiness,
Who lived and died for thee.

[UNISON]   5
All might, all praise, be thine,
Father, co-equal Son,
And Spirit, bond of love divine,
While endless ages run.

BISHOP R. MANT and Compilers

Alternative Tune, St. Michael, 539

FOR ANY SAINT'S DAY

HYMN 532 Woodchurch   Sir S. H. Nicholson, 1875–1947

KEY F

WE praise thee, Lord, for all the martyred throng,
Those who by fire and sword or suffering long
Laid down their lives, but would not yield to wrong:
>> Alleluia!

2

For those who fought to keep the faith secure,
For all whose hearts were selfless, strong and pure,
For those whose courage taught us to endure:
>> Alleluia!

3

For fiery spirits, held and God-controlled,
For gentle natures by his power made bold,
For all whose gracious lives God's love retold.
>> Alleluia!

4

Thanks be to thee, O Lord, for saints unknown,
Who by obedience to thy word have shown
That thou didst call and mark them for thine own.
>> Alleluia!

BISHOP R. HEBER

ST. ANDREW THE APOSTLE

HYMN 533 St. Andrew E. H. Thorne, 1834–1916

KEY C

```
                                                          G. t.
|m  :-.m |r  :m  |f  :m  |l  :s  ||d' :-.d' |t  :l   |s d  :r  |d  :-  ||
|d  :-.d |r  :d  |t, :d  |r  :s  ||m  :-.m  |m  :f   |s d  :t, |s, :-  ||
|s  :-.s |s  :s  |s  :s  |t  :d' ||d' :-.d' |d' :d'  |d'f  :f  |m  :-  ||
|d  :-.d |t, :d  |r  :d  |f  :m  ||l  :-.l  |s  :f   |m l, :s, |d  :-  ||

                                                          f. C.
|d  :-.d |t, :d  |r  :d  |f  :m  ||l  :-.f  |f  :-.r |f d' :t  |d' :-  ||
|l, :-.l,|t, :l, |se,:l, |t, :m  ||d  :-.l, |t, :-.t,|d s  :f  |m  :-  ||
|m  :-.m |m  :m  |m  :m  |se :l  ||f  :-.f  |l  :-.f |l m' :r' |d' :-  ||
|l, :-.l,|se,:l, |t, :l, |r  :d  ||f  :-.f  |r  :-.r |d s  :s  |d  :-  ||
```

mf JESUS calls us! o'er the tumult‿
Of our life's wild restless sea
Day by day his sweet voice soundeth,
Saying, 'Christian, follow me;'

2

As of old Saint Andrew heard it
By the Galilean lake,
Turned from home and toil and kindred,
Leaving all for his dear sake.

3

p Jesus calls us from the worship‿
Of the vain world's golden store,
From each idol that would keep us,
Saying, 'Christian, love me more.'

4

mf In our joys and in our sorrows,
Days of toil and hours of ease,
Still he calls, in cares and pleasures,
That we love him more than these.

5

p Jesus calls us! by thy mercies,
Saviour, make us hear thy call,
Give our hearts to thine obedience,
Serve and love thee best of all.

MRS. C. F. ALEXANDER

Alternative Tune, Merton, 47

ST. THOMAS THE APOSTLE

HYMN 534 Elton   J. Dykes Bower
KEY E♭

[Tonic sol-fa notation]

1
WHO dreads, yet undismayed
  Dares face his terror;
Who errs, yet having strayed
  Avows his error—
Him let Saint Thomas guide,
Who stirred his fellows' pride
To move to death beside
  Their Lord and Master.

2
Who longs for guidance clear
  When doubts assail him,
Nor dares to move for fear
  Lest faith should fail him—
For such let Christ's reply
To his disciple's cry,
'I am the Way,' supply
  The light in darkness.

3
Who grieves that love lies dead
  On fate's wheel broken;
And stands uncomforted
  By any token—
His faith shall be restored
By Christ's compelling word
When Thomas saw the Lord,
And seeing worshipped.

ARCHBISHOP J. R. DARBYSHIRE

ST. STEPHEN

HYMN 535 Evangelists Melody by J. B. König (?), 1691–1758

KEY G

[sol-fa notation]

Heri mundus exultavit

YESTERDAY with exultation
Joined the world in celebration
　Of her promised Saviour's birth;
Yesterday the angel-nation
Poured the strains of jubilation
　O'er the Monarch born on earth:

2

But to-day, O deacon glorious,
By thy faith and deeds victorious,
　Stephen, champion renowned,
Thee we hail who, triumph gaining,
Mid the faithless faith sustaining,
　First of martyr saints wast found.

3

For the crown that fadeth never
Bear thy murderers' brief endeavour;
　Victory waits to end the strife:
Death shall be thy life's beginning,
And life's losing be the winning
　Of the true and better life.

ADAM OF ST. VICTOR
Tr. J. M. Neale and Compilers

See also hymn 529 and accompanying note

ST. JOHN THE EVANGELIST

HYMN 536 St. Thomas Traditional Melody (18th cent.)
KEY D

[sol-fa notation]

    mf WORD supreme, before creation
        Born of God eternally,
    Who didst will for our salvation
        To be born on earth, and die;
    Well thy saints have kept their station,
        Watching till thine hour drew nigh.

2

    Now 'tis come, and faith espies thee:
        Like an eaglet in the morn,
    One in steadfast worship eyes thee,
        Thy beloved, thy latest born;
    In thy glory he decries thee
        Reigning from the Tree of scorn.

3

f Lo, heaven's doors lift up, revealing
        How thy judgements earthward move:
    Scrolls unfolded, trumpets pealing,
        Wine-cups from the wrath above;
p Yet o'er all a soft voice stealing,
        'Little children, trust and love!'

4

f Thee, the almighty King eternal,
        Father of the eternal Word,
    Thee, the Father's Word supernal,
    Thee, of Both, the Breath adored,
    Heaven and earth and realms infernal
        Own, one glorious God and Lord.

                      J. KEBLE

ST. JOHN THE EVANGELIST

HYMN 537 Golden Sheaves Sir A. Sullivan, 1842–1900

KEY **G**

{ :s₁ | m :s | s :f | m :r | d ‖ d r :m | f :l₁ | t₁ :— | d ‖
  :s₁ | d :t₁ | d :r | d :t₁ | d ‖ s₁ l₁ :s₁ | f₁ :f₁ | f₁ :— .m₁ ‖
  :s₁ | s :s | s :s | s :f | m ‖ d l₁ :—.l₁ | l₁ :r | r :— | d ‖
  :s₁ | d :r | m :t₁ | d :s₁ | l₁ ‖ m₁ f₁ :m₁ | r₁ :r₁ | s₁ :— | d₁ ‖ }

D.t.

{ :s₁ | m :s | s :f | m :r | d ‖ ᵐl l :s | l :t | r' :— | d' ‖
  :s₁ | d :t₁ | d :r | d :t₁ | d ‖ ᵈf f :f | f :f | f :— | m ‖
  :s₁ | s :s | s :s | s :f | m ‖ ˢd' t :t | d' :r' | t :— | d' ‖
  :s₁ | d :f | m :t₁ | d :s₁ | l₁ ‖ ¹r s₁ :s₁ | s :s | s :— | d ‖ }

d. f. C.

{ :s | s :—.s | d' :l | ˢl :se | t ‖ m d' :d' | r' :d'.r' | m' :— | m' ‖
  :m | m :—.m | m :m | ʳm :m | m ‖ m m :m | s :s | s :— | s ‖
  :d' | d' :—.d' | d' :d' | ¹t :—.l | se ‖ se l :l | t :l.t | d' :— | d' ‖
  :d | d :—.d | l₁ :d | ʳm :—.ba | se ‖ m l :l | s :s | d' :— | d ‖ }

G.t.

{ :ᵈ'f.s | l :l | s :d | f :f | m ‖ d r :m | f :l₁ | t₁ :— | d ‖
  :ᵐl₁ | d :r | r :d | d :t₁ | d ‖ s₁ l₁ :s₁ | f₁ :l₁ | s₁ :— | s₁ ‖
  :ᵈ'f | f :f | m :l | l :s | d ‖ d l₁ :—.l₁ | l₁ :f | f :— | m ‖
  :ᵈf₁ | f :t₁ | m :m | r :s₁ | l₁ ‖ m₁ f₁ :m₁ | r₁ :r₁ | s₁ :— | d₁ ‖ }

TO you was given, O saint beloved,
    A vision of Christ's glory
Before he lived his earthly life
    Begun with Christmas story:
The glory of the Son of God
    Before the world's creation,
In whom all things that are were made
    And have their consummation.

2

In you he found his closest friend,
    A friend though frail and mortal,
Whose love so pure gave sight so sure
    It pierced beyond heaven's portal:
So to the world you witness gave,
    With prophet's eye descrying
The life of grace and fellowship,
    The life in God undying.

3

O love of God that overflowed
    In glories of creation!
O crowning glory of all life
    In wondrous Incarnation!
All praise to God whose saint and seer
    Declared the love excelling
Now shed abroad in faithful hearts,
    Abounding and indwelling.

F. B. MERRYWEATHER

THE INNOCENTS' DAY

HYMN 538 Puer nobis   Melody by M. Praetorius, 1571–1621
KEY D

[Musical notation in tonic sol-fa]

Salvete, flores martyrum

1
O MARTYRS young and fresh as flowers,
Your day was in its morning hours
When Christ was sought and you were found
Like rain-strewn petals on the ground.

2
How weak to hurt you was the king!
You are Christ's morning offering,
His pretty lambs, his children, gay
With martyr-crowns and palms at play.

3
And you had cheated Herod's rage,
You little boys of Jesus' age;
For he whom Herod sought to slay,
Jesus, untouched escaped away.

[UNISON] 4
Glory, O Christ the Lord, to thee,
Child of the blessèd Virgin, be,
Whom with the Father we adore
And Holy Spirit evermore.

PRUDENTIUS
Tr. J. M. C. Crum

Alternative Tune, Alstone, 435

THE CIRCUMCISION

HYMN 539 St. Michael   *Anglo-Genevan Psalms*, 1561
KEY A♭

[Musical notation in tonic sol-fa]

THE CIRCUMCISION

Debilis cessent elementa legis

1. THE ancient law departs,
And all its fears remove,
For Jesus makes with faithful hearts
A covenant of love.

2. The Light of Light divine,
True brightness undefiled,
He bears for us the pain of sin,
A holy spotless Child.

3. To-day the name is thine
At which we bend the knee;
They call thee Jesus, Child divine:
Our Jesus deign to be.

4. All praise, eternal Son,
For thy redeeming love,
With Father, Spirit, ever One,
In glorious might above.

S. BESNAULT
Tr. Compilers (1904)

THE CONVERSION OF ST. PAUL

HYMN 540 Woolmer's   Sir F. A. G. Ouseley, 1825–89

KEY F

Paule, doctor egregie

1. FROM heaven's height Christ spake to call
The Gentiles' great apostle, Paul,
Whose doctrine, like the thunder, sounds
To the wide world's remotest bounds.

2. O bliss of Paul, beyond all thought,
To Paradise, yet living, caught!
He hears the heavenly mysteries there,
Which mortal tongue cannot declare.

3. The word's good seed abroad he flings;
Straightway a mighty harvest springs,
And fruits of holy deeds supply
God's everlasting granary.

4. The lamp his burning faith displays
Has filled the world with glorious rays;
That darkness' realm may be o'erthrown,
And Christ may reign, and reign alone.

ST. PETER DAMIANI
Tr. J. M. Neale‡

Alternative Tune, Agincourt, 501

THE CONVERSION OF ST. PAUL

HYMN 541 Ellacombe *Würtemburg Gesangbuch, 1784*

KEY B♭

WE sing the glorious conquest
  Before Damascus' gate,
When Saul, the Church's spoiler,
  Came breathing threats and hate;
The ravening wolf rushed forward
  Full early to the prey;
But lo, the Shepherd met him,
  And bound him fast to-day.

2*

O glory most excelling
  That smote across his path!
O light that pierced and blinded
  The zealot in his wrath!
O voice that spake within him
  The calm reproving word!
O love that sought and held him
  The bondman of his Lord!

3

O Wisdom, ordering all things
  In order strong and sweet,
What nobler spoil was ever
  Cast at the Victor's feet?
What wiser master-builder
  E'er wrought at thine employ
Than he, till now so furious
  Thy building to destroy?

4

Lord, teach thy Church the lesson,
  Still in her darkest hour
Of weakness and of danger
  To trust thy hidden power:
Thy grace by ways mysterious
  The wrath of man can bind,
And in thy boldest foeman
  Thy chosen saint can find.

J. ELLERTON

THE CONVERSION OF ST. PAUL

HYMN 542 Stuttgart

C. F. Witt, 1660–1716

KEY **G**

```
{ s₁ :s₁ |d :d    r :r |m :d    s :s |l :f    r :s |m :—  ||
  s₁ :s₁ |s₁ :s₁  t₁ :t₁ |d :d  r :d |d :d    d :t₁|d :—  ||
  s₁ :s₁ |m :m    s :s |s :m    s :m |f :l    s :s |s :—  ||
  s₁ :s₁ |m₁:d₁   s₁ :s₁ |d :d  t₁ :d |f₁:f₁  s₁ :s₁ |d :— ||

{ m :m |r :m      d :r |d :t₁   d :l₁|s₁ :d   d :t₁|d :—  ||
  d :d |t₁ :t₁    l₁ :l₁|s₁ :s₁ s₁ :f₁|m₁ :s₁ s₁ :s₁|s₁:—  ||
  l :m |f :m      m :r |r :r    d :d |d :d    r :r |m :—  ||
  l₁:l₁|l₁:se₁    l₁:fe₁|s₁ :s₁ m₁:f₁|d₁:m₁   s₁:s₁|d₁:—   ||
```

PAUL the preacher, Paul the poet,
   Fearless fighter for the truth,
Mystic, pioneer, and prophet,
   Builder of the Church's youth;

2

Foremost of Gamaliel's pupils,
   Pharisee of Christian fame,
Great apostle of the Gentiles,
   We as Gentiles bless thy name.

3

Loyal Jew, yet born a Roman,
   Citizen, yet slave of Christ,
Wealth, position, kindred, freedom,
   To thy Lord were sacrificed.

4

Still to-day we need thy teaching,
   Stern yet loving, hard yet true:
Only those who share his Passion
   Can their lives in Christ renew.

5

Paul the fiery, Paul the saintly,
   Worship with us at thy feast;
May our love to Christ be strengthened,
   And our faith through thee increased;

6

Till, when faith no more is needed,
   There where faith and sight are one,
We in heaven shall praise the Father
   In the Spirit through the Son.

AMY SAYLE

Alternative Tune, St. Oswald, 292

PRESENTATION OF CHRIST IN THE TEMPLE
COMMONLY CALLED
THE PURIFICATION OF ST. MARY THE VIRGIN

HYMN **543** Bristol T. Ravenscroft, *Psalms*, 1621

KEY **G**

Templi sacratas pande, Sion, fores

1
O SION, open wide thy gates,
  Let symbols disappear:
A Priest and Victim, both in one,
  The Truth himself is here.

2
No more the slaughtered beast must die:
  Behold, the Father's Son
His Temple enters, soon himself
  For sinners to atone.

3
Conscious of hidden Deity,
  The lowly Virgin brings
Her new-born Babe, with two young [doves,
  Her humble offerings.

4
There waiting Simeon sees at last
  The Saviour long desired,
And Anna welcomes Israel's Hope,
  With holy rapture fired.

5
But silent stood the Mother blest
  Of the yet silent Word,
And, pondering in her steadfast heart,
  With speechless praise adored.

[UNISON] 6
All glory to the Father be,
  All glory to the Son,
All glory, Holy Ghost, to thee,
  While endless ages run.

J. B. DE SANTEUIL
Tr. E. Caswall and Compilers

HYMN **544** FIRST TUNE

KEY **D** Old 120th *Psalms*, 1570

THE PURIFICATION OF ST. MARY THE VIRGIN

[Sol-fa notation, f.D.]

SECOND TUNE

KEY A St. Veronica   Sir F. Champneys, 1848–1930

[Sol-fa notation]

* *For verses 2, 3 and 5*

f HAIL to the Lord who comes,
    Comes to his Temple gate!
mf Not with his angel host,
    Not in his kingly state:
    No shouts proclaim him nigh,
    No crowds his coming wait.

2
p But borne upon the throne
    Of Mary's gentle breast,
    Watched by her duteous love,
    In her fond arms at rest;
mf Thus to his Father's house
    He comes, the heavenly guest.

3
There Joseph at her side
    In reverent wonder stands;
And, filled with holy joy,
    Old Simeon in his hands
Takes up the promised Child,
    The glory of all lands.

4
Hail to the great First-born,
    Whose ransom-price they pay!
The Son before all worlds;
    The Child of man to-day,
f That he might ransom us
    Who still in bondage lay.

5
mf O Light of all the earth,
    Thy children wait for thee:
    Come to thy temples here,
    That we, from sin set free,
    Before thy Father's face
    May all presented be.

J. ELLERTON

ST. MATTHIAS THE APOSTLE

HYMN 545 Tallis T. Tallis, c. 1505–85

KEY E♭

```
{ :d  | m :f  | s :s   | l :l  | s    ‖ s  | d' :t  | l :l  | s :— |— ‖
  :d  | d :d  | r :m   | f :f  | m    ‖ m  | m  :r  | r :r  | t₁:— |— ‖
  :d  | s :l  | t :s   | d':d' | d'   ‖ d  | m  :s  | s :fe | s :— |— ‖
  :d  | d :l₁ | s₁:d   | f₁:f₁ | d    ‖ d  | d  :s₁ | r :r  | s₁:— |— ‖ }


{ :d  | m :f  | s :s   | l :l  | s    ‖ d  | f :m   | r :r  | d :— |— ‖
  :d  | d :d  | t₁:s₁  | d :d  | d    ‖ d  | d :d   | d :t₁ | d :— |— ‖
  :s  | s :d  | r :m   | f :f  | m    ‖ m  | l :s   | s :s  | m :— |— ‖
  :d  | d :l₁ | s₁:d   | f₁:f₁ | d    ‖ d  | f₁:d   | s₁:s₁ | d :— |— ‖ }
```

THE highest and the holiest place
Guards not the heart from sin:
The Church that safest seems without
May harbour foes within.

2

Thus in the small and chosen band
Beloved above the rest,
One fell from his apostleship,
A traitor soul unblest.

3

But not the great designs of God
Man's sins shall overthrow;
Another witness to the truth
Forth to the lands shall go.

4

The soul that sinneth, it shall die;
Thy purpose shall not fail:
The word of grace no less shall sound,
The truth no less prevail.

5

Righteous, O Lord, are all thy ways:
Long as the worlds endure,
From foes without and foes within
Thy Church shall stand secure.

H. ALFORD

THE ANNUNCIATION OF THE BLESSED VIRGIN MARY

HYMN **546**   Annunciation   C. A. Barry, 1830–1915

KEY E♭

[Tonic sol-fa notation]

PRAISE we the Lord this day,
This day so long foretold,
Whose promise shone with cheering ray
On waiting saints of old.

2
The prophet gave the sign
For faithful men to read:
A Virgin, born of David's line,
Shall bear the promised Seed.

3
Ask not how this should be,
But worship and adore;
Like her, whom heaven's majesty
Came down to shadow o'er.

4
Meekly she bowed her head
To hear the gracious word,
Mary, the pure and lowly maid,
The favoured of the Lord.

5
Blessèd shall be her name
In all the Church on earth,
Through whom that wondrous mercy came,
The incarnate Saviour's birth.

6
Jesu, the Virgin's Son,
We praise thee and adore,
Who art with God the Father One
And Spirit evermore.

ANON. (1847)

Alternative Tune, St. George, 63

THE ANNUNCIATION OF THE BLESSED VIRGIN MARY

HYMN 547 Angelus ad Virginem
KEY G
Medieval Melody from *Dublin Troper* (c. 1360)

By permission of the Faith Press, Ltd.

Angelus ad Virginem

1
GABRIEL to Mary came,
　She saw him in her chamber;
Mary's heart stood still with fear,
　But gently did he greet her:
'Thou queen of maidens, hail!' he said,
'Thou shalt become a Mother-maid;
Thy Son shall be the Lord of earth and heaven:
　He comes to save mankind
　That men, their sins forgiven,
　　The gate of heaven may find.'

2
'How can I a mother be
　That am a maid unwedded?
How can I a mother be
　That am a maid betrothèd?'
He answered to her questioning:
'The Holy Ghost shall do this thing.
Be not afraid, nor let thy heart be careful:
　God guards thy purity;
　His power shall make thee joyful,
　　And blessèd shalt thou be.'

THE ANNUNCIATION OF THE BLESSED VIRGIN MARY

3
Unto whom our Lady then
　Returned her answer meekly:
'Here am I, the handmaiden
　Of God the Lord almighty;
O messenger of God most high,
　Revealer of this mystery,
With all my heart I long to see fulfilment
　Of what I hear thee tell:
Behold his handmaid ready
　To do his holy will.'

4
Ah, thou Mother of my Lord,
　What peace through thee was given!
Thy dear Child, our Christ adored,
　Makes peace in earth and heaven.
Beseech thy Son for us, that he
Would look upon us graciously,
And, all our shame and misery relieving,
　Would give us grace to come
To comfort out of grieving
　And, out of exile, home.

14th cent. *Tr.* J. M. C. Crum

ST. MARK THE EVANGELIST

Hymn 548 Winchester New　　　　　　*Musikalisch Handbuch*
Key B♭　　　　　　　　　　　　　　　(Hamburg, 1690)

{: s₁ | d :s₁ | l₁ :l₁ | s₁ :f₁ | m₁ ‖ m₁ | f₁ :m₁ | r₁ :s₁ | s₁ :fe₁ | s₁ :— ‖
{: m₁ | s₁ :m₁ | f₁ :d₁ | d₁ :-.t₂| d₁ ‖ d₁ | d₁ :d₁ | t₂ :t₂ | m₁ :r₁ | r₁ :— ‖
{: d | d :d | d :f₁ | s₁ :s₁ | s₁ ‖ s₁ | f₁ :s₁ | s₁ :s₁ | d :l₁ | t₁ :— ‖
{: d₁ | m₁ :d₁ | f₁ :f₁ | m₁ :s₁ | d₁ ‖ d₁ | l₂ :d₁ | s₂ :m₁ | d₁ :r₁ | s₂ :— ‖

{: s₁ | d :r | m :d | f :m | r ‖ m | d :l₁ | s₁ :d | d :t₁ | d :— ‖
{: s₁ | s₁ :f₁ | m₁ :s₁ | f₁ :s₁ | s₁ ‖ s₁ | s₁ :f₁ | s₁ :m₁ | l₁ :s₁ | m₁ :— ‖
{: s₁ | s₁ :l₁.t₁| d :d | l₁.t₁:d | t₁ ‖ d | d :d | d :d | r :r | d :— ‖
{: s₁.f₁| m₁ :r₁ | d₁ :m₁ | r₁ :m₁.f₁| s₁ ‖ d₁ | m₁ :f₁ | m₁ :l₁ | f₁ :s₁ | d₁ :— ‖

From out the cloud of fiery light,
　Borne on the whirlwind from the north,
Four living creatures winged and bright
　Before the prophet's eye came forth.

2
The voice of God was in the four
　Beneath that awful crystal mist,
And every wondrous form they wore
　Foreshadowed an Evangelist.

3
The lion-faced, he told abroad
　The strength of love, the strength of faith;
He showed the almighty Son of God,
　The Man divine who won by death.

4
O Lion of the Royal Tribe,
　Strong Son of God, and strong to save,
All power and honour we ascribe
　To thee who only makest brave.

5
For strength to love, for will to speak,
　For fiery crowns by martyrs won,
For suffering patience, strong and meek,
　We praise thee, Lord, and thee alone.

Mrs. C. F. Alexander†

SS. PHILIP AND JAMES THE APOSTLES

Hymn **549** Montgomery *Magdalen Hospital Hymns, c. 1762*

KEY **D**

Caelestis aulae principes

HAIL! princes of the host of heaven,
To whom by Christ your Chief 'tis given
On shining thrones to sit on high,
And judge the world with equity.

2

Through you was borne the Gospel light
To those who lay in sin's dark night;
That Christ, the Life, the Truth, the Way,
Might lead them to eternal day.

3

Not in the power of earthly sword
Of arts of speech ye preached the Lord:
The Cross, the Cross which men despise,
'Twas this achieved your victories.

4

And now to God, the Three in One,
Be highest praise and glory done,
Who calls us from the gloom of night
To share the glory of his light.

J. B. de Santeuil
Tr. J. Chandler and Compilers

ST. BARNABAS THE APOSTLE

HYMN 550 St. Osyth T. Wood
KEY **C**

With vigour. UNISON

{| s :—| l : s | m :—|—: d | r : m | f : m | s :—| m :— || d' :—| l : s }

{| m : s | l : t | d' : t | l :—| s :—|—:— || l :—| m : f | s :—|—: d | r : m | f : s }

{| l : d' | t : l || r' :—| l : t | d' : t | s : m | f : m | r :—| d :—|—:— ||

By permission of the Oxford University Press

O SON of God, our Captain of Salvation,
   Thyself by suffering schooled to human grief,
We bless thee for thy sons of consolation,
   Who follow in the steps of thee their chief:

2

For all true helpers, patient, kind, and skilful,
   Who shed thy light across our darkened earth,
Counsel the doubting, and restrain the wilful,
   Soothe the sick bed, and share the children's mirth.

3

Such was thy Levite, strong in self-oblation
   To cast his all at thine apostles' feet;
He whose new name, through every Christian nation,
   From age to age our thankful strains repeat.

J. ELLERTON

Alternative Tune, Genevan Psalm xii, 17

ST. JOHN BAPTIST

HYMN 551 FIRST TUNE

KEY **E** Ut queant laxis Mode ii

Ut queant laxis   Resonare fibris

{| d r f r m r r r d r m — m — | m f s }
1. Sing we the prai-ses of the great fore-run-ner, Tell
2. Lo, God's high her-ald, swift from heaven de-scend-ing, Gives
3. Oft had the pro-phets in the time be-fore thee Spo-

{| m r m d r f s l s f m r — r — | s s m f }
1. forth the migh-ty won-ders of his sto-ry: So may his
2. to thy fa-ther ti-dings of thy com-ing, Tell-ing thy
3. ken in vi-sion of the Day-star's com-ing; But when he

{| s r l s l f s l l —| s f m r d m — r — ||
1. Mas-ter cleanse our lips and make them Fit to ex-tol him.
2. name and all the tale of mar-vels That shall be-fall thee.
3. came, 'twas thou that didst pro-claim him Sa-viour of all men.

ST. JOHN BAPTIST

HYMN 551   SECOND TUNE
KEY **D**   Lobet den Herren   J. Crüger, 1598–1662

Ut queant laxis   Resonare fibris

SING we the praises of the great forerunner,
Tell forth the mighty wonders of his story:
So may his Master cleanse our lips and make them
    Fit to extol him.

2
Lo, God's high herald, swift from heaven descending,
Gives to thy father tidings of thy coming,
Telling thy name and all the tale of marvels
    That shall befall thee.

3
Oft had the prophets in the time before thee
Spoken in vision of the Daystar's coming;
But when he came, 'twas thou that didst proclaim him
    Saviour of all men.

                            PAUL THE DEACON   *Tr.* Compilers
    Alternative Tune, Diva servatrix, 519

HYMN 552   FIRST TUNE
KEY **C**   Croft's 148th   W. Croft, 1678–1727

ST. JOHN BAPTIST

```
{| l  :— |d' :— | t  :l   | se :—  || se :— | l  :t  | d' :— |s  :— | m :r.d | d  :— |
 | d  :— |s  :— | f  :f   | m  :—  || m  :— | m  :r  | d  :— |d  :— | d :t₁  | d  :— |
 | d' :— |d' :— | r' :—.d'| t  :—  || t  :— | l  :se | l  :— |s  :— | s :f   | m  :— |
 | f  :— |m  :— | r  :r   | m  :—  || m  :— | d  :t₁ | l₁ :— |m  :— | s :s₁  | d  :— |}
```

SECOND TUNE

KEY C Darwall's 148th   J. Darwall. 1731–89

G.t.
```
{|:d |m:d:d|s :m|d':—|—||t |l :s|f :m|r :—|—||r |m:d|¹r :d |
 |:d |d:d:d|r :m|m :—|—||m |f :d|t₁:d|t₁:—|—||t₁|d:d|ᵐl₁:s₁|
 |:m |s:m:s|s :s|d':—|—||d'|d':s|s :s|s :—|—||s |s:m|ᵈᶠf:m |
 |:d |d:d:d|t₁:d|l :—|—||s |f :m|r :d|s₁:—|—||s₁|d:d|¹¹r₁:m₁.f₁|}
```
f. C.
```
{| t₁:s₁ |s :f |m  :— |r  :— |d  :— |— ||ᵈs |l :— | t  :— |
 | s₁:s₁ |s₁:l₁|s₁ :— |s₁.f₁|m₁ :— |— ||ᶠd |d :— | f  :— |
 | r :t₁ |d :d |d  :— |t₁ :— |d  :— |— ||¹m |f :— | f  :— |
 | s₁:s₁.f₁|m₁:f₁|s₁:— |s₁ :— |d₁ :— |— ||ᶠd |f :— | r  :— |}
```
```
{|d':— |— ||d |r :m|f :s |l :t |d':r'|d':— | t  :— |d':— |— |
 |m :— |— ||d |t₁:d|d :d |d :f|m :r |m :— | r :f |m :— |— |
 |l :— |— ||s |s :s|f :m|f :f|s.:l |s :— | s  :— |s :— |— |
 |l₁:— |— ||m |r :d|l₁:d|f :r|m :f |s :— |s₁ :— |d :— |— |}
```

Nunc suis tandem novus e latebris

mf LO, from the desert homes,
   Where he hath hid so long,
   The new Elijah comes,
   In sternest wisdom strong:
f   The voice that cries
     Of Christ from high,
     And judgement nigh
    From opening skies.

2
mf Your God e'en now doth stand
   At heaven's opening door;
   His fan is in his hand,
   And he will purge his floor;
f   The wheat he claims
     And with him stows,
p   The chaff he throws
    To quenchless flames.

3
f Ye haughty mountains, bow
   Your sky-aspiring heads;
mf Ye valleys, hiding low,
   Lift up your gentle meads;
f   Make his way plain
     Your King before,
     For evermore
    He comes to reign.

4
mf May thy dread voice around,
   Thou harbinger of Light,
   On our dull ears still sound,
   Lest here we sleep in night,
    Till judgement come,
     And on our path
     The Lamb's dread wrath
    Shall burst in doom.

5
O God, with love's sweet might,
   Who dost anoint and arm
Christ's soldier for the fight
   With grace that shields from harm:
f   Thrice blessèd Three,
     Heaven's endless days
     Shall sing thy praise
    Eternally.

                              C. COFFIN *Tr.* I. Williams†

ST. JOHN BAPTIST

HYMN 553 Sedulius *Nürnbergisches Gesangbuch, 1676*

KEY **G**

Praecursor altus luminis

THE great forerunner of the morn,
The herald of the Word, is born;
And faithful hearts shall never fail
With thanks and praise his light to hail.

2
With heavenly message Gabriel came,
That John should be that herald's name,
And with prophetic utterance told
His actions great and manifold.

3
John, still unborn, yet gave aright
His witness to the coming Light;
And Christ, the Sun of all the earth,
Fulfilled that witness at his birth.

4
Of woman-born shall never be
A greater prophet than was he,
Whose mighty deeds exalt his fame
To greater than a prophet's name.

[UNISON] 5
All praise to God the Father be,
All praise, eternal Son, to thee,
Whom with the Spirit we adore
For ever and for evermore.

THE VENERABLE BEDE
Tr. J. M. Neale†

ST. PETER THE APOSTLE

Hymn 554 Commandments L. Bourgeois, *c.* 1500–61

KEY **G**

{|d :— |d :r |m :— :m |f :— :f |m :— |r :— ‖ m :— |f :m |r :d |
|s₁:— |l₁:t₁|d :— :d |d :— :d |d :— |t₁:— ‖ d :— |d :d |t₁:l₁|
|m :— |m :s |s :— :s |l :— :l |s :— |s :— ‖ s :— |l :s |s :m |
|d :— |l₁:s₁|d :— :d |f₁:— :f₁|d :— |s₁:— ‖ d :— |f₁:d |s₁:l₁|}

{|t₁:— |d :— |r :— |— :— ‖ s :— |f :m |r :— |t₁:— |d :t₁|
|se₁:— |l₁:— |t₁:— |— :— ‖ d :— |d :d |l₁:— |s₁:— |s₁:s₁|
|m :— |m :— |s :— |— :— ‖ s :— |l :s |f :— |m :— |m :r |
|m₁:— |l₁:— |s₁:— |— :— ‖ m₁:— |f₁:d₁|r₁:— |m₁:— |d₁:s₁|}

{|l₁:— |s₁:— ‖ m :— |f :m |r :d |m :— |r :— |d :— |— :— ‖
|s₁:fe₁|s₁:— ‖ s₁:— |l₁:s₁|s₁:m₁|s₁:— |s₁:— |m₁:— |— :— ‖
|r :— |t₁:— ‖ d :— |d :d |t₁:d |d :— |d :t₁|d :— |— :— ‖
|r₁:— |s₁:— ‖ d :— |f₁:d₁|s₁:l₁|m₁:f₁|s₁:— |d₁:— |— :— ‖}

O ROCK of ages, one Foundation
  On which the living Church doth rest—
The Church whose walls are strong salvation,
  Whose gates are praise—thy name be blest.

2

Son of the living God, O call us
  Once and again to follow thee;
And give us strength, whate'er befall us,
  Thy true disciples still to be.

3

When fears appal and faith is failing,
  Make thy voice heard o'er wind and wave;
And in thy perfect love prevailing
  Put forth thy hand to help and save.

4

And if our coward hearts deny thee
  In inmost thought, in deed or word,
Let not our hardness still defy thee,
  But with a look subdue us, Lord.

5

O strengthen thou our weak endeavour
  Thee in thy sheep to serve and tend,
To give ourselves to thee for ever,
  And find thee with us to the end.

H. A. MARTIN

ST. PETER THE APOSTLE

HYMN 555 Love Unknown John Ireland
KEY E♭

'THOU art the Christ, O Lord,
 The Son of God most high!'
For ever be adored
 That name in earth and sky,
In which, though mortal strength may fail,
The saints of God at last prevail.

2

O surely he was blest
 With blessedness unpriced,
Who, taught of God, confessed
 The Godhead in the Christ!
For of thy Church, Lord, thou didst own
Thy saint a true foundation-stone.

3

Thrice fallen, thrice restored!
 The bitter lesson learnt,
That heart for thee, O Lord,
 With triple ardour burnt.
The cross he took he laid not down
Until he grasped the martyr's crown.

4

O bright triumphant faith,
 O courage void of fears!
O love most strong in death,
 O penitential tears!
By these, Lord, keep us lest we fall,
And make us go where thou shalt call.

BISHOP W. WALSHAM HOW

ST. MARY MAGDALENE

HYMN 556 Rhuddlan   Welsh Traditional Melody

KEY G

MAGDALENE, thy grief and gladness
Voice and heart in concert sing,
Telling how the risen Saviour
Called thee from thy sorrowing,
Tidings of his Resurrection
To his chosen flock to bring.

2

She beheld him, yet she knew not
In the gardener's seeming guise
Christ, who in her heart was sowing
Seed of heavenly mysteries,
Till his voice, her name pronouncing,
Bade her see and recognize.

3

Weep not, Mary, weep no longer!
Now thy seeking heart may rest;
Christ the heavenly gardener soweth
Light and joy within thy breast:
In the glowing cry 'Rabboni!'
Be thy gratitude confest.

C. S. PHILLIPS
Based on *Collaudemus Magdalenae*
Philippe de Grève

Alternative Tune, Lewes, 64

ST. JAMES THE APOSTLE

Hymn 557 St. James R. Courteville (1697)

KEY G

[sol-fa notation]

FOR all thy saints, a noble throng,
   Who fell by fire and sword,
Who soon were called, or waited long,
   We praise thy name, O Lord;

2

For him who left his father's side,
   Nor lingered by the shore,
When, softer than the weltering tide,
   Thy summons glided o'er;

3

Who stood beside the maiden dead,
   Who climbed the mountain with thee,
And saw the glory round thy head,
   One of thy chosen three;

4

Who knelt beneath the olive shade,
   Who drank thy cup of pain,
And passed from Herod's flashing blade
   To see thy face again.

5

Lord, give us grace, and give us love,
   Like him to leave behind
Earth's cares and joys, and look above
   With true and earnest mind.

6

So shall we learn to drink thy cup,
   So meek and firm be found,
When thou shalt come to take us up
   Where thine elect are crowned.

MRS. C. F. ALEXANDER

THE TRANSFIGURATION

HYMN 558
FIRST TUNE
KEY **E** O nata Lux de Lumine Mode iv

Caelestis formam gloriae

{| f m f s l s   f r   f   m f   m — | s   l t a   l
1. O   won - drous type,   O   vi - sion fair   Of   glo - ry
2. The law   and   pro - phets there have place,   The   cho - sen
3. With shi - ning face   and bright ar - ray,   Christ deigns to
4. And Chris - tian hearts are raised on high   By   that great

{| s f   s   s f   m   m — r — | d r   r   r d   r   f }
1. that the Church shall share,   Which Christ up - on the
2. wit - ness - es   of   grace;   The   Fa - ther's voice from
3. man - i - fest   to - day,   What glo - ry   shall to
4. vi - sion's mys - ter - y,   For   which in thank - ful

{| r m   m m — | s   s l   s   f r   f   m f   m   m — ||
1. moun - tain shows, Where bright - er than the sun   he glows!
2. out   the cloud Pro - claims his on - ly Son a - loud.
3. faith   be given When we   en - joy our God in heaven.
4. strains we raise   On   this glad day the voice of praise.

SECOND TUNE

KEY **A** Sandys Psalm viii Melody and bass by H. Lawes, 1596–1662

{| d :— |t₁:l₁ | d :m₁|f₁:l₁ | s₁:— ‖ s₁:— |l₁:r₁|d :t₁ | l₁:m |r :—
  s₁:— |m₁:l₁ | s₁:m₁|d₁:f₁.m₁| r₁:— ‖ s₁:— |f₁:r₁|d₁:s₁ | f₁:s₁|s₁:—
  m :— |t₁:d | d :d |d :r.d | t₁:— ‖ d :— |d :s |m :m | d :d |t₁:—
  d :— |s₁:f₁ | m₁:d₁|l₁:f₁ | s₁:— ‖ m₁:— |f₁:s₁|l₁:m₁ | f₁:d₁|s₁:—

{| r :f :m | l₁ :t₁ |d :r |m :— ‖ m s :r |f :m |r :r |d :—
  t₁:t₁:d.t₁| l₁:s₁.f₁|m₁:r₁|s₁:— ‖ d ta₁:s₁|d :d |d :t₁|d :—
  s :f :s | s.f:m.r|d :s |s :— ‖ m r :s |f :s |s :—.f|m :—
  s₁:r₁:m₁ | f₁ :s₁ |l₁:t₁ |d :— ‖ d s₁:ta₁|l₁:d |s₁:s₁|d₁:—

Caelestis formam gloriae

O WONDROUS type, O vision fair
Of glory that the Church shall share,
Which Christ upon the mountain shows,
Where brighter than the sun he glows!

2
The law and prophets there have place,
The chosen witnesses of grace;
The Father's voice from out the cloud
Proclaims his only Son aloud.

3
With shining face and bright array,
Christ deigns to manifest to-day
What glory shall to faith be given
When we enjoy our God in heaven.

4
And Christian hearts are raised on high
By that great vision's mystery,
For which in thankful strains we raise
On this glad day the voice of praise.

15th cent.
Tr. COMPILERS (1904)

THE TRANSFIGURATION

HYMN 559 Aurelia
KEY E♭

S. S. Wesley, 1810–76

χορὸς Ἰσραήλ

1
IN days of old on Sinai
  The Lord almighty came
In majesty of terror,
  In thunder-cloud and flame:
On Tabor, with the glory
  Of sunniest light for vest,
The excellence of beauty
  In Jesus was exprest.

2
All light created paled there,
  And did him worship meet;
The sun itself adored him,
  And bowed before his feet;
While Moses and Elijah,
  Upon the holy mount,
The co-eternal glory
  Of Christ our God recount.

3
O holy, wondrous vision!
  But O when, this life past,
The beauty of mount Tabor
  Shall end in heaven at last!
But O when all the glory
  Of uncreated light
Shall be the promised guerdon
  Of them that win the fight!

ST. COSMAS *Tr.* J. M. Neale†

HYMN 560 Carlisle
KEY E♭

C. Lockhart, 1745–1815

Slow

570

THE TRANSFIGURATION

mf 'TIS good, Lord, to be here!
　　Thy glory fills the night;
　Thy face and garments, like the sun,
　　Shine with unborrowed light.

2
'Tis good, Lord, to be here,
　Thy beauty to behold,
Where Moses and Elijah stand,
　Thy messengers of old.

f 3
Fulfiller of the past!
　Promise of things to be!
We hail thy body glorified,
　And our redemption see.

mf 4
Before we taste of death,
　We see thy Kingdom come;
We fain would hold the vision bright,
　And make this hill our home.

5
'Tis good, Lord, to be here!
　Yet we may not remain;
But since thou bidst us leave the mount
Come with us to the plain.

J. A. ROBINSON

Alternative Tune, St. George (Gauntlett), 63

HYMN 561 St. Sepulchre   G. Cooper, 1820–76

KEY E♭

1
NOT always on the mount may we
Rapt in the heavenly vision be;
The shores of thought and feeling know
The Spirit's tidal ebb and flow.

2
'Lord, it is good abiding here,'
We cry, the heavenly presence near:
The vision vanishes, our eyes
Are lifted into vacant skies.

3
Yet hath one such exalted hour
Upon the soul redeeming power,
And in its strength through after days
We travel our appointed ways;

4
Till all the lowly vale grows bright,
Transfigured in remembered light,
And in untiring souls we bear
The freshness of the upper air.

5
The mount for vision: but below
The paths of daily duty go,
And nobler life therein shall own
The pattern on the mountain shown.

F. L. HOSMER

This hymn is suitable for general use

ST. BARTHOLOMEW THE APOSTLE

Hymn 562 Valley

Key D

G. H. Knight

[sol-fa notation]

NOT by far-famed deeds alone
  God's Kingdom comes to birth;
The memory of countless saints
  Has perished from the earth.

2
John and Peter, James and Paul,
  Have left a mighty fame:
Another of their company
  Is nothing but a name.

3
Yet for him no less the call
  And gallant course to run;
His too to hear at journey's end
  The Master's glad 'Well done!'

C. S. PHILLIPS

Hymn 549 may also be used

ST. MATTHEW THE APOSTLE

Hymn 563 Ely

Key G

Bishop T. Turton, 1780–1864

[sol-fa notation]

ST. MATTHEW THE APOSTLE

1
HE sat to watch o'er customs paid,
A man of scorned and hardening trade:
Alike the symbol and the tool
Of foreign masters' hated rule.

2
But grace within his breast had stirred;
There needed but the timely word:
It came, true Lord of souls, from thee,
That royal summons, 'Follow me.'

3
Enough, when thou wast passing by,
To hear thy voice, to meet thy eye:
He rose, responsive to the call,
And left his task, his gains, his all.

4
O wise exchange! with these to part,
And lay up treasure in thy heart;
With twofold crown of light to shine
Amid thy servants' foremost line.

5
Come, Saviour, as in days of old;
Pass where the world has strongest hold,
And faithless care and selfish greed
Are thorns that choke the holy seed.

6
Who keep thy gifts, O bid them claim
The steward's, not the owner's, name:
Who yield all up for thy dear sake,
Let them of Matthew's wealth partake.

W. BRIGHT

Alternative Tune, Illsley, 1

ST. MICHAEL AND ALL ANGELS

HYMN 564　　　　FIRST TUNE

KEY **D**　Christe, sanctorum decus angelorum　　　　Mode viii

Christe, sanctorum decus angelorum

1 Christ, the fair glory of the holy angels, Ruler of all men, author of creation, Grant us in mercy grace to win by patience Joys everlasting.

2 Send thine archangel Michael from thy presence: Peacemaker blessèd, may he hover o'er us, Hallow our dwellings, that for us thy children All things may prosper.

3 Send thine archangel, Gabriel the mighty: On strong wings flying, may he come from heaven, Drive from thy temple Satan the old foeman, Succour our weakness.

4 Send thine archangel, Raphael the healer: Through him with wholesome medicines of salvation, Heal our backsliding, and in paths of goodness Guide our steps daily.

5 Father almighty, Son, and Holy Spirit, Godhead eternal, grant us our petition; Thine be the glory through the whole creation Now and for ever.

ST. MICHAEL AND ALL ANGELS

HYMN 564   SECOND TUNE

KEY **C** Rouen

French Melody
G. t.

Christe, sanctorum decus angelorum

CHRIST, the fair glory of the holy angels,
Ruler of all men, author of creation,
Grant us in mercy grace to win by patience
    Joys everlasting.

2

Send thine archangel Michael from thy presence:
Peacemaker blessèd, may he hover o'er us,
Hallow our dwellings, that for us thy children
    All things may prosper.

3

Send thine archangel, Gabriel the mighty:
On strong wings flying, may he come from heaven,
Drive from thy temple Satan the old foeman,
    Succour our weakness.

4

Send thine archangel, Raphael the healer:
Through him with wholesome medicines of salvation
Heal our backsliding, and in paths of goodness
    Guide our steps daily.

5

Father almighty, Son, and Holy Spirit,
Godhead eternal, grant us our petition;
Thine be the glory through the whole creation
    Now and for ever.

Ascribed to ARCHBISHOP RABANUS MAURUS
Tr. Compilers

ST. MICHAEL AND ALL ANGELS

Hymn 565 Xavier   Sir F. Champneys, 1848–1930

f   PRAISE to God who reigns above,
       Binding earth and heaven in love;
       All the armies of the sky
       Worship his dread sovereignty.

2
Seraphim his praises sing,
Cherubim on fourfold wing,
Thrones, Dominions, Princes, Powers,
Marshalled might that never cowers.

3
mf   Speeds the Archangel from his face,
       Bearing messages of grace;
       Angel hosts his words fulfil,
       Ruling nature by his will.

4
Yet on man they joy to wait,
All that bright celestial state,
For in Man their Lord they see,
Christ, the incarnate Deity.

5
On the throne their Lord who died
Sits in Manhood glorified;
Where his people faint below
Angels count it joy to go.

6
O the depths of joy divine
Thrilling through those orders nine,
When the lost are found again,
When the banished come to reign!

[UNISON] 7
f   Now in faith, in hope, in love,
       We will join the choirs above,
       Praising, with the heavenly host,
       Father, Son, and Holy Ghost.

                                       R. M. Benson

ST. MICHAEL AND ALL ANGELS

HYMN 566 Spetisbury   W. Knapp, 1698-1768

KEY G

f ALL praise be to God,
   Whom all things obey,
From angels and men
   For ever and ay;
Who sendeth on earth
   The powers of his throne,
His providence good
   And love to make known.

2

His angels are they
   Of countenance fair,
The arm of his strength,
   His hand of kind care;
His message of peace
   To us they reveal,
His wisdom most high
   They seal or unseal.

3

mf By martyrs of old
   They stood in the flame,
And bade them not flinch,
   But call on God's name.
Through torment, through shame,
   Through darkness of death,
They led without fear
   The sires of our faith.

4

f They stand with the few,
   They fight for the free,
God's reign to advance
   O'er land and o'er sea;
And when the brave die
   Or fall in the fight,
Their spirits they bear
   To rest in God's sight.

5*

mf For patience and toil
   A crown they prepare;
They found for the meek
   A kingdom full fair;
No famine nor plague
   'Gainst them doth prevail;
Their bread cannot lack,
   Their cruse cannot fail.

6

We pray thee, who art
   Thy angels' reward,
Thy flock to defend
   Forget not, O Lord;
But prosper their aid,
   That us they may bring
To see the true face
   Of Jesus, our King.

R. B. in *Yattendon Hymnal*

Alternative Tune, Hanover, 167

ST. LUKE THE EVANGELIST

HYMN 567 Grasmere   J. A. Freylinghausen, 1670–1739

KEY **G**

SAVIOUR, who didst healing give,
  Still in power go before us;
Thou through death didst bid men live,
  Unto fuller life restore us:
Strength from thee the fainting found,
  Deaf men heard, the blind went seeing;
At thy touch was banished sickness,
  And the leper felt new being.

2

Thou didst work thy deeds of old
  Through the loving hands of others:
Still thy mercies manifold
  Bless men by the hands of brothers;
Angels still before thy face
  Go, sweet health to brothers bringing;
Still, hearts glow to tell his praises
  With whose name the Church is ringing.

3

Loved physician! for his word,
  Lo, the gospel page burns brighter:
Mission servants of the Lord,
  Painter true and faithful writer:
Saviour, of thy bounty send
  Such as Luke of Gospel story,
Friends to all in body's prison
  Till the sufferer see thy glory.

H. D. RAWNSLEY†

SS. SIMON AND JUDE THE APOSTLES

HYMN 568 Alleluia, dulce carmen *Essay on the Church Plain Chant,*
KEY A♭ 1782

THOU who sentest thine apostles
  Two and two before thy face,
Partners in the night of toiling,
  Heirs together of thy grace,
Throned at length, their labours ended,
  Each in his appointed place;

2

Praise to thee for those thy champions
  Whom our hymns to-day proclaim:
One, whose zeal by thee enlightened
  Burned anew with nobler flame;
One, the kinsman of thy childhood,
  Brought at last to know thy name.

3

Praise to thee! thy fire within them
  Spake in love, and wrought in power:
Seen in mighty signs and wonders
  In thy Church's morning hour;
Heard in tones of sternest warning
  When the storms began to lower.

4

God the Father, great and wondrous,
  In thy works, to thee be praise;
King of saints, to thee be glory,
  Just and true in all thy ways;
Praise to thee, from Both proceeding,
  Holy Ghost, through endless days.

J. ELLERTON

Alternative Tune, Rhuddlan, 556

ALL SAINTS' DAY

HYMN 569 FIRST TUNE

KEY E♭ Hic breve vivitur A. Pettet, c. 1785–c. 1845

SECOND TUNE

KEY F St. Alphege H. J. Gauntlett, 1805–76

Caelestis O Jerusalem

1
O HEAVENLY Jerusalem,
 Of everlasting halls,
Thrice blessed are the people
 Thou storest in thy walls.

2
Thou art the golden mansion
 Where saints for ever sing,
The seat of God's own chosen,
 The palace of the King.

3
There God for ever sitteth,
 Himself of all the crown:
The Lamb, the Light that shineth,
 And never goeth down.

4
Naught to this seat approacheth
 Their sweet peace to molest;
They sing their God for ever,
 Nor day nor night they rest.

5
Sure hope doth thither lead us;
 Our longings thither tend:
May short-lived toil ne'er daunt us
 For joys that cannot end.

6
To Christ the Sun that lightens
 His Church above, below,
To Father, and to Spirit,
 All things created bow.

18th cent. *Tr.* I. WILLIAMS†

ALL SAINTS' DAY

HYMN **570** All Saints *Geistreiches Gesangbuch* (Darmstadt, 1698)

KEY **C**

[sol-fa notation music]

Wer sind die vor Gottes Throne

WHO are these like stars appearing,
  These, before God's throne who stand?
Each a golden crown is wearing:
  Who are all this glorious band?
    Alleluia, hark! they sing,
    Praising loud their heavenly King.

2*

Who are these in dazzling brightness,
  Clothed in God's own righteousness,
These, whose robes of purest whiteness
  Shall their lustre still possess,
    Still untouched by time's rude hand?
    Whence came all this glorious band?

3

These are they who have contended
  For their Saviour's honour long,
Wrestling on till life was ended,
  Following not the sinful throng;
    These, who well the fight sustained,
    Triumph by the Lamb have gained.

4*

These are they whose hearts were riven,
  Sore with woe and anguish tried,
Who in prayer full oft have striven
  With the God they glorified;
    Now, their painful conflict o'er,
    God has bid them weep no more.

ALL SAINTS' DAY

5
These, the Almighty contemplating,
Did as priests before him stand,
Soul and body always waiting
Day and night at his command:
Now in God's most holy place
Blest they stand before his face.

H. T. Schenck
Tr. Frances E. Cox‡

HYMN **571** Song 67   E. Prys, *Psalms*, 1621
KEY **D**

mf   GIVE us the wings of faith to rise,
Within the veil, and see
The saints above, how great their joys,
How bright their glories be.

2
p   Once they were mourning here below,
Their couch was wet with tears;
They wrestled hard, as we do now,
With sins and doubts and fears.

3
mf   We ask them whence their victory came:
f   They, with united breath,
Ascribe the conquest to the Lamb,
Their triumph to his Death.

4
p   They marked the footsteps that he trod,
His zeal inspired their breast,
And, following their incarnate God,
They reached the promised rest.

5
f   Our glorious Leader claims our praise
For his own pattern given;
While the great cloud of witnesses
Show the same path to heaven.

I. Watts‡

HYMN **572** Rest — Sir J. Stainer, 1840–1901

KEY D♭

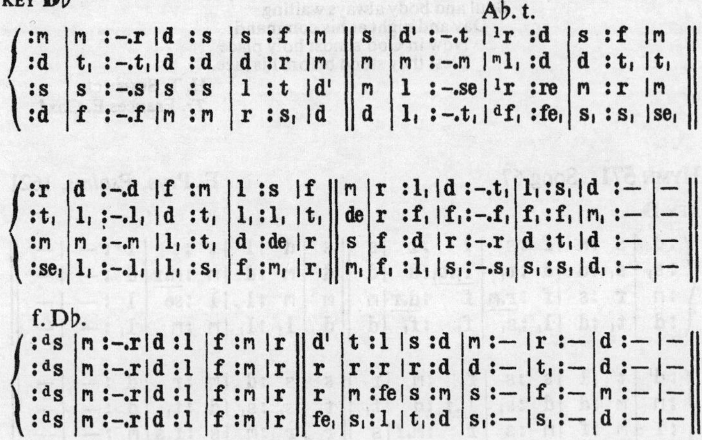

THE saints of God! their conflict past
And life's long battle won at last,
No more they need the shield or sword,
They cast them down before their Lord:
O happy saints! for ever blest,
At Jesus' feet how safe your rest!

2

The saints of God! their wanderings done,
No more their weary course they run,
No more they faint, no more they fall,
No foes oppress, no fears appal:
O happy saints! for ever blest,
In that dear home how sweet your rest!

3

The saints of God! life's voyage o'er,
Safe landed on that blissful shore,
No stormy tempest now they dread,
No roaring billows lift their head:
O happy saints! for ever blest,
In that calm haven of your rest.

4

The saints of God their vigil keep
While yet their mortal bodies sleep,
Till from the dust they too shall rise
And soar triumphant to the skies:
O happy saints! rejoice and sing:
He quickly comes, your Lord and King.

5

O God of saints, to thee we cry;
O Saviour, plead for us on high;
O Holy Ghost, our guide and friend,
Grant us thy grace till life shall end;
That with all saints our rest may be
In that bright Paradise with thee.

ARCHBISHOP W. D. MACLAGAN

Alternative Tune, Colchester, 90

ST. GEORGE, PATRON OF ENGLAND

Hymn 573 Regent Square H. Smart, 1813–79

KEY B♭

[Tonic sol-fa notation]

1

JESUS, Lord of our salvation,
  For thy warrior, bold and true,
Now accept our thankful praises,
  And our strength do thou renew,
That, like George, with courage daunt-
We may all our foes subdue.   [less

2

Blazoned on our country's banner
  England bears the knightly sign:
Lord, our fatherland empower,
  That, endued with strength divine,
She may evermore with courage
  Bear the standard that is thine.

3

Fill her youth with manly spirit,
  Patient, self-restrained, and pure,
Of thy cause the ready champions,
  Never flinching to endure
Hardness for the name of Jesus:
  So their triumph shall be sure.

4

Teach her manhood to confess thee
  As the Master, Lord, and King;
All their powers consecrated
  To thy service may men bring,
And of loyal speech and action
  Make to thee an offering.

5

Jesus, Lord, thou mighty Victor,
  Thy all-glorious name we praise:
Thou art with us, God almighty;
  'Midst our ranks thy shout we raise:
Where thy kingly war-cry soundeth,
  Lead us on through all our days.

F. W. NEWMAN

SAINTS, MARTYRS, AND DOCTORS
OF THE CHURCH OF ENGLAND

HYMN 574 Westminster Abbey
KEY B♭

Adapted from an anthem by
H. Purcell, 1658-95

[musical notation in tonic sol-fa]

1
GOD, whose city's sure foundation
    Stands upon his holy hill,
By his mighty inspiration
    Chose of old and chooseth still
Men of every race and nation
    His good pleasure to fulfil.

2
Here in England through the ages,
    While the Christian years went by,
Saints, confessors, martyrs, sages,
    Strong to live and strong to die,
Wrote their names upon the pages
    Of God's blessèd company.

3
Some there were like lamps of learning
    Shining in a faithless night,
Some on fire with love, and burning
    With a flaming zeal for right,
Some by simple goodness turning
    Souls from darkness unto light.

4
As we now with high thanksgiving
    Their triumphant names record,
Grant that we, like them, believing
    In the promise of thy word,
May, like them, in all good living
    Praise and magnify the Lord.

C. A. ALINGTON

ST. DAVID, PATRON OF WALES

Hymn 575 Claudius
KEY C

Adapted from a song by
G. W. Fink (1783–1846)

[Sol-fa notation]

By permission of the Royal School of Church Music

1
WE praise thy name, all holy Lord,
  For him, the beacon-light
That shone beside our western sea
  Through mists of ancient night;
Who sent to Ireland's fainting Church
  New tidings of thy word:
For David, prince of Cambrian saints,
  We praise thee, holy Lord.

2
For all the saintly band whose prayers
  Still gird our land about,
Of whom, lest men disdain their praise,
  The voiceless stones cry out;
Our hills and vales on every hand
  Their names and deeds record:
For these, thy ancient hero-host,
  We praise thee, holy Lord.

3
Grant us but half their burning zeal,
  But half their iron faith,
But half their charity of heart,
  And fortitude to death;
That we with them and all thy saints
  May in thy truth accord,
And ever in thy holy Church
  May praise thee, holy Lord.

E. J. NEWELL

For ST. PATRICK, PATRON OF IRELAND, *see*

162 I bind unto myself to-day.

585

ST. NICOLAS, PATRON OF CHILDREN AND SAILORS

Hymn 576 St. Nicolas   Sir S. H. Nicholson, 1875–1947

KEY **C**

By permission of the Royal School of Church Music

1
FAR-SHINING names from age to age
Enrich the Church's heritage,
The loyal liegemen of the Lord,
Who found in thee their great reward.

2
One name from that immortal throng
Inspires to-day our festal song:
In loving memory we hold
The bishop and the saint of old,

3
Who, far away in eastern land,
With gentle heart and open hand
Loved all things living, shared his store
With homeless men who sought his door.

4
Friend of the poor, no less was he
The guardian saint of those at sea;
O'er wave-swept rock and sheltered bay
God's churches bear his name to-day.

5
And his the skill, the tender art
That wins the trustful, child-like heart:
His dearest title to the end
'Saint Nicolas, the children's friend.'

6
To thee, O Lord, the praise be given
For this true citizen of heaven:
A star above the stormy sea
To lead the wanderer home to thee.

W. H. SAVILE

For ST. CECILIA, PATRONESS OF MUSIC, *see*
246 Angel-voices, ever singing.

NATIONAL

Hymn 577 National Anthem   *Thesaurus Musicus, c.* 1743

KEY **G**

586

NATIONAL

```
{| f :f :f  | f :-.m:r  | m :f.m:r.d | m  :-.f :s  || l.f:m:r   | d :-:- |
 | t,:r :t, | t,:-.d:t, | d :t,.d:s, | d  :-.t,:d  || d.r:d :t, | d :-:- |
 | s :s :s  | s :-.s:s  | s :s  :s   | s  :-.f :m  || f.l:s :s.f| m :-:- |
 | s,:t,:r  | s,:-.d:s, | d :r.d:t,.l,| s,.f,:m,.r,:d,| f, :s,:s, | d,:-:- |}
```

mf GOD save our gracious Queen,
Long live our noble Queen,
   God save the Queen.
Send her victorious,
Happy and glorious,
Long to reign over us:
   God save the Queen.

2*
O Lord our God, arise,
Scatter our enemies,
   And make them fall;
Confound their politics,
Frustrate their knavish tricks;
On thee our hopes we fix:
   God save us all.

3
Thy choicest gifts in store
On her be pleased to pour,
   Long may she reign.
May she defend our laws,
And ever give us cause
To sing with heart and voice,
   God save the Queen.

ANON.

HYMN 578   Jerusalem   Sir C. H. H. Parry, 1848–1918

KEY **D**

Slow but with animation

```
{|    |    |    |  :.d :m .s | l :-.d':l .s,f | s :-: l .s,f }
 3 bars rest         And did those feet   in an-cient time    Walk up-on

{| s .m : r :d | l, :-.d :m .s | l :-.d': t .l,s }
   Eng-land's moun-tains green? And was the  ho - ly Lamb of

{| l :-.l :t .m | s .fe :m :r | s :-.r :r .m }
   God    On Eng-land's plea-sant pas-tures seen?  And did the

{| f :-.l :s .,r | f :-.r :f .s | l :-.d': ta .s }
   coun - te-nance di - vine   Shine forth up - on   our cloud-ed

{| l :- .f : l .d' | r' ., d' : t : t ., l }
   bills?    And  was Je - ru - sa - lem  build - ed

{| s :-.s :d'.l | s .,l :m :r | d :-: : |}
   here  A-mong those dark sa - tan - ic  mills?  2 bars rest
```

NATIONAL

Hymn 578 (continued)

{| :d |m.s | l:-.d¹:l.s,f | s:- :l.s,f }
Bring me my bow of burn-ing gold! Bring me my

{| s.m:r:d | l,:-.d:m.s | l:d¹:t.l,s }
ar-rows of de-sire! Bring me my spear! O clouds, un-

{| l:-.l:t.m | s.,fe:m:r | s:-.r:r.m }
fold! Bring me my cha-ri-ot of fire! I will not

{| f:-.l:s.,r | f:-.r:f.s | l:d¹:ta.s }
cease from men-tal fight, Nor shall my sword sleep in my

allargando   *ff*   *rit.*
{| l:-.f:l.d¹ | r¹:-.d¹:t.,l | s:-.s:d¹.l }
hand. Till we have built Je-ru-sa-lem In Eng-land's

{| s.l:m:r | d:- :- | - : || }
green and plea-sant land.

By permission of the Executors of the late Sir C. H. H. Parry

WILLIAM BLAKE

Hymn 579 Thaxted

G. Holst, 1874–1934

KEY C

UNISON

{:m.s| l:-.d¹:t.,s |d¹.r¹:d¹:t |l.t:l:s | m:— ||m.s| l:-.d¹:t.,s}

{|d¹.r¹:m¹:m¹|m¹.r¹:d¹:r¹|d¹:—||s.m|r:-.r:d.m|r:s:s.m|r:-.r:m.s|l:—||}

{:l.t| d¹.,d¹: t:l |s:d¹:m | r.d:r:m | s:— || m.s| l:-.d¹:t.,s}

{|d¹.r¹:d¹:t|l.t:l:s|m:—||m.s|l:-.d¹:t.,s|d¹.r¹:m¹:m¹|m¹.r¹:d¹:r¹|d¹:—||}

I VOW to thee, my country, all earthly things above,
Entire and whole and perfect, the service of my love:
The love that asks no question, the love that stands the test,
That lays upon the altar the dearest and the best;
The love that never falters, the love that pays the price,
The love that makes undaunted the final sacrifice.

2

And there's another country, I've heard of long ago,
Most dear to them that love her, most great to them that know;
We may not count her armies, we may not see her King;
Her fortress is a faithful heart, her pride is suffering;
And soul by soul and silently her shining bounds increase,
And her ways are ways of gentleness and all her paths are peace.

SIR CECIL SPRING-RICE

NATIONAL

Hymn 580 Genevan Psalm xii   L. Bourgeois, c. 1500–61

KEY **F**

PART 1
THE Queen, O God, her heart to thee upraiseth;
   With her the nation bows before thy face;
With high thanksgiving thee thy glad Church praiseth,
   Our strength thy spirit, our trust and hope thy grace.

2

Unto great honour, glory undeservèd,
   Hast thou exalted us, and drawn thee nigh;
Nor, from thy judgements when our feet had swervèd,
   Didst thou forsake, nor leave us, Lord most high.

PART 2
3

In thee our fathers trusted and were savèd,
   In thee destroyèd thrones of tyrants proud;
From ancient bondage freed the poor enslavèd;
   To sow thy truth poured out their saintly blood.

4

Unto our minds give freedom and uprightness;
   Let strength and courage lead o'er land and wave;
To our souls' armour grant celestial brightness,
   Joy to our hearts, and faith beyond the grave.

5

Our plenteous nation still in power extending,
   Increase our joy, uphold us by thy word;
Beauty and wisdom all our ways attending,
   Good will to man and peace through Christ our Lord.

Yattendon Hymnal Based on F. R. TAILOUR (1615)

Alternative Tune, St. Osyth, 550

NATIONAL

Hymn 581 Aberdeen
Melody in *Chalmers' Collection* (Aberdeen, *c.* 1749)

KEY **G**

{ :d | r :m | s₁ :d | r :t₁ | d ‖ m | r :s | f :m | r :— | — ‖
  :s₁ | s₁ :s₁ | s₁ :m₁ | l₁ :s₁ | s₁ ‖ s₁ | s₁ :s₁ | l₁ :s₁ | s₁ :— | — ‖
  :m | t₁ :d | r :m | f :r | m ‖ d | t₁ :d | d :d | t₁ :— | — ‖
  :d | s₁ :d | t₁ :l₁ | f₁ :s₁ | d₁ ‖ d | s₁ :m₁ | f₁ :d | s₁ :— | — ‖ }

{ :d | r :m | f :m | r :d | t₁ ‖ s₁ | l₁ :f | m :r | d :— | — ‖
  :m₁ | s₁ :s₁ | l₁ :s₁ | s₁ :s₁.fe₁ | s₁ ‖ s₁ | f₁ :l₁ | s₁ :—.f₁ | m₁ :— | — ‖
  :d | t₁ :d | d :d | r :r | r ‖ d | d :d | d :t₁ | d :— | — ‖
  :d | s₁ :d₁ | f₁ :d | t₁ :l₁ | s₁ ‖ m₁ | f₁ :f₁ | s₁ :s₁ | d₁ :— | — ‖ }

LORD, while for all mankind we pray
  Of every clime and coast,
O hear us for our native land,
  The land we love the most.

2

O guard our shores from every foe,
  With peace our borders bless;
With prosperous times our cities crown,
  Our fields with plenteousness.

3

Unite us in the sacred love
  Of knowledge, truth, and thee;
And let our hills and valleys shout
  The songs of liberty.

4

Lord of the nations, thus to thee
  Our country we commend;
Be thou her refuge and her trust,
  Her everlasting friend.

J. R. WREFORD

Hymn 582 Wareham
W. Knapp, 1698–1768

KEY **A**   E.t.

{ :d | d :t₁ :l₁ | s₁ :— :d | r :d :t₁ | d :— ‖ r s | l₁ :s :f
  :m₁ | f₁ :— :f₁ | s₁ :— :s₁ | l₁ :s₁ :s₁ | s₁ :— ‖ s₁d | d :— :t₁
  :s₁ | s₁ :— :l₁.t₁ | d :— :d | f :m :r | m :— ‖ r s | f :s :s
  :d₁ | r₁ :— :r₁ | m₁ :— :m₁ | f₁ :s₁ :s₁ | d :— ‖ t₁m | f :m :r }

f. **A.**

{ m :f :s | f :m :r | d :— ‖ ᵈs₁ | l₁ :s₁ :l₁.t₁ | d :— :t₁
  d :— :d | l₁ :d :t₁ | d :— ‖ ᶠd₁ | d₁ :— :f₁ | m₁ :s₁ :—
  s :l :s | d :s :f | m :— ‖ ᶠd | d :— :f₁ | s₁ :— :r
  d :l₁ :m₁ | f₁ :s₁ :s₁ | d :— ‖ ¹m₁ | f₁ :m₁ :r₁ | d₁ :m₁ :s₁ }

{ d :— :r | m :— ‖ r.m f :m :r | d :t₁ :d | r :d :t₁ | d :—
  m₁ :— :s₁ | s₁ :— ‖ s₁ f₁ :s₁ :l₁ | s₁ :f₁ :m₁ | l₁ :s₁ :f₁ | m₁ :—
  d :— :t₁ | d :— ‖ r d :— :l₁.t₁ | d :r :s₁ | l₁ :m :r | d :—
  l₁ :— :s₁ | d :— ‖ t₁ l₁ :s₁ :f₁ | m₁ :r₁ :d₁ | f₁ :s₁ :s₁ | d₁ :— }

590

NATIONAL

REJOICE, O land, in God thy might;
His will obey, him serve aright;
For thee the saints uplift their voice:
Fear not, O land, in God rejoice.

2

Glad shalt thou be, with blessing crowned,
With joy and peace thou shalt abound;
Yea, love with thee shall make his home
Until thou see God's Kingdom come.

3

He shall forgive thy sins untold:
Remember thou his love of old;
Walk in his way, his word adore,
And keep his truth for evermore.

Yattendon Hymnal

HYMN 583 Finnart
K. G. Finlay

KEY **D**

{:d |m :r :d |s :—:l |d :—:r |m:— ||m |s :l :s |d¹:—:r¹ |l :—:s |l:—||
 :s₁ |t₁:—:d |d :—:d |l₁:—:t₁|d:— ||d |r :—:s |f :m :r |m :—:m.r|d:—||
 :m |s :f :m |d¹:t :l |s :—:f |s:— ||l |r¹:—:r¹ |d¹:—:s |d¹:t :t |l:—||
 :d |s₁:—:l₁|m₁:—:f₁ |f :m :r |d:— ||d |t₁:—:t₁|l₁:—:t₁ |d.r:m :m|f:—||

{:l |d¹:—:d¹|l :s :l |d¹:—:l |m :r ||d |r :m :s |l :s :m |r :—:d |d:—||
 :d |m :r :d |r :—:m |d :—:d |t₁:— ||d |t₁:d :r |m :— :d |d :t₁:d|d:—||
 :f |s :f :m |r :—:d |f :m :r |s :— ||s |t :l :t |d¹:—.t:d¹|l :f :—|m:—||
 :f |d :—:m |t₁:—:d |l₁:s₁:f₁|s₁:— ||m |s :—:f |m :— :l₁ |f₁:s₁:—|d:—||

ALMIGHTY Father, who dost give
The gift of life to all who live,
Look down on all earth's sin and strife
And lift us to a nobler life.

2

Lift up our hearts, O King of Kings,
To brighten hopes and kindlier things.
To visions of a larger good,
And holier dreams of brotherhood.

3

The world is weary of its pain,
Of selfish greed and fruitless gain,
Of tarnished honour, falsely strong,
And all its ancient deeds of wrong.

4

Hear thou the prayer thy servants pray,
Uprising from all lands to-day,
And, o'er the vanquished powers of sin,
O bring thy great salvation in!

BISHOP J. H. B. MASTERMAN

NATIONAL

Hymn 584   FIRST TUNE

KEY A♭   Julius   Martin Shaw

```
{ :m  |r  :d  |r  :s, |d  :t, |l, :t, |s, :— |— |  ‖ s, |l, :t, 
  :s, |s, :d  |s, :s, |s, :s, |s, :fe, |s, :— |— |     r, |m, :s, 
  :d  |r  :m  |t, :t, |d  :r  |m  :r  |t, :— |— |     t, |d  :r 
  :d  |t, :l, |s, :f, |m, :r, |d, :r, |s, :— |— |     s, |s, :f, }

{ |d  :r  |m  :d  |s  :m  |r  :— |— |  ‖ f  |m  :r  |m  :t, |d  :d  |r :m
  |l, :t, |d  :d  |r  :d  |l, :— |t, |     d  |d  :t, |m, :se, |l, :l, |l, :s,
  |s  :f  |m  :m  |r  :s  |s  :fe |s  |     f  |d  :r  |t, :m  |m  :m  |l, :d
  |m, :r, |d, :l, |t, :d  |r  :— |s, |     l, |l, :t, |se, :m, |l, :s, |f, :m, }

{ |l, :— |— |  ‖ s, |l, :t, |d  :r  |m  :s  |m  :r  |d  :— |— | ‖
  |f, :— |— |     r, |m, :f, |m, :s, |d  :t, |l, :t, |s, :— |— |
  |d  :— |— |     t, |d  :r  |m  :r  |s  :m  |d  :f  |m  :— |— |
  |f, :— |— |     f, |m, :r, |l, :t, |d  :m, |f, :s, |d  :— |— | }
```

By permission of the Royal School of Church Music

SECOND TUNE

KEY A♭   Ellers   E. J. Hopkins, 1818–1901

```
{ s, :s,.l, |s, :d  |d.t, :d.r |m :— ‖ d :d.r |d :m
  m, :f,.f, |m, :l, |s,.l, :s,.f, |m, :— |  l, :s,.se, |l, :l,
  d  :t,.t, |d :r  |m.f :m.r |d :— |  f :m.r |m :s
  d, :r,.r, |m, :f, |s,.s, :l,.t, |d :— |  d :d.t, |l, :d, }

{ m.r :m.fe |s :— ‖ s :d.d |f :f |f.r :m.f
  t,.l, :t,.d |t, :— |  d :d.d |t, :l, |s,.s, :se,.l,
  s.fe :s.r |r :— |  d :s.s |f :—.m |r.r :r.d
  r,.d :t,.l, |s, :— |  m, :m.m |r :d |t,.t, :t,.l, }

{ m :— |d :r.d |d :l, |s,.s, :l,.s, |s, :—  ‖
  t, :— |l, :s,.s, |d, :—.r, |m,.m, :f,.f, |m, :—
  t, :— |d :ta,.ta, |l, :d |d.d :t,.t, |d :—
  se, :— |l, :m,.m, |f, :f, |s,.s, :s,.s, |d, :— }
```

592

NATIONAL

FOR THE FALLEN

mf   O VALIANT hearts, who to your glory came
     Through dust of conflict and through battle flame;
     Tranquil you lie, your knightly virtue proved,
     Your memory hallowed in the land you loved.

2*

f   Proudly you gathered, rank on rank, to war,
    As who had heard God's message from afar;
mf All you had hoped for, all you had, you gave
    To save mankind—yourselves you scorned to save.

3*

f   Splendid you passed, the great surrender made,
    Into the light that never more shall fade;
mf Deep your contentment in that blest abode,
    Who wait the last clear trumpet-call of God.

4

    Long years ago, as earth lay dark and still,
    Rose a loud cry upon a lonely hill,
    While in the frailty of our human clay
    Christ, our Redeemer, passed the self-same way.

5

p   Still stands his Cross from that dread hour to this,
    Like some bright star above the dark abyss;
    Still, through the veil, the Victor's pitying eyes
    Look down to bless our lesser Calvaries.

6

    These were his servants, in his steps they trod,
    Following through death the martyred Son of God:
f   Victor he rose; victorious too shall rise
    They who have drunk his cup of sacrifice.

7

    O risen Lord, O Shepherd of our dead,
    Whose Cross has bought them and whose staff has led,
    In glorious hope their proud and sorrowing land
mf Commits her children to thy gracious hand.

                              Sir John S. Arkwright

NATIONAL

HYMN 585 Emmaus   Greville Cooke

KEY E♭

FOR THE FALLEN

O LORD of Life, whose power sustains
    The world unseen no less than this—
One family in him who reigns,
    Triumphant over death, in bliss;
To thee with thankfulness we pray
For all our valiant dead to-day.

2

As nature's healing through the years
    Reclothes the stricken battle-fields;
So mercy gives us joy for tears,
    And grief to proud remembrance yields,
And mindful hearts are glad to keep
A tryst of love with them that sleep.

3

Not names engraved in marble make
    The best memorials of the dead,
But burdens shouldered for their sake
    And tasks completed in their stead;
A braver faith and stronger prayers,
Devouter worship, nobler cares.

NATIONAL

4

O help us in the silence, Lord,
  To hear the whispered call of love,
And day by day thy strength afford
  Our work to do, our faith to prove.
So be thy blessing richly shed
On our communion with our dead.

ARCHBISHOP J. R. DARBYSHIRE

Alternative Tune, Wrestling Jacob, 343

LITANIES
LITANY FOR LENT

HYMN **586** Attende, Domine Mode v
KEY **D**

Attende, Domine

Chorus   *Fine*

{| d m s s — s d¹ t s l s — | d¹ s r f s m m r d — ||

Hear-ken, O Lord, have mer-cy up-on us, for we have sin-ned a-gainst thee.

{| m m d r r m l l s l f m m — }

1. To thee, Re-deem-er, King of high-est hea-ven,
2. Head of the Cor-ner, right hand of the Fa-ther,
3. Lord, we be-seech thee, from thy throne of glo-ry
4. All our mis-do-ings now we lay be-fore thee,
5. Guilt-less, a cap-tive tak-en un-re-sis-ting,

{| s s s s s m f s l s f m r — }

1. Lift we our eyes in grief and deep a-base-ment;
2. Way of sal-va-tion, gate of life e-ter-nal,
3. Bow down thine ear to hear our cry of sor-row,
4. Un-veil with con-trite heart each guil-ty se-cret:
5. By false ac-cus-ers brought to con-dem-na-tion,

Repeat the refrain

{| s l t d¹ s s r f m m r d — ||

1. Lis-ten, O Sa-viour, to our sup-pli-ca-tions.
2. Wash thou a-way the stain of our of-fen-ces.
3. Look down in mer-cy on our sore trans-gres-sions.
4. Sa-viour, in pi-ty grant us thy for-give-ness.
5. Save, Lord, and help the souls thou hast re-deem-èd.

Tr. COMPILERS

595

LITANIES

LITANY OF THE PASSION

HYMN 587   Litany of the Passion   Sir S. H. Nicholson, 1875–1947
KEY F

mf GOD the Father, God the Son,
    God the Spirit, Three in One,
    Hear us from thy heavenly throne;
        Spare us, holy Trinity.

2
Jesu, who for us didst bear
Scorn and sorrow, toil and care,
Hearken to our lowly prayer,
    We beseech thee, Jesu.

3
p By the hour of agony
Spent while thine apostles three
Slumbered in Gethsemane,
    Hear us, holy Jesu.

4
Jesu, by thy friend betrayed,
Jesu, sport for sinners made,
Jesu, in mock-robes arrayed,
    Hear us, holy Jesu.

5
By the scourging meekly borne,
By the reed and crown of thorn,
By the malice and the scorn,
    Hear us, holy Jesu.

6
mf By the outcry of the Jews,
When a murderer they would choose
And the Prince of Life refuse,
    Hear us, holy Jesu.

7
By the horror of that cry,
'Crucify him, crucify!'
By thy going forth to die,
    Hear us, holy Jesu.

8
p By thy nailing to the Tree,
By the title over thee,
By the gloom of Calvary,
    Hear us, holy Jesu.

9
By thy seven words then said,
By the bowing of thy head,
By thy numbering with the dead.
    Hear us, holy Jesu.

10
mf Jesu, who for us hast died
And, for ever glorified,
Reignest at the Father's side,
    Hear us, holy Jesu.

COMPILERS and others

LITANIES

FOR ROGATIONTIDE OR OTHER OCCASIONS

HYMN 588 Ach Gott und Herr   *Neu-Leipziger Gesangbuch*, 1682

KEY **A**

ὑπὲρ τῆς ἄνωθεν εἰρήνης

THE GREAT COLLECT

LORD, to our humble prayers attend,
Let thou thy peace from heaven descend,
And to our souls salvation send:
    Have mercy, Lord, upon us.

2

Rule in our hearts, thou Prince of Peace,
The welfare of thy Church increase,
And bid all strife and discord cease:
    Have mercy, Lord, upon us.

3

To all who meet for worship here
Do thou in faithfulness draw near;
Inspire with faith and godly fear:
    Have mercy, Lord, upon us.

4

O let thy priests be clothed with might,
To rule within thy Church aright,
That they may serve as in thy sight:
    Have mercy, Lord, upon us.

5

The sovereign ruler of our land
Protect by thine almighty hand,
And all around the throne who stand:
    Have mercy, Lord, upon us.

6

Let clouds and sunshine bless the earth,
Give flowers and fruits a timely birth,
Our harvest crown with peaceful mirth:
    Have mercy, Lord, upon us.

7

Let voyagers by land and sea
In danger's hour in safety be;
The suffering and the captive free:
    Have mercy, Lord, upon us.

8

Around us let thine arm be cast,
Till wrath and danger are o'erpast
And tribulation's bitter blast:
    Have mercy, Lord, upon us.

Tr. J. BROWNLIE

LITANIES

AN EVENING LITANY

Hymn 589 Es ist kein Tag J. Meyer, *Seelenfreud*, 1692
KEY D

By permission of the English Hymnal Co., Ltd.

ἀντιλαβοῦ, σῶσον, ἐλέησον

LITANY OF THE DEACON

1
O GOD of grace, thy mercy send;
Let thy protecting arm defend;
Save us and keep us to the end:
  Have mercy, Lord.

2
And through the coming hours of night
Fill us, we pray, with holy light;
Keep us all sinless in thy sight:
  Grant this, O Lord.

3
May some bright messenger abide
For ever by thy servants' side,
A faithful guardian and our guide:
  Grant this, O Lord.

4
From every sin in mercy free;
Let heart and conscience stainless be,
That we may live henceforth for thee:
  Grant this, O Lord.

5
We would not be by care opprest,
But in thy love and wisdom rest;
Give what thou seest to be best:
  Grant this, O Lord.

6
While we of every sin repent,
Let our remaining years be spent
In holiness and sweet content:
  Grant this, O Lord.

7
And when the end of life is near,
May we, unshamed and void of fear,
Wait for the judgement to appear:
  Grant this, O Lord.

Tr. J. BROWNLIE

LITANY FOR CHILDREN

Hymn 590 Antiphoner *Rheims-Cambrai Antiphoner*, 1871
KEY E♭

LITANIES

```
{| s :-:d' | d':t :l  | s :-:f  | m:-:-  || s :-:d  | f:m :r  | m :r :-  | d:-:- ||
 | t₁:-:m  | m :-:f  | s:d :r  | d:-:-  || d:t₁:l₁ | r:d :r  | d :-:t₁  | d:-:- ||
 | m :-:s  | l :t :d'| d':s :l | l:-:-  || s :-:f  | l :-:l  | s :l :r  | m:-:- ||
 | m :-:d  | l :s :f | m :-:r  | l:-:-  || m :-:f  | r:l₁:f₁ | m₁:f₁:s₁ | d:-:- ||}
```

PART 1

1
GOD the Father, God the Son.
God the Spirit, Three in One,
Hear us from thy heavenly throne;
    Spare us, holy Trinity.

2
Jesu, Saviour meek and mild,
Once for us a little Child
Born of Mary undefiled,
    Hear us, holy Jesu.

3
Jesu, by that blessèd Maid
In thy swaddling-clothes arrayed,
And within a manger laid,
    Hear us, holy Jesu.

4
Jesu, at whose infant feet,
Bending low in worship meet,
Shepherds knelt their Lord to greet,
    Hear us, holy Jesu.

5
Jesu, to thy Temple brought,
Whom the ancient Simeon sought
By thy Holy Spirit taught,
    Hear us, holy Jesu.

6
Jesu, unto whom of yore
Wise men, hasting to adore,
Gold and myrrh and incense bore,
    Hear us, holy Jesu.

7
Jesu, who wast driven to flee
From king Herod's cruelty,
When he sought to murder thee,
    Hear us, holy Jesu.

8
Jesu, whom thy Mother found
'Mid the doctors sitting round,
Marvelling at thy words profound,
    Hear us, holy Jesu.

PART 2

9
From all pride and vain conceit,
From all spite and angry heat,
From all lying and deceit,
    Save us, holy Jesu.

10
From all sloth and idleness,
From hard hearts and selfishness,
From all lust and greediness,
    Save us, holy Jesu.

11
From refusing to obey,
From the love of our own way,
From forgetfulness to pray,
    Save us, holy Jesu.

PART 3

12
By thy birth and early years,
By thine infant wants and fears,
By thy sorrows and thy tears,
    Save us, holy Jesu.

13
By thy pattern bright and pure,
By the pains thou didst endure
Our salvation to procure,
    Save us, holy Jesu.

14
By thy wounds and thorn-crowned head,
By thy Blood for sinners shed,
By thy rising from the dead,
    Save us, holy Jesu.

15
By thy mercies infinite,
By thine all-surpassing might,
By thy glory in the height,
    Save us, holy Jesu.

COMPILERS and others

PROCESSIONAL
CHRISTMAS

HYMN 591 Divinum mysterium   P. Nyland, *Piae Cantiones*, 1582

KEY **E** UNISON

ALTERNATIVE VERSION
FOR VERSES 4 AND 7

KEY **E**

4 O ye heights of heaven adore him; Angel hosts, his praises sing, Powers, dominions, virgins, bow before him. And ex-tol our God and King: Let no tongue on earth be silent, Every voice in concert ringing, Evermore and evermore.

7 Now let old and young men's voices Join with boys' thy name to sing, Ma-trons, little maidens. In glad chorus answering; Let their guileless songs re-ech-o, And the heart its praises bring, Evermore and evermore.

Corde natus ex Parentis

OF the Father's love begotten
Ere the worlds began to be,
He is Alpha and Omega,
He the source, the ending he,
Of the things that are, that have been,
And that future years shall see,
Evermore and evermore.

At his word they were created;
He commanded; it was done:
Heaven and earth and depths of ocean
In their threefold order one;
All that grows beneath the shining
Of the light of moon and sun,
Evermore and evermore.

PROCESSIONAL—CHRISTMAS

3
O that birth for ever blessèd!
 When the Virgin, full of grace,
By the Holy Ghost conceiving,
 Bare the Saviour of our race,
And the Babe, the world's Redeemer,
First revealed his sacred face,
 Evermore and evermore.

4
O ye heights of heaven, adore him;
 Angel-hosts, his praises sing;
Powers, dominions, bow before him,
 And extol our God and King:
Let no tongue on earth be silent,
Every voice in concert ring,
 Evermore and evermore.

5
This is he whom seers and sages
 Sang of old with one accord;
Whom the writings of the Prophets
 Promised in their faithful word;
Now he shines, the long-expected:
Let creation praise its Lord,
 Evermore and evermore.

6*
Hail, thou Judge of souls departed!
 Hail, thou King of them that live!
On the Father's throne exalted
 None in might with thee may strive;
Who at last in judgement coming
Sinners from thy face shalt drive,
 Evermore and evermore.

7
Now let old and young men's voices
 Join with boys' thy name to sing,
Matrons, virgins, little maidens
 In glad chorus answering;
Let their guileless songs re-echo,
And the heart its praises bring,
 Evermore and evermore.

8
Christ, to thee, with God the Father,
 And, O Holy Ghost, to thee,
Hymn and chant and high thanksgiving
 And unwearied praises be,
Honour, glory, and dominion,
And eternal victory,
 Evermore and evermore.

PRUDENTIUS *Tr.* J. M. Neale,
Sir H. W. Baker, and others

At the entrance into the Chancel:

℣. Blessed is he that cometh in the name of the Lord.
℟. God is the Lord who hath shewed us light.

HYMN 592 Oxford New   Isaac Smith's *Collection, c.* 1770

HIGH let us swell our tuneful notes,
 And join the angelic throng,
For angels no such love have known
 To wake a cheerful song.

2
Good will to sinful men is shown,
 And peace on earth is given:
For, lo, the incarnate Saviour comes
 With grace and truth from heaven.

3
Justice and peace with sweet accord
 His rising beams adorn;
Let heaven and earth in concert join:
 To us a Child is born!

P. DODDRIDGE

PROCESSIONAL—CHRISTMAS

HYMN 593 Adeste fideles Probably by J. F. Wade, c. 1711–86

KEY **G**

(VERSES 1–4)   *Adeste fideles*

1. O come, all ye faithful, Joyful and triumphant, O come ye, O come ye to Bethlehem; Come and behold him, Born, the King of angels: O come, let us adore him, O come, let us adore him, O come, let us adore him, Christ the Lord!

2. God of God, Light of Light, Lo, he abhors not the Virgin's womb; Very God, Begotten, not created: O come, let us adore him, ...

3. See how the shepherds Summoned to his cradle, Leaving their flocks, draw nigh to gaze; We too will thither Bend our joyful footsteps: O come, let us adore him, ...

4. Lo, star-led chieftains, Magi, Christ adoring, Offer him incense, gold, and myrrh: We to the Christ-child Bring our hearts' oblations: O come, let us adore him, ...

DESCANT (VERSES 5–7)

5. Child, for us sinners Poor and in the manger,
6. Sing, choirs of angels, Sing in exultation,
7. Yea, Lord, we greet thee, Born this happy morning;

602

PROCESSIONAL—CHRISTMAS

(Tonic Sol-fa notation, D.t. / f.G.)

5. Fain we embrace thee with love and awe; Who would not love thee,
6. Sing, all ye citizens of heaven above: Loving us so dearly?
7. Jesu, to thee.. be.. glory given: 'Glory to God...,
   Father In...the Now in flesh appearing: Word of the highest:'

O come, O come, let us adore him, O come, let us adore him, O come, let us adore him, Christ the Lord!

18th cent. *Tr.* F. OAKELEY,
W. T. BROOKE, and others

KEY **G**   *At the entrance into the Chancel:*

℣. Blessed is he that cometh in the name of the Lord.

℟. God is the Lord who hath shewed us light.

603

PROCESSIONAL—CHRISTMAS

Hymn 594 Shepherds in the field

French or Flemish Melody
Harmonized by Charles Wood

KEY **G**

By permission of A. R. Mowbray & Co., Ltd.

SHEPHERDS, in the field abiding,
  Tell us, when the seraph bright
Greeted you with wondrous tiding,
  What ye saw and heard that night:
    Gloria in excelsis Deo.

2
We beheld (it is no fable)
  God incarnate, King of bliss,
Swathed and cradled in a stable,
  And the angel-strain was this:
    Gloria in excelsis Deo.

3
Quiristers on high were singing
  Jesus and his Virgin-birth;
Heavenly bells the while a-ringing
  'Peace, goodwill to men on earth:'
    Gloria in excelsis Deo.

4
Thanks, good herdmen; true your story;
  Have with you to Bethlehem:
Angels hymn the King of Glory;
  Carol we with you and them:
    Gloria in excelsis Deo.

G. R. WOODWARD

PROCESSIONAL
EPIPHANY

HYMN 595 Evelyns

W. H. Monk, 1823–89

KEY E♭

[musical notation in tonic sol-fa]

1
FROM the eastern mountains
  Pressing on they come,
Wise men in their wisdom,
  To his humble home;
Stirred by deep devotion,
  Hasting from afar,
Ever journeying onward,
  Guided by a star.

2
There their Lord and Saviour
  Meek and lowly lay,
Wondrous Light that led them
  Onward on their way,
Ever now to lighten
  Nations from afar,
As they journey homeward
  By that guiding star.

3
Thou who in a manger
  Once hast lowly lain,
Who dost now in glory
  O'er all kingdoms reign,
Gather in the heathen,
  Who in lands afar
Ne'er have seen the brightness
  Of thy guiding star.

4*
Gather in the outcasts,
  All who've gone astray;
Throw thy radiance o'er them.
  Guide them on their way:
Those who never knew thee,
  Those who've wandered far,
Guide them by the brightness
  Of thy guiding star.

5
Onward through the darkness
  Of the lonely night,
Shining still before them
  With thy kindly light,
Guide them, Jew and Gentile,
  Homeward from afar,
Young and old together,
  By thy guiding star.

6*
Until every nation,
  Whether bond or free,
'Neath thy star-lit banner,
  Jesu, follow thee
O'er the distant mountains
  To that heavenly home,
Where nor sin nor sorrow
  Evermore shall come.

G. THRING

KEY **F**

At the entrance into the Chancel:

℣. All nations whom thou hast made,
℟. Shall come and worship thee, O Lord.

605

PROCESSIONAL—EPIPHANY

Hymn 596 Quem pastores
KEY F *German Medieval Melody*

By permission of the Oxford University Press

Quem pastores laudavere

1
THOU whom shepherds worshipped, hear-
Angels tell their tidings cheering,   [ing_
'Sirs, away with doubt and fearing!
Christ the King is born for all;'

2
Thou to whom came wise men faring
Gold and myrrh and incense bearing,
Heartfelt homage thus declaring
To the King that's born for all:

3
Bending low in adoration
Thee we greet, for our salvation
Given by wondrous Incarnation,
King of Glory born for all.

Tr. C. S. PHILLIPS

PALM SUNDAY

Hymn 597 St. Theodulph
KEY C *M. Teschner (1615)*

Gloria, laus et honor

1
ALL glory, laud, and honour
To thee, Redeemer, King,
To whom the lips of children
Made sweet Hosannas ring.

2
Thou art the King of Israel,
Thou David's royal Son,
Who in the Lord's name comest,
The King and blessèd one.
All glory, etc.

PROCESSIONAL—PALM SUNDAY

3
The company of angels
  Are praising thee on high,
And mortal men and all things
  Created make reply.
    All glory, etc.

4
The people of the Hebrews
  With palms before thee went:
Our praise and prayer and anthems
  Before thee we present.
    All glory, etc.

5
To thee before thy Passion
  They sang their hymns of praise:
To thee the now high exalted
  Our melody we raise.
    All glory, etc.

6
Thou didst accept their praises,
  Accept the prayers we bring,
Who in all good delightest,
  Thou good and gracious King.
    All glory, etc.

7*
Thy sorrow and thy triumph
  Grant us, O Christ, to share,
That to the holy city
  Together we may fare.
    All glory, etc.

8*
For homage may we bring thee
  Our victory o'er the foe,
That in the Conqueror's triumph
  This strain may ever flow:
    All glory, etc.

ST. THEODULPH OF ORLEANS Tr. J. M. Neale‡

HYMN 598 Gloria, laus et honor Mode

KEY D

Gloria, laus et honor

The refrain is first sung by solo voices, then repeated by chorus

1 Glo - ry and hon-our and laud be to thee, Christ, King and Re-deem - er,

1 As when the chil - dren of old sang their Ho-san - nas of praise.

SOLO VOICES

2 Is - ra - el's Mon-arch art thou, the glo - ri-ous off-spring of Da - vid,
3 'Glo - ry to thee in the height,' the hea-ven-ly arm - ies are sing-ing,
4 Bear-ing their branch-es of palm, the He - brews crowd-ed to greet thee;
5 They came to ut - ter thy praise as thou went-est thy way to thy Pas-sion;
6 Thou didst re - joice in their praise: may ours too by thee be ac-cept-ed,

Repeat the refrain

2 Thou that ap-proach-est as King, blest in the name of the Lord.
3 'Glo - ry to thee up-on earth,' men and cre - a - tion re - ply.
4 We with our prayers and our hymns now to thy pre - sence draw nigh.
5 We to the King on his throne lift up our ju - bi - lant hymn.
6 Gra-cious and mer - ci - ful King, who in all good-ness art pleased.

ST. THEODULPH OF ORLEANS
Tr. J. M. Neale and Compilers

KEY G

At the entrance into the Chancel:

℣. O Saviour of the world, who by thy Cross and precious
                           Blood hast redeem - ed us.
℟. Save us and help us, we humbly beseech thee,   O Lord.

PROCESSIONAL—PALM SUNDAY

Hymn 599 Farley Castle   H. Lawes, 1596–1662

KEY **D**

{| d :— | m :f | s :m | f :s | l :t | d¹:— ‖ d¹:— | t :l |
 | s₁:— | d :d | r :d | d :d | f :f | m :— ‖ m :— | m :d |
 | m :— | s :l | t :s | l :s | f :f | s :— ‖ d¹:— | s :l |
 | d :— | d :l₁| s₁:d | f :m | r :r | d :— ‖ l :— | m :f |}

{| d¹:s | l :m | s :fe | s :— ‖ s :— | m :l | s :f | m :f |
 | m :d | d :d | r :r.d| t₁:— ‖ r :— | d :d | d :r | s₁:d |
 | s :d¹| f :s | t :l | s :— ‖ s :— | s :f | s :l.t| d¹:d¹|
 | d :m | f :d | t₁:r | s₁:— ‖ t₁:— | d :f | m :r | d :l₁|}

{| s :d | r :— ‖ r :— | s :m | f :l | s :d¹| d¹:t | d¹:— ‖
 | d :d | t₁:— ‖ t₁:— | r :d | d :t₁| d :m | s :s | m :— ‖
 | s :fe| s :— ‖ s :— | s :s | l :f | s :l | r¹:r¹| d¹:— ‖
 | m₁:l₁| s₁:— ‖ s₁:— | t₁:d | f :r | m :l | s :s | d :— ‖}

RIDE on triumphantly! Behold, we lay
Our lusts and sins and proud will in thy way:
Thy road is ready, and thy paths made straight
With longing expectation seem to wait.

2

Hosanna! Welcome to our hearts! for here
Thou hast a temple too, as Sion dear:
Enter, O Lord, and cleanse that holy place
Where thou dost choose to set thy beauteous face.

Adapted from BISHOP JEREMY TAYLOR

EASTER DAY

Hymn 600 Salve, festa dies   Mode iv

KEY **D**

Salve, festa dies

The refrain is first sung by solo voices, and then repeated by chorus

{| f s m s l f r m— | s l d¹ l s l s f r m — m — |}
  1 Wel-come, morn-ing of joy, glad feast that all a-ges shall hal-low,

{| f m r f l l s m — r — | f s l l f r m — ‖
  1 Day where-in, van-quish-ing hell, God com-eth forth from the grave.

PROCESSIONAL—EASTER DAY

SOLO VOICES   VERSES 2, 4, 6, 8 AND 10

{| s   l   t   d¹   s   f   l — | f̣ ṛ   m   r }

2   Lo, the fresh beau-ty of spring,   re - born from
4   Now, Lord of mer-cy and might,   of thy pro-mise
6* Shame that in dur-ance should lie,   close girt in
8   Meek-ly thou stoop'st to the grave,   who art Au-thor
10 Out of the pri-son of deaths   thou art res-cu-

{| s   s   f   r   ṃd r — | f̣ ṛ   m   f   ṣf   r }

2   the womb of the win-ter,   Tells how, to greet his
4   vouch-safe the ful-fil-ment: Rise, bur-ied Love, from
6* the tomb's rock-y fast-ness,   He who sus-tains the
8   of life and cre-a-tion,   Tread-est the path-way
10 ing souls with-out num-ber;   Free-ly they press to

Repeat the refrain

{| d   m — | m   r   f   r   d   m   m — ||

2   re-turn,   na-ture it - self is re-newed.
4   the tomb;   has-ten, the third day is here.
6* whole world,   held in the grasp of his hand.
8   of death,   win-ning sal-va-tion for men.
10 the goal   whi-ther their Ma-ker lead on.

SOLO VOICES   VERSES 3, 5, 7, 9 AND 11

{| s   l   t   d¹   s   f   l — | f̣ ṛ   m }

3   He who was nailed to the Cross   is reign-
5   Shame would it be that thy limbs   with earth's
7* Fling off the clothes of the grave,   leave them there
9   Give back thy face to the world,   with its sun-
11 Hell's gloom-y cas-tle is stormed,   un-loosed

{| r   s   s   f   r   ṃd r — | f̣ ṛ   m   f   ṣf }

3   ing as God o-ver all things,   While the Cre-a-
5   sor-ry mould should be cov-ered   Or that base rock
7* in the sep-ul-chre ly-ing;   For thou art all
9   shine to glad-den the a-ges;   Give back the light
11 are the chains of its cap-tives: Cha-os and Death

Repeat the refrain

{| r   d   m — | m   r   f   r   d   m   m — ||

3   tor of all   all things cre-a-ted a-dore.
5   should im-mure him   who hath ran-somed the world.
7* that we need,   and with-out thee we have naught.
9   of the day,   fled from our eyes at thy Death.
11 flee a-way,   cowed at the face of the Light.

BISHOP VENANTIUS FORTUNATUS
Tr. C. S. PHILLIPS

KEY A

{| d   *At the entrance into the Chancel:*   l₁ (t₁) — ||

℣. The Lord is risen from   the grave.
℟. Who for our sakes hung on the Tree. Al - le - lu - ia.

PROCESSIONAL—EASTER DAY

HYMN 601 Christ ist erstanden Proper melody of 12th cent. hymn
KEY D

Christ ist erstanden

1
CHRIST is now risen again
From his death and all his pain;
Therefore will we merry be,
And rejoice with him gladly. Alleluia!

2
Since he is risen indeed
Let us love him with all speed;
Therefore glad now will we be,
And rejoice in him only. Alleluia!

Tr. BISHOP MILES COVERDALE†

HYMN 602   FIRST TUNE
KEY E♭ Easter Song   *Catholische Kirchengesänge* (Cologne, 1623)

PROCESSIONAL—EASTER DAY

ALTERNATIVE VERSION FOR VERSES 4, 8 AND 11
KEY E♭
(Melody in the Tenor part)

4 The pains of hell are loosed at last, The days of mourning now are
8 His faithful followers with speed to Galilee forth with pro-
11 Jesu, the King of gentleness, Do thou thyself our hearts pos-

4 past; Alleluia! Alleluia! An angel robed in light hath
8 ceed, Alleluia! Alleluia! That there once more they may be-
11 sess, That we may give thee all our

4 said, 'The Lord is risen from the dead.'
8 hold The Lord's dear face, as he foretold.
11 days The tribute of our grateful praise.

Alleluia! Alleluia!
Alleluia! Alleluia! Alleluia! Alleluia!

PROCESSIONAL—EASTER DAY

HYMN 602 SECOND TUNE
KEY E♭ Devonshire   J. F. Lampe, 1703-51

Aurora lucis rutilat

PART 1

1
LIGHT'S glittering morn bedecks the sky;
Heaven thunders forth its victor-cry:
  [Alleluia!]
The glad earth shouts her triumph high,
And groaning hell makes wild reply:
  [Alleluia!]

2
While he, the King, the mighty King,
Despoiling death of all its sting,
And trampling down the powers of night,
Brings forth his ransomed saints to light.

3
His tomb of late the threefold guard
Of watch and stone and seal had barred;
But now, in pomp and triumph high,
He comes from death to victory.

4
The pains of hell are loosed at last,
The days of mourning now are past;
An angel robed in light hath said,
'The Lord is risen from the dead.'

PART 2

5
O bitter the apostles' pain
For their dear Lord so lately slain,
By rebel servants doomed to die
A death of cruel agony!

6
With gentle voice the angel gave
The women tidings at the grave:
'Fear not, your Master shall ye see;
He goes before to Galilee.'

7
Then, hastening on their eager way
The joyful tidings to convey,
Their Lord they met, their living Lord,
And falling at his feet adored.

8
His faithful followers with speed
To Galilee forthwith proceed,
That there once more they may behold
The Lord's dear face, as he foretold.

PART 3

9
That Eastertide with joy was bright,
The sun shone out with fairer light,
When, to their longing eyes restored,
The glad apostles saw their Lord.

10
He bade them see his hands, his side,
Where yet the glorious wounds abide;
The tokens true which made it plain
Their Lord indeed was risen again.

11
Jesu, the King of gentleness,
Do thou thyself our hearts possess,
That we may give thee all our days
The tribute of our grateful praise.

PROCESSIONAL—EASTER DAY

The following Doxology may be sung at the end of any Part, or of the whole hymn:

12
O Lord of all, with us abide
In this our joyful Eastertide;
From every weapon death can wield
Thine own redeemed for ever shield.

13
All praise be thine, O risen Lord,
From death to endless life restored;
All praise to God the Father be
And Holy Ghost eternally.

Tr. J. M. NEALE and Compilers

KEY E♭   *At the entrance into the Chancel:*

℣. The Lord is risen from the grave.

℟. Who for our sakes hung on the Tree. Al-le-lu-ia.

HYMN 603   Gelobt sei Gott   M. Vulpius, *Gesangbuch*, 1609

KEY C

1
GOOD Christian men, rejoice and sing!
Now is the triumph of our King!
To all the world glad news we bring:
    Alleluia!

2
The Lord of Life is risen for ay:
Bring flowers of song to strew his way;
Let all mankind rejoice and say
    Alleluia!

3
Praise we in songs of victory
That Love, that Life, which cannot die,
And sing with hearts uplifted high
    Alleluia!

4
Thy name we bless, O risen Lord,
And sing to-day with one accord
The life laid down, the life restored:
    Alleluia!

C. A. ALINGTON

PROCESSIONAL—EASTER DAY

HYMN 604 Scientia Salutis Sir J. Stainer, 1840–1901
KEY F

In slow march time. MEN ONLY   C. t.

{| d :— | r : m | r :— | d :— | f : m | r : d |ᵗm : s | d¹ :— }
 Day - star on high, bright har-bin-ger of glad-ness,

  F. f.
{| d¹:—|l : f|r¹:—|—:d¹|d¹:t| l : s|s:—|d¹:—|d¹:s:—|m : m | de:—|l₁:—}
 Pier-cing the clouds of ig-nor-ance and er-ror, Thou hast dis-persed our

{| r :m | f : r | t₁:—|s₁:— | d :— | m : f |s:—|s₁:—| d:—|—:—|—:—|—:— ||
 night of sin and sad - ness; Death has no ter - ror.

HARMONY

| d :— | r : m | r :— | d :— | f : m | r : d |t₁:r | s :— | s :— | m : d |
| s₁:— | s₁:s₁| t₁:— | l₁:— | f₁: s₁|l₁: m₁|s₁:—|t₁:— | d :— | ta₁:ta₁|
 Dark-ness is past, joy com-eth in the morn-ing; Hope springs a-
| m :— | r : d | s :— | m :— | l : s |f : d | r :— | s :— | s :— | s : m |
| d :— | t₁: d | s₁:— | l₁:— | r₁: m₁|f₁: l₁|s₁:—| s :f | m :— | d : d |

| l :—|—: s | s :fe| m : r | r :—|s :— | s :—|m : m | de:—|l₁:— | r : m |
| l₁:—|—: d | d : d | d : d |t₁:—|t₁:— | t₁:—|ta₁:ta₁| l₁:—|l₁:s₁| f₁ : l₁|
 new for sin-ners with-out num-ber: Sleep-ers, a - wake! a bright-er
| f :—|—: s | l : l | s :fe|s :—|r :— | m :—| s : s |m : r|m :— | f : m |
| f :—|—: m | r : r | r₁: r₁|s₁:—|s₁:— | m₁:—|m₁: m₁| l₁:t₁|de:— | r : de|

| f : r | t₁:—|s₁:— | d :— | m : f | s :—|s₁:— | d :—|—:—|—:—|—:— ||
| l₁: l₁| s₁:—|r₁:— | s₁:— | d : d | t₁:—|s₁:— | s₁:—|—:—|—:—|—:— ||
 day is dawn-ing; Shake off your slum - ber.
| r : f | r :—|s : f | m :— | d : d | r :—|f :— | m :—|—:—|—:—|—:— ||
| r : f₁| s₁: l₁|t₁:— | d :— | l₁: l₁| s₁:—|—:— | {d :—|—:—|—:—|—:— ||
                                                   {d₁:—|—:—|—:—|—:— ||

| m :—|r : d | f :—|—: m | r : d |t₁: d | r :—|s₁:— | s :—|—: s |
| s₁:—|t₁: d | t₁:—|d :— | f₁:s₁|s₁:l₁| t₁:—|s₁:— | t₁:—|—: t₁|
 Al - le - lu - ia, Al - le - lu - ia, Al - le -
| m :—|f : s | f :—|s :— | l : s |f : m | r : s |s :— | s :—|—: s |
| d :—|r : m | r :—|d :— | f : m |r : d |t₁: r | s :— | s :—|—: m |

| m :—|fe : s | l :—|—: t | l :—|s :— | s :—|—: s | l :—|s :— |
| d :—|d :— | d :—|—: r | d :—|t₁:— | ta₁:—|—: ta₁| l₁:—|—: l₁|
 lu - ia, Al - le - lu - ia, Al - le - lu - ia,
| l :—|l :— | l :—|s : fe| fe:—|s :— | s :—|s :— | m :—|de :— |
| l :—|—: s | s : fe|m : r | r :—|s :— | s :—|m :— | de:—|l₁:— |

614

PROCESSIONAL—EASTER DAY

{ | f :m | r :l | s :f | m :r | m:f | s :f | m :— | r :— | d :—|—:—|—:—|—:— |
| l₁:s₁| f₁:l₁| r :— | t₁:— | d :— |— :r | d :— | t₁:— | d :—|—:—|—:—|—:— |
| Al - le - lu - ia,   Al   le - lu   ia. |
| f :s | l :f | r :— | s :— | s:f | m :l | s :— |— :f | m :—|—:—|—:—|—:— |
| r :m | f :r | t₁:— | s₁:— | d:— |— :m | f :s | s :— | s₁:— | d :—|—:—|—:—|—:— | }

[MEN]   DAYSTAR on high, bright harbinger of gladness,
         Piercing the clouds of ignorance and error,
         Thou hast dispersed our night of sin and sadness;
           Death has no terror.

[HARMONY]   Darkness is past, joy cometh in the morning;
         Hope springs anew for sinners without number:
         Sleepers, awake! a brighter day is dawning;
           Shake off your slumber.   [FULL] Alleluia!

2

[MEN]   Prophets of old spake darkly of this wonder,
         Psalmist and saints have handed on the story;
         Now he is risen, bursting bonds asunder,
           Risen to glory.

[HARMONY]   Earth's tyrants quail; the mighty make obeisance:
         He hath preferred the innocent and lowly:
         Mercy and truth shine round about his presence:
           His name is Holy.   [FULL] Alleluia!

3

[MEN]   Victor he comes in majesty, revealing
         Promise of life and liberty to mortals:
         Heaven and earth, with hymns of triumph pealing,
           Throw wide their portals.

[HARMONY]   Praise him, ye nations, hearts and voices blending:
         Raise high your song; the Conqueror advances:
         Praise him with cymbals, lute and harp attending,
           Praise him with dances.   [FULL] Alleluia!

4

[MEN]   Hail him the Monarch, Ruler of creation;
         Princes and powers, bow your heads before him;
         This is the Lord, the god of our salvation;
           Let us adore him.

[HARMONY]   Lord God of Hosts, great Deity supernal,
         Be thou our strength, by thee our steps be guided,
         Father and Son and Spirit co-eternal,
           One undivided.   [FULL] Alleluia!

                                              J. R. L. STAINER

KEY F

At the entrance into the Chancel:

{ | d | l₁   (t₁) — |

℣. The Lord is risen from   the   grave.

℟. Who for our sakes hung on the Tree.   Al - le - lu - ia.

PROCESSIONAL—EASTER DAY

HYMN 605 Exodus J. F. Rötscher (1790)

KEY **F**

[tonic sol-fa notation]

Cedant justi signa luctus

1
JESUS Christ from death hath risen!
Lo, his Godhead bursts the prison,
   While his Manhood passes free,
   Vanquishing our misery:
Risen with him to salvation
Through his self-humiliation,
   We may share his victory.

2
Far be sorrow, tears and sadness!
See the dayspring of our gladness!
   Satan's slaves no more are we,
   Children by the Son set free:
Rise, for Life with death hath striven,
All the snares of hell are riven;
   Rise and claim the victory.

H. LINDENBORN (1741)
Tr. Compilers

ROGATIONTIDE

HYMN 606 FIRST TUNE

KEY **D** Croft's 148th W. Croft, 1678–1727

[tonic sol-fa notation]

PROCESSIONAL—ROGATIONTIDE

(Sol-fa notation with musical score)

1

TO thee our God we fly
 For mercy and for grace;
O hear our lowly cry,
 And hide not thou thy face.
O Lord, stretch forth thy mighty hand,
And guard and bless our fatherland.

2

Arise, O Lord of Hosts!
 Be jealous for thy name,
And drive from out our coasts
 The sins that put to shame.
O Lord, stretch forth, etc.

3

Thy best gifts from on high
 In rich abundance pour,
That we may magnify
 And praise thee more and more.
O Lord, stretch forth, etc.

4

The powers ordained by thee
 With heavenly wisdom bless;
May they thy servants be,
 And rule in righteousness.
O Lord, stretch forth, etc.

5

The Church of thy dear Son
 Inflame with love's pure fire,
Bind her once more in one,
 And life and truth inspire.
O Lord, stretch forth, etc.

6*

The pastors of thy fold
 With grace and power endue,
That faithful, pure, and bold,
 They may be pastors true.
O Lord, stretch forth, etc.

7

O let us love thy house,
 And sanctify thy day,
Bring unto thee our vows,
 And loyal homage pay.
O Lord, stretch forth, etc.

8

Give peace, Lord, in our time;
 O let no foe draw nigh,
Nor lawless deed of crime
 Insult thy majesty.
O Lord, stretch forth, etc.

9*

Though vile and worthless, still
 Thy people, Lord, are we;
And for our God we will
 None other have but thee.
O Lord, stretch forth, etc.

BISHOP W. WALSHAM HOW

PROCESSIONAL—ROGATIONTIDE

Hymn 606 SECOND TUNE

Key D Pro Patria   J. Armistead, 1877–1935

Verses 1, 2, 4, 5, 7, 9 in Unison

[tonic sol-fa notation]

O Lord, stretch forth thy mighty hand, And guard and bless our fa-ther-land.

Verses 3, 6, 8 in Harmony

[tonic sol-fa notation in four parts]

O Lord, stretch forth thy mighty hand, And guard and bless our fa-ther-land.

By permission of Novello & Co., Ltd.

TO thee our God we fly
  For mercy and for grace;
O hear our lowly cry,
  And hide not thou thy face.
O Lord, stretch forth thy mighty hand,
And guard and bless our fatherland.

2
Arise, O Lord of Hosts!
  Be jealous for thy name,
And drive from out our coasts
  The sins that put to shame.
O Lord, stretch forth, etc.

3
Thy best gifts from on high
  In rich abundance pour,
That we may magnify
  And praise thee more and more.
O Lord, stretch forth, etc.

4
The powers ordained by thee
  With heavenly wisdom bless;
May they thy servants be,
  And rule in righteousness.
O Lord, stretch forth, etc.

PROCESSIONAL—ROGATIONTIDE

5
The Church of thy dear Son
　Inflame with love's pure fire,
Bind her once more in one,
　And life and truth inspire.
O Lord, stretch forth, etc.

6*
The pastors of thy fold
　With grace and power endue,
That faithful, pure, and bold,
　They may be pastors true.
O Lord, stretch forth, etc.

7
O let us love thy house,
　And sanctify thy day,
Bring unto thee our vows,
　And loyal homage pay.
O Lord, stretch forth, etc.

8
Give peace, Lord, in our time;
　O let no foe draw nigh,
Nor lawless deed of crime
　Insult thy majesty.
O Lord, stretch forth, etc.

9*
Though vile and worthless, still
　Thy people, Lord, are we;
And for our God we will
　None other have but thee.
O Lord, stretch forth, etc.

BISHOP W. WALSHAM HOW

KEY A

At the entrance into the Chancel:

℣. The eyes of all wait upon thee, O Lord.

℟. And thou givest them their meat in due sea - son.

HYMN **607** Northampton　　　　　　　　C. J. KING, 1859–1934
KEY A

KINDLY spring again is here,
Trees and fields in bloom appear;
Hark! the birds with artless lays
Warble their Creator's praise.

2
Where in winter all was snow,
Now the flowers in clusters grow;
And the corn, in green array,
Promises a harvest-day.

3
On thy garden deign to smile,
Raise the plants, enrich the soil;
Soon thy presence will restore
Life to what seemed dead before.

J. NEWTON†

PROCESSIONAL

ASCENSIONTIDE

Hymn 608   Salve, festa dies   Mode iv

KEY D

This refrain is first sung by solo voices then repeated by chorus

{| f s   m   s l   f   r   m — | s l d'   l   s }
1 Wel - come, morn - ing of joy, glad feast that all

{| l   s f   r m   m —   m — | f   m   r }
1 a - ges shall hal - low. Day where - in,

{| f l   l   s   m — r — | f   s   l   l   f   r   m — ||
1 van - quish - ing hell. God to high hea - ven as - cends.

SOLO VOICES   VERSES 2, 4, 6, 8 AND 10

{| s   l   t   d'   s   f   l — | f r   m   r   s }
2 Calm is the breath of the spring that wa - kens the

{| s   f   r   m d   r — | f r   m   f }
2 glo - ry of blos - som, Bright - er the

Repeat the refrain

{| s f   r   d   m — | m   r   f   r   d   m   m — ||
2 sun - light that streams forth from the gates of the sky.

SOLO VOICES   VERSES 3, 5, 7, 9 AND 11

{| s   l   t   d'   s   f   l — | f r   m   r   s }
3 Christ hath trod un - der his feet the king - dom of

{| s   f   r   m d   r — | f r   m   f }
3 tor - ment and sad - ness; Decked is the

Repeat the refrain

{| s f   r   d   m — | m   r   f   r   d   m   m — ||
3 wood - land with leaves, earth strews her flowers at his feet.

Salve, festa dies

WELCOME, morning of joy, glad feast that all ages shall hallow,
Day wherein, vanquishing hell, God to high heaven ascends.   *(Repeat)*

PROCESSIONAL—ASCENSIONTIDE

2
Calm is the breath of the spring that wakens the glory of blossom,
Brighter the sunlight that streams forth from the gates of the sky. Welcome, etc.

3
Christ hath trod under his feet the kingdom of torment and sadness;
Decked is the woodland with leaves, earth strews her flowers at his feet.
Welcome, etc.

4
Trampling the powers of hell he mounts on his journey to heaven:
Heaven's light hails him as God; field, sky and sea tell his praise. Welcome, etc.

5
Strike off the fetters that bind the spirits that hell hath imprisoned,
Call back and lift to the light souls rushing down to the pit. Welcome, etc.

6*
Out of the prison of death thou art rescuing souls without number;
Freely they press to the goal whither their Maker leads on. Welcome, etc.

7*
Now may'st thou nurse in thine arms a people that knows no defilement,
Bear them aloft to be given for a pure hostage to God. Welcome, etc.

8
Two are the crowns that for thee the Father hath laid up in heaven:
One shalt thou wear for thine own, one for a people redeemed. Welcome, etc.

9
Jesu, thou Saviour of all, Creator of men and Redeemer,
Only-begotten of God, sprung from the Deity's fount; Welcome, etc.

10
Equal, co-eval art thou, and in fellowship one with the Father;
Thine was the word of command when all creation began. Welcome, etc.

11
Thou too, beholding in love the depth of humanity's ruin,
Man to deliver from death, Man didst vouchsafe to become. Welcome, etc.

BISHOP VENANTIUS FORTUNATUS
Tr. C. S. Phillips

KEY **A**

At the entrance into the Chancel:

℣. God is gone up with a mer - - ry noise.

℟. And the Lord with the sound of a trumpet. Al - le - lu - ia.

PROCESSIONAL—ASCENSIONTIDE

HYMN 609 Erschienen ist   N. Hermann, *c.* 1485–1561
KEY D

1
OUR Lord is risen from the dead;
  Our Jesus is gone up on high;
The powers of hell are captive led,
  Dragged to the portals of the sky.
      Alleluia!

2
There his triumphant chariot waits,
  And angels chant the solemn lay:
Lift up your heads, ye heavenly gates;
  Ye everlasting doors, give way.
      Alleluia!

3
Loose all your bars of massy light,
  And wide unfold the ethereal scene:
He claims these mansions as his right;
  Receive the King of Glory in.
      Alleluia!

4
Who is this King of Glory? Who?
  The Lord that all our foes o'ercame,
The world, sin, death and hell o'erthrew:
  And Jesus is the Conqueror's name.
      Alleluia!

C. WESLEY

HYMN 610 Chislehurst   Sir S. H. Nicholson, 1875–1947
KEY G
UNISON

Hail the day that sees him rise, Al - le - lu - ia!

To his throne a - bove the skies; A - le - lu - ia!

Christ, the Lamb for sin-ners given, En-ters now the high-est heaven.

PROCESSIONAL—ASCENSIONTIDE

HARMONY

{| r.m | f.m : r : m.f | s.f : m | l | -.s : f :— | m :—:— |
Al-le-	lu - ia! Al-le-	lu - ia!	d	-.d: d :t₁	d :—:—
		Al-	le - lu -	ia!
	: f	-.s: l :s	s :—:—
	: f	-.m: r :s₁	d :—:—

1
HAIL the day that sees him rise,
      Alleluia!
To his throne above the skies;
      Alleluia!
Christ, the Lamb for sinners given,
      [Alleluia!]
Enters now the highest heaven.
      Alleluia!

2
There for him high triumph waits;
      Alleluia!
Lift your heads, eternal gates!
      Alleluia!
He hath conquered death and sin;
      [Alleluia!]
Take the King of Glory in!
      Alleluia!

3*
Circled round with angel-powers,
      Alleluia!
Their triumphant Lord and ours:
      Alleluia!
Wide unfold the radiant scene,
      [Alleluia!]
Take the King of Glory in!
      Alleluia!

4
Lo, the heaven its Lord receives,
      Alleluia!
Yet he loves the earth he leaves;
      Alleluia!
Though returning to his throne,
      [Alleluia!]
Still he calls mankind his own.
      Alleluia!

5
See! he lifts his hands above;
      Alleluia!
See! he shows the prints of love;
      Alleluia!
Hark! his gracious lips bestow
      [Alleluia!]
Blessings on his Church below.
      Alleluia!

6
Still for us he intercedes,
      Alleluia!
His prevailing Death he pleads;
      Alleluia!
Near himself prepares our place,
      [Alleluia!]
He the first-fruits of our race.
      Alleluia!

7
Lord, though parted from our sight,
      Alleluia!
Far above the starry height,
      Alleluia!
Grant our hearts may thither rise,
      [Alleluia!]
Seeking thee above the skies.
      Alleluia!

8*
Ever upward let us move,
      Alleluia!
Wafted on the wings of love;
      Alleluia!
Looking when our Lord shall come,
      [Alleluia!]
Longing, sighing after home.
      Alleluia!

9*
There we shall with thee remain, Alleluia!
Partners of thine endless reign; Alleluia!
There thy face unclouded see, [Alleluia!]
Find our heaven of heavens in thee. Alleluia!

C. WESLEY, T. COTTERILL, and others

Alternative Tunes, Ascension, Llanfair, 147

KEY **G**

{| d   *At the entrance into the Chancel:*   l₁ (t₁) — ||

℣. God is gone up with a mer - - ry noise.
℟. And the Lord with the sound of a trumpet. Al-le-lu - ia.

623

PROCESSIONAL—ASCENSIONTIDE

HYMN 611 Allgütiger, mein Preisgesang   G. P. Weimar, 1734–1800
KEY G

Tu, Christe, nostrum gaudium

O CHRIST our joy, gone up on high
To fill thy throne above the sky,
  How glorious dost thou shine!
Thy sovereign rule the worlds obey,
And earthly joys all fade away
  In that pure light of thine.

2
Ascended up from mortal sight,
Jesu, we praise thee in the height,
  Our joy, our great reward;
Whom with the Father we confess,
And with the Holy Spirit bless,
  One ever-glorious Lord.

Tr. D. T. MORGAN

WHITSUNDAY

HYMN 612 Salve, festa dies   Mode iv
KEY D

This refrain is first sung by solo voices, then repeated by chorus

1 Wel-come, morn-ing of joy, glad feast that all a-ges shall hal-low, Day when to earth out of hea-ven flashed a new glo-ry of grace.

PROCESSIONAL—WHITSUNDAY

SOLO VOICES   VERSES 2, 4 AND 6

{| s l t d' s f l — | f r m r s }
 2 Fling-ing his tor-rents of fire,   the sun rides

{| s f r m d r — | f r m f }
 2 high in the hea-ven;   Forth from the

Repeat the refrain

{| s f r d m — | m r f r d m m — ||
 2 o-cean he comes, sinks to the o-cean at eve.

SOLO VOICES   VERSES 3, 5 AND 7

{| s l t d' s f l — | f r m r s }
 3 Dart-ing his rays as he goes   through the li-quid

{| s f r m d r — | f r m f s f }
 3 air of the sum-mer,   Now doth he short-

Repeat the refrain

{| r d m — | m r f r d m m — ||
 3 en the nights,   draw out the length of the days.

Salve, festa dies

WELCOME, morning of joy, glad feast that all ages shall hallow,
Day when to earth out of heaven flashed a new glory of grace   *(Repeat)*

2

Flinging his torrents of fire, the sun rides high in the heaven;
Forth from the ocean he comes, sinks to the ocean at eve.   Welcome, etc.

3

Darting his rays as he goes through the liquid air of the summer,
Now doth he shorten the nights, draw out the length of the days.   Welcome, etc.

4

Blue is the sky by day, with crystalline radiance glowing;
Night is a glory of stars, singing together for joy.   Welcome, etc.

5

Now doth the country rejoice in all the gay store of its bounty;
Summer returns to the earth bearing her wealth in her hand.   Welcome, etc.

6

Flowers bespangle the field with riot and glitter of colour;
White are the hedgerows with may, green grows the grass in the meads.
　　　　　　　　　　　　　　　　　　　　　　　　　　　　Welcome, etc.

7

One by one open their buds the blossoms of tulip and lily;
Shyly smile from the grass daisies with myriad eyes.   Welcome, etc.

BISHOP VENANTIUS FORTUNATUS   *Tr.* C. S. PHILLIPS

KEY **A**

At the entrance into the Chancel:

{| d   l₁ (t₁) — ||
 ℣. The Spirit of the Lord filleth   the world.
 ℟. And that which containeth all things
    hath knowledge of the voice.   Al-le-lu - ia.

PROCESSIONAL—WHITSUNDAY

HYMN 613 Whitsun B. Luard Selby, 1853–1919
KEY **A**

[tonic sol-fa notation]

TO thee, O Comforter divine,
For all thy grace and power benign,
 Sing we Alleluia!

2
To thee, whose faithful love had place
In God's great covenant of grace,
 Sing we Alleluia!

3
To thee, whose faithful power doth heal,
Enlighten, sanctify, and seal,
 Sing we Alleluia!

4
To thee, our teacher and our friend,
Our faithful leader to the end,
 Sing we Alleluia!

5
To thee, by Jesus Christ sent down,
Of all his gifts the sum and crown,
 Sing we Alleluia!

FRANCES R. HAVERGAL

HYMN 614 Kybald Twychen W. H. Harris
KEY **A**

[tonic sol-fa notation]

PROCESSIONAL—WHITSUNDAY

f.D.

{ | d s :-.s | l :d' | - :t | d' :- || l :-.l | t :r' | r' :de' | r' :- |
  | ₁m :-.m | f :s | s :- | m :- || m :-.m | r :f | m :m | fe :- |
  | f d':-.d'| d' :- | r' :r'| d' :- || de':de' | r' :l | l :l | l :- |
  | f₁d :-.d | f :m | s :s | d :- || l :s | f :r | l :l₁ | r :- | }

A.t.

{ | ʳs₁:-.s₁|l₁:d | f :m | r :- | d :- || s :m | r :d | d :r | t₁:- | d :- | - :- ||
  | ʳs₁:ʳ₁.m₁|f₁:s₁| l₁:- | l₁:t₁| t₁:l₁|| s₁:t₁|l₁:l₁| s₁:- | s₁:- | s₁:- | - :- ||
  | ᶠᵉt₁:-.t₁|d :m | l :s | f :- | m :- || d :s | f :f.m| r :- | r :- | m :- | - :- ||
  | ʳs₁:-.s₁|f₁:m₁| r₁:- | s₁:- | l₁:- || m₁:m₁|f₁:r₁ | s₁:- | s₁:- | d₁:- | - :- || }

HOLY Spirit, gently come,
Raise us from our fallen state,
Fix thy everlasting home
In the hearts thou didst create.
Gift of God most high!
Visit every troubled breast,
Light and life and love supply,
Give our spirits perfect rest.

2

Heavenly unction from above,
Comforter of hearts that faint,
Fountain, life, and fire of love,
Hear and answer our complaint:
Thee we humbly pray,
Finger of the living God,
Now thy sevenfold gift display,
Shed our Saviour's love abroad.

3

Now thy quickening influence bring,
On our spirits sweetly move,
Open every mouth to sing
Jesus' everlasting love:
Lighten every heart;
Drive our enemies away,
Joy and peace to us impart,
Lead us in the heavenly way.

4

Take the things of Christ and show
What our Lord for us hath done;
May we God the Father know
Only in and through the Son:
Nothing will we fear,
Though to wilds and deserts driven,
While we feel thy presence near,
Witnessing our sins forgiven.

5

Glory be to God alone,
God whose hand created all!
Glory be to God the Son,
Who redeemed us from our fall!
To the Holy Ghost
Equal praise and glory be,
When the course of time is lost,
Lost in wide eternity!

W. HAMMOND† Based on *Veni, creator Spiritus*

KEY **A**

At the entrance into the Chancel:

{| d   l₁ (t₁) — ||

℣. The Spirit of the Lord filleth   the world.

℟. And that which containeth all things hath
knowledge of the voice.   Al - le - lu - ia.

PROCESSIONAL—WHITSUNDAY

HYMN 615 Venice   W. Amps, 1824–1910
KEY D

LORD God the Holy Ghost,
In this accepted hour,
As on the day of Pentecost,
Descend in all thy power.

2
The young, the old, inspire
With wisdom from above;
And give us hearts and tongues of fire,
To pray and praise and love.

3
Spirit of truth, be thou
In life and death our guide;
O Spirit of adoption, now
May we be sanctified.

J. MONTGOMERY

TRINITY SUNDAY

HYMN 616 Dolberrow   W. K. Stanton
KEY A

PROCESSIONAL—TRINITY SUNDAY

SOUND aloud Jehovah's praises,
　Tell abroad the aweful Name!
Heaven the ceaseless anthem raises;
　Let the earth her God proclaim,
God, the hope of every nation,
God, the source of consolation,
　　Holy, blessèd Trinity.

2

This the Name from ancient ages
　Hidden in its dazzling light;
This the Name that kings and sages
　Prayed and strove to know aright,
Through God's wondrous Incarnation
Now revealed the world's salvation,
　　Ever blessèd Trinity.

3

Into this great Name and holy
　We all tribes and tongues baptize;
Thus the Highest owns the lowly,
　Homeward, heavenward, bids them rise,
Gathers them from every nation,
Bids them join in adoration
　　Of the blessèd Trinity.

4

In this Name the heart rejoices,
　Pouring forth its secret prayer;
In this Name we lift our voices,
　And our common faith declare,
Offering praise and supplication
And the thankful life's oblation
　　To the blessèd Trinity.

5

Still thy Name o'er earth and ocean
　Shall be carried, 'God is Love,'
Whispered by the heart's devotion,
　Echoed by the choirs above,
Hallowed through all worlds for ever,
Lord, of life the only giver,
　　Blessèd, glorious Trinity.

　　　　　　　　　　H. A. MARTIN

KEY **A**　　　　*At the entrance into the Chancel:*

{|　　d　　　　　　　　　　　　　　　　　1, (t,—) ||

℣. Let us bless the Father and the Son and the Ho - ly　Ghost.

℟. Let us praise and exalt him for ev　　-　　er.

PROCESSIONAL—TRINITY SUNDAY

HYMN **617** Sharon   Sir F. A. G. Ouseley, 1825–89
KEY **A**   E.t.

f.A.

Ave, colenda Trinitas

ALL hail, adorèd Trinity!
All hail, eternal Unity!
O God the Father, God the Son,
And God the Spirit, ever One.

2
To thee upon this festal day
We offer here our thankful lay:
O let our work accepted be,
That blessèd work of praising thee.

3
Three Persons praise we evermore,
One only God our hearts adore:
In thy sure mercy ever kind
May we our strong protection find.

4
O Trinity! O Unity!
Be present as we worship thee;
And with the songs that angels sing
Unite the hymns of praise we bring.

Tr. J. D. CHAMBERS and Compilers

DEDICATION FESTIVAL

HYMN **618** Salve, festa dies   Mode iv
KEY **D**

The refrain is first sung by solo voices, then repeated by chorus

1 Welcome, morning of joy, glad feast that all

1 ages shall hallow, Day when the Bride

1 of the Lamb joyfully weddeth her Spouse.

SOLO VOICES VERSES 2, 4, 6 AND 8

2 This is the palace of God, the dwelling of

PROCESSIONAL—DEDICATION FESTIVAL

{| s f r m d r — | f r m f }
2 peace and re-fresh-ing: Hi-ther the

Repeat the refrain
{| s f r d m — | m r f r d m m — ||
2 poor may re-pair, win-ning a So-lo-mon's wealth.

SOLO VOICES   VERSES 3, 5, 7 AND 9

{| s l t d' s f l — | f r m r s }
3 True Son of Da-vid is he who hath knit us up

{| s f r m d r — | f r m f }
3 in-to his Bo-dy; Here in your

Repeat the refrain
{| s f r d m — | m r f r d m m — ||
3 mo-ther-home, hail him as God and as Man.

Salve, festa dies

WELCOME, morning of joy, glad feast that all ages shall hallow,
Day when the Bride of the Lamb joyfully weddeth her Spouse.   *(Repeat)*

2
This is the palace of God, the dwelling of peace and refreshing:
Hither the poor may repair, winning a Solomon's wealth.   Welcome, etc.

3
True Son of David is he who hath knit us up into his Body;
Here in your mother-home, hail him as God and as Man.   Welcome, etc.

4
Linked by a heavenly bond are ye in the grace of the Spirit,
If ye will honour your troth, seek to be brothers in heart.   Welcome, etc.

5
New-made from heaven descends Jerusalem's mystical city,
Decked with a glory that flows straight from the fountain of light.   Welcome, etc.

6
Here at the laver of grace the King of goodness eternal
Cleanses with water from heaven souls that approach him in faith.   Welcome, etc.

7
Here David's Tower standeth sure: on hasting feet run to its stronghold;
Stored up within ye shall find pledges of heavenly bliss.   Welcome, etc.

8
This is the Ark of the Lord that succour affords to the faithful,
Carrying safe into port them that were tossed on the sea.   Welcome, etc.

9
Ladder of Jacob is here, the ladder that bringeth to heaven
Those who with faith for their guide follow the path of the just.   Welcome, etc.

c. 13th cent. (YORK PROCESSIONAL)   *Tr.* C. S. Phillips

KEY **D**   *At the entrance into the Chancel:*
{| d   l₁ t₁ — ||
℣. Blessed are they that dwell in   thy house.
℟. They will be always prais   ing thee.

PROCESSIONAL—DEDICATION FESTIVAL

HYMN 619 Manchester New R. Wainwright, 1748–82
KEY D

1. THE heaven of heavens cannot contain
The universal Lord;
Yet he in humble hearts will deign
To dwell and be adored.

2
Where'er ascends the sacrifice
Of fervent praise and prayer,
Or in the earth or in the skies,
The heaven of God is there.

3
His presence there is spread abroad
Through realms, through worlds unknown;
Who seeks the mercies of his God
Is ever near his throne.

W. DRENNAN

HYMN 620 Westminster Abbey Adapted from an anthem by
KEY B♭ H. Purcell, 1658–95

632

PROCESSIONAL—DEDICATION FESTIVAL

Urbs beata

PART 1

1
BLESSÈD city, heavenly Salem,
 Vision dear of peace and love,
Who of living stones art builded
 In the height of heaven above,
And, with angel hosts encircled,
 As a bride dost earthward move!

2
From celestial realms descending,
 Bridal glory round thee shed,
Meet for him whose love espoused thee,
 To thy Lord shalt thou be led;
All thy streets and all thy bulwarks
 Of pure gold are fashionèd.

3
Bright thy gates of pearl are shining,
 They are open evermore;
And by virtue of his merits
 Thither faithful souls do soar,
Who for Christ's dear name in this world
 Pain and tribulation bore.

4
Many a blow and biting sculpture
 Polished well those stones elect,
In their places now compacted
 By the heavenly Architect,
Who therewith hath willed for ever
 That his palace should be decked.

PART 2

5
Christ is made the sure Foundation,
 Christ the Head and Corner-stone,
Chosen of the Lord, and precious,
 Binding all the Church in one,
Holy Sion's help for ever,
 And her confidence alone.

6
All that dedicated city,
 Dearly loved of God on high,
In exultant jubilation
 Pours perpetual melody,
God the One in Three adoring
 In glad hymns eternally.

PART 3

7
To this temple, where we call thee,
 Come, O Lord of Hosts, to-day;
With thy wonted loving-kindness
 Hear thy servants as they pray,
And thy fullest benediction
 Shed within its walls alway.

8
Here vouchsafe to all thy servants
 What they ask of thee to gain,
What they gain from thee for ever
 With the blessèd to retain,
And hereafter in thy glory
 Evermore with thee to reign.

The following Doxology may be sung at the end of any Part, or of the whole hymn:

9
Laud and honour to the Father,
 Laud and honour to the Son,
Laud and honour to the Spirit,
 Ever Three, and ever One,
Consubstantial, co-eternal,
 While unending ages run.

Tr. J. M. NEALE and Compilers

KEY B♭

At the entrance into the Chancel:

℣. Blessed are they that dwell in thy house.

℟. They will be always prais ing thee.

PROCESSIONAL—DEDICATION FESTIVAL

HYMN 621 Old 100th L. Bourgeois, c. 1500–61
KEY **G**

[Tonic sol-fa notation]

ETERNAL Power, whose high abode
Becomes the grandeur of a God,
Infinite lengths beyond the bounds
Where stars revolve their little rounds;

2
Thee while the first Archangel sings,
He hides his face behind his wings,
And ranks of shining Thrones around
Fall worshipping and spread the ground

3
Lord, what shall earth and ashes do?
We would adore our Maker too:
From sin and dust to thee we cry,
The great, the holy, and the high!

I. WATTS and J. WESLEY

THANKSGIVING FOR THE INSTITUTION OF HOLY COMMUNION

HYMN 622 Cumulus Sir S. H. Nicholson, 1875–1947
KEY **A♭**
VERSES 1–9

[Tonic sol-fa notation]

PROCESSIONAL—THANKSGIVING FOR HOLY COMMUNION

PART 1

Lauda, Sion, Salvatorem

1
PRAISE, O Sion, praise thy Master,
Praise thy Saviour, praise thy Pastor,
    In a joyous melody:
Put forth all thy strength to sing him,
For the best that thou canst bring him
    Cannot ever worthy be.

2
Tell, O tell in praises glowing
How the living, life-bestowing
    Bread from heaven is given to thee:
Bread which Christ, before he suffered,
At the sacred banquet proffered
    To the Twelve in company.

3*
Lift thy voice in tuneful chorus,
Joyfully in strain sonorous
    Be thy heart's delight outpoured;
While this solemn day we celebrate
How the Saviour first did consecrate
    For his guests the mystic board.

4*
Here, our new King's table gracing,
This new Passover's new blessing
    Hath fulfilled the older rite:
Here is new to old succeeding,
Truth its shadow superseding,
    Darkness swallowed up in light.

5
What he did at supper seated
Christ ordained to be repeated
    In his memory divine;
Wherefore we, his precept heeding,
And his saving Offering pleading,
    Consecrate the bread and wine.

6
'Tis the truth to Christians given,
Bread becomes his Flesh from heaven,
    Wine becomes his holy Blood:
Here, where sight is unavailing,
Faith may seize with grasp unfailing
    What can ne'er be understood.

7
'Neath these diverse signs are hidden
Priceless things to sense forbidden,
    Outward signs are all we see:
Bread for eating, wine for drinking,
Yet, in ways beyond all thinking,
    Christ in each doth deign to be.

8*
Whoso of this feast partaketh,
Christ divideth not nor breaketh—
    He is whole to all that taste:
Whether one this bread receiveth
Or a thousand, still he giveth
    One same food that cannot waste.

9*
Good and bad alike are sharing
One repast, a doom preparing
    All unlike—'tis life or death:
Each a destiny is making—
See ye of the one partaking
    How the issue differeth!

10* When this Sa-cra-ment is bro-ken, Doubt not in each sev-ered to-ken,

Hal-lowed by the bless-ing spo-ken, What is veiled doth whole a-bide:

635

PROCESSIONAL—THANKSGIVING FOR HOLY COMMUNION

Hymn 622 (continued)

d :t₁ | l₁:d	t₁:l₁ | l₁:se₁	l₁:t₁ | d :d	f :m | r :r
m₁:s₁ | l₁:l₁.s₁	f₁:f₁ | m₁:m₁	m₁:s₁ | s₁:f₁.s₁	l₁:s₁.l₁|t₁:l₁
Though the sign is	bro-ken du-ly,	Christ him-self re-	main-eth tru-ly
d :m.r|d :m	r :d |t₁:t₁	d :r | d :d	d.r:m.fe|s :l
l₁ :m₁ | f₁:d₁	r₁:r₁ | m₁:m₁	l₁ :s₁.f₁| m₁:l₁.s₁	f₁ :d | s₁:f₁

m :r | d :m	r :-.d|t₁.l₁:s₁	s :-.f|m.s :f .m	r.d:t₁|d :—
t₁:l₁.t₁ | d :t₁	l₁:l₁ | s₁ :s₁	s₁.l₁:t₁ |d.t₁:l₁	l₁ :s₁ | s₁:—
All un-bro-ken;	pre-sent ful-ly	Here a-bides the	Sig-ni-fied.
se:m | m :m	f :f | r.d:t₁	d :r | m :l₁.d	f.m:r | m :—
m₁:ba₁.se₁|l₁: s₁	f₁:r₁ | s₁ :s₁	m₁ :r₁ | d₁ :r₁.m₁	f₁ :s₁ |d₁:—

PART 2
Ecce, Panis angelorum

m :r | d :m	r :d | d :t₁	d :t₁| l₁: d	t₁ : l₁ | l₁ :se₁
d :t₁ | l₁: t₁	l₁ :l₁ | s₁ :s₁	s₁:s₁|m₁: s₁	s₁ : m₁ | f₁ :m₁
11 Lo, the an-gels'	food is gi-ven	To the pil-grim	who hath stri-ven;
s :s.f|m : s	f :f | m :r	d :r | d :m	r :d | r.d:t₁
d :s₁ | l₁: m₁	f₁ :r₁ | s₁ :f₁	m₁:s₁|l₁: m₁	s₁ : l₁ | r₁ :m₁

l₁:t₁ | d : d	r :m |f :m	r :m |d : t₁	l₁ :l₁ | s₁:—
m₁:s₁ | s₁: m₁	s₁ : s₁ | l₁: s₁	s₁:m₁|m₁: s₁	m₁ :fe₁ | s₁:—
See the chil-dren's	Bread from hea-ven,	Which on dogs may	ne'er be spent;
d :r | d :d	t₁: t₁ |d : d	r :t₁| d :m	m :r.d| t₁:—
l₁:s₁.f₁|m₁: l₁	s₁ : s₁ |f₁: d	t₁ :s₁ | l₁:m₁	d₁ :r₁ | s₁:—

d :t₁ | l₁:d	t₁:l₁ | l₁:se₁	l₁:t₁ | d :d	f :m | r :r
m₁ :s₁ | l₁:l₁.s₁	f₁:f₁ | m₁:m₁	m₁:s₁ | s₁ :f₁.s₁	l₁ :s₁.l₁|t₁: l₁
Christ the old types	is ful-fill-ing,	I-saac bound, a	Vic-tim will-ing,
d :m.r|d :m	r :d |t₁:t₁	d :r | d :d	d.r:m.fe|s : l
l₁ :m₁ | f₁:d₁	r₁:r₁ |m₁:m₁	l₁:s₁.f₁| m₁ :l₁.s₁	f₁ :d | s₁: f₁

m :r | d :m	r :-.d| t₁.l₁:s₁	s -.f|m.s :f .m	r.d:t₁|d :—
t₁:l₁.t₁ | d :t₁	l₁ : l₁ | s₁ :s₁	s₁.l₁:t₁ |d.t₁:l₁	l₁ :s₁ | s₁:—
Pas-chal Lamb its	life-blood spill-ing,	Man-na to the	fa-thers sent.
se:m | m :m	f : f | r.d:t₁	d :r | m :l₁.d	f.m:r | m :—
m₁:ba₁.se₁| l₁ :s₁	f₁ : r₁ | s₁ :s₁	m₁ :r₁ | d₁ :r₁.m₁	f₁ :s₁ |d₁:—

KEY A♭

At the entrance into the Chancel:

{\| d   l₁   (t₁ —)   \|\|

℣. I am the true Bread   of   Life.
℟. He that cometh to me shall never hun - ger.

PROCESSIONAL—THANKSGIVING FOR HOLY COMMUNION

PART 3

KEY A♭ Bone Pastor, Panis vere

12 O true Bread, Good Shepherd, tend us, Jesu, of thy love befriend us,
Thou refresh us, thou defend us, Let thy goodness here attend us
Till the land of life we see; Thou who all things canst and knowest,
Who such food on earth bestowest, Make us, where thy face thou showest,
'Mid thy saints, though least and lowest, Guests and fellow heirs with thee.
A - men.

ST. THOMAS AQUINAS
Tr. C. S. Phillips and others

NOTE. *This hymn in its several parts (but omitting the starred verses) is suitable for general use at Holy Communion.*

PROCESSIONAL

SAINTS' DAYS

Hymn 623 Claudius
KEY C

Adapted from a song by G. W. Fink,
1783–1846

By permission of the Royal School of Church Music

2

JERUSALEM, my happy home,
   When shall I come to thee?
When shall my sorrows have an end?
   Thy joys when shall I see?
O happy harbour of the saints!
   O sweet and pleasant soil!
In thee no sorrow may be found,
   No grief, no care, no toil.

There lust and lucre cannot dwell;
   There envy bears no sway;
There is no hunger, heat, nor cold,
   But pleasure every way:
Thy walls are made of precious stones,
   Thy bulwarks diamonds square;
Thy gates are of right orient pearl,
   Exceeding rich and rare.

3

Ah, my sweet home, Jerusalem,
   Would God I were in thee!
Would God my woes were at an end,
   Thy joys that I might see!
Thy saints are crowned with glory great,
   They see God face to face;
They triumph still, they still rejoice:
   Most happy is their case.

PROCESSIONAL—SAINTS' DAYS

4

Thy vineyards and thy orchards are
　　Most beautiful and fair,
Full furnishèd with trees and fruits
　　Most wonderful and rare;
Thy gardens and thy gallant walks
　　Continually are green;
There grow such sweet and pleasant flowers
　　As nowhere else are seen.

5

Quite through the streets with silver sound
　　The flood of life doth flow,
Upon whose banks on every side
　　The wood of life doth grow:
There trees for evermore bear fruit,
　　And evermore do spring;
There evermore the angels sit,
　　And evermore do sing.

6*

There David stands with harp in hand
　　As master of the choir;
Ten thousand times that man were blest
　　That might this music hear:
Our Lady sings Magnificat
　　With tune surpassing sweet,
And all the virgins bear their parts,
　　Sitting about her feet.

7*

Te Deum doth Saint Ambrose sing,
　　Saint Austin doth the like;
Old Simeon and Zachary
　　Have not their songs to seek:
There Magdalene hath left her moan,
　　And cheerfully doth sing
With blessèd saints, whose harmony
　　In every street doth ring.

8

Jerusalem, my happy home,
　　Would God I were in thee!
Would God my woes were at an end,
　　Thy joys that I might see!
Jerusalem, Jerusalem,
　　God grant I once may see
Thy endless joys, and of the same
　　Partaker ay to be!

'F. B. P.' (c. 1600)

KEY **G**

At the entrance into the Chancel:

℣. Be glad, O ye righteous, and rejoice in the Lord.
℟. And be joyful, all ye that are true of heart.

PROCESSIONAL—SAINTS' DAYS

HYMN 624 Eatington W. Croft, 1678–1727

KEY **G**

[Tonic sol-fa notation]

1
THE Church triumphant in thy love,
  Their mighty joys we know;
They sing the Lamb in hymns above,
  And we in hymns below.

2
Thee in thy glorious realm they praise,
  And bow before thy throne;
We in the kingdom of thy grace:
  The kingdoms are but one.

3
The holy to the Holiest leads:
  From hence our spirits rise,
And he that in thy statutes treads
  Shall meet thee in the skies.

C. WESLEY

HYMN 625 Erfreut euch German Melody (1536)

KEY **A♭**

[Tonic sol-fa notation]

PROCESSIONAL—SAINTS' DAYS

In domo Patris

1
OUR Father's home eternal,
 O Christ, thou dost prepare
With many divers mansions,
 And each one passing fair:
They are the victors' guerdon
 Who, through the hard-won fight,
Have followed in thy footsteps
 And reign with thee in light.

2
Amid the happy number
 The virgins' crown and queen,
The ever-Virgin Mother,
 Is first and foremost seen:
Her one and only gladness,
 That undefilèd one,
To gaze in adoration,
 The Mother, on the Son.

3*
There Adam leads the chorus,
 And tunes the joyous strain
Of all his myriad children
 That follow in thy train:
Victorious over sorrow,
 The countless band to see,
Destroyed through his transgression,
 But raised to life through thee.

4
The patriarchs in their triumph
 Thy praises nobly sing,
Of old their promised offspring,
 And now their Victor-King:
The prophets harp their gladness
 That, whom their strains foretold,
In manifested glory
 They evermore behold.

5
And David calls to memory
 His own especial grace
In such clear prophet-vision
 To see thee face to face:
The apostolic cohort,
 Thy valiant and thine own,
As royal co-assessors
 Are nearest to thy throne.

6
Thy martyrs reign in glory
 Who triumphed as they fell,
And by a thousand tortures
 Defeated death and hell;
And every patient sufferer,
 Who sorrow dared contemn,
For each especial anguish
 Hath one especial gem.

7*
The valiant-souled confessors
 Put on their meet array,
Who bare the heat and burden
 Of many a weary day:
The scorners of life's pleasures,
 Their self-denial ceased,
Sit down with thee and banquet
 At thy eternal feast.

8*
The virgins walk in beauty
 Amidst their lily-bowers,
The coronals assuming
 Of never-fading flowers;
And innocents sport gaily
 Through all the courts of light,
To whom thou gav'st the guerdon
 Before they fought the fight.

9
The soldiers of thine army,
 Their earthly struggles o'er,
With joy put off the armour
 That they shall need no more:
For these, and all that battled
 Beneath their Monarch's eyes,
The harder was the conflict
 The brighter is the prize.

10
The penitent, attaining
 Full pardon in thy sight,
Leave off the vest of sackcloth
 And don the robe of white:
The bondsman and the noble,
 The peasant and the king,
All gird one glorious Monarch
 In one eternal ring.

Ascribed to THOMAS À KEMPIS
Tr. J. M. NEALE†

KEY A♭

At the entrance into the Chancel:

℣. Be glad, O ye righteous, and rejoice in the Lord.
℟. And be joyful, all ye that are true of heart.

PROCESSIONAL—SAINTS' DAYS

HYMN 626 St. Magnus
KEY A♭

J. Clarke, c. 1659–1707

[Tonic sol-fa notation]

HAIL, glorious spirits, heirs of light,
The high-born sons of fire,
Whose souls burn clear, whose flames shine bright:
All joy, yet all desire.

2
Hail, all you happy souls above,
Who make that glorious ring
About the sparkling throne of love,
And there forever sing.

J. AUSTIN†

HYMN 627 Tenbury
KEY C

Sir S. H. Nicholson, 1875–1947

In slow march time

[Tonic sol-fa notation]

G.t.

5. A♭.

D. 6.   d.f.C.

By permission of the Royal School of Church Music

PROCESSIONAL—SAINTS' DAYS

1

LET love arise and praise him
  Who came as Light from heaven,
And shines as light reflected
  In souls of men forgiven:
    Through the dimness of our shadows,
      Through the mist he came;
    For the souls of them that see him
      Blessèd be his name.

2

He cometh as the morning,
  The light of day arisen,
To them that sit in darkness,
  The souls of men in prison:
    Blessèd Light that deigns to visit
      Man in his distress;
    Welcome with thy wings of healing,
      Sun of Righteousness!

3

Behold the sky at evening,
  When day on earth is ending,
What clouds are seen at sunset
  Upon the sun attending:
    Where our sun is sinking from us
      Into skies unknown,
    All the clouds aflame with glory
      Where he passes on.

4

So, where our Christ advances,
  The Lord of Life undying,
He goes with flashing trumpets
  And pomp of banners flying;
    Not in unattended glory,
      Nor in lonely might:
    Multitudes that none can number
      Answer back his light.

5

A burning mist around him,
  A flock of souls unending,
A cloud of flying spirits,
  Ascending and descending,
    Swimming on in light below him,
      Soaring on above,
    Who are these that move in rapture
      Round about his love?

6

O these are souls that pitied,
  Because they knew his pity,
And found him in their neighbour
  And met him in their city:
    These are they whose life among us
      Won the weak from vice;
    These are they who, little knowing,
      Shared his sacrifice.

7

Through them he healed our wounded,
  Through them he led our blindness,
Redeemed our unbelieving,
  Atoned for our unkindness.
    Therefore in the light they follow
      Where the Lamb doth go;
    Therefore shines their dazzling raiment
      White as glistening snow.

8

So Christ his temple enters,
  The Priest that was so wounded,
And makes a new atonement
  As Love by love surrounded:
    Love amazing that transfigures
      Where its light has shone,
    Love that burns upon the altar,
      Love that mounts the throne.

J. M. C. CRUM

KEY **G**

At the entrance into the Chancel:

℣. Be glad, O ye righteous, and rejoice in the Lord.

℟. And be joyful, all ye that are true of heart.

PROCESSIONAL—SAINTS' DAYS

HYMN 628 Dundee *Psalms* (Edinburgh, 1615)
KEY E

COME, let us join our friends above
That have obtained the prize,
And on the eagle wings of love
To joy celestial rise.

2
E'en now by faith we join our hands
With those that went before,
And greet our Captain's ransomed bands
On the eternal shore.

C. WESLEY†

GENERAL

HYMN 629 St. Gertrude Sir A. Sullivan, 1842–1900
KEY F

On-ward, Chris-tian sol - diers! March-ing as to war,
war, With the

644

PROCESSIONAL—GENERAL

```
{ s :s | d':t    d':— | s :—    f :m  | r :-.d    d :— |— :—
  m :m | f :f    m :— | d :—    d :d  | t₁:-.d    d :— |— :— ||
  With the Cross of  Je - sus    Go-ing  on  be -     fore.
  Cross    of    Je - sus
  d':— | s :—    s :— | s :—    l :-.s| f :-.m    m :— |— :—
  d :d | r :r    m :— | m₁:—    f₁: r₁| s₁:-.s₁  { d :— |— :—
                                                  { d₁:— |— :—
  With the Cross of  Je - sus
```

ONWARD, Christian soldiers!
   Marching as to war,
With the Cross of Jesus
   Going on before.
Christ the royal Master
   Leads against the foe;
Forward into battle,
   See, his banners go!
    Onward, Christian soldiers!
      Marching as to war,
    With the Cross of Jesus
      Going on before.

2

At the sign of triumph
   Satan's host doth flee;
On then, Christian soldiers,
   On to victory!
Hell's foundations quiver
   At the shout of praise;
Brother, lift your voices,
   Loud your anthems raise.
    Onward, etc.

3

Like a mighty army
   Moves the Church of God;
Brothers, we are treading
   Where the saints have trod:
We are not divided,
   All one body we,
One in hope and doctrine,
   One in charity.
    Onward, etc.

4

Crowns and thrones may perish,
   Kingdoms rise and wane,
But the Church of Jesus
   Constant will remain:
Gates of hell can never
   'Gainst that Church prevail;
We have Christ's own promise,
   And that cannot fail.
    Onward, etc.

5

Onward, then, ye people,
   Join our happy throng,
Blend with ours your voices
   In the triumph song:
Glory, laud, and honour
   Unto Christ the King,
This through countless ages
   Men and angels sing.
    Onward, etc.

S. BARING-GOULD

KEY B♭   *At the entrance into the Chancel:*

```
{|       d                                    l₁  (t₁) —  ||
```

℣. Be strong and of a good cour   -   age.

℟. And the Lord, he it is that doth go be   -   fore thee.

PROCESSIONAL—GENERAL

HYMN 630 Illsley (*or* Bishop) J. Bishop, 1665–1737
KEY **G**

1
FROM all that dwell below the skies
Let the Creator's praise arise:
Let the Redeemer's name be sung
Through every land by every tongue.

2
Eternal are thy mercies, Lord;
Eternal truth attends thy word:
Thy praise shall sound from shore to shore,
Till suns shall rise and set no more.

I. WATTS

HYMN 631 Leoni Traditional Hebrew Melody
KEY **B♭**

646

PROCESSIONAL—GENERAL

1
THE God of Abraham praise
Who reigns enthroned above,
Ancient of everlasting Days,
And God of love:
Jehovah, great I AM,
By earth and heaven confest;
We bow and bless the sacred name
For ever blest.

2*
The God of Abraham praise,
At whose supreme command
From earth we rise, and seek the joys
At his right hand:
We all on earth forsake,
Its wisdom, fame, and power;
And him our only portion make,
Our Shield and Tower.

3
Though nature's strength decay,
And earth and hell withstand,
To Canaan's bounds we urge our way
At his command:
The watery deep we pass,
With Jesus in our view;
And through the howling wilderness
Our way pursue.

4
The goodly land we see,
With peace and plenty blest:
A land of sacred liberty
And endless rest;
There milk and honey flow,
And oil and wine abound,
And trees of life for ever grow,
With mercy crowned.

5
There dwells the Lord our King,
The Lord our Righteousness,
Triumphant o'er the world of sin,
The Prince of Peace:
On Sion's sacred height
His Kingdom he maintains,
And glorious with his saints in light
For ever reigns.

6*
He keeps his own secure,
He guards them by his side,
Arrays in garment white and pure
His spotless Bride:
With streams of sacred bliss,
Beneath serener skies,
With all the fruits of Paradise,
He still supplies.

7*
Before the great Three-One
They all exulting stand,
And tell the wonders he hath done
Through all their land:
The listening spheres attend,
And swell the growing fame,
And sing in songs which never end
The wondrous name.

8*
The God who reigns on high
The great archangels sing,
And 'Holy, Holy, Holy,' cry,
'Almighty King!
Who was, and is the same,
And evermore shall be:
Jehovah, Father, great I AM,
We worship thee.'

9
Before the Saviour's face
The ransomed nations bow,
O'erwhelmed at his almighty grace
For ever new;
He shows his prints of love—
They kindle to a flame,
And sound through all the worlds above
The slaughtered Lamb.

10
The whole triumphant host
Give thanks to God on high;
'Hail! Father, Son, and Holy Ghost,'
They ever cry:
Hail! Abraham's God, and mine!
(I join the heavenly lays)
All might and majesty are thine,
And endless praise.

T. OLIVERS
Based on the Hebrew Yigdal

KEY B♭

At the entrance into the Chancel:

℣. They will go from strength to strength.

℟. And unto the God of gods appeareth every one of them in Zi - on.

PROCESSIONAL—GENERAL

Hymn 632 Austria   F. J. Haydn, 1732–1809
KEY E♭

WORSHIP, honour, glory, blessing,
Lord, we offer to thy name;
Young and old, thy praise expressing,
Join their Saviour to proclaim.

As the saints in heaven adore thee,
We would bow before thy throne;
As thine angels serve before thee,
So on earth thy will be done.

E. OSLER

Hymn 633 Crucifer   Sir S. H. Nicholson, 1875–1947
KEY D

UNISON

Lift high the Cross, the love of Christ pro-claim

Fine.

Till all the world a-dore his sa-cred name.

HARMONY
A. t.

D.C.

648

PROCESSIONAL—GENERAL

LIFT high the Cross, the love of Christ proclaim
Till all the world adore his sacred name.

2
Come, brethren, follow where our Captain trod,
Our King victorious, Christ the Son of God.
                Lift high the Cross, etc.

3
Led on their way by this triumphant sign,
The hosts of God in conquering ranks combine,
                Lift high the Cross, etc.

4
Each new-born soldier of the Crucified
Bears on his brow the seal of him who died.
                Lift high the Cross, etc.

5
This is the sign which Satan's legions fear
And angels veil their faces to revere.
                Lift high the Cross, etc.

6
Saved by this Cross whereon their Lord was slain,
The sons of Adam their lost home regain.
                Lift high the Cross, etc.

7
From north and south, from east and west they raise
In growing unison their songs of praise.
                Lift high the Cross, etc.

8
O Lord, once lifted on the glorious Tree,
As thou hast promised, draw men unto thee.
                Lift high the Cross, etc.

9
Let every race and every language tell
Of him who saves our souls from death and hell.
                Lift high the Cross, etc.

10
From farthest regions let them homage bring,
And on his Cross adore their Saviour King.
                Lift high the Cross, etc.

11
Set up thy throne, that earth's despair may cease
Beneath the shadow of its healing peace.
                Lift high the Cross, etc.

12
For thy blest Cross which doth for all atone
Creation's praises rise before thy throne.
                Lift high the Cross, etc.

                              G. W. KITCHIN and M. R. NEWBOLT

KEY **A**

At the entrance into the Chancel:

℣. God forbid that I should glo - ry.
℟. Save in the Cross of our Lord Je - sus Christ.

PROCESSIONAL—GENERAL

HYMN 634 Breslau   *Geistliche Gesänge* (Leipzig, 1625)

KEY **A**

{ :d | d :d | l₁ :d | r :t₁ | l₁ ‖ l₁ | t₁ :d | r :s₁.l₁ | t₁ :l₁ | s₁ :— ‖
 :l₁ | s₁ :m₁ | f₁ :s₁ | f₁ :m₁ | d₁ | f₁ | s₁ :s₁ | s₁ :s₁ | s₁ :fe₁ | s₁ :— ‖
 :m | d :d | d :d | l₁ :se₁ | l₁ | d | r :d | s₁ :m | r :d | t₁ :— ‖
 :l₁ | m₁ :d₁ | f₁ :m₁ | r₁ :m₁ | l₂ | f₁ | f₁ :m₁ | t₂ :d₁ | r₁ :r₁ | s₁ :— ‖ }

{ :s₁ | d :r | m :d | f :m | r ‖ r | m :s | f :m | r :r | d :— ‖
 :s₁ | s₁ :s₁ | s₁ :s₁ | f₁ :s₁ | s₁ | s₁ | s₁ :ta₁ | l₁ :l₁ | l₁ :s₁.f₁ | m₁ :— ‖
 :s₁ | m :r | d :d | t₁ :d | t₁ | t₁ | d :d | d :d | d :t₁ | d :— ‖
 :s₁ | l₁ :t₁ | d :m₁ | r₁ :m₁.f₁ | s₁ | s₁ | d :m₁ | f₁ :l₁.s₁ | f₁ :s₁ | d₁ :— ‖ }

'TWAS by thy Blood, immortal Lamb,
  Thine armies trod the tempter down;
'Twas by thy word and powerful name
  They gained the battle and renown.

2

Rejoice, ye heavens! let every star
  Shine with new glories round the sky;
Saints, while ye sing the heavenly war,
  Raise your Deliverer's name on high.

I. WATTS

HYMN 635 Ich halte treulich still   Attributed to J. S. Bach, 1685–1750

KEY **D**

{ :s | m :r.d | s :l.s | s :— | — ‖ d¹ | r :m.s | f.m :r.d | d :— | — ‖
 :d | s₁ :l₁ | s₁ :d | d :— | — ‖ d | t₁ :d | l₁ :t₁ | d :— | — ‖
 :m | d :m | s :f | m :f | s ‖ m.f | s :s.m | l.s :f | m :— | — ‖
 :d | d :l₁ | m :f | d :r | m ‖ d | s₁ :d | f₁ :s₁ | d :— | — ‖ }

A.t.

{ :ʳ s₁ | l₁ :s₁ | l₁ :r | t₁ :d | r ‖ s | m :r.d | r :d.t₁ | d :— | — ‖
 :ᵗ m₁ | f₁ :s₁ | f₁ :l₁ | s₁ :s₁ | s₁ ‖ t₁ | d :s₁ | l₁ :s₁ | s₁ :— | — ‖
 :ˢ d | d :d | d :f | r :m | r ‖ r | m :s | f :r | m :— | — ‖
 :ˢ d₁ | f₁ :m₁ | f₁ :r₁ | s₁ :d | t₁ ‖ s₁ | d :m₁ | f₁ :s₁ | d₁ :— | — ‖ }

f.D.

{ :ᵈ s | f :m | f :s | m :— | — ‖ m | l :t | m :se | l :— | — ‖
 :ˢ r | d :t₁ | d :r | d :— | — ‖ r | d :f | d :r | d :r | m ‖
 :ᵐ t | l :t | l :s | s :— | — ‖ se | l :l | l :t | l :— | — ‖
 :ᵈ s₁ | l₁ :s₁ | l₁ :t₁ | d :r | d ‖ t₁ | l₁ :r | m :m | l₁ :t₁ | d ‖ }

650

PROCESSIONAL—GENERAL

```
{ :d' | s :-.l | s :f  | m :f | s  || d' | r :m.s | f.m:r.d | d :— |— ||
  :d  | r :d  | r :t, | d :t,| d  || m  | r :d   | d :t,   | d :— |—
  :m  | s :d  | s :s  | s :s | s  || s.l| t :s   | l.s:f   | m :— |—
  :l, | t,:l, | t,:s, | d :r | m  || d  | s :m   | r :s,   | d :— |— }
```

REJOICE, ye pure in heart!
Rejoice, give thanks, and sing;
Your festal banner wave on high,
The Cross of Christ your King:
  Still lift your standard high,
  Still march in firm array,
As warriors through the darkness toil
Till dawns the golden day.

2

Yes onward, onward still,
With hymn and chant and song,
Through gate and porch and columned
The hallowed pathways throng: [aisle
  With all the angel choirs,
  With all the saints on earth,
Pour out the strains of joy and bliss,
True rapture, noblest mirth.

3

Your clear Hosannas raise,
And Alleluias loud;
Whilst answering echoes upward float,
Like wreaths of incense cloud:
  With voice as full and strong
  As ocean's surging praise,
Send forth the hymns our fathers loved,
The psalms of ancient days.

4

Yes on, through life's long path,
Still chanting as ye go,
From youth to age, by night and day,
In gladness and in woe:
  At last the march shall end,
  The wearied ones shall rest,
The pilgrims find their Father's house,
Jerusalem the blest.

5

Then on, ye pure in heart!
Rejoice, give thanks, and sing;
Your festal banner wave on high,
The Cross of Christ your King.
  Praise him who reigns on high,
  The Lord whom we adore,
The Father, Son, and Holy Ghost,
One God for evermore.

E. H. PLUMPTRE

KEY **D**

At the entrance into the Chancel:

```
{| d                                          l,  l, —  ||
```

℣. Let thy priests be clothed with right - eous - ness.

℟. And thy saints sing with joy - ful - ness.

PROCESSIONAL—GENERAL

HYMN 636 Waltham   H. Albert, 1604–51

KEY **A**

MAY the grace of Christ our Saviour,
And the Father's boundless love,
With the Holy Spirit's favour,
Rest upon us from above.

2

Thus may we abide in union
With each other and the Lord,
And possess, in sweet communion,
Joys which earth cannot afford.

J. NEWTON